Objects First with Java™

A Practical Introduction Using BlueJ

David J. Barnes and Michael Kölling
University of Kent

Fifth Edition

PEARSON

Boston   Columbus   Indianapolis   New York   San Francisco   Upper Saddle River
Amsterdam   Cape Town   Dubai   London   Madrid   Milan   Munich Paris   Montreal   Toronto
Delhi   Mexico City   Sao Paulo   Sydney   Hong Kong   Seoul   Singapore   Taipei   Tokyo

Editorial Director: *Marcia Horton*
Editor in Chief: *Michael Hirsch*
Acquisitions Editor: *Tracy Dunkelberger*
Editorial Assistant: *Chelsea Bell*
Director of Marketing: *Patrice Jones*
Marketing Manager: *Yez Alayan*
Marketing Coordinator: *Kathryn Ferranti*
Marketing Assistant: *Emma Snider*
Director of Production: *Vince O'Brien*
Managing Editor: *Jeff Holcomb*
Senior Production Project Manager: *Marilyn Lloyd*
Manufacturing Buyer: *Lisa McDowell*
Art Director/Cover Designer: *Anthony Gemmellaro*
Cover Art: © *Photoshot Holdings Ltd / Alamy*
Media Project Manager: *John Cassar*
Full-Service Project Management, Composition, and Art: *Integra*
Printer/Bindery: *Von Hoffman dba R.R. Donnelley/ Jefferson City*
Cover printer: *Lehigh-Phoenix Color/Hagerstown*

If you purchased this book within the United States or Canada, you should be aware that it has been imported without the approval of the Publisher or the Author.

10 9 8 7 6 5 4 3 2 1

PEARSON

ISBN 10:   0-13-283554-1
ISBN 13: 978-0-13-283554-1

To my wife Helen,
thirty years and counting

djb

To Monica, for everything

mk

Contents

Foreword
by James Gosling, creator of Java

Watching my daughter Kate, and her middle school classmates, struggle through a Java course using a commercial IDE was a painful experience. The sophistication of the tool added significant complexity to the task of learning. I wish that I had understood earlier what was happening. As it was, I wasn't able to talk to the instructor about the problem until it was too late. This is exactly the sort of situation for which BlueJ is a perfect fit.

BlueJ is an interactive development environment with a mission: it is designed to be used by students who are learning how to program. It was designed by instructors who have been in the classroom facing this problem every day. It's been refreshing to talk to the folks who developed BlueJ: they have a very clear idea of what their target is. Discussions tended to focus more on what to leave out, than what to throw in. BlueJ is very clean and very targeting.

Nonetheless, this book isn't about BlueJ. It is about programming.

In Java.

Over the past several years Java has become widely used in the teaching of programming. This is for a number of reasons. One is that Java has many characteristics that make it easy to teach: it has a relatively clean definition; extensive static analysis by the compiler informs students of problems early on; and it has a very robust memory model that eliminates most "mysterious" errors that arise when object boundaries or the type system are compromised. Another is that Java has become commercially very important.

This book confronts head-on the hardest concept to teach: objects. It takes students from their very first steps all the way through to some very sophisticated concepts.

It manages to solve one of the stickiest questions in writing a book about programming: how to deal with the mechanics of actually typing in and running a program. Most books silently skip over the issue, or touch it lightly, leaving it up to the instructor to figure out how to solve the problem and leaving the instructor with the burden of relating the material being taught to the steps that students have to go through to work on the exercises. Instead, it assumes the use of BlueJ and is able to integrate the tasks of understanding the concepts with the mechanics of how students can explore them.

I wish it had been around for my daughter last year. Maybe next year…

Preface

New to the fifth edition

This is the fifth edition of this book and we have taken the opportunity to incorporate several significant changes from previous editions.

- Java 7 features have been incorporated where appropriate
    - The "diamond notation" (generic type inference) is covered when introducing generics.
    - Coverage of appropriate new classes from the nio package for I/O.
    - Strings are shown in switch statements.
    - The new exception handling syntax is covered, including multi-catch and try-with-resources.

- New engaging projects using music files and social media have been added throughout the book. Many other examples have been changed, updated and improved.

- Unit testing is now based on JUnit 4.

- BlueJ version is 3.0.5 is available on the accompanying DVD. This version includes scope coloring, JUnit 4, and Java 7 support.

- Includes VideoNotes—short video tutorials to reinforce key concepts throughout the book.

- Expanded coverage of collections and iteration in Chapter 4.

- Access to the *Blueroom*, a BlueJ instructor community and forum designed for resource sharing and collaboration with the authors and other instructors teaching using BlueJ.

Some of these changes are the result of the introduction of language changes in Java 7. We discuss diamond notation, use of strings in switch statements, changes to exception handlers, and some of the nio classes, for instance. But the examples can still be used by those who have not upgraded to Java 7, yet.

The majority of the changes in this edition, however, are the result of the nearly ten years of experience we have now developed from using this material with our students, along with feedback from our fellow instructors and readers. A particular example is the expansion of the coverage of collections and iteration in Chapter 4, but there are many other smaller expansions where we have sought to clarify topics needing a little more explanation. We have also changed the order of Chapters 6 and 7 to give a flow of topics that fits more comfortably into a single semester for the first half of the book.

We have introduced several new projects to freshen up our coverage of existing topics. These include a music-file organizer in Chapter 4, an online shop in Chapter 7, and a social network in Chapters 8 and 9.

Nevertheless, the distinctive concept and style of this book, that have been there from the beginning, remain unchanged because, overall, the book seems to be "working".

Feedback we received from readers of prior editions was overwhelmingly positive, and many people have helped in making this book better by sending in comments and suggestions, finding errors and telling us about them, contributing material to the book's web site, contributing to the discussion forum, or translating the book into foreign languages.

This book is an introduction to object-oriented programming for beginners. The main focus of the book is general object-oriented and programming concepts from a software engineering perspective.

While the first chapters are written for students with no programming experience, later chapters are suitable for more advanced or professional programmers as well. In particular, programmers with experience in a non-object-oriented language who wish to migrate their skills into object orientation should also be able to benefit from the book.

We use two tools throughout the book to enable the concepts introduced to be put into practice: the Java programming language and the Java development environment BlueJ.

Java

Java was chosen because of a combination of two aspects: the language design and its popularity. The Java programming language itself provides a very clean implementation of most of the important object-oriented concepts, and serves well as an introductory teaching language. Its popularity ensures an immense pool of support resources.

In any subject area, having a variety of sources of information available is very helpful, for teachers and students alike. For Java in particular, countless books, tutorials, exercises, compilers, environments, and quizzes already exist, in many different kinds and styles. Many of them are online and many are available free of charge. The large amount and good quality of support material makes Java an excellent choice as an introduction to object-oriented programming.

With so much Java material already available, is there still room for more to be said about it? We think there is, and the second tool we use is one of the reasons...

BlueJ

The second tool, BlueJ, deserves more comment. This book is unique in its completely integrated use of the BlueJ environment.

BlueJ is a Java development environment that is being developed and maintained by the Computing Education Research Group at the University of Kent in Canterbury, UK, explicitly as an environment for teaching introductory object-oriented programming. It is better suited to introductory teaching than other environments for a variety of reasons:

- The user interface is much simpler. Beginning students can typically use the BlueJ environment in a competent manner after 20 minutes of introduction. From then on, instruction can concentrate on the important concepts at hand—object orientation and Java—and no time needs to be wasted talking about environments, file systems, class paths, or DLL conflicts.

- The environment supports important teaching tools not available in other environments. One of them is visualization of class structure. BlueJ automatically displays a UML-like diagram representing the classes and relationships in a project. Visualizing these important concepts is a great help to both teachers and students. It is hard to grasp the concept of an object when all you ever see on the screen is lines of code! The diagram notation is a simple subset of UML, again tailored to the needs of beginning students. This makes it easy to understand, but also allows migration to full UML in later courses.

- One of the most important strengths of the BlueJ environment is the user's ability to directly create objects of any class, and then to interact with their methods. This creates the opportunity for direct experimentation with objects, with little overhead in the environment. Students can almost "feel" what it means to create an object, call a method, pass a parameter, or receive a return value. They can try out a method immediately after it has been written, without the need to write test drivers. This facility is an invaluable aid in understanding the underlying concepts and language details.

- BlueJ includes numerous other tools and characteristics that are specifically designed for learners of software development. Some are aimed at helping with understanding fundamental concepts (such as the scope highlighting in the editor), some are designed to introduce additional tools and techniques, such as integrated testing using JUnit, or teamwork using a version control system, such as Subversion, once the students are ready. Several of these features are unique to the BlueJ environment.

BlueJ is a full Java environment. It is not a cut-down, simplified version of Java for teaching. It runs on top of Oracle's Java Development Kit, and makes use of the standard compiler and virtual machine. This ensures that it always conforms to the official and most up-to-date Java specification.

The authors of this book have many years of teaching experience with the BlueJ environment (and many more years without it before that). We both have experienced how the use of BlueJ has increased the involvement, understanding, and activity of students in our courses. One of the authors is also a developer of the BlueJ system.

Real objects first

One of the reasons for choosing BlueJ was that it allows an approach where teachers truly deal with the important concepts first. "Objects first" has been a battle cry for many textbook authors and teachers for some time. Unfortunately, the Java language does not make this noble goal very easy. Numerous hurdles of syntax and detail have to be overcome before the first experience with a living object arises. The minimal Java program to create and call an object typically includes

- writing a class;
- writing a main method, including concepts such as static methods, parameters, and arrays in the signature;
- a statement to create the object ("new");
- an assignment to a variable;
- the variable declaration, including variable type;
- a method call, using dot notation;
- possibly a parameter list.

As a result, textbooks typically either

- have to work their way through this forbidding list, and only reach objects somewhere around Chapter 4; or
- use a "Hello, world"-style program with a single static main method as the first example, thus not creating any objects at all.

With BlueJ, this is not a problem. A student can create an object and call its methods as the very first activity! Because users can create and interact with objects directly, concepts such as classes, objects, methods, and parameters can easily be discussed in a concrete manner before looking at the first line of Java syntax. Instead of explaining more about this here, we suggest that the curious reader dip into Chapter 1—things will quickly become clear then.

An iterative approach

Another important aspect of this book is that it follows an iterative style. In the computing education community, a well-known educational design pattern exists that states that important concepts should be taught early and often.[1] It is very tempting for textbook authors to try and say everything about a topic at the point where it is introduced. For example, it is common, when introducing types, to give a full list of built-in data types, or to discuss all available kinds of loop when introducing the concept of a loop.

These two approaches conflict: we cannot concentrate on discussing important concepts first, and at the same time provide complete coverage of all topics encountered. Our experience with textbooks is that much of the detail is initially distracting, and has the effect of drowning the important points, thus making them harder to grasp.

In this book we touch on all of the important topics several times, both within the same chapter and across different chapters. Concepts are usually introduced at a level of detail necessary for

---

[1] The "Early Bird" pattern, in J. Bergin: "Fourteen pedagogical patterns for teaching computer science", *Proceedings of the Fifth European Conference on Pattern Languages of Programs* (EuroPLop 2000), Irsee, Germany, July 2000.

understanding and applying the task at hand. They are revisited later in a different context, and understanding deepens as the reader continues through the chapters. This approach also helps to deal with the frequent occurrence of mutual dependencies between concepts.

Some teachers may not be familiar with an iterative approach. Looking at the first few chapters, teachers used to a more sequential introduction will be surprised about the number of concepts touched on this early. It may seem like a steep learning curve.

It is important to understand that this is not the end of the story. Students are not expected to understand everything about these concepts immediately. Instead, these fundamental concepts will be revisited again and again throughout the book, allowing students to get a deeper and deeper understanding over time. Since their knowledge level changes as they work their way forward, revisiting important topics later allows them to gain a deeper understanding overall.

We have tried this approach with students many times. It seems that students have fewer problems dealing with it than some long-time teachers. And remember: a steep learning curve is not a problem as long as you ensure that your students can climb it!

No complete language coverage

Related to our iterative approach is the decision not to try to provide complete coverage of the Java language within the book.

The main focus of this book is to convey object-oriented programming principles in general, not Java language details in particular. Students studying with this book may be working as software professionals for the next 30 or 40 years of their life—it is a fairly safe bet that the majority of their work will not be in Java. Every serious textbook must of course attempt to prepare them for something more fundamental than the language flavor of the day.

On the other hand, many Java details are important for actually doing the practical work. In this book we cover Java constructs in as much detail as is necessary to illustrate the concepts at hand and implement the practical work. Some constructs specific to Java have been deliberately left out of the discussion.

We are aware that some instructors will choose to cover some topics that we do not discuss in detail. That is expected and necessary. However, instead of trying to cover every possible topic ourselves (and thus blowing the size of this book out to 1500 pages), we deal with it using *hooks*. Hooks are pointers, often in the form of questions that raise the topic and give references to an appendix or outside material. These hooks ensure that a relevant topic is brought up at an appropriate time, and leave it up to the reader or the teacher to decide to what level of detail that topic should be covered. Thus, hooks serve as a reminder of the existence of the topic, and as a placeholder indicating a point in the sequence where discussion can be inserted.

Individual teachers can decide to use the book as it is, following our suggested sequence, or to branch out into sidetracks suggested by the hooks in the text.

Chapters also often include several questions suggesting discussion material related to the topic, but not discussed in this book. We fully expect teachers to discuss some of these questions in class, or students to research the answers as homework exercises.

Project-driven approach

The introduction of material in the book is project driven. The book discusses numerous programming projects and provides many exercises. Instead of introducing a new construct and then providing an exercise to apply this construct to solve a task, we first provide a goal and a problem. Analyzing the problem at hand determines what kinds of solutions we need. As a consequence, language constructs are introduced as they are needed to solve the problems before us.

Early chapters provide at least two discussion examples. These are projects that are discussed in detail to illustrate the important concepts of each chapter. Using two very different examples supports the iterative approach: each concept is revisited in a different context after it is introduced.

In designing this book we have tried to use a large number and wide variety of different example projects. This will hopefully serve to capture the reader's interest, but it also helps to illustrate the variety of different contexts in which the concepts can be applied. Finding good example projects is hard. We hope that our projects serve to give teachers good starting points and many ideas for a wide variety of interesting assignments.

The implementation for all our projects is written very carefully, so that many peripheral issues may be studied by reading the projects' source code. We are strong believers in the benefit of learning by reading and imitating good examples. For this to work, however, one must make sure that the examples students read are well written and worth imitating. We have tried to do this.

All projects are designed as open-ended problems. While one or more versions of each problem are discussed in detail in the book, the projects are designed so that further extensions and improvements can be done as student projects. Complete source code for all projects is included. A list of projects discussed in this book is provided on page xxvii.

Concept sequence rather than language constructs

One other aspect that distinguishes this book from many others is that it is structured along fundamental software development tasks and not necessarily according to the particular Java language constructs. One indicator of this is the chapter headings. In this book you will not find many of the traditional chapter titles, such as "Primitive data types" or "Control structures". Structuring by fundamental development tasks allows us to give a much more general introduction that is not driven by intricacies of the particular programming language utilized. We also believe that it is easier for students to follow the motivation of the introduction, and that it makes much more interesting reading.

As a result of this approach, it is less straightforward to use the book as a reference book. Introductory textbooks and reference books have different, partly competing, goals. To a certain extent a book can try to be both, but compromises have to be made at certain points. Our book is clearly designed as a textbook, and wherever a conflict occurred, the textbook style took precedence over its use as a reference book.

We have, however, provided support for use as a reference book by listing the Java constructs introduced in each chapter in the chapter introduction.

Chapter sequence

Chapter 1 deals with the most fundamental concepts of object orientation: objects, classes, and methods. It gives a solid, hands-on introduction to these concepts without going into the details of Java syntax. We briefly introduce the concept of abstraction for the first time. This will necessarily be a thread that runs through many chapters. Chapter 1 also gives a first look at some source code. We do this by using an example of graphical shapes that can be interactively drawn, and a second example of a simple laboratory class enrollment system.

Chapter 2 opens up class definitions and investigates how Java source code is written to create behavior of objects. We discuss how to define fields and implement methods, and point out the crucial role of the constructor in setting up an object's state as embodied in its fields. Here, we also introduce the first types of statement. The main example is an implementation of a ticket machine. We also look back to the laboratory class example from Chapter 1 to investigate that a bit further.

Chapter 3 then enlarges the picture to discuss interaction of multiple objects. We see how objects can collaborate by invoking each other's methods to perform a common task. We also discuss how one object can create other objects. A digital alarm clock display is discussed that uses two number display objects to show hours and minutes. A version of the project that includes a GUI picks up on a running theme of the book—that we often provide additional code for the interested and able student to explore, without covering it in detail in the text. As a second major example, we examine a simulation of an email system in which messages can be sent between mail clients.

In Chapter 4 we continue by building more extensive structures of objects and pick up again on the themes of abstraction and object interaction from the preceding chapters. Most importantly, we start using collections of objects. We implement an organizer for music files and an auction system to introduce collections. At the same time, we discuss iteration over collections, and have a first look at the for-each and while loops. The first collection being used is an `ArrayList`. In the second half of the chapter we introduce arrays as a special form of a collection, and the *for* loop as another form of a loop. We discuss an implementation of a web-log analyzer as an example for array use.

Chapter 5 deals with libraries and interfaces. We introduce the Java library and discuss some important library classes. More importantly, we explain how to read and understand the library documentation. The importance of writing documentation in software development projects is discussed, and we end by practicing how to write suitable documentation for our own classes. `Random`, `Set`, and `Map` are examples of classes that we encounter in this chapter. We implement an *Eliza*-like dialog system and a graphical simulation of a bouncing ball to apply these classes.

In Chapter 6 we discuss more formally the issues of dividing a problem domain into classes for implementation. We introduce issues of designing classes well, including concepts such as responsibility-driven design, coupling, cohesion, and refactoring. An interactive, text-based adventure game (*World of Zuul*) is used for this discussion. We go through several iterations of improving the internal class structure of the game and extending its functionality, and end with a long list of proposals for extensions that may be done as student projects.

Chapter 7, titled "Well-Behaved Objects," deals with a whole group of issues connected to producing correct, understandable, and maintainable classes. It covers issues ranging from writing clear, understandable code—including style and commenting—to testing and debugging. Test strategies are introduced, including formalized regression testing using JUnit, and a number of debugging methods are discussed in detail. We use an example of an online shop and an implementation of an electronic calculator to discuss these topics.

Chapters 8 and 9 introduce inheritance and polymorphism, with many of the related detailed issues. We discuss a part of a social network to illustrate the concepts. Issues of code inheritance, subtyping, polymorphic method calls, and overriding are discussed in detail.

In Chapter 10 we implement a predator/prey simulation. This serves to discuss additional abstraction mechanisms based on inheritance, namely interfaces and abstract classes.

Chapter 11 develops an image viewer and a graphical user interface for the music organizer (Chapter 4). Both examples serve to discuss how to build graphical user interfaces (GUIs).

Chapter 12 then picks up the difficult issue of how to deal with errors. Several possible problems and solutions are discussed, and Java's exception-handling mechanism is discussed in detail. We extend and improve an address book application to illustrate the concepts. Input/output is used as a case study where error-handling is an essential requirement.

Chapter 13 steps back to discuss in more detail the next level of abstraction: How to structure a vaguely described problem into classes and methods. In previous chapters we have assumed that large parts of the application structure already exist, and we have made improvements. Now it is time to discuss how we can get started from a clean slate. This involves detailed discussion of what the classes should be that implement our application, how they interact, and how responsibilities should be distributed. We use class–responsibilities–collaborators (CRC) cards to approach this problem, while designing a cinema booking system.

In Chapter 14 we try to bring everything together and integrate many topics from the previous chapters of the book. It is a complete case study, starting with the application design, through design of the class interfaces, down to discussing many important functional and non-functional characteristics and implementation details. Topics discussed in earlier chapters (such as reliability, data structures, class design, testing, and extendibility) are applied again in a new context.

Supplements

VideoNote

VideoNotes: VideoNotes are Pearson's new visual tool designed to teach students key programming concepts and techniques. These short step-by-step videos demonstrate how to solve problems from design through coding. VideoNotes allow for self-paced instruction with easy navigation including the ability to select, play, rewind, fast-forward, and stop within each VideoNote exercise.

VideoNotes are located at http://www.pearsonhighered.com/barnes_kolling. Six months of prepaid access are included with the purchase of a new textbook. If the access code has already been revealed, it may no longer be valid. If this is the case, you can purchase a subscription by going to **http://www.pearsonhighered.com/barnes_kolling/** and following the on-screen instructions.

Student Resource CD: This book includes all projects used as discussion examples and exercises on a CD. The CD also includes the Java development environment (JDK) and BlueJ for various operating systems.

Companion website for students: The following resources are available to all readers of this book at its Companion Website, located at http://www.pearsonhighered.com/barnes_kolling:

- Program style guide for all examples in the book
- Links to further material of interest
- Complete source code for all projects

Discussion group for students: Students who want to ask questions or discuss issues either concerning material covered in this book, or BlueJ in general, can do so at http://groups.google.com/group/bluej-discuss on the *bluej-discuss* group.

Instructor Resources: The following supplements are available to qualified instructors only:

- Solutions to end-of-chapter exercises
- PowerPoint slides

Visit the Pearson Instructor Resource Center at www.pearsonhighered.com/irc to register for access or contact your local Pearson representative.

Authors' website: In addition to the publisher's Companion website for this book, we maintain a website at http://www.bluej.org/objects-first. On this web site, updates to the examples can be found, and additional material is provided. For instance, the style guide used for all examples in this book is available on the web site in electronic form so that instructors can modify it to meet their own requirements. This web site is not supported by the publisher.

The Blueroom

Perhaps more important than the static web site resources is a very active community forum that exists for instructors who teach with BlueJ and this book. It is called the *Blueroom* and can be found at

```
http://blueroom.bluej.org
```

The Blueroom contains a resource collection with many teaching resources shared by other teachers, as well as a discussion forum where instructors can ask questions, discuss issues, and stay up-to-date with latest developments. Many other teachers, as well as developers of BlueJ and the authors of this book can be contacted in the Blueroom.

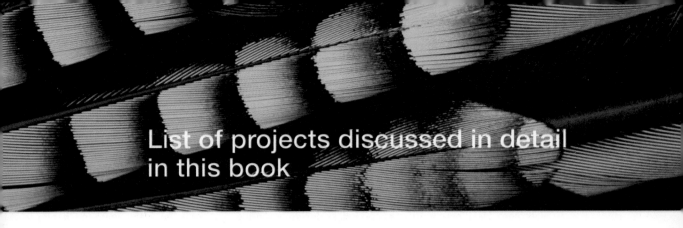
List of projects discussed in detail in this book

scribble   Chapter 5

A shape-drawing program to support learning about classes from their interfaces.

bouncing-balls   Chapter 5

A graphical animation of bouncing balls; demonstrates interface/implementation separation and simple graphics.

world-of-zuul   Chapter 6, Chapter 9

A text-based, interactive adventure game. Highly extendable, makes a great open-ended student project. Used here to discuss good class design, coupling, and cohesion. Used again in Chapter 9 as an example for use of inheritance.

online-shop   Chapter 7

The early stages of an implementation of a part of an online shopping website, dealing with user comments; used to discuss testing and debugging strategies.

calculator   Chapter 7

An implementation of a desk calculator. This example reinforces concepts introduced earlier, and is used to discuss testing and debugging.

bricks   Chapter 7

A simple debugging exercise; models filling pallets with bricks for simple computations.

network   Chapter 8, Chapter 9

Part of a social network application. This project is discussed and then extended in great detail to introduce the foundations of inheritance and polymorphism.

foxes-and-rabbits   Chapter 10

A classic predator–prey simulation; reinforces inheritance concepts and adds abstract classes and interfaces.

image-viewer   Chapter 11

A simple image view and manipulation application. We concentrate mainly on building the GUI.

music-player   Chapter 11

A GUI is added to the *music-organizer* project of Chapter 4 as another example of building GUIs.

address-book   Chapter 12

An implementation of an address book with an optional GUI interface. Lookup is flexible: entries can be searched by partial definition of name or phone number. This project makes extensive use of exceptions.

cinema-booking-system   Chapter 13

A system to manage advance seat bookings in a cinema. This example is used in a discussion of class discovery and application design. No code is provided, as the example represents the development of an application from a blank sheet of paper.

taxi-company   Chapter 14

The taxi example is a combination of a booking system, management system, and simulation. It is used as a case study to bring together many of the concepts and techniques discussed throughout the book.

Acknowledgments

Many people have contributed in many different ways to this book and made its creation possible.

First, and most importantly, John Rosenberg must be mentioned. John is now a Deputy Vice-Chancellor at La Trobe University, Australia. It is by mere coincidence of circumstance that John is not one of the authors of this book. He was one of the driving forces in the development of BlueJ and the ideas and pedagogy behind it from the very beginning, and we talked about the writing of this book for several years. Much of the material in this book was developed in discussions with John. Simply the fact that there are only twenty-four hours in a day, too many of which were already taken up with too much other work, prevented him from actually writing this book. John contributed significantly to the original version of this text and helped improve it in many ways. We have appreciated his friendship and collaboration immensely.

Several other people have helped making BlueJ what it is: Bruce Quig, Davin McCall, and Andrew Patterson in Australia, and Ian Utting, Poul Henriksen, Neil Brown and Philip Stevens in England. All have worked on BlueJ for many years, improving and extending the design and implementation in addition to their other work commitments. Without their work, BlueJ would never have reached the quality and popularity it has today, and this book might never have been written.

Another important contribution that made the creation of BlueJ and this book possible was very generous support first from Sun Microsystems and now from Oracle. Sun has very generously supported BlueJ for many years, and when Oracle acquired Sun this support has continued. We are very grateful for this crucial contribution.

We'd also like to thank the reviewers for this edition: Daniel Rocco, University of West Georgia; Jeanette Allen, University of West Georgia; Katherine Herbert, Montclair State University; Craig A. Piercy. University of Georgia; and Xuemin Chen, Texas Southern University.

The Pearson team also have done a terrific job in making this book happen, managing to bring it into the world and avert every author's worst fear—that his book might go unnoticed. Particular thanks are due to our editor, Tracy Dunkelberger, and editorial assistants Chelsea Bell and Stephanie Sellinger, who supported us through the writing and production process.

David would like to add his personal thanks to both staff and students of the Computer Science Department at the University of Kent. The students who have taken the introductory OO course have always been a privilege to teach. They also provide the essential stimulus and motivation that makes teaching so much fun. Without the valuable assistance of knowledgeable and supportive postgraduate supervisors, running classes would be impossible. Outside university life, various people have supplied a wonderful recreational and social outlet to prevent writing from taking over completely. In particular I would like to thank Tim Hopkins and Maggie Bowman—as sources of good company and limitless amusement—and my fellow members of The River Band: Ian Lithgow, Mick Budd, Olly Jeffery, and Pete Langridge.

Finally, I would like to thank my wife Helen, whose love is so special; and my children, whose lives are so precious.

Michael would like to thank Davin, Neil and Phil who have done such excellent work in building and maintaining BlueJ, Greenfoot, and our community web sites. Without such a great team none of this could work.

I must mention my two little girls, Sophie and Feena, who—admittedly—are not (yet?) terribly interested in this book, but who keep me going. And finally, and most importantly, there is Monica, the love of my life. I don't know where I would be without her.

Part 1
Foundations of object orientation

Main concepts discussed in this chapter:

- objects
- methods
- classes
- parameters

It's time to jump in and get started with our discussion of object-oriented programming. Learning to program requires a mix of some theory and a lot of practice. In this book, we will present both, so that the two reinforce each other.

At the heart of object orientation are two concepts that we have to understand first: *objects* and *classes*. These form the basis of all programming in object-oriented languages. So let us start with a brief discussion of these two foundations.

1.1 Objects and classes

Concept:

Java **objects** model objects from a problem domain.

If you write a computer program in an object-oriented language, you are creating, in your computer, a model of some part of the world. The parts that the model is built up from are the *objects* that appear in the problem domain. These objects must be represented in the computer model being created. The objects from the problem domain vary with the program you are writing. They may be words and paragraphs if you are programming a word processor, users and messages if you are working on a social-network system, or monsters if you are writing a computer game.

Objects may be categorized as—and a class describes, in an abstract way—all objects of a particular kind.

Concept:

Objects are created from **classes**. The class describes the kind of object; the objects represent individual instantiations of the class.

We can make these abstract notions clearer by looking at an example. Assume you want to model a traffic simulation. One kind of entity you then have to deal with is cars. What is a car in our context: Is it a class or an object? A few questions may help us to make a decision.

What color is a car? How fast can it go? Where is it right now?

You will notice that we cannot answer these questions until we talk about one specific car. The reason is that the word "car" in this context refers to the *class* car; we are talking about cars in general, not about one particular car.

If I speak of "My old car that is parked at home in my garage," we can answer the questions above. That car is red, it doesn't go very fast, and it is in my garage. Now I am talking about an object—about one particular example of a car.

We usually refer to a particular object as an *instance*. We shall use the term "instance" quite regularly from now on. "Instance" is roughly synonymous with "object"; we refer to objects as instances when we want to emphasize that they are of a particular class (such as "this object is an instance of class car").

Before we continue this rather theoretical discussion, let us look at an example.

1.2 Creating objects

Start BlueJ and open the example named *figures*.[1] You should see a window similar to that shown in Figure 1.1.

Figure 1.1
The *figures* project in BlueJ

In this window, a diagram should become visible. Every one of the colored rectangles in the diagram represents a class in our project. In this project, we have classes named `Circle`, `Square`, `Triangle`, and `Canvas`.

Right-click on the `Circle` class and choose

```
new Circle()
```

from the pop-up menu. The system asks you for a "name of the instance"; click OK—the default name supplied is good enough for now. You will see a red rectangle toward the bottom of the screen labeled "circle1" (Figure 1.2).

---

[1] We regularly expect you to undertake some activities and exercises while reading this book. At this point, we assume that you already know how to start BlueJ and open the example projects. If not, read Appendix A first.

Figure 1.2
An object on the
object bench

Convention We start names of classes with capital letters (such as Circle) and names of objects with lowercase letters (such as circle1). This helps to distinguish what we are talking about.

Exercise 1.1 Create another circle. Then create a square.

You have just created your first object! "Circle," the rectangular icon in Figure 1.1, represents the class Circle; circle1 is an object created from this class. The area at the bottom of the screen where the object is shown is called the *object bench*.

1.3 Calling methods

Right-click on one of the circle objects (not the class!), and you will see a pop-up menu with several operations (Figure 1.3). Choose makeVisible from the menu—this will draw a representation of this circle in a separate window (Figure 1.4).

Figure 1.3
An object's pop-up
menu, listing its
operations

You will notice several other operations in the circle's menu. Try invoking moveRight and moveDown a few times to move the circle closer to the center of the screen. You may also like to try makeInvisible and makeVisible to hide and show the circle.

Figure 1.4
A drawing of a circle

> **Concept:**
>
> We can communicate with objects by invoking **methods** on them. Objects usually do something if we invoke a method.

Exercise 1.2 What happens if you call moveDown twice? Or three times? What happens if you call makeInvisible twice?

The entries in the circle's menu represent operations that you can use to manipulate the circle. These are called *methods* in Java. Using common terminology, we say that these methods are *called* or *invoked*. We shall use this proper terminology from now on. We might ask you to "invoke the moveRight method of circle1."

1.4 Parameters

Now invoke the moveHorizontal method. You will see a dialog appear that prompts you for some input (Figure 1.5). Type in 50 and click OK. You will see the circle move 50 pixels to the right.[2]

> **Concept:**
>
> Methods can have **parameters** to provide additional information for a task.

The moveHorizontal method that was just called is written in such a way that it requires some more information to execute. In this case, the information required is the distance—how far the circle should be moved. Thus, the moveHorizontal method is more flexible than the moveRight and moveLeft methods. The latter always move the circle a fixed distance, whereas moveHorizontal lets you specify how far you want to move the circle.

Figure 1.5
A method-call dialog

---

[2] A pixel is a single dot on your screen. Your whole screen is made up of a grid of single pixels.

> **Exercise 1.3** Try invoking the moveVertical, slowMoveVertical, and changeSize methods before you read on. Find out how you can use moveHorizontal to move the circle 70 pixels to the left.

Concept:

The header of a method is called its **signature**. It provides information needed to invoke that method.

The additional values that some methods require are called *parameters*. A method indicates what kinds of parameters it requires. When calling, for example, the moveHorizontal method as shown in Figure 1.4, the dialog displays the line near the top.

```
void moveHorizontal(int distance)
```

This is called the *signature* of the method. The signature provides some information about the method in question. The part enclosed by parentheses (int distance) is the information about the required parameter. For each parameter, it defines a *type* and a *name*. The signature above states that the method requires one parameter of type int named distance. The name gives a hint about the meaning of the data expected.

1.5 Data types

A type specifies what kind of data can be passed to a parameter. The type int signifies whole numbers (also called "integer" numbers, hence the abbreviation "int").

Concept:

Parameters have **types**. The type defines what kinds of values a parameter can take.

In the example above, the signature of the moveHorizontal method states that, before the method can execute, we need to supply a whole number specifying the distance to move. The data entry field shown in Figure 1.5 then lets you enter that number.

In the examples so far, the only data type we have seen has been int. The parameters of the move methods and the changeSize method are all of that type.

Closer inspection of the object's pop-up menu shows that the method entries in the menu include the parameter types. If a method has no parameter, the method name is followed by an empty set of parentheses. If it has a parameter, the type and name of that parameter is displayed. In the list of methods for a circle, you will see one method with a different parameter type: the changeColor method has a parameter of type String.

The String type indicates that a section of text (for example, a word or a sentence) is expected. Strings are always enclosed within double quotes. For example, to enter the word *red* as a string, type

```
"red"
```

The method-call dialog also includes a section of text called a *comment* above the method signature. Comments are included to provide information to the (human) reader and are described in Chapter 2. The comment of the changeColor method describes what color names the system knows about.

> **Exercise 1.4** Invoke the changeColor method on one of your circle objects and enter the string "red". This should change the color of the circle. Try other colors.
>
> **Exercise 1.5** This is a very simple example, and not many colors are supported. See what happens when you specify a color that is not known.

> **Exercise 1.6** Invoke the `changeColor` method, and write the color into the parameter field *without* the quotes. What happens?

> **Pitfall** A common error for beginners is to forget the double quotes when typing in a data value of type `String`. If you type `green` instead of `"green"`, you will get an error message saying something like "Error: cannot find symbol - variable green."

Java supports several other data types, including decimal numbers and characters. We shall not discuss all of them right now, but rather come back to this issue later. If you want to find out about them now, look at Appendix B.

1.6 Multiple instances

> **Exercise 1.7** Create several circle objects on the object bench. You can do so by selecting `new Circle()` from the pop-up menu of the `Circle` class. Make them visible, then move them around on the screen using the "move" methods. Make one big and yellow; make another one small and green. Try the other shapes too: create a few triangles, squares, and persons. Change their positions, sizes, and colors.

Concept:

Multiple instances. Many similar objects can be created from a single class.

Once you have a class, you can create as many objects (or instances) of that class as you like. From the class `Circle`, you can create many circles. From `Square`, you can create many squares.

Every one of those objects has its own position, color, and size. You change an attribute of an object (such as its size) by calling a method on that object. This will affect this particular object, but not others.

You may also notice an additional detail about parameters. Have a look at the `changeSize` method of the triangle. Its signature is

```
void changeSize(int newHeight, int newWidth)
```

Here is an example of a method with more than one parameter. This method has two, and a comma separates them in the signature. Methods can, in fact, have any number of parameters.

1.7 State

Concept:

Objects have state. The **state** is represented by storing values in fields.

The set of values of all attributes defining an object (such as *x*-position, *y*-position, color, diameter, and visibility status for a circle) is also referred to as the object's *state*. This is another example of common terminology that we shall use from now on.

In BlueJ, the state of an object can be inspected by selecting the *Inspect* function from the object's pop-up menu. When an object is inspected, an *object inspector* is displayed. The object inspector is an enlarged view of the object that shows the attributes stored inside it (Figure 1.6).

Figure 1.6
An object inspector, showing details of an object

circle1 : Circle

private int diameter	68
private int xPosition	230
private int yPosition	130
private String color	"blue"
private boolean isVisible	true

Inspect
Get
Show static fields
Close

Some methods, when called, change the state of an object. For example, moveLeft changes the xPosition attribute. Java refers to these object attributes as *fields*.

1.8

What is in an object?

On inspecting different objects, you will notice that objects of the *same* class all have the same fields. That is, the number, type, and names of the fields are the same, while the actual value of a particular field in each object may be different. In contrast, objects of a *different* class may have different fields. A circle, for example, has a "diameter" field, while a triangle has fields for "width" and "height."

The reason is that the number, types, and names of fields are defined in a class, not in an object. So the class Circle defines that each circle object will have five fields, named diameter, xPosition, yPosition, color, and isVisible. It also defines the types for these fields. That is, it specifies that the first three are of type int, while the color is of type String and the isVisible flag is of type boolean. (Boolean is a type that can represent two values: true and false. We shall discuss it in more detail later.)

When an object of class Circle is created, the object will automatically have these fields. The values of the fields are stored in the object. That ensures that each circle has a color, for instance, and each can have a different color (Figure 1.7).

The story is similar for methods. Methods are defined in the class of the object. As a result, all objects of a given class have the same methods. However, the methods are invoked on objects. This makes it clear which object to change when, for example, a moveRight method is invoked.

Figure 1.7
A class and its objects with fields and values

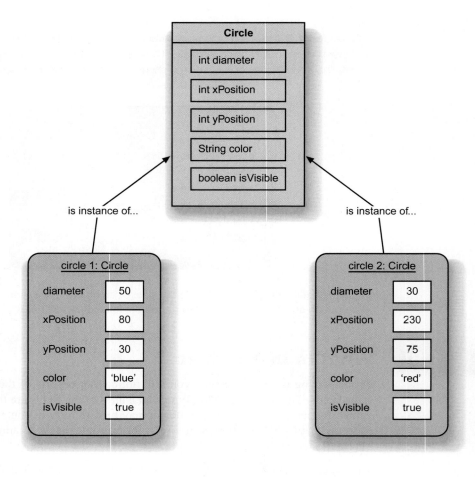

Figure 1.8
Two images created from a set of shape objects

1.9   Java code

When we program in Java, we essentially write down instructions to invoke methods on objects, just as we have done with our figure objects above. However, we do not do this interactively by choosing methods from a menu with the mouse, but instead write the commands down in textual form. We can see what those commands look like in text form by using the BlueJ Terminal.

Exercise 1.10 Select *Show Terminal* from the *View* menu. This shows another window that BlueJ uses for text output. Then select *Record method calls* from the terminal's *Options* menu. This function will cause all our method calls (in their textual form) to be written to the terminal. Now create a few objects, call some of their methods, and observe the output in the terminal window.

Using the terminal's *Record method calls* function, we can see that the sequence of creating a person object and calling its makeVisible and moveRight methods looks like this in Java text form:

```
Person person1 = new Person();

person1.makeVisible();

person1.moveRight();
```

Here, we can observe several things:

- We can see what creating an object and giving it a name looks like. Technically, what we are doing here is *storing the Person object into a variable*; we will discuss this in detail in the next chapter.

- We see that, to call a method on an object, we write the name of the object, followed by a dot, followed by the name of the method. The command ends with a parameter list—an empty pair of parentheses if there are no parameters.

- All Java statements end with a semicolon.

Instead of just looking at Java statements, we can also write them. To do this, we use the *Code Pad*. (You can switch off the *Record method calls* function now and close the terminal.)

Exercise 1.11 Select *Show Code Pad* from the *View* menu. This should display a new pane next to the object bench in your main BlueJ window. This pane is the *Code Pad*. You can type Java code here.

In the Code Pad, we can write Java code that does the same things we did interactively before. The Java code we need to type is exactly like that shown above.

Exercise 1.12 In the Code Pad, type the code shown above to create a person object and call its makeVisible and moveRight methods. Then go on to create some other objects and call their methods.

Typing these commands should have the same effect as invoking the same command from the object's menu. If instead you see an error message, then you have mistyped the command. Check your spelling. You will note that getting even a single character wrong will make the command fail.

Tip You can recall previously used commands in the Code Pad by using the up arrow.

1.10 Object interaction

For the next section, we shall work with a different example project. Close the *figures* project if you still have it open, and open the project called *house*.

> **Exercise 1.13** Open the *house* project. Create an instance of class `Picture` and invoke its `draw` method. Also, try out the `setBlackAndWhite` and `setColor` methods.
>
> **Exercise 1.14** How do you think the `Picture` class draws the picture?

Five of the classes in the *house* project are identical to the classes in the *figures* project. But we now have an additional class: `Picture`. This class is programmed to do exactly what we have done by hand in Exercise 1.9.

In reality, if we want a sequence of tasks done in Java, we would not normally do it by hand as in Exercise 1.9. Instead, we create a class that does it for us. This is the `Picture` class.

The `Picture` class is written so that, when you create an instance, the instance creates two square objects (one for the wall, one for the window), a triangle, and a circle; moves them around; and changes their color and size, until the canvas looks like the picture we see in Figure 1.8.

> **Concept:**
>
> **Method calling.** Objects can communicate by **calling** each other's **methods**.

The important point here is that objects can create other objects, and they can call each other's methods. In a normal Java program, you may well have hundreds or thousands of objects. The user of a program just starts the program (which typically creates a first object), and all other objects are created—directly or indirectly—by that object.

The big question now is this: How do we write the class for such an object?

1.11 Source code

Each class has some *source code* associated with it. The source code is text that defines the details of the class. In BlueJ, the source code of a class can be viewed by selecting the *Open Editor* function from the class's pop-up menu or by double-clicking the class icon.

> **Concept:**
>
> The **source code** of a class determines the structure and behavior (the fields and methods) of each of the objects of that class.

> **Exercise 1.15** Look at the pop-up menu of class `Picture` again. You will see an option labeled *Open Editor*. Select it. This will open a text editor displaying the source code of the class.

The source code is text written in the Java programming language. It defines what fields and methods a class has, and precisely what happens when a method is invoked. In the next chapter, we shall discuss exactly what the source code of a class contains and how it is structured.

A large part of learning the art of programming is learning how to write these class definitions. To do this, we shall learn to use the Java language (although there are many other programming languages that could be used to write code).

When you make a change to the source code and close the editor,[3] the icon for that class appears striped in the diagram. The stripes indicate that the source has been changed. The class

---

[3] In BlueJ, there is no need to explicitly save the text in the editor before closing. If you close the editor, the source code will automatically be saved.

now needs to be compiled by clicking the *Compile* button. (You may like to read the "About compilation" note for more information on what is happening when you compile a class.) Once a class has been compiled, objects can be created again and you can try out your change.

About compilation

When people write computer programs, they typically use a "higher-level" programming language such as Java. A problem with that is that a computer cannot execute Java source code directly. Java was designed to be reasonably easy to read for humans, not for computers. Computers, internally, work with a binary representation of a machine code, which looks quite different from Java. The problem for us is that it looks so complex that we do not want to write it directly. We prefer to write Java. What can we do about this?

The solution is a program called the *compiler*. The compiler translates the Java code into machine code. We can write Java and run the compiler—which generates the machine code—and the computer can then read the machine code. As a result, every time we change the source code, we must first run the compiler before we can use the class again to create an object. Otherwise, the machine code version that the computer needs will not exist.

Exercise 1.16 In the source code of class `Picture`, find the part that actually draws the picture. Change it so that the sun will be blue rather than yellow.

Exercise 1.17 Add a second sun to the picture. To do this, pay attention to the field definitions close to the top of the class. You will find this code:

```
private Square wall;
private Square window;
private Triangle roof;
private Circle sun;
```

You need to add a line here for the second sun. For example:

```
private Circle sun2;
```

Then write the appropriate code for creating the second sun.

Exercise 1.18 *Challenge exercise* (This means that this exercise might not be solved quickly. We do not expect everyone to be able to solve this at the moment. If you do, great. If you don't, then don't worry. Things will become clearer as you read on. Come back to this exercise later.) Add a sunset to the single-sun version of `Picture`. That is, make the sun go down slowly. Remember: The circle has a method `slowMoveVertical` that you can use to do this.

Exercise 1.19 *Challenge exercise* If you added your sunset to the end of the `draw` method (so that the sun goes down automatically when the picture is drawn), change this now. We now want the sunset in a separate method, so that we can call `draw` and see the picture with the sun up, and then call `sunset` (a separate method!) to make the sun go down.

Exercise 1.20 *Challenge exercise* Make a person walk up to the house after the sunset.

1.12 Another example

In this chapter, we have already discussed a large number of new concepts. To help in understanding these concepts, we shall now revisit them in a different context. For this, we use another example. Close the *house* project if you still have it open, and open the *lab-classes* project.

This project is a simplified part of a student database designed to keep track of students in laboratory classes and to print class lists.

> **Exercise 1.21** Create an object of class Student. You will notice that this time you are prompted not only for a name of the instance, but also for some other parameters. Fill them in before clicking OK. (Remember that parameters of type String must be written within double quotes.)

1.13 Return values

As before, you can create multiple objects. And again, as before, the objects have methods that you can call from their pop-up menu.

> **Exercise 1.22** Create some student objects. Call the getName method on each object. Explain what is happening.

Concept:

Result. Methods may return information about an object via a **return value.**

When calling the getName method of the Student class, we notice something new: methods may return a result value. In fact, the signature of each method tells us whether or not it returns a result and what the type of the result is. The signature of getName (as shown in the object's pop-up menu) is defined as

```
String getName()
```

The word String before the method name specifies the return type. In this case, it states that calling this method will return a result of type String. The signature of changeName states:

```
void changeName(String replacementName)
```

The word void indicates that this method does not return any result.

Methods with return values enable us to get information from an object via a method call. This means that we can use methods either to change an object's state or to find out about its state.

1.14 Objects as parameters

> **Exercise 1.23** Create an object of class LabClass. As the signature indicates, you need to specify the maximum number of students in that class (an integer).

Exercise 1.24 Call the `numberOfStudents` method of that class. What does it do?

Exercise 1.25 Look at the signature of the `enrollStudent` method. You will notice that the type of the expected parameter is `Student`. Make sure you have two or three students and a `LabClass` object on the object bench, then call the `enrollStudent` method of the `LabClass` object. With the input cursor in the dialog entry field, click on one of the student objects; this enters the name of the student object into the parameter field of the `enroll-Student` method (Figure 1.9). Click OK and you have added the student to the `LabClass`. Add one or more other students as well.

Exercise 1.26 Call the `printList` method of the `LabClass` object. You will see a list of all the students in that class printed to the BlueJ terminal window (Figure 1.10).

Figure 1.9
Adding a student
to a `LabClass`

Figure 1.10
Output of the
`LabClass` class
listing

```
Blue): Terminal Window - lab-classes
Lab class Fri 10:00
Instructor: M. O. Delmar     Room: 4E
Class list:
Wolfgang Amadeus Mozart, student ID: 547364, credits: 0
Ludwig van Beethoven, student ID: 290034, credits: 0
Johann Sebastian Bach, student ID: 188563, credits: 0
Number of students: 3
```

As the exercises show, objects can be passed as parameters to methods of other objects. In the case where a method expects an object as a parameter, the expected object's class name is specified as the parameter type in the method signature.

Explore this project a bit more. Try to identify the concepts discussed in the *figures* example in this context.

Exercise 1.27 Create three students with the following details:

Snow White, student ID: *A00234*, credits: *24*
Lisa Simpson, student ID: *C22044,* credits: *56*
Charlie Brown, student ID: *A12003*, credits: *6*

Then enter all three into a lab and print a list to the screen.

Exercise 1.28 Use the inspector on a `LabClass` object to discover what fields it has.

Exercise 1.29 Set the instructor, room, and time for a lab, and print the list to the terminal window to check that these new details appear.

1.15 Summary

In this chapter, we have explored the basics of classes and objects. We have discussed the fact that objects are specified by classes. Classes represent the general concept of things, while objects represent concrete instances of a class. We can have many objects of any class.

Objects have methods that we use to communicate with them. We can use a method to make a change to the object or to get information from the object. Methods can have parameters, and parameters have types. Methods have return types, which specify what type of data they return. If the return type is `void`, they do not return anything.

Objects store data in fields (which also have types). All the data values of an object together are referred to as the object's state.

Objects are created from class definitions that have been written in a particular programming language. Much of programming in Java is about learning to write class definitions. A large Java program will have many classes, each with many methods that call each other in many different ways.

To learn to develop Java programs, we need to learn how to write class definitions, including fields and methods, and how to put these classes together well. The rest of this book deals with these issues.

Terms introduced in this chapter

object, class, instance, method, signature, parameter, type, state, source code, return value, compiler

Concept summary

- **object** Java objects model objects from a problem domain.
- **class** Objects are created from classes. The class describes the kind of object; the objects represent individual instantiations of the class.

■ **method** We can communicate with objects by invoking methods on them. Objects usually do something if we invoke a method.

■ **parameter** Methods can have parameters to provide additional information for a task.

■ **signature** The header of a method is called its signature. It provides information needed to invoke that method.

■ **type** Parameters have types. The type defines what kinds of values a parameter can take.

■ **multiple instances** Many similar objects can be created from a single class.

■ **state** Objects have state. The state is represented by storing values in fields.

■ **method calling** Objects can communicate by calling each other's methods.

■ **source code** The source code of a class determines the structure and behavior (the fields and methods) of each of the objects of that class.

■ **result** Methods may return information about an object via a return value.

Exercise 1.30 In this chapter we have mentioned the data types `int` and `String`. Java has more predefined data types. Find out what they are and what they are used for. To do this, you can check Appendix B, or look it up in another Java book or in an online Java language manual. One such manual is at

```
http://download.oracle.com/javase/tutorial/java/nutsandbolts/
datatypes.html
```

Exercise 1.31 What are the types of the following values?

```
0
"hello"
101
-1
true
"33"
3.1415
```

Exercise 1.32 What would you have to do to add a new field, for example one called `name`, to a circle object?

Exercise 1.33 Write the signature for a method named `send` that has one parameter of type `String`, and does not return a value.

Exercise 1.34 Write the signature for a method named `average` that has two parameters, both of type `int`, and returns an `int` value.

Exercise 1.35 Look at the book you are reading right now. Is it an object or a class? If it is a class, name some objects. If it is an object, name its class.

Exercise 1.36 Can an object have several different classes? Discuss.

CHAPTER

2

Understanding class definitions

Main concepts discussed in this chapter:

- fields
- constructors
- parameters

- methods (accessor, mutator)
- assignment and conditional statement

Java constructs discussed in this chapter:

field, constructor, comment, parameter, assignment (=), block, return statement, `void`, compound assignment operators (+=, −=), if statement

In this chapter, we take our first proper look at the source code of a class. We will discuss the basic elements of class definitions: *fields*, *constructors,* and *methods*. Methods contain statements, and initially we look at methods containing only simple arithmetic and printing statements. Later, we introduce *conditional statements* that allow choices between different actions to be made within methods.

We shall start by examining a new project in a fair amount of detail. This project represents a naïve implementation of an automated ticket machine. As we start by introducing the most basic features of classes, we shall quickly find that this implementation is deficient in a number of ways. So we shall then proceed to describe a more sophisticated version of the ticket machine that represents a significant improvement. Finally, in order to reinforce the concepts introduced in this chapter, we take a look at the internals of the *lab-classes* example encountered in Chapter 1.

2.1 Ticket machines

Train stations often provide ticket machines that print a ticket when a customer inserts the correct money for their fare. In this chapter, we shall define a class that models something like these ticket machines. As we shall be looking inside our first Java example classes, we shall keep our simulation fairly simple to start with. That will give us the opportunity to ask some questions about how these models differ from the real-world versions and how we might change our classes to make the objects they create more like the real thing.

Our ticket machines work by customers "inserting" money into them and then requesting a ticket to be printed. Each machine keeps a running total of the amount of money it has collected throughout its operation. In real life, it is often the case that a ticket machine offers a selection of different types of ticket from which customers choose the one they want. Our simplified machines print tickets of only a single price. It turns out to be significantly more complicated to program a class to be able to issue tickets of different values than it does to have a single price. On the other hand, with object-oriented programming it is very easy to create multiple instances of the class, each with its own price setting, to fulfill a need for different types of tickets.

2.1.1 Exploring the behavior of a naïve ticket machine

Open the *naive-ticket-machine* project in BlueJ. This project contains only one class – TicketMachine – which you will be able to explore in a similar way to the examples we discussed in Chapter 1. When you create a TicketMachine instance, you will be asked to supply a number that corresponds to the price of tickets that will be issued by that particular machine. The price is taken to be a number of cents, so a positive whole number such as 500 would be appropriate as a value to work with.

Exercise 2.1 Create a TicketMachine object on the object bench and take a look at its methods. You should see the following: getBalance, getPrice, insertMoney, and printTicket. Try out the getPrice method. You should see a return value containing the price of the tickets that was set when this object was created. Use the insertMoney method to simulate inserting an amount of money into the machine. The machine stores as a balance the amount of money inserted. Use getBalance to check that the machine has kept an accurate record of the amount just inserted. You can insert several separate amounts of money into the machine, just like you might insert multiple coins or bills into a real machine. Try inserting the exact amount required for a ticket, and use getBalance to ensure that the balance is increased correctly. As this is a simple machine, a ticket will not be issued automatically, so once you have inserted enough money, call the printTicket method. A facsimile ticket should be printed in the BlueJ terminal window.

Exercise 2.2 What value is returned if you get the machine's balance after it has printed a ticket?

Exercise 2.3 Experiment with inserting different amounts of money before printing tickets. Do you notice anything strange about the machine's behavior? What happens if you insert too much money into the machine – do you receive any refund? What happens if you do not insert enough and then try to print a ticket?

Exercise 2.4 Try to obtain a good understanding of a ticket machine's behavior by interacting with it on the object bench before we start looking, in the next section, at how the TicketMachine class is implemented.

Exercise 2.5 Create another ticket machine for tickets of a different price; remember that you have to supply this value when you create the machine object. Buy a ticket from that machine. Does the printed ticket look any different from those printed by the first machine?

2.2 Examining a class definition

The exercises at the end of the previous section reveal that TicketMachine objects only really behave in the way we expect them to if we insert exactly the correct amount of money to match the price of a ticket. As we explore the internal details of the class in this section, we shall see why this is so.

Take a look at the source code of the TicketMachine class by double-clicking its icon in the class diagram within BlueJ. It should look something like Figure 2.1.

Figure 2.1
The BlueJ editor window

The complete text of the class is shown in Code 2.1. By looking at the text of the class definition piece by piece, we can flesh out some of the object-oriented concepts that we talked about in Chapter 1. This class definition contains many of the features of Java that we will see over and over again, so it will pay greatly to study it carefully.

Code 2.1
The TicketMachine class

```
/**
 * TicketMachine models a naive ticket machine that issues
 * flat-fare tickets.
 * The price of a ticket is specified via the constructor.
 * It is a naive machine in the sense that it trusts its users
 * to insert enough money before trying to print a ticket.
 * It also assumes that users enter sensible amounts.
 *
```

**Code 2.1
continued**

The TicketMachine
class

```
 * @author David J. Barnes and Michael Kölling
 * @version 2011.07.31
 */
public class TicketMachine
{
    // The price of a ticket from this machine.
    private int price;
    // The amount of money entered by a customer so far.
    private int balance;
    // The total amount of money collected by this machine.
    private int total;

    /**
     * Create a machine that issues tickets of the given price.
     * Note that the price must be greater than zero, and there
     * are no checks to ensure this.
     */
    public TicketMachine(int cost)
    {
        price = cost;
        balance = 0;
        total = 0;
    }

    /**
     * Return the price of a ticket.
     */
    public int getPrice()
    {
        return price;
    }

    /**
     * Return the amount of money already inserted for the
     * next ticket.
     */
    public int getBalance()
    {
        return balance;
    }

    /**
     * Receive an amount of money from a customer.
     */
    public void insertMoney(int amount)
    {
        balance = balance + amount;
    }
```

```
/**
 * Print a ticket
 * Update the total collected and
 * reduce the balance to zero.
 */
public void printTicket()
{
    // Simulate the printing of a ticket.
    System.out.println("##################");
    System.out.println("# The BlueJ Line");
    System.out.println("# Ticket");
    System.out.println("# " + price + " cents.");
    System.out.println("##################");
    System.out.println();

    // Update the total collected with the balance.
    total = total + balance;
    // Clear the balance.
    balance = 0;
}
}
```

2.3   The class header

The text of a class can be broken down into two main parts: a small outer wrapping that simply names the class and a much larger inner part that does all the work. In this case, the outer wrapping appears as follows:

```
public class TicketMachine
{
        Inner part of the class omitted.
}
```

The outer wrappings of different classes all look pretty much the same. The outer wrapping contains the class header, whose main purpose is to provide a name for the class. By a widely

Exercise 2.6 Write out what you think the outer wrappers of the Student and LabClass classes might look like; do not worry about the inner part.

Exercise 2.7 Does it matter whether we write

```
public class TicketMachine
```

or

```
class public TicketMachine
```

in the outer wrapper of a class? Edit the source of the `TicketMachine` class to make the change, and then close the editor window. Do you notice a change in the class diagram?

What error message do you get when you now press the *Compile* button? Do you think this message clearly explains what is wrong?

Change the class back to how it was, and make sure that this clears the error when you compile it.

Exercise 2.8 Check whether or not it is possible to leave out the word `public` from the outer wrapper of the `TicketMachine` class.

Exercise 2.9 Put back the word `public`, and then check whether it is possible to leave out the word `class` by trying to compile again. Make sure that both words are put back as they were originally before continuing.

followed convention, we always start class names with an uppercase letter. As long as it is used consistently, this convention allows class names to be easily distinguished from other sorts of names, such as variable names and method names, which will be described shortly.

2.3.1 Keywords

The words "public" and "class" are part of the Java language, whereas the word "TicketMachine" is not—the person writing the class has chosen that particular name. We call words like "public" and "class" *keywords* or *reserved words* – the terms are used frequently and interchangeably. There are around 50 of these in Java, and you will soon get to recognize most of them. A point worth remembering is that Java keywords never contain uppercase letters, whereas the words we get to choose (like "TicketMachine") are often a mix of upper- and lowercase letters.

2.4 Fields, constructors, and methods

The inner part of the class is where we define the *fields, constructors*, and *methods* that give the objects of that class their own particular characteristics and behavior. We can summarize the essential features of those three components of a class as follows:

■ The fields store data persistently within an object.

■ The constructors are responsible for ensuring that an object is set up properly when it is first created.

■ The methods implement the behavior of an object; they provide its functionality.

In Java there are very few rules about the order in which you choose to define the fields, constructors, and methods within a class. In the `TicketMachine` class, we have chosen to list the fields first, the constructors second, and finally the methods (Code 2.2). This is the order that we shall follow in all of our examples. Other authors choose to adopt different styles, and this is mostly a question of preference. Our style is not necessarily better than all others. However, it is important to choose one style and then use it consistently, because then your classes will be easier to read and understand.

Code 2.2

Our ordering of fields, constructors, and methods

```
public class ClassName
{
    Fields
    Constructors
    Methods
}
```

Exercise 2.10 From your earlier experimentation with the ticket machine objects within BlueJ, you can probably remember the names of some of the methods—printTicket, for instance. Look at the class definition in Code 2.1 and use this knowledge, along with the additional information about ordering we have given you, to make a list of the names of the fields, constructors, and methods in the TicketMachine class. *Hint:* There is only one constructor in the class.

Exercise 2.11 What are the two features of the constructor that make it look significantly different from the methods of the class?

2.4.1 Fields

Concept:

Fields store data for an object to use. Fields are also known as instance variables.

Fields store data persistently within an object. The TicketMachine class has three fields: price, balance, and total. Fields are also known as *instance variables,* because the word *variable* is used as a general term for things that store data in a program. We have defined the fields right at the start of the class definition (Code 2.3). All of these variables are associated with monetary items that a ticket-machine object has to deal with:

■ price stores the fixed price of a ticket;

■ balance stores the amount of money inserted into the machine by a user prior to asking for a ticket to be printed;

■ total stores the total amount of money inserted into the machine by all users since the machine object was constructed (excluding any current balance). The idea is that, when a ticket is printed, any money in the balance is transferred to the total.

Code 2.3

The fields of the TicketMachine class

```
public class TicketMachine
{
    private int price;
    private int balance;
    private int total;

    Constructor and methods omitted.
}
```

Fields are small amounts of space inside an object that can be used to store data persistently. Every object will have space for each field declared in its class. Figure 2.2 shows a diagrammatic representation of a ticket-machine object with its three fields. The fields have not yet been assigned any values; once they have, we can write each value into the box representing the field. The notation is similar to that used in BlueJ to show objects on the object bench, except that we show a bit more detail here. In BlueJ, for space reasons, the fields are not displayed on the object icon. We can, however, see them by opening an inspector window (Section 1.5).

Figure 2.2
An object of class
`TicketMachine`

Each field has its own declaration in the source code. On the line above each in the full class definition, we have added a single line of text—a *comment*—for the benefit of human readers of the class definition:

```
// The price of a ticket from this machine.
private int price;
```

A single-line comment is introduced by the two characters "//", which are written with no spaces between them. More-detailed comments, often spanning several lines, are usually written in the form of multiline comments. These start with the character pair "/*" and end with the pair "*/". There is a good example preceding the header of the class in Code 2.1.

The definitions of the three fields are quite similar:

- All definitions indicate that they are *private* fields of the object; we shall have more to say about what this means in Chapter 5, but for the time being we will simply say that we always define fields to be private.

- All three fields are of type `int` – `int` is another keyword and represents the data type integer. This indicates that each can store a single whole-number value, which is reasonable given that we wish them to store numbers that represent amounts of money in cents.

It is because fields can store values that can vary over time that they are also known as *variables*. The value stored in a field can be changed from its initial value if required. For instance, as more money is inserted into a ticket machine, we shall want to change the value stored in the `balance` field. It is common to have fields whose values change often, such as `balance` and `total`, and others that change rarely or not at all, such as `price`. The fact that the value of `price` doesn't vary once set doesn't alter the fact that it is still called a variable. In the following sections, we shall also meet other kinds of variables in addition to fields, but they will all share the same fundamental purpose of storing data.

The `price`, `balance`, and `total` fields are all the data items that a ticket-machine object needs to fulfill its role of receiving money from a customer, printing tickets, and keeping a running total of all the money that has been put into it. In the following sections, we shall see how the constructor and methods use those fields to implement the behavior of naïve ticket machines.

Exercise 2.12 What do you think is the *type* of each of the following fields?

```
private int count;
private Student representative;
private Server host;
```

Exercise 2.13 What are the *names* of the following fields?

```
private boolean alive;
private Person tutor;
private Game game;
```

Exercise 2.14 From what you know about the naming conventions for classes, which of the type names in Exercises 2.12 and 2.13 would you say are class names?

Exercise 2.15 In the following field declaration from the `TicketMachine` class

```
private int price;
```

does it matter which order the three words appear in? Edit the `TicketMachine` class to try different orderings. After each change, close the editor. Does the appearance of the class diagram after each change give you a clue as to whether or not other orderings are possible? Check by pressing the *Compile* button to see if there is an error message.

Make sure that you reinstate the original version after your experiments!

Exercise 2.16 Is it always necessary to have a semicolon at the end of a field declaration? Once again, experiment via the editor. The rule you will learn here is an important one, so be sure to remember it.

Exercise 2.17 Write in full the declaration for a field of type `int` whose name is `status`.

From the definitions of fields we have seen so far, we can begin to put a pattern together that will apply whenever we define a field variable in a class:

■ They usually start with the reserved word `private`.

■ They include a type name (such as `int`, `String`, `Person`, etc.)

■ They include a user-chosen name for the field variable.

■ They end with a semicolon.

Remembering this pattern will help you when you write your own classes.

Indeed, as we look closely at the source code of different classes, you will see patterns such as this one emerging over and over again. Part of the process of learning to program involves looking out for such patterns and then using them in your own programs. That is one reason why studying source code in detail is so useful at this stage.

2.4.2 Constructors

Concept:

Constructors allow each object to be set up properly when it is first created.

Constructors have a special role to fulfill. They are responsible for ensuring that an object is set up properly when it is first created; in other words, for ensuring that an object is ready to be used immediately following its creation. This construction process is also called *initialization*.

In some respects, a constructor can be likened to a midwife: it is responsible for ensuring that the new object comes into existence properly. Once an object has been created, the constructor plays no further role in that object's life and cannot be called on it. Code 2.4 shows the constructor of the TicketMachine class.

One of the distinguishing features of constructors is that they have the same name as the class in which they are defined—TicketMachine in this case. The constructor's name immediately follows the word public, with nothing in between.[1]

We should expect a close connection between what happens in the body of a constructor and in the fields of the class. This is because one of the main roles of the constructor is to initialize the

Code 2.4

The constructor of the TicketMachine class

```
public class TicketMachine
{
    Fields omitted.

    /**
     * Create a machine that issues tickets of the given price.
     * Note that the price must be greater than zero, and there
     * are no checks to ensure this.
     */
    public TicketMachine(int cost)
    {
        price = cost;
        balance = 0;
        total = 0;
    }

    Methods omitted.
}
```

[1] While this description is a slight simplification of the full Java rule, it fits the general rule we will use in the majority of code in this book.

fields. It will be possible with some fields, such as `balance` and `total`, to set sensible initial values by assigning a constant number – zero in this case. With others, such as the ticket price, it is not that simple, as we do not know the price that tickets from a particular machine will have until that machine is constructed. Recall that we might wish to create multiple machine objects to sell tickets with different prices, so no one initial price will always be right. You will know from experimenting with creating `TicketMachine` objects within BlueJ that you had to supply the cost of the tickets whenever you created a new ticket machine. An important point to note here is that the price of a ticket is initially determined *externally* and then has to be *passed into* the constructor. Within BlueJ you decide the value and enter it into a dialog box. Part of the task of the constructor is to receive that value and store it in the `price` field of the newly created ticket machine so that the machine can remember what that value was without you having to keep reminding it.

We can see from this that one of the most important roles of a field is to remember external information passed into the object so that that information is available to an object throughout its lifetime. Fields, therefore, provide a place to store long-lasting (i.e., persistent) data.

Figure 2.3 shows a ticket-machine object after the constructor has executed. Values have now been assigned to the fields. From this diagram, we can tell that the ticket machine was created by passing in 500 as the value for the ticket price.

Figure 2.3
A `TicketMachine` object after initialization (created for 500-cent tickets)

In the next section, we discuss how values are received by an object from outside.

> **Note** In Java, all fields are automatically initialized to a default value if they are not explicitly initialized. For integer fields, this default value is zero. So, strictly speaking, we could have done without setting balance and total to zero, relying on the default value to give us the same result. However, we prefer to write the explicit assignments anyway. There is no disadvantage to it, and it serves well to document what is actually happening. We do not rely on a reader of the class knowing what the default value is, and we document that we really want this value to be zero and have not just forgotten to initialize it.

2.5 Parameters: receiving data

Constructors and methods play quite different roles in the life of an object, but the way in which both receive values from outside is the same: via *parameters*. You may recall that we briefly encountered parameters in Chapter 1 (Section 1.4). Parameters are another sort of variable, just as fields are, so they are also used to hold data. Parameters are variables that are defined in the header of a constructor or method:

```
public TicketMachine(int cost)
```

This constructor has a single parameter, cost, which is of type int—the same type as the price field it will be used to set. A parameter is used as a sort of temporary messenger, carrying data originating from outside the constructor or method and making it available inside it.

Figure 2.4 illustrates how values are passed via parameters. In this case, a BlueJ user enters the external value into the dialog box when creating a new ticket machine (shown on the left), and that value is then copied into the cost parameter of the new machine's constructor. This is illustrated with the arrow labeled (A). The box in the TicketMachine object in Figure 2.4, labeled "TicketMachine (constructor)," represents additional space for the object that is created only when the constructor executes. We shall call it the *constructor space* of the object (or *method space* when we talk about methods instead of constructors, as the situation there is the same). The constructor space is used to provide space to store the values for the constructor's parameters. In our diagrams, all variables are represented by white boxes.

We distinguish between the parameter *names* inside a constructor or method and the parameter *values* outside by referring to the names as *formal parameters* and the values as *actual parameters*. So cost is a formal parameter, and a user-supplied value such as 500 is an actual parameter.

A formal parameter is available to an object only within the body of a constructor or method that declares it. We say that the *scope* of a parameter is restricted to the body of the constructor or method in which it is declared. In contrast, the scope of a field is the whole of the class definition – it can be accessed from anywhere in the same class. This is a very important difference between these two sorts of variables.

A concept related to variable scope is variable *lifetime.* The lifetime of a parameter is limited to a single call of a constructor or method. When a constructor or method is called, the extra space

> **Concept:**
>
> The **scope** of a variable defines the section of source code from which the variable can be accessed.

> **Concept:**
>
> The **lifetime** of a variable describes how long the variable continues to exist before it is destroyed.

Figure 2.4

Parameter passing (A) and assignment (B)

for the parameter variables is created and the external values copied into that space. Once that call has completed its task, the formal parameters disappear and the values they held are lost. In other words, when the constructor has finished executing, the whole constructor space (see Figure 2.4) is removed, along with the parameter variables held within it.

In contrast, the lifetime of a field is the same as the lifetime of the object to which it belongs. When an object is created, so are the fields, and they persist for the lifetime of the object. It follows that if we want to remember the cost of tickets held in the `cost` parameter, we must store the value somewhere persistent—that is, in the `price` field.

Just as we expect to see a close link between a constructor and the fields of its class, we expect to see a close link between the constructor's parameters and the fields, because external values will often be needed to set the initial values of one or more of those fields. Where this is the case, the parameter types will closely match the types of the corresponding fields.

Exercise 2.18 To what class does the following constructor belong?

```
public Student(String name)
```

Exercise 2.19 How many parameters does the following constructor have, and what are their types?

```
public Book(String title, double price)
```

Exercise 2.20 Can you guess what types some of the `Book` class's fields might be, from the parameters in its constructor? Can you assume anything about the names of its fields?

2.5.1 Choosing variable names

One of the things you might have noticed is that the variable names we use for fields and parameters have a close connection with the purpose of the variable. Names such as `price`, `cost`, `title`, and `alive` all tell you something useful about the information being stored in that variable. This, then, makes it easier to understand what is going on in the program. Given that we have a large degree of freedom in our choice of variable names, it is worth following this principle of choosing names that communicate a sense of purpose rather than arbitrary and meaningless combinations of letters and numbers.

2.6   Assignment

In the previous section, we noted the need to store the short-lived value stored in a parameter variable into somewhere more permanent—a field variable. In order to do this, the body of the constructor contains the following *assignment statement:*

```
price = cost;
```

Assignment statements are used a lot in programming, as a means to store a value into a variable. They can be recognized by the presence of an assignment operator, such as "=" in the example above. Assignment statements work by taking the value of what appears on the right-hand side of the operator and copying that value into the variable on the left-hand side. This is illustrated in Figure 2.4 by the arrow labeled (B). The right-hand side is called an *expression*. In their most general form, expressions are things that compute value, but in this case, the expression consists of just a single variable, whose value is copied into the price variable. We shall see examples of more-complicated expressions later in this chapter.

One rule about assignment statements is that the type of the expression on the right-hand side must match the type of the variable to which it is assigned. We have already met three different, commonly used types: int, String, and (very briefly) boolean. This rule means that we are not allowed to store an int-type expression in a String-type variable, for instance. This same rule also applies between formal parameters and actual parameters: the type of an actual-parameter expression must match the type of the formal-parameter variable. For now, we can say that the types of both must be the same, although we shall see in later chapters that this is not the whole truth.

Exercise 2.21 Suppose that the class Pet has a field called name that is of type String. Write an assignment statement in the body of the following constructor so that the name field will be initialized with the value of the constructor's parameter.

```
public Pet(String petsName)
{
}
```

Exercise 2.22 *Challenge exercise* The following object creation will result in the constructor of the Date class being called. Can you write the constructor's header?

```
new Date("March", 23, 1861)
```

Try to give meaningful names to the parameters.

2.7   Methods

The TicketMachine class has four methods: getPrice, getBalance, insertMoney, and printTicket. We shall start our look at the source code of methods by considering getPrice (Code 2.5).

Methods have two parts: a *header* and a *body*. Here is the method header for getPrice, preceded by a descriptive comment:

```
/**
 * Return the price of a ticket.
 */
public int getPrice()
```

It is important to distinguish between method headers and field declarations, because they can look quite similar. We can tell that getPrice is a method and not a field because method headers always include a pair of parentheses – "(" and ")" – and no semicolon at the end of the header.

Code 2.5

The **getPrice** method

```
public class TicketMachine
{
    Fields omitted.

    Constructor omitted.

    /**
     * Return the price of a ticket.
     */
    public int getPrice()
    {
        return price;
    }

    Remaining methods omitted.
}
```

The method body is the remainder of the method after the header. It is always enclosed by a matching pair of curly brackets: "{" and "}". Method bodies contain the *declarations* and *statements* that define what an object does when that method is called. Declarations are used to create additional, temporary variable space, while statements describe the actions of the method. In getPrice, the method body contains a single statement, but we shall see examples very soon where the method body consists of many lines of both declarations and statements.

Any set of declarations and statements between a pair of matching curly brackets is known as a *block*. So the body of the TicketMachine class and the bodies of the constructor and all of the methods within the class are blocks.

There are at least two significant differences between the headers of the TicketMachine constructor and the getPrice method:

```
public TicketMachine(int cost)
public int getPrice()
```

■ The method has a *return type* of int, but the constructor has no return type. A return type is written just before the method name. This is a difference that applies in all cases.

■ The constructor has a single formal parameter, cost, but the method has none—just a pair of empty parentheses. This is a difference that applies in this particular case.

It is an absolute rule in Java that a constructor may not have a return type. On the other hand, both constructors and methods may have any number of formal parameters, including none.

Within the body of getPrice there is a single statement:

```
return price;
```

This is a called a *return statement*. It is responsible for returning an integer value to match the int return type in the method's header. Where a method contains a return statement, it is always the final statement of that method, because no further statements in the method will be executed once the return statement is executed.

Return types and return statements work together. The `int` return type of `getPrice` is a form of promise that the body of the method will do something that ultimately results in an integer value being calculated and returned as the method's result. You might like to think of a method call as being a form of question to an object and the return value from the method being the object's answer to that question. In this case, when the `getPrice` method is called on a ticket machine, the question is, What do tickets cost? A ticket machine does not need to perform any calculations to be able to answer that, because it keeps the answer in its `price` field. So the method answers by just returning the value of that variable. As we gradually develop more-complex classes, we shall inevitably encounter more-complex questions that require more work to supply their answers.

2.8 Accessor and mutator methods

Concept:

Accessor methods return information about the state of an object.

We often describe methods such as the two "get" methods of `TicketMachine` (`getPrice` and `getBalance`) as *accessor methods* (or just *accessors*). This is because they return information to the caller about the state of an object; they provide access to information about the object's state. An accessor usually contains a return statement in order to pass back that information.

There is often confusion about what "returning a value" actually means in practice. People often think it means that something is printed by the program. This is not the case at all—we shall see how printing is done when we look at the `printTicket` method. Rather, returning a value means that some information is passed internally between two different parts of the program. One part of the program has requested information from an object via a method call, and the return value is the way the object has of passing that information back to the caller.

Exercise 2.23 Compare the header and body of the `getBalance` method with the header and body of the `getPrice` method. What are the differences between them?

Exercise 2.24 If a call to `getPrice` can be characterized as "What do tickets cost?" how would you characterize a call to `getBalance`?

Exercise 2.25 If the name of `getBalance` is changed to `getAmount`, does the return statement in the body of the method also need to be changed for the code to compile? Try it out within BlueJ. What does this tell you about the name of an accessor method and the name of the field associated with it?

Exercise 2.26 Write an accessor method `getTotal` in the `TicketMachine` class. The new method should return the value of the `total` field.

Exercise 2.27 Try removing the return statement from the body of `getPrice`. What error message do you see now when you try compiling the class?

> **Exercise 2.28** Compare the method headers of `getPrice` and `printTicket` in Code 2.1. Apart from their names, what is the main difference between them?
>
> **Exercise 2.29** Do the `insertMoney` and `printTicket` methods have return statements? Why do you think this might be? Do you notice anything about their headers that might suggest why they do not require return statements?

Concept:

Mutator methods change the state of an object.

The `get` methods of a ticket machine perform similar tasks: returning the value of one of their object's fields. The remaining methods—`insertMoney` and `printTicket`—have a much more significant role, primarily because they *change* the value of one or more fields of a ticket-machine object each time they are called. We call methods that change the state of their object *mutator methods* (or just *mutators*).

In the same way as we think of a call to an accessor as a request for information (a question), we can think of a call to a mutator as a request for an object to change its state. The most basic form of mutator is one that takes a single parameter whose value is used to directly overwrite what is stored in one of an object's fields. In a direct complement to "get" methods, these are often called "set" methods, although the `TicketMachine` does not have any of those, at this stage.

One distinguishing effect of a mutator is that an object will often exhibit slightly different behavior before and after it is called. We can illustrate this with the following exercise.

> **Exercise 2.30** Create a ticket machine with a ticket price of your choosing. Before doing anything else, call the `getBalance` method on it. Now call the `insertMoney` method (Code 2.6) and give a non-zero positive amount of money as the actual parameter. Now call `getBalance` again. The two calls to `getBalance` should show different outputs, because the call to `insertMoney` had the effect of changing the machine's state via its `balance` field.

The header of `insertMoney` has a `void` return type and a single formal parameter, `amount`, of type `int`. A `void` return type means that the method does not return any value to its caller. This is significantly different from all other return types. Within BlueJ, the difference is most noticeable in that no return-value dialog is shown following a call to a `void`

Code 2.6
The `insertMoney` method

```
/**
 * Receive an amount of money in cents from a customer.
 */
public void insertMoney(int amount)
{
    balance = balance + amount;
}
```

method. Within the body of a `void` method, this difference is reflected in the fact that there is no return statement.[2]

In the body of `insertMoney`, there is a single statement that is another form of assignment statement. We always consider assignment statements by first examining the calculation on the right-hand side of the assignment symbol. Here, its effect is to calculate a value that is the sum of the number in the `amount` parameter and the number in the `balance` field. This combined value is then assigned to the `balance` field. So the effect is to increase the value in `balance` by the value in `amount`.[3]

Exercise 2.31 How can we tell from just its header that `setPrice` is a method and not a constructor?

```
public void setPrice(int cost)
```

Exercise 2.32 Complete the body of the `setPrice` method so that it assigns the value of its parameter to the `price` field.

Exercise 2.33 Complete the body of the following method, whose purpose is to add the value of its parameter to a field named `score`.

```
/**
 * Increase score by the given number of points.
 */
public void increase(int points)
{
    ...
}
```

Exercise 2.34 Is the increase method a mutator? If so, how could you demonstrate this?

Exercise 2.35 Complete the following method, whose purpose is to subtract the value of its parameter from a field named `price`.

```
/**
 * Reduce price by the given amount.
 */
public void discount(int amount)
{
    ...
}
```

---

[2] In fact, Java does allow `void` methods to contain a special form of return statement in which there is no return value. This takes the form

```
return;
```

and simply causes the method to exit without executing any further code.

[3] Adding an amount to the value in a variable is so common that there is a special **compound assignment operator** to do this: +=. For instance:

```
balance += amount;
```

2.9 Printing from methods

Code 2.7 shows the most complex method of the class: printTicket. To help your understanding of the following discussion, make sure that you have called this method on a ticket machine. You should have seen something like the following printed in the BlueJ terminal window:

```
##################
# The BlueJ Line
# Ticket
# 500 cents.
##################
```

This is the longest method we have seen so far, so we shall break it down into more manageable pieces:

■ The header indicates that the method has a void return type and that it takes no parameters.

■ The body comprises eight statements plus associated comments.

■ The first six statements are responsible for printing what you see in the BlueJ terminal window: five lines of text and a sixth, blank line.

■ The seventh statement adds the balance inserted by the customer (through previous calls to insertMoney) to the running total of all money collected so far by the machine.

■ The eighth statement resets the balance to zero with a basic assignment statement, ready for the next customer.

Code 2.7
The printTicket method

```java
/**
 * Print a ticket and reduce the
 * current balance to zero.
 */
public void printTicket()
{
    // Simulate the printing of a ticket.
    System.out.println("##################");
    System.out.println("# The BlueJ Line");
    System.out.println("# Ticket");
    System.out.println("# " + price + " cents.");
    System.out.println("##################");
    System.out.println();

    // Update the total collected with the balance.
    total = total + balance;
    // Clear the balance.
    balance = 0;
}
```

By comparing the output that appears with the statements that produced it, it is easy to see that a statement such as

```
System.out.println("# The BlueJ Line");
```

literally prints the string that appears between the matching pair of double-quote characters. The basic form of a call to `println` is

```
System.out.println(something-we-want-to-print);
```

where *something-we-want-to-print* can be replaced by any arbitrary string, enclosed between a pair of double-quote characters. For instance, there is nothing significant in the "#" character that is in the string—it is simply one of the characters we wish to be printed.

All of the printing statements in the `printTicket` method are calls to the `println` method of the `System.out` object that is built into the Java language, and what appears between the round brackets is the parameter to each method call, as you might expect. However, in the fourth statement, the actual parameter to `println` is a little more complicated and requires some more explanation:

```
System.out.println("# " + price + " cents.");
```

What it does is print out the price of the ticket, with some extra characters on either side of the amount. The two "+" operators are being used to construct a single actual parameter, in the form of a string, from three separate components:

- the string literal: `"# "` (note the space character after the hash);
- the value of the `price` field (note that there are no quotes around the field name because we want the field's value, not its name);
- the string literal: `" cents."` (note the space character before the word `"cents"`).

When used between a string and anything else, "+" is a string-concatenation operator (i.e., it concatenates or joins strings together to create a new string) rather than an arithmetic-addition operator. So the numeric value of price is converted into a string and joined to its two surrounding strings.

Note that the final call to `println` contains no string parameter. This is allowed, and the result of calling it will be to leave a blank line between this output and any that follows after. You will easily see the blank line if you print a second ticket.

Exercise 2.36 Write down exactly what will be printed by the following statement:

```
System.out.println("My cat has green eyes.");
```

Exercise 2.37 Add a method called `prompt` to the `TicketMachine` class. This should have a `void` return type and take no parameters. The body of the method should print the following single line of output:

```
Please insert the correct amount of money.
```

Exercise 2.38 What do you think would be printed if you altered the fourth statement of `printTicket` so that `price` also has quotes around it, as follows?

```
System.out.println("# " + "price" + " cents.");
```

Exercise 2.39 What about the following version?

```
System.out.println("# price cents.");
```

Exercise 2.40 Could either of the previous two versions be used to show the price of tickets in different ticket machines? Explain your answer.

Exercise 2.41 Add a showPrice method to the TicketMachine class. This should have a void return type and take no parameters. The body of the method should print:

```
The price of a ticket is xyz cents.
```

where xyz should be replaced by the value held in the price field when the method is called.

Exercise 2.42 Create two ticket machines with differently priced tickets. Do calls to their showPrice methods show the same output, or different? How do you explain this effect?

2.10 Method summary

It is worth summarizing a few features of methods at this point, because methods are fundamental to the programs we will be writing and exploring in this book. They implement the core actions of every object.

A method with parameters will receive data passed to it from the method's caller and will then use that data to help it perform a particular task. However, not all methods take parameters; many simply use the data stored in the object's fields to carry out their task.

If a method has a non-void return type, it will return some data to the place it was called from—and that data will almost certainly be used in the caller for further calculations or program manipulations. Many methods, though, have a void return type and return nothing, but they still perform a useful task within the context of their object.

Accessor methods have non-void return types and return information about the object's state. Mutator methods modify an object's state. Mutators often take parameters whose values are used in the modification, although it is still possible to write a mutating method that does not take parameters.

2.11 Summary of the naïve ticket machine

We have now examined the internal structure of the naïve ticket machine class in some detail. We have seen that the class has a small outer layer that gives a name to the class, and a more substantial inner body containing fields, a constructor, and several methods. Fields are used to store data that enable objects to maintain a state that persists between method calls. Constructors are used to set up an initial state when an object is created. Having a proper initial state will enable an object to respond appropriately to method calls immediately following its creation. Methods implement the defined behavior of the class's objects. Accessor methods provide information about an object's state, and mutator methods change an object's state.

We have seen that constructors are distinguished from methods by having the same name as the class in which they are defined. Both constructors and methods may take parameters, but only methods may have a return type. Non-void return types allow us to pass a value out of a method to the place where the method was called from. A method with a non-void return type must have at least one return statement in its body; this will often be the final statement. Constructors never have a return type of any sort—not even void.

Before attempting these exercises, be sure that you have a good understanding of how ticket machines behave and how that behavior is implemented through the fields, constructor, and methods of the class.

Exercise 2.43 Modify the constructor of TicketMachine so that it no longer has a parameter. Instead, the price of tickets should be fixed at 1,000 cents. What effect does this have when you construct ticket-machine objects within BlueJ?

Exercise 2.44 Give the class two constructors. One should take a single parameter that specifies the price, and the other should take no parameter and set the price to be a default value of your choosing. Test your implementation by creating machines via the two different constructors.

Exercise 2.45 Implement a method, empty, that simulates the effect of removing all money from the machine. This method should have a void return type, and its body should simply set the total field to zero. Does this method need to take any parameters? Test your method by creating a machine, inserting some money, printing some tickets, checking the total, and then emptying the machine. Is the empty method a mutator or an accessor?

2.12 Reflecting on the design of the ticket machine

From our study of the internals of the TicketMachine class, you should have come to appreciate how inadequate it would be in the real world. It is deficient in several ways:

■ It contains no check that the customer has entered enough money to pay for a ticket.

■ It does not refund any money if the customer pays too much for a ticket.

■ It does not check to ensure that the customer inserts sensible amounts of money: experiment with what happens if a negative amount is entered, for instance.

■ It does not check that the ticket price passed to its constructor is sensible.

If we could remedy these problems, then we would have a much more functional piece of software that might serve as the basis for operating a real-world ticket machine.

In the next few sections, we shall examine the implementation of an improved ticket machine class that attempts to deal with some of the inadequacies of the naïve implementation. Open the *better-ticket-machine* project. As before, this project contains a single class: TicketMachine. Before looking at the internal details of the class, experiment with it by creating some instances and see whether you notice any differences in behavior between this version and the previous naïve version.

One specific difference is that the new version has an additional method, refundBalance. Take a look at what happens when you call it.

Code 2.8

A more sophisticated
TicketMachine

```java
/**
 * TicketMachine models a ticket machine that issues
 * flat-fare tickets.
 * The price of a ticket is specified via the constructor.
 * Instances will check to ensure that a user only enters
 * sensible amounts of money, and will only print a ticket
 * if enough money has been input.
 * @author David J. Barnes and Michael Kölling
 * @version 2011.07.31
 */
public class TicketMachine
{
    // The price of a ticket from this machine.
    private int price;
    // The amount of money entered by a customer so far.
    private int balance;
    // The total amount of money collected by this machine.
    private int total;

    /**
     * Create a machine that issues tickets of the given price.
     */
    public TicketMachine(int cost)
    {
        price = cost;
        balance = 0;
        total = 0;
    }

    /**
     * Return the price of a ticket.
     */
    public int getPrice()
    {
        return price;
    }

    /**
     * Return the amount of money already inserted for the
     * next ticket.
     */
    public int getBalance()
    {
        return balance;
    }
```

**Code 2.8
continued**

A more sophisticated
TicketMachine

```java
/**
 * Receive an amount of money in cents from a customer.
 * Check that the amount is sensible.
 */
public void insertMoney(int amount)
{
    if(amount > 0) {
        balance = balance + amount;
    }
    else {
        System.out.println("Use a positive amount rather than: " +
                            amount);
    }
}

/**
 * Print a ticket if enough money has been inserted, and
 * reduce the current balance by the ticket price. Print
 * an error message if more money is required.
 */
public void printTicket()
{
    if(balance >= price) {
        // Simulate the printing of a ticket.
        System.out.println("##################");
        System.out.println("# The BlueJ Line");
        System.out.println("# Ticket");
        System.out.println("# " + price + " cents.");
        System.out.println("##################");
        System.out.println();

        // Update the total collected with the price.
        total = total + price;
        // Reduce the balance by the price.
        balance = balance - price;
    }
    else {
        System.out.println("You must insert at least: " +
                            (price - balance) + " cents.");
    }
}

/**
 * Return the money in the balance.
 * The balance is cleared.
 */
```

Code 2.8
continued

A more sophisticated
TicketMachine

```
public int refundBalance()
{
    int amountToRefund;
    amountToRefund = balance;
    balance = 0;
    return amountToRefund;
}
}
```

2.13 # Making choices: the conditional statement

Code 2.8 shows the internal details of the better ticket machine's class definition. Much of this definition will already be familiar to you from our discussion of the naïve ticket machine. For instance, the outer wrapping that names the class is the same, because we have chosen to give this class the same name. In addition, it contains the same three fields to maintain object state, and these have been declared in the same way. The constructor and the two get methods are also the same as before.

The first significant change can be seen in the insertMoney method. We recognized that the main problem with the naïve ticket machine was its failure to check certain conditions. One of those missing checks was on the amount of money inserted by a customer, as it was possible for a negative amount of money to be inserted. We have remedied that failing by making use of a *conditional statement* to check that the amount inserted has a value greater than zero:

```
if(amount > 0) {
    balance = balance + amount;
}
else {
    System.out.println("Use a positive amount rather than: " +
                                amount);
}
```

Concept:

A **conditional statement** takes one of two possible actions based upon the result of a test.

Conditional statements are also known as *if statements*, from the keyword used in most programming languages to introduce them. A conditional statement allows us to take one of two possible actions based upon the result of a check or test. If the test is true, then we do one thing; otherwise, we do something different. This kind of either/or decision should be familiar from situations in everyday life: for instance, if I have enough money left, then I shall go out for a meal; otherwise, I shall stay home and watch a movie. A conditional statement has the general form described in the following *pseudo-code*:

```
if(perform some test that gives a true or false result) {
    Do the statements here if the test gave a true result
}
else {
    Do the statements here if the test gave a false result
}
```

Certain parts of this pseudo-code are proper bits of Java, and those will appear in almost all conditional statements – the keywords `if` and `else`, the round brackets around the test, and the curly brackets marking the two blocks – while the other three italicized parts will be fleshed out differently for each particular situation being coded.

It is important to appreciate that only one of the two blocks of statements following the test will ever be performed following the evaluation of the test. So, in the example from the `insertMoney` method, following the test of an inserted amount we shall only either add the amount to the balance or print the error message. The test uses the *greater-than operator*, "`>`", to compare the value in `amount` against zero. If the value is greater than zero, then it is added to the balance. If it is not greater than zero, then an error message is printed. By using a conditional statement, we have, in effect, protected the change to `balance` in the case where the parameter does not represent a valid amount. Details of other Java operators can be found in Appendix C. The obvious ones to mention at this point are "`<`" (less-than), "`<=`" (less-than or equal-to), and "`>=`" (greater-than or equal-to). All are used to compare two numeric values, as in the `printTicket` method.

The test used in a conditional statement is an example of a *boolean expression*. Earlier in this chapter, we introduced arithmetic expressions that produced numerical results. A boolean expression has only two possible values (`true` or `false`): the value of `amount` is either greater than zero (`true`) or it is not greater (`false`). A conditional statement makes use of those two possible values to choose between two different actions.

> **Concept:**
>
> **Boolean expressions** have only two possible values: true and false. They are commonly found controlling the choice between the two paths through a conditional statement.

Exercise 2.46 Check that the behavior we have discussed here is accurate by creating a `TicketMachine` instance and calling `insertMoney` with various actual parameter values. Check the balance both before and after calling `insertMoney`. Does the balance ever change in the cases when an error message is printed? Try to predict what will happen if you enter the value zero as the parameter, and then see if you are right.

Exercise 2.47 Predict what you think will happen if you change the test in `insertMoney` to use the *greater-than or equal-to operator*:

```
if(amount >= 0)
```

Check your predictions by running some tests. What difference does it make to the behavior of the method?

Exercise 2.48 Rewrite the if-else statement so that the error message is printed if the boolean expression is true but the balance is increased if the expression is false. You will obviously have to rewrite the condition to make things happen this way around.

Exercise 2.49 In the *figures* project we looked at in Chapter 1 we used a `boolean` field to control a feature of the circle objects. What was that feature? Was it well suited to being controlled by a type with only two different values?

2.14 A further conditional-statement example

The `printTicket` method contains a further example of a conditional statement. Here it is in outline:

```java
if(balance >= price) {

    Printing details omitted.

    // Update the total collected with the price.
    total = total + price;
    // Reduce the balance by the price.
    balance = balance - price;

}
else {
    System.out.println("You must insert at least: " +
                       (price - balance) + " more cents.");
}
```

We wish to remedy the fact that the naïve version makes no check that a customer has inserted enough money to be issued a ticket. This version checks that the value in the `balance` field is at least as large as the value in the `price` field. If it is, then it is okay to print a ticket. If it is not, then we print an error message instead.

The printing of the error message follows exactly the same pattern as we saw for printing the price of tickets in the `printTicket` method; it is just a little more verbose.

```java
System.out.println("You must insert at least: " +
                   (price - balance) + " more cents.");
```

The single actual parameter to the `println` method consists of a concatenation of three elements: two string literals on either side of a numeric value. In this case, the numeric value is a subtraction that has been placed in parentheses to indicate that it is the resulting value we wish to concatenate with the two strings.

Exercise 2.50 In this version of `printTicket`, we also do something slightly different with the `total` and `balance` fields. Compare the implementation of the method in Code 2.1 with that in Code 2.8 to see whether you can tell what those differences are. Then check your understanding by experimenting within BlueJ.

Exercise 2.51 Is it possible to remove the else part of the if statement in the `printTicket` method (i.e., remove the word `else` and the block attached to it)? Try doing this and seeing if the code still compiles. What happens now if you try to print a ticket without inserting any money?

The `printTicket` method reduces the value of `balance` by the value of `price`. As a consequence, if a customer inserts more money than the price of the ticket, then some money will be left in the balance that could be used toward the price of a second ticket. Alternatively, the customer could ask to be refunded the remaining balance, and that is what the `refundBalance` method does, as we shall see in the next section.

2.15 Scope highlighting

You will have noticed by now that the BlueJ editor displays source code with some additional decoration: colored boxes around some elements that are not reproduced in the code samples shown in this book (Figure 2.5).

Figure 2.5

Scope highlighting in the BlueJ editor

These colored annotations are known as *scope highlighting*, and they help clarify logical units of your program. A *scope* (also called a *block*) is a unit of code usually indicated by a pair of curly brackets. The whole body of a class is a scope, as is the body of each method and the *if* and *else* parts of an if statement.

As you can see, scopes are often nested: the if statement is inside a method, which is inside a class. BlueJ helps by distinguishing different kinds of scopes with different colors.

One of the most common errors in the code of beginning programmers is getting the curly brackets wrong—either by having them in the wrong place or by having a bracket missing altogether. Two things can greatly help in avoiding this kind of error:

■ Pay attention to proper indentation of your code. Every time a new scope starts (after an open curly bracket), indent the following code one level more. Closing the scope brings the indentation back. If your indentation is completely out, use BlueJ's "Auto-layout" function (find it in the editor menu!) to fix it.

■ Pay attention to the scope highlighting. You will quickly get used to the way well-structured code looks. Try removing a curly bracket in the editor or adding one at an arbitrary location, and observe how the coloring changes. Get used to recognizing when scopes look wrong.

Exercise 2.52 After a ticket has been printed, could the value in the `balance` field ever be set to a negative value by subtracting `price` from it? Justify your answer.

Exercise 2.53 So far, we have introduced you to two arithmetic operators, + and -, that can be used in **arithmetic expressions** in Java. Take a look at Appendix C to find out what other operators are available.

Exercise 2.54 Write an assignment statement that will store the result of multiplying two variables, `price` and `discount`, into a third variable, `saving`.

Exercise 2.55 Write an assignment statement that will divide the value in `total` by the value in `count` and store the result in `mean`.

Exercise 2.56 Write an if statement that will compare the value in `price` against the value in `budget`. If `price` is greater than `budget`, then print the message "Too expensive"; otherwise print the message "Just right".

Exercise 2.57 Modify your answer to the previous exercise so that the message includes the value of your budget if the price is too high.

2.16 Local variables

So far, we have met two different sorts of variables: fields (instance variables) and parameters. We are now going to introduce a third kind. All have in common that they store data, but each sort of variable has a particular role to play.

> **Concept:**
>
> A **local variable** is a variable declared and used within a single method. Its scope and lifetime are limited to that of the method.

Section 2.6 noted that a method body (or, in general, a *block*) can contain both declarations and statements. To this point, none of the methods we have looked at contain any declarations. The `refundBalance` method contains three statements and a single declaration. The declaration introduces a new kind of variable:

```
public int refundBalance()
{
    int amountToRefund;
    amountToRefund = balance;
    balance = 0;
    return amountToRefund;
}
```

What sort of variable is `amountToRefund`? We know that it is not a field, because fields are defined outside methods. It is also not a parameter, as those are always defined in the method header. The `amountToRefund` variable is what is known as a *local variable,* because it is defined *inside* a method body.

Local variable declarations look similar to field declarations, but they never have `private` or `public` as part of them. Constructors can also have local variables. Like formal parameters, local variables have a scope that is limited to the statements of the method to which they belong. Their lifetime is the time of the method execution: they are created when a method is called and destroyed when a method finishes.

You might wonder why there is a need for local variables if we have fields. Local variables are primarily used as temporary storage, to help a single method complete its task; we think of them as data storage for a single method. In contrast, fields are used to store data that persists through the life of a whole object. The data stored in fields is accessible to all of the object's methods. We try to avoid declaring as fields variables that really only have a local (method-level) usage, whose values don't have to be retained beyond a single method call. So even if two or more methods in the same class used local variables for a similar purpose, it would not be appropriate to define them as fields if their values don't need to persist beyond the end of the methods.

In the `refundBalance` method, `amountToRefund` is used briefly to hold the value of the `balance` immediately prior to the latter being set to zero. The method then returns the remembered value of the balance. The following exercises will help to illustrate why a local variable is needed here, as we try to write the `refundBalance` method without one.

Exercise 2.58 Why does the following version of `refundBalance` not give the same results as the original?

```
public int refundBalance()
{
    balance = 0;
    return balance;
}
```

What tests can you run to demonstrate that it does not?

Exercise 2.59 What happens if you try to compile the `TicketMachine` class with the following version of `refundBalance`?

```
public int refundBalance()
{
    return balance;
    balance = 0;
}
```

What do you know about return statements that helps to explain why this version does not compile?

Exercise 2.60 What is wrong with the following version of the constructor of `TicketMachine`?

```
public TicketMachine(int cost)
{
    int price = cost;
    balance = 0;
    total = 0;
}
```

Try out this version in the *better-ticket-machine* project. Does this version compile? Create an object and then inspect its fields. Do you notice something wrong about the value of the `price` field in the inspector with this version? Can you explain why this is?

It is quite common to initialize local variables within their declaration. So we could abbreviate the first two statements of `refundBalance` as

```
int amountToRefund = balance;
```

but it is still important to keep in mind that there are two steps going on here: declaring the variable `amountToRefund` and giving it an initial value.

Pitfall A local variable of the same name as a field will prevent the field being accessed from within a constructor or method. See Section 3.12.2 for a way around this when necessary.

2.17 Fields, parameters, and local variables

With the introduction of `amountToRefund` in the `refundBalance` method, we have now seen three different kinds of variables: fields, formal parameters, and local variables. It is important to understand the similarities and differences between these three kinds. Here is a summary of their features:

■ All three kinds of variables are able to store a value that is appropriate to their defined types. For instance, a defined type of `int` allows a variable to store an integer value.

■ Fields are defined outside constructors and methods.

■ Fields are used to store data that persist throughout the life of an object. As such, they maintain the current state of an object. They have a lifetime that lasts as long as their object lasts.

■ Fields have class scope: their accessibility extends throughout the whole class, so they can be used within any of the constructors or methods of the class in which they are defined.

■ As long as they are defined as `private`, fields cannot be accessed from anywhere outside their defining class.

■ Formal parameters and local variables persist only for the period that a constructor or method executes. Their lifetime is only as long as a single call, so their values are lost between calls. As such, they act as temporary rather than permanent storage locations.

- Formal parameters are defined in the header of a constructor or method. They receive their values from outside, being initialized by the actual parameter values that form part of the constructor or method call.

- Formal parameters have a scope that is limited to their defining constructor or method.

- Local variables are defined inside the body of a constructor or method. They can be initialized and used only within the body of their defining constructor or method. Local variables must be initialized before they are used in an expression—they are not given a default value.

- Local variables have a scope that is limited to the block in which they are defined. They are not accessible from anywhere outside that block.

Exercise 2.61 Add a new method, `emptyMachine`, that is designed to simulate emptying the machine of money. It should reset `total` to be zero but also return the value that was stored in `total` before it was reset.

Exercise 2.62 Rewrite the `printTicket` method so that it declares a local variable, `amountLeftToPay`. This should then be initialized to contain the difference between `price` and `balance`. Rewrite the test in the conditional statement to check the value of `amountLeftToPay`. If its value is less than or equal to zero, a ticket should be printed; otherwise, an error message should be printed stating the amount left to pay. Test your version to ensure that it behaves in exactly the same way as the original version. Make sure that you call the method more than once, when the machine is in different states, so that both parts of the conditional statement will be executed on separate occasions.

Exercise 2.63 *Challenge exercise* Suppose we wished a single `TicketMachine` object to be able to issue tickets of different prices. For instance, users might press a button on the physical machine to select a discounted ticket price. What further methods and/or fields would need to be added to `TicketMachine` to allow this kind of functionality? Do you think that many of the existing methods would need to be changed as well?

Save the *better-ticket-machine* project under a new name, and implement your changes in the new project.

2.18 Summary of the better ticket machine

In developing a better version of the `TicketMachine` class, we have been able to address the major inadequacies of the naïve version. In doing so, we have introduced two new language constructs: the conditional statement and local variables.

- A conditional statement gives us a means to perform a test and then, on the basis of the result of that test, perform one or the other of two distinct actions.

- Local variables allow us to calculate and store temporary values within a constructor or method. They contribute to the behavior that their defining method implements, but their values are lost once that constructor or method finishes its execution.

You can find more details of conditional statements and the form their tests can take in Appendix D.

2.19 Self-review exercises

This chapter has covered a lot of new ground, and we have introduced a lot of new concepts. We will be building on these in future chapters, so it is important that you are comfortable with them. Try the following pencil-and-paper exercises as a way of checking that you are becoming used to the terminology that we have introduced in this chapter. Don't be put off by the fact that we suggest that you do these on paper rather than within BlueJ. It will be good practice to try things out without a compiler.

Exercise 2.64 List the name and return type of this method:

```
public String getCode()
{
    return code;
}
```

Exercise 2.65 List the name of this method and the name and type of its parameter:

```
public void setCredits(int creditValue)
{
    credits = creditValue;
}
```

Exercise 2.66 Write out the outer wrapping of a class called `Person`. Remember to include the curly brackets that mark the start and end of the class body, but otherwise leave the body empty.

Exercise 2.67 Write out definitions for the following fields:

■ a field called `name` of type `String`
■ a field of type `int` called `age`
■ a field of type `String` called `code`
■ a field called `credits` of type `int`

Exercise 2.68 Write out a constructor for a class called `Module`. The constructor should take a single parameter of type `String` called `moduleCode`. The body of the constructor should assign the value of its parameter to a field called `code`. You don't have to include the definition for `code`, just the text of the constructor.

Exercise 2.69 Write out a constructor for a class called `Person`. The constructor should take two parameters. The first is of type `String` and is called `myName`. The second is of type `int` and is called `myAge`. The first parameter should be used to set the value of a field called `name`, and the second should set a field called `age`. You don't have to include the definitions for the fields, just the text of the constructor.

Exercise 2.70 Correct the error in this method:

```
public void getAge()
{
    return age;
}
```

Exercise 2.71 Write an accessor method called `getName` that returns the value of a field called `name`, whose type is `String`.

Exercise 2.72 Write a mutator method called `setAge` that takes a single parameter of type `int` and sets the value of a field called `age`.

Exercise 2.73 Write a method called `printDetails` for a class that has a field of type `String` called `name`. The `printDetails` method should print out a string of the form "The name of this person is", followed by the value of the `name` field. For instance, if the value of the `name` field is "Helen", then `printDetails` would print:

```
The name of this person is Helen
```

If you have managed to complete most or all of these exercises, then you might like to try creating a new project in BlueJ and making up your own class definition for a `Person`. The class could have fields to record the name and age of a person, for instance. If you were unsure how to complete any of the previous exercises, look back over earlier sections in this chapter and the source code of `TicketMachine` to revise what you were unclear about. In the next section, we provide some further review material.

2.20 Reviewing a familiar example

By this point in the chapter, you have met a lot of new concepts. To help reinforce them, we shall now revisit a few in a different but familiar context. Along the way, though, watch out for one or two further new concepts that we will then cover in more detail in later chapters!

Open the *lab-classes* project that we introduced in Chapter 1, and then examine the `Student` class in the editor (Code 2.9).

Code 2.9
The `Student` class

```
/**
 * The Student class represents a student in a
 * student administration system.
 * It holds the student details relevant in our context.
 *
 * @author Michael Kölling and David Barnes
 * @version 2011.07.31
 */
public class Student
{
    // the student's full name
```

Code 2.9
continued
The Student class

```java
private String name;
// the student ID
private String id;
// the amount of credits for study taken so far
private int credits;

/**
 * Create a new student with a given name and ID number.
 */
public Student(String fullName, String studentID)
{
    name = fullName;
    id = studentID;
    credits = 0;
}

/**
 * Return the full name of this student.
 */
public String getName()
{
    return name;
}

/**
 * Set a new name for this student.
 */
public void changeName(String newName)
{
    name = newName;
}

/**
 * Return the student ID of this student.
 */
public String getStudentID()
{
    return id;
}

/**
 * Add some credit points to the student's
 * accumulated credits.
 */
public void addCredits(int newCreditPoints)
{
    credits += newCreditPoints;
}
```

**Code 2.9
continued**
The Student class

```java
/**
 * Return the number of credit points this student
 * has accumulated.
 */
public int getCredits()
{
    return credits;
}

/**
 * Return the login name of this student.
 * The login name is a combination
 * of the first four characters of the
 * student's name and the first three
 * characters of the student's ID number.
 */
public String getLoginName()
{
    return name.substring(0,4) +
            id.substring(0,3);
}

/**
 * Print the student's name and ID number
 * to the output terminal.
 */
public void print()
{
    System.out.println(name + ", student ID: " + id +
                        ", credits: " + credits);
}
}
```

In this small example, the pieces of information we wish to store for a student are their name, their student ID, and the number of course credits they have obtained so far. All of this information is persistent during their time as a student, even if some of it changes during that time (the number of credits). We want to store this information in fields, therefore, to represent each student's state.

The class contains three fields: name, id, and credits. Each of these is initialized in the single constructor. The initial values of the first two are set from parameter values passed into the constructor. Each of the fields has an associated get accessor method, but only name and credits have associated mutator methods. This means that the value of an id field remains fixed once the object has been constructed. If a field's value cannot be changed once initialized, we say that it is *immutable*. Sometimes we make the complete state of an object immutable once it has been constructed; the String class is an important example of this.

2.21 Calling methods

The `getLoginName` method illustrates a new feature that is worth exploring:

```
public String getLoginName()
{
    return name.substring(0,4) +
            id.substring(0,3);
}
```

We are seeing two things in action here:

■ Calling a method on another object, where the method returns a result.

■ Using the value returned as a result as part of an expression.

Both `name` and `id` are `String` objects, and the `String` class has a method, `substring`, with the following header:

```
/**
 * Return a new string containing the characters from
 * beginIndex to (endIndex-1) from this string.
 */
public String substring(int beginIndex, int endIndex)
```

An index value of zero represents the first character of a string, so `getLoginName` takes the first four characters of the `name` string and the first three characters of the `id` string and then concatenates them together to form a new string. This new string is returned as the method's result. For instance, if `name` is the string `"Leonardo da Vinci"` and id is the string `"468366"`, then the string `"Leon468"` would be returned by this method.

We will learn more about method calling between objects in Chapter 3.

Exercise 2.74 Draw a picture of the form shown in Figure 2.3, representing the initial state of a `Student` object following its construction, with the following actual parameter values:

```
new Student("Benjamin Jonson", "738321")
```

Exercise 2.75 What would be returned by `getLoginName` for a student with `name` `"Henry Moore"` and `id` `"557214"`?

Exercise 2.76 Create a `Student` with name `"djb"` and id `"859012"`. What happens when `getLoginName` is called on this student? Why do you think this is?

Exercise 2.77 The `String` class defines a `length` accessor method with the following header:

```
/**
 * Return the number of characters in this string.
 */
public int length()
```

so the following is an example of its use with the `String` variable `fullName`:

```
fullName.length()
```

Add conditional statements to the constructor of `Student` to print an error message if either the length of the `fullName` parameter is less than four characters or the length of the `studentId` parameter is less than three characters. However, the constructor should still use those parameters to set the `name` and `id` fields, even if the error message is printed. *Hint:* Use if statements of the following form (that is, having no `else` part) to print the error messages.

```
if(perform a test on one of the parameters) {
    Print an error message if the test gave a true result
}
```

See Appendix D for further details of the different types of if statements, if necessary.

Exercise 2.78 *Challenge exercise* Modify the `getLoginName` method of `Student` so that it always generates a login name, even if either the `name` or the `id` field is not strictly long enough. For strings shorter than the required length, use the whole string.

2.22 Experimenting with expressions: the Code Pad

In the previous sections, we have seen various expressions to achieve various computations, such as the `total + price` calculation in the ticket machine and the `name.substring(0,4)` expression in the `Student` class.

In the remainder of this book, we shall encounter many more such operations, sometimes written with operator symbols (such as "+") and sometimes written as method calls (such as `substring`). When we encounter new operators and methods, it often helps to try out with different examples what they do.

The Code Pad, which we have briefly used in Chapter 1, can help us experiment with Java expressions (Figure 2.6). Here, we can type in expressions, which will then be immediately evaluated and the results displayed. This is very helpful for trying out new operators and methods.

Figure 2.6

The BlueJ Code Pad

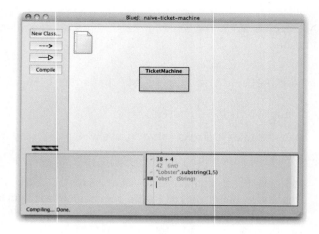

Exercise 2.79 Consider the following expressions. Try to predict their results, and then type them in the Code Pad to check your answers.

```
99 + 3
"cat" + "fish"
"cat" + 9
9 + 3 + "cat"
"cat" + 3 + 9
"catfish".substring(3,4)
"catfish".substring(3,8)
```

Did you learn anything you did not expect from the exercise? If so, what was it?

When the result of an expression in the Code Pad is an object (such as a String), it will be marked with a small red object symbol. You can double-click this symbol to inspect it or drag it onto the object bench for further use. You can also declare variables and write complete statements in the Code Pad.

Whenever you encounter new operators and method calls, it is a good idea to try them out here to get a feel for their behavior.

You can also explore the use of variables in the Code Pad. Try the following:

```
sum = 99 + 3;
```

You will see the following error message:

```
Error: cannot find symbol - variable sum
```

This is because Java requires that every variable (sum, in this case) be given a type before it can be used. Recall that every time a field, parameter, or local variable has been introduced for the first time in the source, it has had a type name in front of it, such as `int` or `String`. In light of this, now try the following in the Code Pad:

```
int sum = 0;
sum = 99 + 3;
```

This time there is no complaint, because `sum` has been introduced with a type and can be used without repeating the type thereafter. If you then type

```
sum
```

on a line by itself (with no semicolon), you will see the value it currently stores.

Now try this in the Code Pad:

```
String swimmer = "cat" + "fish";
swimmer
```

One again, we have given an appropriate type to the variable `swimmer`, allowing us to make an assignment to it and find out what it stores. This time we chose to set it to the value we wanted at the same time as declaring it.

What would you expect to see after the following?

```
String fish = swimmer;
fish
```

Try it out. What do you think has happened in the assignment?

Exercise 2.80 Open the Code Pad in the *better-ticket-machine* project. Type the following in the Code Pad:

```
TicketMachine t1 = new TicketMachine(1000);
t1.getBalance()
t1.insertMoney(500);
t1.getBalance()
```

Take care to type these lines exactly as they appear here; pay particular attention to whether or not there is a semicolon at the end of the line. Note what the calls to `getBalance` return in each case.

Exercise 2.81 Now add the following in the Code Pad:

```
TicketMachine t2 = t1;
```

What would you expect a call to `t2.getBalance()` to return? Try it out.

Exercise 2.82 Add the following:

```
t1.insertMoney(500);
```

What would you expect the following to return? Think carefully about this before you try it, and be sure to use the `t2` variable this time.

```
t2.getBalance()
```

Did you get the answer you expected? Can you find a connection between the variables `t1` and `t2` that would explain what is happening?

2.23 Summary

In this chapter, we have covered the basics of how to create a class definition. Classes contain fields, constructors, and methods that define the state and behavior of objects. Within the body of a constructor or method, a sequence of statements implements that part of its behavior. Local variables can be used as temporary data storage to assist with that. We have covered assignment statements and conditional statements and will be adding further types of statements in later chapters.

Terms introduced in this chapter

field, instance variable, constructor, method, method header, method body, actual parameter, formal parameter, accessor, mutator, declaration, initialization, block, statement, assignment statement, conditional statement, return statement, return type, comment, expression, operator, variable, local variable, scope, lifetime

Concept summary

- **object creation** Some objects cannot be constructed unless extra information is provided.
- **field** Fields store data for an object to use. Fields are also known as instance variables.
- **comment** Comments are inserted into the source code of a class to provide explanations to human readers. They have no effect on the functionality of the class.
- **constructor** Constructors allow each object to be set up properly when it is first created.
- **scope** The scope of a variable defines the section of source code from which the variable can be accessed.
- **lifetime** The lifetime of a variable describes how long the variable continues to exist before it is destroyed.
- **assignment** Assignment statements store the value represented by the right-hand side of the statement in the variable named on the left.
- **accessor method** Accessor methods return information about the state of an object.
- **mutator method** Mutator methods change the state of an object.
- **println** The method `System.out.println` prints its parameter to the text terminal.

- **conditional** A conditional statement takes one of two possible actions based upon the result of a test.

- **boolean expression** Boolean expressions have only two possible values: true and false. They are commonly found controlling the choice between the two paths through a conditional statement.

- **local variable** A local variable is a variable declared and used within a single method. Its scope and lifetime are limited to that of the method.

The following exercises are designed to help you experiment with the concepts of Java that we have discussed in this chapter. You will create your own classes that contain elements such as fields, constructors, methods, assignment statements, and conditional statements.

Exercise 2.83 Below is the outline for a `Book` class, which can be found in the *book-exercise* project. The outline already defines two fields and a constructor to initialize the fields. In this and the next few exercises, you will add features to the class outline.

Add two accessor methods to the class—`getAuthor` and `getTitle`—that return the `author` and `title` fields as their respective results. Test your class by creating some instances and calling the methods.

```java
/**
 * A class that maintains information on a book.
 * This might form part of a larger application such
 * as a library system, for instance.
 *
 * @author (Insert your name here.)
 * @version (Insert today's date here.)
 */
public class Book
{
    // The fields.
    private String author;
    private String title;

    /**
     * Set the author and title fields when this object
     * is constructed.
     */
    public Book(String bookAuthor, String bookTitle)
    {
        author = bookAuthor;
        title = bookTitle;
    }

    // Add the methods here...
}
```

Exercise 2.84 Add two methods, `printAuthor` and `printTitle`, to the outline `Book` class. These should print the `author` and `title` fields, respectively, to the terminal window.

Exercise 2.85 Add a field, `pages`, to the `Book` class to store the number of pages. This should be of type `int`, and its initial value should be passed to the single constructor, along with the `author` and `title` strings. Include an appropriate `getPages` accessor method for this field.

Exercise 2.X Are the `Book` objects you have implemented immutable? Justify your answer.

Exercise 2.86 Add a method, `printDetails`, to the `Book` class. This should print details of the author, title, and pages to the terminal window. It is your choice how the details are formatted. For instance, all three items could be printed on a single line, or each could be printed on a separate line. You might also choose to include some explanatory text to help a user work out which is the author and which is the title, for example

    Title: Robinson Crusoe, Author: Daniel Defoe, Pages: 232

Exercise 2.87 Add a further field, `refNumber`, to the `Book` class. This field can store a reference number for a library, for example. It should be of type `String` and initialized to the zero length string (`""`) in the constructor, as its initial value is not passed in a parameter to the constructor. Instead, define a mutator for it with the following header:

    public void setRefNumber(String ref)

The body of this method should assign the value of the parameter to the `refNumber` field. Add a corresponding `getRefNumber` accessor to help you check that the mutator works correctly.

Exercise 2.88 Modify your `printDetails` method to include printing the reference number. However, the method should print the reference number only if it has been set—that is, the `refNumber` string has a non-zero length. If it has not been set, then print the string `"ZZZ"` instead. *Hint:* Use a conditional statement whose test calls the `length` method on the `refNumber` string.

Exercise 2.89 Modify your `setRefNumber` mutator so that it sets the `refNumber` field only if the parameter is a string of at least three characters. If it is less than three, then print an error message and leave the field unchanged.

Exercise 2.90 Add a further integer field, `borrowed`, to the `Book` class. This keeps a count of the number of times a book has been borrowed. Add a mutator, `borrow`, to the class. This should update the field by 1 each time it is called. Include an accessor, `getBorrowed`, that returns the value of this new field as its result. Modify `printDetails` so that it includes the value of this field with an explanatory piece of text.

Exercise 2.91 Add a further `boolean` field, `courseText`, to the `Book` class. This records whether or not a book is being used as a text book on a course. The field should be set through a parameter to the constructor and the field is immutable. Provide an accessor method for it called isCourseText.

Exercise 2.92 *Challenge exercise* Create a new project, *heater-exercise*, within BlueJ. Edit the details in the project description—the text note you see in the diagram. Create a class, Heater, that contains a single field, temperature whose type is *double-precision floating point*—see Appendix B, section B.1, for the Java type name that corresponds to this description. Define a constructor that takes no parameters. The temperature field should be set to the value 15.0 in the constructor. Define the mutators warmer and cooler, whose effect is to increase or decrease the value of temperature by 5.0° respectively. Define an accessor method to return the value of temperature.

Exercise 2.93 *Challenge exercise* Modify your Heater class to define three new *double-precision floating point* fields: min, max, and increment. The values of min and max should be set by parameters passed to the constructor. The value of increment should be set to 5.0 in the constructor. Modify the definitions of warmer and cooler so that they use the value of increment rather than an explicit value of 5.0. Before proceeding further with this exercise, check that everything works as before.

Now modify the warmer method so that it will not allow the temperature to be set to a value greater than max. Similarly modify cooler so that it will not allow temperature to be set to a value less than min. Check that the class works properly. Now add a method, setIncrement, that takes a single parameter of the appropriate type and uses it to set the value of increment. Once again, test that the class works as you would expect it to by creating some Heater objects within BlueJ. Do things still work as expected if a negative value is passed to the setIncrement method? Add a check to this method to prevent a negative value from being assigned to increment.

Main concepts discussed in this chapter:

- abstraction
- modularization
- object creation
- object diagrams
- method calls
- debuggers

Java constructs discussed in this chapter:

class types, logic operators (&&, ||), string concatenation, modulo operator (%), object construction (`new`), method calls (dot notation), `this`

In the previous chapters, we have examined what objects are and how they are implemented. In particular, we discussed fields, constructors, and methods when we looked at class definitions.

We shall now go one step further. To construct interesting applications, it is not enough to build individual working objects. Instead, objects must be combined so that they cooperate to perform a common task. In this chapter, we shall build a small application from three objects and arrange for methods to call other methods to achieve their goal.

3.1 The clock example

The project we shall use to discuss interaction of objects is a display for a digital clock. The display shows hours and minutes, separated by a colon (Figure 3.1). For this exercise, we shall first build a clock with a European-style 24-hour display. Thus, the display shows the time from 00:00 (midnight) to 23:59 (one minute before midnight). It turns out on closer inspection that building a 12-hour clock is slightly more difficult than it is for a 24-hour clock; we shall leave this to the end of this chapter.

Figure 3.1
A display of a digital clock

11:03

Abstraction and modularization

A first idea might be to implement the whole clock display in a single class. That is, after all, what we have seen so far: how to build classes to do a job.

However, here we shall approach this problem slightly differently. We will see whether we can identify subcomponents in the problem that we can turn into separate classes. The reason is *complexity*. As we progress in this book, the examples we use and the programs we build will get more and more complex. Trivial tasks such as the ticket machine can be solved as a single problem. You can look at the complete task and devise a solution using a single class. For more complex problems, that is too simplistic. As a problem grows larger, it becomes increasingly difficult to keep track of all details at the same time.

> **Concept:**
>
> **Abstraction** is the ability to ignore details of parts, to focus attention on a higher level of a problem.

The solution we use to deal with the complexity problem is *abstraction*. We divide the problem into sub-problems, then again into sub-sub-problems, and so on, until the individual problems are small enough to be easy to deal with. Once we solve one of the sub-problems, we do not think about the details of that part any more, but treat the solution as a single building block for our next problem. This technique is sometimes referred to as *divide and conquer*.

Let us discuss this with an example. Imagine engineers in a car company designing a new car. They may think about the parts of the car, such as the shape of the outer body, the size and location of the engine, the number and size of the seats in the passenger area, the exact spacing of the wheels, and so on. Another engineer, on the other hand, whose job is to design the engine (well, that's a whole team of engineers in reality, but we simplify this a bit here for the sake of the example), thinks of the many parts of an engine: the cylinders, the injection mechanism, the carburetor, the electronics, etc. She will think of the engine not as a single entity, but as a complex work of many parts. One of these parts may be a spark plug.

Then there is an engineer (maybe in a different company) who designs the spark plugs. He will think of the spark plug as a complex artifact of many parts. He might have done complex studies to determine exactly what kind of metal to use for the contacts or what kind of material and production process to use for the insulation.

The same is true for many other parts. A designer at the highest level will regard a wheel as a single part. Another engineer much further down the chain may spend her days thinking about the chemical composition necessary to produce the right materials to make the tires. For the tire engineer, the tire is a complex thing. The car company will just buy the tire from the tire company and then view it as a single entity. This is abstraction.

The engineer in the car company *abstracts from* the details of the tire manufacture to be able to concentrate on the details of the construction of, say, the wheel. The designer designing the body shape of the car abstracts from the technical details of the wheels and the engine to concentrate on the design of the body (he will just be interested in the size of the engine and the wheels).

> **Concept:**
>
> **Modularization** is the process of dividing a whole into well-defined parts that can be built and examined separately and that interact in well-defined ways.

The same is true for every other component. While someone might be concerned with designing the interior passenger space, someone else may work on developing the fabric that will eventually be used to cover the seats.

The point is, if viewed in enough detail, a car consists of so many parts that it is impossible for a single person to know every detail about every part at the same time. If that were necessary, no car could ever be built.

The reason why cars are successfully built is that the engineers use *modularization* and abstraction. They divide the car into independent modules (wheel, engine, gear box, seat, steering wheel, etc.) and get separate people to work on separate modules independently. When a module is built, they use abstraction. They view that module as a single component that is used to build more-complex components.

Modularization and abstraction thus complement each other. Modularization is the process of dividing large things (problems) into smaller parts, while abstraction is the ability to ignore details to focus on the bigger picture.

3.3 Abstraction in software

The same principles of modularization and abstraction discussed in the previous section are used in software development. To help us maintain an overview in complex programs, we try to identify subcomponents that we can program as independent entities. Then we try to use those subcomponents as if they were simple parts, without being concerned about their inner complexities.

In object-oriented programming, these components and subcomponents are objects. If we were trying to construct a car in software, using an object-oriented language, we would try to do what the car engineers do. Instead of implementing the car as a single, monolithic object, we would first construct separate objects for an engine, gearbox, wheel, seat, and so on, and then assemble the car object from those smaller objects.

Identifying what kinds of objects (and with these, classes) you should have in a software system for any given problem is not always easy, and we shall have a lot more to say about that later in this book. For now, we shall start with a relatively simple example. Now, back to our digital clock.

3.4 Modularization in the clock example

Let us have a closer look at the clock-display example. Using the abstraction concepts we have just described, we want to try to find the best way to view this example so that we can write some classes to implement it. One way to look at it is to consider it as consisting of a single display with four digits (two digits for the hours, two for the minutes). If we now abstract away from that very low-level view, we can see that it could also be viewed as two separate two-digit displays (one pair for the hours and one pair for the minutes). One pair starts at 0, increases by 1 each hour, and rolls back to 0 after reaching its limit of 23. The other rolls back to 0 after reaching its limit of 59. The similarity in behavior of these two displays might then lead us to abstract away even further from viewing the hours display and minutes display distinctly. Instead, we might think of them as being objects that can display values from zero up to a given limit. The value can be incremented, but, if the value reaches the limit, it rolls over to zero. Now we seem to have reached an appropriate level of abstraction that we can represent as a class: a two-digit display class.

For our clock display, we shall first program a class for a two-digit number display (Figure 3.2) and then give it an accessor method to get its value and two mutator methods to set the value and to increment it. Once we have defined this class, we can just create two objects of the class with different limits to construct the whole clock display.

Figure 3.2
A two-digit number
display

```
03
```

3.5

Implementing the clock display

As discussed above, in order to build the clock display, we will first build a two-digit number display. This display needs to store two values. One is the limit to which it can count before rolling over to zero. The other is the current value. We shall represent both of these as integer fields in our class (Code 3.1).

Code 3.1
Class for a two-digit
number display

```java
public class NumberDisplay
{
    private int limit;
    private int value;

    Constructor and methods omitted.

}
```

Concept:

Classes define types. A class name can be used as the type for a variable. Variables that have a class as their type can store objects of that class.

We shall look at the remaining details of this class later. First, let us assume that we can build the class NumberDisplay, and then let us think a bit more about the complete clock display. We would build a complete clock display by having an object that has, internally, two number displays (one for the hours and one for the minutes). Each of the number displays would be a field in the clock display (Code 3.2). Here, we make use of a detail that we have not mentioned before: *classes define types*.

Code 3.2
The ClockDisplay
class containing two
NumberDisplay fields

```java
public class ClockDisplay
{
    private NumberDisplay hours;
    private NumberDisplay minutes;

    Constructor and methods omitted.

}
```

When we discussed fields in Chapter 2, we said that the word "private" in the field declaration is followed by a type and a name for the field. Here we use the class NumberDisplay as the type for the fields named hours and minutes. This shows that class names can be used as types.

The type of a field specifies what kind of values can be stored in the field. If the type is a class, the field can hold objects of that class.

3.6   Class diagrams versus object diagrams

The structure described in the previous section (one ClockDisplay object holding two NumberDisplay objects) can be visualized in an *object diagram* as shown in Figure 3.3a. In this diagram, you see that we are dealing with three objects. Figure 3.3b shows the *class diagram* for the same situation.

Figure 3.3
Object diagram and class diagram for the ClockDisplay

a)

b)

Note that the class diagram shows only two classes, whereas the object diagram shows three objects. This has to do with the fact that we can create multiple objects from the same class. Here, we create two NumberDisplay objects from the NumberDisplay class.

These two diagrams offer different views of the same application. The class diagram shows the *static view*. It depicts what we have at the time of writing the program. We have two classes, and the arrow indicates that the class ClockDisplay makes use of the class NumberDisplay (NumberDisplay is mentioned in the source code of ClockDisplay). We also say that ClockDisplay *depends on* NumberDisplay.

To start the program, we will create an object of class ClockDisplay. We will program the clock display so that it automatically creates two NumberDisplay objects for itself. Thus, the object diagram shows the situation at *runtime* (when the application is running). This is also called the *dynamic view.*

The object diagram also shows another important detail: when a variable stores an object, the object is not stored in the variable directly, but rather an *object reference* is stored in the variable. In the diagram, the variable is shown as a white box, and the object reference is shown as an arrow. The object referred to is stored outside the referring object, and the object reference links the two.

It is very important to understand these two different diagrams and different views. BlueJ displays only the static view. You see the class diagram in its main window. In order to plan and understand Java programs, you need to be able to construct object diagrams on paper or in your head. When we think about what our program will do, we will think about the object structures it creates and how these objects interact. Being able to visualize the object structures is essential.

> **Exercise 3.1** Think again about the *lab-classes* project that we discussed in Chapter 1 and Chapter 2. Imagine that we create a LabClass object and three Student objects. We then enroll all three students in that lab. Try to draw a class diagram and an object diagram for that situation. Identify and explain the differences between them.
>
> **Exercise 3.2** At what time(s) can a class diagram change? How is it changed?
>
> **Exercise 3.3** At what time(s) can an object diagram change? How is it changed?
>
> **Exercise 3.4** Write a definition of a field named tutor that can hold a reference to an object of type Instructor.

3.7 Primitive types and object types

Java knows two very different kinds of type: *primitive types* and *object types*. Primitive types are all predefined in the Java language. They include int and boolean. A complete list of primitive types is given in Appendix B. Object types are those defined by classes. Some classes are defined by the standard Java system (such as String); others are those classes we write ourselves.

Both primitive types and object types can be used as types, but there are situations in which they behave differently. One difference is how values are stored. As we could see from our diagrams, primitive values are stored directly in a variable (we have written the value directly into the variable box—for example, in Chapter 2, Figure 2.3). Objects, on the other hand, are not stored directly in the variable, but instead a reference to the object is stored (drawn as an arrow in our diagrams, as in Figure 3.3a).

We will see other differences between primitive types and object types later.

Concept:

The **primitive types** in Java are the non-object types. Types such as int, boolean, char, double, and long are the most common primitive types. Primitive types have no methods.

3.8 The ClockDisplay source code

Before we start to analyze the source code, it will help if you have a look at the example.

> **Exercise 3.5** Start BlueJ, open the *clock-display* example, and experiment with it. To use it, create a ClockDisplay object using the constructor that takes no parameters, then open an inspector window for this object. With the inspector open, call the object's methods. Watch the displayString field in the inspector. Read the project comment (by double-clicking the text note icon on the main screen) to get more information.

3.8.1 Class `NumberDisplay`

We shall now analyze a complete implementation of this task. The project *clock-display* in the examples attached to this book contains the solution. First, we shall look at the implementation of the class `NumberDisplay`. Code 3.3 shows the complete source code. Overall, this class is fairly straightforward. It has the two fields discussed above (Section 3.5), one constructor, and four methods (`getValue`, `setValue`, `getDisplayValue`, and `increment`).

The constructor receives the roll-over limit as a parameter. If, for example, 24 is passed in as the roll-over limit, the display will roll over to 0 at that value. Thus, the range for the display value would be 0 to 23. This feature allows us to use this class for both hour and minute displays. For the hour display, we will create a `NumberDisplay` with limit 24; for the minute display, we will create one with limit 60.

The constructor then stores the roll-over limit in a field and sets the current value of the display to 0.

Code 3.3

Implementation of the `NumberDisplay` class

```java
/**
 * The NumberDisplay class represents a digital number
 * display that can hold values from zero to a given limit.
 * The limit can be specified when creating the display. The
 * values range from zero (inclusive) to limit-1. If used, for
 * example, for the seconds on a digital clock, the limit
 * would be 60, resulting in display values from 0 to 59.
 * When incremented, the display automatically rolls over to
 * zero when reaching the limit.
 *
 * @author Michael Kölling and David J. Barnes
 * @version 2011.07.31
 */
public class NumberDisplay
{
    private int limit;
    private int value;

    /**
     * Constructor for objects of class NumberDisplay
     */
    public NumberDisplay(int rollOverLimit)
    {
        limit = rollOverLimit;
        value = 0;
    }

    /**
     * Return the current value.
     */
```

**Code 3.3
continued**

Implementation of the
`NumberDisplay`
class

```java
public int getValue()
{
    return value;
}


/**
 * Set the value of the display to the new specified
 * value. If the new value is less than zero or over the
 * limit, do nothing.
 */
public void setValue(int replacementValue)
{
    if((replacementValue >= 0) &&
            (replacementValue < limit)) {
        value = replacementValue;
    }
}


/**
 * Return the display value (that is, the current value
 * as a two-digit String. If the value is less than ten,
 * it will be padded with a leading zero).
 */
public String getDisplayValue()
{
    if(value < 10) {
        return "0" + value;
    }
    else {
        return "" + value;
    }
}


/**
 * Increment the display value by one, rolling over to zero if
 * the limit is reached.
 */
public void increment()
{
    value = (value + 1) % limit;
}
}
```

Next follows a simple accessor method for the current display value (getValue). This allows other objects to read the current value of the display.

The following mutator method setValue is more interesting. It reads:

```
public void setValue(int replacementValue)
{
    if((replacementValue >= 0) && (replacementValue < limit)) {
        value = replacementValue;
    }
}
```

Here, we pass the new value for the display as a parameter into the method. However, before we assign the value, we have to check whether the value is legal. The legal range for the value, as discussed above, is 0 to 1 below the limit. We use an if statement to check that the value is legal before we assign it. The symbol "&&" is a logical "and" operator. It causes the condition in the if statement to be true if both the conditions on either side of the "&&" symbol are true. See the "Logic operators" note that follows for details. Appendix C shows a complete table of logic operators in Java.

Logic operators Logic operators operate on boolean values (true or false) and produce a new boolean value as a result. The three most important logical operators are **and, or**, and **not**. They are written in Java as:

&& (and)

|| (or)

! (not)

The expression

a && b

is true if both a and b are true, and false in all other cases. The expression

a || b

is true if either a or b or both are true, and false if they are both false. The expression

!a

is true if a is false and false if a is true.

Exercise 3.6 What happens when the setValue method is called with an illegal value? Is this a good solution? Can you think of a better solution?

Exercise 3.7 What would happen if you replaced the ">=" operator in the test with ">" so that it reads

```
if((replacementValue > 0) && (replacementValue < limit))
```

Exercise 3.8 What would happen if you replaced the **&&** operator in the test with **||** so that it reads

```
if((replacementValue >= 0) || (replacementValue < limit))
```

Exercise 3.9 Which of the following expressions return *true*?

```
! (4 < 5)
! false
(2 > 2) || ((4 == 4) && (1 < 0))
(2 > 2) || (4 == 4) && (1 < 0)
(34 != 33) && ! false
```

After writing your answers on paper, open the Code Pad in BlueJ and try it out. Check your answers.

Exercise 3.10 Write an expression using boolean variables a and b that evaluates to *true* when a and b are either both *true* or both *false*.

Exercise 3.11 Write an expression using boolean variables a and b that evaluates to *true* when only one of a and b is *true*, and that is *false* if a and b are both *false* or both *true*. (This is also called an *exclusive or*.)

Exercise 3.12 Consider the expression (a && b). Write an equivalent expression (one that evaluates to *true* at exactly the same values for a and b) without using the && operator.

The next method, `getDisplayValue`, also returns the display's value, but in a different format. The reason is that we want to display the value as a two-digit string. That is, if the current time is 3:05 a.m., we want the display to read `03:05`, and not `3:5`. To enable us to do this easily, we have implemented the `getDisplayValue` method. This method returns the current value as a string, and it adds a leading 0 if the value is less than 10. Here is the relevant section of the code:

```
if(value < 10) {
    return "0" + value;
}
else {
    return "" + value;
}
```

Note that the zero (`"0"`) is written in double quotes. Thus, we have written the *string* 0, not the *integer number* 0. Then the expression

```
"0" + value
```

"adds" a string and an integer (because the type of `value` is integer). The plus operator, therefore, represents string concatenation again, as seen in Section 2.9. Before continuing, we will now look at string concatenation a little more closely.

3.8.2 String concatenation

The plus operator (+) has different meanings, depending on the type of its operands. If both operands are numbers, it represents addition, as we would expect. Thus,

```
42 + 12
```

adds those two numbers and the result is 54. However, if the operands are strings, then the meaning of the plus sign is string concatenation, and the result is a single string that consists of both operands stuck together. For example, the result of the expression

```
"Java" + "with BlueJ"
```

is the single string

```
"Javawith BlueJ"
```

Note that the system does not automatically add a space between the strings. If you want a space, you have to include it yourself within one of the strings.

If one of the operands of a plus operation is a string and the other is not, then the other operator is automatically converted to a string, and then a string concatenation is performed. Thus,

```
"answer: " + 42
```

results in the string

```
"answer: 42"
```

This works for all types. Whatever type is "added" to a string is automatically converted to a string and then concatenated.

Back to our code in the getDisplayValue method. If value contains 3, for example, then the statement

```
return "0" + value;
```

will return the string "03". In the case where the value is greater than 9, we have used a little trick:

```
return "" + value;
```

Here, we concatenate value with an empty string. The result is that the value will be converted to a string and no other characters will be prefixed to it. We are using the plus operator for the sole purpose of forcing a conversion of the integer value to a value of type String.

Exercise 3.13 Does the getDisplayValue method work correctly in all circumstances? What assumptions are made within it? What happens if you create a number display with limit 800, for instance?

Exercise 3.14 Is there any difference in the result of writing

```
return value + "";
```

rather than

```
return "" + value;
```

in the getDisplayValue method?

3.8.3 The modulo operator

The last method in the NumberDisplay class increments the display value by 1. It takes care that the value resets to 0 when the limit is reached:

```
public void increment()
{
    value = (value + 1) % limit;
}
```

This method uses the *modulo* operator (%). The modulo operator calculates the remainder of an integer division. For example, the result of the division

```
27 / 4
```

can be expressed in integer numbers as

```
result = 6, remainder = 3
```

The modulo operator returns just the remainder of such a division. Thus, the result of the expression (27 % 4) would be 3.

> **Exercise 3.15** Explain the modulo operator. You may need to consult more resources (online Java language resources, other Java books, etc.) to find out the details.
>
> **Exercise 3.16** What is the result of the expression (8 % 3)?
>
> **Exercise 3.17** Try out the expression (8 % 3) in the Code Pad. Try other numbers. What happens when you use the modulo operator with negative numbers?
>
> **Exercise 3.18** What are all possible results of the expression (n % 5), where n is an integer variable?
>
> **Exercise 3.19** What are all possible results of the expression (n % m), where n and m are integer variables?
>
> **Exercise 3.20** Explain in detail how the increment method works.
>
> **Exercise 3.21** Rewrite the increment method without the modulo operator, using an if statement. Which solution is better?
>
> **Exercise 3.22** Using the *clock-display* project in BlueJ, test the NumberDisplay class by creating a few NumberDisplay objects and calling their methods.

3.8.4 Class ClockDisplay

Now that we have seen how we can build a class that defines a two-digit number display, we shall look in more detail at the ClockDisplay class—the class that will create two number displays to create a full time display. Code 3.4 shows the complete source code of the ClockDisplay class.

As with the NumberDisplay class, we shall briefly discuss all fields, constructors, and methods.

Code 3.4

Implementation of the
`ClockDisplay`
class

```java
/**
 * The ClockDisplay class implements a digital clock display
 * for a European-style 24-hour clock. The clock shows hours
 * and minutes.
 * The range of the clock is 00:00 (midnight) to 23:59 (one
 * minute before midnight).
 *
 * The clock display receives "ticks" (via the timeTick
 * method) every minute and reacts by incrementing the
 * display. This is done in the usual clock fashion: the hour
 * increments when the minutes roll over to zero.
 *
 * @author Michael Kölling and David J. Barnes
 * @version 2011.07.31
 */
public class ClockDisplay
{
    private NumberDisplay hours;
    private NumberDisplay minutes;
    private String displayString; // simulates the actual display

    /**
     * Constructor for ClockDisplay objects. This constructor
     * creates a new clock set at 00:00.
     */
    public ClockDisplay()
    {
        hours = new NumberDisplay(24);
        minutes = new NumberDisplay(60);
        updateDisplay();
    }

    /**
     * Constructor for ClockDisplay objects. This constructor
     * creates a new clock set at the time specified by the
     * parameters.
     */
    public ClockDisplay(int hour, int minute)
    {
        hours = new NumberDisplay(24);
        minutes = new NumberDisplay(60);
        setTime(hour, minute);
    }

    /**
     * This method should get called once every minute - it
     * makes the clock display go one minute forward.
     */
```

**Code 3.4
continued**

Implementation of the
`ClockDisplay`
class

```java
public void timeTick()
{
    minutes.increment();
    if(minutes.getValue() == 0) { // it just rolled over!
        hours.increment();
    }
    updateDisplay();
}

/**
 * Set the time of the display to the specified hour and
 * minute.
 */
public void setTime(int hour, int minute)
{
    hours.setValue(hour);
    minutes.setValue(minute);
    updateDisplay();
}

/**
 * Return the current time of this display in the format
 * HH:MM.
 */
public String getTime()
{
    return displayString;
}

/**
 * Update the internal string that represents the
 * display.
 */
private void updateDisplay()
{
    displayString = hours.getDisplayValue() + ":" +
                    minutes.getDisplayValue();
}
}
```

In this project, we use the field `displayString` to simulate the actual display device of the clock (as you could see in Exercise 3.5). Were this software to run in a real clock, we would present the output on the real clock display instead. So this string serves as our software simulation for the clock's output device.[1]

---

[1] The book projects folder also includes a version of this project with a simple graphical user interface (GUI), named *clock-display-with-GUI*. The curious reader may like to experiment with this project; however, it will not be discussed in this book.

To achieve this, we use one string field and a method:

```
public class ClockDisplay
{
    private String displayString;

    Other fields and methods omitted.

    /**
     * Update the internal string that represents the display.
     */
    private void updateDisplay()
    {
        Method implementation omitted.
    }
}
```

Whenever we want the display of the clock to change, we shall call the internal method up-dateDisplay. In our simulation, this method will change the display string (we will examine the source code to do this below). In a real clock, this method would also exist; there it would change the real clock display.

Apart from the display string, the ClockDisplay class has only two more fields: hours and minutes. Each of these fields can hold an object of type NumberDisplay. The logical value of the clock's display (the current time) is stored in these NumberDisplay objects. Figure 3.4 shows an object diagram of this application when the current time is 15:23.

Figure 3.4
Object diagram
of the clock display

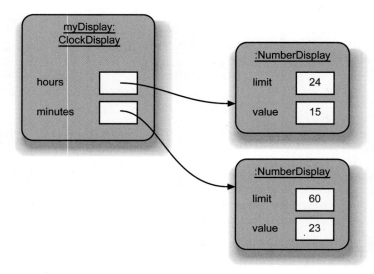

3.9 Objects creating objects

The first question we have to ask ourselves is: Where do these three objects come from? When we want to use a clock display, we might create a ClockDisplay object. We then assume that our clock display has hours and minutes. So by simply creating a clock display, we expect that we have implicitly created two number displays for the hours and minutes.

As writers of the ClockDisplay class, we have to make this happen. We simply write code in the constructor of the ClockDisplay that creates and stores two NumberDisplay objects. Because the constructor is automatically executed when a ClockDisplay object is created, the NumberDisplay objects will automatically be created at the same time. Here is the code of the ClockDisplay constructor that makes this work:

```
public class ClockDisplay
{
    private NumberDisplay hours;
    private NumberDisplay minutes;

    Remaining fields omitted.

    public ClockDisplay()
    {
        hours = new NumberDisplay(24);
        minutes = new NumberDisplay(60);
        updateDisplay();
    }

    Methods omitted.

}
```

Each of the first two lines in the constructor creates a new NumberDisplay object and assigns it to a variable. The syntax of an operation to create a new object is

new ClassName (parameter-list)

The new operation does two things:

1 It creates a new object of the named class (here, NumberDisplay).

2 It executes the constructor of that class.

If the constructor of the class is defined to have parameters, then the actual parameters must be supplied in the new statement. For instance, the constructor of class NumberDisplay was defined to expect one integer parameter:

```
public NumberDisplay (int rollOverLimit)
```

Thus, the new operation for the NumberDisplay class, which calls this constructor, must provide one actual parameter of type int to match the defined constructor header:

```
new NumberDisplay (24);
```

This is the same as for methods discussed in Section 2.4. With this constructor, we have achieved what we wanted: if someone now creates a `ClockDisplay` object, the `ClockDisplay` constructor will automatically execute and create two `NumberDisplay` objects. Then the clock display is ready to go.

Exercise 3.23 Create a `ClockDisplay` object by selecting the following constructor:

```
new ClockDisplay()
```

Call its `getTime` method to find out the initial time the clock has been set to. Can you work out why it starts at that particular time?

Exercise 3.24 How many times would you need to call the `timeTick` method on a newly created `ClockDisplay` object to make its time reach 01:00? How else could you make it display that time?

Exercise 3.25 Create a `NumberDisplay` object with limit 80 in the Code Pad by typing

```
NumberDisplay nd = new NumberDisplay(80);
```

Then call its `getValue()`, `setValue(int value)`, and `increment()` methods in the Code Pad (e.g., by typing `nd.getValue()`). Note that statements (mutators) need a semicolon at the end, while expressions (accessors) do not.

Exercise 3.26 Write the signature of a constructor that matches the following object creation instruction:

```
new Editor("readme.txt", -1)
```

Exercise 3.27 Write Java statements that define a variable named `window` of type `Rectangle`, and then create a rectangle object and assign it to that variable. The rectangle constructor has two `int` parameters.

3.10 Multiple constructors

You might have noticed when you created a `ClockDisplay` object that the pop-up menu offered you two ways to do that:

```
new ClockDisplay()
new ClockDisplay(int hour, int minute)
```

Concept:

Overloading. A class may contain more than one constructor, or more than one method of the same name, as long as each has a distinctive set of parameter types.

This is because the `ClockDisplay` class contains two constructors. What they provide are alternative ways of initializing a `ClockDisplay` object. If the constructor with no parameters is used, then the starting time displayed on the clock will be 00:00. If, on the other hand, you want to have a different starting time, you can set that up by using the second constructor. It is common for class definitions to contain alternative versions of constructors or methods that provide various ways of achieving a particular task via their distinctive sets of parameters. This is known as *overloading* a constructor or method.

Exercise 3.28 Look at the second constructor in `ClockDisplay`'s source code. Explain what it does and how it does it.

Exercise 3.29 Identify the similarities and differences between the two constructors. Why is there no call to `updateDisplay` in the second constructor, for instance?

3.11 Method calls

3.11.1 Internal method calls

The last line of the first `ClockDisplay` constructor consists of the statement

```
updateDisplay();
```

This statement is a *method call*. As we have seen above, the `ClockDisplay` class has a method with the following signature:

```
private void updateDisplay()
```

Concept:

Methods can call other methods of the same class as part of their implementation. This is called an **internal method call**.

The method call above invokes this method. Because this method is in the same class as the call of the method, we also call it an *internal method call*. Internal method calls have the syntax

```
methodName ( parameter-list )
```

In our example, the method does not have any parameters, so the parameter list is empty. This is signified by the pair of parentheses with nothing between them.

When a method call is encountered, the matching method is executed, and then execution returns to the method call and continues at the next statement after the call. For a method signature to match the method call, both the name and the parameter list of the method must match. Here, both parameter lists are empty, so they match. This need to match against both method name and parameter lists is important, because there may be more than one method of the same name in a class—if that method is overloaded.

In our example, the purpose of this method call is to update the display string. After the two number displays have been created, the display string is set to show the time indicated by the number display objects. The implementation of the `updateDisplay` method will be discussed below.

3.11.2 External method calls

Now let us examine the next method: `timeTick`. The definition is:

```
public void timeTick()
{
    minutes.increment();
    if(minutes.getValue() == 0) { // it just rolled over!
        hours.increment();
    }
    updateDisplay();
}
```

Were this display connected to a real clock, this method would be called once every 60 seconds by the electronic timer of the clock. For now, we just call it ourselves to test the display.

When the `timeTick` method is called, it first executes the statement

```
minutes.increment();
```

This statement calls the `increment` method of the `minutes` object. Thus, when one of the methods of the `ClockDisplay` object is called, it in turn calls a method of another object to do part of the task. A method call to a method of another object is referred to as an *external method call*. The syntax of an external method call is

```
object . methodName ( parameter-list )
```

This syntax is known as *dot notation*. It consists of an object name, a dot, the method name, and parameters for the call. It is particularly important to appreciate that we use the name of an *object* here and not the name of a class. We use the name `minutes` rather than `NumberDisplay`.

The `timeTick` method then has an if statement to check whether the hours should also be incremented. As part of the condition in the if statement, it calls another method of the minutes object: `getValue`. This method returns the current value of the minutes. If that value is zero, then we know that the display just rolled over and we should increment the hours. That is exactly what the code does.

If the value of the minutes is not zero, then we're done. We don't have to change the hours in that case. Thus, the if statement does not need an *else* part.

We should now also be able to understand the remaining three methods of the `ClockDisplay` class (see Code 3.4). The method `setTime` takes two parameters—the hour and the minute—and sets the clock to the specified time. Looking at the method body, we can see that it does so by calling the `setValue` methods of both number displays (the one for the hours and the one for the minutes). Then it calls `updateDisplay` to update the display string accordingly, just as the constructor does.

The `getTime` method is trivial—it just returns the current display string. Because we always keep the display string up to date, this is all there is to do.

Finally, the `updateDisplay` method is responsible for updating the display string so that the string correctly reflects the time as represented by the two number display objects. It is called every time the time of the clock changes. It works by calling the `getDisplayValue` methods of each of the `NumberDisplay` objects. These methods return the value of each separate number display. It then uses string concatenation to concatenate these two values, with a colon in the middle, to a single string.

Exercise 3.30 Given a variable

```
Printer p1;
```

which currently holds a reference to a printer object, and two methods inside the `Printer` class with the headers

```
public void print(String filename, boolean doubleSided)
public int getStatus(int delay)
```

write two possible calls to each of these methods.

3.11.3   Summary of the clock display

It is worth looking for a minute at the way this example uses abstraction to divide the problem into smaller parts. Looking at the source code of the class `ClockDisplay`, you will notice that we just create a `NumberDisplay` object without being particularly interested in what that object looks like internally. We can then call methods (`increment`, `getValue`) of that object to make it work for us. At this level, we simply assume that increment will correctly increment the display's value, without being concerned with how it does it.

In real-world projects, these different classes are often written by different people. You might already have noticed that all these two people have to agree on is what method signatures the class should have and what they should do. Then one person can concentrate on implementing the methods, while the other person can just use them.

The set of methods an object makes available to other objects is called its *interface*. We shall discuss interfaces in much more detail later in this book.

Exercise 3.31 *Challenge exercise* Change the clock from a 24-hour clock to a 12-hour clock. Be careful: This is not as easy as it might at first seem. In a 12-hour clock, the hours after midnight and after noon are not shown as 00:30, but as 12:30. Thus, the minute display shows values from 0 to 59, while the hour display shows values from 1 to 12!

Exercise 3.32 There are (at least) two ways in which you can make a 12-hour clock. One possibility is to just store hour values from 1 to 12. On the other hand, you can simply leave the clock to work internally as a 24-hour clock but change the display string of the clock display to show `4:23` or `4.23pm` when the internal value is `16:23`. Implement both versions. Which option is easier? Which is better? Why?

3.12   Another example of object interaction

We shall now examine the same concepts with a different example, using different tools. We are still concerned with understanding how objects create other objects and how objects call each other's methods. In the first half of this chapter, we have used the most fundamental technique to analyze a given program: code reading. The ability to read and understand source code is one of the most essential skills for a software developer, and we will need to apply it in every project we work on. However, sometimes it is beneficial to use additional tools in order to help us gain a deeper understanding about how a program executes. One tool we will now look at is a *debugger*.

Concept:

A **debugger** is a software tool that helps in examining how an application executes. It can be used to find bugs.

A debugger is a program that lets programmers execute an application one step at a time. It typically provides functions to stop and start a program at selected points in the source code, and to examine the values of variables.

The name "debugger" Errors in computer programs are commonly known as "bugs." Thus programs that help in the removal of errors are known as "debuggers."

It is not entirely clear where the term "bug" comes from. There is a famous case of what is known as "the first computer bug"—a real bug (a moth, in fact)—which was found inside the Mark II computer by Grace Murray Hopper, an early computing pioneer, in 1945. A logbook still exists in the National Museum of American History of the Smithsonian Institute that shows an entry with this moth taped into the book and the remark "first actual case of a bug being found." The wording, however, suggests that the term "bug" had been in use before this real one caused trouble in the Mark II.

To find out more, do a web search for "first computer bug"—you will even find pictures of the moth!

Debuggers vary widely in complexity. Those for professional developers have a large number of functions useful for sophisticated examination of many facets of an application. BlueJ has a built-in debugger that is much simpler. We can use it to stop our program, step through it one line of code at a time, and examine the values of our variables. Despite the debugger's apparent lack of sophistication, this is enough to give us a great deal of information.

Before we start experimenting with the debugger, we will take a look at the example we will use for debugging: a simulation of an e-mail system.

3.12.1   The mail-system example

We start by investigating the functionality of the *mail-system* project. At this stage, it is not important to read the source, but mainly to execute the existing project to get an understanding of what it does.

Exercise 3.33 Open the *mail-system* project, which you can find in the book's support material. The idea of this project is to simulate the act of users sending mail items to each other. A user uses a mail client to send mail items to a server, for delivery to another user's mail client. First create a `MailServer` object. Now create a `MailClient` object for one of the users. When you create the client, you will need to supply a `MailServer` instance as a parameter. Use the one you just created. You also need to specify a username for the mail client. Now create a second `MailClient` in a similar way, with a different username.

Experiment with the `MailClient` objects. They can be used for sending mail items from one mail client to another (using the `sendMailItem` method) and receiving messages (using the `getNextMailItem` or `printNextMailItem` methods).

Examining the mail system project, we see that:

- It has three classes: `MailServer`, `MailClient`, and `MailItem`.
- One mail-server object must be created that is used by all mail clients. It handles the exchange of messages.
- Several mail-client objects can be created. Every mail client has an associated user name.
- Mail items can be sent from one mail client to another via a method in the mail-client class.
- Mail items can be received by a mail client from the server one at a time, using a method in the mail client.
- The `MailItem` class is never explicitly instantiated by the user. It is used internally in the mail clients and server to create, store, and exchange messages.

Exercise 3.34 Draw an object diagram of the situation you have after creating a mail server and three mail clients. Object diagrams were discussed in Section 3.6.

The three classes have different degrees of complexity. `MailItem` is fairly trivial. We shall discuss only one small detail and leave the rest up to the reader to investigate. `MailServer` is quite complex at this stage; it makes use of concepts discussed only much later in this book. We shall not investigate that class in detail here. Instead, we just trust that it does its job—another example of the way abstraction is used to hide detail that we do not need to be aware of.

The `MailClient` class is the most interesting, and we shall examine it in some detail.

3.12.2   The `this` keyword

The only section we will discuss from the `MailItem` class is the constructor. It uses a Java construct that we have not encountered before. The source code is shown in Code 3.5.

Code 3.5

Fields and constructor of the `MailItem` class

```
public class MailItem
{
    // The sender of the item.
    private String from;
    // The intended recipient.
    private String to;
    // The text of the message.
    private String message;

    /**
     * Create a mail item from sender to the given recipient,
     * containing the given message.
     * @param from    The sender of this item.
     * @param to      The intended recipient of this item.
     * @param message The text of the message to be sent.
     */
```

Code 3.5 continued

Fields and constructor of the MailItem class

```
        public MailItem(String from, String to, String message)
        {
            this.from = from;
            this.to = to;
            this.message = message;
        }
        Methods omitted.
    }
```

The new Java feature in this code fragment is the use of the this keyword:

```
    this.from = from;
```

The whole line is an assignment statement. It assigns the value on the right-hand side (from) to the variable on the left (this.from).

The reason for using this construct is that we have a situation known as *name overloading*—the same name being used for two different entities. The class contains three fields, named from, to, and message. The constructor has three parameters, also named from, to, and message!

So while we are executing the constructor, how many variables exist? The answer is six: three fields and three parameters. It is important to understand that the fields and the parameters are separate variables that exist independently of each other, even though they share similar names. A parameter and a field sharing a name is not really a problem in Java.

The problem we do have, though, is how to reference the six variables so as to be able to distinguish between the two sets. If we simply use the variable name "from" in the constructor (for example, in a statement System.out.println(from)), which variable will be used—the parameter or the field?

The Java specification answers this question. It specifies that the definition originating in the closest enclosing block will always be used. Because the from parameter is defined in the constructor and the from field is defined in the class, the parameter will be used. Its definition is "closer" to the statement that uses it.

Now all we need is a mechanism to access a field when there is a more closely defined variable with the same name. That is what the this keyword is used for. The expression this refers to the current object. Writing this.from refers to the from field in the current object. Thus, this construct gives us a means to refer to the field instead of the parameter with the same name. Now we can read the assignment statement again:

```
    this.from = from;
```

This statement, as we can see now, has the following effect:

field named from = *parameter named* from;

In other words, it assigns the value from the parameter to the field with the same name. This is, of course, exactly what we need to do to initialize the object properly.

One last question remains: Why are we doing this at all? The whole problem could easily be avoided just by giving the fields and the parameters different names. The reason is readability of source code.

Sometimes there is one name that perfectly describes the use of a variable—it fits so well that we do not want to invent a different name for it. We want to use it for the parameter, where it serves as a hint to the caller, indicating what needs to be passed; and we want to use it for the field, where it is useful as a reminder for the implementer of the class, indicating what the field is used for. If one name perfectly describes the use, it is reasonable to use it for both and to go through the trouble of using the `this` keyword in the assignment to resolve the name conflict.

3.13 Using a debugger

The most interesting class in the mail-system example is the mail client. We shall now investigate it in more detail by using a debugger. The mail client has three methods: `getNextMailItem`, `printNextMailItem`, and `sendMailItem`. We will first investigate the `printNextMailItem` method.

Before we start with the debugger, set up a scenario we can use to investigate (Exercise 3.35).

> **Exercise 3.35** Set up a scenario for investigation: Create a mail server, then create two mail clients for the users `"Sophie"` and `"Juan"` (you should name the instances `sophie` and `juan` as well so that you can better distinguish them on the object bench). Then use Sophie's `sendMailItem` method to send a message to Juan. Do not read the message yet.

After the setup in Exercise 3.35, we have a situation where one mail item is stored on the server for Juan, waiting to be picked up. We have seen that the `printNextMailItem` method picks up this mail item and prints it to the terminal. Now we want to investigate exactly how this works.

3.13.1 Setting breakpoints

To start our investigation, we set a breakpoint (Exercise 3.36). A breakpoint is a flag attached to a line of source code that will stop the execution of a method at that point when it is reached. It is represented in the BlueJ editor as a small stop sign (Figure 3.5).

You can set a breakpoint by opening the BlueJ editor, selecting the appropriate line (in our case, the first line of the `printNextMailItem` method) and then selecting Set/Clear Breakpoint from the *Tools* menu of the editor. Alternatively, you can also simply click into the area next to the line of code where the breakpoint symbol appears, to set or clear breakpoints. Note that the class has to be compiled to do this.

> **Exercise 3.36** Open the editor for the `MailClient` class and set a breakpoint at the first line of the `printNextMailItem` method, as shown in Figure 3.5.

Figure 3.5
A breakpoint
in the BlueJ editor

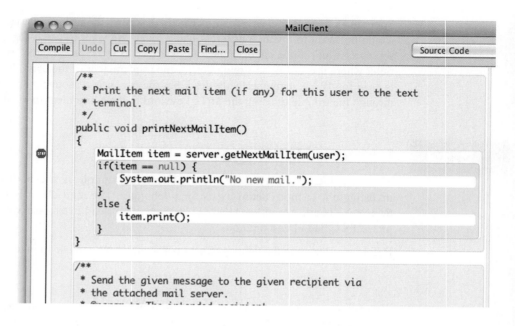

Once you have set the breakpoint, invoke the `printNextMailItem` method on Juan's mail client. The editor window for the `MailClient` class and a debugger window will pop up (Figure 3.6).

Along the bottom of the debugger window are some control buttons. They can be used to continue or interrupt the execution of the program. (For a more detailed explanation of the debugger controls, see Appendix F.)

On the right-hand side of the debugger window are three areas for variable display, titled *static variables*, *instance variables*, and *local variables*. We will ignore the static-variable area for now. We will discuss static variables later, and this class does not have any.

Figure 3.6
The debugger window,
execution stopped
at a breakpoint

We see that this object has two instance variables (or fields), `server` and `user`, and we can see the current values. The `user` variable stores the string `"Juan"`, and the `server` variable stores a reference to another object. The object reference is what we have drawn as an arrow in the object diagrams.

Note that there is no local variable yet. This is because execution stops *before* the line with the breakpoint is executed. Because the line with the breakpoint contains the declaration of the only local variable and that line has not yet been executed, no local variable exists at the moment.

The debugger not only allows us to interrupt the execution of the program and inspect the variables, it also lets us step forward slowly.

3.13.2 Single stepping

When stopped at a breakpoint, clicking the *Step* button executes a single line of code and then stops again.

> **Exercise 3.37** Step one line forward in the execution of the `printNextMailItem` method by clicking the *Step* button.

The result of executing the first line of the `printNextMailItem` method is shown in Figure 3.7. We can see that execution has moved on by one line (a small black arrow next to the line of source code indicates the current position), and the local variable list in the debugger window indicates that a local variable item has been created and an object assigned to it.

Figure 3.7
Stopped again after
a single step

> **Exercise 3.38** Predict which line will be marked as the next line to execute after the next step. Then execute another single step and check your prediction. Were you right or wrong? Explain what happened and why.

We can now use the *Step* button repeatedly to step to the end of the method. This allows us to see the path the execution takes. This is especially interesting in conditional statements: we can clearly see which branch of an if statement is executed and use this to see whether it matches our expectations.

Exercise 3.39 Call the same method (`printNextMailItem`) again. Step through the method again, as before. What do you observe? Explain why this is.

3.13.3 Stepping into methods

When stepping through the `printNextMailItem` method, we have seen two method calls to objects of our own classes. The line

```
MailItem item = server.getNextMailItem(user);
```

includes a call to the `getNextMailItem` method of the `server` object. Checking the instance variable declarations, we can see that the `server` object is declared of class `MailServer`.

The line

```
item.print();
```

calls the `print` method of the `item` object. We can see in the first line of the `printNextMailItem` method that `item` is declared to be of class `MailItem`.

Using the *Step* command in the debugger, we have used abstraction: we have viewed the `print` method of the `item` class as a single instruction, and we could observe that its effect is to print out the details (sender, recipient, and message) of the mail item.

If we are interested in more detail, we can look further into the process and see the print method itself execute step by step. This is done by using the *Step Into* command in the debugger instead of the *Step* command. *Step Into* will step into the method being called and stop at the first line inside that method.

Exercise 3.40 Set up the same test situation as we did before. That is, send a message from Sophie to Juan. Then invoke the `printNextMailItem` message of Juan's mail client again. Step forward as before. This time, when you reach the line

```
item.print();
```

use the *Step Into* command instead of the *Step* command. Make sure you can see the text terminal window as you step forward. What do you observe? Explain what you see.

3.14 Method calling revisited

In the experiments in Section 3.13, we have seen another example of object interaction similar to one we saw before: objects calling methods of other objects. In the `printNextMailItem` method, the `MailClient` object made a call to a `MailServer` object to retrieve the next mail item. This method (`getNextMailItem`) returned a value—an object of type

MailItem. Then there was a call to the print method of the mail item. Using abstraction, we can view the print method as a single command. Or, if we are interested in more detail, we can go to a lower level of abstraction and look inside the print method.

In a similar style, we can use the debugger to observe one object creating another. The send-Message method in the MailClient class shows a good example. In this method, a MailItem object is created in the first line of code:

```
MailItem item = new MailItem(user, to, message);
```

The idea here is that the mail item is used to encapsulate a mail message. The mail item contains information about the sender, the recipient, and the message itself. When sending a message, a mail client creates a mail item with all this information and then stores the mail item on the mail server. There it can later be picked up by the mail client of the recipient.

In the line of code above, we see the new keyword being used to create the new object, and we see the parameters being passed to the constructor. (Remember: Constructing an object does two things—the object is being created and the constructor is executed.) Calling the constructor works in a very similar fashion to calling methods. This can be observed by using the *Step Into* command at the line where the object is being constructed.

> **Exercise 3.41** Set a breakpoint in the first line of the sendMailItem method in the MailClient class. Then invoke this method. Use the *Step Into* function to step into the constructor of the mail item. In the debugger display for the MailItem object, you can see the instance variables and local variables that have the same names, as discussed in Section 3.12.2. Step further to see the instance variables get initialized.

> **Exercise 3.42** Use a combination of code reading, execution of methods, breakpoints, and single stepping to familiarize yourself with the MailItem and MailClient classes. Note that we have not yet discussed enough for you to understand the implementation of the MailServer class, so you can ignore this for now. (You can, of course, look at it if you feel adventurous, but don't be surprised if you find it slightly baffling...) Explain in writing how the MailClient and MailItem classes interact. Draw object diagrams as part of your explanations.

3.15 Summary

In this chapter, we have discussed how a problem can be divided into sub-problems. We can try to identify subcomponents in those objects that we want to model, and we can implement subcomponents as independent classes. Doing so helps in reducing the complexity of implementing larger applications, because it enables us to implement, test, and maintain individual classes separately.

We have seen how this results in structures of objects working together to solve a common task. Objects can create other objects, and they can invoke each other's methods. Understanding these object interactions is essential in planning, implementing, and debugging applications.

We can use pen-and-paper diagrams, code reading, and debuggers to investigate how an application executes or to track down bugs.

Terms introduced in this chapter

abstraction, modularization, divide and conquer, class diagram, object diagram, object reference, overloading, internal method call, external method call, dot notation, debugger, breakpoint

Concept summary

- **abstraction** Abstraction is the ability to ignore details of parts, to focus attention on a higher level of a problem.

- **modularization** Modularization is the process of dividing a whole into well-defined parts that can be built and examined separately and that interact in well-defined ways.

- **classes define types** A class name can be used as the type for a variable. Variables that have a class as their type can store objects of that class.

- **class diagram** The class diagram shows the classes of an application and the relationships between them. It gives information about the source code and presents the static view of a program.

- **object diagram** The object diagram shows the objects and their relationships at one moment in time during the execution of an application. It gives information about objects at runtime and presents the dynamic view of a program.

- **object references** Variables of object types store references to objects.

- **primitive type** The primitive types in Java are the non-object types. Types such as `int`, `boolean`, `char`, `double`, and `long` are the most common primitive types. Primitive types have no methods.

- **object creation** Objects can create other objects, using the `new` operator.

- **overloading** A class may contain more than one constructor, or more than one method of the same name, as long as each has a distinctive set of parameter types.

- **internal method call** Methods can call other methods of the same class as part of their implementation. This is called an internal method call.

- **external method call** Methods can call methods of other objects using dot notation. This is called an external method call.

- **debugger** A debugger is a software tool that helps in examining how an application executes. It can be used to find bugs.

Exercise 3.43 Use the debugger to investigate the *clock-display* project. Set breakpoints in the `ClockDisplay` constructor and each of the methods, and then single-step through them. Does it behave as you expected? Did this give you new insights? If so, what were they?

Exercise 3.44 Use the debugger to investigate the `insertMoney` method of the *better-ticket-machine* project from Chapter 2. Conduct tests that cause both branches of the if statement to be executed.

Exercise 3.45 Add a subject line for an e-mail to mail items in the *mail-system* project. Make sure printing messages also prints the subject line. Modify the mail client accordingly.

Exercise 3.46 Given the following class (only shown in fragments here),

```
public class Screen
{
    public Screen(int xRes, int yRes)
    { ...
    }

    public int numberOfPixels()
    { ...
    }

    public void clear(boolean invert)
    { ...
    }
}
```

write some lines of Java code that create a `Screen` object. Then call its `clear` method if (and only if) its number of pixels is greater than two million. (Don't worry about things being logical here; the goal is only to write something that is syntactically correct—i.e., that would compile if we typed it in.)

Grouping objects

Main concepts discussed in this chapter:

- collections
- loops
- iterators
- arrays

Java constructs discussed in this chapter:

`ArrayList`, `Iterator`, while loop, `null`, cast, anonymous objects, array, for loop, for-each loop, ++

The main focus of this chapter is to introduce some of the ways in which objects may be grouped together into collections. In particular, we discuss the `ArrayList` class as an example of flexible-size collections and the use of array objects for fixed-size collections. Closely associated with collections is the need to iterate over the elements they contain. For this purpose, we introduce three new control structures: two versions of the for loop, and the while loop.

This chapter is both long and important. You will not succeed in becoming a good programmer without fully understanding the contents of this chapter. You will need longer to study it than was the case for previous chapters. Do not be tempted to rush through it; take your time and study it thoroughly.

4.1 Building on themes from Chapter 3

As well as introducing new material on collections and iteration, we will also be revisiting two of the key themes that were introduced in Chapter 3: *abstraction* and *object interaction*. There we saw that abstraction allows us to simplify a problem by identifying discrete components that can be viewed as a whole, rather than being concerned with their detail. We will see this principle in action when we start making use of the *library classes* that are available in Java. While these classes are not, strictly speaking, a part of the language, some of them are so closely associated with writing most Java programs that they are often thought of in that way. Most people writing Java programs will constantly check the libraries to see if someone has already written a class that they can make use of. That way, they save a huge amount of effort that can be better used in working on other parts of the program. The same principle applies with most other programming languages, which also tend to have libraries of useful classes. So it pays to become familiar with the contents of the library and how to use the most common classes. The power of abstraction is that we don't usually need to know much (if anything, indeed!) about what the class looks like inside to be able to use it effectively.

If we use a library class, it follows that we will be writing code that creates instances of those classes, and then our objects will be interacting with the library objects. Object interaction will also figure highly in this chapter, therefore.

You will find that the chapters in this book continually revisit and build on themes that have been introduced in previous chapters. We refer to this in the preface as an "iterative approach." One particular advantage of the approach is that it will help you to gradually deepen your understanding of topics as you work your way through the book.

In this chapter, we also extend our understanding of abstraction to see that it does not just mean hiding detail but also means seeing the common features and patterns that recur again and again in programs. Recognizing these patterns means that we can often reuse in a new situation part or all of a method or class we have previously written. This particular applies when looking at collections and iteration.

4.2   The collection abstraction

One of the abstractions we wish to explore in this chapter is the idea of a *collection*—the notion of grouping things so that we can refer to them and manage them all together. A collection might be: large (all the students in a university); small (the courses one of the students is taking); or empty even (the paintings by Picasso that I own!).

If we own a collection of stamps, autographs, concert posters, ornaments, music, or whatever, then there are some common things we will want to do to the collection from time to time, regardless of what it is we collect. For instance, we will likely want to *add to* the collection, but we also might want to *cut it down*—say if we have duplicates or want to raise money for additional purchases. We also might want to *arrange it* in some way—by date of acquisition or value, perhaps. What we are describing here are typical *operations* on a collection.

In a programming context, the collection abstraction becomes a class of some sort, and the operations would be methods of that class. A particular collection (my music collection) would be an instance of the class. Furthermore, the items stored in a collection instance would, themselves, be objects.

Here are some further collection examples that are more obviously related to a programming context:

Concept:

Collection
A collection object can store an arbitrary number of other objects.

- Electronic calendars store event notes about appointments, meetings, birthdays, and so on. New notes are added as future events are arranged, and old notes are deleted as details of past events are no longer needed.

- Libraries record details about the books and journals they own. The catalog changes as new books are bought and old ones are put into storage or discarded.

- Universities maintain records of students. Each academic year adds new records to the collection, while the records of those who have left are moved to an archive collection. Listing subsets of the collection will be common: all the students taking first-year CS or all the students due to graduate this year, for instance.

It is typical that the number of items stored in a collection will vary from time to time. So far, we have not met any features of Java that would allow us to group together arbitrary numbers of items. We could, perhaps, define a class with a lot of individual fields to cover a fixed but very large number of items, but programs typically have a need for a more general solution than this provides. A proper solution would not require us either to know in advance how many items we wish to group together, or to fix an upper limit to that number.

So we will start our exploration of the Java library by looking at a class that provides the simplest possible way of grouping objects, an unsorted but ordered flexible-sized list: ArrayList. In the next few sections, we shall use the example of keeping track of a personal music collection to illustrate how we can group together an arbitrary number of objects in a single container object.

4.3 An organizer for music files

We are going to write a class that can help us organize our music files stored on a computer. Our class won't actually store the file details; instead, it will delegate that responsibility to the standard ArrayList library class, which will save us a lot of work. So, why do we need to write our own class at all? An important point to bear in mind when dealing with library classes is that they have not been written for any particular application scenario—they are general-purpose classes. One ArrayList might store student-record objects, while another stores event reminders. This means that it is the classes that we write for using the library classes that provide the scenario-specific operations, such as the fact that we are dealing with music files or playing a file that is stored in the collection.

For the sake of simplicity, the first version of this project will simply work with the file names of individual music tracks. There will be no separate details of title, artist, playing time, etc. That means we will just be asking the ArrayList to store String objects representing the file names. Keeping things simple at this stage will help to avoid obscuring the key concepts we are trying to illustrate, which are the creation and usage of a collection object. Later in the chapter, we will add further sophistication to make a more viable music organizer and player.

We will assume that each music file represents a single music track. The example files we have provided with the project have both the artist's name and the track's title embedded in the file name, and we will use this feature later. For the time being, here are the basic operations we will have in the initial version of our organizer:

■ It allows tracks to be added to the collection.

■ It has no predetermined limit on the number of tracks it can store, aside from the memory limit of the machine on which it is run.

■ It will tell us how many tracks are in the collection.

■ It will list all the tracks.

We shall find that the `ArrayList` class makes it very easy to provide this functionality from our own class.

Notice that we are not being too ambitious in this first version. These features will be sufficient for illustrating the basics of creating and using the `ArrayList` class, and later versions will then build further features incrementally until we have something more sophisticated. (Most importantly, perhaps, we will later add the possibility of playing the music files. Our first version will not be able to do that yet.) This modest, incremental approach is much more likely to lead to success than trying to implement everything all at once.

Before we analyze the source code needed to make use of such a class, it is helpful to explore the starting behavior of the music organizer.

Exercise 4.1 Open the *music-organizer-v1* project in BlueJ and create a `MusicOrganizer` object. Store the names of a few audio files into it—they are simply strings. As we are not going to play the files at this stage, any file names will do, although there is a sample of audio files in the *audio* sub-folder of the project that you might like to use.

Check that the number of files returned by `numberOfFiles` matches the number you stored. When you use the `listFile` method, you will need to use a parameter value of 0 (zero) to print the first file, 1 (one) to print the second, and so on. We shall explain the reason for this numbering in due course.

Exercise 4.2 What happens if you create a new `MusicOrganizer` object and then call `removeFile(0)` before you have added any files to it? Do you get an error? Would you expect to get an error?

Exercise 4.3 Create a `MusicOrganizer` and add two file names to it. Call `listFile(0)` and `listFile(1)` to show the two files. Now call `removeFile(0)` and then `list-File(0)`. What happened? Is that what you expected? Can you find an explanation of what might have happened when you removed the first file name from the collection?

4.4 Using a library class

Code 4.1 shows the full definition of our `MusicOrganizer` class, which makes use of the library class `ArrayList`. Note that library classes do not appear in the BlueJ class diagram.

Class libraries One of the features of object-oriented languages that makes them powerful is that they are often accompanied by *class libraries*. These libraries typically contain many hundreds or thousands of different classes that have proved useful to developers on a wide range of different projects. Java calls its libraries *packages*. Library classes are used in exactly the same way as we would use our own classes. Instances are constructed using `new`, and the classes have fields, constructors, and methods.

Code 4.1

The `MusicOrganizer`
class

```java
import java.util.ArrayList;

/**
 * A class to hold details of audio files.
 *
 * @author David J. Barnes and Michael Kölling
 * @version 2011.07.31
 */
public class MusicOrganizer
{
    // An ArrayList for storing the file names of music files.
    private ArrayList<String> files;

    /**
     * Create a MusicOrganizer
     */
    public MusicOrganizer()
    {
        files = new ArrayList<String>();
    }

    /**
     * Add a file to the collection.
     * @param filename The file to be added.
     */
    public void addFile(String filename)
    {
        files.add(filename);
    }

    /**
     * Return the number of files in the collection.
     * @return The number of files in the collection.
     */
    public int getNumberOfFiles()
    {
        return files.size();
    }

    /**
     * List a file from the collection.
     * @param index The index of the file to be listed.
     */
```

**Code 4.1
continued**

The `MusicOrganizer`
class

```java
    public void listFile(int index)
    {
        if(index >= 0 && index < files.size()) {
            String filename = files.get(index);
            System.out.println(filename);
        }
    }


    /**
     * Remove a file from the collection.
     * @param index The index of the file to be removed.
     */
    public void removeFile(int index)
    {
        if(index >= 0 && index < files.size()) {
            files.remove(index);
        }
    }
}
```

4.4.1 Importing a library class

The very first line of the class file illustrates the way in which we gain access to a library class in Java, via an *import statement:*

```java
import java.util.ArrayList;
```

This makes the `ArrayList` class from the `java.util` package available to our class definition. Import statements must always be placed before class definitions in a file. Once a class name has been imported from a package in this way, we can use that class just as if it were one of our own classes. So we use `ArrayList` at the head of the `MusicOrganizer` class to define a `files` field:

```java
private ArrayList<String> files;
```

Here, we see a new construct: the mention of `String` in angle brackets: `<String>`. The need for this was alluded to in Section 4.3, where we noted that `ArrayList` is a *general-purpose* collection class—i.e., not restricted in what it can store. When we create an `ArrayList` object, however, we have to be specific about the type of objects that will be stored in that particular instance. We can store whatever type we choose, but we have to designate that type when declaring an `ArrayList` variable. Classes such as `ArrayList`, which get parameterized with a second type, are called *generic classes* (we will discuss them in more detail later).

When using collections, therefore, we always have to specify two types: the type of the collection itself (here: `ArrayList`) and the type of the elements that we plan to store in the collection (here: `String`). We can read the complete type definition `ArrayList<String>` as "*ArrayList of String.*" We use this type definition as the type for our `files` variable.

As you should now have come to expect, we see a close connection between the body of the constructor and the fields of the class, because the constructor is responsible for initializing the fields of each instance. So, just as the `ClockDisplay` created `NumberDisplay` objects for its two fields, here we see the constructor of the `MusicOrganizer` creating an object of type `ArrayList<String>` and storing it in the `files` field.

4.4.2   Diamond notation

Note that when creating the `ArrayList` instance, we have specified the complete type again with the element type in angle brackets, followed by parentheses for the (empty) parameter list:

```
files = new ArrayList<String>();
```

In all versions of Java prior to version 7, using the full form of the generic type when creating an instance was a necessity, but from Java 7 onwards it is possible for the Java compiler to infer the parameterized type of the object being created from the type of the variable being assigned to. This allows us to use the so-called *diamond notation* as follows:

```
files = new ArrayList<>();
```

Using this form doesn't change the fact that the object being created will only be able to store `String` objects; it is just a convenience for the programmer.

In this book, however, we will retain the older-style notation, both for compatibility with the majority of Java source code you are likely to see and because, at the time of writing, not everyone using the book will have access to a Java 7 compiler.

4.4.3   Key methods of `ArrayList`

The `ArrayList` class defines quite a lot of methods, but we shall make use of only four at this stage, to support the functionality we require: `add`, `size`, `get`, and `remove`.

The first two are illustrated in the relatively straightforward `addFile` and `getNumberOf-Files` methods, respectively. The `add` method of an `ArrayList` stores an object in the list, and the `size` method tells us how many items are currently stored in it. We will look at how the `get` and `remove` methods work in Section 4.7, though you will probably get some idea beforehand simply by reading through the code of the `listFile` and `removeFile` methods.

4.5   Object structures with collections

To understand how a collection object such as an `ArrayList` operates, it is helpful to examine an object diagram. Figure 4.1 illustrates how a `MusicOrganizer` object might look with two filename strings stored in it. Compare Figure 4.1 with Figure 4.2, where a third file name has been stored.

There are at least three important features of the `ArrayList` class that you should observe:

■ It is able to increase its internal capacity as required: as more items are added, it simply makes enough room for them.

■ It keeps its own private count of how many items it is currently storing. Its `size` method returns that count.

■ It maintains the order of items you insert into it. The `add` method stores each new item at the end of the list. You can later retrieve them in the same order.

Figure 4.1
A MusicOrganizer containing two file names

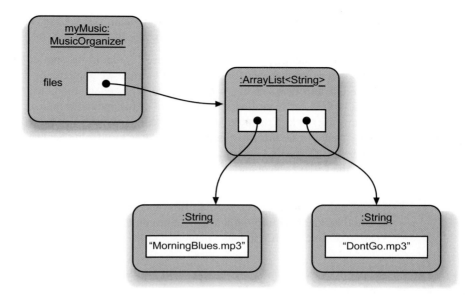

Figure 4.2
A MusicOrganizer containing three file names

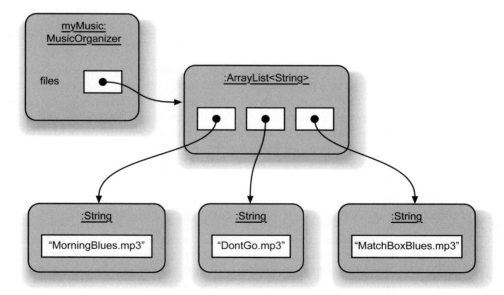

We notice that the MusicOrganizer object looks quite simple—it has only a single field that stores an object of type ArrayList<String>. All the difficult work is done in the ArrayList object. This is one of the great advantages of using library classes: someone has invested time and effort to implement something useful, and we are getting access to this functionality almost for free by using this class.

At this stage, we do not need to worry about *how* an ArrayList is able to support these features. It is sufficient to appreciate just how useful this ability is. Remember: This suppression of detail is a benefit that abstraction gives us; it means that we can utilize `ArrayList` to write any number of different classes that require storage of an arbitrary number of objects.

The second feature—the `ArrayList` object keeping its own count of inserted objects—has important consequences for the way in which we implement the `MusicOrganizer` class. Although an organizer has a `getNumberOfFiles` method, we have not actually defined a specific field for recording this information. Instead, an organizer *delegates* the responsibility for keeping track of the number of items to its `ArrayList` object. This means that an organizer does not duplicate information that is available to it from elsewhere. If a user requests from the organizer information about the number of file names in it, the organizer will pass the question on to the `files` object and then return whatever answer it gets from there.

Duplication of information or behavior is something that we often work hard to avoid. Duplication can represent wasted effort and can lead to inconsistencies where two things that should be identical turn out not to be, through error. We will have a lot more to say about duplication of functionality in later chapters.

4.6 Generic classes

The new notation using the angle brackets deserves a little more discussion. The type of our `files` field was declared as

```
ArrayList<String>
```

The class we are using here is called simply `ArrayList`, but it requires a second type to be specified as a parameter when it is used to declare fields or other variables. Classes that require such a type parameter are called *generic classes*. Generic classes, in contrast to other classes we have seen so far, do not define a single type in Java, but potentially many types. The `ArrayList` class, for example, can be used to specify an *ArrayList of String*, an *ArrayList of Person*, an *ArrayList of Rectangle*, or an `ArrayList` of any other class that we have available. Each particular `ArrayList` is a separate type that can be used in declarations of fields, parameters, and return values. We could, for example, define the following two fields:

```
private ArrayList<Person> members;
private ArrayList<TicketMachine> machines;
```

These definitions state that `members` refers to an `ArrayList` that can store `Person` objects, while `machines` can refer to an `ArrayList` to store `TicketMachine` objects. Note that `ArrayList<Person>` and `ArrayList<TicketMachine>` are different types. The fields cannot be assigned to each other even though their types were derived from the same `ArrayList` class.

Exercise 4.4 Write a declaration of a private field named `library` that can hold an `ArrayList`. The elements of the `ArrayList` are of type `Book`.

Exercise 4.5 Write a declaration of a local variable called `cs101` that can hold an `ArrayList` of `Student`.

> **Exercise 4.6** Write a declaration of a private field called `tracks` for storing a collection of `MusicTrack` objects.
>
> **Exercise 4.7** Write assignments to the `library`, `cs101`, and `track` variables (which you defined in the previous three exercises) to create the appropriate `ArrayList` objects. Write them once without using diamond notation and once with diamond notation if you are using a Java 7 compiler.

Generic classes are used for a variety of purposes; we will encounter more of them later in the book. For now, collections such as `ArrayList`, and some other collections that we shall encounter shortly, are the only generic classes we need to deal with.

4.7 Numbering within collections

When exploring the *music-organizer-v1* project in the first few exercises, we noted that it was necessary to use parameter values starting at 0 to list and remove file names in the collection. The reason behind this requirement is that items stored in `ArrayList` collections have an implicit numbering, or positioning, that starts from 0. The position of an object in a collection is more commonly known as its *index*. The first item added to a collection is given index number 0, the second is given index number 1, and so on. Figure 4.3 illustrates the same situation as above, with index numbers shown in the `ArrayList` object.

It is important to be aware that this means that the last item in a collection has the index *size-1*. For example, in a list of 20 items, the last one will be at index 19.

Figure 4.3
Index numbers of elements in a collection

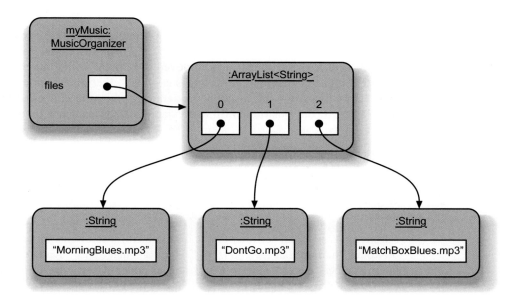

The `listFile` and `removeFile` methods both illustrate the way in which an index number is used to gain access to an item in an `ArrayList`: one via its `get` method and the other via its `remove` method. Note that both methods make sure that their parameter value is in the range of valid index values [0 . . . size()-1] before passing the index on to the `ArrayList` methods. This is a good stylistic validation habit to adopt, as it prevents failure of a library-class method call when passing on parameter values that could be invalid.

> **Pitfall** If you are not careful, you may try to access a collection element that is outside the valid indices of the `ArrayList`. When you do this, you will get an error message and the program will terminate. Such an error is called an *index-out-of-bounds* error. In Java, you will see a message about an `IndexOutOfBoundsException`.

> **Exercise 4.8** If a collection stores 10 objects, what value would be returned from a call to its `size` method?
>
> **Exercise 4.9** Write a method call using `get` to return the fifth object stored in a collection called items.
>
> **Exercise 4.10** What is the index of the last item stored in a collection of 15 objects?
>
> **Exercise 4.11** Write a method call to add the object held in the variable `favoriteTrack` to a collection called `files`.

4.7.1 The effect of removal on numbering

As well as adding items to a collection, it is common to want to remove items, as we saw with the `removeFile` method in Code 4.1. The `ArrayList` class has a `remove` method that takes the index of the object to be removed. One detail of the removal process to be aware of is that it can change the index values at which other objects in the collection are stored. If an item with a low index number is removed, then the collection moves all subsequent items along by one position to fill in the gap. As a consequence, their index numbers will be decreased by 1.

Figure 4.4 illustrates the way in which some of the index values of items in an `ArrayList` are changed by the removal of an item from the middle of the list. Starting with the situation depicted in Figure 4.3, the object with index 1 has been removed. As a result, the object originally at index number 2 has changed to 1, whereas the object at index number 0 remains unchanged.

Furthermore, we shall see later that it is possible to insert items into an `ArrayList` at a position other than right at the end of it. This means that items already in the list may have their index numbers increased when a new item is added. Users have to be aware of this possible change of indices when adding or removing elements.

Figure 4.4
Index number
changes following
removal of an item

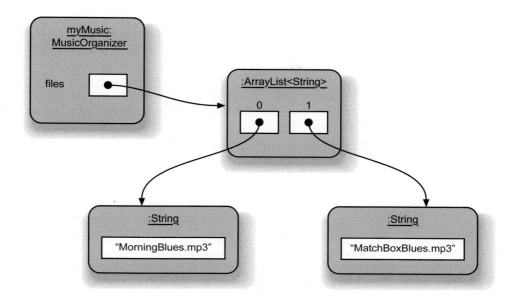

4.7.2 The general utility of numbering with collections

The use of integer index values to access objects in a collection is something that we will see over and over again—not just with ArrayLists but also with several different types of collections. So it is important to understand what we have seen of this so far: that the index values start at zero; that the objects are numbered sequentially; and that there are usually no gaps in the index values of consecutive objects in the collection.

Using integer values as indices also makes it very easy to express in program code expressions such as "the next item" and "the previous item" with respect to an item in the collection. If an item is at index p, then "the next" one will be at index (p+1) and "the previous" one is now at index (p-1). We can also map natural-language selections such as "the first three" to program-related terminology. For example, "the items at indices 0, 1, and 2" or "the last four" could be "the items at indices (list.size()-4) to (list.size()-1)". We could even imagine working our way through the entire collection by having an integer index variable whose value is initially set to zero and is then successively increased by 1, passing its value to the get method to access each item in the list in order (stopping when it goes beyond the final index value of the list).

But we are getting a little ahead of ourselves. Nevertheless, in a little while we will see how all this works out in practice when we look at *loops* and *iteration*.

> **Exercise 4.12** Write a method call to remove the third object stored in a collection called dates.
>
> **Exercise 4.13** Suppose that an object is stored at index 6 in a collection. What will be its index immediately after the objects at index 0 and index 9 are removed?

Exercise 4.14 Add a method called checkIndex to the MusicOrganizer class. It takes a single integer parameter and checks whether it is a valid index for the current state of the collection. To be valid, the parameter must lie in the range 0 to size()-1.

If the parameter is not valid, then it should print an error message saying what the valid range is. If the index is valid, then it prints nothing. Test your method on the object bench with both valid and invalid parameters. Does your method still work when you check an index if the collection is empty?

Exercise 4.15 Write an alternative version of checkIndex called validIndex. It takes an integer parameter and returns a boolean result. It does not print anything, but returns *true* if the parameter's value is a valid index for the current state of the collection and *false* otherwise. Test your method on the object bench with both valid and invalid parameters. Test the empty case too.

Exercise 4.16 Rewrite both the listFile and removeFile methods in MusicOrganizer so that they use your validIndex method to check their parameter, instead of the current boolean expression. They should only call get or remove on the ArrayList if validIndex returns *true*.

4.8 Playing the music files

It would be a nice feature of our organizer if it not only kept a list of music files but also allowed us to play them. Once again, we can use abstraction to help us here. If we have a class that has been written specifically to play audio files, then our organizer class would not need to know anything about how to do that; it could simply hand over the name of the file to the player class and leave it to do the rest.

Unfortunately, the standard Java library does not have a class that is suitable for playing MP3 files, which is the audio format we want to work with. However, many individual programmers are constantly writing their own useful classes and making them available for other people to use. These are often called "third-party libraries," and they are imported and used in exactly the same way as are standard Java library classes.

For the next version of our project, we have made use of a set of classes from javazoom.net to write our own music-player class. You can find this in the version called *music-organizer-v2*. The three methods of the MusicPlayer class we shall be using are playSample, startPlaying, and stop. The first two take the name of the audio file to play. The first plays some seconds of the beginning of the file and returns when it has finished playing, while the second starts its playing in the background and then immediately returns control back to the organizer—hence the need for the stop method, in case you want to cancel playing. Code 4.2 shows the new elements of the MusicOrganizer class that access some of this playing functionality.

Code 4.2

Playing functionality of
the `MusicOrganizer`
class

```java
import java.util.ArrayList;

/**
 * A class to hold details of audio files.
 * This version can play the files.
 *
 * @author David J. Barnes and Michael Kölling
 * @version 2011.07.31
 */
public class MusicOrganizer
{
    // An ArrayList for storing the file names of music files.
    private ArrayList<String> files;
    // A player for the music files.
    private MusicPlayer player;

    /**
     * Create a MusicOrganizer
     */
    public MusicOrganizer()
    {
        files = new ArrayList<String>();
        player = new MusicPlayer();
    }

    /**
     * Start playing a file in the collection.
     * Use stopPlaying() to stop it playing.
     * @param index The index of the file to be played.
     */
    public void startPlayingFile(int index)
    {
        String filename = files.get(index);
        player.startPlaying(filename);
    }

    /**
     * Stop the player.
     */
    public void stopPlaying()
    {
        player.stop();
    }

    Other details omitted.
}
```

Exercise 4.17 Create a `MusicOrganizer` object in the second version of our project. Experiment with adding some files to it and playing them.

If you want to use the files provided in the *audio* folder within the project, you must include the folder name in the filename parameter, as well as the file name and suffix. For example, to use the file *BlindBlake-EarlyMorningBlues.mp3* from the *audio* folder, you must pass the string `"audio/BlindBlake-EarlyMorningBlues.mp3"` to the `addFile` method.

You can use your own mp3 files by placing them into the *audio* folder. Remember to use the folder name as part of the file name.

Also experiment with file names that do not exist. What happens when you use those?

4.8.1 Summary of the music organizer

We have made good progress with the basics of organizing our music collection. We can store the names of any number of music files and even play them. We have done this with relatively little coding effort, because we have been able to piggyback on the functionality provided by library classes: `ArrayList` from the standard Java library and a music player that uses a third-party class library. We have also been able to do this with relatively little knowledge of the internal workings of these library classes; it was sufficient to know the names, parameter types, and return types of the key methods.

However, there is still some key functionality missing if we want a genuinely useful program—most obvious is the lack of any way to list the whole collection, for instance. This will be the topic of the next section, as we introduce the first of several Java loop-control structures.

4.9 Processing a whole collection

At the end of the last section, we said that it would be useful to have a method in the music organizer that lists all of the file names stored in the collection. Knowing that each file name in the collection has a unique index number, one way to express what we want would be to say that we wish to show the file name stored at consecutive, increasing index numbers starting from zero. Before reading further, try the following exercises to see whether we can easily write such a method with the Java that we already know.

Exercise 4.18 What might the header of a `listAllFiles` method in the `MusicOrganizer` class look like? What sort of return type should it have? Does it need to take any parameters?

Exercise 4.19 We know that the first file name is stored at index zero in the `ArrayList` and the list stores the file names as strings, so could we write the body of `listAllFiles` along the following lines?

```
System.out.println(files.get(0));
System.out.println(files.get(1));
System.out.println(files.get(2));
```

etc. How many `println` statements would be required to complete the method?

You have probably appreciated that it is not really possible to complete Exercise 4.19, because it depends on how many file names are in the list at the time they are printed. If there are three, then three `println` statements would be required; if there are four, then four statements would be needed; and so on. The `listFile` and `removeFile` methods illustrate that the range of valid index numbers at any one time is [0 to (`size()`-1)]. So a `listAllFiles` method would also have to take that dynamic size into account in order to do its job.

What we have here is the requirement to do something several times, but the number of times depends upon circumstances that may vary—in this case, the size of the collection. We shall meet this sort of requirement in nearly every program we write, and most programming languages have several ways to deal with it through the use of *loop statements*, which are also known as *iterative control structures*.

The first loop we will introduce to list the files is a special one for use with collections, one that completely avoids the need to use an index variable at all: it is called a *for-each loop*.

4.9.1 The for-each loop

Concept:

A **loop** can be used to execute a block of statements repeatedly without having to write them multiple times.

A *for-each loop* is one way to perform a set of actions repeatedly on the items in a collection, but without having to write out those actions more than once, as we saw was a problem in Exercise 4.19. We can summarize the Java syntax and actions of a for-each loop in the following pseudo-code:

```
for(ElementType element : collection) {
    loop body
}
```

The main new piece of Java is the word `for`. The Java language has two variations of the `for` loop: one is the *for-each loop*, which we are discussing here; the other one is simply called a *for loop* and will be discussed later in this chapter.

A for-each loop has two parts: a loop header (the first line of the loop statement) and a loop body following the header. The body contains those statements that we wish to perform over and over again.

The for-each loop gets its name from the way we can read this loop: if we read the keyword `for` as "for each" and the colon in the loop header as "in," then the code structure shown above slowly starts to make more sense, as in this non-Java pseudo-code:

```
for each element in collection do: {
    loop body
}
```

When you compare this version to the original pseudo-code in the first version, you notice that *element* was written in the form of a variable declaration as ElementType element. This section does indeed declare a variable that is then used for each collection element in turn. Before discussing further, let us look at an example of real Java code.

Code 4.3 shows an implementation of a listAllFiles method that lists all file names currently in the organizer's ArrayList that use such a for-each loop.

Code 4.3

Using a for-each loop to list the file names

```
/**
 * Show a list of all the files in the collection.
 */
public void listAllFiles()
{
    for(String filename : files) {
        System.out.println(filename);
    }
}
```

In this for-each loop, the loop body—consisting of a single System.out.println statement —is executed repeatedly, once for each element in the files ArrayList. If, for example, there were four strings in the list, the println statement would be executed four times.

Each time before the statement is executed, the variable filename is set to hold one of the list elements: first the one at index 0, then the one at index 1, and so on. Thus, each element in the list gets printed out.

Let us dissect the loop in a little more detail. The keyword for introduces the loop. It is followed by a pair of parentheses, within which the loop details are defined. The first of the details is the declaration String filename; this declares a new local variable filename that will be used to hold the list elements in order. We call this variable the *loop variable*. We can choose the name of this variable just as we can that of any other variable; it does not have to be called "filename." The type of the loop variable must be the same as the declared element type of the collection we are going to use—String in our case.

Then follows a colon and the variable holding the collection that we wish to process. From this collection, each element will be assigned to the loop variable in turn; and for each of those assignments, the loop body is executed once. In the loop body, we then use the loop variable to refer to each element.

To test your understanding of how this loop operates, try the following exercises.

Exercise 4.20 Implement the listAllFiles method in your version of the music-organizer project. (A solution with this method implemented is provided in the *music-organizer-v3* version of this project, but to improve your understanding of the subject, we recommend that you write this method yourself.)

Exercise 4.21 Create a `MusicOrganizer` and store a few file names in it. Use the `listAllFiles` method to print them out; check that the method works as it should.

Exercise 4.22 Create an `ArrayList<String>` in the Code Pad by typing the following two lines:

```
import java.util.ArrayList;
new ArrayList<String>()
```

If you write the last line without a trailing semicolon, you will see the small red object icon. Drag this icon onto the object bench. Examine its methods and try calling some (such as `add`, `remove`, `size`, `isEmpty`). Also try calling the same methods from the Code Pad. You can access objects on the object bench from the Code Pad by using their names. For example, if you have an `ArrayList` named `all` on the object bench, in the Code Pad you can type:

```
all.size()
```

Exercise 4.23 If you wish, you could use the debugger to help you understand how the statements in the body of the loop in `listAllFiles` are repeated. Set a breakpoint just before the loop, and step through the method until the loop has processed all elements and exits.

Exercise 4.24 *Challenge exercise* The for-each loop does not use an explicit integer variable to access successive elements of the list. Thus, if we want to include the index of each file name in the listing, then we would have to declare our own local integer variable (`position`, say) so that we can write in the body of the loop something like:

```
System.out.println(position + ": " + filename);
```

See if you can complete a version of `listAllFiles` to do this. *Hint:* You will need a local variable declaration of `position` in the method, as well as a statement to update its value by one inside the for-each loop.

One of the things this exercise illustrates is that the for-each loop is not really intended to be used with a separate index variable.

We have now seen how we can use a for-each loop to perform some operation (the loop body) on every element of a collection. This is a big step forward, but it does not solve all our problems. Sometimes we need a little more control, and Java provides a different loop construct to let us do more: the *while loop*.

4.9.2 Selective processing of a collection

The `listAllFiles` method illustrates the fundamental usefulness of a for-each loop: it provides access to every element of a collection, in order, via the variable declared in the loop's header. It does not provide us with the index position of an element, but we don't always need that, so that is not necessarily a problem.

Having access to every item in the collection, however, does not mean we have to do the same thing to every one; we can be more selective than that. For instance, we might want to only list the music by a particular artist or need to find all the music with a particular phrase in the title. There is nothing to stop us doing this, because the body of a for-each loop is just an ordinary block, and we can use whatever Java statements we wish inside it. So using an if-statement in the body to select the files we want should be easy.

Code 4.4 shows a method to list only those file names in the collection that contain a particular string.

Code 4.4

Printing selected items from the collection

```
/**
 * List the names of files matching the given search string.
 * @param searchString The string to match.
 */
public void listMatching(String searchString)
{
    for(String filename : files) {
        if(filename.contains(searchString)) {
            // A match.
            System.out.println(filename);
        }
    }
}
```

Using an if statement and the `boolean` result of the `contains` method of the `String` class, we can "filter" which file names are to be printed and which are not. If the file name does not match, then we just ignore it—no `else` part is needed. The filtering criterion (the test in the if statement) can be whatever we want.

Exercise 4.25 Add the `listMatching` method in Code 4.4 to your version of the project. (Use *music-organizer-v3* if you do not already have your own version.) Check that the method only lists matching files. Also try it with a search string that matches none of the file names. Is anything at all printed in this case?

Exercise 4.26 *Challenge exercise* In `listMatching`, can you find a way to print a message, once the for-each loop has finished, if no file names matched the search string? *Hint:* Use a `boolean` local variable.

Exercise 4.27 Write a method in your version of the project that plays samples of all the tracks by a particular artist, one after the other. The `listMatching` method illustrates the basic structure you need for this method. Make sure that you choose an artist with more than one file. Use the `playAndWait` method of the `MusicPlayer`, rather than the `startPlaying` method; otherwise, you will end up playing all the matching tracks at the same time. The `playAndWait` method plays the beginning of a track (about 15 seconds) and then returns.

Exercise 4.28 Write out the header of a for-each loop to process an `ArrayList<Track>` called `tracks`. Don't worry about the loop's body.

4.9.3 A limitation of using strings

Of course, by this point we can see that simply having file name strings containing all the details of the music track is not really satisfactory. For instance, suppose we wanted to find all tracks with the word "love" in the title. Using the unsophisticated matching technique described above, we will also find tracks by artists whose names happen to have that sequence of characters in them (e.g., Glover). While that might not seem like a particularly big problem, it does have a rather "cheap" feel about it, and it should be possible to do better with just a little more effort. What we really need is a separate class—`Track`, say—that stores the details of artist and title independently of the file name. Then we could more easily match titles separately from artists. The `ArrayList<String>` in the organizer would then become an `ArrayList<Track>`.

As we develop the music-organizer project in later sections, we will eventually move towards a better structure by introducing a `Track` class.

4.9.4 Summary of the for-each loop

The for-each loop is always used to iterate over a collection. It provides us with a way to access every item in the collection in sequence, one by one, and process those items in whatever way we want. We can choose to do the same thing to each item (as we did when printing the full listing) or we can be selective and filter the list (as we did when we printed only a subset of the collection). The body of the loop can be as complicated as we like.

With its essential simplicity necessarily come some limitations. For instance, one restriction is that we cannot change what is stored in the collection while iterating over it, either by adding new items to it or removing items from it. That doesn't mean, however, that we cannot change the states of objects already within the collection.

We have also seen that the for-each loop does not provide us with an index value for the items in the collection. If we want one, then we have to declare and maintain our own local variable. The reason for this has to do with abstraction, again. When dealing with collections and iterating over them, it is worth bearing two things in mind:

■ A for-each loop provides a general control structure for iterating over different types of collection.

■ There are some types of collections that do not naturally associate integer indices with the items they store. We will meet some of these in Chapter 5.

So the for-each loop abstracts the task of processing a complete collection, element by element, and is able to handle different types of collection. We do not need to know the details of how it manages that.

One of the questions we have not asked is whether a for-each loop can be used if we want to stop partway through processing the collection. For instance, suppose that instead of playing every track by our chosen artist, we just wanted to find the first one and play it, without going any further. While in principle it *is* possible to do this using a for-each loop, our practice and advice is not to use a for-each loop for tasks that might not need to process the whole collection. In other words, we recommend using a for-each loop only if you *definitely* want to process *the whole collection*. Again, stated in another way, once the loop starts, you know for sure how many times the body will be executed—this will be equal to the size of the collection. This style is often called *definite iteration.* For tasks where you might want to stop partway through, there are more appropriate loops to use—for instance, the *while loop*, which we will introduce next. In these cases, the number of times the loop's body will be executed is less certain; it typically depends on what happens during the iteration. This style is often called *indefinite iteration,* and we explore it next.

4.10 Indefinite iteration

Using a for-each loop has given us our first experience with the principle of carrying out some actions repeatedly. The statements inside the loop body are repeated for each item in the associated collection, and the iteration stops when we reach the end of the collection. A for-each loop provides *definite iteration*; given the state of a particular collection, the loop body will be executed the number of times that exactly matches the size of that collection. But there are many situations where we want to repeat some actions but we cannot predict in advance exactly how many times that might be. A for-each loop does not help us in those cases.

Imagine, for instance, that you have lost your keys and you need to find them before you can leave the house. Your search will model an indefinite iteration, because there will be many different places to look, and you cannot predict in advance how many places you will have to search before you find the keys; after all, if you could predict that, you would go straight to where they are! So you will do something like mentally composing a list of possible places they could be and then visit each place in turn until you find them. Once found, you want to stop looking rather than complete the list (which would be pointless).

What we have here is an example of *indefinite iteration*: the (search) action will be repeated an unpredictable number of times, until the task is complete. Scenarios similar to key searching are common in programming situations. While we will not always be searching for something, situations in which we want to keep doing something until the repetition is no longer necessary are frequently encountered. Indeed, they are so common that most programming languages provide at least one—and commonly more than one—loop construct to express them. Because what we are trying to do with these loop constructs is typically more complex than just iterating over a complete collection from beginning to end, they require a little more effort to understand. But this effort will be well rewarded from the greater variety of things we can achieve with them. Our focus here will be on Java's *while loop*, which is similar to loops found in other programming languages.

4.10.1   The while loop

A *while loop* consists of a header and a body; the body is intended to be executed repeatedly. Here is the structure of a while loop where *boolean condition* and *loop body* are pseudo-code but all the rest is the Java syntax:

```
while(boolean condition) {
    loop body
}
```

The loop is introduced with the keyword `while`, which is followed by a boolean condition. The condition is ultimately what controls how many times a particular loop will iterate. The condition is evaluated when program control first reaches the loop, and it is reevaluated each time the loop body has been executed. This is what gives a while loop its indefinite character—the reevaluation process. If the condition evaluates to *true*, then the body is executed; and once it evaluates to *false*, the iteration is finished. The loop's body is then skipped over and execution continues with whatever follows immediately after the loop. Note that the condition could actually evaluate to *false* on the very first time it is tested. If this happens, the body won't be executed at all. This is an important feature of the while loop: the body might be executed zero times, rather than always at least once.

Before we look at a proper Java example, let's look at a pseudo-code version of the key hunt described above, to try to develop a feel for how a while loop works. Here is one way to express the search:

```
while(the keys are missing) {
    look in the next place
}
```

When we arrive at the loop for the first time, the condition is evaluated and the keys are missing. That means we enter the body of the loop and look in the next place on our mental list. Having done that, we return to the condition and reevaluate it. If we have found the keys, the loop is finished and we can skip over the loop and leave the house. If the keys are still missing, then we go back into the loop body and look in the next place. This repetitive process continues until the keys are no longer missing.[1]

Note that we could equally well express the loop's condition the other way around, as follows:

```
while(not (the keys have been found)) {
    look in the next place
}
```

The distinction is subtle—one expressed as a status to be changed and the other as a goal that has not yet been achieved. Take some time to read the two versions carefully to be sure you understand how each works. Both are equally valid and reflect choices of expression we will have to make when writing real loops. In both cases, what we write inside the loop when the keys are finally found will mean the loop conditions "flip" from *true* to *false* the next time they are evaluated.

Exercise 4.29 Suppose we express the first version of the key search in pseudo-code as follows:

```
boolean missing = true;
while(missing) {
    if(the keys are in the next place) {
        missing = false;
    }
}
```

---

[1] At this stage, we will ignore the possibility that the keys are not found, but taking this kind of possibility into account will actually become very important when we look at real Java examples.

Try to express the second version by completing the following outline:

```
boolean found = false;
while(...) {
    if(the keys are in the next place) {
        ...
    }
}
```

4.10.2 Iterating with an index variable

For our first while loop in correct Java code, we shall write a version of the `listAllFiles` method shown in Code 4.3. This does not really illustrate the indefinite character of while loops, but it does provide a useful comparison with the equivalent, familiar for-each example. The while-loop version is shown in Code 4.5. A key feature is the way that an integer variable (`index`) is used both to access the list's elements and to control the length of the iteration.

Code 4.5

Using a while loop
to list the tracks

```
/**
 * Show a list of all the files in the collection.
 */
public void listAllFiles()
{
    int index = 0;
    while(index < files.size()) {
        String filename = files.get(index);
        System.out.println(filename);
        index++;
    }
}
```

It is immediately obvious that the while-loop version requires more effort on our part to program it. Consider:

■ We have to declare a variable for the list index, and we have to initialize it ourselves to 0 for the first list element. The variable must be declared outside the loop.

■ We have to work out how to express the loop's condition in order to ensure that the loop stops at the right time.

■ The list elements are not automatically fetched out of the collection and assigned to a variable for us. Instead, we have to do this ourselves, using the `get` method of the `ArrayList`. The variable `filename` will be local to the body of the loop.

■ We have to remember to increment the counter variable (`index`) ourselves, in order to ensure that the loop condition will eventually become *false* when we have reached the end of the list.

The final statement in the body of the while loop illustrates a special operator for incrementing a numerical variable by 1:

```
index++;
```

This is equivalent to

```
index = index + 1;
```

So far, the for-each loop is clearly nicer for our purpose. It was less trouble to write, and it is safer. The reason it is safer is that it is always guaranteed to come to an end. In our while-loop version, it is possible to make a mistake that results in an *infinite loop*. If we were to forget to increment the index variable (the last line in the loop body), the loop condition would never become *false*, and the loop would iterate indefinitely. This is a typical programming error that catches out even experienced programmers from time to time. The program will then run forever. If the loop in such a situation does not contain an output statement, the program will appear to "hang": it seems to do nothing, and does not respond to any mouse clicks or key presses. In reality, the program does a lot. It executes the loop over and over, but we cannot see any effect of this, and the program seems to have died. In BlueJ, this can often be detected by the fact that the red-and-white-striped "running" indicator remains on while the program appears to be doing nothing.

So what are the benefits of a while loop over a for-each loop? They are twofold: first, the while loop does not need to be related to a collection (we can loop on any condition that we can write as a boolean expression); second, even if we are using the loop to process the collection, we do not need to process every element—instead, we could stop earlier if we wanted to by including another component in the loop's condition that expresses why we would want to stop. Of course, strictly speaking, the loop's condition actually expresses whether we want to continue, and it is the negation of this that causes the loop to stop.

A benefit of having an explicit index variable is that we can use its value both inside and outside the loop, which was not available to us in the for-each examples. So we can include the index in the listing if we wish. That will make it easier to choose a track by its position in the list. For instance:

```
int index = 0;
while(index < files.size()) {
    String filename = files.get(index);
    // Prefix the file name with the track's index.
    System.out.println(index + ": " + filename);
    index++;
}
```

Having a local index variable can be particularly important when searching a list, because it can provide a record of where the item was located, which is still available once the loop has finished. We shall see this in the next section.

4.10.3 Searching a collection

Searching is one of the most important forms of iteration you will encounter. It is vital, therefore, to have a good grasp of its essential elements. The sort of loop structures that result occur again and again in practical programming situations.

The key characteristic of a search is that it involves *indefinite iteration*; this is necessarily so, because if we knew exactly where to look, we would not need a search at all! Instead, we have to initiate a search, and it will take an unknown number of iterations before we succeed. This implies that a for-each loop is inappropriate for use when searching, because it will complete its full set of iterations.[2]

In real search situations, we have to take into account the fact that the search might fail: we might run out of places to look. That means that we typically have two finishing possibilities to consider when writing a searching loop:

- The search succeeds after an indefinite number of iterations.
- The search fails after exhausting all possibilities.

Both of these must be taken into account when writing the loop's condition. As the loop's condition should evaluate to *true* if we want to iterate one more time, each of the finishing criteria should, on their own, make the condition evaluate to *false* to stop the loop.

The fact that we end up searching the whole list when the search fails does not turn a failed search into an example of definite iteration. The key characteristic of definite iteration is that you can determine the number of iterations *when the loop starts*. This won't be the case with a search.

If we are using an index variable to work our way through successive elements of a collection, then a failed search is easy to identify: the index variable will have been incremented beyond the final item in the list. That's exactly the situation that is covered in the `listAllFiles` method in Code 4.5, where the condition is:

```
while(index < files.size())
```

The condition expresses that we want to continue as long as the index is within the valid index range of the collection; as soon as it has been incremented out of range, then we want the loop to stop. It is worth pointing out that this condition even works if the list is completely empty. In this case, `index` will have been initialized to zero and the call to the `size` method will return zero too. Because zero is not less than zero, the loop's body will not be executed at all, which is what we want.

We also need to add a second part to the condition that indicates whether we have found the search item yet and stops the search when we have. We saw in Section 4.10.1 and Exercise 4.29 that we can often express this positively or negatively, via appropriately set boolean variables:

- A variable called `searching` (or `missing`, say) initially set to *true* could keep the search going until it is set to *false* inside the loop when the item is found.
- A variable called `found`, initially set to *false* and used in the condition as `!found` could keep the search going until set to *true* when the item is found.

Here are the two corresponding code fragments that express the full condition in both cases:

```
int index = 0;
boolean searching = true;
while(index < files.size() && searching)
```

---

[2] While there are ways to subvert this characteristic of a for-each loop, and they are used quite commonly, we consider them to be bad style and do not use them in our examples.

and

```
int index = 0;
boolean found = false;
while(index < files.size() && !found)
```

Take some time to make sure you understand these two fragments, which accomplish exactly the same loop control, but expressed in slightly different ways. Remember that the condition *as a whole* must evaluate to *true* if we want to continue looking, and *false* if we want to stop looking, for any reason. We discussed the "and" operator && in Chapter 3, which only evaluates to *true* if *both* of its operands are *true*.

The full version of a method to search for the first file name matching a given search string can be seen in Code 4.6 (*music-organizer-v4*). The method returns the index of the item as its result. Note that we need to find a way to indicate to the method's caller if the search has failed. In this case, we choose to return a value that cannot possibly represent a valid location in the collection—a negative value. This is a commonly used technique in search situations: the return of an *out-of-bounds* value to indicate failure.

Code 4.6

Finding the first matching item in a list

```
/**
 * Find the index of the first file matching the given
 * search string.
 * @param searchString The string to match.
 * @return The index of the first occurrence, or -1 if
 *          no match is found.
 */
public int findFirst(String searchString)
{
    int index = 0;
    // Record that we will be searching until a match is found.
    boolean searching = true;

    while(searching && index < files.size()) {
        String filename = files.get(index);
        if(filename.contains(searchString)) {
            // A match. We can stop searching.
            searching = false;
        }
        else {
            // Move on.
            index++;
        }
    }
    if(searching) {
        // We didn't find it.
        return -1;
    }
```

Code 4.6 continued

Finding the first matching item in a list

```
    else {
        // Return where it was found.
        return index;
    }
}
```

It might be tempting to try to have just one condition in the loop, even though there are two distinct reasons for ending the search. A way to do this would be to arrange artificially for the value of index to be too large if we find what we are looking for. This is a practice we discourage, because it makes the termination criteria of the loop misleading, and clarity is always to be preferred.

4.10.4 Some non-collection examples

Loops are not only used with collections. There are many situations were we want to repeat a block of statements that does not involve a collection at all. Here is an example that prints out all even numbers from 0 up to 30:

```
int index = 0;
while(index <= 30) {
    System.out.println(index);
    index = index + 2;
}
```

In fact, this is the use of a while loop for definite iteration, because it is clear at the start how many numbers will be printed. However, we cannot use a for-each loop, because they can only be used when iterating over collections. Later we will meet a third, related loop—the *for loop*—that would be more appropriate for this particular example.

To test your own understanding of while loops aside from collections, try the following exercises.

Exercise 4.30 Write a while loop (for example, in a method called `multiplesOfFive`) that prints out all multiples of 5 between 10 and 95.

Exercise 4.31 Write a while loop to sum the values 1 to 10 and print the sum once the loop has finished.

Exercise 4.32 Write a method called `sum` with a while loop that adds up all numbers between two numbers `a` and `b`. The values for `a` and `b` can be passed to the `sum` method as parameters.

Exercise 4.33 *Challenge task* Write a method `isPrime(int n)` that returns *true* if the parameter `n` is a prime number, and *false* if it is not. To implement the method, you can write a while loop that divides n by all numbers between 2 and (n-1) and tests whether the division yields a whole number. You can write this test by using the modulo operator (%) to check whether the integer division leaves a remainder of 0 (see the discussion of the modulo operator in Section 3.8.3).

Exercise 4.34 In the findFirst method, the loop's condition repeatedly asks the files collection how many files it is storing. Does the value returned by size vary from one check to the next? If you think the answer is no, then rewrite the method so that the number of files is determined only once and stored in a local variable prior to execution of the loop. Then use the local variable in the loop's condition rather than the call to size. Check that this version gives the same results. If you have problems completing this exercise, try using the debugger to see where things are going wrong.

4.11 Improving structure—the Track class

We have seen in a couple of places that using strings to store all of the track details is not entirely satisfactory and gives our music player a rather cheap feel. Any commercial player would allow us to search for tracks by artist, title, album, genre, etc., and would likely include further details, such as track playing time and track number. One of the powers of object orientation is that it allows us to design classes that closely model the inherent structure and behaviors of the real-world entities we are often trying to represent. This is achieved through writing classes whose fields and methods match those of the attributes. We know enough already about how to write basic classes with fields, constructors, and accessor and mutator methods that we can easily design a Track class that has fields for storing separate artist and title information, for instance. In this way, we will be able to interact with the objects in the music organizer in a way that feels more natural.

So it is time to move away from storing the track details as strings, because having a separate Track class is the most appropriate way to represent the main data items—music tracks—that we are using in the program. However, we will not be too ambitious. One of the obvious hurdles to overcome is how to obtain the separate pieces of information we wish to store in each Track object. One way would be to ask the user to input the artist, title, genre, etc., each time they add a music file to the organizer. However, that would be fairly slow and laborious, so, for this project, we have chosen a set of music files that have the artist and title as part of the file name, and we have written a helper class for our application (called TrackReader) that will look for any music files in a particular folder and use their file names to fill in parts of the corresponding Track objects. We won't worry about the details of how this is done at this stage. (Later in this book, we will discuss the techniques and library classes used in the TrackReader class.) An implementation of this design is in *music-organizer-v5*.

Here are some of the key points to look for in this version:

■ The main thing to review is the changes we have made to the MusicOrganizer class, in going from storing String objects in the ArrayList to storing Track objects (Code 4.7). This has affected most of the methods we developed previously.

- When listing details of the tracks in listAllTracks, we request the Track object to return a String containing its details. This shows that we have designed the Track class to be responsible for formatting the details to be printed, such as artist and title. This is an example of what is called *responsibility-driven design*, which we cover in more detail in a later chapter.

- In the playTrack method, we now have to retrieve the file name from the selected Track object before passing it on to the player.

- In the music library, we have added code to automatically read from the *audio* folder and some print statements to display some information.

Code 4.7

Using Track in the MusicOrganizer class

```java
import java.util.ArrayList;

/**
 * A class to hold details of audio tracks.
 * Individual tracks may be played.
 *
 * @author David J. Barnes and Michael Kölling
 * @version 2011.07.31
 */
public class MusicOrganizer
{
    // An ArrayList for storing music tracks.
    private ArrayList<Track> tracks;
    // A player for the music tracks.
    private MusicPlayer player;
    // A reader that can read music files and load them as tracks.
    private TrackReader reader;

    /**
     * Create a MusicOrganizer
     */
    public MusicOrganizer()
    {
        tracks = new ArrayList<Track>();
        player = new MusicPlayer();
        reader = new TrackReader();
        readLibrary("audio");
        System.out.println("Music library loaded. " +
                          getNumberOfTracks() + " tracks.");
        System.out.println();
    }

    /**
     * Add a track to the collection.
     * @param track The track to be added.
     */
```

**Code 4.7
continued**

Using Track in the
MusicOrganizer
class

```
    public void addTrack(Track track)
    {
        tracks.add(track);
    }

    /**
     * Show a list of all the tracks in the collection.
     */
    public void listAllTracks()
    {
        System.out.println("Track listing: ");
        for(Track track : tracks) {
            System.out.println(track.getDetails());
        }
        System.out.println();
    }

    /**
     * Play a track in the collection.
     * @param index The index of the track to be played.
     */
    public void playTrack(int index)
    {
        if(indexValid(index)) {
            Track track = tracks.get(index);
            player.startPlaying(track.getFilename());
            System.out.println("Now playing: " + track.getArtist() +
                               " - " + track.getTitle());
        }
    }

    Other methods omitted.
}
```

While we can see that introducing a Track class has made some of the old methods slightly more complicated, working with specialized Track objects ultimately results in a much better structure for the program as a whole and allows us to develop the Track class to the most appropriate level of detail for representing more than just music file names.

With a better structuring of track information, we can now do a much better job of searching for tracks that meet particular criteria. For instance, if we want to find all tracks that contain the word "love" in their title, we can do so as follows without risking mismatches on artists' names:

```
    /**
     * List all tracks containing the given search string.
     * @param searchString The search string to be found.
     */
```

```
public void findInTitle(String searchString)
{
    for(Track track : tracks) {
        String title = track.getTitle();
        if(title.contains(searchString)) {
            System.out.println(track.getDetails());
        }
    }
}
```

Exercise 4.35 Add a `playCount` field to the `Track` class. Provide methods to reset the count to zero and to increment it by one.

Exercise 4.36 Have the `MusicOrganizer` increment the play count of a track whenever it is played.

Exercise 4.37 Add a further field, of your choosing, to the `Track` class, and provide accessor and mutator methods to query and manipulate it. Find a way to use this information in your version of the project; for instance, include it in a track's details string, or allow it to be set via a method in the `MusicOrganizer` class.

Exercise 4.38 If you play two tracks without stopping the first one, both will play simultaneously. This is not very useful. Change your program so that a playing track is automatically stopped when another track is started.

4.12 The Iterator type

Concept:

An **iterator** is an object that provides functionality to iterate over all elements of a collection.

Iteration is a vital tool in almost every programming project, so it should come as no surprise to discover that programming languages typically provide a wide range of features that support it, each with their own particular characteristics suited for different situations.

We will now discuss a third variation for how to iterate over a collection that is somewhat in the middle between the while loop and the for-each loop. It uses a while loop to perform the iteration and an *Iterator object* instead of an integer index variable to keep track of the position in the list. We have to be very careful with naming at this point, because `Iterator` (note the uppercase *I*) is a Java *type*, but we will also encounter a *method* called `iterator` (lowercase *i*), so be sure to pay close attention to these differences when reading this section and when writing your own code.

Examining every item in a collection is so common that we have already seen a special control structure—the for-each loop—that is custom made for this purpose. In addition, Java's various collection library classes provide a custom-made common type to support iteration, and `ArrayList` is typical in this respect.

The `iterator` method of `ArrayList` returns an `Iterator` object. `Iterator` is also defined in the `java.util` package, so we must add a second import statement to the class file to use it:

```
import java.util.ArrayList;
import java.util.Iterator;
```

An `Iterator` provides just three methods, and two of these are use to iterate over a collection: `hasNext` and `next`. Neither takes a parameter, but both have non-void return types, so they are used in expressions. The way we usually use an `Iterator` can be described in pseudo-code as follows:

```
Iterator<ElementType> it = myCollection.iterator();
while(it.hasNext()) {
        call it.next() to get the next element
        do something with that element
}
```

In this code fragment, we first use the `iterator` method of the `ArrayList` class to obtain an `Iterator` object. Note that `Iterator` is also a generic type, so we parameterize it with the type of the elements in the collection we are iterating over. Then we use that `Iterator` to repeatedly check whether there are any more elements, `it.hasNext()`, and to get the next element, `it.next()`. One important point to note is that it is the `Iterator` object that we ask to return the next item, and not the collection object. Indeed, we tend not to refer directly to the collection at all in the body of the loop; all interaction with the collection is done via the `Iterator`.

Using an `Iterator`, we can write a method to list the tracks, as shown in Code 4.8. In effect, the `Iterator` starts at the beginning of the collection and progressively works its way through, one object at a time, each time we call its `next` method.

Code 4.8

Using an `Iterator` to list the tracks

```
/**
 * List all the tracks.
 */
public void listAllTracks()
{
    Iterator<Track> it = tracks.iterator();
    while(it.hasNext()) {
        Track t = it.next();
        System.out.println(t.getDetails());
    }
}
```

Take some time to compare this version to the one using a for-each loop in Code 4.7 and the two versions of `listAllFiles` shown in Code 4.3 and Code 4.5. A particular point to note about the latest version is that we use a while loop, but we do not need to take care of the `index` variable. This is because the `Iterator` keeps track of how far it has gotten through the collection, so that it knows both whether there are any more items left (`hasNext`) and which one to return (`next`) if there is another.

One of the keys to understanding how `Iterator` works is that the call to `next` causes the `Iterator` to return the next item in the collection *and then move past that item*. Therefore, successive calls to `next` on an `Iterator` will always return distinct items; you cannot go back to the previous item once `next` has been called. Eventually, the `Iterator` reaches the end of the collection and then returns *false* from a call to `hasNext`. Once `hasNext` has returned *false*, it would be an error to try to call `next` on that particular `Iterator` object—in effect, the `Iterator` object has been "used up" and has no further use.

Figure 4.5
An iterator, after one
iteration, pointing to
the next item to be
processed

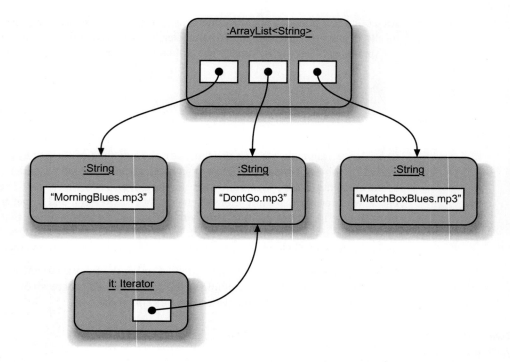

On the face of it, Iterator seems to offer no obvious advantages over the previous ways we have seen to iterate over a collection, but the following two sections provide reasons why it is important to know how to use it.

4.12.1 Index access versus iterators

We have seen that we have at least three different ways in which we can iterate over an ArrayList. We can use a for-each loop (as seen in Section 4.9.1), the get method with an integer index variable (Section 4.10.2), or an Iterator object (this section).

From what we know so far, all approaches seem about equal in quality. The first one was maybe slightly easier to understand, but the least flexible.

The first approach, using the for-each loop, is the standard technique used if all elements of a collection are to be processed (i.e., definite iteration), because it is the most concise for that case. The two latter versions have the benefit that iteration can more easily be stopped in the middle of processing (indefinite iteration), so they are preferable when processing only a part of the collection.

For an ArrayList, the two latter methods (using the while loops) are in fact equally good. This is not always the case, though. Java provides many more collection classes besides the ArrayList. We shall see several of them in the following chapters. For some collections, it is either impossible or very inefficient to access individual elements by providing an index. Thus, our first while loop version is a solution particular to the ArrayList collection and may not work for other types of collections.

The most recent solution, using an `Iterator`, is available for all collections in the Java class library and thus is an important code pattern that we shall use again in later projects.

4.12.2 Removing elements

Another important consideration when choosing which looping structure to use comes in when we have to remove elements from the collection while iterating. An example might be that we want to remove all tracks from our collection that are by an artist we are no longer interested in.

We can quite easily write this in pseudo-code:

```
for each track in the collection {
    if track.getArtist() is the out-of-favor artist:
        collection.remove(track)
}
```

It turns out that this perfectly reasonable operation is not possible to achieve with a for-each loop. If we try to modify the collection using one of the collection's `remove` methods while in the middle of an iteration, the system will report an error (called a `ConcurrentModificationException`). This happens because changing the collection in the middle of an iteration has the potential to thoroughly confuse the situation. What if the removed element was the one we were currently working on? If it has now been removed, how should we find the next element? There are no generally good answers to these potential problems, so using the collection's `remove` method is just not allowed during an iteration with the for-each loop.

The proper solution to removing while iterating is to use an `Iterator`. Its third method (in addition to `hasNext` and `next`) is `remove`. It takes no parameter and has a `void` return type. Calling `remove` will remove the item that was returned by the most recent call to `next`. Here is some sample code:

```
Iterator<Track> it = tracks.iterator();
while(it.hasNext()) {
    Track t = it.next();
    String artist = t.getArtist();
    if(artist.equals(artistToRemove)) {
        it.remove();
    }
}
```

Once again, note that we do not use the `tracks` collection variable in the body of the loop. While both `ArrayList` and `Iterator` have `remove` methods, we must use the `Iterator`'s `remove` method, not the `ArrayList`'s.

Using the `Iterator`'s `remove` is less flexible: we cannot remove arbitrary elements, but only the last element we retrieved from the `Iterator`'s `next` method. On the other hand, using the `Iterator`'s `remove` is allowed during an iteration. Because the `Iterator` itself is informed of the removal (and does it for us), it can keep the iteration properly in sync with the collection.

Such removal is not possible with the for-each loop, because we do not have an `Iterator` there to work with. In this case, we need to use the while loop with an `Iterator`.

Technically, we can also remove elements by using the collection's get method with an index for the iteration. This is not recommended, however, because the element indices can change when we add or delete elements and it is quite easy to get the iteration with indices wrong when we modify the collection during iteration. Using an Iterator protects us from such errors.

> **Exercise 4.39** Implement a method in your music organizer that lets you specify a string as a parameter and then removes all tracks whose titles contain that string.

4.13 Summary of the music-organizer project

In the music organizer we have seen how we can use an ArrayList object, created from a class out of the class library, to store an arbitrary number of objects in a collection. We do not have to decide in advance how many objects we want to store, and the ArrayList object automatically keeps track of the number of items stored in it.

We have discussed how we can use a loop to iterate over all elements in the collection. Java has several loop constructs—the two we have used here are the *for-each loop* and the *while loop*. We typically use a for-each loop when we want to process the whole collection and the while loop when we cannot predetermine how many iterations we need or when we need to remove elements during iteration.

With an ArrayList, we can access elements either by index or we can iterate over all elements using an Iterator object. It will be worthwhile for you to review the different circumstances under which the different types of loop (for-each and while) are appropriate and why an Iterator is to be preferred over an integer index, because these sorts of decisions will have to be made over and over again. Getting them right can make a big difference to the ease with which a particular problem can be solved.

> **Exercise 4.40** Use the *club* project to complete the following exercises. Your task is to complete the Club class, an outline of which has been provided in the project. The Club class is intended to store Membership objects in a collection.
>
> Within Club, define a field for an ArrayList. Use an appropriate import statement for this field, and think carefully about the element type of the list. In the constructor, create the collection object and assign it to the field. Make sure that all the files in the project compile before moving on to the next exercise.
>
> **Exercise 4.41** Complete the numberOfMembers method to return the current size of the collection. Until you have a method to add objects to the collection, this will always return zero, of course, but it will be ready for further testing later.
>
> **Exercise 4.42** Membership of a club is represented by an instance of the Membership class. A complete version of Membership is already provided for you in the *club* project, and it should not need any modification. An instance contains details of a person's name and the

month and year in which they joined the club. All membership details are filled out when an instance is created. A new `Membership` object is added to a `Club` object's collection via the `Club` object's `join` method, which has the following description:

```
/**
 * Add a new member to the club's collection of members.
 * @param member The member object to be added.
 */
public void join (Membership member)
```

Complete the `join` method.

When you wish to add a new `Membership` object to the `Club` object from the object bench, there are two ways you can do this. Either create a new `Membership` object on the object bench, call the `join` method on the `Club` object, and click on the `Membership` object to supply the parameter or call the `join` method on the `Club` object and type into the method's parameter dialog box:

```
new Membership ("member name ...", month, year)
```

Each time you add one, use the `numberOfMembers` method to check both that the `join` method is adding to the collection and that the `numberOfMembers` method is giving the correct result.

We shall continue to explore this project with some further exercises later in the chapter.

Exercise 4.43 *Challenge exercise* The following exercises present a challenge because they involve using some things that we have not covered explicitly. Nevertheless, you should be able to make a reasonable attempt at them if you have a comfortable grasp of the material covered so far. They involve adding something that most music players have: a "shuffle," or "random-play," feature.

The `java.util` package contains the `Random` class whose `nextInt` method will generate a positive random integer within a limited range. Write a method in the `MusicOrganizer` class to select a single random track from its list and play it.

Hint: You will need to import `Random` and create a `Random` object, either directly in the new method or in the constructor and stored in a field. You will need to find the API documentation for the `Random` class and check its methods to choose the correct version of `nextInt`. Alternatively, we cover the `Random` class in the next chapter.

Exercise 4.44 *Challenge exercise* Consider how you might play multiple tracks in a random order. Would you want to make sure that all tracks are played equally or prefer favorite tracks? How might a "play count" field in the `Track` class help with this task? Discuss the various options.

Exercise 4.45 *Challenge exercise* Write a method to play every track in the track list exactly once in random order.

Hint: One way to do this would be to shuffle the order of the tracks in the list—or, perhaps better, a copy of the list—and then play through from start to finish. Another way would be to make a copy of the list and then repeatedly choose a random track from the list, play it, and remove it from the list until the list is empty. Try to implement one of these approaches. If you try the first, how easy is it to shuffle the list so that it is genuinely in a new random order? Are there any library methods that could help with this?

4.14 Another example: an auction system

In this section, we will follow up some of the new ideas we have introduced in this chapter by looking at them again in a different context.

The *auction* project models part of the operation of an online auction system. The idea is that an auction consists of a set of items offered for sale. These items are called "lots," and each is assigned a unique lot number by the program. A person can try to buy a lot they want by bidding an amount of money for it. Our auctions are slightly different from other auctions because ours offer all lots for a limited period.[3] At the end of that period, the auction is closed. At the close of the auction, the person who bid the highest amount for a lot is considered to have bought it. Any lots for which there are no bids remain unsold at the close. Unsold lots might be offered in a later auction, for instance.

Figure 4.6
The class structure
of the *auction* project

---

[3] For the sake of simplicity, the time-limit aspects of auctions are not implemented within the classes we are considering here.

The *auction* project contains the following classes: `Auction`, `Bid`, `Lot`, and `Person`. A close look at the class diagram for this project (Figure 4.6) reveals that the relationships between the various classes are a little more complicated than we have seen in previous projects, and this will have a bearing on the way in which information is accessed during the auction activities. For instance, the diagram shows that `Auction` objects know about all the other types of objects: `Bid`, `Lot`, and `Person`. `Lot` objects know about `Bid` objects, and `Bid` objects know about `Person` objects. What the diagram cannot tell us is exactly how information stored in a `Bid` object, say, is accessed by an `Auction` object. For that, we have to look at the code of the various classes.

4.14.1 Getting started with the project

At this stage, it would be worth opening the *auction* project and exploring the source code before reading further. As well as seeing familiar use of an `ArrayList` and loops, you will likely encounter several things that you do not quite understand at first, but that is to be expected as we move on to new ideas and new ways of doing things.

An `Auction` object is the starting point for the project. People wishing to sell items enter them into the auction via the `enterLot` method, but they only supply a string description. The `Auction` object then creates a `Lot` object for each entered lot. This models the way things work in the real world: it is the auction site, rather than the sellers, for instance, that assigns lot numbers or identification codes to items. So a `Lot` object is the auction site's representation of an item for sale.

In order to bid for lots, people must register with the auction house. In our program, a potential bidder is represented by a `Person` object. These objects must be created independently on BlueJ's object bench. In our project, a `Person` object simply contains the person's name. When someone wants to bid for a lot, they call the `bidFor` method of the `Auction` object, entering the lot number they are interested in and how much they want to bid for it. Notice that they pass the lot number rather than the `Lot` object; `Lot` objects remain internal to the `Auction` object and are always referenced externally by their lot number.

Just as the `Auction` object creates `Lot` objects, it also transforms a monetary bid amount into a `Bid` object, which records the amount and the person who bid that amount. This is why we see a link from the `Bid` class to the `Person` class on the class diagram. However, note that there is no link from `Bid` to `Lot`; the link on the diagram is the other way around, because a `Lot` records which is currently the highest bid for that lot. This means that the `Lot` object will replace the `Bid` object it stores each time a higher bid is made.

What we have described here reveals quite a nested chain of object references. `Auction` objects store `Lot` objects; each `Lot` object can store a `Bid` object; each `Bid` object stores a `Person` object. Such chains are very common in programs, so this project offers a good opportunity to explore how they work in practice.

Exercise 4.46 Create an auction with a few lots, persons, and bids. Then use the object inspector to investigate the object structure. Start with the auction object, and continue by inspecting any further object references you encounter in the objects' fields.

Because neither the `Person` class nor the `Bid` class initiates any activity within the auction system, we shall not discuss them here in detail, and so studying these classes is left as an exercise to the reader. Instead, we shall focus on the source code of the `Lot` and `Auction` classes.

4.14.2   The `null` keyword

Concept:

The Java reserved word `null` is used to mean "no object" when an object variable is not currently referring to a particular object. A field that has not explicitly been initialized will contain the value `null` by default.

From the discussion above, it should be clear that a `Bid` object is only created when someone actually makes a bid for a `Lot`. The newly created `Bid` object then stores the `Person` making the bid. This means that the `Person` field of every `Bid` object can be initialized in the `Bid` constructor, and the field will always contain a valid `Person` object.

In contrast, when a `Lot` object is created, this simply means it has been entered into the auction and it has no bidders yet. Nevertheless, it still has a `Bid` field, `highestBid`, for recording the highest bid for the lot. What value should be used to initialize this field in the `Lot` constructor?

What we need is a value for the field that makes it clear that there is currently "no object" being referred to by that variable. In some sense, the variable is "empty." To indicate this, Java provides the `null` keyword. Hence, the constructor of `Lot` has the following statement in it:

```
highestBid = null;
```

A very important principle is that, if a variable contains the `null` value, a method call should not be made on it. The reason for this should be clear: as methods belong to objects, we cannot call a method if the variable does not refer to an object. This means that we sometimes have to use an if statement to test whether a variable contains `null` or not before calling a method on that variable. Failure to make this test will lead to the very common runtime error called a `NullPointerException`. You will see some examples of this test in both the `Lot` and `Auction` classes.

In fact, if we fail to initialize an object-type field, it will be given the value `null` automatically. In this particular case, however, we prefer to make the assignment explicitly so that there is no doubt in the mind of the reader of the code that we expect `highestBid` to be `null` when a `Lot` object is created.

4.14.3   The `Lot` class

The `Lot` class stores a description of the lot, a lot number, and details of the highest bid received for it so far. The most complex part of the class is the `bidFor` method (Code 4.9). This deals with what happens when a person makes a bid for the lot. When a bid is made, it is necessary to check that the new bid is higher in value than any existing bid on that lot. If it is higher, then the new bid will be stored as the current highest bid within the lot.

Code 4.9

Handle a bid for a lot

```
public class Lot
{
    // The current highest bid for this lot.
    private Bid highestBid;

    Other fields and constructor omitted.
```

Code 4.9
continued

Handle a bid for a lot

```
/**
 * Attempt to bid for this lot. A successful bid
 * must have a value higher than any existing bid.
 * @param bid A new bid.
 * @return true if successful, false otherwise
 */
public boolean bidFor(Bid bid)
{
    if(highestBid == null) {
        // There is no previous bid.
        highestBid = bid;
        return true;
    }
    else if(bid.getValue() > highestBid.getValue()) {
        // The bid is better than the previous one.
        highestBid = bid;
        return true;
    }
    else {
        // The bid is not better.
        return false;
    }
}

Other methods omitted.
}
```

Here, we first check whether this bid is the highest bid. This will be the case if there has been no previous bid or if the current bid is higher than the best bid so far. The first part of the check involves the following test:

```
highestBid == null
```

This is a test for whether the `highestBid` variable is currently referring to an object or not. As described in the previous section, until a bid is received for this lot, the `highestBid` field will contain the `null` value. If it is still `null`, then this is the first bid for this particular lot and it must clearly be the highest one. If it is not `null`, then we have to compare its value with the new bid. Note that the failure of the first test gives us some very useful information: we now know for sure that `highestBid` is not `null`, so we know that it is safe to call a method on it. We do not need to make a `null` test again in this second condition. Comparing the values of the two bids allows us to choose a higher new bid or reject the new bid if it is no better.

4.14.4   The `Auction` class

The `Auction` class (Code 4.10) provides further illustration of the `ArrayList` and for-each loop concepts we discussed earlier in the chapter.

Code 4.10

The Auction class

```java
import java.util.ArrayList;
/**
 * A simple model of an auction.
 * The auction maintains a list of lots of arbitrary length.
 * @author David J. Barnes and Michael Kölling.
 * @version 2011.07.31
 */
public class Auction
{
    // The list of Lots in this auction.
    private ArrayList<Lot> lots;
    // The number that will be given to the next lot entered
    // into this auction.
    private int nextLotNumber;

    /**
     * Create a new auction.
     */
    public Auction()
    {
        lots = new ArrayList<Lot>();
        nextLotNumber = 1;
    }

    /**
     * Enter a new lot into the auction.
     * @param description A description of the lot.
     */
    public void enterLot(String description)
    {
        lots.add(new Lot(nextLotNumber, description));
        nextLotNumber++;
    }

    /**
     * Show the full list of lots in this auction.
     */
    public void showLots()
    {
        for(Lot lot : lots) {
            System.out.println(lot.toString());
        }
    }

    /**
     * Make a bid for a lot.
     * A message is printed indicating whether the bid is
     * successful or not.
```

Code 4.10
continued

The Auction class

```java
     * @param lotNumber The lot being bid for.
     * @param bidder The person bidding for the lot.
     * @param value The value of the bid.
     */
    public void makeABid(int lotNumber, Person bidder, long value)
    {
        Lot selectedLot = getLot(lotNumber);
        if(selectedLot != null) {
            Bid bid = new Bid(bidder, value);
            boolean successful = selectedLot.bidFor(bid);
            if(successful) {
                System.out.println("The bid for lot number " +
                                    lotNumber + " was successful.");
            }
            else {
                // Report which bid is higher.
                Bid highestBid = selectedLot.getHighestBid();
                System.out.println("Lot number: " + lotNumber +
                                " already has a bid of: " +
                                highestBid.getValue());
            }
        }
    }

    /**
     * Return the lot with the given number. Return null
     * if a lot with this number does not exist.
     * @param lotNumber The number of the lot to return.
     */
    public Lot getLot(int lotNumber)
    {
        if((lotNumber >= 1) && (lotNumber < nextLotNumber)) {
            // The number seems to be reasonable.
            Lot selectedLot = lots.get(lotNumber - 1);
            // Include a confidence check to be sure we have the
            // right lot.
            if(selectedLot.getNumber() != lotNumber) {
                System.out.println("Internal error: Lot number " +
                                selectedLot.getNumber() +
                                " was returned instead of " +
                                lotNumber);
                selectedLot = null;
            }
            return selectedLot;
        }
```

```
        else {
            System.out.println("Lot number: " + lotNumber +
                                " does not exist.");
            return null;
        }
    }
}
```

The lots field is an ArrayList used to hold the lots offered in this auction. Lots are entered in the auction by passing a simple description to the enterLot method. A new lot is created by passing the description and a unique lot number to the constructor of Lot. The new Lot object is added to the collection. The following sections discuss some additional, commonly found features illustrated in the Auction class.

4.14.5   Anonymous objects

The enterLot method in Auction illustrates a common idiom—anonymous objects. We see this in the following statement:

```
lots.add(new Lot(nextLotNumber, description));
```

Here, we are doing two things:

■ We are creating a new Lot object.

■ We are also passing this new object to the ArrayList's add method.

We could have written the same statement in two lines, to make the separate steps more explicit:

```
Lot furtherLot = new Lot(nextLotNumber, description);
lots.add(furtherLot);
```

Both versions are equivalent, but if we have no further use for the furtherLot variable, then the original version avoids defining a variable with such a limited use. In effect, we create an anonymous object—an object without a name—by passing it straight to the method that uses it.

Exercise 4.47 The makeABid method includes the following two statements:

```
Bid bid = new Bid(bidder, value);
boolean successful = selectedLot.bidFor(bid);
```

The bid variable is only used here as a placeholder for the newly created Bid object before it is passed immediately to the lot's bidFor method. Rewrite these statements to eliminate the bid variable by using an anonymous object as seen in the enterLot method.

4.14.6 Chaining method calls

In our introduction to the *auction* project, we noted a chain of object references: `Auction` objects store `Lot` objects; each `Lot` object can store a `Bid` object; each `Bid` object stores a `Person` object. If the `Auction` object needs to identify who currently has the highest bid on a `Lot`, then it would need to ask the `Lot` to return the `Bid` object for that lot and then ask the `Bid` object for the `Person` who made the bid.

Ignoring the possibility of `null` object references, we might see something like the following sequence of statement in order to print the name of a bidder:

```
Bid bid = lot.getHighestBid();
Person bidder = bid.getBidder();
String name = bidder.getName();
System.out.println(name);
```

Because the `bid`, `bidder`, and `name` variables are being used here simply as staging posts to get to the bidder's name, it is common to see sequences like this compressed through the use of anonymous object references. For instance, we can achieve the same effect with the following:

```
System.out.println(lot.getHighestBid().getBidder().getName());
```

This looks as if methods are calling methods, but that is not how this must be read. Bearing in mind that the two sets of statements are equivalent, the chain of method calls must be read strictly from left to right:

```
lot.getHighestBid().getBidder().getName()
```

The call to `getHighestBid` returns an anonymous `Bid` object, and the `getBidder` method is then called on that object. Similarly, `getBidder` returns an anonymous `Person` object, so `getName` is called on that person.

Such chains of method calls can look complicated, but they can be unpicked if you understand the underlying rules. Even if you choose not to write your code in this more concise fashion, you should learn how to read it, because you may come across it in other programmers' code.

Exercise 4.48 Add a `close` method to the `Auction` class. This should iterate over the collection of lots and print out details of all the lots. Use a for-each loop. Any lot that has had at least one bid for it is considered to be sold, so what you are looking for is `Lot` objects whose `highestBid` field is not `null`. Use a local variable inside the loop to store the value returned from calls to the `getHighestBid` method, and then test that variable for the `null` value.

For lots with a bidder, the details should include the name of the successful bidder and the value of the winning bid. For lots with no bidder, print a message that indicates this.

Exercise 4.49 Add a `getUnsold` method to the `Auction` class with the following header:

```
public ArrayList<Lot> getUnsold()
```

This method should iterate over the `lots` field, storing unsold lots in a new `ArrayList` local variable. What you are looking for is `Lot` objects whose `highestBid` field is `null`. At the end of the method, return the list of unsold lots.

Exercise 4.50 Suppose that the `Auction` class includes a method that makes it possible to remove a lot from the auction. Assuming that the remaining lots do not have their `lotNumber` fields changed when a lot is removed, write down what you think the impact would be on the `getLot` method.

Exercise 4.51 Rewrite `getLot` so that it does not rely on a lot with a particular number being stored at index (`number-1`) in the collection. For instance, if lot number 2 has been removed, then lot number 3 will have been moved from index 2 to index 1, and all higher lot numbers will also have been moved by one index position. You may assume that lots are always stored in increasing order according to their lot numbers.

Exercise 4.52 Add a `removeLot` method to the `Auction` class, having the following header:

```
/**
 * Remove the lot with the given lot number.
 * @param number The number of the lot to be removed.
 * @return The Lot with the given number, or null if
 * there is no such lot.
 */
public Lot removeLot(int number)
```

This method should not assume that a lot with a given number is stored at any particular location within the collection.

Exercise 4.53 The `ArrayList` class is found in the `java.util` package. That package also includes a class called `LinkedList`. Find out what you can about the `LinkedList` class, and compare its methods with those of `ArrayList`. Which methods do they have in common, and which are different?

4.14.7 Using collections

The `ArrayList` collection class (and others like it) is an important programming tool, because many programming problems involve working with variable-sized collections of objects. Before moving on to the rest of this chapter, it is important that you become thoroughly familiar and comfortable with how to work with them. The following exercises will help you do this.

Exercise 4.54 Continue working with the *club* project from Exercise 4.40. Define a method in the `Club` class with the following description:

```
/**
 * Determine the number of members who joined in the
 * given month.
 * @param month The month we are interested in.
```

```
    * @return The number of members who joined in that month.
    */
  public int joinedInMonth(int month)
```

If the `month` parameter is outside the valid range of 1 to 12, print an error message and return zero.

Exercise 4.55 Define a method in the `Club` class with the following description:

```
/**
  * Remove from the club's collection all members who
  * joined in the given month, and return them stored
  * in a separate collection object.
  * @param month The month of the membership.
  * @param year The year of the membership.
  * @return The members who joined in the given month and year.
  */
  public ArrayList<Membership> purge(int month, int year)
```

If the `month` parameter is outside the valid range of 1 to 12, print an error message and return a collection object with no objects stored in it.

Note: The `purge` method is significantly harder to write than any of the others in this class.

Exercise 4.56 Open the *product* project and complete the `StockManager` class through this and the next few exercises. `StockManager` uses an `ArrayList` to store `Product` items. Its `addProduct` method already adds a product to the collection, but the following methods need completing: `delivery`, `findProduct`, `printProductDetails`, and `numberInStock`.

Each product sold by the company is represented by an instance of the `Product` class, which records a product's ID, name, and how many of that product are currently in stock. The `Product` class defines the `increaseQuantity` method to record increases in the stock level of that product. The `sellOne` method records that one item of that product has been sold, by reducing the quantity field level by 1. `Product` has been provided for you, and you should not need to make any alterations to it.

Start by implementing the `printProductDetails` method to ensure that you are able to iterate over the collection of products. Just print out the details of each `Product` returned, by calling its `toString` method.

Exercise 4.57 Implement the `findProduct` method. This should look through the collection for a product whose `id` field matches the ID argument of this method. If a matching product is found, it should be returned as the method's result. If no matching product is found, return `null`.

This differs from the `printProductDetails` method in that it will not necessarily have to examine every product in the collection before a match is found. For instance, if the first product in the collection matches the product ID, iteration can finish and that first `Product` object can be returned. On the other hand, it is possible that there might be no match in the collection. In that case, the whole collection will be examined without finding a product to return. In this case, the `null` value should be returned.

When looking for a match, you will need to call the `getID` method on a `Product`.

Exercise 4.58 Implement the `numberInStock` method. This should locate a product in the collection with a matching ID and return the current quantity of that product as a method result. If no product with a matching ID is found, return zero. This is relatively simple to implement once the `findProduct` method has been completed. For instance, `numberInStock` can call the `findProduct` method to do the searching and then call the `getQuantity` method on the result. Take care over products that cannot be found, though.

Exercise 4.59 Implement the `delivery` method using a similar approach to that used in `numberInStock`. It should find the product with the given ID in the list of products and then call its `increaseQuantity` method.

Exercise 4.60 *Challenge exercises* Implement a method in `StockManager` to print details of all products with stock levels below a given value (passed as a parameter to the method).

Modify the `addProduct` method so that a new product cannot be added to the product list with the same ID as an existing one.

Add to `StockManager` a method that finds a product from its name rather than its ID:

    public Product findProduct(String name)

In order to do this, you need to know that two `String` objects, `s1` and `s2`, can be tested for equality with the boolean expression

    s1.equals(s2)

More details can be found on this in Chapter 5.

4.15 Flexible-collection summary

We have seen that classes such as ArrayList conveniently allow us to create collections containing an arbitrary number of objects. The Java library contains more collections like this, and we shall look at some of the others in the next chapter. You will find that being able to use collections confidently is an important skill in writing interesting programs. There is hardly an application we shall see from now on that does not use collections of some form.

4.16   Fixed-size collections

Flexible-size collections are powerful both because we do not need to know in advance how many items will be stored in them and because it is possible to vary the number of items they hold. However, some applications are different in that we *do* know in advance how many items we wish to store in a collection, and that number typically remains fixed for the life of the collection. In such circumstances, we have the option of choosing to use a specialized fixed-size collection object to store the items.

A fixed-size collection is called an *array*. Although the fixed-size nature of arrays can be a significant disadvantage in many situations, they do have at least two compensating advantages over the flexible-size collection classes:

Concept:

An **array** is a special type of collection that can store a fixed number of items.

- Access to the items held in an array is often more efficient than access to the items in a comparable flexible-size collection.

- Arrays are able to store either objects or primitive-type values. Flexible-size collections can store only objects.[4]

Another distinctive feature of arrays is that they have special syntactic support in Java; they can be accessed using a custom syntax different from the usual method calls. The reason for this is mostly historical: arrays are the oldest collection structure in programming languages, and syntax for dealing with arrays has developed over many decades. Java uses the same syntax established in other programming languages to keep things simple for programmers who are used to arrays already, even though it is not consistent with the rest of the language syntax.

In the following sections, we shall show how arrays can be used to maintain collections of fixed size. We shall also introduce a new loop structure that is often closely associated with arrays—the *for loop*. (Note that the *for loop* is different from the *for-each loop*.)

4.16.1   A log-file analyzer

Web servers typically maintain log files of client accesses to the web pages that they store. Given suitable tools, these logs enable web service managers to extract and analyze useful information such as:

- which are the most popular pages they provide

- which sites brought users to this one

- whether other sites appear to have broken links to this site's pages

- how much data is being delivered to clients

- the busiest periods over the course of a day, a week, or a month

Such information might help managers to determine, for instance, whether they need to upgrade to more-powerful server machines or when the quietest periods are in order to schedule maintenance activities.

---

[4] A Java construct called "auto-boxing" provides a mechanism that also lets us store primitive values in flexible-size collections. It is, however, true that only arrays can directly store them.

The *weblog-analyzer* project contains an application that performs an analysis of data from such a web server. The server writes a line to a log file each time an access is made. A sample log file called *weblog.txt* is provided in the project folder. Each line records the date and time of the access in the following format:

```
year month day hour minute
```

For instance, the line below records an access at 03:45am on 7 June 2011:

```
2011 06 07 03 45
```

The project consists of five classes: `LogAnalyzer`, `LogfileReader`, `LogEntry`, `LoglineTokenizer`, and `LogfileCreator`. We shall spend most of our time looking at the `LogAnalyzer` class, as it contains examples of both creating and using an array (Code 4.11). Later exercises will encourage you to examine and modify `LogEntry`, because it also uses an array. The `LogReader` and `LogLineTokenizer` classes use features of the Java language that we have not yet covered, so we shall not explore those in detail. The `LogfileCreator` class allows you to create your own log files containing random data.

Code 4.11

The log-file analyzer

```java
/**
 * Read web server data and analyze
 * hourly access patterns.
 *
 * @author David J. Barnes and Michael Kölling.
 * @version 2011.07.31
 */
public class LogAnalyzer
{
    // Array to store the hourly access counts.
    private int[] hourCounts;
    // Use a LogfileReader to access the data.
    private LogfileReader reader;

    /**
     * Create an object to analyze hourly web accesses.
     */
    public LogAnalyzer()
    {
        // Create the array object to hold the hourly
        // access counts.
        hourCounts = new int[24];
        // Create the reader to obtain the data.
        reader = new LogfileReader();
    }

    /**
     * Analyze the hourly access data from the log file.
     */
```

**Code 4.11
continued**

The log-file analyzer

```java
public void analyzeHourlyData()
{
    while(reader.hasNext()) {
        LogEntry entry = reader.next();
        int hour = entry.getHour();
        hourCounts[hour]++;
    }
}

/**
 * Print the hourly counts.
 * These should have been set with a prior
 * call to analyzeHourlyData.
 */
public void printHourlyCounts()
{
    System.out.println("Hr: Count");
    for(int hour = 0; hour < hourCounts.length; hour++) {
        System.out.println(hour + ": " + hourCounts[hour]);
    }
}

/**
 * Print the lines of data read by the LogfileReader
 */
public void printData()
{
    reader.printData();
}
}
```

The analyzer currently uses only part of the data stored in a server's log line. It provides information that would allow us to determine which hours of the day, on average, tend to be the busiest or quietest for the server. It does this by counting how many accesses were made in each one-hour period over the duration covered by the log.

Exercise 4.61 Explore the *weblog-analyzer* project by creating a `LogAnalyzer` object and calling its `analyzeHourlyData` method. Follow that with a call to its `printHourlyCounts` method, which will print the results of the analysis. Which are the busiest times of the day?

Over the course of the next few sections, we shall examine how this class uses an array to accomplish this task.

4.16.2   Declaring array variables

The `LogAnalyzer` class contains a field that is of an array type:

```
private int[] hourCounts;
```

The distinctive feature of an array variable's declaration is a pair of square brackets as part of the type name: `int[]`. This indicates that the `hourCounts` variable is of type *integer array*. We say that `int` is the *base type* of this particular array, which means that the array object will store values of type `int`. It is important to distinguish between an array-variable declaration and a similar-looking simple-variable declaration:

```
int hour; // A single int variable.
int[] hourCounts; // An int-array variable.
```

Here, the variable `hour` is able to store a single integer value, whereas `hourCounts` will be used to refer to an array object once that object has been created. An array-variable declaration does not itself create the array object. That takes place in a separate stage using the `new` operator, as with other objects.

It is worth looking at the unusual syntax again for a moment. The declaration `int[]` would in more conventional syntax appear, maybe, as `Array<int>`. That it does not has historical rather than logical reasons. You should still get used to reading it in the same way: as "array of int."

> **Exercise 4.62** Write a declaration for an array variable `people` that could be used to refer to an array of `Person` objects.
>
> **Exercise 4.63** Write a declaration for an array variable `vacant` that could be used to refer to an array of boolean values.
>
> **Exercise 4.64** Read through the `LogAnalyzer` class and identify all the places where the `hourCounts` variable is used. At this stage, do not worry about what all the uses mean, as they will be explained in the following sections. Note how often a pair of square brackets is used with the variable.
>
> **Exercise 4.65** What is wrong with the following array declarations? Correct them.
>
> ```
> []int counts;
> boolean[5000] occupied;
> ```

4.16.3   Creating array objects

The next thing to look at is how an array variable is associated with an array object.

The constructor of the `LogAnalyzer` class includes a statement to create an `int` array object:

```
hourCounts = new int[24];
```

Once again, notice how different the syntax is from that of normal object creation. For instance, there are no round brackets for a constructor's parameters, because an array object does not have a constructor. This statement creates an array object that is able to store 24 separate integer values and makes the `hourCounts` array variable refer to that object. The value of 24 is the size of the array, and not a constructor parameter. Figure 4.7 illustrates the result of this assignment.

Figure 4.7

An array of
24 integers

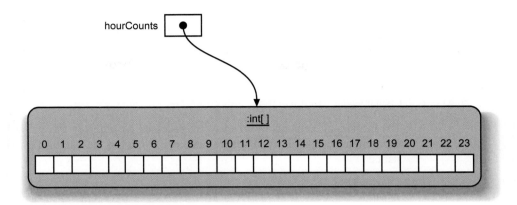

The general form of an array object's construction is

```
new type[integer-expression]
```

The choice of *type* specifies what type of items are to be stored in the array. The *integer expression* specifies the size of the array—that is, the fixed number of items that can be stored in it.

When an array object is assigned to an array variable, the type of the array object must match the declared type of the variable. The assignment to `hourCounts` is allowed because the array object is an integer array, and `hourCounts` is an integer-array variable. The following declares a string-array variable and makes it refer to an array that has a capacity of 10 strings:

```
String[] names = new String[10];
```

It is important to note that the creation of the array assigned to `names` does not actually create 10 strings. Rather, it creates a fixed-size collection that is able to have 10 strings stored within it. Those strings will probably be created in another part of the class to which `names` belongs. Immediately following its creation, an array object can be thought of as empty. If it is an array for objects, then the array will contain `null` values for all elements. If it is an `int` array, then all elements will be set to zero. In the next section we shall look at the way in which items are stored into (and retrieved from) arrays.

Exercise 4.66 Given the following variable declarations,

```
double[] readings;
String[] urls;
TicketMachine[] machines;
```

write assignments that accomplish the following tasks: (a) Make the `readings` variable refer to an array that is able to hold sixty `double` values; (b) Make the `urls` variable refer to an array that is able to hold ninety `String` objects; (c) Make the `machines` variable refer to an array that is able to hold five `TicketMachine` objects.

Exercise 4.67 How many `String` objects are created by the following declaration?

```
String[] labels = new String[20];
```

> **Exercise 4.68** What is wrong with the following array creation? Correct it.
>
> ```
> double[] prices = new double(50);
> ```

4.16.4 Using array objects

The individual elements of an array are accessed by *indexing* the array. An index is an integer expression written between square brackets following the name of an array variable. For instance:

```
labels[6]
machines[0]
people[x + 10 - y]
```

The valid values for an index expression depend upon the length of the array on which they are used. As with other collections, array indices always start at zero and go up to one less than the length of the array. So the valid indices for the hourCounts array are 0 to 23, inclusive.

> **Pitfall** Two very common errors are to think that the valid indices of an array start at 1, and to use the value of the length of the array as an index. Using indices outside the bounds of an array will lead to a runtime error called an ArrayIndexOutOfBoundsException.

Expressions that select an element from an array can be used anywhere that a variable of the base type of the array could be used. This means that we can use them on both sides of assignments, for instance. Here are some examples that use array expressions in different places:

```
labels[5] = "Quit";
double half = readings[0] / 2;
System.out.println(people[3].getName());
machines[0] = new TicketMachine(500);
```

Using an array index on the left-hand side of an assignment is the array equivalent of a mutator (or set method), because the contents of the array will be changed. Using one anywhere else represents the equivalent of an accessor (or get method).

4.16.5 Analyzing the log file

The hourCounts array created in the constructor of LogAnalyzer is used to store an analysis of the access data. The data is stored into it in the analyzeHourlyData method and displayed from it in the printHourlyCounts method. As the task of the analyze method is to count how many accesses were made during each hour period, the array needs 24 locations—one for each hour period in a 24-hour day. The analyzer delegates the task of reading its log file to a LogfileReader.

The LogfileReader class is quite complex, and we suggest that you do not spend too much time investigating its implementation. Its role is to handle the task of breaking up each log line into separate data values, but we can abstract from the implementation details by considering just the headers of two of its methods:

```
public boolean hasNext()
public LogEntry next()
```

These exactly match the methods we have seen with the Iterator type, and a LogfileReader can be used in exactly the same way, except that we do not permit the remove method to be used. The hasNext method tells the analyzer whether there is at least one more entry in the log file, and the next method then returns a LogEntry object containing the values from the next log line.

From each LogEntry, the analyzeHourlyData method of the analyzer obtains the value of the hour field:

```
int hour = entry.getHour();
```

We know that the value stored in the local variable hour will always be in the range 0 to 23, which exactly matches the valid range of indices for the hourCounts array. Each location in the array is used to represent an access count for the corresponding hour. So each time an hour value is read, we wish to update the count for that hour by 1. We have written this as

```
hourCounts[hour]++;
```

Note that it is the value stored in the array element that is being incremented and not the hour variable. The following alternatives are both equivalent, as we can use an array element in exactly the same way as we would an ordinary variable:

```
hourCounts[hour] = hourCounts[hour] + 1;
hourCounts[hour] += 1;
```

By the end of the analyzeHourlyData method, we have a complete set of cumulative counts for each hour of the log period.

In the next section, we look at the printHourlyCounts method, as it introduces a new control structure that is well suited to iterating over an array.

4.16.6 The for loop

Java defines two variations of for loops, both of which are indicated by the keyword *for* in source code. In Section 4.9, we introduced the first variant, the *for-each loop*, as a convenient means to iterate over a flexible-size collection. The second variant, the *for loop*, is an alternative iterative control structure[5] that is particularly appropriate when:

■ we wish to execute a set of statements a fixed number of times

■ we need a variable inside the loop whose value changes by a fixed amount—typically increasing by 1—on each iteration

---

[5] Sometimes, if people want to make clearer the distinction between the for loop and the for-each loop, they also talk about the former as the "old-style for loop," because it has been in the Java language longer than the for-each loop. The for-each loop is sometimes referred to as the "enhanced for loop."

The for loop is well suited to situations requiring *definite iteration*. For instance, it is common to use a for loop when we wish to do something to every element in an array, such as printing out the contents of each element. This fits the criteria, as the fixed number of times corresponds to the length of the array and the variable is needed to provide an incrementing index into the array.

A for loop has the following general form:

```
for(initialization; condition; post-body action) {
    statements to be repeated
}
```

The following concrete example is taken from the `printHourlyCounts` method of the `LogAnalyzer`:

```
for(int hour = 0; hour < hourCounts.length; hour++) {
    System.out.println(hour + ": " + hourCounts[hour]);
}
```

The result of this will be that the value of each element in the array is printed, preceded by its corresponding hour number. For instance:

```
0: 149
1: 149
2: 148
...
23: 166
```

When we compare this for loop to the for-each loop, we notice that the syntactic difference is in the section between the parentheses in the loop header. In this for loop, the parentheses contain three separate sections, separated by semicolons.

From a programming-language design point of view, it would have been nicer to use two different keywords for these two loops, maybe `for` and `foreach`. The reason that `for` is used for both of them is, again, a historical accident. Older versions of the Java language did not contain the for-each loop, and when it was finally introduced, Java designers did not want to introduce a new keyword at this stage, because this could cause problems with existing programs. So they decided to use the same keyword for both loops. This makes it slightly harder for us to distinguish these loops, but we will get used to recognizing the different header structures.

Even though the for loop is often used for definite iteration, the fact that it is controlled by a general boolean expression means that it is actually closer to the while loop than to the for-each loop. We can illustrate the way that a for loop executes by rewriting its general form as an equivalent while loop:

```
initialization;
while(condition) {
    statements to be repeated
    post-body action
}
```

So the alternative form for the body of `printHourlyCounts` would be

```
int hour = 0;
while(hour < hourCounts.length) {
    System.out.println(hour + ": " + hourCounts[hour]);
    hour++;
}
```

From this rewritten version, we can see that the post-body action is not actually executed until after the statements in the loop's body, despite the action's position in the for loop's header. In addition, we can see that the initialization part is executed only once—immediately before the condition is tested for the first time.

In both versions, note in particular the condition

```
hour < hourCounts.length
```

This illustrates two important points:

- All arrays contain a field `length` that contains the value of the fixed size of that array. The value of this field will always match the value of the integer expression used to create the array object. So the value of `length` here will be 24.

- The condition uses the less-than operator, <, to check the value of `hour` against the length of the array. So in this case the loop will continue as long as `hour` is less than 24. In general, when we wish to access every element in an array, a for-loop header will have the following general form:

```
for(int index = 0; index < array.length; index++)
```

This is correct, because we do not wish to use an index value that is equal to the array's length; such an element will never exist.

4.16.7 Arrays and the for-each loop

Could we also rewrite the for loop shown above with a for-each loop? The answer is: almost. Here is an attempt:

```
for(int value : hourCounts) {
    System.out.println(": " + value);
}
```

This code will compile and execute. (Try it out!) From this fragment, we can see that arrays can, in fact, be used in for-each loops just like other collections. We have, however, one problem: we cannot easily print out the hour in front of the colon. This code fragment simply omits printing the hour, and just prints the colon and the value. This is because the for-each loop does not provide access to a loop-counter variable, which we need in this case for printing the hour.

To fix this, we would need to define our own counter variable (similar to what we did in the while loop example). Instead of doing this, we prefer using the old-style for loop because it is more concise.

4.16.8 The for loop and iterators

In Section 4.12.2, we showed the necessity of using an `Iterator` if we wished to remove elements from a collection. There is a special use of the for loop with an `Iterator` when we want to do something like this. Suppose that we wished to remove every music track by a particular artist from our music organizer. The point here is that we need to examine every track in the collection, so a for-each loop would seem appropriate, but we know already that we cannot use it in this particular case. However, we can use a for loop as follows:

```
for(Iterator<Track> it = tracks.iterator(); it.hasNext(); ) {
    Track t = it.next();
    if(t.getArtist().equals(artist)) {
        it.remove();
    }
}
```

The important point here is that there is no post-body action in the loop's header—it is just blank. This is allowed, but we must still include the semicolon after the loop's condition. By using a for loop instead of a while loop, it is a little clearer that we intend to examine every item in the list.

Which loop should I use? We have discussed three different loops: the for-each loop, the while loop, and the for loop. As you have seen, in many situations you have a choice of using either one of these to solve your task. Usually, one loop could be rewritten using another. So how do you decide which one to use at any given point? Here are some guidelines:

■ If you need to iterate over all elements in a collection, the for-each loop is almost always the most elegant loop to use. It is clear and concise (but it does not give you a loop counter).

■ If you have a loop that is not related to collections (but instead performs some other action repeatedly), the for-each loop is not useful. Your choice will be between the for loop and the while loop. The for-each loop is only for collections.

■ The for loop is good if you know at the start of the loop how many iterations you need (that is, how often you need to loop around). This information can be in a variable but should not change during the loop execution. It is also very good if you need to use the loop counter explicitly.

■ The while loop should be preferred if, at the start of the loop, you don't know how often you need to loop. The end of the loop can be determined on the fly by some condition (for example, repeatedly read one line from a file until we reach the end of the file).

■ If you need to remove elements from the collection while looping, use a for loop with an `Iterator` if you want to examine the whole collection, or a while loop if you might finish before reaching the end of the collection.

Exercise 4.69 Check to see what happens if the for loop's condition is incorrectly written using the `<=` operator in `printHourlyCounts`:

```
for(int hour = 0; hour <= hourCounts.length; hour++)
```

Exercise 4.70 Rewrite the body of `printHourlyCounts` so that the for loop is replaced by an equivalent while loop. Call the rewritten method to check that it prints the same results as before.

Exercise 4.71 Correct all the errors in the following method.

```java
/**
 * Print all the values in the marks array that are
 * greater than mean.
 * @param marks An array of mark values.
 * @param mean The mean (average) mark.
 */
public void printGreater(double marks, double mean)
{
    for(index = 0; index <= marks.length; index++) {
        if(marks[index] > mean) {
            System.out.println(marks[index]);
        }
    }
}
```

Exercise 4.72 Modify the `LogAnalyzer` class so that it has a constructor that can take the name of the log file to be analyzed. Have this constructor pass the file name to the constructor of the `LogfileReader` class. Use the `LogfileCreator` class to create your own file of random log entries, and analyze the data.

Exercise 4.73 Complete the `numberOfAccesses` method, below, to count the total number of accesses recorded in the log file. Complete it by using a for loop to iterate over `hourCounts`:

```java
/**
 * Return the number of accesses recorded in the log
 * file.
 */
public int numberOfAccesses()
{
    int total = 0;
    // Add the value in each element of hourCounts
    // to total.
    ...
    return total;
}
```

Exercise 4.74 Add your `numberOfAccesses` method to the `LogAnalyzer` class and check that it gives the correct result. *Hint*: You can simplify your checking by having the analyzer read log files containing just a few lines of data. That way you will find it easier to determine whether or not your method gives the correct answer. The `LogfileReader` class has a constructor with the following header, to read from a particular file:

```java
/**
 * Create a LogfileReader that will supply data
 * from a particular log file.
```

```
   * @param filename The file of log data.
   */
  public LogfileReader(String filename)
```

Exercise 4.75 Add a method `busiestHour` to `LogAnalyzer` that returns the busiest hour. You can do this by looking through the `hourCounts` array to find the element with the biggest count. *Hint:* Do you need to check every element to see if you have found the busiest hour? If so, use a for loop or a for-each loop. Which one is better in this case?

Exercise 4.76 Add a method `quietestHour` to `LogAnalyzer` that returns the number of the least busy hour. *Note:* This sounds almost identical to the previous exercise, but there is a small trap for the unwary here. Be sure to check your method with some data in which every hour has a non-zero count.

Exercise 4.77 Which hour is returned by your `busiestHour` method if more than one hour has the biggest count?

Exercise 4.78 Add a method to `LogAnalyzer` that finds which two-hour period is the busiest. Return the value of the first hour of this period.

Exercise 4.79 *Challenge exercise* Save the *weblog-analyzer* project under a different name so that you can develop a new version that performs a more extensive analysis of the available data. For instance, it would be useful to know which days tend to be quieter than others, Are there any seven-day cyclical patterns, for instance? In order to perform analysis of daily, monthly, or yearly data, you will need to make some changes to the `LogEntry` class. This already stores all the values from a single log line, but only the hour and minute values are available via accessors. Add further methods that make the remaining fields available in a similar way. Then add a range of additional analysis methods to the analyzer.

Exercise 4.80 *Challenge exercise* If you have completed the previous exercise, you could extend the log-file format with additional numerical fields. For instance, servers commonly store a numerical code that indicates whether an access was successful or not. The value 200 stands for a successful access, 403 means that access to the document was forbidden, and 404 means that the document could not be found. Have the analyzer provide information on the number of successful and unsuccessful accesses. This exercise is likely to be very challenging, as it will require you to make changes to every class in the project.

4.17 Summary

In this chapter, we have discussed mechanisms to store collections of objects, rather than single objects in separate fields. We have looked at two different collections in detail: the `ArrayList` as an example of a collection with flexible size, and arrays as a fixed-size collection.

Using collections such as these will be very important in all projects from now on. You will see that almost every application has a need somewhere for some form of collection. They are fundamental to writing programs.

When using collections, the need arises to iterate over all elements in a collection to make use of the objects stored in them. For this purpose, we have seen the use of loops and iterators.

Loops are also a fundamental concept in computing that you will be using in every project from now on. Make sure you familiarize yourself sufficiently with writing loops—you will not get very far without them. When deciding on the type of loop to use in a particular situation, it is often useful to consider whether the task involves definite iteration or indefinite iteration. Is there certainty or uncertainty about the number of iterations that will be required?

As an aside, we have mentioned the Java class library, a large collection of useful classes that we can use to make our own classes more powerful. We shall need to study the library in some more detail to see what else is in it that we should know about. This will be the topic of the next chapter.

Terms introduced in this chapter

collection, array, iterator, for-each loop, while loop, for loop, index, import statement, library, package, anonymous object, definite iteration, indefinite iteration

Concept summary

- **collection** A collection object can store an arbitrary number of other objects.

- **loop** A loop can be used to execute a block of statements repeatedly without having to write them multiple times.

- **iterator** An iterator is an object that provides functionality to iterate over all elements of a collection.

- **null** The Java reserved word `null` is used to mean "no object" when an object variable is not currently referring to a particular object. A field that has not explicitly been initialized will contain the value `null` by default.

- **array** An array is a special type of collection that can store a fixed number of elements.

Exercise 4.81 In the *lab-classes* project that we have discussed in previous chapters, the `LabClass` class includes a `students` field to maintain a collection of `Student` objects. Read through the `LabClass` class in order to reinforce some of the concepts we have discussed in this chapter.

Exercise 4.82 The `LabClass` class enforces a limit to the number of students who may be enrolled in a particular tutorial group. In view of this, do you think it would be more appropriate to use a fixed-size array rather than a flexible-size collection for the `students` field? Give reasons both for and against the alternatives.

Exercise 4.83 Rewrite the listAllFiles method in the MusicOrganizer class from *music-organizer-v3* by using a for loop rather than a for-each loop.

Exercise 4.84 Java provides another type of loop: the *do-while loop*. Find out how this loop works and describe it. Write an example of a do-while loop that prints out the numbers from 1 to 10. To find out about this loop, find a description of the Java language (for example, at

http://download.oracle.com/javase/tutorial/java/nutsandbolts/
in the section "Control Flow Statements").

Exercise 4.85 Rewrite the listAllFiles method in the MusicOrganizer class from music-organizer-v3 by using a do-while loop rather than a for-each loop. Test your solution carefully. Does it work correctly if the collection is empty?

Exercise 4.86 *Challenge exercise* Rewrite the findFirst method in the MusicOrganizer class from *music-organizer-v4* by using a do-while loop rather than a while loop. Test your solution carefully. Try searches that will succeed and others that will fail. Try searches where the file to be found is first in the list and also where it is last in the list.

Exercise 4.87 Find out about Java's *switch-case statement*. What is its purpose? How is it used? Write an example. (This is also a *control flow statement*, so you will find information in similar locations as for the *do-while loop*.)

CHAPTER 5

More-sophisticated behavior

Main concepts discussed in this chapter:

- using library classes
- writing documentation
- reading documentation

Java constructs discussed in this chapter:

```
String, ArrayList, Random, HashMap, HashSet, Iterator, Arrays,
static, final
```

In Chapter 4, we introduced the class `ArrayList` from the Java class library. We discussed how this enabled us to do something that would otherwise be hard to achieve (in this case, storing an arbitrary number of objects).

This was just a single example of a useful class from the Java library. The library consists of thousands of classes, many of which are generally useful for your work and many of which you will probably never use.

For a good Java programmer, it is essential to be able to work with the Java library and make informed choices about which classes to use. Once you have started work with the library, you will quickly see that it enables you to perform many tasks more easily than you would otherwise have been able to. Learning to work with library classes is the main topic of this chapter.

The items in the library are not just a set of unrelated, arbitrary classes that we all have to learn individually, but are often arranged in relationships, exploiting common characteristics. Here, we again encounter the concept of abstraction to help us deal with a large amount of information. Some of the most important parts of the library are the collections, of which the `ArrayList` class is one. We will discuss other sorts of collections in this chapter and see that they share many attributes among themselves, so that we can often abstract from the individual details of a specific collection and talk about collection classes in general.

New collection classes, as well as some other useful classes, will be introduced and discussed. Throughout this chapter, we will work on the construction of a single application (the *TechSupport* system), which makes use of various different library classes. A complete implementation containing all the ideas and source code discussed here, as well as several intermediate versions, is included in the book projects. While this enables you to study the complete solution, you are encouraged to follow the path through the exercises in this chapter. These will, after a brief look at the complete program, start with a very simple initial version of the project and then gradually develop and implement the complete solution.

The application makes use of several new library classes and techniques—each requiring study individually—such as hash maps, sets, string tokenization, and further use of random numbers. You should be aware that this is not a chapter to be read and understood in a single day, but that it contains several sections that deserve a few days of study each. Overall, when you finally reach the end and have managed to undertake the implementation suggested in the exercises, you will have learned about a good variety of important topics.

5.1 Documentation for library classes

The Java library is big. It consists of thousands of classes, each of which has many methods, both with and without parameters, and with and without return types. It is impossible to memorize them all and all of the details that go with them. Instead, a good Java programmer should know:

■ some of the most important classes and their methods from the library by name (`ArrayList` is one of those important ones) and

■ how to find out about other classes and look up the details (such as methods and parameters).

In this chapter, we will introduce some of the important classes from the class library, and further library classes will be introduced throughout the book. But, more importantly, we will show you how you can explore and understand the library on your own. This will enable you to write much more interesting programs. Fortunately, the Java library is quite well documented. This documentation is available in HTML format (so that it can be read in a web browser). This is what we shall use to find out about the library classes.

Reading and understanding the documentation is the first part of our introduction to library classes. We will take this approach a step further and also discuss how to prepare our own classes so that other people can use them in the same way as they would use standard library classes. This is important for real-world software development, where teams have to deal with large projects and maintenance of software over time.

One thing you may have noted about the `ArrayList` class is that we used it without ever looking at the source code. We did not check how it was implemented. That was not necessary for utilizing its functionality. All we needed to know was the name of the class, the names of the methods, the parameters and return types of those methods, and what exactly these methods do. We did not really care how the work was done. This is typical for the use of library classes.

The same is also true for other classes in larger software projects. Typically, several people work together on a project by working on different parts. Each programmer should concentrate on her own area and need not understand the details of all the other parts (we discussed this in Section 3.2 where we talked about abstraction and modularization). In effect, each programmer should be able to use the classes of other team members as if they were library classes, making informed use of them without the need to know how they work internally.

For this to work, each team member must write documentation about his class similar to the documentation for the Java standard library, which enables other people to use the class without the need to read the code. This topic will also be discussed in this chapter.

5.2 The TechSupport system

As always, we shall explore these issues with an example. This time, we shall use the *TechSupport* application. You can find it in the book projects under the name *tech-support1*.

TechSupport is a program intended to provide technical support for customers of the fictitious DodgySoft software company. Some time ago, DodgySoft had a technical support department with people sitting at telephones. Customers could call to get advice and help with their technical problems with the DodgySoft software products. Recently, though, business has not been going so well, and DodgySoft decided to get rid of the technical support department to save money. They now want to develop the *TechSupport* system to give the impression that support is still provided. The system is supposed to mimic the responses a technical-support person might give. Customers can communicate with the technical-support system online.

5.2.1 Exploring the TechSupport system

Exercise 5.1 Open and run the project *tech-support-complete*. You run it by creating an object of class `SupportSystem` and calling its `start` method. Enter some problems you might be having with your software, to try out the system. See how it behaves. Type "bye" when you are done. You do not need to examine the source code at this stage. This project is the complete solution that we will have developed by the end of this chapter. The purpose of this exercise is only to give you an idea of what we plan to achieve.

Eliza The idea of the TechSupport project is based on the groundbreaking artificial intelligence program, Eliza, developed by Joseph Weizenbaum at Massachusetts Institute of Technology in the 1960s. You can find out more about the original program by searching the web for "Eliza" and "Weizenbaum."

We will now start our more detailed exploration by using the *tech-support1* project. It is a first, rudimentary implementation of our system. We will improve it throughout the chapter. This way, we should arrive at a better understanding of the whole system than we would by just reading the complete solution.

In Exercise 5.1 you have seen that the program essentially holds a dialog with the user. The user can type in a question, and the system responds. Try the same with our prototype version of the project, *tech-support1*.

In *TechSupport*'s complete version, the system manages to produce reasonably varied responses— sometimes they even seem to make sense! In the prototype version we are using as a starting point, the responses are much more restricted (Figure 5.1). You will notice very quickly that the response is always the same:

"That sounds interesting. Tell me more..."

Figure 5.1
A first
TechSupport
dialog

```
○ ○ ○              BlueJ: Terminal Window – tech-support1
Welcome to the DodgySoft Technical Support System.

Please tell us about your problem.
We will assist you with any problem you might have.
Please type 'bye' to exit our system.
> My system crashes all the time.
That sounds interesting. Tell me more...
> I am using Windows 9. Should your program run on Windows 9?
That sounds interesting. Tell me more...
> I really need help! It's not working.
That sounds interesting. Tell me more...
> Why are you always saying "That sounds interesting"?
That sounds interesting. Tell me more...
> I hate you.
That sounds interesting. Tell me more...
> bye
Nice talking to you. Bye...
```

This is, in fact, not very interesting at all and not very convincing when trying to pretend that we have a technical-support person sitting at the other end of the dialog. We will shortly try to improve this. However, before we do this, we shall explore further what we have so far.

The project diagram shows us three classes: SupportSystem, InputReader, and Responder (Figure 5.2). SupportSystem is the main class, which uses the InputReader to get some input from the terminal and the Responder to generate a response.

Figure 5.2
TechSupport class
diagram

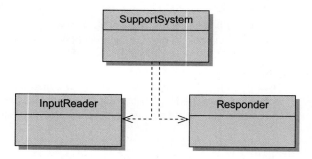

Examine the InputReader further by creating an object of this class and then looking at the object's methods. You will see that it has only a single method available, called getInput, which returns a string. Try it out. This method lets you type a line of input in the terminal and then returns whatever you typed as a method result. We will not examine how this works internally at this point, but just note that the InputReader has a getInput method that returns a string.

Do the same with the Responder class. You will find that it has a generateResponse method that always returns the string "That sounds interesting. Tell me more...". This explains what we saw in the dialog earlier.

Now let us look at the SupportSystem class a bit more closely.

5.2.2 Reading the code

The complete source code of the SupportSystem class is shown in Code 5.1. Code 5.2 shows the source code of class Responder.

Code 5.1

The SupportSystem source code

```java
/**
 * This class implements a technical support system. It is
 * the top-level class in this project. The support system
 * communicates via text input/output in the text terminal.
 * This class uses an object of class InputReader to read
 * input from the user and an object of class Responder to
 * generate responses.
 * It contains a loop that repeatedly reads input and
 * generates output until the user wants to leave.
 *
 * @author    Michael Kölling and David J. Barnes
 * @version   0.1 (2011.07.31)
 */
public class SupportSystem
{
    private InputReader reader;
    private Responder responder;

    /**
     * Creates a technical support system.
     */
    public SupportSystem()
    {
        reader = new InputReader();
        responder = new Responder();
    }

    /**
     * Start the technical support system. This will print a
     * welcome message and enter into a dialog with the user,
     * until the user ends the dialog.
     */
    public void start()
    {
        boolean finished = false;

        printWelcome();
        while(!finished) {
            String input = reader.getInput();

            if(input.startsWith("bye")) {
                finished = true;
            }
```

**Code 5.1
continued**

The SupportSystem
source code

```
            else {
                String response = responder.generateResponse();
                System.out.println(response);
            }
        }
        printGoodbye();
    }

    /**
     * Print a welcome message to the screen.
     */
    private void printWelcome()
    {
        System.out.println(
            "Welcome to the DodgySoft Technical Support System.");
        System.out.println();
        System.out.println("Please tell us about your problem.");
        System.out.println(
            "We will assist you with any problem you might have.");
        System.out.println(
            "Please type 'bye' to exit our system.");
    }

    /**
     * Print a good-bye message to the screen.
     */
    private void printGoodbye()
    {
        System.out.println("Nice talking to you. Bye...");
    }
}
```

Code 5.2

The Responder
source code

```
/**
 * The responder class represents a response generator object.
 * It is used to generate an automatic response to an input string.
 *
 * @author     Michael Kölling and David J. Barnes
 * @version    0.1 (2011.07.31)
 */
public class Responder
{
    /**
     * Construct a Responder - nothing to do
     */
```

**Code 5.2
continued**

The Responder
source code

```
public Responder()
{
}

/**
 * Generate a response.
 * @return   A string that should be displayed as the
 *           response
 */
public String generateResponse()
{
    return "That sounds interesting. Tell me more...";
}
}
```

Looking at Code 5.2, we see that the Responder class is trivial. It has only one method, and that always returns the same string. This is something we shall improve later. For now, we will concentrate on the SupportSystem class.

SupportSystem declares two instance fields to hold an InputReader and a Responder object, and it assigns those two objects in its constructor.

At the end, it has two methods called printWelcome and printGoodbye. These simply print out some text—a welcome message and a good-bye message, respectively.

The most interesting piece of code is the method in the middle: start. We will discuss this method in some more detail.

Toward the top of the method is a call to printWelcome, and at the end is a call to print-Goodbye. These two calls take care of printing out these sections of text at the appropriate times. The rest of this method consists of a declaration of a boolean variable and a while loop. The structure is

```
boolean finished = false;

while(!finished) {

    do something

    if(exit condition) {
        finished = true;
    }
    else {
        do something more
    }
}
```

This code pattern is a variation of the while-loop idiom discussed in Section 4.10. We use finished as a flag that becomes true when we want to end the loop (and with it, the whole program). We make sure that it is initially `false`. (Remember that the exclamation mark is a *not* operator!)

The main part of the loop—the part that is done repeatedly while we wish to continue—consists of three statements if we strip it of the check for the exit condition:

```
String input = reader.getInput();
...
String response = responder.generateResponse();
System.out.println(response);
```

Thus, the loop repeatedly

- reads some user input,

- asks the responder to generate a response, and

- prints out that response.

(You may have noticed that the response does not depend on the input at all! This is certainly something we shall have to improve later.)

The last part to examine is the check of the exit condition. The intention is that the program should end once a user types the word 'bye'. The relevant section of source code we find in the class reads

```
String input = reader.getInput();

if(input.startsWith("bye")) {
    finished = true;
}
```

If you understand these pieces in isolation, then it is a good idea to look again at the complete `start` method in Code 5.1 and see whether you can understand everything together.

In the last code fragment examined above, a method called `startsWith` is used. Because that method is called on the `input` variable, which holds a `String` object, it must be a method of the `String` class. But what does this method do? And how do we find out?

We might guess, simply from seeing the name of the method, that it tests whether the input string starts with the word "bye". We can verify this by experiment. Run the *TechSupport* system again and type "bye bye" or "bye everyone". You will notice that both versions cause the system to exit. Note, however, that typing "Bye" or " bye"—starting with a capital letter or with a space in front of the word—is not recognized as starting with "bye". This could be slightly annoying for a user, but it turns out that we can solve these problems if we know a bit more about the `String` class.

How do we find out more information about the `startsWith` method or other methods of the `String` class?

5.3 Reading class documentation

The class `String` is one of the classes of the standard Java class library. We can find out more details about it by reading the library documentation for the `String` class.

Concept:

The Java **class library documentation** shows details about all classes in the library. Using this documentation is essential in order to make good use of library classes.

Figure 5.3
The Java class library documentation

To do this, choose the *Java Class Libraries* item from the BlueJ *Help* menu. This will open a web browser displaying the main page of the Java API (Application Programming Interface) documentation.[1]

The web browser will display three frames. In the one at the top left, you see a list of packages. Below that is a list of all classes in the Java library. The large frame on the right is used to display details of a selected package or class.

In the list of classes on the left, find and select the class `String`. The frame on the right then displays the documentation of the `String` class (Figure 5.3).

Exercise 5.2 Investigate the `String` documentation. Then look at the documentation for some other classes. What is the structure of class documentation? Which sections are common to all class descriptions? What is their purpose?

---

[1] By default, this function accesses the documentation through the Internet. This will not work if your machine does not have network access. However, BlueJ can be configured to use a local copy of the Java API documentation. This is recommended, because it speeds up access and can work without an Internet connection. For details, see Appendix A.

Exercise 5.3 Look up the startsWith method in the documentation for String. There are two versions. Describe in your own words what they do and the differences between them.

Exercise 5.4 Is there a method in the String class that tests whether a string ends with a given suffix? If so, what is it called and what are its parameters and return type?

Exercise 5.5 Is there a method in the String class that returns the number of characters in the string? If so, what is it called and what are its parameters?

Exercise 5.6 If you found methods for the two tasks above, how did you find them? Is it easy or hard to find methods you are looking for? Why?

5.3.1 Interfaces versus implementation

You will see that the documentation includes different pieces of information. They are, among other things:

Concept:

The **interface** of a class describes what a class does and how it can be used without showing the implementation.

■ the name of the class;

■ a general description of the purpose of the class;

■ a list of the class's constructors and methods;

■ the parameters and return types for each constructor and method;

■ a description of the purpose of each constructor and method.

This information, taken together, is called the *interface* of a class. Note that the interface does *not* show the source code that implements the class. If a class is well described (that is, if its interface is well written) then a programmer does not need to see the source code to be able to use the class. Seeing the interface provides all the information needed. This is abstraction in action again.

Concept:

The complete source code that defines a class is called the **implementation** of that class.

The source code behind the scene, which makes the class work, is called the *implementation* of the class. Usually a programmer works on the implementation of one class at a time, while making use of several other classes via their interfaces.

This distinction between the interface and the implementation is a very important concept, and it will surface repeatedly in this and later chapters of this book.

Note The word *interface* has several meanings in the context of programming and Java. It is used to describe the publicly visible part of a class (which is how we have just been using it here), but it also has other meanings. The user interface (often a graphical user interface) is sometimes referred to as just *the interface*, but Java also has a language construct called interface (discussed in Chapter 10) that is related but distinct from our meaning here.

It is important to be able to distinguish between the different meanings of the word *interface* in a particular context.

The interface terminology is also used for individual methods. For example, the `String` documentation shows us the interface of the `length` method:

```
public int length()
```

> *Returns the length of this string. The length is equal to the number of Unicode code units in the string.*

> *Specified by:*

> *length in interface CharSequence*

> *Returns:*

> *the length of the sequence of characters represented by this object.*

The interface of a method consists of the *signature* of the method and a comment (shown here in italics). The signature of a method includes (in this order):

■ an access modifier (here `public`), which we shall discuss below;

■ the return type of the method (here `int`);

■ the method name;

■ a list of parameters (which is empty in this example).

The interface provides everything we need to know to make use of this method.

5.3.2 Using library-class methods

Back to our *TechSupport* system. We now want to improve the processing of input a little. We have seen in the discussion above that our system is not very tolerant: if we type "Bye" or " bye" instead of "bye", for instance, the word is not recognized. We want to change that by adjusting the text read in from a user so that these variations are all recognized as "bye".

The documentation of the `String` class tells us that it has a method called `trim` to remove spaces at the beginning and the end of the string. We can use that method to handle the second problem case.

Concept:

Immutable objects. An object is said to be immutable if its contents or state cannot be changed once it has been created. Strings are an example of immutable objects.

Exercise 5.7 Find the `trim` method in the `String` class's documentation. Write down the signature of that method. Write down an example call to that method on a `String` variable called `text`.

One important detail about String objects is that they are *immutable*—that is, they cannot be modified once they have been created. Note carefully that the `trim` method, for example, returns a new string; it does not modify the original string. Pay close attention to the following "Pitfall" comment.

> **Pitfall** It is a common error in Java to try to modify a string—for example by writing
>
> ```
> input.toUpperCase();
> ```
>
> This is incorrect (strings cannot be modified), but this unfortunately does not produce an error. The statement simply has no effect, and the input string remains unchanged.
>
> The `toUpperCase` method, as well as other string methods, does not modify the original string, but instead returns a *new* string that is similar to the original one, with some changes applied (here, with characters changed to uppercase). If we want our input variable to be changed, then we have to assign this new object back into the variable (discarding the original one), like this:
>
> ```
> input = input.toUpperCase();
> ```
>
> The new object could also be assigned to another variable or processed in other ways.

After studying the interface of the `trim` method, we can see that we can remove the spaces from an input string with the following line of code:

```
input = input.trim();
```

This code will request the `String` object stored in the `input` variable to create a new, similar string with the leading and trailing spaces removed. The new `String` is then stored in the `input` variable because we have no further use for the old one. Thus, after this line of code, `input` refers to a string without spaces at either end.

We can now insert this line into our source code so that it reads

```
String input = reader.getInput();
input = input.trim();

if(input.startsWith("bye")) {
    finished = true;
}
else {
    ...    Code omitted.
}
```

The first two lines can also be merged into a single line:

```
String input = reader.getInput().trim();
```

The effect of this line of code is identical to that of the first two lines above. The right-hand side should be read as if it were parenthesized as follows:

```
(reader.getInput()) . trim()
```

Which version you prefer is mainly a matter of taste. The decision should be made mainly on the basis of readability: use the version that you find easier to read and understand. Often, novice programmers will prefer the two-line version, whereas more experienced programmers get used to the one-line style.

> **Exercise 5.8** Implement this improvement in your version of the *tech-support1* project. Test it to confirm that it is tolerant of extra space around the word 'bye'.

Now we have solved the problem caused by spaces surrounding the input, but we have not yet solved the problem with capital letters. However, further investigation of the String class's documentation suggests a possible solution, because it describes a method named toLowerCase.

> **Exercise 5.9** Improve the code of the SupportSystem class in the *tech-support1* project so that case in the input is ignored. Use the String class's toLowerCase method to do this. Remember that this method will not actually change the String it is called on, but result in the creation of a new one being created with slightly different contents.

5.3.3 Checking string equality

An alternative solution would have been to check whether the input string *is* the string 'bye' instead of whether it *starts with* the string 'bye.' An (incorrect!) attempt to write this code could look as follows:

```
if(input == "bye") { // does not always work!
    ...
}
```

The problem here is that it is possible for several independent String objects to exist that all represent the same text. Two String objects, for example, could both contain the characters 'bye'. The equality operator (==) checks whether each side of the operator refers to *the same object*, not whether they have the same value! That is an important difference.

In our example, we are interested in the question of whether the input variable and the string constant 'bye' represent the same value, not whether they refer to the same object. Thus, using the == operator is wrong. It could return false, even if the value of the input variable is 'bye'.[2]

The solution is to use the equals method, defined in the String class. This method correctly tests whether the contents of two String objects are the same. The correct code reads:

```
if(input.equals("bye")) {
    ...
}
```

This can, of course, also be combined with the trim and toLowerCase methods.

> **Pitfall** Comparing strings with the == operator can lead to unintended results. As a general rule, strings should almost always be compared with equals, rather than with the == operator.

---

[2] Unfortunately, Java's implementation of strings means that using == will often misleadingly give the 'right' answer when comparing two different String objects with identical contents. However, you should *never* use == between String objects when you want to compare their contents.

Exercise 5.10 Find the `equals` method in the documentation for class `String`. What is the return type of this method?

Exercise 5.11 Change your implementation to use the `equals` method instead of `startsWith`.

5.4 Adding random behavior

So far, we have made a small improvement to the *TechSupport* project, but overall it remains very basic. One of the main problems is that it always gives the same response, independent of the user's input. We shall now improve this by defining a set of plausible phrases with which to respond. We will then have the program randomly choose one of them each time it is expected to reply. This will be an extension of the `Responder` class in our project.

To do this, we will use an `ArrayList` to store some response strings, generate a random integer number, and use the random number as an index into the response list to pick one of our phrases. In this version, the response will still not depend on the user's input (we'll do that later), but at least it will vary the response and look a lot better.

First, we have to find out how to generate a random integer number.

Random and pseudo-random Generating random numbers on a computer is actually not as easy to do as one might initially think. Because computers operate in a very well-defined, deterministic way that relies on the fact that all computation is predictable and repeatable, they provide little space for real random behavior.

Researchers have, over time, proposed many algorithms to produce seemingly random sequences of numbers. These numbers are typically not really random, but follow complicated rules. They are therefore referred to as *pseudo-random* numbers.

In a language such as Java, the pseudo-random number generation has fortunately been implemented in a library class, so all we have to do to receive a pseudo-random number is to make some calls to the library.

If you want to read more about this, do a web search for "pseudo random numbers."

5.4.1 The `Random` class

The Java class library contains a class named `Random` that will be helpful for our project.

Exercise 5.12 Find the class `Random` in the Java class library documentation. Which package is it in? What does it do? How do you construct an instance? How do you generate a random number? Note that you will probably not understand everything that is stated in the documentation. Just try to find out what you need to know.

Exercise 5.13 Write a small code fragment (on paper) that generates a random integer number using this class.

To generate a random number, we have to:

▪ create an instance of class `Random` and

▪ make a call to a method of that instance to get a number.

Looking at the documentation, we see that there are various methods called next*Something* for generating random values of various types. The one that generates a random integer number is called `nextInt`.

The following illustrates the code needed to generate and print a random integer number:

```
Random randomGenerator;

randomGenerator = new Random();
int index = randomGenerator.nextInt();
System.out.println(index);
```

This code fragment creates a new instance of the `Random` class and stores it in the `randomGenerator` variable. It then calls the `nextInt` method to receive a random number, stores it in the `index` variable, and eventually prints it out.

> **Exercise 5.14** Write some code (in BlueJ) to test the generation of random numbers. To do this, create a new class called `RandomTester`. You can create this class in the *tech-support1* project, or you can create a new project for it—it doesn't matter. In class `RandomTester`, implement two methods: `printOneRandom` (which prints out one random number) and `printMultiRandom(int howMany)` (which has a parameter to specify how many numbers you want, and then prints out the appropriate number of random numbers).

Your class should create only a single instance of class `Random` (in its constructor) and store it in a field. Do not create a new `Random` instance every time you want a new number.

5.4.2 Random numbers with limited range

The random numbers we have seen so far were generated from the whole range of Java integers (–2147483648 to 2147483647). That is okay as an experiment, but seldom useful. More often, we want random numbers within a given limited range.

The `Random` class also offers a method to support this. It is again called `nextInt`, but it has a parameter to specify the range of numbers that we would like to use.

> **Exercise 5.15** Find the `nextInt` method in class `Random` that allows the target range of random numbers to be specified. What are the possible random numbers that are generated when you call this method with 100 as its parameter?
>
> **Exercise 5.16** Write a method in your `RandomTester` class called `throwDice` that returns a random number between 1 and 6 (inclusive).

Exercise 5.17 Write a method called `getResponse` that randomly returns one of the strings `"yes"`, `"no"`, or `"maybe"`.

Exercise 5.18 Extend your `getResponse` method so that it uses an `ArrayList` to store an arbitrary number of responses and randomly returns one of them.

When using a method that generates random numbers from a specified range, care must be taken to check whether the boundaries are *inclusive* or *exclusive*. The `nextInt(int n)` method in the Java library `Random` class, for example, specifies that it generates a number from 0 (inclusive) to n (exclusive). That means that the value 0 is included in the possible results, whereas the specified value for n is not. The highest number possibly returned by this call is `n-1`.

Exercise 5.19 Add a method to your `RandomTester` class that takes a parameter `max` and generates a random number in the range 1 to `max` (inclusive).

Exercise 5.20 Add a method to your `RandomTester` class that takes two parameters, `min` and `max`, and generates a random number in the range `min` to `max` (inclusive). Rewrite the body of the method you wrote for the previous exercise so that it now calls this new method to generate its result. Note that it should not be necessary to use a loop in this method.

5.4.3 Generating random responses

Now we can look at extending the `Responder` class to select a random response from a list of predefined phrases. Code 5.2 shows the source code of class `Responder` as it is in our first version.

We shall now add code to this first version to:

■ declare a field of type `Random` to hold the random number generator;

■ declare a field of type `ArrayList` to hold our possible responses;

■ create the `Random` and `ArrayList` objects in the `Responder` constructor;

■ fill the responses list with some phrases;

■ select and return a random phrase when `generateResponse` is called.

Code 5.3 shows a version of the `Responder` source code with these additions.

Code 5.3

The Responder
source code with
random responses

```java
import java.util.ArrayList;
import java.util.Random;

/**
 * The responder class represents a response-generator object.
 * It is used to generate an automatic response by randomly
 * selecting a phrase from a predefined list of responses.
 *
```

Code 5.3
continued

The Responder
source code with
random responses

```java
 * @author      Michael Kölling and David J. Barnes
 * @version     0.2 (2011.07.31)
 */
public class Responder
{
    private Random randomGenerator;
    private ArrayList<String> responses;

    /**
     * Create a responder.
     */
    public Responder()
    {
        randomGenerator = new Random();
        responses = new ArrayList<String>();
        fillResponses();
    }

    /**
     * Generate a response.
     * @return  A string that should be displayed as the
     *          response
     */
    public String generateResponse()
    {
        // Pick a random number for the index in the default response
        // list. The number will be between 0 (inclusive) and the size
        // of the list (exclusive).
        int index = randomGenerator.nextInt(responses.size());
        return responses.get(index);
    }

    /**
     * Build up a list of default responses from which we can
     * pick one if we don't know what else to say.
     */
    private void fillResponses()
    {
        responses.add("That sounds odd. Could you describe \n" +
                      "that problem in more detail?");
        responses.add("No other customer has ever \n" +
                      "complained about this before. \n" +
                      "What is your system configuration?");
        responses.add("That's a known problem with Vista." +
                      "Windows 7 is much better.");
        responses.add("I need a bit more information on that.");
        responses.add("Have you checked that you do not \n" +
                      "have a dll conflict?");
```

**Code 5.3
continued**
The Responder
source code with
random responses

```
                    responses.add("That is explained in the manual. \n" +
                                   "Have you read the manual?");
                    responses.add("Your description is a bit \n" +
                                   "wishy-washy. Have you got an expert \n" +
                                   "there with you who could describe \n" +
                                   "this more precisely?");
                    responses.add("That's not a bug, it's a feature!");
                    responses.add("Could you elaborate on that?");
            }
    }
```

In this version, we have put the code that fills the response list into its own method, named
fillResponses, which is called from the constructor. This ensures that the responses list will
be filled as soon as a Responder object is created, but the source code for filling the list is kept
separate to make the class easier to read and understand.

The most interesting code segment in this class is in the generateResponse method. Leaving
out the comments, it reads

```
public String generateResponse()
{
    int index = randomGenerator.nextInt(responses.size());
    return responses.get(index);
}
```

The first line of code in this method does three things:

■ It gets the size of the response list by calling its size method.

■ It generates a random number between 0 (inclusive) and the size (exclusive).

■ It stores that random number in the local variable index.

If this seems a lot of code for one line, you could also write

```
int listSize = responses.size();
int index = randomGenerator.nextInt(listSize);
```

This code is equivalent to the first line above. Which version you prefer, again, depends on
which one you find easier to read.

It is important to note that this code segment will generate a random number in the range
0 to listSize-1 (inclusive). This fits perfectly with the legal indices for an ArrayList.
Remember that the range of indices for an ArrayList of size listSize is 0 to listSize-1.
Thus, the computed random number gives us a perfect index to randomly access one from the
complete set of the list's elements.

The last line in the method reads

```
return responses.get(index);
```

This line does two things:

■ It retrieves the response at position index using the get method.

■ It returns the selected string as a method result, using the return statement.

If you are not careful, your code may generate a random number that is outside the valid indices of the ArrayList. When you then try to use it as an index to access a list element, you will get an IndexOutOfBoundsException.

5.4.4 Reading documentation for parameterized classes

So far, we have asked you to look at the documentation for the String class from the java.lang package and the Random class from the java.util package. You might have noticed when doing this that some class names in the documentation list look slightly different, such as ArrayList<E> or HashMap<K, V>. That is, the class name is followed by some extra information in angle brackets. Classes that look like this are called *parameterized classes* or *generic classes*. The information in the brackets tells us that when we use these classes, we must supply one or more type names in angle brackets to complete the definition. We have already seen this idea in practice in Chapter 4, where we used ArrayList by parameterizing it with type names such as String. They can also be parameterized with any other type:

```
private ArrayList<String> notes;
private ArrayList<Student> students;
```

Because we can parameterize an ArrayList with any other class type that we choose, this is reflected in the API documentation. So if you look at the list of methods for ArrayList<E>, you will see methods such as:

```
boolean add(E o)
E get(int index)
```

This tells us that the type of objects we can add to an ArrayList depends on the type used to parameterize it, and the type of the objects returned from its get method depends on this type in the same way. In effect, if we create an ArrayList<String> object and then the documentation tells us that the object has the following two methods:

```
boolean add(String o)
String get(int index)
```

whereas if we create an ArrayList<Student> object, then it will have these two methods:

```
boolean add(Student o)
Student get(int index)
```

We will ask you to look at the documentation for further parameterized types in later sections in this chapter.

5.5 **Packages and import**

There are still two lines at the top of the source file that we need to discuss:

```
import java.util.ArrayList;
import java.util.Random;
```

We encountered the import statement for the first time in Chapter 4. Now is the time to look at it a little more closely.

Java classes that are stored in the class library are not automatically available for use, like the other classes in the current project. Rather, we must state in our source code that we would like to use a class from the library. This is called *importing* the class and is done using the `import` statement. The `import` statement has the form

```
import qualified-class-name;
```

Because the Java library contains several thousand classes, some structure is needed in the organization of the library to make it easier to deal with the large number of classes. Java uses *packages* to arrange library classes into groups that belong together. Packages can be nested (that is, packages can contain other packages).

The classes `ArrayList` and `Random` are both in the package `java.util`. This information can be found in the class documentation. The *full name* or *qualified name* of a class is the name of its package, followed by a dot followed by the class name. Thus, the qualified names of the two classes we used here are `java.util.ArrayList` and `java.util.Random`.

Java also allows us to import complete packages with statements of the form

```
import package-name.*;
```

So the following statement would import all class names from the `java.util` package:

```
import java.util.*;
```

Listing all used classes separately, as in our first version, is a little more work in terms of typing but serves well as a piece of documentation. It clearly indicates which classes are actually used by our class. Therefore, in this book, we shall tend to use the style of the first example, listing all imported classes separately.

There is one exception to these rules: some classes are used so frequently that almost every class would import them. These classes have been placed in the package `java.lang`, and this package is automatically imported into every class. So we do not need to write import statements for classes in `java.lang`. The class `String` is an example of such a class.

> **Exercise 5.21** Implement in your version of the *tech-support* system the random-response solution discussed here.
>
> **Exercise 5.22** What happens when you add more (or fewer) possible responses to the responses list? Will the selection of a random response still work properly? Why or why not?

The solution discussed here is also in the book projects under the name *tech-support2*. We recommend, however, that you implement it yourself as an extension of the base version.

5.6 Using maps for associations

We now have a solution to our technical-support system that generates random responses. This is better than our first version, but is still not very convincing. In particular, the input of the user does not influence the response in any way. It is this area that we now want to improve.

The plan is that we shall have a set of words that are likely to occur in typical questions and we will associate these words with particular responses. If the input from the user contains one of our known words, we can generate a related response. This is still a very crude method, because it does not pick up any of the meaning of the user's input, nor does it recognize a context, but it can be surprisingly effective. And it is a good next step.

To do this, we will use a HashMap. You will find the documentation for the class HashMap in the Java library documentation. HashMap is a specialization of a Map, which you will also find documented. You will see that you need to read the documentation of both to understand what a HashMap is and how it works.

> **Exercise 5.23** What is a HashMap? What is its purpose and how do you use it? Answer these questions in writing, and use the Java library documentation of Map and HashMap for your responses. Note that you will find it hard to understand everything, as the documentation for these classes is not very good. We will discuss the details later in this chapter, but see what you can find out on your own before reading on.
>
> **Exercise 5.24** HashMap is a parameterized class. List those of its methods that depend on the types used to parameterize it. Do you think the same type could be used for both of its parameters?

5.6.1 The concept of a map

Concept:

A **map** is a collection that stores key/value pairs as entries. Values can be looked up by providing the key.

A map is a collection of key/value pairs of objects. As with the ArrayList, a map can store a flexible number of entries. One difference between the ArrayList and a Map is that with a Map each entry is not an object, but a *pair* of objects. This pair consists of a *key* object and a *value* object.

Instead of looking up entries in this collection using an integer index (as we did with the ArrayList), we use the key object to look up the value object.

An everyday example of a map is a telephone directory. A telephone directory contains entries, and each entry is a pair: a name and a phone number. You use a phone book by looking up a name and getting a phone number. We do not use an index—the position of the entry in the phone book—to find it.

A map can be organized in such a way that looking up a value for a key is easy. In the case of a phone book, this is done using alphabetical sorting. By storing the entries in the alphabetical order of their keys, finding the key and looking up the value is easy. Reverse lookup (finding the key for a value—i.e., finding the name for a given phone number) is not so easy with a map. As with a phone book, reverse lookup in a map is possible, but it takes a comparatively long time. Thus, maps are ideal for a one-way lookup, where we know the lookup key and need to know a value associated with this key.

5.6.2 Using a HashMap

HashMap is a particular implementation of Map. The most important methods of the HashMap class are put and get.

The put method inserts an entry into the map, and get retrieves the value for a given key. The following code fragment creates a HashMap and inserts three entries into it. Each entry is a key/value pair consisting of a name and a telephone number.

```
HashMap<String, String> phoneBook = new HashMap<String, String>();

phoneBook.put("Charles Nguyen", "(531) 9392 4587");
phoneBook.put("Lisa Jones", "(402) 4536 4674");
phoneBook.put("William H. Smith", "(998) 5488 0123");
```

As we saw with ArrayList, when declaring a HashMap variable and creating a HashMap object, we have to say what type of objects will be stored in the map and, additionally, what type of objects will be used for the key. For the phone book, we will use strings for both the keys and the values, but the two types will sometimes be different.

As we have seen in Section 4.4.2 if we are using Java 7 (or newer), the generic type specification on the right-hand side of the assignment may be left out, like this:

```
HashMap<String, String> phoneBook = new HashMap<>();
```

This is known as the "diamond operator" because of the two empty angle brackets: <>.

In Java 7, this line is equivalent to the first line above (but in Java 6 it does not compile). If you leave out the generic parameters, the compiler will just assume the same parameters used on the left-hand side of the assignment. Thus, the effect is exactly the same—we just save a little bit of typing.

The following code will find the phone number for Lisa Jones and print it out.

```
String number = phoneBook.get("Lisa Jones");
System.out.println(number);
```

Note that you pass the key (the name "Lisa Jones") to the get method in order to receive the value (the phone number).

Read the documentation of the get and put methods of class HashMap again and see whether the explanation matches your current understanding.

Exercise 5.25 How do you check how many entries are contained in a map?

Exercise 5.26 Create a class MapTester (either in your current project or in a new project). In it, use a HashMap to implement a phone book similar to the one in the example above. (Remember that you must import java.util.HashMap.) In this class, implement two methods:

```
public void enterNumber(String name, String number)
```

and

```
public String lookupNumber(String name)
```

The methods should use the put and get methods of the HashMap class to implement their functionality.

Exercise 5.27 What happens when you add an entry to a map with a key that already exists in the map?

Exercise 5.28 What happens when you add an entry to a map with two different keys?

Exercise 5.29 How do you check whether a given key is contained in a map? (Give a Java code example.)

Exercise 5.30 What happens when you try to look up a value and the key does not exist in the map?

Exercise 5.31 How do you check how many entries are contained in a map?

Exercise 5.32 How do you print out all keys currently stored in a map?

5.6.3 Using a map for the TechSupport system

In the TechSupport system, we can make good use of a map by using known words as keys and associated responses as values. Code 5.4 shows an example in which a `HashMap` named `response-Map` is created and three entries are made. For example, the word "slow" is associated with the text

> *"I think this has to do with your hardware. Upgrading your processor should solve all performance problems. Have you got a problem with our software?"*

Now, whenever somebody enters a question containing the word "slow," we can look up and print out this response. Note that the response string in the source code spans several lines but is concatenated with the + operator, so a single string is entered as a value into the `HashMap`.

Code 5.4

Associating selected words with possible responses

```java
private HashMap<String, String> responseMap;

...

public Responder()
{
    responseMap = new HashMap<String, String>();
    fillResponseMap();
}

/**
 * Enter all the known keywords and their associated
 * responses into our response map.
 */
private void fillResponseMap()
{
    responseMap.put("slow",
        "I think this has to do with your hardware. \n" +
        "Upgrading your processor should solve all " +
        "performance problems. \n" +
        "Have you got a problem with our software?");
    responseMap.put("bug",
```

Code 5.4 continued

Associating selected words with possible responses

```
            "Well, you know, all software has some bugs. \n" +
            "But our software engineers are working very " +
            "hard to fix them. \n" +
            "Can you describe the problem a bit further?");
        responseMap.put("expensive",
            "The cost of our product is quite competitive. \n" +
            "Have you looked around and " +
            "really compared our features?");
    }
```

A first attempt at writing a method to generate the responses could now look like the `gener-ateResponse` method below. Here, to simplify things for the moment, we assume that only a single word (for example, "slow") is entered by the user.

```
public String generateResponse(String word)
{
    String response = responseMap.get(word);
    if(response != null) {
        return response;
    }
    else {
        // If we get here, the word was not recognized. In
        // this case, we pick one of our default responses.
        return pickDefaultResponse();
    }
}
```

In this code fragment, we look up the word entered by the user in our response map. If we find an entry, we use this entry as the response. If we don't find an entry for that word, we call a method called `pickDefaultResponse`. This method can now contain the code of our previous version of `generateResponse`, which randomly picks one of the default responses (as shown in Code 5.3). The new logic, then, is that we pick an appropriate response if we recognize a word, or a random response out of our list of default responses if we don't.

Exercise 5.33 Implement the changes discussed here in your own version of the TechSupport system. Test it to get a feel for how well it works.

This approach of associating keywords with responses works quite well as long as the user does not enter complete questions, but only single words. The final improvement to complete the application is to let the user enter complete questions again and then pick matching responses if we recognize any of the words in the questions.

This poses the problem of recognizing the keywords in the sentence that was entered by the user. In the current version, the user input is returned by the `InputReader` as a single string. We shall now change this to a new version in which the `InputReader` returns the input as a set of words. Technically, this will be a set of strings, where each string in the set represents a single word that was entered by the user.

If we can do that, then we can pass the whole set to the Responder, which can then check every word in the set to see whether it is known and has an associated response.

To achieve this in Java, we need to know about two things: how to cut a single string containing a whole sentence into words and how to use sets. These two issues are discussed in the next two sections.

5.7 Using sets

The Java standard library includes different variations of sets implemented in different classes. The class we shall use is called HashSet.

> **Exercise 5.34** What are the similarities and differences between a HashSet and an ArrayList? Use the descriptions of Set, HashSet, List, and ArrayList in the library documentation to find out, because HashSet is a special case of a Set and ArrayList is a special case of a List.

The two types of functionality that we need are the ability to enter elements into the set and retrieve the elements later. Fortunately, these tasks contain hardly anything new for us. Consider the following code fragment:

```
import java.util.HashSet;
...
HashSet<String> mySet = new HashSet<String>();

mySet.add("one");
mySet.add("two");
mySet.add("three");
```

Compare this code with the statements needed to enter elements into an ArrayList. There is almost no difference, except that we create a HashSet this time instead of an ArrayList. Now let us look at iterating over all elements:

```
for(String item : mySet) {
    do something with that item
}
```

Again, these statements are the same as the ones we used to iterate over an ArrayList in Chapter 4.

In short, using collections in Java is quite similar for different types of collections. Once you understand how to use one of them, you can use them all. The differences really lie in the behavior of each collection. A list, for example, will keep all elements entered in the desired order, provides access to elements by index, and can contain the same element multiple times.

Concept:

A **set** is a collection that stores each individual element at most once. It does not maintain any specific order.

A set, on the other hand, does not maintain any specific order (the elements may be returned in a for-each loop in a different order from that in which they were entered) and ensures that each element is in the set at most once. Entering an element a second time simply has no effect.

> **List, Map, and Set** It is tempting to assume that a HashSet must be used in a similar way to a HashMap. In fact, as we have illustrated, a HashSet is actually much closer in usage to an ArrayList.
>
> When trying to understand how the various collection classes are used, it helps to pay close attention to their names. The names consist of two parts, e.g.: "Array" "List." The second half tells us what kind of collection we are dealing with (List, Map, Set), and the first tells us how it is implemented (for instance, using an array).
>
> For using collections, the type of the collection (the second part) is the more important. We have discussed before that we can often abstract from the implementation; we do not need to think about it much. Thus, for our purposes, a HashSet and a TreeSet are very similar. They are both sets, so they behave in the same way. The difference is only in their implementation, which is important only when we start thinking about efficiency: one implementation will perform some operations much faster than another. However, efficiency concerns come much later, and only when we have either very large collections or applications in which performance is critical.

5.8 Dividing strings

Now that we have seen how to use a set, we can investigate how we can cut the input string into separate words to be stored in a set of words. The solution is shown in a new version of the InputReader's getInput method (Code 5.5).

Code 5.5
The getInput method returning a set of words

```java
/**
 * Read a line of text from standard input (the text
 * terminal), and return it as a set of words.
 *
 * @return  A set of Strings, where each String is one of the
 *          words typed by the user
 */
public HashSet<String> getInput()
{
    System.out.print("> ");                      // print prompt
    String inputLine = reader.nextLine().trim().toLowerCase();
    String[] wordArray = inputLine.split(" ");

    // add words from array into hashset
    HashSet<String> words = new HashSet<String>();
    for(String word : wordArray) {
        words.add(word);
    }

    return words;
}
```

Here, in addition to using a HashSet, we also use the split method, which is a standard method of the String class.

The split method can divide a string into separate substrings and return those in an array of strings. The parameter to the split method defines at what kind of characters the original string should be split. We have defined that we want to cut our string at every space character.

The next few lines of code create a HashSet and copy the words from the array into the set before returning the set.[3]

Exercise 5.35 The split method is more powerful than it first seems from our example. How can you define exactly how a string should be split? Give some examples.

Exercise 5.36 How would you call the split method if you wanted to split a string at either space or tab characters? How might you break up a string in which the words are separated by colon characters (:)?

Exercise 5.37 What is the difference in the result of returning the words in a HashSet compared with returning them in an ArrayList?

Exercise 5.38 What happens if there is more than one space between two words (e.g., two or three spaces)? Is there a problem?

Exercise 5.39 *Challenge exercises* Read the footnote about the Arrays.asList method. Find and read the sections in this book about class variables and class methods. Explain in your own words how this works.

What are examples of other methods that the Arrays class provides?

Create a class called SortingTest. In it, create a method that accepts an array of int values as a parameter and prints out to the terminal the elements sorted (smallest element first).

5.9 Finishing the TechSupport system

To put everything together, we also have to adjust the SupportSystem and Responder classes to deal correctly with a set of words rather than a single string. Code 5.6 shows the new version of the start method from the SupportSystem class. It has not changed a great deal. The changes are:

---

[3] There is a shorter, more elegant way of doing this. One could write

```
HashSet<String> words = new HashSet<String>(Arrays.asList(wordArray));
```

to replace all four lines of code. This uses the Arrays class from the standard library and a *static method* (also known as *class method*) that we do not really want to discuss just yet. If you are curious, read about *class methods* in Section 6.15, and try to use this version.

- The `input` variable receiving the result from `reader.getInput()` is now of type `HashSet`.

- The check for ending the application is done using the `contains` method of the `HashSet` class, rather than a `String` method. (Look this method up in the documentation.)

- The `HashSet` class has to be imported using an `import` statement (not shown here).

Finally, we have to extend the `generateResponse` method in the `Responder` class to accept a set of words as a parameter. It then has to iterate over these words and check each of them with our map of known words. If any of the words is recognized, we immediately return the associated response. If we do not recognize any of the words, as before, we pick one of our default responses. Code 5.7 shows the solution.

Code 5.6

Final version of the `start` method

```java
public void start()
{
    boolean finished = false;

    printWelcome();

    while(!finished) {
        HashSet<String> input = reader.getInput();

        if(input.contains("bye")) {
            finished = true;
        }
        else {
            String response = responder.generateResponse(input);
            System.out.println(response);
        }
    }
    printGoodbye();
}
```

Code 5.7

Final version of the generate Response method

```java
public String generateResponse(HashSet<String> words)
{
    for(String word : words) {
        String response = responseMap.get(word);
        if(response != null) {
            return response;
        }
    }
    // If we get here, none of the words from the input line was
    // recognized. In this case, we pick one of our default
    // responses.

    return pickDefaultResponse();
}
```

This is the last change to the application discussed here in this chapter. The solution in the project *tech-support-complete* contains all these changes. It also contains more associations of words to responses than are shown in this chapter.

Many more improvements to this application are possible. We shall not discuss them here. Instead, we suggest some, in the form of exercises, left to the reader. Some of these are quite challenging programming exercises.

Exercise 5.40 Implement the final changes discussed above in your own version of the program.

Exercise 5.41 Add more word/response mappings into your application. You could copy some out of the solutions provided and add some yourself.

Exercise 5.42 Ensure that the same default response is never repeated twice in a row.

Exercise 5.43 Sometimes two words (or variations of a word) are mapped to the same response. Deal with this by mapping synonyms or related expressions to the same string so that you do not need multiple entries in the response map for the same response.

Exercise 5.44 Identify multiple matching words in the user's input, and respond with a more appropriate answer in that case.

Exercise 5.45 When no word is recognized, use other words from the user's input to pick a well-fitting default response: for example, words such as "why," "how," and "who."

5.10 Writing class documentation

When working on your projects, it is important to write documentation for your classes as you develop the source code. It is quite common for programmers not to take documentation seriously enough, and very frequently this creates serious problems later.

If you do not supply sufficient documentation, it may be very hard for another programmer (or yourself some time later!) to understand your classes. Typically, what you have to do in that case is to read the class's implementation and figure out what it does. This may work with a small student project, but it creates serious problems in real-world projects.

It is not uncommon for commercial applications to consist of hundreds of thousands of lines of code in several thousand classes. Imagine that you had to read all that in order to understand how an application works! You would never succeed.

When we used the Java library classes, such as HashSet or Random, we relied exclusively on the documentation to find out how to use them. We never looked at the implementation of those classes. This worked because these classes were sufficiently well documented (although even this documentation could be improved). Our task would have been much harder had we been required to read the classes' implementation before using them.

In a software development team, the implementation of classes is typically shared between multiple programmers. While you might be responsible for implementing the SupportSystem

Concept:

The **documentation** of a class should be detailed enough for other programmers to use the class without the need to read the implementation.

class from our last example, someone else might implement the InputReader. Thus, you might write one class while making calls to methods of other classes.

The same argument discussed for library classes holds true for classes that you write: if we can use the classes without having to read and understand the complete implementation, our task becomes a lot easier. As with library classes, we want to see just the public interface of the class, instead of the implementation. It is therefore important to write good class documentation for our own classes as well.

Java systems include a tool called javadoc that can be used to generate such an interface description from source files. The standard library documentation that we have used, for example, was created from the classes' source files by javadoc.

5.10.1   Using javadoc in BlueJ

The BlueJ environment uses javadoc to let you create documentation for your class in two ways:

■ You can view the documentation for a single class by switching the pop-up selector at the top right of the editor window from *Source Code* to *Documentation* (or by using *Toggle Documentation View* from the editor's *Tools* menu).

■ You can use the *Project Documentation* function from the main window's *Tools* menu to generate documentation for all classes in the project.

The BlueJ tutorial provides more detail if you are interested. You can find the BlueJ tutorial in BlueJ's *Help* menu.

5.10.2   Elements of class documentation

The documentation of a class should at least include:

■ the class name

■ a comment describing the overall purpose and characteristics of the class

■ a version number

■ the author's name (or authors' names)

■ documentation for each constructor and each method

The documentation for each constructor and method should include:

■ the name of the method

■ the return type

■ the parameter names and types

■ a description of the purpose and function of the method

■ a description of each parameter

■ a description of the value returned

In addition, each complete project should have an overall project comment, often contained in a "ReadMe" file. In BlueJ, this project comment is accessible through the text note displayed in the top left corner of the class diagram.

Exercise 5.46 Use BlueJ's *Project Documentation* function to generate documentation for your TechSupport project. Examine it. Is it accurate? Is it complete? Which parts are useful? Which are not? Do you find any errors in the documentation?

Some elements of the documentation, such as names and parameters of methods, can always be extracted from the source code. Other parts, such as comments describing the class, methods, and parameters, need more attention, as they can easily be forgotten, be incomplete, or be incorrect.

In Java, javadoc comments are written with a special comment symbol at the beginning:

```
/**
    This is a javadoc comment.
 */
```

The comment start symbol must have two asterisks to be recognized as a javadoc comment. Such a comment immediately preceding the class declaration is read as a class comment. If the comment is directly above a method signature, it is considered a method comment.

The exact details of how documentation is produced and formatted are different in different programming languages and environments. The content, however, should be more or less the same.

In Java, using javadoc, several special key symbols are available for formatting the documentation. These key symbols start with the @ symbol and include

```
@version
@author
@param
@return
```

Exercise 5.47 Find examples of javadoc key symbols in the source code of the *TechSupport* project. How do they influence the formatting of the documentation?

Exercise 5.48 Find out about and describe other javadoc key symbols. One place where you can look is the online documentation of Oracle's Java distribution. It contains a document called *javadoc – The Java API Documentation Generator* (for example, at http://download.oracle.com/javase/6/docs/technotes/tools/windows/javadoc.html). In this document, the key symbols are called *javadoc tags*.

Exercise 5.49 Properly document all classes in your version of the *TechSupport* project.

5.11 Public versus private

It is time to discuss in more detail one aspect of classes that we have encountered several times already without saying much about it: *access modifiers*.

Access modifiers are the keywords `public` or `private` at the beginning of field declarations and method signatures. For example:

```
// field declaration
private int numberOfSeats;

// methods
public void setAge(int replacementAge)
{ ...
}

private int computeAverage()
{ ...
}
```

Fields, constructors, and methods can all be either public or private, although so far we have seen mostly private fields and public constructors and methods. We shall come back to this below.

Access modifiers define the visibility of a field, constructor, or method. If a method, for example, is public, it can be invoked from within the same class or from any other class. Private methods, on the other hand, can be invoked only from within the class in which they are declared. They are not visible to other classes.

Now that we have discussed the difference between the interface and the implementation of a class (Section 5.3.1), we can more easily understand the purpose of these keywords.

Remember: The interface of a class is the set of details that another programmer using the class needs to see. It provides information about how to use the class. The interface includes constructor and method signatures and comments. It is also referred to as the *public* part of a class. Its purpose is to define *what* the class does.

The implementation is the section of a class that defines precisely *how* the class works. The method bodies, containing the Java statements, and most fields are part of the implementation. The implementation is also referred to as the *private* part of a class. The user of a class does not need to know about the implementation. In fact, there are good reasons why a user *should be prevented from knowing* about the implementation (or at least from making use of this knowledge). This principle is called *information hiding*.

The `public` keyword declares an element of a class (a field or method) to be part of the interface (i.e., publicly visible); the `private` keyword declares it to be part of the implementation (i.e., hidden from outside access).

> **Concept:**
>
> **Access modifiers** define the visibility of a field, constructor, or method. Public elements are accessible from inside the same class and from other classes; private elements are accessible only from within the same class.

5.11.1   Information hiding

In many object-oriented programming languages, the internals of a class—its implementation—are hidden from other classes. There are two aspects to this. First, a programmer making use of a class should *not need to know* the internals; second, a user should *not be allowed to know* the internals.

The first principle—*need to know*—has to do with abstraction and modularization as discussed in Chapter 3. If it were necessary to know all internals of all classes we need to use, we would never finish implementing large systems.

Concept:

information hiding
is a principle that
states that internal
details of a class's
implementation
should be hidden
from other classes.
It ensures better
modularization of an
application.

The second principle—*not being allowed to know*—is different. It also has to do with modularization, but in a different context. The programming language does not allow access to the private section of one class by statements in another class. This ensures that one class does not depend on exactly how another class is implemented.

This is very important for maintenance work. It is a very common task for a maintenance programmer to later change or extend the implementation of a class to make improvements or fix bugs. Ideally, changing the implementation of one class should not make it necessary to change other classes as well. This issue is known as *coupling*. If changes in one part of a program do not make it necessary to also make changes in another part of the program, this is known as weak coupling or loose coupling. Loose coupling is good, because it makes a maintenance programmer's job much easier. Instead of understanding and changing many classes, she may only need to understand and change one class. For example, if a Java systems programmer makes an improvement to the implementation of the ArrayList class, you would hope that you would not need to change your code using this class. This will work, because you have not made any references to the implementation of ArrayList in your own code.

So, to be more precise, the rule that a user should not be allowed to know the internals of a class does not refer to the programmer of another class, but to the class itself. It is not usually a problem if a programmer knows the implementation details, but a class should not "know" (depend on) the internal details of another class. The programmer of both classes might even be the same person, but the classes should still be loosely coupled.

The issues of coupling and information hiding are very important, and we shall have more to say about them in later chapters.

For now, it is important to understand that the private keyword enforces information hiding by not allowing other classes access to this part of the class. This ensures loose coupling and makes an application more modular and easier to maintain.

5.11.2   Private methods and public fields

Most methods we have seen so far were public. This ensures that other classes can call these methods. Sometimes, though, we have made use of private methods. In the SupportSystem class of the *TechSupport* system, for instance, we saw the methods printWelcome and printGoodbye declared as private methods.

The reason for having both options is that methods are actually used for different purposes. They are used to provide operations to users of a class (public methods), and they are used to break up a larger task into several smaller ones to make the large task easier to handle. In the second case, the subtasks are not intended to be invoked directly from outside the class, but are placed in separate methods purely to make the implementation of a class easier to read. In this case, such methods should be private. The printWelcome and printGoodbye methods are examples of this.

Another good reason for having a private method is for a task that is needed (as a subtask) in several of a class's methods. Instead of writing the code multiple times, we can write it once in a single private method and then call this method from several different places. We shall see an example of this later.

In Java, fields can also be declared private or public. So far, we have not seen examples of public fields, and there is a good reason for this. Declaring fields public breaks the information-hiding principle. It makes a class that is dependent upon that information vulnerable to incorrect operation if the implementation changes. Even though the Java language allows us to declare public fields, we consider this bad style and will not make use of this option. Some other object-oriented languages do not allow public fields at all.

A further reason for keeping fields private is that it allows an object to maintain greater control over its state. If access to a private field is channeled through accessor and mutator methods, then an object has the ability to ensure that the field is never set to a value that would be inconsistent with its overall state. This level of integrity is not possible if fields are made public.

In short, fields should always be private.

Java has two more access levels. One is declared by using the `protected` keyword as access modifier; the other one is used if no access modifier at all is declared. We shall discuss these in later chapters.

5.12 Learning about classes from their interfaces

We shall briefly discuss another project to revisit and practice the concepts discussed in this chapter. The project is named *scribble*, and you can find it in the Chapter 5 folder of the book projects. This section does not introduce any new concepts, so it consists in large part of exercises, with some commentary sprinkled in.

5.12.1 The *scribble* demo

The *scribble* project provides three classes: `DrawDemo`, `Pen`, and `Canvas` (Figure 5.4).

Figure 5.4

The *scribble* project

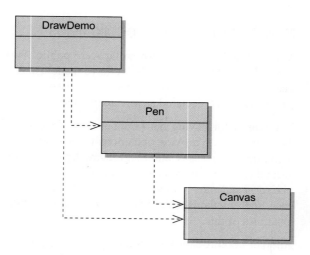

The `Canvas` class provides a window on screen that can be used to draw on. It has operations for drawing lines, shapes, and text. A canvas can be used by creating an instance interactively or from another object. The `Canvas` class should not need any modification. It is probably best to treat it as a library class: open the editor and switch to the documentation view. This displays the class's interface with the `javadoc` documentation.

The `Pen` class provides a pen object that can be used to produce drawings on the canvas by moving the pen across the screen. The pen itself is invisible, but it will draw a line when moved on the canvas.

The `DrawDemo` class provides a few small examples of how to use a pen object to produce a drawing on screen.

The best starting point for understanding and experimenting with this project is the `DrawDemo` class.

Exercise 5.50 Create a `DrawDemo` object and experiment with its various methods. Read the `DrawDemo` source code and describe (in writing) how each method works.

Exercise 5.51 Create a `Pen` object interactively using its default constructor (the constructor without parameters). Experiment with its methods. While you do this, make sure to have a window open showing you the documentation of the `Pen` class (either the editor window in *Documentation* view or a web-browser window showing the project documentation). Refer to the documentation to be certain what each method does.

Exercise 5.52 Interactively create an instance of class `Canvas` and try some of its methods. Again, refer to the class's documentation while you do this.

Some of the methods in the classes `Pen` and `Canvas` refer to parameters of type `Color`. This type is defined in class `Color` in the `java.awt` package (thus, its fully qualified name is `java.awt.Color`). The `Color` class defines some color constants, which we can refer to as follows:

```
Color.RED
```

Using these constants requires the `Color` class to be imported in the using class.

Exercise 5.53 Find some uses of the color constants in the code of class `DrawDemo`.

Exercise 5.54 Write down four more color constants that are available in the `Color` class. Refer to the class's documentation to find out what they are.

When calling methods interactively that expect parameters of the `Color` class, we have to refer to the class slightly differently. Because the interactive dialog has no import statement (and thus the `Color` class is not automatically known), we have to write the fully qualified class name to refer to the class (Figure 5.5). This enables the Java system to find the class without using an import statement.

Figure 5.5

Now that we know how to change the color for pens and canvases, we can do some more exercises.

Exercise 5.55 Create a canvas. Using the canvas's methods interactively, draw a red circle near the center of the canvas. Now draw a yellow rectangle.

Exercise 5.56 How do you clear the whole canvas?

As you have seen, we can either draw directly on to the canvas or we can use a pen object to draw. The pen provides us with an abstraction that holds a current position, rotation, and color, and this makes producing some kinds of drawings easier. Let us experiment with this a bit more, this time by writing code in a class instead of using interactive calls.

Exercise 5.57 In class `DrawDemo`, create a new method named `drawTriangle`. This method should create a pen (as in the `drawSquare` method) and then draw a green triangle.

Exercise 5.58 Write a method `drawPentagon` that draws a pentagon.

Exercise 5.59 Write a method `drawPolygon(int n)` that draws a regular polygon with n sides (thus, n=3 draws a triangle, n=4 draws a square, etc.).

Exercise 5.60 Write a method called `spiral` that draws a spiral (see Figure 5.6).

Figure 5.6
A spiral drawn on the canvas

5.12.2 Code completion

Often, we are reasonably familiar with a library class that we are using but we still cannot remember the exact names of all methods or the exact parameters. For this situation, development environments commonly offer some help: code completion.

Code completion is a function that is available in BlueJ's editor when the cursor is behind the dot of a method call. In this situation, typing *CTRL-space* will bring up a pop-up listing all methods in the interface of the object we are using in the call (Figure 5.7).

When the code completion pop-up is displayed, we can type the beginning of the method name to narrow down the method list. Hitting *Return* enters the selected method call into our source code. Code completion can also be used without a preceding object to call local methods.

Using code completion should not be a replacement for reading the documentation of a class, because it does not include all information (such as the introductory class comment). But once we are reasonably familiar with a class in general, code completion is a great aid for more easily recalling details of a method and entering the call into our source.

> **Exercise 5.61** Add a method to your `DrawDemo` class that produces a picture on the canvas directly (without using a pen object). The picture can show anything you like, but should at least include some shapes, different colors, and text. Use code completion in the process of entering your code.

5.12.3 The *bouncing-balls* demo

Open the *bouncing-balls* project and find out what it does. Create a `BallDemo` object and execute its `bounce` method.

Exercise 5.62 Change the method `bounce` in class `BallDemo` to let the user choose how many balls should be bouncing.

For this exercise, you should use a collection to store the balls. This way, the method can deal with 1, 3, or 75 balls—any number you want. The balls should initially be placed in a row along the top of the canvas.

Which type of collection should you choose? So far, we have seen an `ArrayList`, a `HashMap`, and a `HashSet`. Try the next exercises first, before you write your implementation.

Exercise 5.63 Which type of collection (`ArrayList`, `HashMap`, or `HashSet`) is most suitable for storing the balls for the new `bounce` method? Discuss in writing, and justify your choice.

Exercise 5.64 Change the `bounce` method to place the balls randomly anywhere in the top half of the screen.

Exercise 5.65 Write a new method named `boxBounce`. This method draws a rectangle (the "box") on screen and one or more balls inside the box. For the balls, do not use `BouncingBall`, but create a new class `BoxBall` that moves around inside the box, bouncing off the walls of the box so that the ball always stays inside. The initial position and speed of the ball should be random. The `boxBounce` method should have a parameter that specifies how many balls are in the box.

Exercise 5.66 Give the balls in `boxBounce` random colors.

5.13 Class variables and constants

So far, we have not looked at the `BouncingBall` class. If you are interested in really understanding how this animation works, you may want to study this class as well. It is reasonably simple. The only method that takes some effort to understand is `move`, where the ball changes its position to the next position in its path.

We shall leave it largely to the reader to study this method, except for one detail that we want to discuss here. We start with an exercise.

Exercise 5.67 In class `BouncingBall`, you will find a definition of gravity (a simple integer). Increase or decrease the gravity value; compile and run the bouncing ball demo again. Do you observe a change?

The most interesting detail in this class is the line

```
private static final int GRAVITY = 3;
```

This is a construct we have not seen yet. This one line, in fact, introduces two new keywords, which are used together: `static` and `final`.

5.13.1 The `static` keyword

The keyword `static` is Java's syntax to define *class variables*. Class variables are fields that are stored in a class itself, not in an object. This makes them fundamentally different from instance variables (the fields we have dealt with so far). Consider this segment of code (a part of the `BouncingBall` class):

> **Concept:**
>
> Classes can have fields. These are known as **class variables** or static variables. Exactly one copy exists of a class variable at all times, independent of the number of created instances.

```
public class BouncingBall
{
    // Effect of gravity.
    private static final int GRAVITY = 3;

    private int xPosition;
    private int yPosition;

    Other fields and method omitted.
}
```

Now imagine that we create three `BouncingBall` instances. The resulting situation is shown in Figure 5.8.

Figure 5.8
Instance variables and a class variable

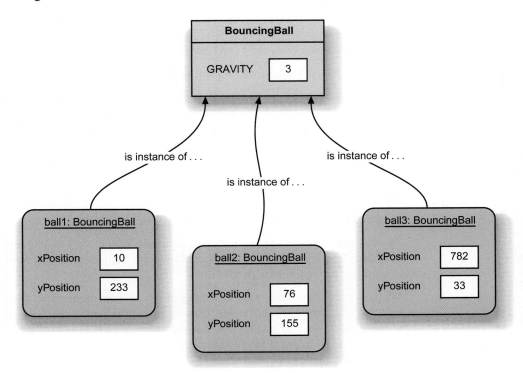

As we can see from the diagram, the instance variables (xPosition and yPosition) are stored in each object. Because we have created three objects, we have three independent copies of these variables.

The class variable GRAVITY, on the other hand, is stored in the class itself. As a result, there is always exactly one copy of this variable, independent of the number of created instances.

Source code in the class can access (read and set) this kind of variable just as it can an instance variable. The class variable can be accessed from any of the class's instances. As a result, the objects share this variable.

Class variables are frequently used if a value should always be the same for all instances of a class. Instead of storing one copy of the same value in each object, which would be a waste of space and might be hard to coordinate, a single value can be shared among all instances.

Java also supports *class methods* (also known as *static methods*), which are methods that belong to a class. We shall discuss those later.

5.13.2 Constants

One frequent use for the static keyword is to define *constants*. Constants are similar to variables, but they cannot change their value during the execution of an application. In Java, constants are defined with the keyword final. For example:

```
private final int SIZE = 10;
```

Here, we define a constant named SIZE with the value 10. We notice that constant declarations look similar to field declarations, with two differences:

■ they include the keyword final before the type name; and

■ they must be initialized with a value at the point of declaration.

If a value is intended not to change, it is a good idea to declare it final. This ensures that it cannot accidentally be changed later. Any attempt to change a constant field will result in a compile-time error message. Constants are, by convention, often written in capital letters. We will follow that convention in this book.

In practice, it is frequently the case that constants apply to all instances of a class. In this situation, we declare *class constants*. Class constants are constant class fields. They are declared by using a combination of the static and final keywords. For example:

```
private static final int SIZE = 10;
```

The definition of GRAVITY from our bouncing-ball project is another example of such a constant. This is the style in which constants are defined most of the time. Instance-specific constants are much less frequently used.

We have encountered two more examples of constants in the *scribble* project. The first example was two constants used in the Pen class to define the size of the "random squiggle" (go back to the project and find them!). The second example was the use of the color constants in that project, such as Color.RED. In that case, we did not define the constants, but instead used constants defined in another class.

The reason we could use the constants from class Color is that they were declared public. As opposed to other fields (about which we commented earlier that they should never be declared public), declaring constants public is generally unproblematic and sometimes useful.

Exercise 5.68 Write constant declarations for the following:

- A public variable that is used to measure tolerance, with the value 0.001.
- A private variable that is used to indicate a pass mark, with the integer value of 40.
- A public character variable that is used to indicate that the help command is 'h'.

Exercise 5.69 Take a look at the LogEntry class in the *weblog-analyzer* project from Chapter 4. How have constants been used in that class? Do you think that this is a good use of constants?

Exercise 5.70 Suppose that a change to the *weblog-analyzer* project meant that it was no longer necessary to store year values in the dataValues array in the LogEntry class. How much of the class would need to be altered if the month value were now to be stored at index 0, the day value at index 1, and so on? Do you see how the use of named constants for special values simplifies this sort of process?

5.14 Summary

Dealing with class libraries and class interfaces is essential for a competent programmer. There are two aspects to this topic: reading class library descriptions (especially class interfaces) and writing them.

It is important to know about some essential classes from the standard Java class library and to be able to find out more when necessary. In this chapter, we have presented some of the most important classes and have discussed how to browse the library documentation.

It is also important to be able to document any class that is written, in the same style as the library classes, so that other programmers can easily use the class without the need to understand the implementation. This documentation should include good comments for every project, class, and method. Using javadoc with Java programs will help you to do this.

Terms introduced in this chapter

interface, implementation, map, set, javadoc, access modifier, information hiding, coupling, class variable, static, constant, final

Concept summary

- **Java library** The Java standard class library contains many classes that are very useful. It is important to know how to use the library.

- **library documentation** The Java class library documentation shows details about all classes in the library. Using this documentation is essential in order to make good use of library classes.

- **interface** The interface of a class describes what a class does and how it can be used without showing the implementation.

- **implementation** The complete source code that defines a class is called the implementation of that class.

- **immutable** An object is said to be immutable if its contents or state cannot be changed once it has been created. Strings are an example of immutable objects.

- **map** A map is a collection that stores key/value pairs as entries. Values can be looked up by providing the key.

- **set** A set is a collection that stores each individual element at most once. It does not maintain any specific order.

- **documentation** The documentation of a class should be detailed enough for other programmers to use the class without the need to read the implementation.

- **access modifier** Access modifiers define the visibility of a field, constructor, or method. Public elements are accessible from inside the same class and from other classes; private elements are accessible only from within the same class.

- **information hiding** Information hiding is a principle that states that internal details of a class's implementation should be hidden from other classes. It ensures better modularization of an application.

- **class variable, static variable** Classes can have fields. These are known as class variables or static variables. Exactly one copy exists of a class variable at all times, independent of the number of created instances.

Exercise 5.71 There is a rumor circulating on the Internet that George Lucas (the creator of the *Star Wars* movies) uses a formula to create the names for the characters in his stories (Jar Jar Binks, ObiWan Kenobi, etc.). The formula—allegedly—is this:

Your Star Wars *first name:*
1 Take the first three letters of your last name.
2 Add to that the first two letters of your first name.

Your Star Wars *last name:*
1 Take the first two letters of your mother's maiden name.
2 Add to this the first three letters of the name of the town or city where you were born.

And now your task: Create a new BlueJ project named *star-wars*. In it create a class named `NameGenerator`. This class should have a method named `generateStarWarsName` that generates a *Star Wars* name, following the method described above. You will need to find out about a method of the `String` class that generates a substring.

Exercise 5.72 The following code fragment attempts to print out a string in uppercase letters:

```
public void printUpper(String s)
{
    s.toUpperCase();
    System.out.println(s);
}
```

This code, however, does not work. Find out why, and explain. How should it be written properly?

Exercise 5.73 Assume that we want to swap the values of two integer variables, a and b. To do this, we write a method

```
public void swap(int i1, int i2)
{
    int tmp = i1;
    i1 = i2;
    i2 = tmp;
}
```

Then we call this method with our a and b variables:

```
swap(a, b);
```

Are a and b swapped after this call? If you test it, you will notice that they are not! Why does this not work? Explain in detail.

CHAPTER

6

Designing classes

Main concepts discussed in this chapter:

- responsibility-driven design
- coupling
- cohesion
- refactoring

Java constructs discussed in this chapter:

`static` (for methods), `Math`, enumerated types, `switch`

In this chapter, we look at some of the factors that influence the design of a class. What makes a class design either good or bad? Writing good classes can take more effort in the short term than writing bad classes, but in the long term that extra effort will often be justified. To help us write good classes, there are some principles that we can follow. In particular, we introduce the view that class design should be responsibility-driven, and that classes should encapsulate their data.

This chapter is, like many of the chapters before, structured around a project. It can be studied by just reading it and following our line of argument, or it can be studied in much more depth by doing the project exercises in parallel with working through the chapter.

The project work is divided into three parts. In the first part, we discuss the necessary changes to the source code and develop and show complete solutions to the exercises. The solution for this part is also available in a project accompanying this book. The second part suggests more changes and extensions, and we discuss possible solutions at a high level (the class-design level) but leave it to readers to do the lower-level work and to complete the implementation.

The third part suggests even more improvements in the form of exercises. We do not give solutions—the exercises apply the material discussed throughout the chapter.

Implementing all parts makes a good programming project over several weeks. It can also be used very successfully as a group project.

6.1   Introduction

It is possible to implement an application and get it to perform its task with badly designed classes. Just executing a finished application does not usually indicate whether it is well structured internally or not.

The problems typically surface when a maintenance programmer wants to make some changes to an existing application. If, for example, a programmer attempts to fix a bug or wants to add new functionality to an existing program, a task that might be easy and obvious with well-designed classes may well be very hard and involve a great deal of work if the classes are badly designed.

In larger applications, this effect occurs earlier on, during the original implementation. If the implementation starts with a bad structure, then finishing it might later become overly complex, and the complete program may either not be finished, or contain bugs, or take a lot longer to build than necessary. In reality, companies often maintain, extend, and sell an application over many years. It is not uncommon that an implementation for software that we can buy in a software store today was started more than ten years ago. In this situation, a software company cannot afford to have badly structured code.

Because many of the effects of bad class design become most obvious when trying to adapt or extend an application, we shall do exactly that. In this chapter, we will use an example called *world-of-zuul*, which is a simple, rudimentary implementation of a text-based adventure game. In its original state, the game is not actually very ambitious—for one thing, it is incomplete. By the end of this chapter, however, you will be in a position to exercise your imagination and design and implement your own game and make it really fun and interesting.

world-of-zuul   Our *world-of-zuul* game is modeled on the original *Adventure* game that was developed in the early 1970s by Will Crowther and expanded by Don Woods. The original game is also sometimes known as the *Colossal Cave Adventure*. This was a wonderfully imaginative and sophisticated game for its time, involving finding your way through a complex cave system, locating hidden treasure, using secret words, and other mysteries, all in an effort to score the maximum number of points. You can read more about it at sites such as `http://jerz.setonhill.edu/if/canon/Adventure.htm` and `http://www.rickadams.org/adventure/`, or try doing a web search for "Colossal Cave Adventure."

While we work on extending the original application, we will take the opportunity to discuss aspects of its existing class design. We will see that the implementation we start with contains examples of bad design, and we will be able to appreciate how this impacts on our tasks and how we can fix them.

In the project examples for this book, you will find two versions of the *zuul* project: *zuul-bad* and *zuul-better*. Both implement exactly the same functionality, but some of the class structure is different, representing bad design in one project and better design in the other. The fact that we can implement the same functionality in either a good way or a bad way illustrates the fact that bad design is not usually a consequence of having a difficult problem to solve. Bad design has more to do with the decisions that we make when solving a particular problem. We cannot use the argument that there was no other way to solve the problem as an excuse for bad design.

So, we will use the project with the bad design so that we can explore why it is bad and then improve it. The better version is an implementation of the changes we discuss here.

Exercise 6.1 Open the project *zuul-bad*. (This project is called "bad" because its implementation contains some bad design decisions, and we want to leave no doubt that this should not be used as an example of good programming practice!) Execute and explore the application. The project comment gives you some information about how to run it.

While exploring the application, answer the following questions:

■ What does this application do?
■ What commands does the game accept?
■ What does each command do?
■ How many rooms are in the scenario?
■ Draw a map of the existing rooms.

Exercise 6.2 After you know what the whole application does, try to find out what each individual class does. Write down for each class its purpose. You need to look at the source code to do this. Note that you might not (and need not) understand all of the source code. Often, reading through comments and looking at method headers is enough.

6.2 The *world-of-zuul* game example

From Exercise 6.1, you have seen that the *zuul* game is not yet very adventurous. It is, in fact, quite boring in its current state. But it provides a good basis for us to design and implement our own game, which will hopefully be more interesting.

We start by analyzing the classes that are already there in our first version and trying to find out what they do. The class diagram is shown in Figure 6.1.

Figure 6.1

Zuul class diagram

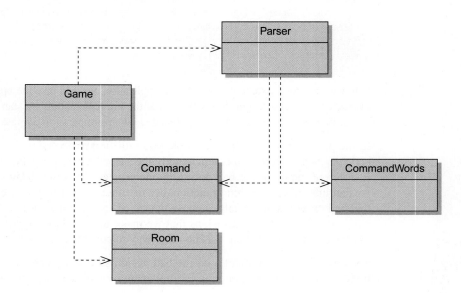

The project shows five classes. They are `Parser`, `CommandWords`, `Command`, `Room`, and `Game`. An investigation of the source code shows, fortunately, that these classes are quite well documented, and we can get an initial overview of what they do by just reading the class comment at the top of each class. (This fact also serves to illustrate that bad design involves something deeper than simply the way a class looks or how good its documentation is.) Our understanding of the game will be assisted by having a look at the source code to see what methods each class has and what some of the methods appear to do. Here, we summarize the purpose of each class:

- *CommandWords* The `CommandWords` class defines all valid commands in the game. It does this by holding an array of `String` objects representing the command words.

- *Parser* The parser reads lines of input from the terminal and tries to interpret them as commands. It creates objects of class `Command` that represent the command that was entered.

- *Command* A `Command` object represents a command that was entered by the user. It has methods that make it easy for us to check whether this was a valid command and to get the first and second words of the command as separate strings.

- *Room* A `Room` object represents a location in a game. Rooms can have exits that lead to other rooms.

- *Game* The `Game` class is the main class of the game. It sets up the game and then enters a loop to read and execute commands. It also contains the code that implements each user command.

Exercise 6.3 Design your own game scenario. Do this away from the computer. Do not think about implementation, classes, or even programming in general. Just think about inventing an interesting game. This could be done with a group of people.

The game can be anything that has as its base structure a player moving through different locations. Here are some examples:

- You are a white blood cell traveling through the body in search of viruses to attack...
- You are lost in a shopping mall and must find the exit...
- You are a mole in its burrow and you cannot remember where you stored your food reserves before winter...
- You are an adventurer who searches through a dungeon full of monsters and other characters...
- You are from the bomb squad and must find and defuse a bomb before it goes off...

Make sure that your game has a goal (so that it has an end and the player can "win"). Try to think of many things to make the game interesting (trap doors, magic items, characters that help you only if you feed them, time limits... whatever you like). Let your imagination run wild.

At this stage, do not worry about how to implement these things.

6.3 Introduction to coupling and cohesion

If we are to justify our assertion that some designs are better than others, then we need to define some terms that will allow us to discuss the issues that we consider to be important in class design. Two terms are central when talking about the quality of a class design: *coupling* and *cohesion*.

The term *coupling* refers to the interconnectedness of classes. We have already discussed in earlier chapters that we aim to design our applications as a set of cooperating classes that communicate via well-defined interfaces. The degree of coupling indicates how tightly these classes are connected. We strive for a low degree of coupling, or *loose coupling*.

The degree of coupling determines how hard it is to make changes in an application. In a tightly coupled class structure, a change in one class can make it necessary to change several other classes as well. This is what we try to avoid, because the effect of making one small change can quickly ripple through a complete application. In addition, finding all the places where changes are necessary and actually making the changes can be difficult and time consuming.

In a loosely coupled system, on the other hand, we can often change one class without making any changes to other classes, and the application will still work. We shall discuss particular examples of tight and loose coupling in this chapter.

The term *cohesion* relates to the number and diversity of tasks for which a single unit of an application is responsible. Cohesion is relevant for units of a single class and an individual method.[1]

Ideally, one unit of code should be responsible for one cohesive task (that is, one task that can be seen as a logical unit). A method should implement one logical operation, and a class should represent one type of entity. The main reason behind the principle of cohesion is reuse: if a method or a class is responsible for only one well-defined thing, then it is much more likely that it can be used again in a different context. A complementary advantage of following this principle is that, when change *is* required to some aspect of an application, we are likely to find all the relevant pieces located in the same unit.

We shall discuss with examples below how cohesion influences the quality of class design.

> **Concept:**
>
> The term **coupling** describes the interconnectedness of classes. We strive for loose coupling in a system—that is, a system where each class is largely independent and communicates with other classes via a small, well-defined interface.

> **Concept:**
>
> The term **cohesion** describes how well a unit of code maps to a logical task or entity. In a highly cohesive system, each unit of code (method, class, or module) is responsible for a well-defined task or entity. Good class design exhibits a high degree of cohesion.

Exercise 6.4 Draw (on paper) a map for the game you invented in Exercise 6.3. Open the *zuul-bad* project and save it under a different name (e.g., *zuul*). This is the project you will use for making improvements and modifications throughout this chapter. You can leave off the *-bad* suffix, because it will (hopefully) soon not be that bad anymore.

As a first step, change the `createRooms` method in the `Game` class to create the rooms and exits you invented for your game. Test!

---

[1] We sometimes also use the term *module* (or *package* in Java) to refer to a multi-class unit. *Cohesion* is relevant at this level too.

6.4 Code duplication

Code duplication is an indicator of bad design. The Game class shown in Code 6.1 contains a case of code duplication. The problem with code duplication is that any change to one version must also be made to another if we are to avoid inconsistency. This increases the amount of work a maintenance programmer has to do, and it introduces the danger of bugs. It very easily happens that a maintenance programmer finds one copy of the code and, having changed it, assumes that the job is done. There is nothing indicating that a second copy of the code exists, and it might incorrectly remain unchanged.

Concept:

Code duplication (having the same segment of code in an application more than once) is a sign of bad design. It should be avoided.

Code 6.1

Selected sections of the (badly designed) Game class

```java
public class Game
{
    // ... some code omitted ...

    private void createRooms()
    {
        Room outside, theater, pub, lab, office;

        // create the rooms
        outside = new Room(
                "outside the main entrance of the university");
        theater = new Room("in a lecture theater");
        pub = new Room("in the campus pub");
        lab = new Room("in a computing lab");
        office = new Room("in the computing admin office");

        // initialize room exits
        outside.setExits(null, theater, lab, pub);
        theatre.setExits(null, null, null, outside);
        pub.setExits(null, outside, null, null);
        lab.setExits(outside, office, null, null);
        office.setExits(null, null, null, lab);

        currentRoom = outside; // start game outside
    }

    // ... some code omitted ...
    /**
     * Print out the opening message for the player.
     */
    private void printWelcome()
    {
        System.out.println();
        System.out.println("Welcome to the World of Zuul!");
```

**Code 6.1
continued**

Selected sections of the
(badly designed) Game
class

```
        System.out.println(
            "Zuul is a new, incredibly boring adventure game.");
        System.out.println("Type 'help' if you need help.");
        System.out.println();
        System.out.println("You are " +
                            currentRoom.getDescription());
        System.out.print("Exits: ");
        if(currentRoom.northExit != null) {
            System.out.print("north ");
        }
        if(currentRoom.eastExit != null) {
            System.out.print("east ");
        }
        if(currentRoom.southExit != null) {
            System.out.print("south ");
        }
        if(currentRoom.westExit != null) {
            System.out.print("west ");
        }
        System.out.println();
    }

    // ... some code omitted ...

    /**
     * Try to go in one direction. If there is an exit, enter
     * the new room; otherwise print an error message.
     */
    private void goRoom(Command command)
    {
        if(!command.hasSecondWord()) {
            // if there is no second word,
            // we don't know where to go
            System.out.println("Go where?");
            return;
        }
        String direction = command.getSecondWord();

        // Try to leave current room.
        Room nextRoom = null;
        if(direction.equals("north")) {
            nextRoom = currentRoom.northExit;
        }
        if(direction.equals("east")) {
            nextRoom = currentRoom.eastExit;
        }
```

**Code 6.1
continued**

Selected sections of the
(badly designed) Game
class

```java
            if(direction.equals("south")) {
                nextRoom = currentRoom.southExit;
            }
            if(direction.equals("west")) {
                nextRoom = currentRoom.westExit;
            }
            if(nextRoom == null) {
                System.out.println("There is no door!");
            }
            else {
                currentRoom = nextRoom;
                System.out.println("You are " +
                                    currentRoom.getDescription());
                System.out.print("Exits: ");
                if(currentRoom.northExit != null) {
                    System.out.print("north ");
                }
                if(currentRoom.eastExit != null) {
                    System.out.print("east ");
                }
                if(currentRoom.southExit != null) {
                    System.out.print("south ");
                }
                if(currentRoom.westExit != null) {
                    System.out.print("west ");
                }
                System.out.println();
            }
        }

    //  ... some code omitted ...
}
```

Both the printWelcome and goRoom methods contain the following lines of code:

```java
System.out.println("You are " + currentRoom.getDescription());
System.out.print("Exits: ");
if(currentRoom.northExit != null) {
    System.out.print("north ");
}
if(currentRoom.eastExit != null) {
    System.out.print("east ");
}
if(currentRoom.southExit != null) {
    System.out.print("south ");
}
```

```
    if(currentRoom.westExit != null) {
        System.out.print("west ");
    }
    System.out.println();
```

Code duplication is usually a symptom of bad cohesion. The problem here has its roots in the fact that both methods in question do two things: printWelcome prints the welcome message and prints the information about the current location, while goRoom changes the current location and then prints information about the (new) current location.

Both methods print information about the current location, but neither can call the other, because they also do other things. This is bad design.

A better design would use a separate, more cohesive method whose sole task is to print the current location information (Code 6.2). Both the printWelcome and goRoom methods can then make calls to this method when they need to print this information. This way, writing the code twice is avoided, and when we need to change it, we need to change it only once.

Code 6.2

printLocation
Info as a separate
method

```
private void printLocationInfo()
{
    System.out.println("You are " + currentRoom.getDescription());
    System.out.print("Exits: ");
    if(currentRoom.northExit != null) {
        System.out.print("north ");
    }
    if(currentRoom.eastExit != null) {
        System.out.print("east ");
    }
    if(currentRoom.southExit != null) {
        System.out.print("south ");
    }
    if(currentRoom.westExit != null) {
        System.out.print("west ");
    }
    System.out.println();
}
```

Exercise 6.5 Implement and use a separate printLocationInfo method in your project, as discussed in this section. Test your changes.

6.5 Making extensions

The *zuul-bad* project does work. We can execute it, and it correctly does everything that it was intended to do. However, it is in some respects quite badly designed. A well-designed alternative would perform in the same way; we would not notice any difference just by executing the program.

Once we try to make modifications to the project, however, we will notice significant differences in the amount of work involved in changing badly designed code, compared with changes to a well-designed application. We will investigate this by making some changes to the project. While we are doing this, we will discuss examples of bad design when we see them in the existing source, and we will improve the class design before we implement our extensions.

6.5.1   The task

The first task we will attempt is to add a new direction of movement. Currently, a player can move in four directions: *north*, *east*, *south*, and *west*. We want to allow for multilevel buildings (or cellars, or dungeons, or whatever you later want to add to your game) and add *up* and *down* as possible directions. A player can then type **"go down"** to move, say, down into a cellar.

6.5.2   Finding the relevant source code

Inspection of the given classes shows us that at least two classes are involved in this change: Room and Game.

Room is the class that stores (among other things) the exits of each room, and, as we saw in Code 6.1, in the Game class the exit information from the current room is used to print out information about exits and to move from one room to another.

The Room class is fairly short. Its source code is shown in Code 6.3. Reading the source, we can see that the exits are mentioned in two different places: they are listed as fields at the top of the class, and they get assigned in the setExits method. To add two new directions, we would need to add two new exits (upExit and downExit) in these two places.

Code 6.3

Source code of the (badly designed) Room class

```
public class Room
{
    public String description;
    public Room northExit;
    public Room southExit;
    public Room eastExit;
    public Room westExit;

    /**
     * Create a room described "description "Initially, it
     * has no exits. "description" is something like
     *  "a kitchen" or "an open courtyard".
     */
    public Room(String description)
    {
        this.description = description;
    }
```

**Code 6.3
continued**

Source code of the
(badly designed) Room
class

```java
/**
 * Define the exits of this room. Every direction either
 * leads to another room or is null (no exit there).
 */
public void setExits(Room north, Room east, Room south,
                         Room west)
{
    if(north != null) {
        northExit = north;
    }
    if(east != null) {
        eastExit = east;
    }
    if(south != null) {
        southExit = south;
    }
    if(west != null) {
        westExit = west;
    }
}

/**
 * Return the description of the room (the one that was
 * defined in the constructor).
 */
public String getDescription()
{
    return description;
}
}
```

It is a bit more work to find all relevant places in the Game class. The source code is somewhat longer (it is not fully shown here), and finding all the relevant places takes some patience and care.

Reading the code shown in Code 6.1, we can see that the Game class makes heavy use of the exit information of a room. The Game object holds a reference to one room in the current-Room variable and frequently accesses this room's exit information.

■ In the createRoom method, the exits are defined.

■ In the printWelcome method, the current room's exits are printed out so that the player knows where to go when the game starts.

■ In the goRoom method, the exits are used to find the next room. They are then used again to print out the exits of the next room we have just entered.

If we now want to add two new exit directions, we will have to add the *up* and *down* options in all these places. However, read the following section before you do this.

6.6 Coupling

The fact that there are so many places where all exits are enumerated is symptomatic of poor class design. When declaring the exit variables in the Room class, we need to list one variable per exit; in the setExits method, there is one if statement per exit; in the goRoom method, there is one if statement per exit; in the printLocationInfo method, there is one if statement per exit; and so on. This design decision now creates work for us: when adding new exits, we need to find all these places and add two new cases. Imagine the effect if we decided to use directions such as northwest, southeast, etc.!

To improve the situation, we decide to use a HashMap to store the exits, rather than separate variables. Doing this, we should be able to write code that can cope with any number of exits and does not need so many modifications. The HashMap will contain a mapping from a named direction (e.g., "north") to the room that lies in that direction (a Room object). Thus, each entry has a String as the key and a Room object as the value.

This is a change in the way a room stores information internally about neighboring rooms. Theoretically, this is a change that should affect only the *implementation* of the Room class (*how* the exit information is stored), not the *interface* (*what* the room stores).

Ideally, when only the implementation of a class changes, other classes should not be affected. This would be a case of *loose* coupling.

In our example, this does not work. If we remove the exit variables in the Room class and replace them with a HashMap, the Game class will not compile any more. It makes numerous references to the room's exit variables, which all would cause errors.

We see that we have a case here of *tight* coupling. In order to clean this up, we will decouple these classes before we introduce the HashMap.

6.6.1 Using encapsulation to reduce coupling

Concept:

Proper **encapsulation** in classes reduces coupling and thus leads to a better design.

One of the main problems in this example is the use of public fields. The exit fields in the Room class have all been declared public. Clearly, the programmer of this class did not follow the guidelines we have set out earlier in this book ("Never make fields public!"). We shall now see the result! The Game class in this example can make direct accesses to these fields (and it makes extensive use of this fact). By making the fields public, the Room class has exposed in its interface not only the fact that it has exits, but also exactly how the exit information is stored. This breaks one of the fundamental principles of good class design: *encapsulation.*

The encapsulation guideline (hiding implementation information from view) suggests that only information about *what* a class can do should be visible to the outside, not about *how* it does it. This has a great advantage: if no other class knows how our information is stored, then we can easily change how it is stored without breaking other classes.

We can enforce this separation of *what* and *how* by making the fields private and using an accessor method to access them. The first stage of our modified Room class is shown in Code 6.4.

Code 6.4

Using an accessor method to decrease coupling

```
public class Room
{
    private String description;
    private Room northExit;
    private Room southExit;
    private Room eastExit;
    private Room westExit;

    //  existing methods unchanged

    public Room getExit(String direction)
    {
        if(direction.equals("north")) {
            return northExit;
        }
        if(direction.equals("east")) {
            return eastExit;
        }
        if(direction.equals("south")) {
            return southExit;
        }
        if(direction.equals("west")) {
            return westExit;
        }
        return null;
    }
}
```

Having made this change to the Room class, we need to change the Game class as well. Wherever an exit variable was accessed, we now use the accessor method. For example, instead of writing

```
nextRoom = currentRoom.eastExit;
```

we now write

```
nextRoom = currentRoom.getExit("east");
```

This makes coding one section in the Game class much easier as well. In the goRoom method, the replacement suggested here will result in the following code segment:

```
Room nextRoom = null;
if(direction.equals("north")) {
    nextRoom = currentRoom.getExit("north");
}
if(direction.equals("east")) {
    nextRoom = currentRoom.getExit("east");
}
```

```
if(direction.equals("south")) {
    nextRoom = currentRoom.getExit("south");
}
if(direction.equals("west")) {
    nextRoom = currentRoom.getExit("west");
}
```

Instead, this whole code segment can now be replaced with:

```
Room nextRoom = currentRoom.getExit(direction);
```

Exercise 6.6 Make the changes we have described to the Room and Game classes.

Exercise 6.7 Make a similar change to the printLocationInfo method of Game so that details of the exits are now prepared by the Room rather than the Game. Define a method in Room with the following signature:

```
/**
 * Return a description of the room's exits,
 * for example, "Exits: north west".
 * @return A description of the available exits.
 */
public String getExitString()
```

So far, we have not changed the representation of the exits in the Room class. We have only cleaned up the interface. The *change* in the Game class is minimal—instead of an access of a public field, we use a method call—but the *gain* is dramatic. We can now make a change to the way exits are stored in the room, without any need to worry about breaking anything in the Game class. The internal representation in Room has been completely decoupled from the interface. Now that the design is the way it should have been in the first place, exchanging the separate exit fields for a HashMap is easy. The changed code is shown in Code 6.5.

Code 6.5
Source code of the
Room class

```
import java.util.HashMap;

// class comment omitted

public class Room
{
    private String description;
    private HashMap<String, Room> exits;

    /**
     * Create a room described "description "Initially, it
     * has no exits. "description" is something like "a
     * kitchen" or "an open courtyard".
     */
```

Code 6.5 continued

Source code of the Room class

```java
    public Room(String description)
    {
        this.description = description;
        exits = new HashMap<String, Room>();
    }


    /**
     * Define the exits of this room. Every direction either
     * leads to another room or is null (no exit there).
     */
    public void setExits(Room north, Room east, Room south,
                            Room west)
    {
        if(north != null)
            exits.put("north", north);
        if(east != null)
            exits.put("east", east);
        if(south != null)
            exits.put("south", south);
        if(west != null)
            exits.put("west", west);
    }


    /**
     * Return the room that is reached if we go from this
     * room in direction "direction "If there is no room in
     * that direction, return null.
     */
    public Room getExit(String direction)
    {
        return exits.get(direction);
    }


    /**
     * Return the description of the room (the one that was
     * defined in the constructor).
     */
    public String getDescription()
    {
        return description;
    }
}
```

It is worth emphasizing again that we can make this change now without even checking whether anything will break elsewhere. Because we have changed only private aspects of the Room class, which, by definition, cannot be used in other classes, this change does not impact on other classes. The interface remains unchanged.

A by-product of this change is that our Room class is now even shorter. Instead of listing four separate variables, we have only one. In addition, the getExit method is considerably simplified.

Recall that the original aim that set off this series of changes was to make it easier to add the two new possible exits in the *up* and *down* direction. This has already become a lot easier. Because we now use a HashMap to store exits, storing these two additional directions will work without any change. We can also obtain the exit information via the getExit method without any problem.

The only place where knowledge about the four existing exits (*north, east, south, west*) is still coded into the source is in the setExits method. This is the last part that needs improvement. At the moment, the method's signature is

```
public void setExits(Room north, Room east, Room south, Room west)
```

This method is part of the interface of the Room class, so any change we make to it will inevitably affect some other classes by virtue of coupling. It is worth noting that we can never completely decouple the classes in an application; otherwise objects of different classes would not be able to interact with one another. Rather, we try to keep the degree of coupling as low as possible. If we have to make a change to setExits anyway, to accommodate additional directions, then our preferred solution is to replace it entirely with this method:

```
/**
 * Define an exit from this room.
 * @param direction The direction of the exit.
 * @param neighbor The room in the given direction.
 */
public void setExit(String direction, Room neighbor)
{
    exits.put(direction, neighbor);
}
```

Now, the exits of this room can be set one exit at a time, and any direction can be used for an exit. In the Game class, the change that results from modifying the interface of Room is as follows. Instead of writing

```
lab.setExits(outside, office, null, null);
```

we now write

```
lab.setExit("north", outside);
lab.setExit("east", office);
```

We have now completely removed the restriction from Room that it can store only four exits. The Room class is now ready to store *up* and *down* exits, as well as any other direction you might think of (northwest, southeast, etc.).

Exercise 6.8 Implement the changes described in this section in your own *zuul* project.

6.7 Responsibility-driven design

Concept:

Responsibility-driven design is the process of designing classes by assigning well-defined responsibilities to each class. This process can be used to determine which class should implement which part of an application function.

We have seen in the previous section that making use of proper encapsulation reduces coupling and can significantly reduce the amount of work needed to make changes to an application. Encapsulation, however, is not the only factor that influences the degree of coupling. Another aspect is known by the term *responsibility-driven design*.

Responsibility-driven design expresses the idea that each class should be responsible for handling its own data. Often, when we need to add some new functionality to an application, we need to ask ourselves in which class we should add a method to implement this new function. Which class should be responsible for the task? The answer is that the class that is responsible for storing some data should also be responsible for manipulating it.

How well responsibility-driven design is used influences the degree of coupling and, therefore, again, the ease with which an application can be modified or extended. As usual, we will discuss this in more detail with our example.

6.7.1 Responsibilities and coupling

The changes to the Room class that we discussed in Section 6.6.1 make it quite easy now to add the new directions for up and down movement in the Game class. We investigate this with an example. Assume that we want to add a new room (the cellar) under the office. All we have to do to achieve this is to make some small changes to the Game's createRooms method to create the room and to make two calls to set the exits:

```
private void createRooms()
{
    Room outside, theater, pub, lab, office, cellar;
    ...
    cellar = new Room("in the cellar");
    ...
    office.setExit("down", cellar);
    cellar.setExit("up", office);
}
```

Because of the new interface of the Room class, this will work without problems. The change is now very easy and confirms that the design is getting better.

Further evidence of this can be seen if we compare the original version of the printLocationInfo method shown in Code 6.2 with the getExitString method shown in Code 6.6 that represents a solution to Exercise 6.7.

Code 6.6
The getExitString method of Room

```
/**
 * Return a description of the room's exits,
 * for example, "Exits: north west".
 * @return A description of the available exits.
 */
```

Code 6.6 continued

The getExitString method of Room

```
public String getExitString()
{
    String exitString = "Exits: ";
    if(northExit != null)
        exitString += "north ";
    if(eastExit != null)
        exitString += "east ";
    if(southExit != null)
        exitString += "south ";
    if(westExit != null)
        exitString += "west ";
    return exitString;
}
```

Because information about its exits is now stored only in the room itself, it is the room that is responsible for providing that information. The room can do this much better than any other object, because it has all the knowledge about the internal storage structure of the exit data. Now, inside the Room class, we can make use of the knowledge that exits are stored in a HashMap, and we can iterate over that map to describe the exits.

Consequently, we replace the version of getExitString shown in Code 6.6 with the version shown in Code 6.7. This method finds all the names for exits in the HashMap (the keys in the HashMap are the names of the exits) and concatenates them to a single String, which is then returned. (We need to import Set from java.util for this to work.)

Exercise 6.9 Look up the keySet method in the documentation of HashMap. What does it do?

Exercise 6.10 Explain, in detail and in writing, how the getExitString method shown in Code 6.7 works.

Code 6.7

A revised version of getExitString

```
/**
 * Return a description of the room's exits,
 * for example "Exits: north west".
 * @return A description of the available exits.
 */
public String getExitString()
{
    String returnString = "Exits:";
    Set<String> keys = exits.keySet();
    for(String exit : keys) {
        returnString += " " + exit;
    }
    return returnString;
}
```

Our goal to reduce coupling demands that, as far as possible, changes to the Room class do not require changes to the Game class. We can still improve this.

Currently, we have still encoded in the Game class the knowledge that the information we want from a room consists of a description string and the exit string:

```
System.out.println("You are " + currentRoom.getDescription());
System.out.println(currentRoom.getExitString());
```

What if we add items to rooms in our game? Or monsters? Or other players?

When we describe what we see, the list of items, monsters, and other players should be included in the description of the room. We would need not only to make changes to the Room class to add these things, but also to change the code segment above where the description is printed out.

This is again a breach of the responsibility-driven design rule. Because the Room class holds information about a room, it should also produce a description for a room. We can improve this by adding to the Room class the following method:

```
/**
 * Return a long description of this room, of the form:
 *      You are in the kitchen.
 *      Exits: north west
 * @return A description of the room, including exits.
 */
public String getLongDescription()
{
    return "You are " + description + ".\n" + getExitString();
}
```

In the Game class, we then write

```
System.out.println(currentRoom.getLongDescription());
```

The "long description" of a room now includes the description string and information about the exits and may in the future include anything else there is to say about a room. When we make these future extensions, we will have to make changes to only a single class: the Room class.

Exercise 6.11 Implement the changes described in this section in your own *zuul* project.

Exercise 6.12 Draw an object diagram with all objects in your game, the way they are just after starting the game.

Exercise 6.13 How does the object diagram change when you execute a *go* command?

6.8 Localizing change

Another aspect of the decoupling and responsibility principles is that of *localizing change*. We aim to create a class design that makes later changes easy by localizing the effects of a change.

Concept:

One of the main goals of a good class design is that of **localizing change**: making changes to one class should have minimal effects on other classes.

Ideally, only a single class needs to be changed to make a modification. Sometimes several classes need change, but we then aim at this being as few classes as possible. In addition, the changes needed in other classes should be obvious, easy to detect, and easy to carry out.

To a large extent, we can achieve this by following good design rules such as using responsibility-driven design and aiming for loose coupling and high cohesion. In addition, however, we should have modification and extension in mind when we create our applications. It is important to anticipate that an aspect of our program might change, in order to make this change easy.

6.9 Implicit coupling

We have seen that the use of public fields is one practice that is likely to create an unnecessarily tight form of coupling between classes. With this tight coupling, it may be necessary to make changes to more than one class for what should have been a simple modification. Therefore, public fields should be avoided. However, there is an even worse form of coupling: *implicit coupling*.

Implicit coupling is a situation where one class depends on the internal information of another, but this dependence is not immediately obvious. The tight coupling in the case of the public fields was not good, but at least it was obvious. If we change the public fields in one class and forget about the other, the application will not compile any more and the compiler will point out the problem. In cases of implicit coupling, omitting a necessary change can go undetected.

We can see the problem arising if we try to add further command words to the game.

Suppose that we want to add the command *look* to the set of legal commands. The purpose of *look* is merely to print out the description of the room and the exits again (we "look around the room"). This could be helpful if we have entered a sequence of commands in a room so that the description has scrolled out of view and we cannot remember where the exits of the current room are.

We can introduce a new command word simply by adding it to the array of known words in the validCommands array in the CommandWords class:

```
// a constant array that holds all valid command words
private static final String validCommands[] = {
    "go", "quit", "help", "look"
};
```

This, by the way, shows an example of good cohesion: instead of defining the command words in the parser, which would have been one obvious possibility, the author created a separate class just to define the command words. This makes it very easy for us to now find the place where command words are defined, and it is easy to add one. The author was obviously thinking ahead, assuming that more commands might be added later, and created a structure that makes this very easy.

We can test this already. When we make this change and then execute the game and type the command look, nothing happens. This contrasts with the behavior of an unknown command word; if we type any unknown word, we see the reply

```
I don't know what you mean...
```

Thus, the fact that we do not see this reply indicates that the word was recognized, but nothing happens because we have not yet implemented an action for this command.

We can fix this by adding a method for the *look* command to the Game class:

```
private void look()
{
    System.out.println(currentRoom.getLongDescription());
}
```

You should, of course, also add a comment for this method. After this, we only need to add a case for the *look* command in the processCommand method, which will invoke the look method when the *look* command is recognized:

```
if(commandWord.equals("help")) {
    printHelp();
}
else if(commandWord.equals("go")) {
    goRoom(command);
}
else if(commandWord.equals("look")) {
    look();
}
else if(commandWord.equals("quit")) {
    wantToQuit = quit(command);
}
```

Try this out, and you will see that it works.

Exercise 6.14 Add the *look* command to your version of the zuul game.

Exercise 6.15 Add another command to your game. For a start, you could choose something simple, such as a command *eat* that, when executed, just prints out "*You have eaten now and you are not hungry any more.*" Later, we can improve this so that you really get hungry over time and you need to find food.

Coupling between the Game, Parser, and CommandWords classes so far seems to have been very good—it was easy to make this extension, and we got it to work quickly.

The problem that was mentioned before—implicit coupling—becomes apparent when we now issue a help command. The output is

```
You are lost. You are alone. You wander
around at the university.
Your command words are:
  go quit help
```

Now we notice a small problem. The help text is incomplete: the new command, *look*, is not listed.

This seems easy to fix: we can just edit the help text string in the Game's printHelp method. This is quickly done and does not seem a great problem. But suppose we had not noticed this error now. Did you think of this problem before you just read about it here?

This is a fundamental problem, because every time a command is added, the help text needs to be changed, and it is very easy to forget to make this change. The program compiles and runs, and everything seems fine. A maintenance programmer may well believe that the job is finished and release a program that now contains a bug.

This is an example of implicit coupling. When commands change, the help text must be modified (coupling), but nothing in the program source clearly points out this dependence (thus implicit).

A well-designed class will avoid this form of coupling by following the rule of responsibility-driven design. Because the CommandWords class is responsible for command words, it should also be responsible for printing command words. Thus, we add the following method to the CommandWords class:

```java
/**
 * Print all valid commands to System.out.
 */
public void showAll()
{
    for(String command : validCommands) {
        System.out.print(command + " ");
    }
    System.out.println();
}
```

The idea here is that the printHelp method in Game, instead of printing a fixed text with the command words, invokes a method that asks the CommandWords class to print all its command words. Doing this ensures that the correct command words will always be printed, and adding a new command will also add it to the help text without further change.

The only remaining problem is that the Game object does not have a reference to the CommandWords object. You can see in the class diagram (Figure 6.1) that there is no arrow from Game to CommandWords. This indicates that the Game class does not even know of the existence of the CommandWords class. Instead, the game just has a parser, and the parser has command words.

We could now add a method to the parser that hands the CommandWords object to the Game object so that they could communicate. This would, however, increase the degree of coupling in our application. Game would then depend on CommandWords, which it currently does not. Also, we would see this effect in the class diagram: Game would then have an arrow to CommandWords.

The arrows in the diagram are, in fact, a good first indication of how tightly coupled a program is—the more arrows, the more coupling. As an approximation of good class design, we can aim at creating diagrams with few arrows.

Thus, the fact that Game did not have a reference to CommandWords is a good thing! We should not change this. From Game's viewpoint, the fact that the CommandWords class exists is an implementation detail of the parser. The parser returns commands, and whether it uses a CommandWords object to achieve this or something else is entirely up to the parser's implementation.

It follows that a better design just lets the Game talk to the Parser, which in turn may talk to CommandWords. We can implement this by adding the following code to the printHelp method in Game:

```java
System.out.println("Your command words are:");
parser.showCommands();
```

All that is missing, then, is the `showCommands` method in the `Parser`, which delegates this task to the `CommandWords` class. Here is the complete method (in class `Parser`):

```
/**
 * Print out a list of valid command words.
 */
public void showCommands()
{
    commands.showAll();
}
```

> **Exercise 6.16** Implement the improved version of printing out the command words, as described in this section.
>
> **Exercise 6.17** If you now add another new command, do you still need to change the `Game` class? Why?

The full implementation of all changes discussed in this chapter so far is available in your code examples in a project named *zuul-better*. If you have done the exercises so far, you can ignore this project and continue to use your own. If you have not done the exercises but want to do the following exercises in this chapter as a programming project, you can use the *zuul-better* project as your starting point.

6.10 Thinking ahead

The design we have now is an important improvement to the original version. It is, however, possible to improve it even more.

One characteristic of a good software designer is the ability to think ahead. What might change? What can we safely assume will stay unchanged for the life of the program?

One assumption that we have hard-coded into most of our classes is that this game will run as a text-based game with terminal input and output. But will it always be like this?

It might be an interesting extension later to add a graphical user interface with menus, buttons, and images. In that case, we would not want to print the information to the text terminal anymore. We might still have command words, and we might still want to show them when a player enters a help command. But we might then show them in a text field in a window, rather than using `System.out.println`.

It is good design to try to encapsulate all information about the user interface in a single class or a clearly defined set of classes. Our solution from Section 6.9, for example—the `showAll` method in the `CommandWords` class—does not follow this design rule. It would be nicer to define that `CommandWords` is responsible for *producing* (but not *printing*!) the list of command words, but that the `Game` class should decide how it is presented to the user.

We can easily achieve this by changing the `showAll` method so that it returns a string containing all command words instead of printing them out directly. (We should probably rename it `getCommandList` when we make this change.) This string can then be printed in the `printHelp` method in `Game`.

Note that this does not gain us anything right now, but we might profit from the improved design in the future.

Exercise 6.18 Implement the suggested change. Make sure that your program still works as before.

Exercise 6.19 Find out what the *model-view-controller* pattern is. You can do a web search to get information, or you can use any other sources you find. How is it related to the topic discussed here? What does it suggest? How could it be applied to this project? (Only *discuss* its application to this project, as an actual implementation would be an advanced-challenge exercise.)

6.11 Cohesion

We introduced the idea of cohesion in Section 6.3: a unit of code should always be responsible for one, and only one, task. We shall now investigate the cohesion principle in more depth and analyze some examples.

The principle of cohesion can be applied to classes and methods: classes should display a high degree of cohesion, and so should methods.

6.11.1 Cohesion of methods

Concept:

Method cohesion. A cohesive method is responsible for one, and only one, well-defined task.

When we talk about cohesion of methods, we seek to express the ideal that any one method should be responsible for one, and only one, well-defined task.

We can see an example of a cohesive method in the `Game` class. This class has a private method named `printWelcome` to show the opening text, and this method is called when the game starts in the `play` method (Code 6.8).

Code 6.8
Two methods with a good degree of cohesion

```
/**
 * Main play routine. Loops until end of play.
 */
public void play()
{
    printWelcome();

    // Enter the main command loop. Here we repeatedly read
    // commands and execute them until the game is over.
```

**Code 6.8
continued**

Two methods with a
good degree of
cohesion

```
        boolean finished = false;
        while (! finished) {
            Command command = parser.getCommand();
            finished = processCommand(command);
        }
        System.out.println("Thank you for playing.  Good bye.");
}


/**
 * Print out the opening message for the player.
 */
private void printWelcome()
{
    System.out.println();
    System.out.println("Welcome to The World of Zuul!");
    System.out.println(
            "Zuul is a new, incredibly boring adventure game.");
    System.out.println("Type 'help' if you need help.");
    System.out.println();
    System.out.println(currentRoom.getLongDescription());
}
```

From a functional point of view, we could have just entered the statements from the `print-Welcome` method directly into the `play` method and achieved the same result without defining an extra method and making a method call. The same can, by the way, be said for the `processCommand` method that is also invoked in the `play` method: this code, too, could have been written directly into the `play` method.

It is, however, much easier to understand what a segment of code does and to make modifications if short, cohesive methods are used. In the chosen method structure, all methods are reasonably short and easy to understand, and their names indicate their purposes quite clearly. These characteristics represent valuable help for a maintenance programmer.

6.11.2   Cohesion of classes

Concept:

Class cohesion
A cohesive class
represents one
well-defined entity.

The rule of cohesion of classes states that each class should represent one single, well-defined entity in the problem domain.

As an example of class cohesion, we now discuss another extension to the *zuul* project. We now want to add *items* to the game. Each room may hold an item, and each item has a description and a weight. An item's weight can be used later to determine whether it can be picked up or not.

A naïve approach would be to add two fields to the Room class: `itemDescription` and `item-Weight`. This could work. We could now specify the item details for each room, and we could print out the details whenever we enter a room.

This approach, however, does not display a good degree of cohesion: the Room class now describes both a room and an item. It also suggests that an item is bound to a particular room, which we might not wish to be the case.

A better design would create a separate class for items, probably called Item. This class would have fields for a description and weight, and a room would simply hold a reference to an item object.

> **Exercise 6.20** Extend either your adventure project or the *zuul-better* project so that a room can contain a single item. Items have a description and a weight. When creating rooms and setting their exits, items for this game should also be created. When a player enters a room, information about an item present in this room should be displayed.

> **Exercise 6.21** How should the information be produced about an item present in a room? Which class should produce the string describing the item? Which class should print it? Why? Explain in writing. If answering this exercise makes you feel you should change your implementation, go ahead and make the changes.

The real benefits of separating rooms and items in the design can be seen if we change the specification a little. In a further variation of our game, we want to allow not only a single item in each room, but an unlimited number of items. In the design using a separate Item class, this is easy: we can create multiple Item objects and store them in a collection of items in the room.

With the first, naïve approach, this change would be almost impossible to implement.

> **Exercise 6.22** Modify the project so that a room can hold any number of items. Use a collection to do this. Make sure the room has an addItem method that places an item into the room. Make sure all items get shown when a player enters a room.

6.11.3 Cohesion for readability

There are several ways in which high cohesion benefits a design. The two most important ones are *readability* and *reuse*.

The example discussed in Section 6.11.1, cohesion of the printWelcome method, is clearly an example in which increasing cohesion makes a class more readable and thus easier to understand and maintain.

The class-cohesion example in Section 6.11.2 also has an element of readability. If a separate Item class exists, a maintenance programmer will easily recognize where to start reading code if a change to the characteristics of an item is needed. Cohesion of classes also increases readability of a program.

6.11.4 Cohesion for reuse

The second great advantage of cohesion is a higher potential for reuse.

The class-cohesion example in Section 6.11.2 also shows an example of this: by creating a separate Item class, we can create multiple items and thus use the same code for more than a single item.

Reuse is also an important aspect of method cohesion. Consider a method in the Room class with the following signature:

```
public Room leaveRoom(String direction)
```

This method could return the room in the given direction (so that it can be used as the new currentRoom) and also print out the description of the new room that we just entered.

This seems like a possible design, and it can indeed be made to work. In our version, however, we have separated this task into two methods:

```
public Room getExit(String direction)
public String getLongDescription()
```

The first one is responsible for returning the next room, whereas the second one produces the room's description.

The advantage of this design is that the separate tasks can be reused more easily. The getLongDescription method, for example, is now used not only in the goRoom method, but also in printWelcome and the implementation of the *look* command. This is only possible because it displays a high degree of cohesion. Reusing it would not be possible in the version with the leaveRoom method.

Exercise 6.23 Implement a *back* command. This command does not have a second word. Entering the *back* command takes the player into the previous room he/she was in.

Exercise 6.24 Test your new command. Does it work as expected? Also test cases where the command is used incorrectly. For example, what does your program do if a player types a second word after the *back* command? Does it behave sensibly?

Exercise 6.25 What does your program do if you type "back" twice? Is this behavior sensible?

Exercise 6.26 *Challenge exercise* Implement the *back* command so that using it repeatedly takes you back several rooms, all the way to the beginning of the game if used often enough. Use a Stack to do this. (You may need to find out about stacks. Look at the Java library documentation.)

6.12 Refactoring

Concept:

Refactoring is the activity of restructuring an existing design to maintain a good class design when the application is modified or extended.

When designing applications, we should attempt to think ahead, anticipate possible changes in the future, and create highly cohesive, loosely coupled classes and methods that make modifications easy. This is a noble goal, but of course we cannot always anticipate all future adaptations, and it is not feasible to prepare for all possible extensions we can think of.

This is why *refactoring* is important.

Refactoring is the activity of restructuring existing classes and methods to adapt them to changed functionality and requirements. Often in the lifetime of an application, functionality is gradually added. One common effect is that, as a side-effect of this, methods and classes slowly grow in length.

It is tempting for a maintenance programmer to add some extra code to existing classes or methods. Doing this for some time, however, decreases the degree of cohesion. When more and more code is added to a method or a class, it is likely that at some stage it will represent more than one clearly defined task or entity.

Refactoring is the rethinking and redesigning of class and method structures. Most commonly, the effect is that classes are split in two or that methods are divided into two or more methods. Refactoring can also include the joining of multiple classes or methods into one, but that is less common than splitting.

6.12.1 Refactoring and testing

Before we provide an example of refactoring, we need to reflect on the fact that, when we refactor a program, we are usually proposing to make some potentially large changes to something that already works. When something is changed, there is a likelihood that errors will be introduced. Therefore, it is important to proceed cautiously; and, prior to refactoring, we should establish that a set of tests exists for the current version of the program. If tests do not exist, then we should first decide how we can reasonably test the functionality of the program and record those tests (for instance, by writing them down) so that we can repeat the same tests later. We will discuss testing more formally in the next chapter. If you are already familiar with automated testing, use automated tests. Otherwise, manual (but systematic) testing is sufficient for now.

Once a set of tests has been decided, the refactoring can start. Ideally, the refactoring should then follow in two steps:

■ The first step is to refactor in order to improve the internal structure of the code, but without making any changes to the functionality of the application. In other words, the program should, when executed, behave exactly as it did before. Once this stage is completed, the previously established tests should be repeated to ensure that we have not introduced unintended errors.

■ The second step is taken only once we have reestablished the baseline functionality in the re-factored version. Then we are in a safe position to enhance the program. Once that has been done, of course, testing will need to be conducted on the new version.

Making several changes at the same time (refactoring and adding new features) makes it harder to locate the source of problems when they occur.

Exercise 6.27 What sort of baseline functionality tests might we wish to establish in the current version of the game?

6.12.2 An example of refactoring

As an example, we shall continue with the extension of adding items to the game. In Section 6.11.2, we started adding items, suggesting a structure in which rooms can contain any number of items. A logical extension to this arrangement is that a player should be able to pick up items and carry them around. Here is an informal specification of our next goal:

■ The player can pick up items from the current room.

■ The player can carry any number of items, but only up to a maximum weight.

■ Some items cannot be picked up.

■ The player can drop items in the current room.

To achieve these goals, we can do the following:

■ If not already done, we add a class `Item` to the project. An item has, as discussed above, a description (a string) and a weight (an integer).

■ We should also add a field `name` to the `Item` class. This will allow us to refer to the item with a name shorter than that of the description. If, for instance, there is a book in the current room, the field values of this item might be:

name: `book`
description: `an old, dusty book bound in gray leather`
weight: `1200`

If we enter a room, we can print out the item's description to tell the player what is there. But for commands, the name will be easier to use. For instance, the player might then type *take book* to pick up the book.

■ We can ensure that some items cannot be picked up, by just making them very heavy (more than a player can carry). Or should we have another `boolean` field `canBePickedUp`? Which do you think is the better design? Does it matter? Try answering this by thinking about what future changes might be made to the game.

■ We add commands *take* and *drop* to pick up and drop items. Both commands have an item name as a second word.

■ Somewhere we have to add a field (holding some form of collection) to store the items currently carried by the player. We also have to add a field with the maximum weight the player can carry, so that we can check it each time we try to pick up something. Where should these go? Once again, think about future extensions to help you make the decision.

This last task is what we will discuss in more detail now, in order to illustrate the process of refactoring.

The first question to ask ourselves when thinking about how to enable players to carry items is: Where should we add the fields for the currently carried items and the maximum weight? A quick look over the existing classes shows that the `Game` class is really the only place where it can be fitted in. It cannot be stored in `Room`, `Item`, or `Command`, because there are many different instances of these classes over time, which are not all always accessible. It does not make sense in `Parser` or `CommandWords` either.

Reinforcing the decision to place these changes in the `Game` class is the fact that it already stores the current room (information about where the player is right now), so adding the current items (information about what the player has) seems to fit with this quite well.

This approach could be made to work. It is, however, not a solution that is well designed. The `Game` class is fairly big already, and there is a good argument that it contains too much as it is. Adding even more does not make this better.

We should ask ourselves again which class or object this information should belong to. Thinking carefully about the type of information we are adding here (carried items, maximum weight), we realize that this is information about a *player*! The logical thing to do (following responsibility-driven design guidelines) is to create a Player class. We can then add these fields to the Player class and create a Player object at the start of the game, to store the data.

The existing field currentRoom also stores information about the player: the player's current location. Consequently, we should now also move this field into the Player class.

Analyzing it now, it is obvious that this design better fits the principle of responsibility-driven design. Who should be responsible for storing information about the player? The Player class, of course.

In the original version, we had only a single piece of information for the player: the current room. Whether we should have had a Player class even back then is up for discussion. There are arguments both ways. It would have been nice design, so, yes, maybe we should. But having a class with only a single field and no methods that do anything of significance might be regarded as overkill.

Sometimes there are gray areas such as this one, where either decision is defensible. But after adding our new fields, the situation is quite clear. There is now a strong argument for a Player class. It would store the fields and have methods such as dropItem and pickUpItem (which can include the weight check and might return false if we cannot carry it).

What we did when we introduced the Player class and moved the currentRoom field from Game into Player was refactoring. We have restructured the way we represent our data, to achieve a better design under changed requirements.

Programmers not as well trained as us (or just being lazy) might have left the currentRoom field where it was, seeing that the program worked as it was and there did not seem to be a great need to make this change. They would end up with a messy class design.

The effect of making the change can be seen if we think one step further ahead. Assume that we now want to extend the game to allow for multiple players. With our nice new design, this is suddenly very easy. We already have a Player class (the Game holds a Player object), and it is easy to create several Player objects and store in Game a collection of players instead of a single player. Each player object would hold its own current room, items, and maximum weight. Different players could even have different maximum weights, opening up the even wider concept of having players with quite different capabilities—their carrying capability being just one of possibly many.

The lazy programmer who left currentRoom in the Game class, however, has a serious problem now. Because the whole game has only a single current room, current locations of multiple players cannot easily be stored. Bad design usually bites back later to create more work for us in the end.

Doing good refactoring is as much about thinking in a certain mindset as it is about technical skills. While we make changes and extensions to applications, we should regularly question whether an original class design still represents the best solution. As the functionality changes, arguments for or against certain designs change. What was a good design for a simple application might not be good any more when some extensions are added.

Recognizing these changes and actually making the refactoring modifications to the source code usually saves a lot of time and effort in the end. The earlier we clean up our design, the more work we usually save.

We should be prepared to *factor out* methods (turn a sequence of statements from the body of an existing method into a new, independent method) and classes (take parts of a class and create a new class from it). Considering refactoring regularly keeps our class design clean and saves work in the end. Of course, one of the things that will actually mean that refactoring makes life harder in the long run is if we fail to adequately test the refactored version against the original. Whenever we embark on a major refactoring task, it is essential to ensure that we test well, before and after the change. Doing these tests manually (by creating and testing objects interactively) will get tedious very quickly. We shall investigate how we can improve our testing—by automating it—in the next chapter.

Exercise 6.28 Refactor your project to introduce a separate `Player` class. A `Player` object should store at least the current room of the player, but you may also like to store the player's name or other information.

Exercise 6.29 Implement an extension that allows a player to pick up one single item. This includes implementing two new commands: *take* and *drop*.

Exercise 6.30 Extend your implementation to allow the player to carry any number of items.

Exercise 6.31 Add a restriction that allows the player to carry items only up to a specified maximum weight. The maximum weight a player can carry is an attribute of the player.

Exercise 6.32 Implement an *items* command that prints out all items currently carried and their total weight.

Exercise 6.33 Add a *magic cookie* item to a room. Add an *eat cookie* command. If a player finds and eats the magic cookie, it increases the weight that the player can carry. (You might like to modify this slightly to better fit into your own game scenario.)

6.13 Refactoring for language independence

One feature of the *zuul* game that we have not commented on yet is that the user interface is closely tied to commands written in English. This assumption is embedded in both the `CommandWords` class, where the list of valid commands is stored, and the `Game` class, where the `processCommand` method explicitly compares each command word against a set of English words. If we wish to change the interface to allow users to use a different language, then we would have to find all the places in the source code where command words are used and change them. This is a further example of a form of implicit coupling, which we discussed in Section 6.9.

If we want to have language independence in the program, then ideally we should have just one place in the source code where the actual text of command words is stored and have everywhere else refer to commands in a language-independent way. A programming language feature that makes this possible is *enumerated types*, or *enums*. We will explore this feature of Java via the *zuul-with-enums* projects.

6.13.1   Enumerated types

Code 6.9 shows a Java enumerated type definition called `CommandWord`.

Code 6.9

An enumerated type for
command words

```java
/**
 * Representations for all the valid command words for the game.
 *
 * @author Michael Kölling and David J. Barnes
 * @version 2011.08.09
 */
public enum CommandWord
{
    // A value for each command word, plus one for unrecognized
    // commands.
    GO, QUIT, HELP, UNKNOWN;
}
```

In its simplest form, an enumerated type definition consists of an outer wrapper that uses the word `enum` rather than `class` and a body that is simply a list of variable names denoting the set of values that belong to this type. By convention, these variable names are fully capitalized. We never create objects of an enumerated type. In effect, each name within the type definition represents a unique instance of the type that has already been created for us to use. We refer to these instances as `CommandWord.GO`, `CommandWord.QUIT`, etc. Although the syntax for using them is similar, it is important to avoid thinking of these values as being like the numeric class constants we discussed in Section 5.13. Despite the simplicity of their definition, enumerated type values are proper objects and are not the same as integers.

How can we use the `CommandWord` type to make a step toward decoupling the game logic of *zuul* from a particular natural language? One of the first improvements we can make is to the following series of tests in the `processCommand` method of `Game`:

```java
if(command.isUnknown()) {
    System.out.println("I don't know what you mean...");
    return false;
}
String commandWord = command.getCommandWord();
if(commandWord.equals("help")) {
    printHelp();
}
else if(commandWord.equals("go")) {
    goRoom(command);
}
else if(commandWord.equals("quit")) {
    wantToQuit = quit(command);
}
```

If commandWord is made to be of type CommandWord rather than String, then this can be rewritten as:

```
if(commandWord == CommandWord.UNKNOWN) {
    System.out.println("I don't know what you mean...");
}
else if(commandWord == CommandWord.HELP) {
    printHelp();
}
else if(commandWord == CommandWord.GO) {
    goRoom(command);
}
else if(commandWord == CommandWord.QUIT) {
    wantToQuit = quit(command);
}
```

In fact, now that we changed the type to CommandWord, we could also use a *switch statement* instead of the series of if statements. This expresses the intent of this code segment a little more clearly.[2]

```
switch (commandWord) {
    case UNKNOWN:
        System.out.println("I don't know what you mean...");
        break;
    case HELP:
        printHelp();
        break;
    case GO:
        goRoom(command);
        break;
    case QUIT:
        wantToQuit = quit(command);
        break;
}
```

The switch statement takes the variable in the parentheses following the switch keyword (commandWord in our case) and compares it to each of the values listed after the case keywords. When a case matches, the code following it is executed. The break statement causes the switch statement to abort at that point, and execution continues after the switch statement. For a fuller description of the switch statement, see Appendix D.

Now we just have to arrange for the user's typed commands to be mapped to the corresponding CommandWord values. Open the *zuul-with-enums-v1* project to see how we have done this. The most significant change can be found in the CommandWords class. Instead of using an array of strings to define the valid commands, we now use a map between strings and CommandWord objects:

```
public CommandWords()
{
    validCommands = new HashMap<String, CommandWord>();
    validCommands.put("go", CommandWord.GO);
```

---

[2] As of Java 7, strings can also be used as values in switch statements. In Java 6 and earlier, strings cannot be used in switch statements.

```
        validCommands.put("help", CommandWord.HELP);
        validCommands.put("quit", CommandWord.QUIT);
    }
```

The command typed by a user can now easily be converted to its corresponding enumerated type value.

Exercise 6.34 Review the source code of the *zuul-with-enums-v1* project to see how it uses the `CommandWord` type. The classes `Command`, `CommandWords`, `Game`, and `Parser` have all been adapted from the *zuul-better* version to accommodate this change. Check that the program still works as you would expect.

Exercise 6.35 Add a *look* command to the game, along the lines described in Section 6.9.

Exercise 6.36 "Translate" the game to use different command words for the `GO` and `QUIT` commands. These could be from a real language or just made-up words. Do you only have to edit the `CommandWords` class to make this change work? What is the significance of this?

Exercise 6.37 Change the word associated with the HELP command and check that it works correctly. After you have made your changes, what do you notice about the welcome message that is printed when the game starts?

Exercise 6.38 In a new project, define your own enumerated type called `Position` with values `TOP`, `MIDDLE`, and `BOTTOM`.

6.13.2 Further decoupling of the command interface

The enumerated `CommandWord` type has allowed us to make a significant decoupling of the user interface language from the game logic, and it is almost completely possible to translate the commands into another language just by editing the `CommandWords` class. (At some stage, we should also translate the room descriptions and other output strings, probably by reading them from a file, but we shall leave this until later.) There is one further piece of decoupling of the command words that we would like to perform. Currently, whenever a new command is introduced into the game, we must add a new value to the `CommandWord` and an association between that value and the user's text in the `CommandWords` classes. It would be helpful if we could make the `CommandWord` type self-contained—in effect, move the text:value association from `CommandWords` to `CommandWord`.

Java allows enumerated type definitions to contain much more than a list of the type's values. We will not explore this feature in much detail but just give you a flavor of what is possible. Code 6.10 shows an enhanced `CommandWord` type that looks quite similar to an ordinary class definition. This can be found in the *zuul-with-enums-v2* project.

Code 6.10

Associating command
strings with enumerated
type values

```java
/**
 * Representations for all the valid command words for the game
 * along with a string in a particular language.
 *
 * @author Michael Kölling and David J. Barnes
 * @version 2011.08.10
 */
public enum CommandWord
{
    // A value for each command word along with its
    // corresponding user interface string.
    GO("go"), QUIT("quit"), HELP("help"), UNKNOWN("?");

    // The command string.
    private String commandString;

    /**
     * Initialize with the corresponding command string.
     * @param commandString The command string.
     */
    CommandWord(String commandString)
    {
        this.commandString = commandString;
    }

    /**
     * @return The command word as a string.
     */
    public String toString()
    {
        return commandString;
    }
}
```

The main points to note about this new version of CommandWord are that:

■ Each type value is followed by a parameter value—in this case, the text of the command associated with that value.

■ The type definition includes a constructor. This does not have the word public in its header. Enumerated type constructors are never public, because we do not create the instances. The parameter associated with each type value is passed to this constructor.

■ The type definition includes a field, commandString. The constructor stores the command string in this field.

■ A toString method has been used to return the text associated with a particular type value.

With the text of the commands stored in the `CommandWord` type, the `CommandWords` class in *zuul-with-enums-v2* uses a different way to create its map between text and enumerated values:

```
validCommands = new HashMap<String, CommandWord>();
for(CommandWord command : CommandWord.values()) {
    if(command != CommandWord.UNKNOWN) {
        validCommands.put(command.toString(), command);
    }
}
```

Every enumerated type defines a `values` method that returns an array filled with the value objects from the type. The code above iterates over the array and calls the `toString` method to obtain the command `String` associated with each value.

> **Exercise 6.39** Add your own *look* command to *zuul-with-enums-v2*. Do you only need to change the `CommandWord` type?
>
> **Exercise 6.40** Change the word associated with the *help* command in `CommandWord`. Is this change automatically reflected in the welcome text when you start the game? Take a look at the `printWelcome` method in the `Game` class to see how this has been achieved.

6.14 Design guidelines

An often-heard piece of advice to beginners about writing good object-oriented programs is, "Don't put too much into a single method" or "Don't put everything into one class." Both suggestions have merit but frequently lead to the counter-questions, "How long should a method be?" or "How long should a class be?"

After the discussion in this chapter, these questions can now be answered in terms of cohesion and coupling. A method is too long if it does more than one logical task. A class is too complex if it represents more than one logical entity.

You will notice that these answers do not give clear-cut rules that specify exactly what to do. Terms such as *one logical task* are still open to interpretation, and different programmers will decide differently in many situations.

These are *guidelines* (not cast-in-stone rules). Keeping these in mind, though, will significantly improve your class design and enable you to master more complex problems and write better and more interesting programs.

> It is important to understand the following exercises as suggestions, not as fixed specifications. This game has many possible ways in which it can be extended, and you are encouraged to invent your own extensions. You do not need to do all the exercises here to create an interesting game; you may want to do more, or you may want to do different ones. Here are some suggestions to get you started.

Exercise 6.41 Add some form of time limit to your game. If a certain task is not completed in a specified time, the player loses. A time limit can easily be implemented by counting the number of moves or the number of entered commands. You do not need to use real time.

Exercise 6.42 Implement a trapdoor somewhere (or some other form of door that you can only cross one way).

Exercise 6.43 Add a *beamer* to the game. A beamer is a device that can be *charged* and *fired*. When you charge the beamer, it memorizes the current room. When you fire the beamer, it transports you immediately back to the room it was charged in. The beamer could either be standard equipment or an item that the player can find. Of course, you need commands to charge and fire the beamer.

Exercise 6.44 Add locked doors to your game. The player needs to find (or otherwise obtain) a key to open a door.

Exercise 6.45 Add a transporter room. Whenever the player enters this room, he/she is randomly transported into one of the other rooms. Note: Coming up with a good design for this task is not trivial. It might be interesting to discuss design alternatives for this with other students. (We discuss design alternatives for this task at the end of Chapter 9. The adventurous or advanced reader may want to skip ahead and have a look.)

Exercise 6.46 *Challenge exercise* In the `processCommand` method in `Game`, there is a switch statement (or a sequence of if statements) to dispatch commands when a command word is recognized. This is not a very nice design, because every time we add a command, we have to add a case here. Can you improve this design? Design the classes so that handling of commands is more modular and new commands can be added more easily. Implement it. Test it.

Exercise 6.47 Add characters to the game. Characters are similar to items, but they can talk. They speak some text when you first meet them, and they may give you some help if you give them the right item.

Exercise 6.48 Add moving characters. These are like other characters, but every time the player types a command, these characters can move into an adjoining room.

6.15 Executing without BlueJ

When our game is finished, we may want to pass it on to others to play. To do this, it would be nice if people could play the game without the need to start BlueJ. To be able to do this, we need one more thing: *class methods,* which in Java are also referred to as *static methods*.

6.15.1 Class methods

So far, all methods we have seen have been *instance methods*: they are invoked on an instance of a class. What distinguishes class methods from instance methods is that class methods can be invoked without an instance—having the class is enough.

In Section 5.13, we discussed class variables. Class methods are conceptually related and use a related syntax (the keyword `static` in Java). Just as class variables belong to the class rather than to an instance, so do class methods.

A class method is defined by adding the keyword `static` in front of the type name in the method's signature:

```
public static int getNumberOfDaysThisMonth()
{
    ...
}
```

Such a method can then be called by specifying the name of the class in which it is defined, before the dot in the usual dot notation. If, for instance, the above method is defined in a class called `Calendar`, the following call invokes it:

```
int days = Calendar.getNumberOfDaysThisMonth();
```

Note that the name of the class is used before the dot—no object has been created.

Exercise 6.49 Read the class documentation for class `Math` in the package `java.lang`. It contains many static methods. Find the method that computes the maximum of two integer numbers. What is its signature?

Exercise 6.50 Why do you think the methods in the `Math` class are static? Could they be written as instance methods?

Exercise 6.51 Write a test class that has a method to test how long it takes to count from 1 to 100 in a loop. You can use the method `currentTimeMillis` from class `System` to help with the time measurement.

6.15.2 The main method

If we want to start a Java application without BlueJ, we need to use a class method. In BlueJ, we typically create an object and invoke one of its methods, but without BlueJ an application starts without any object in existence. Classes are the only things we have initially, so the first method that can be invoked must be a class method.

The Java definition for starting applications is quite simple: the user specifies the class that should be started, and the Java system will then invoke a method called `main` in that class. This method must have a specific signature. If such a method does not exist in that class, an error is reported. Appendix E describes the details of this method and the commands needed to start the Java system without BlueJ.

Exercise 6.52 Find out the details of the `main` method and add such a method to your `Game` class. The method should create a `Game` object and invoke the `play` method on it. Test the `main` method by invoking it from BlueJ. Class methods can be invoked from the class's pop-up menu.

Exercise 6.53 Execute your game without BlueJ.

6.15.3   Limitations of class methods

Because class methods are associated with a class rather than an instance, they have two important limitations. The first limitation is that a class method may not access any instance fields defined in the class. This is logical, because instance fields are associated with individual objects. Instead, class methods are restricted to accessing class variables from their class. The second limitation is like the first: a class method may not call an instance method from the class. A class method may only invoke other class methods defined in its class.

You will find that we make very little use of class methods in the examples in this book.

6.16   Summary

In this chapter, we have discussed what are often called the *nonfunctional aspects* of an application. Here, the issue is not so much to get a program to perform a certain task, but to do this with well-designed classes.

Good class design can make a huge difference when an application needs to be corrected, modified, or extended. It also allows us to reuse parts of the application in other contexts (for example, for other projects) and thus creates benefits later.

There are two key concepts under which class design can be evaluated: coupling and cohesion. Coupling refers to the interconnectedness of classes, cohesion to modularization into appropriate units. Good design exhibits loose coupling and high cohesion.

One way to achieve a good structure is to follow a process of responsibility-driven design. Whenever we add a function to the application, we try to identify which class should be responsible for which part of the task.

When extending a program, we use regular refactoring to adapt the design to changing requirements and to ensure that classes and methods remain cohesive and loosely coupled.

Terms introduced in this chapter

code duplication, coupling, cohesion, encapsulation, responsibility-driven design, implicit coupling, refactoring, class method

Concept summary

- **coupling** The term *coupling* describes the interconnectedness of classes. We strive for *loose coupling* in a system—that is, a system where each class is largely independent and communicates with other classes via a small, well-defined interface.

- **cohesion** The term *cohesion* describes how well a unit of code maps to a logical task or entity. In a *highly cohesive* system, each unit of code (method, class, or module) is responsible for a well-defined task or entity. Good class design exhibits a high degree of cohesion.

■ **code duplication** Code duplication (having the same segment of code in an application more than once) is a sign of bad design. It should be avoided.

■ **encapsulation** Proper encapsulation in classes reduces coupling and thus leads to a better design.

■ **responsibility-driven design** Responsibility-driven design is the process of designing classes by assigning well-defined responsibilities to each class. This process can be used to determine which class should implement which part of an application function.

■ **localizing change** One of the main goals of a good class design is that of localizing change: making changes to one class should have minimal effects on other classes.

■ **method cohesion** A cohesive method is responsible for one, and only one, well-defined task.

■ **class cohesion** A cohesive class represents one well-defined entity.

■ **refactoring** Refactoring is the activity of restructuring an existing design to maintain a good class design when the application is modified or extended.

■ **switch statement** A switch statement selects a sequence of statements for execution from multiple different options.

Exercise 6.54 Without using BlueJ, edit your *TechSupport* project from Chapter 5 so that it can execute without BlueJ. Then run it from a command line.

Exercise 6.55 Can you call a static method from an instance method? Can you call an instance method from a static method? Can you call a static method from a static method? Answer these questions on paper, then create a test project to check your answers and try it. Explain in detail your answers and observations.

Exercise 6.56 Can a class count how many instances have been created of that class? What is needed to do this? Write some code fragments that illustrate what needs to be done. Assume that you want a static method called `numberOfInstances` that returns the number of instances created.

CHAPTER
7

Well-behaved objects

Main concepts discussed in this chapter:

- testing
- debugging

- unit testing
- test automation

Java constructs introduced in this chapter:

(No new Java constructs are introduced in this chapter.)

7.1 Introduction

If you have followed the previous chapters in this book and if you have implemented the exercises we have suggested, then you have written a good number of classes by now. One observation that you will likely have made is that a class you write is rarely perfect after the first attempt to write its source code. Usually, it does not work correctly at first, and some more work is needed to complete it.

The problems you are dealing with will shift over time. Beginners typically struggle with Java *syntax errors*. Syntax errors are errors in the structure of the source code itself. They are easy to spot, because the compiler will highlight them and display some sort of error message.

More-experienced programmers who tackle more-complicated problems usually have less difficulty with the language syntax. They are more concerned with *logical errors* instead.

A logical error is a problem where the program compiles and executes without an obvious error but delivers the wrong result. Logical problems are much more severe and harder to find than syntax errors. In fact, it is sometimes not easy to detect that there even is an error in the first place.

Writing syntactically correct programs is relatively easy to learn, and good tools (such as compilers) exist to detect syntax errors and point them out. Writing logically correct programs, on the other hand, is very difficult for any nontrivial problem, and proof that a program is correct cannot, in general, be automated. It is so hard, in fact, that most software that is sold commercially is known to contain a significant number of bugs.

Thus, it is essential for a competent software engineer to learn how to deal with correctness and how to reduce the number of errors in a class.

In this chapter, we shall discuss a variety of activities that are related to improving the correctness of a program. These include testing, debugging, and writing for maintainability.

Testing is an activity that is concerned with finding out whether a segment of code contains any errors. Testing well is not easy, and there is much to think about when testing a program.

Debugging comes after testing. If tests have shown that an error is present, we use debugging techniques to find out exactly where the error is and how to fix it. There can be a significant amount of work between knowing that an error exists and finding the cause and fixing it.

Writing for maintainability is maybe the most fundamental topic. It is about trying to write code in such a way that errors are avoided in the first place and, if they still slip in, that they can be found as easily as possible. Code style and commenting are part of it, as are the code quality principles that we have discussed in the previous chapter. Ideally, code should be easy to understand so that the original programmer avoids introducing errors and a maintenance programmer can easily find possible errors.

In practice, this is not always simple. But there are big differences between few and many errors and also between the effort it takes to debug well-written code and not-so-well-written code.

Concept:

Testing is the activity of finding out whether a piece of code (a method, class, or program) produces the intended behavior.

Concept:

Debugging is the attempt to pinpoint and fix the source of an error.

7.2 Testing and debugging

Testing and debugging are crucial skills in software development. You will often need to check your programs for errors and then locate the source of those errors when they occur. In addition, you might also be responsible for testing other people's programs or modifying them. In the latter case, the debugging task is closely related to the process of understanding someone else's code, and there is a lot of overlap in the techniques you might use to do both. In the sections that follow, we shall investigate the following testing and debugging techniques:

- manual unit testing within BlueJ
- test automation
- manual walkthroughs
- print statements
- debuggers

We shall look at the first two testing techniques in the context of some classes that you might have written for yourself, and the remaining debugging techniques in the context of understanding someone else's source code.

7.3 Unit testing within BlueJ

The term *unit testing* refers to a test of the individual parts of an application, as opposed to *application testing*, which is testing of the complete application. The units being tested can be of various sizes. They may be a group of classes, a single class, or even a single method. It is worth observing that unit testing can be done long before an application is complete. Any single method, once written and compiled, can (and should) be tested.

Because BlueJ allows us to interact directly with individual objects, it offers unique ways to conduct testing on classes and methods. One of the points we want to stress in this section is that it is never too early to start testing. There are several benefits in early experimentation and testing. First, they give us valuable experience with a system; this can make it possible to spot problems early enough to fix them, and at a much lower cost than if they had not been uncovered until much later in the development. Second, we can start to build up a series of test cases and results that can be used over and over again as the system grows. Each time we make a change to the system, these test cases allow us to check that we have not inadvertently introduced errors into the rest of the system as a result of the changes.

In order to illustrate this form of testing within BlueJ, we shall use the *online-shop* project, which represents an early stage in the development of software for an online sales shop (such as Amazon.com). Our project contains only a very small part of this application, namely the part that deals with customer comments for sales items.

Open the *online-shop* project. Currently, it contains only two classes: `SalesItem` and `Comment`. The intended functionality of this part of the application—concentrating solely on handling customer comments—is as follows:

- Sales items can be created with a description and price.

- Customer comments can be added to and removed from sales items.

- Comments include a comment text, an author's name, and a rating. The rating is in the range of 1 to 5 (inclusive).

- Each person may leave only one comment. Subsequent attempts to leave a comment by the same author are rejected.

- The user interface (not implemented in this project yet) will include a question asking, "Was this comment helpful to you?" with Yes and No buttons. A user clicking Yes or No is known as *upvoting* or *downvoting* the comment. The balance of up and down votes is kept for comments, so that the most useful comments (the ones with the highest vote balance) can be displayed at the top.

The `Comment` class in our project stores information about a single comment. For our testing, we shall concentrate on the `SalesItem` class, shown in Code 7.1. Objects of this class represent a single sales item, including all comments left for this item.

As part of our testing, we should check several parts of the intended functionality, including:

- Can comments be added and removed from a sales item?

- Does the `showInfo` method correctly show all the information stored about a sales item?

- Are the constraints (ratings must be 1 to 5, only one comment per person) enforced correctly?

- Can we correctly find the most helpful comment (the one with the most votes)?

We shall find that all of these can be tested conveniently using the object bench within BlueJ. In addition, we shall see that the interactive nature of BlueJ makes it possible to simplify some of the testing by making controlled alterations to a class under test.

Code 7.1

The SalesItem class

```java
import java.util.ArrayList;
import java.util.Iterator;

/**
 * The class represents sales items on an online e-commerce site (such
 * as Amazon.com). SalesItem objects store all information relevant to
 * this item, including description, price, customer comments, etc.
 *
 * NOTE: The current version is incomplete! Currently, only code
 * dealing with customer comments is here.
 *
 * @author Michael Kölling and David J. Barnes
 * @version 0.1 (2011-07-31)
 */
public class SalesItem
{
    private String name;
    private int price;  // in cents
    private ArrayList<Comment> comments;

    /**
     * Create a new sales item.
     */
    public SalesItem(String name, int price)
    {
        this.name = name;
        this.price = price;
        comments = new ArrayList<Comment>();
    }

    /**
     * Return the name of this item.
     */
    public String getName()
    {
        return name;
    }

    /**
     * Return the price of this item.
     */
    public int getPrice()
    {
        return price;
    }
```

Code 7.1 continued

The `SalesItem` class

```java
/**
 * Return the number of customer comments for this item.
 */
public int getNumberOfComments()
{
    return comments.size();
}

/**
 * Add a comment to the comment list of this sales item. Return
 * true if successful, false if the comment was rejected.
 *
 * The comment will be rejected if the same author has already
 * left a comment or if the rating is invalid. Valid ratings are
 * numbers between 1 and 5 (inclusive).
 */
public boolean addComment(String author, String text, int rating)
{
    if(ratingInvalid(rating)) {  // reject invalid ratings
        return false;
    }

    if(findCommentByAuthor(author) != null) {
        // reject multiple comments by same author
        return false;
    }

    comments.add(new Comment(author, text, rating));
    return true;
}

/**
 * Remove the comment stored at the index given. If the index is
 * invalid, do nothing.
 */
public void removeComment(int index)
{
    if(index >=0 && index < comments.size()) { // index is valid
        comments.remove(index);
    }
}

/**
 * Upvote the comment at 'index'. That is: count this comment as
 * more helpful. If the index is invalid, do nothing.
 */
```

**Code 7.1
continued**

The SalesItem class

```java
public void upvoteComment(int index)
{
    if(index >=0 && index < comments.size()) { // index is valid
        comments.get(index).upvote();
    }
}


/**
 * Downvote the comment at 'index'. That is: count this comment as
 * less helpful. If the index is invalid, do nothing.
 */
public void downvoteComment(int index)
{
    if(index >=0 && index < comments.size()) { // index is valid
        comments.get(index).downvote();
    }
}

/**
 * Show all comments on screen. (Currently, for testing purposes:
 * print to the terminal. Modify later for web display.)
 */
public void showInfo()
{
    System.out.println("*** " + name + " ***");
    System.out.println("Price: " + priceString(price));
    System.out.println();
    System.out.println("Customer comments:");
    for(Comment comment : comments) {
        System.out.println("------------------------------------------");
        System.out.println(comment.getFullDetails());
    }
    System.out.println();
    System.out.println("===========================================");
}


/**
 * Return the most helpful comment. The most useful comment is the
 * one with the highest vote balance. If there are multiple
 * comments with equal highest balance, return any one of them.
 */
public Comment findMostHelpfulComment()
{
    Iterator<Comment> it = comments.iterator();
    Comment best = it.next();
```

**Code 7.1
continued**

The SalesItem class

```
        while(it.hasNext()) {
            Comment current = it.next();
            if(current.getVoteCount() > best.getVoteCount()) {
                best = current;
            }
        }
        return best;
    }


    /**
     * Check whether the given rating is invalid. Return true if it is
     * invalid. Valid ratings are in the range [1..5].
     */
    private boolean ratingInvalid(int rating)
    {
        return rating < 0 || rating > 5;
    }


    /**
     * Find the comment by the author with the given name.
     *
     * @return The comment if it exists, null if it doesn'>t.
     */
    private Comment findCommentByAuthor(String author)
    {
        for(Comment comment : comments) {
            if(comment.getAuthor().equals(author)) {
                return comment;
            }
        }
        return null;
    }


    /**
     * For a price given as an int, return a readable String
     * representing the same price. The price is given in whole cents.
     * For example for price==12345, the following String
     * is returned: $123.45
     */
    private String priceString(int price)
    {
        int dollars = price / 100;
        int cents = price - (dollars*100);
```

Code 7.1
continued
The SalesItem class

```
        if(cents <= 9) {
            return "$" + dollars + ".0" + cents;  // zero padding
        }
        else {
            return "$" + dollars + "." + cents;
        }
    }
}
```

7.3.1 Using inspectors

When testing interactively, using object inspectors is often very helpful. In preparation for our testing, create a SalesItem object on the object bench and open its inspector by selecting the *Inspect* function from the object's menu. Select the comments field and open its inspector as well (Figure 7.1). Check that the list has been created (is not null) and is initially of size 0. Check also that the size grows as you add comments. Leave the comment-list inspector open to assist with subsequent tests.

Figure 7.1
Inspector for the comments list

An essential component of testing classes that use data structures is checking that they behave properly both when the data structures are empty and—if appropriate—when they are full. Testing for full data structures only applies to those that have a fixed limit, such as arrays. In our case, where we use an ArrayList, testing for the list being full does not apply, because the list expands as needed. However, making tests with an empty list is important, as this is a special case that needs special treatment.

A first test that can be performed on SalesItem is to call its showInfo method before any comments have been added. This should correctly show the item's description and price, and no comments.

A key feature of good testing is to ensure that *boundaries* are checked, because these are often the points at which things go wrong. The boundaries associated with the SalesItem class are, for example, the empty comment list. Boundaries set for the Comment class include the restriction of the rating to the range 1 to 5. Ratings at the top and bottom of this range are boundary cases. It will be important to check not only ratings in the middle of this range, but also the maximum and minimum possible rating.

In order to conduct tests along these lines, create a `SalesItem` object on the object bench and try the following as initial tests of the comment functionality. If you do these tests carefully, they should uncover two errors in our code.

Exercise 7.1 Add several comments to the sales item while keeping an eye on the inspector for the comments list. Make sure the list behaves as expected (that is, its size should increase). You may also like to inspect the *elementData* field of the ArrayList object.

Exercise 7.2 Check that the `showInfo` method correctly prints the item information, including the comments. Try this both for items with and without comments.

Exercise 7.3 Check that the `getNumberOfComments` method works as expected.

Exercise 7.4 Now check that duplicate authors are correctly handled—i.e., that further comments by the same author are rejected. When trying to add a comment with an author name for whom a comment already exists, the `addComment` method should return `false`. Check also that the comment was not added to the list.

Exercise 7.5 Perform boundary checking on the rating value. That is, create comments not only with medium ratings, but also with top and bottom ratings. Does this work correctly?

Exercise 7.6 Good boundary testing also involves testing values that lie just beyond the valid range of data. Test 0 and 6 as rating values. In both cases, the comment should be rejected (`addComment` should return `false`, and the comment should not be added to the comment list).

Exercise 7.7 Test the `upvoteComment` and `downvoteComment` methods. Make sure that the vote balance is correctly counted.

Exercise 7.8 Use the `upvoteComment` and `downvoteComment` methods to mark some comments as more or less helpful. Then test the `findMostHelpfulComment` method. This method should return the comment that was voted most helpful. You will notice that the method returns an object reference. You can use the *Inspect* function in the method result dialog to check whether the correct comment was returned. Of course, you will need to know which is the correct comment in order to check whether you get the right result!

Exercise 7.9 Do boundary testing of the `findMostHelpfulComment` method. That is, call this method when the comments list is empty (no comments have been added). Does this work as expected?

Exercise 7.10 The tests in the exercises above should have uncovered two bugs in our code. Fix them. After fixing these errors, is it safe to assume that all previous tests will still work as before? Section 7.4 will discuss some of the testing issues that arise when software is corrected or enhanced.

From these exercises, it is easy to see how valuable interactive method invocations and inspectors are in giving immediate feedback on the state of an object, often avoiding the need to add print statements to a class when testing or debugging it.

7.3.2 Positive versus negative testing

Concept:

Positive testing is the testing of cases that are expected to succeed.

When deciding about what to test, we generally distinguish *positive* and *negative* test cases. Positive testing is the testing of functionality that we expect to work. For example, adding a comment by a new author with a valid rating is a positive test. When testing positive test cases, we have to convince ourselves that the code did indeed work as expected.

Concept:

Negative testing is the testing of cases that are expected to fail.

Negative testing is the test of cases that we expect to fail. Using an invalid rating or attempting to store a second comment from the same author are both negative tests. When testing negative cases, we expect the program to handle this error in some specified, controlled way.

> **Pitfall** It is a very common error for inexperienced testers to conduct only positive tests. Negative tests—testing that what should go wrong indeed does go wrong, and does so in a well-defined manner—are crucial for a good test procedure.

> **Exercise 7.11** Which of the test cases mentioned in the previous exercises are positive tests and which are negative? Make a table of each category. Can you think of further positive tests? Can you think of further negative ones?

7.4 Test automation

One reason why thorough testing is often neglected is that it is both a time consuming and a relatively boring activity if done manually. You will have noticed, if you did all exercises in the previous section, that testing thoroughly can become tedious very quickly. This particularly becomes an issue when tests have to be run not just once but possibly many hundreds or thousands of times. Fortunately, there are techniques available that allow us to automate repetitive testing, and so remove much of the drudgery associated with it. The next section looks at test automation in the context of *regression testing*.

7.4.1 Regression testing

It would be nice if we could assume that correcting errors only ever improves the quality of a program. Sadly, experience shows that it is all too easy to introduce further errors when modifying software. Thus, fixing an error at one spot may introduce another error at the same time.

As a consequence, it is desirable to run *regression tests* whenever a change is made to software. Regression testing involves rerunning tests that have previously passed, to ensure that the new version still passes them. It is much more likely to be performed if it can be automated. One of the easiest ways to automate regression tests is to write a program that acts as a *test rig*, or *test harness*.

7.4.2   Automated testing using JUnit

Support for regression testing is integrated in BlueJ (and many other development environments) using a testing system called JUnit. JUnit is a testing framework devised by Erich Gamma and Kent Beck for the Java language, and similar systems are now available for many other programming languages.

> **JUnit, www.junit.org** JUnit is a popular testing framework to support organized unit testing and regression testing in Java. It is available independent of specific development environments, as well as integrated in many environments. JUnit was developed by Erich Gamma and Kent Beck. You can find the software and a lot of information about it at `http://www.junit.org`.

To start investigating regression testing with our example, open the *online-shop-junit* project. This project contains the same classes as the previous one, plus an additional class, `SalesItemTest`.

`SalesItemTest` is a test class. The first thing to note is that its appearance is different from what we have seen previously (Figure 7.2). It is annotated as a `<<unit test>>`, its color is different from that of the ordinary classes in the diagram, and it is attached to the `SalesItem` class (it will be moved with this class if `SalesItem` is moved in the diagram).

You will note that Figure 7.2 also shows some additional controls in the main window, below the *Compile* button. These allow you to use the built-in regression testing tools. If you have not used JUnit in BlueJ before, the testing tools are switched off, and the buttons will not yet be visible on your system. You should switch on these testing tools now. To do this, open the *Miscellaneous* tab in your *Preferences* dialog and ensure that the *Show unit testing tools* option is selected.

Figure 7.2
A project with a test class

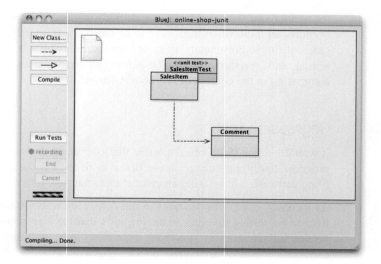

A further difference is apparent in the menu that appears when we right-click the test class (Figure 7.3). There are three new sections in the menu instead of a list of constructors.

Figure 7.3
The pop-up menu
for a test class

```
Test All

void testAddComment()
void testIllegalRating()
void testInit()

Create Test Method...
Object Bench to Test Fixture
Test Fixture to Object Bench

Open Editor
Compile
Inspect
Remove
```

Using test classes, we can automate regression testing. The test class contains code to perform a number of prepared tests and check their results. This makes repeating the same tests many times much easier.

A test class is usually associated with an ordinary project class. In this case, `SalesItemTest` is associated with the `SalesItem` class, and we say that `SalesItem` is the *reference class* for `SalesItemTest`.

In our project, the test class has already been created, and it already contains some tests. We can now execute these tests by clicking the *Run Tests* button.

> **Exercise 7.12** Run the tests in your project, using the *Run Tests* button. You should see a window similar to Figure 7.4, summarizing the results of the tests.

Figure 7.4
The Test Results
window

```
BlueJ:  Test Results

  SalesItemTest.testAddComment (10ms)
  SalesItemTest.testIllegalRating (1ms)
  SalesItemTest.testInit (1ms)




Runs: 3/3      X Errors: 0      X Failures: 0      Total Time: 12ms




Show Source                                              Close
```

Figure 7.4 shows the result of running three tests named `testAddComment`, `testIllegal-Rating`, and `testInit`, which are defined in the test class. The ticks immediately to the left of the test names indicate that the tests succeeded. You can achieve the same result by selecting the *Test All* option from the pop-up menu associated with the test class or running the tests individually by selecting them from the same menu.

Test classes are clearly different in some way from ordinary classes, and if you open the source code of `SalesItemTest`, you will notice that it has some new features. At this stage of the book, we are not going to discuss in detail how test classes work internally, but it is worth noting that although the source code of `SalesItemTest` could have been written by a person, it was, in fact, *automatically generated* by BlueJ. Some of the comments were then added afterwards to document the purpose of the tests.

Each test class typically contains tests for the functionality of its reference class. It is created by using the right mouse button over a potential reference class and selecting *Create Test Class* from the pop-up menu. Note that `SalesItem` already has a test class, so this additional menu item does not appear in its class menu, but the one for `Comment` does have this option, as it currently has no associated test class.

The test class contains source code both to run tests on a reference class and to check whether the tests were successful or not. For instance, here is one of the statements from `testInit` that checks that the price of the item is 1000 at that point:

```
assertEquals(1000, salesIte1.getPrice());
```

When such tests are run, BlueJ is able to display the results in the window shown in Figure 7.4.

In the next section, we shall discuss how BlueJ supports creation of tests so that you can create your own automated tests.

> **Exercise 7.13** Create a test class for the `Comment` class in the *online-shop-junit* project.
>
> **Exercise 7.14** What methods are created automatically when a new test class is created?

7.4.3 Recording a test

As we discussed at the beginning of Section 7.4, test automation is desirable because manually creating and re-creating tests is a time-consuming process. BlueJ makes it possible to combine the effectiveness of manual unit testing with the power of test automation by enabling us to record manual tests and then replay them later for the purposes of regression testing. The `SalesItemTest` class was created via this process.

Suppose that we wanted to thoroughly test the `addComment` method of the `SalesItem` class. This method, as we have seen, adds customer comments if they are valid. There are several tests we would like to make, such as:

■ adding a first comment to an empty comment list (positive)

■ adding further comments when other comments already exist (positive)

- attempting to add a comment with an author who has already submitted a comment (negative)

- attempting to add a comment with an invalid rating (negative)

The first of these already exists in the `SalesItemTest` class. We will now describe how to create the next one using the *online-shop-junit* project.

A test is recorded by telling BlueJ to start recording, performing the test manually, and then signaling the end of the test. The first step is done via the menu attached to a test class. This tells BlueJ which class you wish the new test to be stored in. Select *Create Test Method...* from the `SalesItemTest` class's pop-up menu. You will be prompted for a name for the test method. By convention, we start the name with the prefix "test." For example, to create a method that tests adding two comments, we might call that method `testTwoComments`.[1]

Once you have entered a name and clicked *OK,* a red recording indicator appears to the left of the class diagram, and the *End* and *Cancel* buttons become available. *End* is used to indicate the end of the test-creation process and *Cancel* to abandon it.

Once recording is started, we just carry out the actions that we would with a normal manual test:

- Create a `SalesItem` object.

- Add a comment to the sales item.

Once `addComment` has been called, a new dialog window will appear (Figure 7.5). This is an extended version of the normal method result window, and it is a crucial part of the automated testing process. Its purpose is to allow you to specify what the result of the method call *should be.* This is called an *assertion.*

Figure 7.5
The Method Result dialog with assertion facility

---

[1] Earlier versions of JUnit, up to version 3, required the method names to start with the prefix "test." This is not a requirement anymore in current versions.

Concept:

An **assertion** is an expression that states a condition that we expect to be true. If the condition is false, we say that the assertion fails. This indicates an error in our program.

In this case, we expect the method return value to be *true*, and we want to include a check in our test to make sure that this is really the case. We can now make sure that the *Assert that* check-box is checked, enter *true* in the dialog, and select the *Close* button.

■ Add a second comment to your sales item. Make sure the comments are valid (they have unique authors and the rating is valid). Assert that the result is true for the second comment addition as well.

■ We now expect two comments to exist. To test that this is indeed the case, call the getNumberOfComments method and assert that the result is 2.

This is the final stage of the test. We then press the *End* button to stop the recording. At that point, BlueJ adds source code to the SalesItemTest class for our new method, testTwoComments, then compiles the class and clears the object bench. The resulting generated method is shown in Code 7.2.

Code 7.2

An automatically generated test method

```
@Test
public void testTwoComments()
{
    SalesItem salesIte1 = new SalesItem("Java Book", 12345);
    assertEquals(true, salesIte1.addComment("James Duckling",
                 "Great book. ...", 4));
    assertEquals(true, salesIte1.addComment("Fred", "Like it", 2));
    assertEquals(2, salesIte1.getNumberOfComments());
}
```

As can be seen, the method contains statements that reproduce the actions made when recording it: a SalesItem object is created, and the addComment and getNumberOfComments methods are called. The call to assertEquals is what checks that the result returned by these methods matches the expected value. You can also see a new construct, @Test, before the method. This is an annotation that identifies this method as a test method.

The exercises below are provided so that you can try this process out for yourself. They include an example to show what happens if the actual value does not match the expected value.

Exercise 7.15 Create a test to check that addComment returns false when a comment from the same author already exists.

Exercise 7.16 Create a test that performs negative testing on the boundaries of the rating range. That is, test the values 0 and 6 as a rating (the values just outside the legal range). We expect these to return false, so assert false in the result dialog. You will notice that one of these actually (incorrectly) returns true. This is the bug we uncovered earlier in manual testing. Make sure that you assert false anyway. The assertion states the *expected* result, not the *actual* result.

Exercise 7.17 Run all tests again. Explore how the *Test Result* dialog displays the failed test. Select the failed test in the list. What options do you have available to explore the details of the failed test?

Exercise 7.18 Create a test class that has `Comment` as its reference class. Create a test that checks whether the author and rating details are stored correctly after creation. Record separate tests that check whether the `upvote` and `downvote` methods work as expected.

Exercise 7.19 Create tests for `SalesItem` that test whether the `findMostHelpfulComment` method works as expected. Note that this method returns a `Comment` object. During your testing, you can use the *Get* button in the method result dialog to get the result object onto the object bench, which then allows you to make further method calls and add assertions for this object. This allows you to identify the comment object returned (e.g., by checking its author). You can also assert that the result is *null* or *not null*, depending on what you expect.

7.4.4 Fixtures

Concept:

A **fixture** is a set of objects in a defined state that serves as a basis for unit tests.

As a set of test methods is built up, it is common to find yourself creating similar objects for each one. For instance, every test of the `SalesItem` class will involve creating at least one `SalesItem` and initializing it, often by adding one or more comments. An object or a group of objects that is used in more than one test is known as a *fixture*. Two menu items associated with a test class enable us to work with fixtures in BlueJ: *Object Bench to Test Fixture* and *Test Fixture to Object Bench.* In your project, create two `SalesItem` objects on the object bench. Leave one without any comments, and add two comments to the other. Now select *Object Bench to Test Fixture* from `SalesItemTest`. The objects will disappear from the object bench, and if you examine the source code of `SalesItemTest`, you will see that its `setUp` method looks something like Code 7.3, where `salesIte1` and `salesIte2` have been defined as fields.

Code 7.3

Creating a fixture

```
/**
 * Sets up the test fixture.
 *
 * Called before every test case method.
 */
@Before
public void setUp()
{
    salesIte1 = new SalesItem("Java Book", 12345);
    salesIte2 = new SalesItem("Other", 123);
    salesIte2.addComment("Fred", "too expensive", 1);
}
```

The significance of the `setUp` method is that it is automatically called immediately before every test method is called. (The `@Before` annotation above the method header ensures this.) This means that the individual test methods no longer need to create their own versions of the fixture objects.

Once we have a fixture associated with a test class, recording tests becomes significantly simpler. Whenever we create a new test method, the objects from the fixture will automatically appear on the object bench—there is no longer a need to create new test objects manually each time.

Should we wish to add further objects to the fixture at any time, one of the easiest ways is to select *Test Fixture to Object Bench*, add further objects to the object bench in the usual way, and then select *Object Bench to Test Fixture*. We could also edit the setUp method in the editor and add further fields directly to the test class.

Test automation is a powerful concept because it makes it more likely that tests will be written in the first place, and more likely that they will be run and rerun as a program develops. You should try to get into the habit of starting to write unit tests early in the development of a project, and of keeping them up to date as the project progresses. In Chapter 12, we shall return to the subject of assertions in the context of error handling.

Exercise 7.20 Add further automated tests to your project until you reach a point where you are reasonably confident of the correct operation of the classes. Use both positive and negative tests. If you discover any errors, be sure to record tests that guard against recurrence of these errors in later versions.

In the next section, we look at debugging—the activity that starts when we have noticed the existence of an error and we need to find and fix it.

7.5 Debugging

Testing is important, and testing well helps uncover the existence of errors. However, testing alone is not enough. After detecting the existence of an error, we also have to find its cause and fix it. That's where debugging comes in.

To discuss various approaches to debugging, we use a hypothetical scenario. Imagine that you have been asked to join an existing project team that is working on an implementation of a software calculator (Figure 7.6). You have been drafted in because a key member of the programming team, Hacker T. Largebrain, has just been promoted to a management position on another project. Before leaving, Hacker assured the team you are joining that his implementation of the part of the calculator he was responsible for was finished and fully tested. He had even written some test software to verify that this was the case. You have been asked to take over the class and simply ensure that it is properly commented prior to integration with the classes being written by other members of the team.

The software for the calculator has been carefully designed to separate the user interface from the calculator logic so that the calculator might be used in different contexts later on. The first version, which we are looking at here, will run with a graphical user interface, shown in Figure 7.6. However, in later extensions to the project, it is intended that the same calculator implementation should be able to run in a web browser or on a mobile device. In preparation for this, the application has been split into separate classes, most importantly UserInterface, to implement the graphical user interface, and CalcEngine, to implement the calculation logic. It is this latter class that Hacker was responsible for. This class should remain unchanged when the calculator runs with a different user interface.

Figure 7.6
The user interface of a software calculator

To investigate how the CalcEngine class is used by other classes, it is useful to look at its *interface*. Confusingly, we are now not talking about the *user interface*, but about the *class interface*. This double meaning of the term *interface* is unfortunate, but it is important to understand both meanings.

The class interface is the summary of the public-method headers that other classes can use. It is what other classes can see and how they can interact with our class. The interface is shown in the javadoc documentation of a class and in the *Documentation* view in the editor. Code 7.4 shows the interface of the CalcEngine class.

Code 7.4
The interface of the arithmetic logic unit

```
// Return the value to be displayed.
public int getDisplayValue();

// Call when a digit button is pressed.
public void numberPressed(int number);

// Call when a plus operator is pressed.
public void plus();

// Call when a minus operator is pressed.
public void minus();

// Call to complete a calculation.
public void equals();

// Call to reset the calculator.
public void clear();
```

Such an interface can be written before the full classes are implemented. It represents a simple form of contract between the CalcEngine class and other parts of the program that wish to use it. The CalcEngine class provides the implementation of this interface. The interface describes a minimum set of methods that will be implemented in the logic component, and for each method the return type and parameters are fully defined. Note that the interface gives no details of exactly what its implementing class will do internally when notified that a plus operator has been pressed, for instance; that is left to its implementers. In addition, the implementing class might well have additional methods not listed here.

In the sections that follow, we shall look at Hacker's attempt to implement this interface. In this case, we decide that the best way to understand Hacker's software prior to documenting it is to explore its source and the behavior of its objects.

7.6 Commenting and style

Open the *calculator-engine* project to view the classes. This is Hacker's own version of the project, containing only the calculator engine and a test class, but not the user interface class. The `CalcEngineTester` class takes the place of the user interface at this stage of development. This illustrates another positive feature of defining interfaces between classes: it becomes easier to develop mock-ups of the other classes for the purpose of testing.

If you take a look at the `CalcEngine` class, you will find that its author has paid attention to some important areas of good style:

- The class has been given a multiline comment at the top, indicating the purpose of the class. Also included are annotations indicating author and version number.

- Each method of the interface has a comment indicating its purpose, parameters, and return type. This will certainly make it easier to generate project documentation for the interface, as discussed in Chapter 5.

- The layout of the class is consistent, with appropriate amounts of white-space indentation used to indicate the distinct levels of nested blocks and control structures.

- Expressive variable names and method names have been chosen.

Although these conventions may seem time consuming during implementation, they can be of enormous benefit in helping someone else to understand your code (as we have to in this scenario) or in helping you to remember what a class does if you have taken a break from working on it.

We also note another detail that looks less promising: Hacker has not used a specialized unit test class to capture his tests, but has written his own test class. As we know about unit test support in BlueJ, we wonder why.

This does not necessarily have to be bad. Handwritten test classes may be just as good, but it makes us a little suspicious. Did Hacker really know what he was doing? We shall come back to this point a bit later.

So, maybe Hacker's abilities are as great as he thinks they are, and in that case you will not have much to do to make the class ready for integration with the others?! Try the following exercises to see if this is the case.

> **Exercise 7.21** Make sure the classes in the project are compiled, and then create a `CalcEngineTester` object within BlueJ. Call the `testAll` method. What is printed in the terminal window? Do you believe the final line of what it says?

Exercise 7.22 Using the object you created in the previous exercise, call the `testPlus` method. What result does it give? Is that the same result as was printed by the call to `testAll`? Call `testPlus` one more time. What result does it give now? Should it always give the same answer? If so, what should that answer be? Take a look at the source of the `testPlus` method to check.

Exercise 7.23 Repeat the previous exercise with the `testMinus` method. Does it always give the same result?

The experiments above should have alerted you to the fact that not all seems to be right with the `CalcEngine` class. It looks like it contains some errors. But what are they, and how can we find them? In the sections that follow, we shall consider a number of different ways in which we can try to locate where errors are occurring in a class.

7.7 Manual walkthroughs

Concept:

A **walkthrough** is an activity of working through a segment of code line by line while observing changes of state and other behavior of the application.

Manual walkthroughs are a relatively underused technique, perhaps because they are a particularly "low-tech" debugging and testing technique. However, do not let this fool you into thinking that they are not useful. A manual walkthrough involves printing copies of the classes you are trying to understand or debug and then getting right away from your computer! It is all too easy to spend a lot of time sitting in front of a computer screen not making much progress in trying to deal with a programming problem. Relocating and refocusing your efforts can often free your mind to attack a problem from a completely different direction. We have often found that going off to lunch or cycling home from the office brings enlightenment that has otherwise eluded us through hours of slogging away at the keyboard!

A walkthrough involves both reading classes and tracing the flow of control between classes and objects. This aids understanding both the ways in which objects interact with one another and how they behave internally. In effect, a walkthrough is a pencil-and-paper simulation of what happens inside the computer when you run a program. In practice, it is best to focus on a narrow portion of an application, such as a single logical grouping of actions or even a single method call.

7.7.1 A high-level walkthrough

We shall illustrate the walkthrough technique with the *calculator-engine* project. You might find it useful to print out copies of the `CalcEngine` and `CalcEngineTester` classes in order to follow through the steps of this technique.

We shall start by examining the `testPlus` method of the `CalcEngineTester` class, as it contains a single logical grouping of actions that should help us gain an understanding of how several methods of the `CalcEngine` class work together to fulfill the computation role of a calculator. As we work our way through it, we shall often make penciled notes of questions that arise in our minds.

1   For this first stage, we do not want to delve into too much detail. We simply want to look at how the `testPlus` method uses an engine object, without exploring the internal details of the engine. From earlier experimentation, it would appear that there are some errors to be

found, but we do not know whether the errors are in the tester or the engine. So the first step is to check that the tester appears to be using the engine appropriately.

2   We note that the first statement of `testPlus` assumes that the `engine` field already refers to a valid object:

```
engine.clear();
```

We can verify that this is the case by checking the tester's constructor. It is a common error for an object's fields not to have been initialized properly, either in their declarations or in a constructor. If we attempt to use a field with no associated object, then a `NullPointerException` is a likely runtime error.

3   The first statement's call to `clear` appears to be an attempt to put the calculator engine into a valid starting state, ready to receive instructions to perform a calculation. This looks like a reasonable thing to do, equivalent to pressing a "reset" or "clear" key on a real calculator. At this stage, we do not look at the engine class to check exactly what the `clear` method does. That can wait until we have achieved a level of confidence that the tester's actions are reasonable. Instead, we simply make a penciled note to check that `clear` puts the engine into a valid starting state as expected.

4   The next statement in `testPlus` is the entry of a digit via the `numberPressed` method:

```
engine.numberPressed(3);
```

This too is reasonable, as the first step in making a calculation is to enter the first operand. Once again, we do not look to see what the engine does with the number. We simply assume that it stores it somewhere for later use in the calculation.

5   The next statement calls `plus`, so we now know that the full value of the left operand is 3. We could make a penciled note of this fact on the printout, or make a tick against this assertion in one of the comments of `testPlus`. Similarly, we should note or confirm that the operation being executed is addition. This seems like a trivial thing to do, but it is all too easy for a class's comments to get out of step with the code they are supposed to document. So checking the comments at the same time as we read the code can help us avoid being misled by them later.

6   Next, another single digit is entered as the right operand by a further call to `numberPressed`.

7   Completion of the addition is requested by a call to the `equals` method. We might make a penciled note that, from the way it has been used in `testPlus`, the `equals` method appears not to return the result of the calculation, as we might have expected otherwise. This is something else that we can check when we look at `CalcEngine`.

8   The final statement of `testPlus` obtains the value that should appear in the calculator's display:

```
return engine.getDisplayValue();
```

Presumably, this is the result of the addition, but we cannot know that for sure without looking in detail at `CalcEngine`. Once again, we shall make a note to check that this is indeed the case.

With our examination of `testPlus` completed, we have gained a reasonable degree of confidence that it uses the engine appropriately: that is, simulating a recognizable sequence of key presses to complete a simple calculation. We might remark that the method is not particularly ambitious—both operands are single-digit numbers, and only a single operator is used. However, that is not unusual in test methods, because it is important to test for the most basic functionality before testing more complex combinations. Nevertheless, it is useful to observe that some more complex tests should be added to the tester at some stage.

> **Exercise 7.24** Perform a similar walkthrough of your own with the `testMinus` method. Does that raise any further questions in your mind about things you might like to check when looking at `CalcEngine` in detail?

Before looking at the `CalcEngine` class, it is worth walking through the `testAll` method to see how it uses the `testPlus` and `testMinus` methods we have been looking at. From this we observe the following:

1 The `testAll` method is a straight-line sequence of print statements.

2 It contains one call to each of `testPlus` and `testMinus`, and the values they return are printed out for the user to see. We might note that there is nothing to tell the user what the results should be. This makes it hard for the user to confirm that the results are correct.

3 The final statement boldly states:

```
All tests passed.
```

but the method contains no tests to establish the truth of this assertion! There really should be a proper means of establishing both what the result values should be and whether they have been calculated correctly or not. This is something we should remedy as soon as we have the chance to get back to the source of this class.

At this stage, we should not be distracted by the final point into making changes that do not directly address the errors we are looking for. If we make those sorts of changes, we could easily end up masking the errors. One of the crucial requirements for successful debugging is to be able to trigger the error you are looking for easily and reproducibly. When that is the case, it is much easier to assess the effect of an attempted correction.

Having checked over the test class, we are in a position to examine the source of the `CalcEngine` class. We can do so armed with a reasonable sequence of method calls to explore from the walkthrough of the `testPlus` method, as well as with a set of questions thrown up by it.

7.7.2 Checking state with a walkthrough

A `CalcEngine` object is quite different in style from its tester. This is because the engine is a completely passive object. It initiates no activity of its own, but simply responds to external method calls. This is typical of the server style of behavior. Server objects often rely heavily on their state to determine how they should respond to method calls. This is particularly true of the calculator engine. So an important part of conducting the walkthrough is to be sure that we always have an accurate representation of its state. One way to do this on paper is by making up a table of an object's fields and their values (Figure 7.7). A new line can be entered to keep a running log of the values following each method call.

Figure 7.7
Informal tabulation
of an object's state

Method called	displayValue	leftOperand	previousOperator
initial state	0	0	' '
clear	0	0	' '
numberPressed(3)	3	0	' '

This technique makes it quite easy to check back if something appears to go wrong. It is also possible to compare the states after two calls to the same method.

1 As we start the walkthrough of CalcEngine, we document the initial state of the engine, as in the first row of values in Figure 7.7. All of its fields are initialized in the constructor. As we observed when walking through the tester, object initialization is important, and we might make a note here to check that the default initialization is sufficient—particularly as the default value of previousOperator would appear not to represent a meaningful operator. Furthermore, this might make us think about whether it really is meaningful to have a *previous* operator before the first real operator in a calculation. In noting down these questions, we do not necessarily have to try to discover the answers right away, but they provide prompts as we discover more about the class.

2 The next step is to see how a call to clear changes the engine's state. As shown in the second data row of Figure 7.7, the state remains unchanged at this point because display-Value is already set to 0. But we might note another question here: Why is the value of only one of the fields set by this method? If this method is supposed to implement a form of reset, why not clear all of the fields?

3 Next, a call to numberPressed with an actual parameter of 3 is investigated. The method multiplies an existing value of displayValue by 10 and then adds in the new digit. This correctly models the effect of appending a new digit onto the right-hand end of an existing number. It relies on displayValue having a sensible initial value of 0 when the first digit of a new number is entered, and our investigation of the clear method gives us confidence that this will be the case. So this method looks all right.

4 Continuing to follow the order of calls in the testPlus method, we next look at plus. Its first statement calls the applyPreviousOperator method. Here we have to decide whether to continue ignoring nested method calls or whether to break off and see what it does. Taking a quick look at the applyPreviousOperator method, we can see that it is fairly short. Furthermore, it is clearly going to alter the state of the engine, and we shall not be able to continue documenting the state changes unless we follow it up. So we would certainly decide to follow the nested call. It is important to remember where we came from, so we would mark the listing just inside the plus method before following through the applyPreviousOperator method. If following a nested method call is likely to lead to further nested calls, we should need to use something more than a simple mark to help us find our way back to the caller. In that case, it is better to mark the call points with ascending numerical values, reusing previous values as calls return.

5 The applyPreviousOperator method gives us some insights into how the previous-Operator field is used. It also appears to answer one of our earlier questions: whether having a space as the initial value for the previous operator was all right. The method

explicitly checks to see that `previousOperator` contains either a + or a − before applying it. So another value will not result in an incorrect operation being applied. By the end of this method, the value of `leftOperand` will have been changed, so we would note its new value in the state table.

6 Returning to the `plus` method, the remaining two fields have their values set, so the next row of the state table will contain the following values:

```
plus  0  3  '+'
```

The walkthrough of the engine can be continued in a similar fashion, documenting the state changes, gaining insights into its behavior, and raising questions along the way. The following exercises should help you complete the walkthrough.

Exercise 7.25 Complete the state table based on the following subsequent calls found in the `testPlus` method:

```
numberPressed(4);
equals();
getDisplayValue();
```

Exercise 7.26 When walking through the `equals` method, did you feel the same reassurances that we felt in `applyPreviousOperator` about the default value of `previousOperator`?

Exercise 7.27 Walk through a call to `clear` immediately following the call to `getDisplayValue` at the end of your state table, and record the new state. Is the engine in the same state as it was at the previous call to `clear`? If not, what impact do you think this could have on any subsequent calculations?

Exercise 7.28 In the light of your walkthrough, what changes do you think should be made to the `CalcEngine` class? Make those changes to a paper version of the class, and then try the walkthrough all over again. You should not need to walk through the `CalcEngineTester` class, just repeat the actions of its `testAll` method.

Exercise 7.29 Try a walkthrough of the following sequence of calls on your corrected version of the engine:

```
clear();
numberPressed(9);
plus();
numberPressed(1);
minus();
numberPressed(4);
equals();
```

What should the result be? Does the engine appear to behave correctly and leave the correct answer in `displayValue`?

7.7.3 Verbal walkthroughs

Another way in which the walkthrough technique can be used to find errors in a program is to try explaining to another person what a class or method does. This works in two completely different ways:

■ The person you explain the code to might spot the error for you.

■ You will often find that the simple act of trying to put into words what a piece of code should do is enough to trigger in your own mind an understanding of why it does not.

This latter effect is so common that it can often be worth explaining a piece of code to someone who is completely unfamiliar with it—not in anticipation that *they* will find the error, but that *you* will!

7.8 Print statements

Probably the most common technique used to understand and debug programs—even amongst experienced programmers—is to annotate methods temporarily with print statements. Print statements are popular because they exist in most languages, they are available to everyone, and they are very easy to add with any editor. No additional software or language features are required to make use of them. As a program runs, these additional print statements will typically provide a user with information such as:

■ which methods have been called

■ the values of parameters

■ the order in which methods have been called

■ the values of local variables and fields at strategic points

Code 7.5 shows an example of how the numberPressed method might look with print statements added. Such information is particularly helpful in providing a picture of the way in which the state of an object changes as mutators are called. To help support this, it is often worth including a debugging method that prints out the current values of all the fields of an object. Code 7.6 shows such a reportState method for the CalcEngine class.

Code 7.5
A method with debugging print statements added

```java
/**
 * A number button was pressed.
 * @param number The number that was pressed.
 */
public void numberPressed(int number)
{
    System.out.println("numberPressed called with: " +
                         number);

    displayValue = displayValue * 10 + number;

    System.out.println("displayValue is: " + displayValue +
                        " at end of numberPressed.");
}
```

Code 7.6

A state-reporting method

```java
/**
 * Print the values of this object's fields.
 * @param where Where this state occurs.
 */
public void reportState(String where)
{
    System.out.println("displayValue: " + displayValue +
                       " leftOperand: " + leftOperand +
                       " previousOperator: " +
                       previousOperator + " at " + where);
}
```

If each method of `CalcEngine` contained a print statement at its entry point and a call to `reportState` at its end, Figure 7.8 shows the output that might result from a call to the tester's `testPlus` method. (This was generated from a version of the calculator engine that can be found in the *calculator-engine-print* project.) Such output allows us to build up a picture of how control flows between different methods. For instance, we can see from the order in which the state values are reported that a call to `plus` contains a nested call to `applyPreviousOperator`.

Figure 7.8

Debugging output from a call to `testPlus`

```
clear called
displayValue: 0 leftOperand: 0 previousOperator: at end of clear
numberPressed called with: 3
displayValue: 3 leftOperand: 0 previousOperator: at end of number...
plus called
applyPreviousOperator called
displayValue: 3 leftOperand: 3 previousOperator: at end of apply...
displayValue: 0 leftOperand: 3 previousOperator: + at end of plus
numberPressed called with: 4
displayValue: 4 leftOperand: 3 previousOperator: + at end of number...
equals called
displayValue: 7 leftOperand: 0 previousOperator: + at end of equals
```

Print statements can be very effective in helping us understand programs or locate errors, but there are a number of disadvantages:

■ It is not usually practical to add print statements to every method in a class. So they are only fully effective if the right methods have been annotated.

■ Adding too many print statements can lead to information overload. A large amount of output can make it difficult to identify what you need to see. Print statements inside loops are a particular source of this problem.

■ Once their purpose has been served, it can be tedious to remove them.

■ There is also the chance that, having removed them, they will be needed again later. It can be very frustrating to have to put them back in again!

Exercise 7.30 Open the *calculator-engine-print* project and complete the addition of print statements to each method and the constructor.

Exercise 7.31 Create a `CalcEngineTester` in the project and run the `testAll` method. Does the output that results help you identify where the problem lies?

Exercise 7.32 Do you feel that the amount of output produced by the fully annotated `CalcEngine` class is too little, too much, or about right? If you feel that it is too little or too much, either add further print statements or remove some until you feel that you have the right level of detail.

Exercise 7.33 What are the respective advantages and disadvantages of using manual walkthroughs or print statements for debugging? Discuss.

7.8.1 Turning debugging information on or off

If a class is still under development when print statements are added, we often do not want to see the output every time the class is used. It is best if we can find a way to turn the printing on or off as required. The most common way to achieve this is to add an extra `boolean` debugging field to the class and then make printing dependent upon the value of the field. Code 7.7 illustrates this idea.

Code 7.7

Controlling whether debugging information is printed or not

```java
/**
 * A number button was pressed.
 * @param number The number that was pressed.
 */
public void numberPressed(int number)
{
    if(debugging) {
        System.out.println("numberPressed called with: " +
                                number);
    }

    displayValue = displayValue * 10 + number;
    if(debugging) {
        reportState();
    }
}
```

A more economical variation on this theme is to replace the direct calls to print statements with calls to a specialized printing method added to the class.[2] The printing method would print only if the `debugging` field is `true`. Therefore, calls to the printing method would not need to be

---

[2] In fact, we could move this method to a specialized debugging class, but we shall keep things simple in this discussion.

guarded by an if statement. Code 7.8 illustrates this approach. Note that this version assumes that `reportState` either tests the `debugging` field itself or also calls the new `printDebugging` method.

Code 7.8

A method for selectively printing debugging information

```java
/**
 * A number button was pressed.
 * @param number The number that was pressed.
 */
public void numberPressed(int number)
{
    printDebugging("numberPressed called with: " + number);

    displayValue = displayValue * 10 + number;
    reportState();
}

/**
 * Only print the debugging information if debugging
 * is true.
 * @param info The debugging information.
 */
public void printDebugging(String info)
{
    if(debugging) {
        System.out.println(info);
    }
}
```

As you can see from these experiments, it takes some practice to find the best level of detail to print out to be useful. In practice, print statements are often added to one or a small number of methods at a time, when we have a rough idea in what area of our program an error might be hiding.

7.9 Debuggers

In Chapter 3, we introduced the use of a debugger to understand how an existing application operates and how its objects interact. In a very similar manner, we can use the debugger to track down errors.

The debugger is essentially a software tool that provides support for performing a walkthrough on a segment of code. We typically set a breakpoint at the statement where we want to start our walkthrough and then use the *Step* or *Step Into* functions to do the actual walking.

One advantage is that the debugger automatically takes care of keeping track of every object's state, and, thus, doing this is quicker and less error prone than doing the same manually.

A disadvantage is that debuggers typically do not keep a permanent record of state changes, so it is harder to go back and check the state as it was a few statements earlier.

A debugger typically also gives you information about the *call sequence* (or *stack*) at each point in time. The call sequence shows the name of the method containing the current statement, the name of the method that the current method was called from, and the name of the method that *that* method was called from, and so on. Thus, the call sequence contains a record of all currently active, unfinished methods—similar to what we have done manually during our walk-through by writing marks next to method-call statements.

In BlueJ, the call sequence is displayed on the left-hand side of the debugger window (Figure 7.9). Every method name in that sequence can be selected to inspect the current values of that method's local variables.

Figure 7.9
The BlueJ debugger window, with execution stopped at a breakpoint

Exercise 7.34 Using the *calculator-engine* project, set a breakpoint in the first line of the `testPlus` method in the `CalcEngineTester` class. Execute this method. When the debugger appears, walk through the code step by step. Experiment with both the *Step* and *Step Into* buttons.

Exercise 7.35 *Challenge exercise* In practice, you will probably find that Hacker T. Largebrain's attempt to program the `CalcEngine` class is too full of errors to be worth trying to fix. Instead, write your own version of the class from scratch. The *calculator-gui* project contains classes that provide the GUI shown in Figure 7.6. You can use this project as the basis for your own implementation of the `CalcEngine` class. Be sure to document your class thoroughly and to create a thorough set of tests for your implementation so that your experience with Hacker's code will not have to be repeated by your successor! Make sure to use dedicated unit test classes for your testing, instead of writing tests into standard classes; as you have seen, this makes asserting the correct results much easier.

7.10 Choosing a debugging strategy

We have seen that several different debugging and testing strategies exist: written and verbal walkthroughs, use of print statements (either temporary or permanent, with enabling switches), interactive testing using the object bench, writing your own test class, and using a dedicated unit test class.

In practice, we would use different strategies at different times. Walkthroughs, print statements, and interactive testing are useful techniques for initial testing of newly written code, to investigate how a program segment works, or for debugging. Their advantage is that they are quick and easy to use, they work in any programming language, and they are (except for the interactive testing) independent of the environment. Their main disadvantage is that the activities are not easily repeatable. This is okay for debugging, but for testing we need something better: we need a mechanism that allows easy repetition for regression testing. Using unit test classes has the advantage—once they have been set up—that tests can be replayed any number of times.

So Hacker's way of testing—writing his own test class—was one step in the right direction, but was, of course, flawed. We know now that his problem was that although his class contained reasonable method calls for testing, it did not include any assertions on the method results, and thus did not detect test failure. Using a dedicated unit test class can solve these problems.

> **Exercise 7.36** Open your project again and add better testing by replacing Hacker's test class with a unit test class attached to the `CalcEngine`. Add similar tests to those Hacker used (and any others you find useful), and include correct assertions.

7.11 Putting the techniques into practice

This chapter has described several techniques that can be used either to understand a new program or to test for errors in a program. The *bricks* project provides a chance for you to try out those techniques with a new scenario. The project contains part of an application for a company producing bricks. Bricks are delivered to customers on pallets (stacks of bricks). The `Pallet` class provides methods telling the height and weight of an individual pallet, according to the number of bricks on it.

> **Exercise 7.37** Open the *bricks* project. Test it. There are at least four errors in this project. See if you can find them and fix them. What techniques did you use to find the errors? Which technique was most useful?

7.12 Summary

When writing software, we should anticipate that it will contain logical errors. Therefore, it is essential to consider both testing and debugging to be normal activities within the overall development process. BlueJ is particularly good at supporting interactive unit testing of both methods and classes. We have also looked at some basic techniques for automating the testing process and performing simple debugging.

Writing good JUnit tests for our classes ensures that errors are detected early, and they give a good indication which part of the system an error originates in, making the resulting debugging task much easier.

Terms introduced in this chapter

syntax error, logical error, testing, debugging, unit testing, JUnit, positive testing, negative testing, regression testing, manual walkthrough, call sequence

Concept summary

- **testing** Testing is the activity of finding out whether a piece of code (a method, class, or program) produces the intended behavior.

- **debugging** Debugging is the attempt to pinpoint and fix the source of an error.

- **positive testing** Positive testing is the testing of cases that are expected to succeed.

- **negative testing** Negative testing is the testing of cases that are expected to fail.

- **assertion** An assertion is an expression that states a condition that we expect to be true. If the condition is false, we say that the assertion fails. This indicates an error in our program.

- **fixture** A fixture is a set of objects in a defined state that serves as a basis for unit tests.

- **walkthrough** A walkthrough is an activity of working through a segment of code line by line while observing changes of state and other behavior of the application.

Part 2
Application structures

Improving structure with inheritance

Main concepts discussed in this chapter:

- inheritance
- subtyping
- substitution
- polymorphic variables

Java constructs discussed in this chapter:

`extends`, `super` (in constructor), cast, `Object`, autoboxing, wrapper classes

---

In this chapter, we introduce some additional object-oriented constructs to improve the general structure of our applications. The main concepts we shall use to design better program structures are *inheritance* and *polymorphism*.

Both of these concepts are central to the idea of object orientation, and you will discover later how they appear in various forms in everything we discuss from now on. However, it is not only the following chapters that rely heavily on these concepts. Many of the constructs and techniques discussed in earlier chapters are influenced by aspects of inheritance and polymorphism, and we shall revisit some issues introduced earlier and gain a fuller understanding of the interconnections between different parts of the Java language.

Inheritance is a powerful construct that can be used to create solutions to a variety of different problems. As always, we will discuss the important aspects using an example. In this example, we will first introduce only some of the problems that are addressed by using inheritance structures and discuss further uses and advantages of inheritance and polymorphism as we progress through this chapter.

The example we discuss to introduce these new structures is called *network*.

8.1 The *network* example

The *network* project implements a prototype of a small part of a social-network application like Facebook or Google+. The part we are concentrating on is the *news feed*—the list of messages that should appear on screen when a user opens the network's main page.

Here, we will start small and simple, with a view to extending and growing the application later. Initially, we have only two types of post appearing in our news feed: text posts (which we call *messages*) and photo posts consisting of a photo and a caption.

The part of the application that we are prototyping here is the engine that stores and displays these posts. The functionality that we want to provide with this prototype should at least include the following:

■ It should allow us to create text and photo posts.

■ Text posts consist of a message of arbitrary length, possibly spanning multiple lines. Photo posts consist of an image and a caption. Some additional details are stored with each post.

■ It should store this information permanently so that it can be used later.

■ It should provide a search function that allows us to find, for example, all posts by a certain user or all photos within a given date range.

■ It should allow us to display lists of posts, such as a list of the most recent posts or a list of all posts by a given user.

■ It should allow us to remove information.

The details we want to store for each message post are:

■ the username of the author

■ the text of the message

■ a time stamp (time of posting)

■ how many people like this post

■ a list of comments on this post by other users

The details we want to store for each photo post are:

■ the username of the author

■ the filename of the image to display

■ the caption for the photo (one line of text)

■ a time stamp (time of posting)

■ how many people like this post

■ a list of comments on this post by other users

8.1.1 The *network* project: classes and objects

To implement the application, we first have to decide what classes to use to model this problem. In this case, some of the classes are easy to identify. It is quite straightforward to decide that we should have a class MessagePost to represent message posts and a class PhotoPost to represent photo posts.

Objects of these classes should then encapsulate all the data we want to store about these objects (Figure 8.1).

Figure 8.1
Fields in
MessagePost and
PhotoPost objects

Figure 8.2
Details of the
MessagePost and
PhotoPost classes

Some of these data items should probably also have accessor and mutator methods (Figure 8.2).[1] For our purpose, it is not important to decide on the exact details of all the methods right now, but just to get a first impression of the design of this application. In this figure, we have defined accessor and mutator methods for those fields that may change over time ("liking" or "unliking" a post and adding a comment) and assume for now that the other fields are set in the constructor. We have also added a method called display that will show details of a MessagePost or PhotoPost object.

---

[1] The notation style for class diagrams that is used in this book and in BlueJ is a subset of a widely used notation called UML. Although we do not use everything from UML (by far), we attempt to use UML notation for those things that we show. The UML style defines how fields and methods are shown in a class diagram. The class is divided into three parts that show (in this order from the top) the class name, the fields, and the methods.

Once we have defined the MessagePost and PhotoPost classes, we can create as many post objects as we need—one object per message post or photo post that we want to store. Apart from this, we then need another object: an object representing the complete news feed that can hold a collection of message posts and a collection of photo posts. For this, we shall create a class called NewsFeed.

The NewsFeed object could itself hold two collection objects (for example, of types ArrayList <MessagePost> and ArrayList<PhotoPost>). One of these collections can then hold all message posts, the other all photo posts. An object diagram for this model is shown in Figure 8.3.

Figure 8.3
Objects in the *network* application

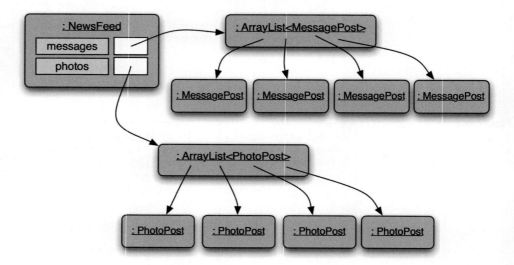

The corresponding class diagram, as BlueJ displays it, is shown in Figure 8.4. Note that BlueJ shows a slightly simplified diagram: classes from the standard Java library (ArrayList in this case) are not shown. Instead, the diagram focuses on user-defined classes. Also, BlueJ does not show field and method names in the diagram.

Figure 8.4
BlueJ class diagram of *network*

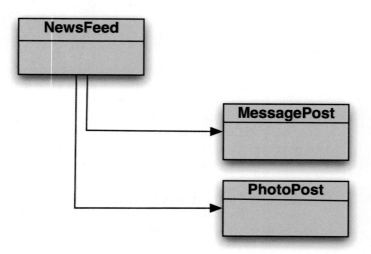

In practice, to implement the full *network* application, we would have more classes to handle things such as saving the data to a database and providing a user interface, most likely through a web browser. These are not very relevant to the present discussion, so we shall skip describing those for now and concentrate on a more detailed discussion of the core classes mentioned here.

8.1.2 *Network* source code

So far, the design of the three current classes (`MessagePost`, `PhotoPost`, and `NewsFeed`) has been very straightforward. Translating these ideas into Java code is equally easy. Code 8.1 shows the source code of the `MessagePost` class. It defines the appropriate fields, sets in its constructor all the data items that are not expected to change over time, and provides accessor and mutator methods where appropriate. It also implements the `display` method to show the post in the text terminal.

Code 8.1

Source code of the
`MessagePost` class

```java
import java.util.ArrayList;

/**
 * This class stores information about a post on a social network.
 * The main part of the post consists of a (possibly multiline)
 * text message. Other data such as author and time are also stored.
 *
 * @author Michael Kölling and David J. Barnes
 * @version 0.1
 */
public class MessagePost
{
    private String username; // username of the post's author
    private String message;  // an arbitrarily long, multiline message
    private long timestamp;
    private int likes;
    private ArrayList<String> comments;

    /**
     * Constructor for objects of class MessagePost.
     *
     * @param author    The username of the author of this post.
     * @param text      The text of this post.
     */
    public MessagePost(String author, String text)
    {
        username = author;
        message = text;
        timestamp = System.currentTimeMillis();
        likes = 0;
        comments = new ArrayList<String>();
    }
```

Code 8.1 continued

Source code of the `MessagePost` class

```java
/**
 * Record one more 'Like' indication from a user.
 */
public void like()
{
    likes++;
}

/**
 * Record that a user has withdrawn his/her 'Like' vote.
 */
public void unlike()
{
    if (likes > 0) {
        likes--;
    }
}

/**
 * Add a comment to this post.
 *
 * @param text   The new comment to add.
 */
public void addComment(String text)
{
    comments.add(text);
}

/**
 * Return the text of this post.
 *
 * @return The post's text.
 */
public String getText()
{
    return message;
}

/**
 * Return the time of creation of this post.
 *
 * @return The post's creation time, as a system time value.
 */
public long getTimeStamp()
{
    return timestamp;
}
```

**Code 8.1
continued**

Source code of the
`MessagePost` class

```java
/**
 * Display the details of this post.
 *
 * (Currently: Print to the text terminal. This is simulating
 * display in a web browser for now.)
 */
public void display()
{
    System.out.println(username);
    System.out.println(message);
    System.out.print(timeString(timestamp));
    if(likes > 0) {
        System.out.println("  -  " + likes + " people like this.");
    }
    else {
        System.out.println();
    }
    if(comments.isEmpty()) {
        System.out.println("   No comments.");
    }
    else {
        System.out.println("    " + comments.size() +
                                " comment(s). Click here to view.");
    }
}


/**
 * Create a string describing a time point in the past in relative
 * terms, such as "30 seconds ago" or "7 minutes ago".
 * Currently, only seconds and minutes are used for the string.
 *
 * @param time  The time value to convert (in system milliseconds)
 * @return      A relative time string for the given time
 */
private String timeString(long time)
{
    long current = System.currentTimeMillis();
    long pastMillis = current - time; // time passed in millisecs
    long seconds = pastMillis / 1000;
    long minutes = seconds / 60;
    if(minutes > 0) {
        return minutes + " minutes ago";
    }
```

Code 8.1 continued

Source code of the MessagePost class

```
        else {
            return seconds + " seconds ago";
        }
    }
}
```

Some details are worth mentioning briefly:

■ Some simplifications have been made. For example, comments for a post are stored as strings. In a more complete version, we would probably use a custom class for comments, as comments also have additional detail such as an author and a time. The "like" count is stored as a simple integer. We are currently not recording which user liked a post. While these simplifications make our prototype incomplete, they are not relevant for our main discussion here, and we shall leave them as they are for now.

■ The time stamp is stored as a single number, of type long. This reflects common practice. We can easily get the system time from the Java system, as a long value in milliseconds. We have also written a short method, called timeString, to convert this number into a relative time string, such as "5 minutes ago." In our final application, the system would have to use real time rather than system time, but again, system time is good enough for our prototype for now.

Note that we do not intend right now to make the implementation complete in any sense. It serves to provide a feel for what a class such as this might look like. We will use this as the basis for our following discussion of inheritance.

Now let us compare the MessagePost source code with the source code of class PhotoPost, shown in Code 8.2. Looking at both classes, we quickly notice that they are very similar. This is not surprising, because their purpose is similar: both are used to store information about newsfeed posts, and the different types of post have a lot in common. They differ only in their details, such as some of their fields and corresponding accessors and the bodies of the display method.

Code 8.2

Source code of the PhotoPost class

```
import java.util.ArrayList;

/**
 * This class stores information about a post on a social network.
 * The main part of the post consists of a photo and a caption.
 * Other data such as author and time are also stored.
 *
 * @author Michael Kölling and David J. Barnes
 * @version 0.1
 */
public class PhotoPost
{
    private String username;  // username of the post's author
    private String filename;  // the name of the image file
```

**Code 8.2
continued**

Source code of the
PhotoPost class

```java
private String caption;    // a one-line image caption
private long timestamp;
private int likes;
private ArrayList<String> comments;

/**
 * Constructor for objects of class PhotoPost.
 *
 * @param author    The username of the author of this post.
 * @param filename  The filename of the image in this post.
 * @param caption   A caption for the image.
 */
public PhotoPost(String author, String filename, String caption)
{
    username = author;
    this.filename = filename;
    this.caption = caption;
    timestamp = System.currentTimeMillis();
    likes = 0;
    comments = new ArrayList<String>();
}

/**
 * Record one more 'Like' indication from a user.
 */
public void like()
{
    likes++;
}

/**
 * Record that a user has withdrawn his/her 'Like' vote.
 */
public void unlike()
{
    if (likes > 0) {
        likes--;
    }
}

/**
 * Add a comment to this post.
 *
 * @param text  The new comment to add.
 */
```

**Code 8.2
continued**
Source code of the
PhotoPost class

```java
public void addComment(String text)
{
    comments.add(text);
}

/**
 * Return the filename of the image in this post.
 *
 * @return The post's image filename.
 */
public String getImageFile()
{
    return filename;
}

/**
 * Return the caption of the image of this post.
 *
 * @return The image's caption.
 */
public String getCaption()
{
    return caption;
}

/**
 * Return the time of creation of this post.
 *
 * @return The post's creation time, as a system time value.
 */
public long getTimeStamp()
{
    return timestamp;
}

/**
 * Display the details of this post.
 *
 * (Currently: Print to the text terminal. This is simulating
 * display in a web browser for now.)
 */
public void display()
{
    System.out.println(username);
    System.out.println("   [" + filename + "]");
    System.out.println("    " + caption);
    System.out.print(timeString(timestamp));
```

Code 8.2 continued

Source code of the PhotoPost class

```java
        if(likes > 0) {
            System.out.println("  -  " + likes + " people like this.");
        }
        else {
            System.out.println();
        }
        if(comments.isEmpty()) {
            System.out.println("   No comments.");
        }
        else {
            System.out.println("    " + comments.size() +
                                " comment(s). Click here to view.");
        }
    }

    /**
     * Create a string describing a time point in the past in relative
     * terms, such as "30 seconds ago" or "7 minutes ago".
     * Currently, only seconds and minutes are used for the string.
     *
     * @param time  The time value to convert (in system milliseconds)
     * @return      A relative time string for the given time
     */

    private String timeString(long time)
    {
        long current = System.currentTimeMillis();
        long pastMillis = current - time;  // time passed in millisecs
        long seconds = pastMillis / 1000;
        long minutes = seconds / 60;
        if(minutes > 0) {
            return minutes + " minutes ago";
        }
        else {
            return seconds + " seconds ago";
        }
    }
}
```

Next, let us examine the source code of the NewsFeed class (Code 8.3). It too is quite simple. It defines two lists (each based on class ArrayList) to hold the collection of message posts and the collection of photo posts. The constructor is where the empty lists are created. It then provides two methods for adding items: one for adding message posts, one for adding photo posts. The last method, named show, prints a list of all message and photo posts to the text terminal.

Code 8.3
Source code of the
NewsFeed class

```java
import java.util.ArrayList;

/**
 * The NewsFeed class stores news posts for the news feed in a
 * social-network application (like FaceBook or Google+).
 *
 * Display of the posts is currently simulated by printing the
 * details to the terminal. (Later, this should display in a browser.)
 *
 * This version does not save the data to disk, and it does not
 * provide any search or ordering functions.
 *
 * @author Michael Kölling and David J. Barnes
 * @version 0.1
 */
public class NewsFeed
{
    private ArrayList<MessagePost> messages;
    private ArrayList<PhotoPost> photos;

    /**
     * Construct an empty news feed.
     */
    public NewsFeed()
    {
        messages = new ArrayList<MessagePost>();
        photos = new ArrayList<PhotoPost>();
    }

    /**
     * Add a text post to the news feed.
     *
     * @param text  The text post to be added.
     */
    public void addMessagePost(MessagePost message)
    {
        messages.add(message);
    }

    /**
     * Add a photo post to the news feed.
     *
     * @param photo  The photo post to be added.
     */
    public void addPhotoPost(PhotoPost photo)
    {
        photos.add(photo);
    }
```

Code 8.3 continued

Source code of the NewsFeed class

```
    /**
     * Show the news feed. Currently: print the news feed details
     * to the terminal. (To do: replace this later with display
     * in web browser.)
     */
    public void show()
    {
        // display all text posts
        for(MessagePost message : messages) {
            message.display();
            System.out.println();    // empty line between posts
        }

        // display all photos
        for(PhotoPost photo : photos) {
            photo.display();
            System.out.println();    // empty line between posts
        }
    }
}
```

This is by no means a complete application. It has no user interface yet (so it will not be usable outside BlueJ), and the data entered is not stored to the file system or in a database. This means that all data entered will be lost each time the application ends. There are no functions to sort the displayed list of posts—for example, by date and time or by relevance. Currently, we will always get messages first, in the order in which they were entered, followed by the photos. Also, the functions for entering and editing data, as well as searching for data and displaying it, are not flexible enough for what we would want from a real program.

However, this does not matter in our context. We can work on improving the application later. The basic structure is there, and it works. This is enough for us to discuss design problems and possible improvements.

Exercise 8.1 Open the project *network-v1*. It contains the classes exactly as we have discussed them here. Create some MessagePost objects and some PhotoPost objects. Create a NewsFeed object. Enter the posts into the news feed, and then display the feed's contents.

Exercise 8.2 Try the following. Create a MessagePost object. Enter it into the news feed. Display the news feed. You will see that the post has no associated comments. Add a comment to the MessagePost object on the object bench (the one you entered into the news feed). When you now list the news feed again, will the post listed there have a comment attached? Try it. Explain the behavior you observe.

8.1.3 Discussion of the *network* application

Even though our application is not yet complete, we have done the most important part. We have defined the core of the application—the data structure that stores the essential information.

This was fairly straightforward so far, and we could now go ahead and design the rest that is still missing. Before doing that, though, we will discuss the quality of the solution so far.

There are several fundamental problems with our current solution. The most obvious one is *code duplication*.

We have noticed above that the `MessagePost` and `PhotoPost` classes are very similar. In fact, the majority of the classes' source code is identical, with only a few differences. We have already mentioned the problems associated with code duplication in Chapter 6. Apart from the annoying fact that we have to write everything twice (or copy and paste, then go through and fix all the differences), there are often problems associated with maintaining duplicated code. Many possible changes would have to be done twice. If, for example, the type of the comment list is changed from `ArrayList<String>` to `ArrayList<Comment>` (so that more details can be stored), this change has to be made once in the `MessagePost` class and again in the `PhotoPost` class. In addition, associated with maintenance of code duplication is always the danger of introducing errors, because the maintenance programmer might not realize that an identical change is needed at a second (or third) location.

There is another spot where we have code duplication: in the `NewsFeed` class. We can see that everything in that class is done twice—once for message posts and once for photo posts. The class defines two list variables, then creates two list objects, defines two `add` methods, and has two almost-identical blocks of code in the `show` method to print out the lists.

The problems with this duplication become clear when we analyze what we would have to do to add another type of post to this program. Imagine that we want to store not only text messages and photo posts, but also activity posts. Activity posts can be automatically generated and inform us about an activity of one of our contacts, such as "Fred has changed his profile picture" or "Ava is now friends with Feena." Activity posts seem similar enough that it should be easy to modify our application to do this. We would introduce another class, `ActivityPost`, and essentially write a third version of the source code that we already have in the `MessagePost` and `PhotoPost` classes. Then we have to work through the `NewsFeed` class and add another list variable, another list object, another `add` method, and another loop in the `show` method.

We would have to do the same for a fourth type of post. The more we do this, the more the code-duplication problem increases and the harder it becomes to make changes later. When we feel uncomfortable about a situation such as this one, it is often a good indicator that there may be a better alternative approach. For this particular case, the solution is found in object-oriented languages. They provide a distinctive feature that has a big impact on programs involving sets of similar classes. In the following sections, we will introduce this feature, which is called *inheritance*.

8.2 Using inheritance

Inheritance is a mechanism that provides us with a solution to our problem of duplication. The idea is simple: instead of defining the `MessagePost` and `PhotoPost` classes completely independently, we first define a class that contains everything these two have in common. We shall call this class `Post`. Then we can declare that a `MessagePost` is a `Post` and a `PhotoPost` is a `Post`. Finally, we add those extra details needed for a message post to the `MessagePost` class, and those for a photo post to the `PhotoPost` class. The essential feature of this technique is that we need to describe the common features only once.

Figure 8.5 shows a class diagram for this new structure. At the top, it shows the class `Post`, which defines all fields and methods that are common to all posts (messages and photos). Below the `Post` class, it shows the `MessagePost` and `PhotoPost` classes, which hold only those fields and methods that are unique to each particular class.

Figure 8.5
`MessagePost` and `PhotoPost` inheriting from `Post`

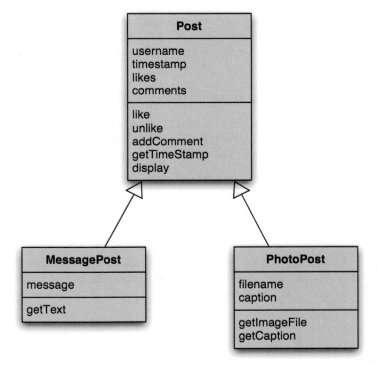

This new feature of object-oriented programming requires some new terminology. In a situation such as this one, we say that the class `MessagePost` *inherits from* class `Post`. Class `PhotoPost` also inherits from `Post`. In the vernacular of Java programs, the expression "class `MessagePost` *extends* class `Post`" could be used, because Java uses an `extends` keyword to define the inheritance relationship (as we shall see shortly). The arrows in the class diagram (usually drawn with hollow arrow heads) represent the inheritance relationship.

Class `Post` (the class that the others inherit from) is called the *parent class* or *superclass*. The inheriting classes (`MessagePost` and `PhotoPost` in this example) are referred to as *child classes* or *subclasses*. In this book, we will use the terms "superclass" and "subclass" to refer to the classes in an inheritance relationship.

Inheritance is sometimes also called an *is-a* relationship. The reason is that a subclass is a specialization of a superclass. We can say that "a message post *is a* post" and "a photo post *is a* post."

The purpose of using inheritance is now fairly obvious. Instances of class `MessagePost` will have all fields defined in class `MessagePost` *and* in class `Post`. (`MessagePost` inherits the fields from `Post`.) Instances of `PhotoPost` will have all fields defined in `PhotoPost` and in `Post`. Thus, we achieve the same as before, but we need to define the fields `username`, `timestamp`, `likes`, and `comments` only once, while being able to use them in two different places).

The same holds true for methods: instances of subclasses have all methods defined in both the superclass and the subclass. In general, we can say: because a message post is a post, a message-post object has everything that a post has, and more. And because a photo post is also a post, it has everything that a post has, and more.

Thus, inheritance allows us to create two classes that are quite similar, while avoiding the need to write the identical part twice. Inheritance has a number of other advantages, which we discuss below. First, however, we will take another, more general look at inheritance hierarchies.

8.3   Inheritance hierarchies

Concept:

Classes that are linked through inheritance relationships form an **inheritance hierarchy**.

Inheritance can be used much more generally than shown in the example above. More than two subclasses can inherit from the same superclass, and a subclass can, in turn, be a superclass to other subclasses. The classes then form an *inheritance hierarchy*.

The best-known example of an inheritance hierarchy is probably the classification of species used by biologists. A small part is shown in Figure 8.6. We can see that a poodle is a dog, which is a mammal, which is an animal.

We know some things about poodles—for example, that they are alive, they can bark, they eat meat, and they give birth to live young. On closer inspection, we see that we know some of these things not because they are poodles, but because they are dogs, mammals, or animals. An instance of class `Poodle` (an actual poodle) has all the characteristics of a poodle, a dog, a mammal, and an animal, because a poodle is a dog, which is a mammal, and so on.

Figure 8.6

An example of an inheritance hierarchy

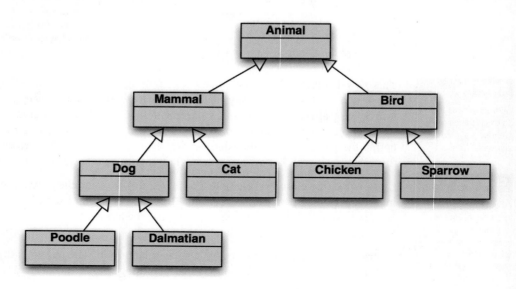

The principle is simple: inheritance is an abstraction technique that lets us categorize classes of objects under certain criteria and helps us specify the characteristics of these classes.

> **Exercise 8.3** Draw an inheritance hierarchy for the people in your place of study or work. For example, if you are a university student, then your university probably has students (first-year students, second-year students, ...), professors, tutors, office personnel, etc.

8.4 Inheritance in Java

Before discussing more details of inheritance, we will have a look at how inheritance is expressed in the Java language. Here is a segment of the source code of the Post class:

```java
public class Post
{
    private String username;   // username of the post's author
    private long timestamp;
    private int likes;
    private ArrayList<String> comments;
    // Constructors and methods omitted.
}
```

There is nothing special about this class so far. It starts with a normal class definition and defines Post's fields in the usual way. Next, we examine the source code of the MessagePost class:

```java
public class MessagePost extends Post
{
    private String message;
    // Constructors and methods omitted.
}
```

There are two things worth noting here. First, the keyword extends defines the inheritance relationship. The phrase "extends Post" specifies that this class is a subclass of the Post class. Second, the MessagePost class defines only those fields that are unique to MessagePost objects (only message in this case). The fields from Post are inherited and do not need to be listed here. Objects of class MessagePost will nonetheless have fields for username, timestamp, and so on.

Next, let us have a look at the source code of class PhotoPost:

```java
public class PhotoPost extends Post
{
    private String filename;
    private String caption;
    // Constructors and methods omitted.
}
```

This class follows the same pattern as the MessagePost class. It uses the extends keyword to define itself as a subclass of Post and defines its own additional fields.

8.4.1 Inheritance and access rights

To objects of other classes, `MessagePost` or `PhotoPost` objects appear just like all other types of objects. As a consequence, members defined as `public` in either the superclass or subclass portions will be accessible to objects of other classes, but members defined as `private` will be inaccessible.

In fact, the rule on privacy also applies between a subclass and its superclass: a subclass cannot access private members of its superclass. It follows that if a subclass method needed to access or change private fields in its superclass, then the superclass would need to provide appropriate accessor and/or mutator methods. However, an object of a subclass may call any public methods defined in its superclass as if they were defined locally in the subclass—no variable is needed, because the methods are all part of the same object.

This issue of access rights between super- and subclasses is one we will discuss further in Chapter 9 when we introduce the `protected` modifier.

Exercise 8.4 Open the project *network-v2*. This project contains a version of the *network* application, rewritten to use inheritance, as described above. Note that the class diagram displays the inheritance relationship. Open the source code of the `MessagePost` class and remove the "`extends Post`" phrase. Close the editor. What changes do you observe in the class diagram? Add the "`extends Post`" phrase again.

Exercise 8.5 Create a `MessagePost` object. Call some of its methods. Can you call the inherited methods (for example, `addComment`)? What do you observe about the inherited methods?

Exercise 8.6 In order to illustrate that a subclass can access non-private elements of its superclass without any special syntax, try the following slightly artificial modification to the `MessagePost` and `Post` classes. Create a method called `printShortSummary` in the `MessagePost` class. Its task is to print just the phrase "Message post from *NAME*", where *NAME* should show the name of the author. However, because the `username` field is private in the `Post` class, it will be necessary to add a public `getUserName` method to `Post`. Call this method from `printShortSummary` to access the name for printing. Remember that no special syntax is required when a subclass calls a superclass method. Try out your solution by creating a `MessagePost` object. Implement a similar method in the `PhotoPost` class.

8.4.2 Inheritance and initialization

When we create an object, the constructor of that object takes care of initializing all object fields to some reasonable state. We have to look more closely at how this is done in classes that inherit from other classes.

When we create a `MessagePost` object, we pass two parameters to the message post's constructor: the name of the author and the message text. One of these contains a value for a field defined in class `Post`, and the other a value for a field defined in class `MessagePost`. All of these fields must be correctly initialized, and Code 8.4 shows the code segments that are used to achieve this in Java.

Code 8.4

Initialization of subclass and superclass fields

```java
public class Post
{
    private String username;   // username of the post's author
    private long timestamp;
    private int likes;
    private ArrayList<String> comments;

    /**
     * Constructor for objects of class Post.
     *
     * @param author     The username of the author of this post.
     */
    public Post(String author)
    {
        username = author;
        timestamp = System.currentTimeMillis();
        likes = 0;
        comments = new ArrayList<String>();
    }

    // Methods omitted.
}

public class MessagePost extends Post
{
    private String message;   // an arbitrarily long, multi-line message

    /**
     * Constructor for objects of class MessagePost.
     *
     * @param author     The username of the author of this post.
     * @param text       The text of this post.
     */
    public MessagePost(String author, String text)
    {
        super(author);
        message = text;
    }

    // Methods omitted.
}
```

Several observations can be made here. First, the class `Post` has a constructor, even though we do not intend to create an instance of class `Post` directly.[2] This constructor receives the parameters needed to initialize the `Post` fields, and it contains the code to do this initialization. Second, the `MessagePost` constructor receives parameters needed to initialize both `Post` and `MessagePost` fields. It then contains the following line of code:

```
super(author);
```

The keyword `super` is a call from the subclass constructor to the constructor of the superclass. Its effect is that the `Post` constructor is executed as part of the `MessagePost` constructor's execution. When we create a message post, the `MessagePost` constructor is called, which, in turn, as its first statement, calls the `Post` constructor. The `Post` constructor initializes the post's fields, and then returns to the `MessagePost` constructor, which initializes the remaining field defined in the `MessagePost` class. For this to work, those parameters needed for the initialization of the post fields are passed on to the superclass constructor as parameters to the `super` call.

> **Concept:**
>
> **Superclass constructor** The constructor of a subclass must always invoke the constructor of its superclass as its first statement. If the source code does not include such a call, Java will attempt to insert a call automatically.

In Java, a subclass constructor must always call the *superclass constructor* as its first statement. If you do not write a call to a superclass constructor, the Java compiler will insert a superclass call automatically, to ensure that the superclass fields get properly initialized. The inserted call is equivalent to writing

```
super();
```

Inserting this call automatically works only if the superclass has a constructor without parameters (because the compiler cannot guess what parameter values should be passed). Otherwise, an error will be reported.

In general, it is a good idea to always include explicit superclass calls in your constructors, even if it is one that the compiler could generate automatically. We consider this good style, because it avoids the possibility of misinterpretation and confusion in case a reader is not aware of the automatic code generation.

> **Exercise 8.7** Set a breakpoint in the first line of the `MessagePost` class's constructor. Then create a `MessagePost` object. When the debugger window pops up, use *Step Into* to step through the code. Observe the instance fields and their initialization. Describe your observations.

8.5 *Network*: adding other post types

Now that we have our inheritance hierarchy set up for the *network* project so that the common elements of the items are in the `Post` class, it becomes a lot easier to add other types of posts. For instance, we might want to add event posts, which consist of a description of a standard event (e.g., "Fred has joined the 'Neal Stephenson fans' group."). Standard events might be a user joining a group, a user becoming friends with another, or a user changing their profile picture. To

---

[2] Currently, there is nothing actually preventing us from creating a `Post` object, although that was not our intention when we designed these classes. In Chapter 10, we shall see some techniques that allow us to make sure that `Post` objects cannot be created directly, but only `MessagePost` or `PhotoPost` objects.

achieve this, we can now define a new subclass of Post named EventPost (Figure 8.7). Because EventPost is a subclass of Post, it automatically inherits all fields and methods that we have already defined in Post. Thus, EventPost objects already have a username, a time stamp, a likes counter, and comments. We can then concentrate on adding attributes that are specific to event posts, such as the event type. The event type might be stored as an enumeration constant (see Chapter 6) or as a string describing the event.

Figure 8.7
Network items with an
EventPost class

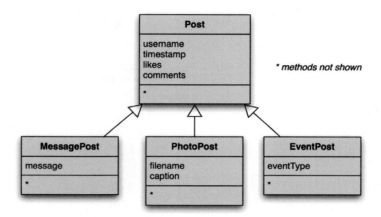

This is an example of how inheritance enables us to *reuse* existing work. We can reuse the code that we have written for photo posts and message posts (in the Post class) so that it also works for the EventPost class. The ability to reuse existing software components is one of the great benefits that we get from the inheritance facility. We will discuss this in more detail later.

Concept:

Inheritance allows us to **reuse** previously written classes in a new context.

This reuse has the effect that a lot less new code is needed when we now introduce additional post types. Because new post types can be defined as subclasses of Post, only the code that is actually different from Post has to be added.

Now imagine that we change the requirements a bit: event posts in our *network* application will not have a "Like" button or comments attached. They are for information only. How do we achieve this? Currently, because EventPost is a subclass of Post, it automatically inherits the likes and comments fields. Is this a problem?

We could leave everything as it is and decide to never display the likes count or comments for event posts—just ignore the fields. This does not feel right. Having the fields present but unused invites problems. Someday a maintenance programmer will come along who does not realize that these fields should not be used and try to process them.

Or we could write EventPost without inheriting from Post. But then we are back to code duplication for the username and timestamp fields and their methods.

The solution is to refactor the class hierarchy. We can introduce a new superclass for all posts that have comments attached (named CommentedPost), which is a subclass of Post (Figure 8.8). We then shift the likes and comments fields from the Post class to this new class. MessagePost and PhotoPost are now subclasses of our new CommentedPost class, while EventPost inherits from `Posts` directly. `MessagePost` objects inherit everything from both superclasses and have the same fields and methods as before. Objects of class `EventPost` will inherit the `username` and `timestamp`, but not the comments.

Figure 8.8
Adding more post
types to *network*

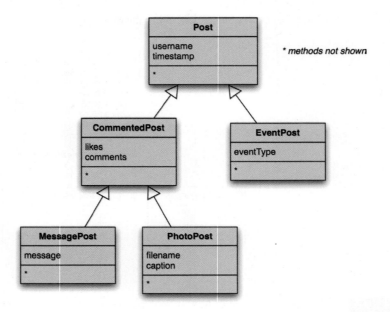

This is a very common situation in designing class hierarchies. When the hierarchy does not seem to fit properly, we have to refactor the hierarchy.

Classes that are not intended to be used to create instances, but whose purpose is exclusively to serve as superclasses for other classes (such as `Post` and `CommentedPost`), are called *abstract classes*. We shall investigate this in more detail in Chapter 10.

Exercise 8.8 Open the *network-v2* project. Add a class for event posts to the project. Create some event-post objects and test that all methods work as expected.

8.6 Advantages of inheritance (so far)

We have seen several advantages of using inheritance for the *network* application. Before we explore other aspects of inheritance, we shall summarize the general advantages we have encountered so far:

■ **Avoiding code duplication** The use of inheritance avoids the need to write identical or very similar copies of code twice (or even more often).

■ **Code reuse** Existing code can be reused. If a class similar to the one we need already exists, we can sometimes subclass the existing class and reuse some of the existing code rather than having to implement everything again.

■ **Easier maintenance** Maintaining the application becomes easier, because the relationship between the classes is clearly expressed. A change to a field or a method that is shared between different types of subclasses needs to be made only once.

■ **Extendibility** Using inheritance, it becomes much easier to extend an existing application in certain ways.

Exercise 8.9 Order these items into an inheritance hierarchy: apple, ice cream, bread, fruit, food item, cereal, orange, dessert, chocolate mousse, baguette.

Exercise 8.10 In what inheritance relationship might a *touch pad* and a *mouse* be? (We are talking about computer input devices here, not small furry mammals.)

Exercise 8.11 Sometimes things are more difficult than they first seem. Consider this: In what kind of inheritance relationship are *Rectangle* and *Square*? What are the arguments? Discuss.

8.7 Subtyping

The one thing we have not yet investigated is how the code in the NewsFeed class was changed when we modified our project to use inheritance. Code 8.5 shows the full source code of class NewsFeed. We can compare this with the original source shown in Code 8.3.

Code 8.5

Source code of the NewsFeed class (second version)

```java
import java.util.ArrayList;

/**
 * The NewsFeed class stores news posts for the news feed in a
 * social-network application (like FaceBook or Google+).
 *
 * Display of the posts is currently simulated by printing the
 * details to the terminal. (Later, this should display in a browser.)
 *
 * This version does not save the data to disk, and it does not
 * provide any search or ordering functions.
 *
 * @author Michael Kölling and David J. Barnes
 * @version 0.2
 */
public class NewsFeed
{
    private ArrayList<Post> posts;
```

Code 8.5 continued

Source code of the NewsFeed class (second version)

```java
/**
 * Construct an empty news feed.
 */
public NewsFeed()
{
    posts = new ArrayList<Post>();
}

/**
 * Add a post to the news feed.
 *
 * @param post  The post to be added.
 */
public void addPost(Post post)
{
    posts.add(post);
}

/**
 * Show the news feed. Currently: print the news feed details
 * to the terminal. (To do: replace this later with display
 * in web browser.)
 */
public void show()
{
    // display all posts
    for(Post post : posts) {
        post.display();
        System.out.println();    // empty line between posts
    }
}
}
```

As we can see, the code has become significantly shorter and simpler since our change to use inheritance. Where in the first version (Code 8.3) everything had to be done twice, it now exists only once. We have only one collection, only one method to add posts, and one loop in the show method.

The reason why we could shorten the source code is that, in the new version, we can use the type Post where we previously used MessagePost and PhotoPost. We investigate this first by examining the addPost method.

In our first version, we had two methods to add posts to the news feed. They had the following headers:

```java
public void addMessagePost(MessagePost message)
public void addPhotoPost(PhotoPost photo)
```

In our new version, we have a single method to serve the same purpose:

```
public void addPost(Post post)
```

The parameters in the original version are defined with the types `MessagePost` and `PhotoPost`, ensuring that we pass `MessagePost` and `PhotoPost` objects to these methods, because actual parameter types must match the formal parameter types. So far, we have interpreted the requirement that parameter types must match as meaning "must be of the same type"—for instance, that the type name of an actual parameter must be the same as the type name of the corresponding formal parameter. This is only part of the truth, in fact, because an object of a subclass can be used wherever its superclass type is required.

8.7.1 Subclasses and subtypes

We have discussed earlier that classes define types. The type of an object that was created from class `MessagePost` is `MessagePost`. We also just discussed that classes may have subclasses. Thus, the types defined by the classes can have subtypes. In our example, the type `MessagePost` is a subtype of type `Post`.

8.7.2 Subtyping and assignment

When we want to assign an object to a variable, the type of the object must match the type of the variable. For example,

```
Car myCar = new Car();
```

is a valid assignment, because an object of type `Car` is assigned to a variable declared to hold objects of type `Car`. Now that we know about inheritance, we must state the typing rule more completely: a variable can hold objects of its declared type or of any subtype of its declared type.

Imagine that we have a class `Vehicle` with two subclasses, `Car` and `Bicycle` (Figure 8.9). In this case, the typing rule admits that the following assignments are all legal:

```
Vehicle v1 = new Vehicle();
Vehicle v2 = new Car();
Vehicle v3 = new Bicycle();
```

Figure 8.9
An inheritance hierarchy

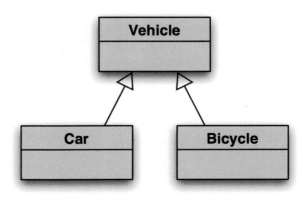

The type of a variable declares what it can store. Declaring a variable of type `Vehicle` states that this variable can hold vehicles. But because a car is a vehicle, it is perfectly legal to store a car in a variable that is intended for vehicles. (Think of the variable as a garage: if someone tells you that you may park a vehicle in a garage, you would think that parking either a car or a bicycle in the garage would be okay.)

This principle is known as *substitution*. In object-oriented languages, we can substitute a subclass object where a superclass object is expected, because the subclass object is a special case of the superclass. If, for example, someone asks us to give them a pen, we can fulfill the request perfectly well by giving them a fountain pen or a ballpoint pen. Both fountain pen and ballpoint pen are subclasses of pen, so supplying either where an object of class `Pen` was expected is fine.

However, doing it the other way is not allowed:

```
Car c1 = new Vehicle(); // this is an error!
```

This statement attempts to store a `Vehicle` object in a `Car` variable. Java will not allow this, and an error will be reported if you try to compile this statement. The variable is declared to be able to store cars. A vehicle, on the other hand, may or may not be a car—we do not know. Thus, the statement may be wrong and is not allowed.

Similarly:

```
Car c2 = new Bicycle(); // this is an error!
```

This is also an illegal statement. A bicycle is not a car (or, more formally, the type `Bicycle` is not a subtype of `Car`), and thus the assignment is not allowed.

Exercise 8.12 Assume that we have four classes: `Person`, `Teacher`, `Student`, and `PhDStudent`. `Teacher` and `Student` are both subclasses of `Person`. `PhDStudent` is a subclass of `Student`.

a. Which of the following assignments are legal, and why or why not?

```
Person p1 = new Student();
Person p2 = new PhDStudent();
PhDStudent phd1 = new Student();
Teacher t1 = new Person();
Student s1 = new PhDStudent();
```

b. Suppose that we have the following legal declarations and assignments:

```
Person p1 = new Person();
Person p2 = new Person();
PhDStudent phd1 = new PhDStudent();
Teacher t1 = new Teacher();
Student s1 = new Student();
```

Based on those just mentioned, which of the following assignments are legal, and why or why not?

```
s1 = p1;
s1 = p2;
p1 = s1;
```

```
t1 = s1;
s1 = phd1;
phd1 = s1;
```

Exercise 8.13 Test your answers to the previous question by creating bare-bones versions of the classes mentioned in that exercise and trying it out in BlueJ.

8.7.3 Subtyping and parameter passing

Passing a parameter (that is, assigning an actual parameter to a formal parameter variable) behaves in exactly the same way as an assignment to a variable. This is why we can pass an object of type `MessagePost` to a method that has a parameter of type `Post`. We have the following definition of the `addPost` method in class `NewsFeed`:

```
public class NewsFeed
{
    public void addPost(Post post)
    {
        . . .
    }
}
```

We can now use this method to add message posts and photo posts to the feed:

```
NewsFeed feed = new NewsFeed();
MessagePost message = new MessagePost(...);
PhotoPost photo = new PhotoPost(...);

feed.addPost(message);
feed.addPost(photo);
```

Because of subtyping rules, we need only one method (with a parameter of type `Post`) to add both `MessagePost` and `PhotoPost` objects.

We will discuss subtyping in more detail in the next chapter.

8.7.4 Polymorphic variables

Variables holding object types in Java are *polymorphic* variables. The term "polymorphic" (literally, *many shapes*) refers to the fact that a variable can hold objects of different types (namely, the declared type or any subtype of the declared type). Polymorphism appears in object-oriented languages in several contexts—polymorphic variables are just the first example. We will discuss other incarnations of polymorphism in more detail in the next chapter.

For now, we just observe how the use of a polymorphic variable helps us simplify our show method. The body of this method is

```
for(Post post : posts) {
    post.display();
    System.out.println();    // empty line between posts
}
```

Here, we iterate through the list of posts (held in an `ArrayList` in the `posts` variable). We get out each post and then invoke its `display` method. Note that the actual posts that we get out of the list are of type `MessagePost` or `PhotoPost`, not of type `Post`. We can, however, use a loop variable of type `Post`, because variables are polymorphic. The `post` variable is able to hold `MessagePost` and `PhotoPost` objects, because these are subtypes of `Post`.

Thus, the use of inheritance in this example has removed the need for two separate loops in the `show` method. Inheritance avoids code duplication not only in the server classes, but also in clients of those classes.

Note When doing the exercises, you may have noticed that the `show` method has a problem: not all details are printed out. Solving this problem requires some more explanation. We will provide this in the next chapter.

Exercise 8.14 What has to change in the `NewsFeed` class when another `Post` subclass (for example, a class `EventPost`) is added? Why?

8.7.5 Casting

Sometimes the rule that we cannot assign from a supertype to a subtype is more restrictive than necessary. If we know that the supertype variable holds a subtype object, the assignment could actually be allowed. For example:

```
Vehicle v;
Car c = new Car();
v = c; // correct
c = v; // error
```

The above statements would not compile: we get a compiler error in the last line, because assigning a `Vehicle` variable to a `Car` variable (supertype to subtype) is not allowed. However, if we execute these statements in sequence, we know that we could actually allow this assignment. We can see that the variable v actually contains an object of type `Car`, so the assignment to c would be okay. The compiler is not that smart. It translates the code line by line, so it looks at the last line in isolation without knowing what is currently stored in variable v. This is called type loss. The type of the object in v is actually `Car`, but the compiler does not know this.

We can get around this problem by explicitly telling the type system that the variable v holds a `Car` object. We do this using a *cast operator*:

```
c = (Car) v; // okay
```

The cast operator consists of the name of a type (here, `Car`) written in parentheses in front of a variable or an expression. Doing this will cause the compiler to believe that the object is a `Car`, and it will not report an error. At runtime, however, the Java system will check that it really is a `Car`. If we were careful, and it is truly is a `Car`, everything is fine. If the object in v is of another type, the runtime system will indicate an error (called a `ClassCastException`), and the program will stop.[3]

---

[3] Exceptions are discussed in detail in Chapter 12.

Now consider this code fragment, in which Bicycle is also a subclass of Vehicle:

```
Vehicle v;
Car c;
Bicycle b;
c = new Car();
v = c; // okay
b = (Bicycle) c; // compile time error!
b = (Bicycle) v; // runtime error!
```

The last two assignments will both fail. The attempt to assign c to b (even with the cast) will be a compile-time error. The compiler notices that Car and Bicycle do not form a subtype/supertype relationship, so c can never hold a Bicycle object—the assignment could never work.

The attempt to assign v to b (with the cast) will be accepted at compile time but will fail at runtime. Vehicle is a superclass of Bicycle, and thus v can potentially hold a Bicycle object. At runtime, however, it turns out that the object in v is not a Bicycle but a Car, and the program will terminate prematurely.

Casting should be avoided wherever possible, because it can lead to runtime errors, and that is clearly something we do not want. The compiler cannot help us to ensure correctness in this case.

In practice, casting is very rarely needed in a well-structured object-oriented program. In almost all cases, when you use a cast in your code, you could restructure your code to avoid this cast and end up with a better-designed program. This usually involves replacing the cast with a polymorphic method call (more about this in the next chapter).

8.8 The Object class

All classes have a superclass. So far, it has appeared as if most classes we have seen do not have a superclass. In fact, while we can declare an explicit superclass for a class, all classes that have no superclass declaration implicitly inherit from a class called Object.

Concept:

All classes with no explicit superclass have Object as their superclass.

Object is a class from the Java standard library that serves as a superclass for all objects. Writing a class declaration such as

```
public class Person
{
    . . .
}
```

is equivalent to writing

```
public class Person extends Object
{
    . . .
}
```

The Java compiler automatically inserts the Object superclass for all classes without an explicit extends declaration, so it is never necessary to do this for yourself. Every single class (with the sole exception of the Object class itself) inherits from Object, either directly or indirectly. Figure 8.10 shows some randomly chosen classes to illustrate this.

Figure 8.10
All classes inherit from
`Object`

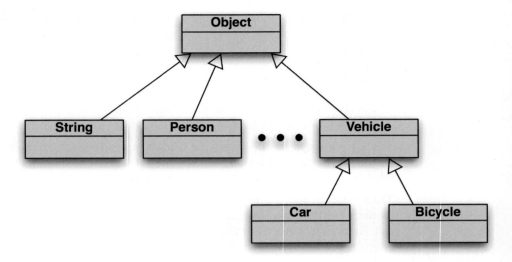

Having a common superclass for all objects serves two purposes: First, we can declare polymorphic variables of type `Object` to hold any object. Having variables that can hold any object type is not often useful, but there are some situations where this can help. Second, the `Object` class can define some methods that are then automatically available for every existing object. Of particular importance are the methods `toString`, `equals`, and `hashCode` which `Object` defines. This second point becomes interesting a bit later, and we shall discuss this in more detail in the next chapter.

8.9 Autoboxing and wrapper classes

We have seen that, with suitable parameterization, the collection classes can store objects of any object type. There remains one problem: Java has some types that are not object types.

As we know, the simple types—such as `int`, `boolean`, and `char`—are separate from object types. Their values are not instances of classes, and they do not inherit from the `Object` class. Because of this, they are not subtypes of `Object`, and it would not normally be possible to add them into a collection.

Concept:

Autoboxing is performed automatically when a primitive-type value is used in a context requiring a wrapper type.

This is unfortunate. There are situations in which we might want to create a list of `int` values or a set of `char` values, for instance. What can we do?

Java's solution to this problem is *wrapper classes*. Every primitive type in Java has a corresponding wrapper class that represents the same type but is a real object type. The wrapper class for `int`, for example, is called `Integer`. A complete list of simple types and their wrapper classes is given in Appendix B.

The following statement explicitly wraps the value of the primitive `int` variable `ix` in an `Integer` object:

```
Integer iwrap = new Integer(ix);
```

And now `iwrap` could obviously easily be stored in an `ArrayList<Integer>` collection, for instance. However, storing of primitive values into an object collection is made even easier through a compiler feature known as *autoboxing*.

Whenever a value of a primitive type is used in a context that requires a wrapper type, the compiler automatically wraps the primitive-type value in an appropriate wrapper object. This means that primitive-type values can be added directly to a collection:

```
private ArrayList<Integer> markList;
...
public void storeMarkInList(int mark)
{
    markList.add(mark);
}
```

The reverse operation—*unboxing*—is also performed automatically, so retrieval from a collection might look like this:

```
int firstMark = markList.remove(0);
```

Autoboxing is also applied whenever a primitive-type value is passed as a parameter to a method that expects a wrapper type and when a primitive-type value is stored in a wrapper-type variable. Similarly, unboxing is applied when a wrapper-type value is passed as a parameter to a method that expects a primitive-type value and when stored in a primitive-type variable. It is worth noting that this almost makes it appear as if primitive types can be stored in collections. However, the type of the collection must still be declared using the wrapper type (e.g., `ArrayList<Integer>`, not `ArrayList<int>`).

8.10 The collection hierarchy

The Java library uses inheritance extensively in the definition of the collections classes. Class `ArrayList`, for example, inherits from a class called `AbstractList`, which, in turn, inherits from `AbstractCollection`. We shall not discuss this hierarchy here, because it is described in detail at various easily accessible places. One good description is at Oracle's web site at `http://download.oracle.com/javase/tutorial/collections/index.html`.

Note that some details of this hierarchy require an understanding of Java *interfaces*. We discuss those in Chapter 10.

Exercise 8.15 Use the documentation of the Java standard class libraries to find out about the inheritance hierarchy of the collection classes. Draw a diagram showing the hierarchy.

8.11 Summary

This chapter has presented a first view of inheritance. All classes in Java are arranged in an inheritance hierarchy. Each class may have an explicitly declared superclass, or it inherits implicitly from the class `Object`.

Subclasses usually represent specializations of superclasses. Because of this, the inheritance relationship is also referred to as an is-a relationship (a car *is-a* vehicle).

Subclasses inherit all fields and methods of a superclass. Objects of subclasses have all fields and methods declared in their own classes, as well as those from all superclasses. Inheritance relationships can be used to avoid code duplication, to reuse existing code, and to make an application more maintainable and extendable.

Subclasses also form subtypes, which leads to polymorphic variables. Subtype objects may be substituted for supertype objects, and variables are allowed to hold objects that are instances of subtypes of their declared type.

Inheritance allows the design of class structures that are easier to maintain and more flexible. This chapter contains only an introduction to the use of inheritance for the purpose of improving program structures. More uses of inheritance and their benefits will be discussed in the following chapters.

Terms introduced in this chapter

inheritance, superclass (parent), subclass (child), is-a, inheritance hierarchy, abstract class, subtype substitution, polymorphic variable, type loss, cast, autoboxing, wrapper classes

Concept summary

- **inheritance** Inheritance allows us to define one class as an extension of another.

- **superclass** A superclass is a class that is extended by another class.

- **subclass** A subclass is a class that extends (inherits from) another class. It inherits all fields and methods from its superclass.

- **inheritance hierarchy** Classes that are linked through inheritance relationships form an inheritance hierarchy.

- **superclass constructor** The constructor of a subclass must always invoke the constructor of its superclass as its first statement. If the source code does not include such a call, Java will attempt to insert a call automatically.

- **reuse** Inheritance allows us to reuse previously written classes in a new context.

- **subtype** As an analog to the class hierarchy, types form a type hierarchy. The type defined by a subclass definition is a subtype of the type of its superclass.

- **variables and subtypes** Variables may hold objects of their declared type or of any subtype of their declared type.

- **substitution** Subtype objects may be used wherever objects of a supertype are expected. This is known as substitution.

- **Object** All classes with no explicit superclass have `Object` as their superclass.

- **autoboxing** Autoboxing is performed automatically when a primitive-type value is used in a context requiring a wrapper type.

Exercise 8.16 Go back to the *lab-classes* project from Chapter 1. Add instructors to the project (every lab class can have many students and a single instructor). Use inheritance to avoid code duplication between students and instructors (both have a name, contact details, etc.).

Exercise 8.17 Draw an inheritance hierarchy representing parts of a computer system (processor, memory, disk drive, DVD drive, printer, scanner, keyboard, mouse, etc.).

Exercise 8.18 Look at the code below. You have four classes (O, X, T, and M) and a variable of each of these.

```
O o;
X x;
T t;
M m;
```

The following assignments are all legal (assume that they all compile):

```
m = t;
m = x;
o = t;
```

The following assignments are all illegal (they cause compiler errors):

```
o = m;
o = x;
x = o;
```

What can you say about the relationships of these classes? Draw a class diagram.

Exercise 8.19 Draw an inheritance hierarchy of `AbstractList` and all its (direct and indirect) subclasses as they are defined in the Java standard library.

More about inheritance

Main concepts discussed in this chapter:

- method polymorphism
- overriding
- static and dynamic type
- dynamic method lookup

Java constructs discussed in this chapter:

`super` (in method), `toString`, `protected`, `instanceof`

The last chapter introduced the main concepts of inheritance by discussing the *network* example. While we have seen the foundations of inheritance, there are still numerous important details that we have not yet investigated. Inheritance is central to understanding and using object-oriented languages, and understanding it in detail is necessary to progress from here.

In this chapter, we shall continue to use the *network* example to explore the most important of the remaining issues surrounding inheritance and polymorphism.

9.1 The problem: *network's* display method

When you experimented with the *network* examples in Chapter 8, you probably noticed that the second version—the one using inheritance—has a problem: the `display` method does not show all of a post's data.

Let us look at an example. Assume that we create a `MessagePost` and a `PhotoPost` object with the following data:

The message post:

Leonardo da Vinci

Had a great idea this morning.
But now I forgot what it was. Something to do with flying ...

40 seconds ago. 2 people like this.

No comments.

The photo post:

Alexander Graham Bell

[experiment.jpg]   I think I might call this thing 'telephone'.

12 minutes ago. 4 people like this.

No comments.

If we enter these objects into the news feed[1] and then invoke the first version of the news feed's show method (the one without inheritance), it prints

```
Leonardo da Vinci
Had a great idea this morning.
But now I forgot what it was. Something to do with flying ...
40 seconds ago  -  2 people like this.
  No comments.

Alexander Graham Bell
[experiment.jpg]
I think I might call this thing 'telephone'.
12 minutes ago  -  4 people like this.
  No comments.
```

While the formatting isn't pretty (because, in the text terminal, we don't have formatting options available), all the information is there, and we can imagine how the show method might be adapted later to show the data in a nicer formatting in a different user interface.

Compare this with the second *network* version (with inheritance), which prints only

```
Leonardo da Vinci
40 seconds ago  -  2 people like this.
  No comments.

Alexander Graham Bell
12 minutes ago  -  4 people like this.
  No comments.
```

We note that the message post's text, as well as the photo post's image filename and caption, are missing. The reason for this is simple. The display method in this version is implemented in the Post class, not in MessagePost and PhotoPost (Figure 9.1). In the methods of Post, only the fields declared in Post are available. If we tried to access the MessagePost's message field from Post's display method, an error would be reported. This illustrates the important principle that inheritance is a one-way street: MessagePost inherits the fields of Post, but Post still does not know anything about fields in its subclasses.

---

[1] The text for the message post is a two-line string. You can enter a multiline text into a string by using "\n" in the string for the line break.

Figure 9.1
Display, version 1:
display method in
superclass

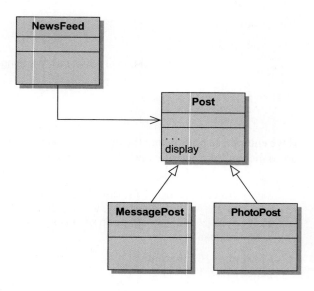

9.2 Static type and dynamic type

Trying to solve the problem of developing a complete polymorphic display method leads us into a discussion of *static* and *dynamic types* and *method lookup*. But let us start at the beginning.

A first attempt to solve the display problem might be to move the display method to the sub-classes (Figure 9.2). That way, because the method would now belong to the MessagePost and PhotoPost classes, it could access the specific fields of MessagePost and PhotoPost. It could also access the inherited fields by calling accessor methods defined in the Post class. That should enable it to display a complete set of information again. Try out this approach by completing Exercise 9.1.

Figure 9.2
Display, version 2:
display method
in subclasses

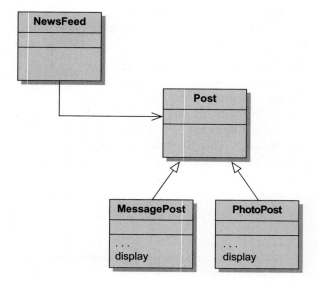

Exercise 9.1 Open your last version of the *network* project. (You can use *network-v2* if you do not have your own version yet.) Remove the `display` method from class `Post` and move it into the `MessagePost` and `PhotoPost` classes. Compile. What do you observe?

When we try to move the `display` method from `Post` to the subclasses, we notice that we have some problems: the project does not compile any more. There are two fundamental issues:

- We get errors in the `MessagePost` and `PhotoPost` classes, because we cannot access the superclass fields.

- We get an error in the `NewsFeed` class, because it cannot find the `display` method.

The reason for the first sort of error is that the fields in `Post` have private access and so are inaccessible to any other class—including subclasses. Because we do not wish to break encapsulation and make these fields public, as was suggested above, the easiest way to solve this is to define public accessor methods for them. However, in Section 9.9, we shall introduce a further type of access designed specifically to support the superclass–subclass relationship.

The reason for the second sort of error requires a more detailed explanation, and this is explored in the next section.

9.2.1 Calling `display` from `NewsFeed`

First, we investigate the problem of calling the `display` method from `NewsFeed`. The relevant lines of code in the `NewsFeed` class are:

```
for(Post post : posts) {
    post.display();
    System.out.println();
}
```

The for-each statement retrieves each post from the collection; the first statement inside its body tries to invoke the `display` method on the post. The compiler informs us that it cannot find a `display` method for the post.

On the one hand, this seems logical; `Post` does not have a `display` method any more (see Figure 9.2).

On the other hand, it seems illogical and is annoying. We know that every `Post` object in the collection is in fact a `MessagePost` or a `PhotoPost` object, and both have `display` methods. This should mean that `post.display()` ought to work, because, whatever it is— `MessagePost` or `PhotoPost`—we know that it does have a `display` method.

To understand in detail why it doesn't work, we need to look more closely at types. Consider the following statement:

```
Car c1 = new Car();
```

We say that the type of c1 is `Car`. Before we encountered inheritance, there was no need to distinguish whether by "type of c1" we meant "the type of the variable c1" or "the type of the object stored in c1." It did not matter, because the type of the variable and the type of the object were always the same.

Now that we know about subtyping, we need to be more precise. Consider the following statement:

```
Vehicle v1 = new Car();
```

What is the type of v1? That depends on what precisely we mean by "type of v1." The type of the variable v1 is Vehicle; the type of the object stored in v1 is Car. Through subtyping and substitution rules, we now have situations where the type of the variable and the type of the object stored in it are not exactly the same.

Let us introduce some terminology to make it easier to talk about this issue:

Concept:

The **static type** of a variable v is the type as declared in the source code in the variable declaration statement.

Concept

The **dynamic type** of a variable v is the type of the object that is currently stored in v.

- We call the declared type of the variable the *static type,* because it is declared in the source code—the static representation of the program.

- We call the type of the object stored in a variable the *dynamic type,* because it depends on assignments at runtime—the dynamic behavior of the program.

Thus, looking at the explanations above, we can be more precise: the static type of v1 is Vehicle, the dynamic type of v1 is Car. We can now also rephrase our discussion about the call to the post's display method in the NewsFeed class. At the time of the call

```
post.display();
```

the static type of post is Post, while the dynamic type is either MessagePost or PhotoPost (Figure 9.3). We do not know which one of these it is, assuming that we have entered both MessagePost and PhotoPost objects into the feed.

Figure 9.3
Variable of type Post containing an object of type PhotoPost

Post post

The compiler reports an error because, for type checking, the static type is used. The dynamic type is often only known at runtime, so the compiler has no other choice but to use the static type if it wants to do any checks at compile time. The static type of post is Post, and Post does not have a display method. It makes no difference that all known subtypes of Post do have a display method. The behavior of the compiler is reasonable in this respect, because it has no guarantee that *all* subclasses of Post will, indeed, define a display method, and this is impossible to check in practice.

In other words, to make this call work, class Post must have a display method, so we appear to be back to our original problem without having made any progress.

> **Exercise 9.2** In your *network* project, add a display method in class Post again. For now, write the method body with a single statement that prints out only the username. Then modify the display methods in MessagePost and PhotoPost so that the MessagePost version prints out only the message and the PhotoPost version prints only the caption. This removes the other errors encountered above (we shall come back to those below).

You should now have a situation corresponding to Figure 9.4, with display methods in three classes. Compile your project. (If there are errors, remove them. This design should work.)

Before executing, predict which of the display methods will get called if you execute the news feed's show method.

Try it out. Enter a message post and a photo post into the news feed and call the news feed's show method. Which display methods were executed? Was your prediction correct? Try to explain your observations.

Figure 9.4

Display, version 3: display method in subclasses and superclass

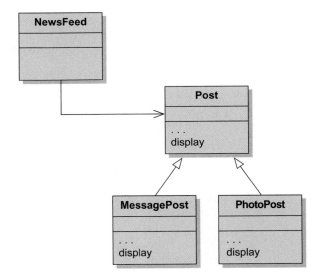

9.3 Overriding

The next design we shall discuss is one where both the superclass and the subclasses have a display method (Figure 9.4). The header of all the display methods is exactly the same.

Code 9.1 shows the relevant details of the source code of all three classes. Class Post has a display method that prints out all the fields that are declared in Post (those common to message posts and photo posts), and the subclasses MessagePost and PhotoPost print out the fields specific to MessagePost and PhotoPost objects, respectively.

Code 9.1

Source code of the display methods in all three classes

```java
public class Post
{
    ...
    public void display()
    {
        System.out.println(username);
        System.out.print(timeString(timestamp));
```

**Code 9.1
continued**

Source code of the
`display` methods
in all three classes

```java
        if(likes > 0) {
            System.out.println("  -  " + likes + " people like this.");
        }
        else {
            System.out.println();
        }

        if(comments.isEmpty()) {
            System.out.println("   No comments.");
        }
        else {
            System.out.println("   " + comments.size() +
                                " comment(s). Click here to view.");
        }
    }
}

public class MessagePost extends Post
{
    ...
    public void display()
    {
        System.out.println(message);
    }
}

public class PhotoPost extends Post
{
    ...
    public void display()
    {
        System.out.println("  [" + filename + "]");
        System.out.println("  " + caption);
    }
}
```

Concept:

Overriding A
subclass can over-
ride a method
implementation.
To do this, the
subclass declares
a method with the
same signature
as the superclass,
but with a different
method body. The
overriding method
takes precedence
for method calls on
subclass objects.

This design works a bit better. It compiles, and it can be executed (even though it is not perfect yet). An implementation of this design is provided in the project *network-v3*. (If you have done Exercise 9.2, you already have a similar implementation of this design in your own version.)

The technique we are using here is called *overriding* (sometimes it is also referred to as *redefinition*). Overriding is a situation where a method is defined in a superclass (method `display` in class `Post` in this example), and a method with exactly the same signature is defined in the subclass.

In this situation, objects of the subclass have two methods with the same name and header: one inherited from the superclass and one from the subclass. Which one will be executed when we call this method?

9.4 Dynamic method lookup

One surprising detail is what exactly is printed once we execute the news feed's show method. If we again create and enter the objects described in Section 9.1, the output of the show method in our new version of the program is

```
Had a great idea this morning.
But now I forgot what it was. Something to do with flying ...

[experiment.jpg]
I think I might call this thing 'telephone'.
```

We can see from this output that the display methods in MessagePost and in PhotoPost were executed, but not the one in Post.

This may seem strange at first. Our investigation in Section 9.2 has shown that the compiler insisted on a display method in class Post—methods in the subclasses were not enough. This experiment now shows that the method in class Post is then not executed at all, but the subclass methods are. In short:

■ Type checking uses the static type, but at runtime, the methods from the dynamic type are executed.

This is a fairly important statement. To understand it better, we look in more detail at how methods are invoked. This procedure is known as *method lookup*, *method binding*, or *method dispatch*. We will use the term "method lookup" in this book.

We start with a simple method-lookup scenario. Assume that we have an object of a class PhotoPost stored in a variable v1 declared of type PhotoPost (Figure 9.5). The PhotoPost class has a display method and no declared superclass. This is a very simple situation—there is no inheritance or polymorphism involved here. We then execute the statement

```
v1.display();
```

Figure 9.5
Method lookup with
a simple object

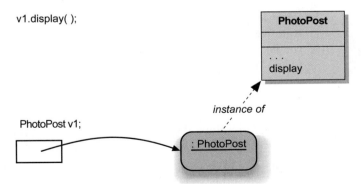

When this statement executes, the display method is invoked in the following steps:

1 The variable v1 is accessed.

2 The object stored in that variable is found (following the reference).

3   The class of the object is found (following the "instance of" reference).

4   The implementation of the display method is found in the class and executed.

This is all very straightforward and not surprising.

Next, we look at method lookup with inheritance. This scenario is similar, but this time the PhotoPost class has a superclass Post and the display method is defined only in the superclass (Figure 9.6).

Figure 9.6
Method lookup
with inheritance

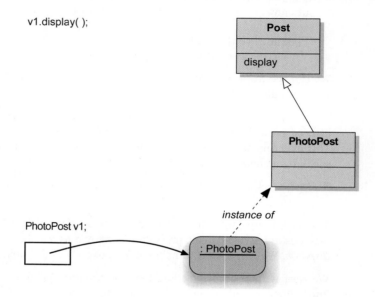

We execute the same statement. The method invocation then starts in a similar way: steps 1 to 3 from the previous scenario are executed again, but then it continues differently:

4   No display method is found in class PhotoPost.

5   Because no matching method was found, the superclass is searched for a matching method. If no method is found in the superclass, the next superclass (if it exists) is searched. This continues all the way up the inheritance hierarchy to the Object class, until a method is found. Note that at runtime a matching method should definitely be found, or else the class would not have compiled.

6   In our example, the display method is found in class Post, and will be executed.

This scenario illustrates how objects inherit methods. Any method found in a superclass can be invoked on a subclass object and will correctly be found and executed.

Next, we come to the most interesting scenario: method lookup with a polymorphic variable and method overriding (Figure 9.7). The scenario is again similar to the one before, but there are two changes:

■ The declared type of the variable v1 is now Post, not PhotoPost.

■ The display method is defined in class Post and then redefined (overridden) in class PhotoPost.

Figure 9.7
Method lookup with
polymorphism and
overriding

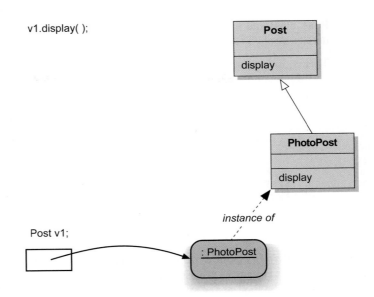

This scenario is the most important one for understanding the behavior of our *network* application and in finding a solution to our `display` method problem.

The steps in which method execution takes place are exactly the same as steps 1 through 4 from scenario 1. Read them again.

Some observations are worth noting:

■ No special lookup rules are used for method lookup in cases where the dynamic type is not equal to the static type. The behavior we observe is a result of the general rules.

■ Which method is found first and executed is determined by the dynamic type, not the static type. In other words, the fact that the declared type of the variable `v1` is now `Post` does not have any effect. The instance we are dealing with is of class `PhotoPost`—that is all that counts.

■ Overriding methods in subclasses take precedence over superclass methods. Because method lookup starts in the dynamic class of the instance (at the bottom of the inheritance hierarchy), the last redefinition of a method is found first, and this is the one that is executed.

■ When a method is overridden, only the last version (the one lowest in the inheritance hierarchy) is executed. Versions of the same method in any superclasses are not also automatically executed.

This explains the behavior that we observe in our *network* project. Only the `display` methods in the subclasses (`MessagePost` and `PhotoPost`) are executed when posts are printed out, leading to incomplete listings. In the next section, we discuss how to fix this.

9.5 Super call in methods

Now that we know in detail how overridden methods are executed, we can understand the solution to the problem. It is easy to see that what we would want to achieve is for every call to a `display` method of, say, a `PhotoPost` object, to result in both the `display` method of the

Post class and that of the PhotoPost class being executed for the same object. Then all the details would be printed out. (A different solution will be discussed later in this chapter.)

This is, in fact, quite easy to achieve. We can simply use the super construct, which we have already encountered in the context of constructors in Chapter 8. Code 9.2 illustrates this idea with the display method of the PhotoPost class.

Code 9.2

Redefining method with super call

```
public void display()
{
    super.display();
    System.out.println("   [" + filename + "]");
    System.out.println("   " + caption);
}
```

When display is now called on a PhotoPost object, initially the display method in the PhotoPost class will be invoked. As its first statement, this method will in turn invoke the display method of the superclass, which prints out the general post information. When control returns from the superclass method, the remaining statements of the subclass method print the distinctive fields of the PhotoPost class.

There are three details worth noting:

- Contrary to the case of super calls in constructors, the method name of the superclass method is explicitly stated. A super call in a method always has the form

    super.*method-name* (*parameters*)

  The parameter list can, of course, be empty.

- Again, contrary to the rule for super calls in constructors, the super call in methods may occur anywhere within that method. It does not have to be the first statement.

- And contrary to the case of super calls in constructors, no automatic super call is generated and no super call is required; it is entirely optional. So the default behavior gives the effect of a subclass method completely hiding (i.e., overriding) the superclass version of the same method.

Exercise 9.3 Modify your latest version of the *network* project to include the super call in the display method. Test it. Does it behave as expected? Do you see any problems with this solution?

It is worth reiterating what was illustrated in Exercise 8.6: that in the absence of method overriding, the non-private members of a superclass are directly accessible from its subclasses without any special syntax. A super call only has to be made when it is necessary to access the superclass version of an *overridden* method.

If you completed Exercise 9.3, you will have noticed that this solution works but is not perfect yet. It prints out all details, but in a different order from what we wanted. We will fix this last problem later in the chapter.

9.6 Method polymorphism

What we have just discussed in the previous sections (Sections 9.2–9.5) is yet another form of polymorphism. It is what is known as *polymorphic method dispatch* (or *method polymorphism* for short).

Remember that a polymorphic variable is one that can store objects of varying types (every object variable in Java is potentially polymorphic). In a similar manner, Java method calls are polymorphic, because they may invoke different methods at different times. For instance, the statement

```
post.display();
```

could invoke the `MessagePost`'s `display` method at one time and the `PhotoPost`'s `display` method at another, depending on the dynamic type of the `post` variable.

9.7 Object methods: `toString`

In Chapter 8, we mentioned that the universal superclass, `Object`, implements some methods that are then part of all objects. The most interesting of these methods is `toString`, which we introduce here (if you are interested in more detail, you can look up the interface for `Object` in the standard library documentation).

Exercise 9.4 Look up `toString` in the library documentation. What are its parameters? What is its return type?

The purpose of the `toString` method is to create a string representation of an object. This is useful for any objects that are ever to be textually represented in the user interface, but also helps for all other objects; they can then easily be printed out for debugging purposes, for instance.

The default implementation of `toString` in class `Object` cannot supply a great amount of detail. If, for example, we call `toString` on a `PhotoPost` object, we receive the string similar to this:

```
PhotoPost@6acdd1
```

The return value simply shows the object's class name and a magic number.[2]

Exercise 9.5 You can easily try this out. Create an object of class `PhotoPost` in your project, and then invoke the `toString` method from the `Object` submenu in the object's pop-up menu.

---

[2] The magic number is in fact the memory address where the object is stored. It is not very useful except to establish identity. If this number is the same in two calls, we are looking at the same object. If it is different, we have two distinct objects.

To make this method more useful, we would typically override it in our own classes. We can, for example, define the Post's display method in terms of a call to its toString method. In this case, the toString method would not print out the details, but just create a string with the text. Code 9.3 shows the changed source code.

Code 9.3

toString method for Post and MessagePost

```java
public class Post
{
    ...
    public String toString()
    {
        String text = username + "\n" + timeString(timestamp);
        if(likes > 0) {
            text += "  -  " + likes + " people like this.\n";
        }
        else {
            text += "\n";
        }

        if(comments.isEmpty()) {
            return text + "   No comments.\n";
        }
        else {
            return text + "    " + comments.size() +
                    " comment(s). Click here to view.\n";
        }
    }

    public void display()
    {
        System.out.println(toString());
    }
}

public class MessagePost extends Post
{
    ...
    public String toString()
    {
        return super.toString() + message + "\n";
    }

    public void display()
    {
        System.out.println(toString());
    }
}
```

Ultimately, we would plan on removing the `display` methods completely from these classes. A great benefit of defining just a `toString` method is that we do not mandate in the `Post` classes what exactly is done with the description text. The original version always printed the text to the output terminal. Now, any client (e.g., the `NewsFeed` class) is free to do whatever it chooses with this text. It might show the text in a text area in a graphical user interface; save it to a file; send it over a network; show it in a web browser; or, as before, print it to the terminal.

The statement used in the client to print the post could now look as follows:

```
System.out.println(post.toString());
```

In fact, the `System.out.print` and `System.out.println` methods are special in this respect: if the parameter to one of the methods is not a `String` object, then the method automatically invokes the object's `toString` method. Thus we do not need to write the call explicitly and could instead write

```
System.out.println(post);
```

Now consider the modified version of the `show` method of class `NewsFeed` shown in Code 9.4. In this version, we have removed the `toString` call. Would it compile and run correctly?

Code 9.4

New version of
`NewsFeed` show
method

```
public class NewsFeed
{
    // fields, constructors, and other methods omitted

    /**
     * Show the news feed. Currently: print the news feed details
     * to the terminal. (To do: replace this later with display
     * in web browser.)
     */
    public void show()
    {
        for(Post post : posts) {
            System.out.println(post);
        }
    }
}
```

In fact, the method *does* work as expected. If you can explain this example in detail, then you probably already have a good understanding of most of the concepts that we have introduced in this and the previous chapter! Here is a detailed explanation of the single `println` statement inside the loop.

- The for-each loop iterates through all posts and places them in a variable with the static type `Post`. The dynamic type is either `MessagePost` or `PhotoPost`.

- Because this object is being printed to `System.out` and it is not a `String`, its `toString` method is automatically invoked.

- Invoking this method is valid only because the class `Post` (the static type!) has a `toString` method. (Remember: Type checking is done with the static type. This call would not be allowed if class `Post` had no `toString` method. However, the `toString` method in class `Object` guarantees that this method is always available for any class.)

■ The output appears properly with all details, because each possible dynamic type (`MessagePost` and `PhotoPost`) overrides the `toString` method and the dynamic method lookup ensures that the redefined method is executed.

The `toString` method is generally useful for debugging purposes. Often, it is very convenient if objects can easily be printed out in a sensible format. Most of the Java library classes override `toString` (all collections, for instance, can be printed out like this), and often it is a good idea to override this method for our classes as well.

9.8 Object equality: `equals` and `hashCode`

It is often necessary to determine whether two objects are "the same." The `Object` class defines two methods, `equals` and `hashCode`, that have a close link with determining similarity. We actually have to be careful when using phrases such as "the same"; this is because it can mean two quite different things when talking about objects. Sometimes we wish to know whether two different variables are referring to the same object. This is exactly what happens when an object variable is passed as a parameter to a method: there is only one object, but both the original variable and the parameter variable refer to it. The same thing happens when any object variable is assigned to another. These situations produce what is called *reference equality*. Reference equality is tested for using the `==` operator. So the following test will return `true` if both `var1` and `var2` are referring to the same object (or are both `null`), and `false` if they are referring to anything else:

```
var1 == var2
```

Reference equality takes no account at all of the *contents* of the objects referred to, just whether there is one object referred to by two different variables or two distinct objects. That is why we also define *content equality*, as distinct from reference equality. A test for content equality asks whether two objects are the same internally—that is, whether the internal states of two objects are the same. This is why we rejected using reference equality for making string comparisons in Chapter 5.

What content equality between two particular objects means is something that is defined by the objects' class. This is where we make use of the `equals` method that every class inherits from the `Object` superclass. If we need to define what it means for two objects to be equal according to their internal states, then we must override the `equals` method, which then allows us to write tests such as

```
var1.equals(var2)
```

This is because the `equals` method inherited from the `Object` class actually makes a test for reference equality. It looks something like this:

```
public boolean equals(Object obj)
{
    return this == obj;
}
```

Because the `Object` class has no fields, there is no state to compare, and this method obviously cannot anticipate fields that might be present in subclasses.

The way to test for content equality between two objects is to test whether the values of their two sets of fields are equal. Notice, however, that the parameter of the `equals` method is of type `Object`, so a test of the fields will make sense only if we are comparing fields of the same type. This means that we first have to establish that the type of the object passed as a parameter is the same as that of the object it is being compared with. Here is how we might think of writing the method in the `Student` class of the *lab-classes* project from Chapter 1:

```
public boolean equals(Object obj)
{
    if(this == obj) {
        return true;    // Reference equality.
    }
    if(!(obj instanceof Student)) {
        return false;    // Not the same type.
    }
    // Gain access to the other student's fields.
    Student other = (Student) obj;
    return name.equals(other.name) &&
            id.equals(other.id) &&
            credits == other.credits;
}
```

The first test is just an efficiency improvement; if the object has been passed a reference to itself to compare against, then we know that content equality must be true. The second test makes sure that we are comparing two students. If not, then we decide that the two objects cannot be equal. Having established that we have another student, we use a cast and another variable of the right type so that we can access its details properly. Finally, we make use of the fact that the private elements of an object are directly accessible to an instance of the same class; this is essential in situations such as this one, because there will not necessarily be accessor methods defined for every private field in a class. Notice that we have consistently used content-equality tests rather than reference-equality tests on the object fields `name` and `id`.

It will not always be necessary to compare every field in two objects in order to establish that they are equal. For instance, if we know for certain that every `Student` is assigned a unique `id`, then we need not test the `name` and `credits` fields as well. It would then be possible to reduce the final statement above to

```
return id.equals(other.id);
```

Whenever the `equals` method is overridden, the `hashCode` method should also be overridden. The `hashCode` method is used by data structures such as `HashMap` and `HashSet` to provide efficient placement and lookup of objects in these collections. Essentially, the `hashCode` method returns an integer value that represents an object. From the default implementation in `Object`, distinct objects have distinct `hashCode` values.

There is an important link between the `equals` and `hashCode` methods in that two objects that are the same as determined by a call to `equals` must return identical values from `hashCode`. This stipulation, or contract, can be found in the description of `hashCode` in the API documentation of the `Object` class.[3] It is beyond the scope of this book to describe in detail a suitable

---

[3] Note that it is not essential that unequal objects always return distinct hash codes.

technique for calculating hash codes, but we recommend the interested reader to see Joshua Bloch's *Effective Java*, whose technique we use here.[4] Essentially, an integer value should be computed making use of the values of the fields that are compared by the overridden `equals` method. Here is a hypothetical `hashCode` method that uses the values of an integer field called `count` and a `String` field called `name` to calculate the code:

```java
public int hashCode()
{
    int result = 17;    // An arbitrary starting value.
    // Make the computed value depend on the order in which
    // the fields are processed.
    result = 37 * result + count;
    result = 37 * result + name.hashCode();
    return result;
}
```

9.9 Protected access

Concepts:

Declaring a field or a method **protected** allows direct access to it from (direct or indirect) subclasses.

In Chapter 8, we noted that the rules on public and private visibility of class members apply between a subclass and its superclass, as well as between classes in different inheritance hierarchies. This can be somewhat restrictive, because the relationship between a superclass and its subclasses is clearly closer than it is with other classes. For this reason, object-oriented languages often define a level of access that lies between the complete restriction of private access and the full availability of public access. In Java, this is called *protected access* and is provided by the `protected` keyword as an alternative to `public` and `private`. Code 9.5 shows an example of a protected accessor method, which we could add to class `Post`.

Code 9.5

An example of a protected method

```java
protected long getTimeStamp()
{
    return timestamp;
}
```

Protected access allows access to the fields or methods within a class itself and from all its subclasses, but not from other classes.[5] The `getTimeStamp` method shown in Code 9.5 can be called from class `Post` or any subclasses, but not from other classes. Figure 9.8 illustrates this. The oval areas in the diagram show the group of classes that are able to access members in class `SomeClass`.

---

[4] At the time of writing, sample chapters that contain material relevant to this topic are available at `http://java.sun.com/developer/Books/effectivejava/`.

[5] In Java, this rule is not as clear-cut as described here, because Java includes an additional level of visibility, called *package level*, but with no associated keyword. We will not discuss this further, and it is more general to consider protected access as intended for the special relationship between superclass and subclass.

Figure 9.8
Access levels: private, protected, and public

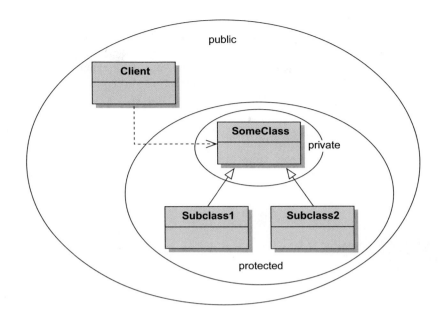

While protected access can be applied to any member of a class, it is usually reserved for methods and constructors. It is not usually applied to fields, because that would be a weakening of encapsulation. Wherever possible, mutable fields in superclasses should remain private. There are, however, occasional valid cases where direct access by subclasses is desirable. Inheritance represents a much closer form of coupling than does a normal client relationship.

Inheritance binds the classes closer together, and changing the superclass can more easily break the subclass. This should be taken into consideration when designing classes and their relationships.

Exercise 9.6 The version of `display` shown in Code 9.2 produces the output shown in Figure 9.9. Reorder the statements in the method in your version of the *network* project so that it prints the details as shown in Figure 9.10.

Figure 9.9
Possible output from `display`: superclass call at the beginning of `display` (shaded areas printed by superclass method)

```
Leonardo da Vinci
40 seconds ago - 2 people like this.
  No comments.
Had a great idea this morning.
But now I forgot what it was. Something to do with flying...
```

Figure 9.10
Alternative output from `display` (shaded areas printed by superclass method)

```
Had a great idea this morning.
But now I forgot what it was. Something to do with flying...
Leonardo da Vinci
40 seconds ago - 2 people like this.
  No comments.
```

Exercise 9.7 Having to use a superclass call in `display` is somewhat restrictive in the ways in which we can format the output, because it is dependent on the way the superclass formats its fields. Make any necessary changes to the `Post` class and to the `display` method of `MessagePost` so that it produces the output shown in Figure 9.11. Any changes you make to the `Post` class should be visible only to its subclasses. *Hint:* You could add protected accessors to do this.

Figure 9.11
Output from `display`
mixing subclass and
superclass details
(shaded areas represent
superclass details)

```
Leonardo da Vinci
Had a great idea this morning.
But now I forgot what it was. Something to do with flying...
40 seconds ago - 2 people like this.
  No comments.
```

9.10 The `instanceof` operator

One of the consequences of the introduction of inheritance into the *network* project has been that the `NewsFeed` class knows only about `Post` objects and cannot distinguish between message posts and photo posts. This has allowed all types of post to be stored in a single list.

However, suppose that we wish to retrieve just the message posts or just the photo posts from the list; how would we do that? Or perhaps we wish to look for a message by a particular author? That is not a problem if the `Post` class defines a `getAuthor` method, but this will find both message and photo posts. Will it matter which type is returned?

There are occasions when we need to rediscover the distinctive dynamic type of an object rather than dealing with a shared supertype. For this, Java provides the `instanceof` operator. The `instanceof` operator tests whether a given object is, directly or indirectly, an instance of a given class. The test

```
obj instanceof MyClass
```

returns `true` if the dynamic type of `obj` is `MyClass` or any subclass of `MyClass`. The left operand is always an object reference, and the right operand is always the name of a class. So

```
post instanceof MessagePost
```

returns `true` only if `post` is a `MessagePost`, as opposed to a `PhotoPost`, for instance.

Use of the `instanceof` operator is often followed immediately by a cast of the object reference to the identified type. For instance, here is some code to identify all of the message posts in a list of posts and to store them in a separate list.

```
ArrayList<MessagePost> messages = new ArrayList<MessagePost>();
for(Post post : posts) {
    if(post instanceof MessagePost) {
        messages.add((MessagePost) post);
    }
}
```

It should be clear that the cast here does not alter the post object in any way, because we have just established that it already is a `MessagePost` object.

9.11 Another example of inheritance with overriding

To discuss another example of a similar use of inheritance, we go back to a project from Chapter 6: the *zuul* project. In the *world-of-zuul* game, we used a set of Room objects to create a scene for a simple game. One of the exercises toward the end of the chapter suggested that you implement a transporter room (a room that beams you to a random location in the game if you try to enter or leave it). We revisit this exercise here, because its solution can greatly benefit from inheritance. If you don't remember this project well, have a quick read through Chapter 6 again, or look at your own *zuul* project.

There is no single solution to this task. Many different solutions are possible and can be made to work. Some are better than others, though. They may be more elegant, easier to read, and easier to maintain and to extend.

Assume that we want to implement this task so that the player is automatically transported to a random room when she tries to leave the magic transporter room. The most straightforward solution that comes to mind first for many people is to deal with this in the Game class, which implements the player's commands. One of the commands is "go," which is implemented in the goRoom method. In this method, we used the following statement as the central section of code:

```
nextRoom = currentRoom.getExit(direction);
```

This statement retrieves from the current room the neighboring room in the direction we want to go. To add our magic transportation, we could modify this in a form similar to the following:

```
if(currentRoom.getName().equals("Transporter room")) {
    nextRoom = getRandomRoom();
}
else {
    nextRoom = currentRoom.getExit(direction);
}
```

The idea here is simple: we just check whether we are in the transporter room. If we are, then we find the next room by getting a random room (of course, we have to implement the getRandomRoom method somehow); otherwise, we just do the same as before.

While this solution works, it has several drawbacks. The first is that it is a bad idea to use text strings, such as the room's name, to identify the room. Imagine that someone wanted to translate your game into another language—say, to German. They might change the names of the rooms—"Transporter room" becomes "Transporterraum"—and suddenly the game does not work any more! This is a clear case of a maintainability problem.

The second solution, which is slightly better, would be to use an instance variable instead of the room's name to identify the transporter room. Similar to this:

```
if(currentRoom == transporterRoom) {
    nextRoom = getRandomRoom();
}
else {
    nextRoom = currentRoom.getExit(direction);
}
```

This time, we assume that we have an instance variable `transporterRoom` of class Room, where we store the reference to our transporter room.[6] Now the check is independent of the room's name. That is a bit better.

There is still a case for further improvement, though. We can understand the shortcomings of this solution when we think about another maintenance change. Imagine that we want to add two more transporter rooms so that our game has three different transporter locations.

A very nice aspect of our existing design was that we could set up the floor plan in a single spot, and the rest of the game was completely independent of it. We could easily change the layout of the rooms, and everything would still work—high score for maintainability! With our current solution, though, this is broken. If we add two new transporter rooms, we have to add two more instance variables or an array (to store references to those rooms), and we have to modify our goRoom method to add a check for those rooms. In terms of easy changeability, we have gone backwards.

The question, therefore, is: Can we find a solution that does not require a change to the command implementation each time we add a new transporter room? Following is our next idea.

We can add a method `isTransporterRoom` in the Room class. This way, the Game object does not need to remember all the transporter rooms—the rooms themselves do. When rooms are created, they could receive a boolean flag indicating whether a given room is a transporter room. The goRoom method could then use the following code segment:

```
if(currentRoom.isTransporterRoom()) {
    nextRoom = getRandomRoom();
}
else {
    nextRoom = currentRoom.getExit(direction);
}
```

Now we can add as many transporter rooms as we like; there is no need for any more changes to the Game class. However, the Room class has an extra field whose value is really needed only because of the nature of one or two of the instances. Special-case code such as this is a typical indicator of a weakness in class design. This approach also does not scale well should we decide to introduce further sorts of special rooms, each requiring its own flag field and accessor method.[7]

With inheritance, we can do better and implement a solution that is even more flexible than this one. We can implement a class `TransporterRoom` as a subclass of class Room. In this new class, we override the `getExit` method and change its implementation so that it returns a random room:

```
public class TransporterRoom extends Room
{
    /**
     * Return a random room, independent of the direction
     * parameter.
     * @param direction Ignored.
     * @return A random room.
     */
```

---

[6] Make sure that you understand why a test for reference equality is the most appropriate here.

[7] We might also think of using `instanceof`, but the point here is that none of these ideas is the best.

```
    public Room getExit(String direction)
    {
        return findRandomRoom();
    }

    /*
     * Choose a random room.
     * @return A random room.
     */
    private Room findRandomRoom()
    {
        . . .    // implementation omitted
    }
}
```

The elegance of this solution lies in the fact that no change at all is needed in either the original Game or Room classes! We can simply add this class to the existing game, and the goRoom method will continue to work as it is. Adding the creation of a TransporterRoom to the setup of the floor plan is (almost) enough to make it work. Note, too, that the new class does not need a flag to indicate its special nature—its very type and distinctive behavior supply that information.

Because TransporterRoom is a subclass of Room, it can be used everywhere a Room object is expected. Thus, it can be used as a neighboring room for another room or be held in the Game object as the current room.

What we have left out, of course, is the implementation of the findRandomRoom method. In reality, this is probably better done in a separate class (say RoomRandomizer) than in the TransporterRoom class itself. We leave this open as an exercise for the reader.

Exercise 9.8 Implement a transporter room with inheritance in your version of the *zuul* project.

Exercise 9.9 Discuss how inheritance could be used in the *zuul* project to implement a player and a monster class.

Exercise 9.10 Could (or should) inheritance be used to create an inheritance relationship (super-, sub-, or sibling class) between a character in the game and an item?

9.12 Summary

When we deal with classes with subclasses and polymorphic variables, we have to distinguish between the static and dynamic type of a variable. The static type is the declared type, while the dynamic type is the type of the object currently stored in the variable.

Type checking is done by the compiler using the static type, whereas at runtime method lookup uses the dynamic type. This enables us to create very flexible structures by overriding methods. Even when using a supertype variable to make a method call, overriding enables us to ensure that specialized methods are invoked for every particular subtype. This ensures that objects of different classes can react distinctly to the same method call.

When implementing overriding methods, the super keyword can be used to invoke the super-class version of the method. If fields or methods are declared with the protected access modifier, subclasses are allowed to access them, but other classes are not.

Terms introduced in this chapter

static type, dynamic type, overriding, redefinition, method lookup, method dispatch, method polymorphism, protected

Concept summary

- **static type** The static type of a variable *v* is the type as declared in the source code in the variable declaration statement.

- **dynamic type** The dynamic type of a variable *v* is the type of the object that is currently stored in *v*.

- **overriding** A subclass can override a method implementation. To do this, the subclass declares a method with the same signature as the superclass, but with a different method body. The overriding method takes precedence for method calls on subclass objects.

- **method polymorphism** Method calls in Java are polymorphic. The same method call may at different times invoke different methods, depending on the dynamic type of the variable used to make that call.

- **toString** Every object in Java has a toString method that can be used to return a string representation of itself. Typically, to make it useful, a class should override this method.

- **protected** Declaring a field or a method protected allows direct access to it from (direct or indirect) subclasses.

Exercise 9.11 Assume that you see the following lines of code:

```
Device dev = new Printer();
dev.getName();
```

Printer is a subclass of Device. Which of these classes must have a definition of method getName for this code to compile?

Exercise 9.12 In the same situation as in the previous exercise, if both classes have an implementation of getName, which one will be executed?

Exercise 9.13 Assume that you write a class Student that does not have a declared superclass. You do not write a toString method. Consider the following lines of code:

```
Student st = new Student();
String s = st.toString();
```

Will these lines compile? If so, what exactly will happen when you try to execute?

Exercise 9.14 In the same situation as before (class `Student`, no `toString` method), will the following lines compile? Why?

```
Student st = new Student();
System.out.println(st);
```

Exercise 9.15 Assume that your class `Student` overrides `toString` so that it returns the student's name. You now have a list of students. Will the following code compile? If not, why not? If yes, what will it print? Explain in detail what happens.

```
for(Object st : myList) {
    System.out.println(st);
}
```

Exercise 9.16 Write a few lines of code that result in a situation where a variable x has the static type T and the dynamic type D.

Main concepts discussed in this chapter:

- abstract classes
- interfaces
- multiple inheritance

Java constructs discussed in this chapter:

`abstract`, `implements`, `interface`

In this chapter, we examine further inheritance-related techniques that can be used to enhance class structures and improve maintainability and extendibility. These techniques introduce an improved method of representation of abstractions in object-oriented programs.

The previous two chapters have discussed the most important aspects of inheritance in application design, but several more advanced uses and problems have been ignored so far. We will now complete the picture with a more advanced example.

The project we use for this chapter is a simulation. We use it to discuss inheritance again and see that we run into some new problems. Abstract classes and interfaces are then introduced to deal with these problems.

10.1 Simulations

Computers are frequently used to simulate real systems. These include systems that model traffic flows in a city, forecast weather, simulate the spread of infection, analyze the stock market, do environmental simulations, and much more. In fact, many of the most powerful computers in the world are used for running some sort of simulation.

When creating a computer simulation, we try to model the behavior of a subset of the real world in a software model. Every simulation is necessarily a simplification of the real thing. Deciding which details to leave out and which to include is often a challenging task. The more detailed a simulation is, the more accurate it may be in forecasting the behavior of the real system. But more detail increases the complexity of the model and the requirements for both more computing power and more programmer time. A well-known example is weather forecasting: climate models in weather simulations have been improved by adding more and more detail over the last few decades. As a result, weather forecasts have improved significantly in accuracy (but are far from perfect, as we all have experienced at some time). Much of this improvement has been made possible through advances in computer technology.

The benefit of simulations is that we can undertake experiments that we could not do with the real system, either because we have no control over the real thing (for instance, the weather) or because it is too costly, too dangerous, or irreversible in case of disaster. We can use the simulation to investigate the behavior of the system under certain circumstances or to investigate "what if" questions.

An example of the use of environmental simulations is to try to predict the effects of human activity on natural habitats. Consider the case of a national park containing endangered species and a proposal to build a freeway through the middle of it, completely separating the two halves. The supporters of the freeway proposal claim that splitting the park in half will lead to little actual land loss and make no difference to the animals in it, but environmentalists claim otherwise. How can we tell what the effect is likely to be without building the freeway? Simulation is one option. An essential question in all cases of this kind will be, of course, "How good is the simulation?" One can "prove" just about anything with an ill-designed simulation. Gaining trust in it through controlled experiments will be essential.

The issue in this particular case boils down to whether it is significant for the survival of a species to have a single, connected habitat area or whether two disjoint areas (with the same total size as the other) are just as good. Rather than building the freeway first and then observing what happens, we will try to simulate the effect in order to make a well-informed decision.[1]

Our simulation will necessarily be simpler than the scenario we have described, because we are using it mainly to illustrate new features of object-oriented design and implementation. Therefore, it will not have the potential to simulate accurately many aspects of nature, but some of the simulation's characteristics are nonetheless interesting. In particular, it will demonstrate the structure of typical simulations. In addition, its accuracy may surprise you; it would be a mistake to equate greater complexity with greater accuracy. It is often the case that a simplified model of something can provide greater insight and understanding than a more complex one, from which it is often difficult to isolate the underlying mechanisms—or even be sure that the model is valid.

10.2 The foxes-and-rabbits simulation

The simulation scenario we have chosen to work with in this chapter uses the freeway example from above as its basis. It involves tracking populations of foxes and rabbits within an enclosed field. This is just one particular example of what are known as *predator–prey simulations*. Such simulations are often used to model the variation in population sizes that result from a predator species feeding on a prey species. A delicate balance exists between such species. A large population of prey will potentially provide plenty of food for a small population of predators. However, too many predators could kill off all the prey and leave the hunters with nothing to eat. Population sizes could also be affected by the size and nature of the environment. For instance, a small, enclosed environment could lead to overcrowding and make it easy for the predators to locate their prey, or a polluted environment could reduce the stock of prey and prevent even a modest population of predators from surviving. Because predators in one context are themselves often prey for other species (think of cats, birds, and worms, for instance), loss of one part of the food chain can have dramatic effects on the survival of other parts.

---

[1] In this particular case, by the way, size does matter: the size of a natural park has a significant impact on its usefulness as a habitat for animals.

As we have done in previous chapters, we will start with a version of an application that works perfectly well from a user's point of view but whose internal view is not so good when judged by the principles of good object-oriented design and implementation. We will use this base version to develop several improved versions that progressively introduce new abstraction techniques.

One particular problem that we wish to address in the base version is that it does not make good use of the inheritance techniques that were introduced in Chapter 8. However, we will start by examining the mechanism of the simulation, without being too critical of its implementation. Once we understand how it works, we shall be in a good position to make some improvements.

> **Predator–prey modeling** There is a long history of trying to model predator–prey relationships mathematically before the invention of the computer, because they have economic, as well as environmental, importance. For instance, mathematical models were used in the early twentieth century to explain variations in the level of fish stocks in the Adriatic Sea as a side effect of World War I. To find out more about the background of this topic, and perhaps gain an understanding of population dynamics, do a web search for the Lotka-Volterra model.

10.2.1 The *foxes-and-rabbits* project

Open the *foxes-and-rabbits-v1* project. The class diagram is shown in Figure 10.1.

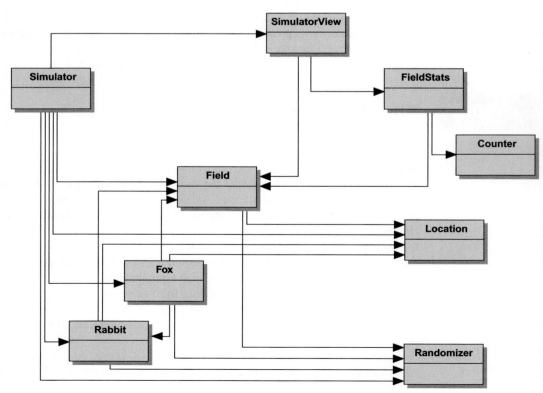

Figure 10.1
Class diagram of the *foxes-and-rabbits* project

The main classes we will focus on in our discussion are Simulator, Fox, and Rabbit. The Fox and Rabbit classes provide simple models of the behavior of a predator and prey, respectively. In this particular implementation, we have not tried to provide an accurate biological model of real foxes and rabbits; rather, we are simply trying to illustrate the principles of typical predator–prey simulations. Our main concerns will be on the aspects that most affect population size: birth, death, and food supply.

The Simulator class is responsible for creating the initial state of the simulation, and then controlling and executing it. The basic idea is simple: the simulator holds collections of foxes and rabbits, and it repeatedly gives those animals an opportunity to live through one step[2] of their life cycle. At each step, each fox and each rabbit is allowed to carry out the actions that characterize their behaviors. After each step (when all the animals have had the chance to act), the new current state of the field is displayed on screen.

We can summarize the purpose of the remaining classes as follows:

■ Field represents a two-dimensional enclosed field. The field is composed of a fixed number of locations, which are arranged in rows and columns. At most, one animal may occupy a single location within the field. Each field location can hold an animal or it can be empty.

■ Location represents a two-dimensional position within the field, specified by a row and a column value.

■ These five classes together (Simulator, Fox, Rabbit, Field, and Location) provide the model for the simulation. They completely determine the simulation behavior.

■ The Randomizer class provides us with a degree of control over random aspects of the simulation, such as when new animals are born.

■ The classes SimulatorView, FieldStats, and Counter provide a graphical display of the simulation. The display shows an image of the field and counters for each species (the current number of rabbits and foxes).

■ SimulatorView provides a visualization of the state of the field. An example can be seen in Figure 10.2.

■ FieldStats provides to the visualization counts of the numbers of foxes and rabbits in the field.

■ A Counter stores a current count for one type of animal to assist with the counting.

Try the following exercises to gain an understanding of how the simulation operates before reading about its implementation.

Exercise 10.1 Create a Simulator object, using the constructor without parameters, and you should see an initial state of the simulation similar to that in Figure 10.2. The more numerous rectangles represent the rabbits. Does the number of foxes change if you call the simulateOneStep method just once?

---

[2] We won't define how much time a "step" actually represents. In practice, this has to be decided by a combination of such things as what we are trying to discover, what events we are simulating, and how much real time is available to run the simulation.

Figure 10.2

The initial state of the *foxes-and-rabbits* simulation

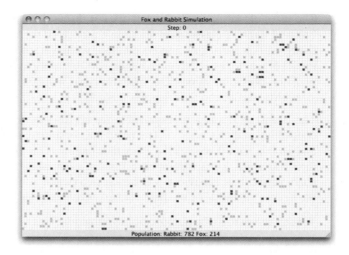

Exercise 10.2 Does the number of foxes change on every step? What natural processes do you think we are modeling that cause the number of foxes to increase or decrease?

Exercise 10.3 Call the `simulate` method with a parameter to run the simulation continuously for a significant number of steps, such as 50 or 100. Do the numbers of foxes and rabbits increase or decrease at similar rates?

Exercise 10.4 What changes do you notice if you run the simulation for a much longer time, say for 4,000 steps? You can use the `runLongSimulation` method to do this.

Exercise 10.5 Use the `reset` method to create a new starting state for the simulation, and then run it again. Is an identical simulation run this time? If not, do you see broadly similar patterns emerging anyway?

Exercise 10.6 If you run a simulation for long enough, do all of the foxes or all of the rabbits ever die off completely? If so, can you pinpoint any reasons why that might be occurring?

Exercise 10.7 Make a note of the numbers of foxes and rabbits at each of the first few steps and at the end of a long run. It will be useful to have a record of these when we come to make changes later on and perform regression testing.

Exercise 10.8 After having run the simulation for a while, reset it and also call the static `reset` method of the `Randomizer` class. Now run the first few steps again, and you should see the original simulation repeated. Take a look at the code of the `Randomizer` class to see if you can work out why this might be. You might need to look at the API for the `java.util.Random` class to help you with this.

Exercise 10.9 Check to see that setting the useShared field in Randomizer to false breaks the repeatability of the simulations seen in Exercise 10.8. Be sure to restore it to true afterwards, because repeatability will be an important element in later testing.

Now that we have a broad, external understanding of what this project does, we will look in detail at the implementation of the Rabbit, Fox, and Simulator classes.

10.2.2 The Rabbit class

The source code of the Rabbit class is shown in Code 10.1.

Code 10.1

The Rabbit class

```
// import statements and class comment omitted

public class Rabbit
{
    // Characteristics shared by all rabbits (class variables).

    // The age at which a rabbit can start to breed.
    private static final int BREEDING_AGE = 5;
    // The age to which a rabbit can live.
    private static final int MAX_AGE = 40;
    // The likelihood of a rabbit breeding.
    private static final double BREEDING_PROBABILITY = 0.12;
    // The maximum number of births.
    private static final int MAX_LITTER_SIZE = 4;
    // A shared random number generator to control breeding.
    private static final Random rand = Randomizer.getRandom();

    // Individual characteristics (instance fields).

    // The rabbit's age.
    private int age;
    // Whether the rabbit is alive or not.
    private boolean alive;
    // The rabbit's position.
    private Location location;
    // The field occupied.
    private Field field;

    /**
     * Create a new rabbit. A rabbit may be created with age
     * zero (a newborn) or with a random age.
     *
```

Code 10.1 continued

The Rabbit class

```java
 * @param randomAge If true, the rabbit will have a random age.
 * @param field The field currently occupied.
 * @param location The location within the field.
 */
public Rabbit(boolean randomAge, Field field, Location location)
{
    // body of constructor omitted
}


/**
 * This is what the rabbit does most of the time: it runs
 * around. Sometimes it will breed or die of old age.
 * @param newRabbits A list to return newly born rabbits.
 */
public void run(List<Rabbit> newRabbits)
{
    incrementAge();
    if(alive) {
        giveBirth(newRabbits);
        // Try to move into a free location.
        Location newLocation =
            field.freeAdjacentLocation(location);
        if(newLocation ! = null) {
            setLocation(newLocation);
        }
        else {
            // Overcrowding.
            setDead();
        }
    }
}


/**
 * Indicate that the rabbit is no longer alive.
 * It is removed from the field.
 */
public void setDead()
{
    alive = false;
    if(location != null) {
        field.clear(location);
        location = null;
        field = null;
    }
}
```

Code 10.1 continued

The Rabbit class

```java
/**
 * Increase the age.
 * This could result in the rabbit's death.
 */
private void incrementAge()
{
    age++;
    if(age > MAX_AGE) {
        setDead();
    }
}

/**
 * Check whether or not this rabbit is to give birth at this step.
 * New births will be made into free adjacent locations.
 * @param newRabbits A list to return newly born rabbits.
 */
private void giveBirth(List<Rabbit> newRabbits)
{
    // New rabbits are born into adjacent locations.
    // Get a list of adjacent free locations.
    List<Location> free = field.getFreeAdjacentLocations(location);
    int births = breed();
    for(int b = 0; b < births && free.size() > 0; b++) {
        Location loc = free.remove(0);
        Rabbit young = new Rabbit(false, field, loc);
        newRabbits.add(young);
    }
}

/**
 * Generate a number representing the number of births,
 * if it can breed.
 * @return The number of births (may be zero).
 */
private int breed()
{
    int births = 0;
    if(canBreed() && rand.nextDouble() <= BREEDING_PROBABILITY) {
        births = rand.nextInt(MAX_LITTER_SIZE) + 1;
    }
    return births;
}

// other methods omitted
}
```

The `Rabbit` class contains a number of class variables that define configuration settings that are common to all rabbits. These include values for the maximum age to which a rabbit can live (defined as a number of simulation steps) and the maximum number of offspring it can produce at any one step. Centralized control of random aspects of the simulation is provided through a single, shared `Random` object supplied by the `Randomizer` class. This is what makes possible the repeatability seen in Exercise 10.8. In addition, each individual rabbit has four instance variables that describe its state: its age as a number of steps, whether it is still alive, and its location in a particular field.

> **Exercise 10.10** Do you feel that omitting gender as an attribute in the `Rabbit` class is likely to lead to an inaccurate simulation? Write down the arguments for and against including it.
>
> **Exercise 10.11** Are there other simplifications that you feel are present in our implementation of the `Rabbit` class, compared with real life? Discuss whether these could have a significant impact on the accuracy of the simulation.
>
> **Exercise 10.12** Experiment with the effects of altering some or all of the values of the class variables in the `Rabbit` class. For instance, what effect does it have on the populations if the breeding probability of rabbits is much higher or much lower than it currently is?

A rabbit's behavior is defined in its `run` method, which in turn uses the `giveBirth` and `incrementAge` methods and implements the rabbit's movement. At each simulation step, the `run` method will be called and a rabbit will increase its age; if old enough, it might also breed, and it will then try to move. Both the movement and the breeding behaviors have random components. The direction in which the rabbit moves is randomly chosen, and breeding occurs randomly, controlled by the class variable `BREEDING_PROBABILITY`.

You can already see some of the simplifications that we have made in our model of rabbits: there is no attempt to distinguish males from females, for instance, and a rabbit could potentially give birth to a new litter at every simulation step once it is old enough.

10.2.3 The `Fox` class

There is a lot of similarity between the `Fox` and the `Rabbit` classes, so only the distinctive elements of `Fox` are shown in Code 10.2.

Code 10.2

The `Fox` class

```
// import statements and class comment omitted

public class Fox
{
    // Characteristics shared by all foxes (class variables).

    // The food value of a single rabbit. In effect, this is the
    // number of steps a fox can go before it has to eat again.
    private static final int RABBIT_FOOD_VALUE = 9;
```

Code 10.2 continued

The Fox class

```
// other static fields omitted

// Individual characteristics (instance fields).

// The fox's age.
private int age;
// Whether the fox is alive or not.
private boolean alive;
// The fox's position.
private Location location;
// The field occupied.
private Field field;
// The fox's food level, which is increased by eating rabbits.
private int foodLevel;

/**
 * Create a fox. A fox can be created as a newborn (age zero
 * and not hungry) or with a random age and food level.
 *
 * @param randomAge If true, the fox will have random age
 *                  and hunger level.
 * @param field The field currently occupied.
 * @param location The location within the field.
 */
public Fox(boolean randomAge, Field field, Location location)
{
     // body of constructor omitted
}

/**
 * This is what the fox does most of the time: it hunts for
 * rabbits. In the process, it might breed, die of hunger,
 * or die of old age.
 * @param field The field currently occupied.
 * @param newFoxes A list to return newly born foxes.
 */
public void hunt(List<Fox> newFoxes)
{
    incrementAge();
    incrementHunger();
    if(alive) {
        giveBirth(newFoxes);
        // Move towards a source of food if found.
        Location newLocation = findFood();
        if(newLocation == null) {
            // No food found - try to move to a free location.
            newLocation = field.freeAdjacentLocation(location);
        }
```

**Code 10.2
continued**

The Fox class

```
                    // See if it was possible to move.
                    if(newLocation != null) {
                        setLocation(newLocation);
                    }
                    else {
                        // Overcrowding.
                        setDead();
                    }
                }
            }


    /**
     * Look for rabbits adjacent to the current location.
     * Only the first live rabbit is eaten.
     * @return Where food was found, or null if it wasn't.
     */
    private Location findFood()
    {
        List<Location> adjacent = field.adjacentLocations(location);
        Iterator<Location> it = adjacent.iterator();
        while(it.hasNext()) {
            Location where = it.next();
            Object animal = field.getObjectAt(where);
            if(animal instanceof Rabbit) {
                Rabbit rabbit = (Rabbit) animal;
                if(rabbit.isAlive()) {
                    rabbit.setDead();
                    foodLevel = RABBIT_FOOD_VALUE;
                    return where;
                }
            }
        }
        return null;
    }

    // other methods omitted
}
```

For foxes, the `hunt` method is invoked at each step and defines their behavior. In addition to aging
and possibly breeding at each step, a fox searches for food (using `findFood`). If it is able to find a
rabbit in an adjacent location, then the rabbit is killed and the fox's food level is increased. As with
rabbits, a fox that is unable to move is considered dead through overcrowding.

Exercise 10.13 As you did for rabbits, assess the degree to which we have simplified the model
of foxes and evaluate whether you feel the simplifications are likely to lead to an inaccurate simulation.

Exercise 10.14 Does increasing the maximum age for foxes lead to a significantly higher numbers of foxes throughout a simulation, or is the rabbit population more likely to be reduced to zero as a result?

Exercise 10.15 Experiment with different combinations of settings (breeding age, maximum age, breeding probability, litter size, etc.) for foxes and rabbits. Do species always disappear completely in some configurations? Are there configurations that are stable—i.e., that produce a balance of numbers for a significant length of time?

Exercise 10.16 Experiment with different sizes of fields. (You can do this by using the second constructor of `Simulator`.) Does the size of the field affect the likelihood of species surviving?

Exercise 10.17 Compare the results of running a simulation with a single large field and two simulations with fields that each have half the area of the single field. This models something close to splitting an area in half with a freeway. Do you notice any significant differences in the population dynamics between the two scenarios?

Exercise 10.18 Repeat the investigations of the previous exercise, but vary the proportions of the two, smaller fields. For instance, try three-quarters and one quarter, or two-thirds and one-third. Does it matter at all how the single field is split?

Exercise 10.19 Currently, a fox will eat at most one rabbit at each step. Modify the `find-Food` method so that rabbits in all adjacent locations are eaten at a single step. Assess the impact of this change on the results of the simulation. Note that the `findFood` method currently returns the location of the single rabbit that is eaten, so you will need to return the location of one of the eaten rabbits in your version. However, don't forget to return `null` if there are no rabbits to eat.

Exercise 10.20 Following on from the previous exercise, if a fox eats multiple rabbits at a single step, there are several different possibilities as to how we can model its food level. If we add all the rabbit's food values, the fox will have a very high food level, making it unlikely to die of hunger for a very long time. Alternatively, we could impose a ceiling on the fox's food level. This models the effect of a predator that kills prey regardless of whether it is hungry or not. Assess the impacts on the resulting simulation of implementing this choice.

Exercise 10.21 *Challenge exercise* Given the random elements in the simulation, argue why the population numbers in an apparently stable simulation could ultimately collapse.

10.2.4   The `Simulator` class: setup

The `Simulator` class is the central part of the application that coordinates all the other pieces. Code 10.3 illustrates some of its main features.

Code 10.3

Part of the `Simulator` class

```java
// import statements and class comment omitted

public class Simulator
{
    // static variables omitted

    // Lists of animals in the field.
    private List<Rabbit> rabbits;
    private List<Fox> foxes;
    // The current state of the field.
    private Field field;
    // The current step of the simulation.
    private int step;
    // A graphical view of the simulation.
    private SimulatorView view;

    /**
     * Create a simulation field with the given size.
     * @param depth Depth of the field.
     *              Must be greater than zero.
     * @param width Width of the field.
     *              Must be greater than zero.
     */
    public Simulator(int depth, int width)
    {
        if(width <= 0 || depth <= 0) {
            System.out.println(
                    "The dimensions must be greater than zero.");
            System.out.println( "Using default values.");
            depth = DEFAULT_DEPTH;
            width = DEFAULT_WIDTH;
        }
        rabbits = new ArrayList<Rabbit>();
        foxes = new ArrayList<Fox>();
        field = new Field(depth, width);

        // Create a view of the state of each location in the
        // field.
        view = new SimulatorView(depth, width);
        view.setColor(Rabbit.class, Color.ORANGE);
        view.setColor(Fox.class, Color.BLUE);

        // Set up a valid starting point.
        reset();
    }

    /**
     * Run the simulation from its current state for the
```

Code 10.3
continued

Part of the Simulator
class

```java
 * given number of steps.
 * Stop before the given number of steps if it ceases to
 * be viable.
 * @param numSteps The number of steps to run for.
 */
public void simulate(int numSteps)
{
    for(int step = 1; step <= numSteps &&
                        view.isViable(field); step++) {
        simulateOneStep();
    }
}


/**
 * Run the simulation from its current state for a single
 * step.
 * Iterate over the whole field, updating the state of
 * each fox and rabbit.
 */
public void simulateOneStep()
{
    // method body omitted
}


/**
 * Reset the simulation to a starting position.
 */
public void reset()
{
    step = 0;
    rabbits.clear();
    foxes.clear();
    field.clear();
    populate();

    // Show the starting state in the view.
    view.showStatus(step, field);
}


/**
 * Populate the field with foxes and rabbits.
 */
private void populate()
{
    Random rand = Randomizer.getRandom();
    field.clear();
```

Code 10.3 continued

Part of the `Simulator` class

```
                 for(int row = 0; row < field.getDepth(); row++) {
                     for(int col = 0; col < field.getWidth(); col++) {
                         if(rand.nextDouble() <= FOX_CREATION_PROBABILITY) {
                             Location location = new Location(row, col);
                             Fox fox = new Fox(true, field, location);
                             foxes.add(fox);
                         }
                         else if(rand.nextDouble() <=
                                         RABBIT_CREATION_PROBABILITY) {
                             Location location = new Location(row, col);
                             Rabbit rabbit = new Rabbit(true, field, location);
                             rabbits.add(rabbit);
                         }
                         // else leave the location empty.
                     }
                 }
             }
             // other methods omitted
         }
```

The `Simulator` has three important parts: its constructor, the `populate` method, and the `simulateOneStep` method. (The body of `simulateOneStep` is shown below.)

When a `Simulator` object is created, all other parts of the simulation are constructed by it (the field, the lists to hold the different types of animals, and the graphical interface). Once all these have been set up, the simulator's `populate` method is called (indirectly, via the `reset` method) to create the initial populations. Different probabilities are used to decide whether a particular location will contain one of these animals. Note that animals created at the start of the simulation are given a random initial age. This serves two purposes:

■ It represents more accurately a mixed-age population that should be the normal state of the simulation.

■ If all animals were to start with an age of zero, no new animals would be created until the initial population had reached their respective breeding ages. With foxes eating rabbits regardless of the fox's age, there is a risk that either the rabbit population will be killed off before it has a chance to reproduce or that the fox population will die of hunger.

Exercise 10.22 Modify the `populate` method of `Simulator` to determine whether setting an initial age of zero for foxes and rabbits is always catastrophic. Make sure that you run it a sufficient number of times—with different initial states, of course!

Exercise 10.23 If an initial random age is set for rabbits but not foxes, the rabbit population will tend to grow large while the fox population remains very small. Once the foxes do become old enough to breed, does the simulation tend to behave again like the original version? What does this suggest about the relative sizes of the initial populations and their impact on the outcome of the simulation?

10.2.5 The `Simulator` class: a simulation step

The central part of the `Simulator` class is the `simulateOneStep` method shown in Code 10.4. It uses separate loops to let each type of animal move (and possibly breed or do whatever it is programmed to do). Because each animal can give birth to new animals, lists for these to be stored in are passed as parameters to the `hunt` and `run` methods of `Fox` and `Rabbit`. The newly born animals are then added to the master lists at the end of the step. Running longer simulations is trivial. To do this, the `simulateOneStep` method is called repeatedly in a simple loop.

In order to let each animal act, the simulator holds separate lists of the different types of animals. Here, we make no use of inheritance, and the situation is reminiscent of the first version of the *network* project introduced in Chapter 8.

Code 10.4

Inside the `Simulator` class: simulating one step

```
public void simulateOneStep()
{
    step++;
    // Provide space for newborn rabbits.
    List<Rabbit> newRabbits = new ArrayList<Rabbit>();
    // Let all rabbits act.
    for(Iterator<Rabbit> it = rabbits.iterator(); it.hasNext(); ) {
        Rabbit rabbit = it.next();
        rabbit.run(newRabbits);
        if(!rabbit.isAlive()) {
            it.remove();
        }
    }

    // Provide space for newborn foxes.
    List<Fox> newFoxes = new ArrayList<Fox> ();
    // Let all foxes act.
    for(Iterator<Fox> it = foxes.iterator(); it.hasNext(); ) {
        Fox fox = it.next();
        fox.hunt(newFoxes);
        if(!fox.isAlive()) {
            it.remove();
        }
    }

    // Add the newly born foxes and rabbits to the main lists.
    rabbits.addAll(newRabbits);
    foxes.addAll(newFoxes);
    view.showStatus(step, field);
}
```

Exercise 10.24 Each animal is always held in two different data structures: the `Field` and the `Simulator`'s `rabbits` and `foxes` lists. There is a risk that they could be inconsistent with each other. Check that you thoroughly understand how the `Field` and the animal lists are kept consistent between the `simulateOneStep` method in `Simulator`, `hunt` in `Fox`, and `run` in `Rabbit`.

Exercise 10.25 Do you think it would be better for `Simulator` not to keep separate lists of foxes and rabbits but to generate these lists again from the contents of the field at the beginning of each simulation step? Discuss this.

Exercise 10.26 Write a test to ensure that, at the end of a simulation step, there is no animal (dead or alive) in the field that is not in one of the lists and vice versa. Should there be any dead animals in any of those places at that stage?

10.2.6 Taking steps to improve the simulation

Now that we have examined how the simulation operates, we are in a position to make improvements to its internal design and implementation. Making progressive improvements through the introduction of new programming features will be the focus of subsequent sections. There are several points at which we could start, but one of the most obvious weaknesses is that no attempt has been made to exploit the advantages of inheritance in the implementation of the `Fox` and `Rabbit` classes, which share a lot of common elements. In order to do this, we shall introduce the concept of an *abstract class*.

Exercise 10.27 Identify the similarities and differences between the `Fox` and `Rabbit` classes. Make separate lists of the fields, methods, and constructors, and distinguish between the class variables (static fields) and instance variables.

Exercise 10.28 Candidate methods for placement in a superclass are those that are identical in all subclasses. Which methods are truly identical in the `Fox` and `Rabbit` classes? In reaching a conclusion, you might like to consider the effect of substituting the values of class variables into the bodies of the methods that use them.

Exercise 10.29 In the current version of the simulation, the values of all similarly named class variables are different. If the two values of a particular class variable (`BREEDING_AGE`, say) were identical, would it make any difference to your assessment of which methods are truly identical?

10.3 Abstract classes

Chapter 8 introduced concepts such as inheritance and polymorphism that we ought to be able to exploit in the simulation application. For instance, the `Fox` and `Rabbit` classes share many similar characteristics that suggest they should be subclasses of a common superclass, such as `Animal`. In this section, we will start to make such changes in order to improve the design and implementation of the simulation as a whole. As with the project in Chapter 8, using a common superclass should avoid code duplication in the subclasses and simplify the code in the client class (here, `Simulator`). It is important to note that we are undertaking a process of refactoring and that these changes should not change the essential characteristics of the simulation as seen from a user's viewpoint.

10.3.1   The `Animal` superclass

For the first set of changes, we will move the identical elements of `Fox` and `Rabbit` to an `Animal` superclass. The project *foxes-and-rabbits-v1* provides a copy of the base version of the simulation for you to follow through the changes we make.

- Both `Fox` and `Rabbit` define `age`, `alive`, `field`, and `location` attributes. However, at this point we will only move `alive`, `location`, and `field` to the `Animal` superclass and come back to discuss the `age` field later. As is our normal practice with instance fields, we will keep all of these private in the superclass. The initial values are set in the constructor of `Animal`, with `alive` set to `true`, and `field` and `location` passed via `super` calls from the constructors of `Fox` and `Rabbit`.

- These fields will need accessors and mutators, so we can move the existing `getLocation`, `setLocation`, `isAlive`, and `setDead` from `Fox` and `Rabbit`. We will also need to add a `getField` method in `Animal` so that direct access to `field` from the subclass methods `run`, `hunt`, `giveBirth`, and `findFood` can be replaced.

- In moving these methods, we have to think about the most appropriate visibility for them. For instance, `setLocation` is private in both `Fox` and `Rabbit`, but cannot be kept private in `Animal` because `Fox` and `Rabbit` would not be able to call it. So we should raise it to `protected` visibility, to indicate that it is for subclasses to call.

- In a similar vein, notice that `setDead` was public in `Rabbit` but private in `Fox`. Should it therefore be public in `Animal`? It was public in `Rabbit` because a fox needs to be able to call a rabbit's `setDead` method when it eats its prey. Now that they are sibling classes of a shared superclass, a more appropriate visibility is `protected`, again indicating that this is a method that is not a part of an animal's general interface—at least at this stage of the project's development.

Making these changes is a first step toward eliminating code duplication through the use of inheritance, in much the same way as we did this in Chapter 8.

Exercise 10.30 What sort of regression-testing strategy could you establish before undertaking the process of refactoring on the simulation? Is this something you could conveniently automate?

Exercise 10.31 The `Randomizer` class provides us with a way to control whether the "random" elements of the simulation are repeatable or not. If its `useShared` field is set to `true`, then a single `Random` object is shared between all of the simulation objects. In addition, its `reset` method resets the starting point for the shared `Random` object. Use these features as you work on the following exercise, to check that you do not change anything fundamental about the overall simulation as you introduce an `Animal` class.

Create the `Animal` superclass in your version of the project. Make the changes discussed above. Ensure that the simulation works in a similar manner as before. You should be able to check this by having the old and new versions of the project open side by side, for instance, and making identical calls on `Simulator` objects in both, expecting identical outcomes.

Exercise 10.32 How has using inheritance improved the project so far? Discuss this.

10.3.2   Abstract methods

So far, use of the `Animal` superclass has helped to avoid a lot of the code duplication in the `Rabbit` and `Fox` classes, and has potentially made it easier to add new animal types in the future. However, as we have seen in Chapter 8, intelligent use of inheritance should also simplify the client class—in this case, `Simulator`. We shall investigate this now.

In the `Simulator` class, we have used separate typed lists of foxes and rabbits and per-list iteration code to implement each simulation step. The relevant code is shown in Code 10.4. Now that we have the `Animal` class, we can improve this. Because all objects in our animal collections are a subtype of `Animal`, we can merge them into a single collection and hence iterate just once using the `Animal` type. However, one problem with this is evident from the single-list solution in Code 10.5. Although we know that each item in the list is an `Animal`, we still have to work out which type of animal it is in order to call the correct action method for its type—`run` or `hunt`. We determine the type using the `instanceof` operator.

The fact that in Code 10.5 each type of animal must be tested for and cast separately and that special code exists for each animal class is a good sign that we have not taken full advantage of what inheritance has to offer. A better solution is to place a method in the superclass (`Animal`),

Code 10.5

An unsatisfactory single-list solution to making animals act

```
for(Iterator<Animal> it = animals.iterator(); it.hasNext(); ) {
    Animal animal = it.next();
    if(animal instanceof Rabbit) {
        Rabbit rabbit = (Rabbit) animal;
        rabbit.run(newAnimals);
    }
    else if(animal instanceof Fox) {
        Fox fox = (Fox) animal;
        fox.hunt(newAnimals);
    }
    else {
        System.out.println("found unknown animal");
    }
    // Remove dead animals from the simulation.
    if(! animal.isAlive()) {
        it.remove();
    }
}
```

letting an animal act, and then override it in each subclass so that we have a polymorphic method call to let each animal act appropriately, without the need to test for the specific animal types. This is a standard refactoring technique in situations like this, where we have subtype-specific behavior invoked from a context that only deals with the supertype.

Let us assume that we create such a method, called `act`, and investigate the resulting source code. Code 10.6 shows the code implementing this solution.

Code 10.6

The fully improved solution to animal action

```
// Let all animals act.
for(Iterator<Animal> it = animals.iterator(); it.hasNext(); ) {
    Animal animal = it.next();
    animal.act(newAnimals);
    // Remove dead animals from the simulation.
    if(! animal.isAlive()) {
      it.remove();
    }
}
```

Several observations are important at this point:

■ The variable we are using for each collection element (`animal`) is of type `Animal`. This is legal, because all objects in the collection are foxes or rabbits and are all subtypes of Animal.

■ We assume that the specific action methods (`run` for `Rabbit`, `hunt` for `Fox`) have been renamed `act`. This is more appropriate than previously. Instead of telling each animal exactly what to do, we are just telling it to "act," and we leave it up to the animal itself to decide what exactly it wants to do. This reduces coupling between `Simulator` and the individual animal subclasses.

■ Because the dynamic type of the variable determines which method is actually executed (as discussed in Chapter 9), the fox's action method will be executed for foxes and the rabbit's method for rabbits.

■ Because type checking is done using the static type, this code will compile only if class `Animal` has an `act` method with the right header.

The last of these points is the only remaining problem. Because we are using the statement

```
animal.act(newAnimals);
```

and the variable `animal` is of type `Animal`, this will compile only if `Animal` defines an `act` method—as we saw in Chapter 9. However, the situation here is rather different from the situation we encountered with the `display` method in Chapter 9. There, the superclass version of `display` had a useful job to do: print the fields defined in the superclass. Here, although each particular animal has a specific set of actions to perform, we cannot describe in any detail the actions for animals in general. The particular actions depend on the specific subtype.

Our problem is to decide how we should define `Animal`'s `act` method.

The problem is a reflection of the fact that no instance of class `Animal` will ever exist. There is no object in our simulation (or in nature) that is just an animal and not also an instance of a more specific subclass. These kinds of classes, which are not intended for creating objects but serve only as superclasses, are known as *abstract classes.* For animals, for example, we can say that each animal can act, but we cannot describe exactly how it acts without referring to a more specific subclass. This is typical for abstract classes, and it is reflected in Java constructs.

For the `Animal` class, we wish to state that each animal has an `act` method, but we cannot give a reasonable implementation in class `Animal`. The solution in Java is to declare the method *abstract.* Here is an example of an abstract `act` method:

```
abstract public void act(List<Animal> newAnimals);
```

An abstract method is characterized by two details:

- It is prefixed with the keyword `abstract`.

- It does not have a method body. Instead, its header is terminated with a semicolon.

Because the method has no body, it can never be executed. But we have already established that we do not want to execute an `Animal`'s `act` method, so that is not a problem.

Before we investigate in detail the effects of using an abstract method, we shall introduce more formally the concept of an abstract class.

> **Concept:**
>
> An **abstract method** definition consists of a method header without a method body. It is marked with the keyword `abstract`.

10.3.3 Abstract classes

It is not only methods that can be declared abstract; classes can be declared abstract as well. Code 10.7 shows an example of class `Animal` as an abstract class. Classes are declared abstract by inserting the keyword `abstract` into the class header.

Classes that are not abstract (all classes we have seen previously) are called *concrete classes.*

Declaring a class abstract serves several purposes:

- No instances can be created of abstract classes. Trying to use the `new` keyword with an abstract class is an error and will not be permitted by the compiler. This is mirrored in BlueJ: right-clicking on an abstract class in the class diagram will not list any constructors in the

> **Concept:**
>
> An **abstract class** is a class that is not intended for creating instances. Its purpose is to serve as a superclass for other classes. Abstract classes may contain abstract methods.

Code 10.7

`Animal` as an abstract class

```
public abstract class Animal
{
    // fields omitted

    /**
     * Make this animal act - that is, make it do whatever
     * it wants/needs to do.
     * @param newAnimals A list to return newly born animals.
     */
    abstract public void act(List<Animal> newAnimals);

    // other methods omitted
}
```

pop-up menu. This serves our intention discussed above: we stated that we did not want instances of class `Animal` created directly—this class serves only as a superclass. Declaring the class abstract enforces this restriction.

■ Only abstract classes can have abstract methods. This ensures that all methods in concrete classes can always be executed. If we allowed an abstract method in a concrete class, we would be able to create an instance of a class that lacked an implementation for a method.

■ Abstract classes with abstract methods force subclasses to override and implement those methods declared abstract. If a subclass does not provide an implementation for an inherited abstract method, it is itself abstract, and no instances may be created. For a subclass to be concrete, it must provide implementations for *all* inherited abstract methods.

Now we can start to see the purpose of abstract methods. Although they do not provide an implementation, they nonetheless ensure that all concrete subclasses have an implementation of this method. In other words, even though class `Animal` does not implement the `act` method, it ensures that all existing animals have an implemented `act` method. This is done by ensuring that

■ no instance of class `Animal` can be created directly, and

■ all concrete subclasses must implement the `act` method.

Although we cannot create an instance of an abstract class directly, we can otherwise use an abstract class as a type in the usual ways. For instance, the normal rules of polymorphism allow us to handle foxes and rabbits as instances of the `Animal` class. So those parts of the simulation that do not need to know whether they are dealing with a specific subclass can use the superclass type instead.

Exercise 10.33 Although the body of the loop in Code 10.6 no longer deals with the `Fox` and `Rabbit` types, it still deals with the `Animal` type. Why is it not possible for it to treat each object in the collection simply using the `Object` type?

Exercise 10.34 Is it necessary for a class with one or more abstract methods to be defined as abstract? If you are not sure, experiment with the source of the `Animal` class in the *foxes-and-rabbits-v2* project.

Exercise 10.35 Is it possible for a class that has no abstract methods to be defined as abstract? If you are not sure, change `act` to be a concrete method in the `Animal` class by giving it a method body with no statements.

Exercise 10.36 Could it ever make sense to define a class as abstract if it has no abstract methods? Discuss this.

Exercise 10.37 Which classes in the `java.util` package are abstract? Some of them have `Abstract` in the class name, but is there any other way to tell from the documentation? Which concrete classes extend them?

Exercise 10.38 Can you tell from the API documentation for an abstract class which (if any) of its methods are abstract? Do you *need* to know which methods are abstract?

Exercise 10.39 Review the overriding rules for methods and fields discussed in Chapter 9. Why are they particularly significant in our attempts to introduce inheritance into this application?

Exercise 10.40 The changes made in this section have removed the dependences (couplings) of the simulateOneStep method on the Fox and Rabbit classes. The Simulator class, however, is still coupled to Fox and Rabbit, because these classes are referenced in the populate method. There is no way to avoid this; when we create animal instances, we have to specify exactly what kind of animal to create.

This could be improved by splitting the Simulator into two classes: one class, Simulator, that runs the simulation and is completely decoupled from the concrete animal classes, and another class, PopulationGenerator (created and called by the simulator), that creates the population. Only this class is coupled to the concrete animal classes, making it easier for a maintenance programmer to find places where change is necessary when the application is extended. Try implementing this refactoring step. The PopulationGenerator class should also define the colors for each type of animal.

The project *foxes-and-rabbits-v2* provides an implementation of our simulation with the improvements discussed here. It is important to note that the change in Simulator to processing all the animals in a single list, rather than in separate lists, means that the simulation results in version 2 will not be identical to those in version 1.

In the book projects, you will find a third version of this project: *foxes-and-rabbits-graph*. This project is identical to *foxes-and-rabbits-v2* in its model (i.e., the animal/fox/rabbit/simulator implementations), but it adds a second view to the project: a graph showing population numbers over time. We will discuss some aspects of its implementation a little later in this chapter; for now, just experiment with this project.

Exercise 10.41 Open and run the *foxes-and-rabbits-graph* project. Pay attention to the *Graph View* output. Explain, in writing, the meaning of the graph you see, and try to explain why it looks the way it looks. Is there a relationship between the two curves?

Exercise 10.42 Repeat some of your experiments with different sizes of fields (especially smaller fields). Does the graph view give you any new insights or help you understand or explain what you see?

If you have done all the exercises in this chapter so far, then your version of the project will be the same as *foxes-and-rabbits-v2* and similar to *foxes-and-rabbits-graph*, except for the graph display. You can continue the exercises from here on with either version of these projects.

10.4 More abstract methods

When we created the Animal superclass in Section 10.3, we did this by identifying common elements of the subclasses, but we chose not to move the age field and the methods associated with it. This might be overly conservative. We could, in fact, have quite easily moved the age field to Animal and provided for it there an accessor and a mutator that were called by subclass methods, such as incrementAge. Why didn't we move incrementAge and canBreed into Animal, then? The reason for not moving these is that, although several of the remaining method bodies in Fox and Rabbit contain textually identical statements, their use of class variables with different values means that they cannot be moved directly to the superclass. In the case of canBreed, the problem is the BREEDING_AGE variable, while breed depends on BREEDING_PROBABILITY and MAX_LITTER_SIZE. If canBreed is moved to Animal, for instance, then the compiler will need to have access to a value for the subtype-specific breeding age in class Animal. It is tempting to define a BREEDING_AGE field in the Animal class and assume that its value will be overridden by similarly named fields in the subclasses. However, fields are handled differently from methods in Java: they cannot be overridden by subclass versions.[3] This means that a canBreed method in Animal would use a meaningless value defined in that class rather than one that is specific to a particular subclass.

The fact that the field's value would be meaningless gives us a clue as to how we can get around this problem and, as a result, move more of the similar methods from the subclasses to the superclass.

Remember that we defined act as abstract in Animal because having a body for the method would be meaningless. If we access the breeding age with a method rather than a field, we can get around the problems associated with the age-dependent properties. This approach is shown in Code 10.8.

Code 10.8

The canBreed method of Animal

```
/**
 * An animal can breed if it has reached the breeding age.
 * @return true if the animal can breed
 */
public boolean canBreed()
{
    return age >= getBreedingAge();
}

/**
 * Return the breeding age of this animal.
 * @return The breeding age of this animal.
 */
abstract protected int getBreedingAge();
```

The canBreed method has been moved to Animal and rewritten to use the value returned from a method call rather than the value of a class variable. For this to work, a method getBreedingAge must be defined in class Animal. Because we cannot specify a breeding age for animals in general, we can again use an abstract method in the Animal class and concrete

[3] This rule applies regardless of whether a field is static or not.

Concept:

Superclass method calls. Calls to non-private instance methods from within a superclass are always evaluated in the wider context of the object's dynamic type.

redefinitions in the subclasses. Both `Fox` and `Rabbit` will define their own versions of `get-BreedingAge` to return their particular values of `BREEDING_AGE`:

```
/**
 * @return The age at which a rabbit starts to breed.
 */
public int getBreedingAge()
{
    return BREEDING_AGE;
}
```

So even though the call to `getBreedingAge` originates in the code of the superclass, the method called is defined in the subclass. This may seem mysterious at first but it is based on the same principles we described in Chapter 9 in using the dynamic type of an object to determine which version of a method is called at runtime. The technique illustrated here makes it possible for each instance to use the value appropriate to its subclass type. Using the same approach, we can move the remaining methods, `incrementAge` and `breed`, to the superclass.

Exercise 10.43 Using your latest version of the project (or the *foxes-and-rabbits-v2* project in case you have not done all the exercises), record the number of foxes and rabbits over a small number of steps, to prepare for regression testing of the changes to follow.

Exercise 10.44 Move the `age` field from `Fox` and `Rabbit` to `Animal`. Initialize it to zero in the constructor. Provide accessor and mutator methods for it and use these in `Fox` and `Rabbit` rather than in direct accesses to the field. Make sure the program compiles and runs as before.

Exercise 10.45 Move the `canBreed` method from `Fox` and `Rabbit` to `Animal`, and rewrite it as shown in Code 10.8. Provide appropriate versions of `getBreedingAge` in `Fox` and `Rabbit` that return the distinctive breeding age values.

Exercise 10.46 Move the `incrementAge` method from `Fox` and `Rabbit` to `Animal` by providing an abstract `getMaxAge` method in `Animal` and concrete versions in `Fox` and `Rabbit`.

Exercise 10.47 Can the `breed` method be moved to `Animal`? If so, make this change.

Exercise 10.48 In light of all the changes you have made to these three classes, reconsider the visibility of each method and make any changes you feel are appropriate.

Exercise 10.49 Was it possible to make these changes without having any impact on any other classes in the project? If so, what does this suggest about the degrees of encapsulation and coupling that were present in the original version?

Exercise 10.50 *Challenge exercise* Define a completely new type of animal for the simulation, as a subclass of `Animal`. You will need to decide what sort of impact its existence will have on the existing animal types. For instance, your animal might compete with foxes as a predator on the rabbit population, or your animal might prey on foxes but not on rabbits. You will probably find that you need to experiment quite a lot with the configuration settings you use for it. You will need to modify the `populate` method to have some of your animals created at the start of a simulation.

You should also define a new color for your new animal class. You can find a list of predefined color names on the API page documenting the `Color` class in the `java.awt` package.

Exercise 10.51 *Challenge exercise* The text of the `giveBirth` methods in `Fox` and `Rabbit` is very similar. The only difference is that one creates new `Fox` objects and the other creates new `Rabbit` objects. Is it possible to use the technique illustrated with `canBreed` to move the common code into a shared `giveBirth` method in `Animal`? If you think it is, try it out. *Hint*: The rules on polymorphic substitution apply to values returned from methods as well as in assignment and parameter passing.

10.5 Multiple inheritance

10.5.1 An `Actor` class

In this section, we discuss some possible future extensions and some programming constructs to support these extensions.

The first obvious extension for our simulation is the addition of new animals. If you have attempted Exercise 10.50 then you will have touched on this already. We should, however, generalize this a bit: maybe not all participants in the simulation will be animals. Our current structure assumes that all acting participants in the simulation are animals and that they inherit from the `Animal` superclass. One enhancement that we might like to make is the introduction of human predators to the simulation, as either hunters or trappers. They do not neatly fit the existing assumption of purely animal-based actors. We might also extend the simulation to include plants eaten by the rabbits, or even some aspects of the weather. The plants as food would influence the population of rabbits (in effect, rabbits become predators of the plants), and the growth of the plants might be influenced by the weather. All these new components would act in the simulation, but they are clearly not animals, so it would be inappropriate to have them as subclasses of `Animal`.

As we consider the potential for introducing further actors into the simulation, it is worth revealing why we chose to store details of the animals in both a `Field` object and an `Animal` list. Visiting each animal in the list is what constitutes a single simulation step. Placing all participants in a single list keeps the basic simulation step simple. However, this clearly duplicates information, which risks creating inconsistency. One reason for this design decision is that it allows us to consider participants in the simulation that are not actually within the field—a representation for the weather might be one example of this.

To deal with more general actors, it seems like a good idea to introduce an Actor super-class. The Actor class would serve as a superclass to all kinds of simulation participants, independent of what they are. Figure 10.3 shows a class diagram for this part of the simulation. The Actor and Animal classes are abstract, while Rabbit, Fox, and Hunter are concrete classes.

Figure 10.3
Simulation structure
with Actor

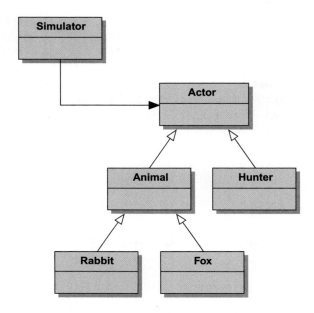

The Actor class would include the common part of all actors. One thing all possible actors have in common is that they perform some kind of action. We will also need to know whether an actor is still active or not. So the only definitions in class Actor are those of abstract act and isActive methods:

```
// all comments omitted

public abstract class Actor
{
    abstract public void act(List<Actor> newActors);
    abstract public boolean isActive();
}
```

This should be enough to rewrite the actor loop in the Simulator (Code 10.6), using class Actor instead of class Animal. (Either the isAlive method could be renamed to isActive or a separate isActive method in Animal could simply call the existing isAlive method.)

> **Exercise 10.52** Introduce the Actor class into your simulation. Rewrite the simulate-OneStep method in Simulator to use Actor instead of Animal. You can do this even if you have not introduced any new participant types. Does the Simulator class compile? Or is there something else that is needed in the Actor class?

This new structure is more flexible because it allows easier addition of non-animal actors. In fact, we could even rewrite the statistics-gathering class, FieldStats, as an Actor—it too acts once every step. Its action would be to update its current count of animals.

10.5.2 Flexibility through abstraction

By moving towards the notion of the simulation being responsible for managing actor objects, we have succeeded in abstracting quite a long way away from our original very specific scenario of foxes and rabbits in a rectangular field. This process of abstraction has brought with it an increased flexibility that may allow us to widen even further the scope of what we might do with a general simulation framework. If we think through the requirements of other similar simulation scenarios, then we might come up with ideas for additional features that we could introduce.

For instance, it might be useful to simulate other predator–prey scenarios such as a marine simulation involving fish and sharks, or fish and fishing fleets. If the marine simulation were to involve modeling food supplies for the fish, then we would probably not want to visualize plankton populations—either because the numbers are too vast or because their size is too small. Other environmental simulations might involve modeling the weather, which, while it is clearly an actor, also might not require visualization.

In the next section, we shall investigate the separation of visualization from acting, as a further extension to our simulation framework.

10.5.3 Selective drawing

One way to implement the separation of visualization from acting is to change the way it is performed in the simulation. Instead of iterating over the whole field every time and drawing actors in every position, we could iterate over a separate collection of drawable actors. The code in the simulator class would look similar to this:

```
// Let all actors act.
for(Actor actor : actors) {
    actor.act(...);
}

// Draw all drawables.
for(Drawable item : drawables) {
    item.draw(...);
}
```

All of the actors would be in the actors collection, and those actors we want to show on screen would also be in the drawables collection. For this to work, we need another superclass called Drawable, which declares an abstract draw method. Drawable actors must then inherit from both Actor and Drawable. (Figure 10.4 shows an example where we assume that we have ants, which act but are too numerous to visualize.)

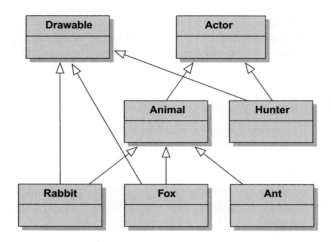

10.5.4 Drawable actors: multiple inheritance

Concept:

Multiple inheritance. A situation in which a class inherits from more than one superclass is called multiple inheritance.

The scenario presented here uses a structure known as *multiple inheritance*. Multiple inheritance exists in cases where one class has more than one immediate superclass.[4] The subclass then has all the features of both superclasses and those defined in the subclass itself.

Multiple inheritance is quite easy to understand in principle but can lead to significant complications in the implementation of a programming language. Different object-oriented languages vary in their treatment of multiple inheritance: some languages allow the inheritance of multiple superclasses; others do not. Java lies somewhere in the middle. It does not allow multiple inheritance of classes but provides another construct, called an "interface," that allows a limited form of multiple inheritance. Interfaces are discussed in the next section.

10.6   Interfaces

Up to this point in the book, we have used the term "interface" in an informal sense, to represent that part of a class that couples it to other classes. Java captures this concept more formally by allowing *interface types* to be defined.

At first glance, interfaces are similar to classes, with the most obvious difference being that none of their method definitions includes a method body. Thus, they are similar to abstract classes in which all methods are abstract.

---

[4] Don't confuse this case with the regular situation where a single class might have several superclasses in its inheritance hierarchy, such as `Fox`, `Animal`, `Actor`, and `Object`. This is not what is meant by multiple inheritance.

10.6.1 An `Actor` interface

Code 10.9 shows `Actor` defined as an interface type.

Code 10.9

The `Actor` interface

```
/**
 * The interface to be extended by any class wishing
 * to participate in the simulation.
 */
public interface Actor
{
    /**
     * Perform the actor's regular behavior.
     * @param newActors A list for receiving newly created actors.
     */
    void act(List<Actor> newActors);

    /**
     * Is the actor still active?
     * @return true if still active, false if not.
     */
    boolean isActive();
}
```

Concepts:

A Java **interface** is a specification of a type (in the form of a type name and a set of methods) that does not define any implementation for the methods.

Java interfaces have a number of significant features:

- The keyword `interface` is used instead of `class` in the header of the declaration.
- All methods in an interface are abstract; no method bodies are permitted. The `abstract` keyword is not needed, therefore.
- Interfaces do not contain any constructors.
- All method headers in an interface have public visibility, so the `public` keyword is not needed.
- Only `public` constant class fields (`static` and `final`) are allowed in an interface. The `public`, `static`, and `final` keywords may be omitted, therefore.

A class can inherit from an interface in a similar way to that for inheriting from a class. However, Java uses a different keyword—`implements`—for inheriting interfaces.

A class is said to *implement* an interface if it includes an *implements clause* in its class header. For instance:

```
public class Fox extends Animal implements Drawable
{
    // Body of class omitted.
}
```

As in this case, if a class both extends a class and implements an interface, then the extends clause must be written first in the class header.

Two of our abstract classes in the example above, `Actor` and `Drawable`, are good candidates for being written as interfaces. Both of them contain only the definition of methods, without method implementations. Thus, they already fit the definition of an interface perfectly: they contain no instance fields, no constructors, and no method bodies.

The class `Animal` is a different case. It is a real abstract class that provides a partial implementation (many methods have method bodies) and only a single abstract method in its original version. So it must remain as a class rather than becoming an interface.

Exercise 10.53 Redefine as an interface the abstract class `Actor` in your project. Does the simulation still compile? Does it run? Make any changes necessary to make it runnable again.

Exercise 10.54 Are the fields in the following interface class fields or instance fields?

```
public interface Quiz
{
    int CORRECT = 1;
    int INCORRECT = 0;
    ...
}
```

What visibility do they have?

Exercise 10.55 What are the errors in the following interface?

```
public interface Monitor
{
    private static final int THRESHOLD = 50;
    public Monitor (int initial);
    public int getThreshold()
    {
        return THRESHOLD;
    }
    ...
}
```

10.6.2 Multiple inheritance of interfaces

As mentioned above, Java allows any class to extend at most one other class. However, it allows a class to implement any number of interfaces (in addition to possibly extending one class). Thus, if we define both `Actor` and `Drawable` as interfaces instead of abstract classes, we can define class `Hunter` (Figure 10.4) to implement both of them:

```
public class Hunter implements Actor, Drawable
{
    // Body of class omitted.
}
```

The class `Hunter` inherits the methods of all interfaces (`act` and `draw`, in this case) as abstract methods. It must, then, provide method definitions for both of them by overriding the methods, or the class itself must be declared abstract.

The `Animal` class shows an example where a class does not implement an inherited interface method. `Animal`, in our new structure in Figure 10.4, inherits the abstract method `act` from `Actor`. It does not provide a method body for this method, which makes `Animal` itself abstract (it must include the `abstract` keyword in the class header).

The `Animal` subclasses then implement the `act` method and become concrete classes.

> **Exercise 10.56** *Challenge exercise* Add a non-animal actor to the simulation. For instance, you could introduce a `Hunter` class with the following properties. Hunters have no maximum age and neither feed nor breed. At each step of the simulation, a hunter moves to a random location anywhere in the field and fires a fixed number of shots into random target locations around the field. Any animal in one of the target locations is killed.
>
> Place just a small number of hunters in the field at the start of the simulation. Do the hunters remain in the simulation throughout, or do they ever disappear? If they do disappear, why might that be, and does that represent realistic behavior?
>
> What other classes required changing as a result of introducing hunters? Is there a need to introduce further decoupling to the classes?

10.6.3 Interfaces as types

When a class implements an interface, it does not inherit any implementation from it, because interfaces cannot contain method bodies. The question, then, is: What do we actually gain by implementing interfaces?

When we introduced inheritance in Chapter 8, we emphasized two great benefits of inheritance:

- The subclass inherits the code (method implementations and fields) from the superclass. This allows reuse of existing code and avoids code duplication.

- The subclass becomes a subtype of the superclass. This allows polymorphic variables and method calls. In other words, it allows different special cases of objects (instances of subclasses) to be treated uniformly (as instances of the supertype).

Interfaces do not provide the first benefit (because they do not contain implementations), but they do provide the second. An interface defines a type just as a class does. This means that variables can be declared to be of interface types even though no objects of that type can exist (only subtypes).

In our example, even though `Actor` is now an interface, we can still declare an `Actor` variable in the `Simulator` class. The simulation loop still works unchanged.

Interfaces can have no direct instances, but they serve as supertypes for instances of other classes.

10.6.4 Interfaces as specifications

In this chapter, we have introduced interfaces as a means to implement multiple inheritance in Java. This is one important use of interfaces, but there are others.

The most important characteristic of interfaces is that they completely separate the definition of the functionality (the class's "interface" in the wider sense of the word) from its implementation. A good example of how this can be used in practice can be found in the Java collection hierarchy.

The collection hierarchy defines (among other types) the interface List and the classes ArrayList and LinkedList (Figure 10.5). The List interface specifies the full functionality of a list, without giving any implementation. The subclasses (LinkedList and ArrayList) provide two different implementations of the same interface. This is interesting, because the two implementations differ greatly in the efficiency of some of their functions. Random access to elements in the middle of the list, for example, is much faster with the ArrayList. Inserting or deleting elements, however, can be much faster in the LinkedList.

Figure 10.5
The List interface and its subclasses

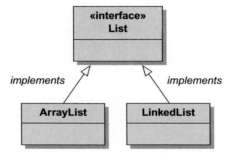

Which implementation is better in any given application can be hard to judge in advance. It depends a lot on the relative frequency with which certain operations are performed and on some other factors. In practice, the best way to find out is often to try it out: implement the application with both alternatives and measure the performance.

The existence of the List interface makes it very easy to do this. If, instead of using ArrayList or LinkedList as variable and parameter types, we always use List, our application will work independently of the specific type of list we are currently using. Only when we create a new list do we really have to use the name of the specific implementation. We would, for instance, write

```
List<Type> myList = new ArrayList<Type>();
```

Note that the polymorphic variable's type is just List of Type. This way, we can change the whole application to use a linked list by just changing ArrayList to LinkedList in a single location when the list is being created.

Exercise 10.57 Which methods do ArrayList and LinkedList have that are not defined in the List interface? Why do you think that these methods are not included in List?

Exercise 10.58 Write a class that can make comparisons between the efficiency of the common methods from the List interface in the ArrayList and LinkedList classes such as add, get, and remove. Use the polymorphic-variable technique described above to write the class so that it only knows it is performing its tests on objects of the interface type List rather than on the concrete types ArrayList and LinkedList. Use large lists of objects for the tests, to make the results significant. You can use the currentTimeMillis method of the System class for getting hold of the start and finish time of your test methods.

Exercise 10.59 Read the API description for the sort methods of the Collections class in the java.util package. Which interfaces are mentioned in the descriptions?

Exercise 10.60 *Challenge exercise* Investigate the Comparable interface. This is a *parameterized* interface. Define a simple class that implements Comparable. Create a collection containing objects of this class and sort the collection. *Hint*: The LogEntry class of the *weblog-analyzer* project in Chapter 4 implements this interface.

10.6.5 Library support through abstract classes and interfaces

In Chapter 5, we pointed out the importance of paying attention to the names of the collection classes: ArrayList, LinkedList, HashSet, TreeSet, etc. Now that we have been introduced to abstract classes and interfaces, we can see why these particular names have been chosen. The java.util package defines several important collection abstractions in the form of interfaces, such as List, Map and Set. The concrete class names have been chosen to communicate information about both what kind of interface they conform to and some of the underlying implementation detail. This information is very useful when it comes to making informed decisions about the right concrete class to use in a particular setting. However, by using the highest-level abstract type (be it abstract class or interface) for our variables, wherever possible, our code will remain flexible in light of future library changes—such as the addition of a new Map or Set implementation, for instance.

In Chapter 11, where we introduce the Java GUI libraries, we will be making enormous use of abstract classes and interfaces as we see how to create quite sophisticated functionality with very little additional code.

10.7 A further example of interfaces

In the previous section, we have discussed how interfaces can be used to separate the specification of a component from its implementation so that different implementations can be "plugged in," thus making it easy to replace components of a system. This is often done to separate parts of a system that are logically only loosely coupled.

We have seen an example of this (without discussing it explicitly) at the end of Section 10.3. There, we investigated the *foxes-and-rabbits-graph* project, which added another view of the populations in the form of a line graph. Looking at the class diagram for this project, we can see that the addition also makes use of a Java interface (Fig 10.6).

Figure 10.6
The SimulatorView
interface and
implementing
classes

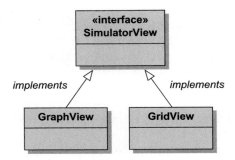

The previous versions of the *foxes-and-rabbits* project contained only one SimulatorView class. This was a concrete class, and it provided the implementation of a grid-based view of the field. As we have seen, the visualization is quite separate from the simulation logic (the field and the actors), and different visualization views are possible.

For this project, SimulatorView was changed from a class to an interface, and the implementation of this view was moved into a class named GridView.

GridView is identical to the previous SimulatorView class. The new SimulatorView interface was constructed by searching through the Simulator class to find all methods that are actually called from outside and then defining an interface that specifies exactly those methods. They are:

```
view.setColor(classObject, color);
view.isViable(field);
view.showStatus(step, field);
view.reset();
```

We can now easily define the complete SimulatorView interface:

```
import java.awt.Color;

public interface SimulatorView
{
    void setColor(Class animalClass, Color color);
    boolean isViable(Field field);
    void showStatus(int step, Field field);
    void reset();
}
```

The one, slightly tricky detail in the definition above is the use of the type Class as the first parameter of the setColor method. We will explain that in the next section.

The previous SimulatorView class, now called GridView, is specified to implement the new SimulatorView interface:

```
public class GridView extends JFrame implements SimulatorView

{
    ...
}
```

It does not require any additional code, because it already implements the interface's methods. However, after making these changes, it becomes fairly easy to "plug in" other views for the simulation by providing further implementations of the SimulatorView interface. The new class GraphView, which produces the line graph, is an example of this.

Once we have more than one view implementation, we can easily replace the current view with another or, as we have in our example, even display two views at the same time. In the Simulator class, the concrete subclasses GridView and GraphView are only mentioned once when each view was constructed. Thereafter, they are stored in a collection holding elements of the SimulatorView supertype, and only the interface type is used to communicate with them.

The implementations of the GridView and GraphView classes are fairly complex, and we do not expect you to fully understand them at this stage. The pattern of providing two implementations for a single interface, however, is important here, and you should make sure that you understand this aspect.

Exercise 10.61 Review the source code of the Simulator class. Find all occurrences of the view classes and interfaces, and trace all variables declared using any of these types. Explain exactly how the views are used in the Simulator class.

Exercise 10.62 Implement a new class TextView that implements SimulatorView. TextView provides a textual view of the simulation. After every simulation step, it prints out one line in the form

```
Foxes: 121 Rabbits: 266
```

Use TextView instead of GridView for some tests. (Do not delete the GridView classes. We want to have the ability to change between different views!)

Exercise 10.63 Can you manage to have all three views active at the same time?

10.8 The Class class

In Chapter 8, we described the paradoxically named Object class. It shouldn't surprise you, therefore, that there is also a Class class! This is where talking about classes and objects can become very confusing.

We used the Class type in defining the SimulatorView interface in the previous section. The Class class has nothing specifically to do with interfaces; it is a general feature of Java, but we just happen to be meeting it for the first time here. The idea is that each type has a Class object associated with it.

The Object class defines the method getClass to return the Class associated with an object. Another way to get the Class object for a type is to write ".class" after the type name: for instance, Fox.class or int.class—notice that even the primitive types have Class objects associated with them.

Class objects are particularly useful if we want to know whether the type of two objects is the same. We use this feature in the original SimulatorView class to associate each animal type with a color in the field. SimulatorView has the following field to map one to the other:

```
private Map<Class, Color> colors;
```

When the view is set up, the constructor of `Simulator` has the following calls to its `setColor` method:

```
view.setColor(Rabbit.class, Color.ORANGE);
view.setColor(Fox.class, Color.BLUE);
```

We won't go into any further detail about `Class`, but this description should be sufficient to enable you to understand the code shown in the previous section.

10.9 Abstract class or interface?

In some situations, a choice has to be made between whether to use an abstract class or an interface. Sometimes the choice is easy: when the class is intended to contain implementations for some methods, we need to use an abstract class. In other cases, either abstract classes or interfaces can do the job.

If we have a choice, interfaces are usually preferable. If we provide a type as an abstract class, then subclasses cannot extend any other classes. Because interfaces allow multiple inheritance, the use of an interface does not create such a restriction. Therefore, using interfaces leads to a more flexible and more extendible structure.

10.10 Event-driven simulations

The style of simulation we have used in this chapter has the characteristic of time passing in discrete, equal-length steps. At each time step, each actor in the simulation was asked to act— i.e., take the actions appropriate to its current state. This style of simulation is sometimes called *time-based*, or *synchronous*, simulation. In this particular simulation, most of the actors will have had something to do at each time step: move, breed, and eat. In many simulation scenarios, however, actors spend large numbers of time steps doing nothing—typically, waiting for something to happen that requires some action on their part. Consider the case of a newly born rabbit in our simulation, for instance. It is repeatedly asked whether it is going to breed, even though it takes several time steps before this is possible. Isn't there a way to avoid asking this unnecessary question until it is actually ready?

There is also the question of the most appropriate size of the time step. We deliberately left vague the issue of how much real time a time step represents, and the various actions actually require significantly different amounts of time (eating and movement should occur much more frequently than giving birth, for instance). Is there a way to decide on a time-step size that is not so small that most of the time nothing will be happening or too long that different types of actions are not distinguished clearly enough between time steps?

An alternative approach is to use an *event-based*, or *asynchronous*, simulation style. In this style, the simulation is driven by maintaining a schedule of future events. The most obvious difference between the two styles is that, in an event-based simulation, time passes in uneven amounts. For instance, one event might occur at time t and the next two events occur at times $t+2$ and time $t+8$, while the following three events might all occur at time $t+9$.

For a fox-and-rabbits simulation, the sort of events we are talking about would be birth, movement, hunting, and death from natural causes. What typically happens is that, as each event occurs, a fresh event is scheduled for some point in the future. For instance, when a birth event occurs, the event marking that animal's death from old age will be scheduled. All future events are stored in an ordered queue, where the next event to take place is held at the head of the queue. It is important to appreciate that newly scheduled events will not always be placed at the end of the current queue; they will often have to be inserted somewhere before the end, in order to keep the queue in time order. In addition, some future events will be rendered obsolete by events that occur before them—an obvious example is that the natural-death event for a rabbit will not take place if the rabbit is eaten beforehand!

Event-driven simulations lend themselves particularly well to the techniques we have described in this chapter. For instance, the concept of an event is likely to be implemented as an Event abstract class containing concrete details of when the event will occur, but only abstract details of what the event involves. Concrete subclasses of Event will then supply the specific details for the different event types. Typically, the main simulation loop will not need to be concerned with the concrete event types, but will be able to use polymorphic method calls when an event occurs.

Event-based simulations are often more efficient and are preferable where large systems and large amounts of data are involved, while synchronous simulations are better for producing time-based visualizations (such as animations of the actors) because time flows more evenly.

> **Exercise 10.64** Find out some more about how event-driven simulations differ from time-based simulations.
>
> **Exercise 10.65** Look at the java.util package to see if there are any classes that might be well suited to storing an event queue in an event-based simulation.
>
> **Exercise 10.66** *Challenge exercise* Rewrite the foxes-and-rabbits simulation in the event-based style.

10.11 Summary of inheritance

In the past three chapters, we have discussed many different aspects of inheritance techniques. These include code inheritance and subtyping as well as inheriting from interfaces, abstract classes, and concrete classes.

In general, we can distinguish two main purposes of using inheritance: we can use it to inherit code (code inheritance), and we can use it to inherit the type (subtyping). The first is useful for code reuse, the second for polymorphism and specialization.

When we inherit from ("extend") concrete classes, we do both: we inherit the implementation and the type. When we inherit from ("implement") interfaces, we separate the two: we inherit a type but no implementation. For cases where parts of both are useful, we can inherit from abstract classes; here, we inherit the type and a partial implementation.

When inheriting a complete implementation, we can choose to add or override methods. When no or only partial implementation of a type is inherited, the subclass must provide the implementation before it can be instantiated.

Some other object-oriented languages also provide mechanisms to inherit code without inheriting the type. Java does not provide such a construct.

10.12 Summary

In this chapter, we have discussed the fundamental structure of computer simulations. We have then used this example to introduce abstract classes and interfaces as constructs that allow us to create further abstractions and develop more-flexible applications.

Abstract classes are classes that are not intended to have any instances. Their purpose is to serve as superclasses to other classes. Abstract classes may have both abstract methods—methods that have a header but no body—and full method implementations. Concrete subclasses of abstract classes must override abstract methods to provide the missing method implementations.

Another construct for defining types in Java is the interface. Java interfaces are similar to completely abstract classes: they define method headers but provide no implementation. Interfaces define types that can be used for variables.

Interfaces can be used to provide a specification for a class (or part of an application) without stating anything about the concrete implementation.

Java allows multiple inheritance of interfaces (which it calls "implements" relationships) but only single inheritance for classes ("extends" relationships).

Terms introduced in this chapter

abstract method, abstract class, concrete class, abstract subclass, multiple inheritance, interface (Java construct), implements

---

Concept summary

- **abstract method** An abstract method definition consists of a method header without a method body. It is marked with the keyword `abstract`.

- **abstract class** An abstract class is a class that is not intended for creating instances. Its purpose is to serve as a superclass for other classes. Abstract classes may contain abstract methods.

- **abstract subclass** For a subclass of an abstract class to become concrete, it must provide implementations for all inherited abstract methods. Otherwise, it will itself be abstract.

■ **superclass method calls** Calls to non-private instance methods from within a superclass are always evaluated in the wider context of the object's dynamic type.

■ **multiple inheritance** A situation in which a class inherits from more than one superclass is called multiple inheritance.

■ **interface** A Java interface is a specification of a type (in the form of a type name and a set of methods) that does not define any implementation for the methods.

Exercise 10.67 Can an abstract class have concrete (non-abstract) methods? Can a concrete class have abstract methods? Can you have an abstract class without abstract methods? Justify your answers.

Exercise 10.68 Look at the code below. You have five types—classes or interfaces—(U, G, B, Z, and X) and a variable of each of these types.

```
U u;
G g;
B b;
Z z;
X x;
```

The following assignments are all legal (assume that they all compile).

```
u = z;
x = b;
g = u;
x = u;
```

The following assignments are all illegal (they cause compiler errors).

```
u = b;
x = g;
b = u;
z = u;
g = x;
```

What can you say about the types and their relationships? (What relationship are they to each other?)

Exercise 10.69 Assume that you want to model people in a university to implement a course management system. There are different people involved: staff members, students, teaching staff, support staff, tutors, technical-support staff, and student technicians. Tutors and student technicians are interesting: tutors are students who have been hired to do some teaching, and student technicians are students who have been hired to help with the technical support.

Draw a type hierarchy (classes and interfaces) to represent this situation. Indicate which types are concrete classes, abstract classes, and interfaces.

Exercise 10.70 *Challenge exercise* Sometimes class/interface pairs exist in the Java standard library that define exactly the same methods. Often, the interface name ends with *Listener* and the class name with *Adapter*. An example is `PrintJobListener` and `PrintJobAdapter`. The interface defines some method headers, and the adapter class defines the same methods, each with an empty method body. What might the reason be for having them both?

Exercise 10.71 The collection library has a class named `TreeSet`, which is an example of a sorted set. Elements in this set are kept in order. Carefully read the description of this class, and then write a class `Person` that can be inserted into a `TreeSet`, which will then sort the `Person` objects by age.

Exercise 10.72 Use the API documentation for the `AbstractList` class to write a concrete class that maintains an unmodifiable list.

CHAPTER 11

Building graphical user interfaces

Main concepts discussed in this chapter:

- constructing GUIs
- interface components
- GUI layout
- event handling

Java constructs discussed in this chapter:

JFrame, JLabel, JButton, JMenuBar, JMenu, JMenuItem, ActionEvent, Color, FlowLayout, BorderLayout, GridLayout, BoxLayout, Box, JOptionPane, EtchedBorder, EmptyBorder, anonymous inner classes, final variables

11.1 Introduction

So far in this book, we have concentrated on writing applications with text-based interfaces. The reason is not that text-based interfaces have any great advantage in principle; they just have the one advantage that they are easier to create.

We did not want to distract too much attention from the important software-development issues in the early stages of learning about object-oriented programming. These were issues such as object structure and interaction, class design, and code quality.

Graphical user interfaces (GUIs) are also constructed from interacting objects, but they have a very specialized structure, and we avoided introducing them before discussing object structures in more general terms. Now, however, we are ready to have a look at the construction of GUIs.

GUIs give our applications an interface consisting of windows, menus, buttons, and other graphical components. They make the applications look much more like the "typical" application most people are used to nowadays.

Note that we are stumbling about the double meaning of the word *interface* again here. The interfaces we are talking about now are neither interfaces of classes nor the Java interface construct. We are now talking about *user interfaces*—the part of an application that is visible on screen for the user to interact with.

Once we know how to create GUIs with Java, we can develop much better-looking programs.

11.2 Components, layout, and event handling

The details involved in creating GUIs are extensive. In this book, we shall not be able to cover all details of all possible things you can do with them, but we shall discuss the general principles and a good number of examples.

All GUI programming in Java is done through the use of dedicated standard class libraries. Once we understand the principles, we can find out all the necessary details by working with the standard library documentation.

The principles we need to understand can be divided into three topic areas:

■ What kinds of elements can we show on screen?

■ How do we arrange those elements?

■ How do we react to user input?

We shall discuss these questions under the keywords *components, layout,* and *event handling.*

> **Concept:**
>
> A GUI is built by arranging **components** on screen. Components are represented by objects.

Components are the individual parts that a GUI is built from. They are things such as buttons, menus, menu items, checkboxes, sliders, text fields, and so on. The Java library contains a good number of ready-made components, and we can also write our own. We shall have to learn what the important components are, how to create them, and how to make them look the way we want them to look.

> **Concept:**
>
> Arranging the **layout** of components is achieved by using layout managers.

Layout deals with the issue of how to arrange the components on screen. Older, more primitive GUI systems handled this with two-dimensional coordinates: the programmer specified x- and y-coordinates (in pixels) for the position and the size of each component. In more modern GUI systems, this is too simplistic. We have to take into account different screen resolutions, different fonts, users resizing windows, and many other aspects that make layout more difficult. The solution will be a scheme where we can specify the layout in more general terms. We can, for example, specify that a particular component should be below this other one or that this component should be stretched if the window gets resized but this other should always have a constant size. We shall see that this is done using *layout managers.*

> **Concept:**
>
> The term **event handling** refers to the task of reacting to user events, such as mouse-button clicks or keyboard input.

Event handling refers to the technique we shall use to deal with user input. Once we have created our components and positioned them on screen, we also have to make sure that something happens when a user clicks a button. The model used by the Java library for this is event-based: if a user activates a component (e.g., clicks a button or selects a menu item) the system will generate an event. Our application can then receive a notification of the event (by having one of its methods invoked), and we can take appropriate action.

We shall discuss each of these areas in much more detail later in this chapter. First, however, we shall briefly introduce a bit more background and terminology.

11.3 AWT and Swing

Java has two GUI libraries. The older one is called *AWT* (Abstract Window Toolkit) and was introduced as part of the original Java API. Later, a much-improved GUI library, called *Swing,* was added to Java.

Swing makes use of some of the AWT classes, replaces some AWT classes with its own versions, and adds many new classes (Figure 11.1).

Figure 11.1
AWT and Swing

In this book, we shall use the Swing libraries. This means that we shall use some AWT classes that are still used with Swing programs but use the Swing versions of all classes that exist in both libraries.

Wherever there are equivalent classes in AWT and Swing, the Swing versions have been identified by adding the letter *J* to the start of the class name. You will, for example, see classes named `Button` and `JButton`, `Frame` and `JFrame`, `Menu` and `JMenu`, and so on. The classes starting with a *J* are the Swing versions; these are the ones we shall use, and the two should not be mixed in an application.

That is enough background for a start. Let us look at some code.

11.4 The ImageViewer example

As always, we shall discuss the new concepts by using an example. The application we shall build in this chapter is an image viewer (Figure 11.2). This is a program that can open and display image files in JPEG and PNG formats, perform some image transformations, and save the images back to disk.

As part of this, we shall use our own image class to represent an image while it is in memory, implement various filters to change the image's appearance, and use Swing components to build a user interface. While doing this, we shall concentrate our discussion on the GUI aspects of the program.

If you are curious to see what we shall build, you can open and try out the *imageviewer1-0* project—that is the version displayed in Figure 11.2; just create an `ImageViewer` object. There are some sample images in the *images* folder inside the *chapter11* folder (one level up from the project folder). You can, of course, also open your own images. Here, we start slowly, initially with something much simpler, and we shall work our way to the final application step by step.

Concept:

Image format Images can be stored in different formats. The differences primarily affect file size and the quality of the image.

11.4.1 First experiments: creating a frame

Almost everything you see in a GUI is contained in a top-level window. A top-level window is one that is under the control of the operating system's window management and which typically can be moved, resized, minimized, and maximized independently.

Figure 11.2
A simple
image-viewer
application

Java calls these top-level windows *frames*. In Swing, they are represented by a class called
JFrame.

Code 11.1
A first version of an
ImageViewer class

```java
import java.awt.*;
import java.awt.event.*;
import javax.swing.*;

// Comment omitted.

public class ImageViewer
{
    private JFrame frame;

    /**
     * Create an ImageViewer and show it on screen.
     */
    public ImageViewer()
    {
        makeFrame();
    }

    /**
     * Create the Swing frame and its content.
     */
    private void makeFrame()
```

Code 11.1
continued

A first version of an
ImageViewer class

```
        {
            frame = new JFrame("ImageViewer");
            Container contentPane = frame.getContentPane();

            JLabel label = new JLabel("I am a label.");
            contentPane.add(label);

            frame.pack();
            frame.setVisible(true);
        }
    }
```

To get a GUI on screen, the first thing we have to do is create and display a frame. Code 11.1 shows a complete class (already named ImageViewer in preparation for things to come) that shows a frame on screen. This class is available in the book projects as *imageviewer0-1* (the number stands for version 0.1).

> **Exercise 11.1** Open the *imageviewer0-1* project. (This will become the basis of your own image viewer.) Create an instance of class ImageViewer. Resize the resulting frame (make it larger). What do you observe about the placement of the text in the frame?

We shall now discuss the ImageViewer class shown in Code 11.1 in some detail.

The first three lines in that class are import statements of all classes in the packages java.awt, java.awt.event, and javax.swing.[1] We need many of the classes in these packages for all Swing applications we create, so we shall always import the three packages completely in our GUI programs.

Looking at the rest of the class shows very quickly that all the interesting stuff is in the make-Frame method. This method takes care of constructing the GUI. The class's constructor contains only a call to this method. We have done this so that all the GUI construction code is at a well-defined place and is easy to find later (cohesion!). We shall do this in all our GUI examples.

The class has one instance variable of type JFrame. This is used to hold the frame that the image viewer wants to show on screen. Let us now take a closer look at the makeFrame method.

The first line in this method is

```
    frame = new JFrame("ImageViewer");
```

This statement creates a new frame and stores it in our instance variable for later use.

As a general principle, you should, in parallel with studying the examples in this book, look at the class documentation for all classes we encounter. This applies to all the classes we use; we shall not point this out every time from now on, but just expect you to do it.

---

[1] The swing package is really in a package called javax (ending with an *x*), not java. The reason for this is largely historic—there does not seem to be a logical explanation for it.

Exercise 11.2 Find the documentation for class `JFrame`. What is the purpose of the `"ImageViewer"` parameter that we used in the constructor call above?

A frame consists of three parts: the *title bar*, an optional *menu bar,* and the *content pane* (Figure 11.3). The exact appearance of the title bar depends on the underlying operating system. It usually contains the window title and a few window controls.

Figure 11.3
Different parts of a frame

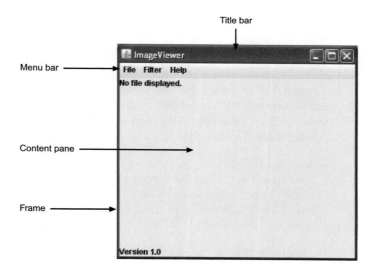

The menu bar and the content pane are under the control of the application. To both, we can add some components to create a GUI. We shall concentrate on the content pane first.

11.4.2 Adding simple components

Immediately following creation of the `JFrame`, the frame will be invisible and its content pane will be empty. We continue by adding a label to the content pane:

```
Container contentPane = frame.getContentPane();

JLabel label = new JLabel("I am a label.");
contentPane.add(label);
```

The first line gets the content pane from the frame. We always have to do this; GUI components are added to a frame by adding them to the frame's content pane.[2]

The content pane itself is of type `Container`. A container is a Swing component that can hold arbitrary groups of other components—rather like an `ArrayList` can hold an arbitrary collection of objects. We shall discuss containers in more detail later.

---

[2] Java also has an `add` method for adding components directly in the `JFrame` class, which will also add the component to the content pane. However, we need access to the content pane for other reasons later anyway, so we do the adding of components to the content pane at this point as well.

We then create a label component (type `JLabel`) and add it to the content pane. A label is a component that can display text and/or an image.

Finally, we have the two lines

```
frame.pack();
frame.setVisible(true);
```

The first line causes the frame to arrange the components inside it properly and to size itself appropriately. We always have to call the `pack` method on the frame after we have added or resized components.

The last line finally makes the frame visible on screen. We always start out with the frame being invisible so that we can arrange all the components inside the frame without the construction process being visible on screen. Then, when the frame is built, we can show it in a completed state.

> **Exercise 11.3** Another often-used Swing component is a button (type `JButton`). Replace the label in the example above with a button.
>
> **Exercise 11.4** What happens when you add two labels (or two buttons) to the content pane? Can you explain what you observe? Experiment with resizing the frame.

11.4.3   An alternative structure

We have chosen to develop our application by creating a `JFrame` object as an attribute of the `ImageViewer` and populating it with further GUI components that are created outside the frame object. An alternative structure for this top level would be to define `ImageViewer` as a subclass of `JFrame` and populate internally. This style is also commonly seen. Code 11.2 shows the equivalent of Code 11.1 in this style. This version is available as the project *imageviewer0-1a*. While it is worth being familiar with both styles, neither is obviously superior to the other, and we will continue with our original version in the rest of this chapter.

Code 11.2

An alternative structure for the `ImageViewer` class

```
import java.awt.*;
import java.awt.event.*;
import javax.swing.*;
// Comment omitted.
public class ImageViewer extends JFrame
{
    /**
     * Create an ImageViewer and show it on screen.
     */
    public ImageViewer()
```

**Code 11.2
continued**

An alternative structure
for the `ImageViewer`
class

```
    {
        super("ImageViewer");
        makeFrame();
        setVisible(true);
    }

    /**
     * Create the Swing frame and its content.
     */
    private void makeFrame()
    {
        Container contentPane = getContentPane();
        JLabel label = new JLabel("I am a label.");
        contentPane.add(label);
        pack();
    }
}
```

11.4.4 Adding menus

Our next step toward building a GUI is to add menus and menu items. This is conceptually easy but contains one tricky detail: How do we arrange to react to user actions, such as the selection of a menu item? We discuss this below.

First, we create the menus. Three classes are involved:

■ JMenuBar—An object of this class represents a menu bar that can be displayed below the title bar at the top of a window (see Figure 11.3). Every window has at most one JMenuBar.[3]

■ JMenu—Objects of this class represent a single menu (such as the common *File, Edit, or Help* menus). Menus are often held in a menu bar. They could also appear as pop-up menus, but we shall not do that now.

■ JMenuItem—Objects of this class represent a single menu item inside a menu (such as *Open* or *Save*).

For our image viewer, we shall create one menu bar and several menus and menu items.

The class JFrame has a method called setJMenuBar. We can create a menu bar and use this method to attach our menu bar to the frame:

```
JMenuBar menubar = new JMenuBar();
frame.setJMenuBar(menubar);
```

---

[3] In Mac OS, the native display is different: the menu bar is at the top of the screen, not the top of each window. In Java applications, the default behavior is to attach the menu bar to the window. It can be placed at the top of the screen with Java applications by using a Mac OS–specific property.

Now we are ready to create a menu and add it to the menu bar:

```
JMenu fileMenu = new JMenu("File");
menubar.add(fileMenu);
```

These two lines create a menu labeled *File* and insert it into our menu bar. Finally, we can add menu items to the menu. The following lines add two items, labeled *Open* and *Quit*, to the *File* menu:

```
JMenuItem openItem = new JMenuItem("Open");
fileMenu.add(openItem);

JMenuItem quitItem = new JMenuItem("Quit");
fileMenu.add(quitItem);
```

> **Exercise 11.5** Add the menu and menu items discussed here to your image-viewer project. What happens when you select a menu item?
>
> **Exercise 11.6** Add another menu called *Help* that contains a menu item named *About ImageViewer*. (Note: To increase readability and cohesion, it may be a good idea to move the creation of the menus into a separate method, perhaps named `makeMenuBar`, which is called from our `makeFrame` method.)

So far, we have achieved half of our task; we can create and display menus. But the second half is missing—nothing happens yet when a user selects a menu. We now have to add code to react to menu selections. This is discussed in the next section.

11.4.5 Event handling

Swing uses a very flexible model to deal with GUI input: an *event-handling* model with *event listeners.*

The Swing framework itself and some of its components raise events when something happens that other objects may be interested in. There are different types of events caused by different types of actions. When a button is clicked or a menu item is selected, the component raises an `ActionEvent`. When a mouse is clicked or moved, a `MouseEvent` is raised. When a frame is closed or iconified, a `WindowEvent` is generated. There are many other types of events.

Concept:

An object can listen to component events by implementing an **event-listener** interface.

Any of our objects can become an event listener for any of these events. When it is a listener, it will get notified about any of the events it listens to. An object becomes an event listener by implementing one of several existing listener interfaces. If it implements the right interface, it can register itself with a component it wants to listen to.

Let us look at an example. A menu item (class `JMenuItem`) raises an `ActionEvent` when it is activated by a user. Objects that want to listen to these events must implement the `ActionListener` interface from the `java.awt.event` package.

There are two alternative styles for implementing event listeners: either a single object listens for events from many different event sources, or each distinct event source is assigned its own unique listener. We shall discuss both styles in the next two sections.

11.4.6 Centralized receipt of events

In order to make our `ImageViewer` object be the single listener to all events from the menu, we have to do three things:

1. We must declare in the class header that it implements the `ActionListener` interface.

2. We have to implement a method with the signature

   ```
   public void actionPerformed(ActionEvent e)
   ```

   This is the only method declared in the `ActionListener` interface.

3. We must call the `addActionListener` method of the menu item to register the `ImageViewer` object as a listener.

Numbers 1 and 2—implementing the interface and defining its method—ensure that our object is a subtype of `ActionListener`. Number 3 then registers our own object as a listener for the menu items. Code 11.3 shows the source code for this in context.

Code 11.3

Adding an action
listener to a menu item

```java
public class ImageViewer
    implements ActionListener
{

    // Fields and constructor omitted.

    public void actionPerformed(ActionEvent event)
    {
        System.out.println("Menu item: " + event.getActionCommand());
    }

    /**
     * Create the Swing frame and its content.
     */
    private void makeFrame()
    {
        frame = new JFrame("ImageViewer");
        makeMenuBar(frame);

        // Other GUI building code omitted.
    }

    /**
     * Create the main frame's menu bar.
     * @param frame The frame the menu bar should be added to.
     */
    private void makeMenuBar(JFrame frame)
    {
        JMenuBar menubar = new JMenuBar();
        frame.setJMenuBar(menubar);
```

**Code 11.3
continued**

Adding an action
listener to a menu item

```java
    // create the File menu
    JMenu fileMenu = new JMenu("File");
    menubar.add(fileMenu);

    JMenuItem openItem = new JMenuItem("Open");
    openItem.addActionListener(this);
    fileMenu.add(openItem);

    JMenuItem quitItem = new JMenuItem("Quit");
    quitItem.addActionListener(this);
    fileMenu.add(quitItem);
    }
}
```

Note especially the lines

```java
JMenuItem openItem = new JMenuItem("Open");
openItem.addActionListener(this);
```

in the code example. Here, a menu item is created, and the current object (the `ImageViewer` object itself) is registered as an action listener by passing `this` as a parameter to the `addActionListener` method.

The effect of registering our object as a listener with the menu item is that our own `actionPerformed` method will be called by the menu item each time the item is activated. When our method is called, the menu item will pass along a parameter of type `ActionEvent` that provides some details about the event that has occurred. These details include the exact time of the event, the state of the modifier keys (the shift, control, and meta keys), a "command string," and more.

The command string is a string that somehow identifies the component that caused the event. For menu items, this is by default the label text of the item.

In our example in Code 11.3, we register the same action object for both menu items. This means that both menu items will invoke the same `actionPerformed` method when they are activated.

In the `actionPerformed` method, we simply print out the command string of the item to demonstrate that this scheme works. Here, we could now add code to properly handle the menu invocation.

This code example, as discussed this far, is available in the book projects as project *imageviewer0-2*.

Exercise 11.7 Implement the menu-handling code, discussed above, in your own image-viewer project. Alternatively, open the *imageviewer0-2* project and carefully examine the source code. Describe in writing and in detail the sequence of events that results from activating the *Quit* menu item.

Exercise 11.8 Add another menu item called *Save*.

Exercise 11.9 Add three private methods to your class, named `openFile`, `saveFile`, and `quit`. Change the `actionPerformed` method so that it calls the corresponding method when a menu item is activated.

Exercise 11.10 If you have done Exercise 11.6 (adding a *Help* menu), make sure that its menu item also gets handled appropriately.

We note that this approach works.

We can now implement methods to handle menu items to do our various program tasks. There is, however, one other aspect we should investigate: the current solution is not very nice in terms of maintainability and extendibility.

Examine the code that you had to write in the `actionPerformed` method for Exercise 11.9. There are several problems. They are:

■ You probably used an if statement and the `getActionCommand` method to find out which item was activated. For example, you could write:

```
if(event.getActionCommand().equals("Open")) ...
```

Depending on the item label string for performing the function is not a good idea. What if you now translated the interface into another language? Just changing the text on the menu item would have the effect that the program does not work anymore. (Or you would have to find all places in the code where this string was used and change them all—a tedious and error-prone procedure.)

■ Having a central dispatch method (such as our `actionPerformed`) is not a nice structure at all. We essentially make every separate item call a single method, only to write tedious code in that method to call separate methods for every item from there. This is annoying in maintenance terms (for every additional menu item we have to add a new if statement in `actionPerformed`); it also seems a waste of effort. It would be much nicer if we could make every menu item call a separate method directly.

In the next section, we introduce a new language construct that allows us to do just that.

11.4.7 Inner classes

To solve the problems with centralized event dispatch mentioned above, we use a new construct that we have not discussed before: *inner classes*. Inner classes are classes that are declared textually inside another class:

```
class EnclosingClass
{
    ...
    class InnerClass
    {
        ...
    }
}
```

Instances of the inner class are attached to instances of the enclosing class; they can only exist together with an enclosing instance, and they exist conceptually *inside* the enclosing instance. One interesting detail is that statements in methods of the inner class can see and access private fields and methods of the enclosing class. There is obviously a very tight coupling between the two, therefore. The inner class is considered to be a part of the enclosing class just as are any of the enclosing class's methods.

We can now use this construct to make a separate action-listener class for every menu item we like to listen to. As they are separate classes, they can each have a separate `actionPerformed` method so that each of these methods handles only a single item's activation. The structure is this:

```
class ImageViewer
{
    ...
    class OpenActionListener implements ActionListener
    {
        public void actionPerformed(ActionEvent event)
        {
            // perform open action
        }
    }
    class QuitActionListener implements ActionListener
    {
        public void actionPerformed(ActionEvent event)
        {
            // perform quit action
        }
    }
}
```

(As a style guide, we usually write inner classes at the end of the enclosing class—after the methods.)

Once we have done this, we can now create instances of these inner classes in exactly the same way as for those of any other class. Note also that `ImageViewer` does not implement `ActionListener` anymore (we remove its `actionPerformed` method), but the two inner classes do. This now allows us to use instances of the inner classes as action listeners for the menu items.

```
JMenuItem openItem = new JMenuItem("Open");
openItem.addActionListener(new OpenActionListener());
...
JMenuItem quitItem = new JMenuItem("Quit");
quitItem.addActionListener(new QuitActionListener());
```

In summary, instead of having the image-viewer object listen to all action events, we create separate listener objects for each possible event, where each listener object listens to one single event type. As every listener has its own `actionPerformed` method, we can now write specific handling code in these methods. Also, because the listener classes are in the scope of the enclosing class (they can access the enclosing class's private fields and methods), they can make full use of the enclosing class in the implementation of the `actionPerformed` methods.

Notice a couple of characteristics of these listener objects:

■ We don't bother storing them in variables—so, in effect, they are anonymous objects. Only the menu items have a reference to the listener objects, so that they can call their `action-Performed` methods.

■ We only create a single object from each of the inner classes, because each is highly specialized for a particular menu item.

These characteristics will lead us to explore a further feature of Java in the next section.

Exercise 11.11 Implement menu-item handling with inner classes, as discussed here, in your own version of the image viewer.

Inner classes can generally be used in some cases to improve cohesion in larger projects. The *foxes-and-rabbits* project from Chapter 10, for example, has a class `SimulatorView` that includes an inner class `FieldView`. You may like to study this example to deepen your understanding.

11.4.8 Anonymous inner classes

The solution to the action dispatch problem using inner classes is fairly good, but we want to take it one step further: we can use *anonymous inner classes*. The project *imageviewer0-3* shows an implementation using this construct.

Exercise 11.12 Open the *imageviewer0-3* project and examine it; that is, test it and read its source code. Don't worry about understanding everything, because some new features are the subject of this section. What do you notice about the use of inner classes to enable `ImageViewer` to listen for and handle events?

Exercise 11.13 You will notice that activating the *Quit* menu item now quits the program. Examine how this is done. Look up the library documentation for any classes and methods involved.

At the center of the changes in this version is the way the action listeners are set up to listen to menu-item action events. The relevant code looks like this:

```
JMenuItem openItem = new JMenuItem("Open");
openItem.addActionListener(new ActionListener() {
        public void actionPerformed(ActionEvent e) { openFile(); }
    });
```

This code fragment looks quite mysterious when you encounter it for the first time, and you will probably have trouble interpreting it, even if you have understood everything we have discussed in this book so far. This construct is probably syntactically the most confusing example that you will ever see in the Java language. But don't worry—we shall investigate this slowly.

What you are seeing here is an anonymous inner class. The idea for this construct is based on the observations from our previous version that we only use each inner class exactly once to create a single, unnamed instance. For this situation, anonymous inner classes provide a syntactical shortcut: they let us define a class and create a single instance of this class, all in one step.

The effect is identical to the inner-class version above, with the difference that we do not need to define separate named classes for the listeners and that the definition of the listener method is closer to the registration of the listener with the menu item.

The scope coloring in BlueJ's editor gives us some hints that may help in understanding this structure (Figure 11.4). The green shading indicates a class, the yellowish color shows a method definition, and the white background identifies a method body. We can see that the body of the makeMenuBar method contains, very tightly packed, two (strange-looking) class definitions, which each have a single method definition with a short body.

Figure 11.4

Scope coloring with two anonymous inner classes

```java
/**
 * Create the main frame's menu bar.
 * @param frame    The frame that the menu bar should be added to.
 */
private void makeMenuBar(JFrame frame)
{
    JMenuBar menubar = new JMenuBar();
    frame.setJMenuBar(menubar);

    // create the File menu
    JMenu fileMenu = new JMenu("File");
    menubar.add(fileMenu);

    JMenuItem openItem = new JMenuItem("Open");
        openItem.addActionListener(new ActionListener() {
                    public void actionPerformed(ActionEvent e) { openFile(); }
            });
    fileMenu.add(openItem);

    JMenuItem quitItem = new JMenuItem("Quit");
        quitItem.addActionListener(new ActionListener() {
                    public void actionPerformed(ActionEvent e) { quit(); }
            });
    fileMenu.add(quitItem);
}
```

When using an anonymous inner class, we create an inner class *without naming it* and immediately create a single instance of the class. In the action-listener code above, this is done with the code fragment

```java
new ActionListener() {
        public void actionPerformed(ActionEvent e) { openFile(); }
    }
```

An anonymous inner class is created by naming a supertype (often an abstract class or an interface—here ActionListener), followed by a block that contains an implementation for its abstract methods. This looks unusual, because it is not otherwise permitted to create an instance of an abstract class or interface directly.

In this example, we create a new subtype of ActionListener that implements the action-Performed method. This new class does not receive a name. Instead, we precede it with the new keyword to create a single instance of this class.

In our example, this single instance is an action-listener object (it is of a subtype of ActionListener). It can be passed to a menu item's addActionListener method and will invoke the `openFile` method of its enclosing class when activated. Each subtype of `ActionListener` created in this way represents a unique anonymous class.

Just like named inner classes, anonymous inner classes are able to access the fields and methods of their enclosing classes. In addition, because they are defined inside a method, they are able to access the local variables and parameters of that method. However, an important rule is that local variables accessed in this way must be declared as final variables. You will see an example of this in the *imageviewer2-0* project, discussed in Section 11.6.

It is worth emphasizing some observations about anonymous inner classes. First, for our concrete problem, using anonymous inner classes is very useful. It allows us to completely remove the central `actionPerformed` method from our `ImageViewer` class. Instead, we create a separate, custom-made action listener (class and object) for each menu item. This action listener can directly call the method implementing the corresponding function.

This structure is nicely cohesive and extendable. If we need an additional menu item, we just add code to create the item and its listener, as well as the method that handles its function. No listing in a central method is required.

> **Concept:**
>
> **Anonymous inner classes** are a useful construct for implementing event listeners.

Second, using anonymous inner classes can make code quite hard to read. It is strongly recommended to use them only for very short classes and for well-established code idioms. For us, implementing event listeners is the only example in this book where we use this construct.[4]

Third, we often use anonymous classes where only a single instance of the implementation will be required—where the actions associated with each menu item are unique to that particular item. In addition, the instance will always be referred to via its supertype. Both reasons mean there is less need for a name for the new class; hence, it can be anonymous.

For all our following work, we shall avoid the central `actionPerformed` method and use anonymous inner classes instead. So you should leave the *imageviewer0-2* project behind and use the structure from *imageviewer0-3* as a basis for your further work.

11.4.9 Summary of key GUI elements

At the beginning of this chapter, we listed the three areas of GUI construction: components, layout, and event handling. So far, we have concentrated on two of these areas. We have encountered a small number of components (labels, buttons, menus, menu items), and we have discussed the handling of action events in quite some detail.

Getting to the current state (showing a frame with a label and a few menus) was hard work, and we had to discuss a lot of background concepts. It gets easier from now on—really! Understanding the event handling for menu items was probably the most difficult detail we had to master for our example.

Adding more menus and other components to the frame will now be quite easy—just more of the same. The one entirely new area we shall have to look at is *layout*: how to arrange the components in the frame.

---

[4] If you'd like to find out more about inner classes, have a look at these two sections of the online Java tutorial: `http://download.oracle.com/javase/tutorial/java/javaOO/nested.html` and `http://download.oracle.com/javase/tutorial/java/javaOO/innerclasses.html`.

11.5   ImageViewer 1.0: the first complete version

We shall now work on creating the first complete version—one that can really accomplish the main task: display some images.

11.5.1   Image-processing classes

On the way to the solution, we shall investigate one more interim version: *imageviewer0-4*. Its class structure is shown in Figure 11.5.

Figure 11.5
The class structure
of the image
viewer application

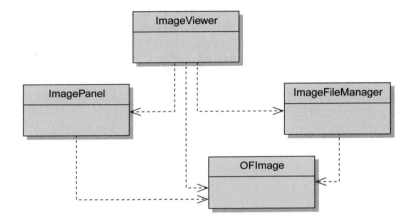

As you can see, we have added three new classes: OFImage, ImagePanel, and ImageFileManager. OFImage is a class to represent an image that we want to display and manipulate. ImageFileManager is a helper class that provides static methods to read an image file (in JPEG or PNG format) from disk and return it in OFImage format and then save the OFImage back to disk. ImagePanel is a custom Swing component to show the image in our GUI.

We shall briefly discuss the most important aspects of each of these classes in some more detail. We shall not, however, explain them completely—that is left as an investigation for the curious reader.

The OFImage class is our own custom format for representing an image in memory. You can think of an OFImage as a two-dimensional array of pixels. Each of the pixels can have a color. We use the standard class Color (from package java.awt) to represent each pixel's color. (Have a look at the documentation of class Color as well; we shall need it later.)

OFImage is implemented as a subclass of the Java standard class BufferedImage (from package java.awt.image). BufferedImage gives us most of the functionality we want (it also represents an image as a two-dimensional array), but it does not have methods to set or get a pixel using a Color object (it uses different formats for this, which we do not want to use). So we made our own subclass that adds these two methods.

For this project, we can treat OFImage like a library class; you will not need to modify this class.

The most important methods from OFImage for us are:

■ getPixel and setPixel to read and modify single pixels

■ getHeight and getWidth to find out about the image's size.

The ImageFileManager class offers three methods: one to read a named image file from disk and return it as an OFImage, one to write an OFImage file to disk, and one to open a file-chooser dialog to let a user select an image to open. The methods can read files in the standard JPEG and PNG formats, and the save method will write files in JPEG format. This is done using the standard Java image I/O methods from the ImageIO class (package javax.imageio).

The ImagePanel class implements a custom-made Swing component to display our image. Custom-made Swing components can easily be created by writing a subclass of an existing component. As such, they can be inserted into a Swing container and displayed in our GUI like any other Swing component. ImagePanel is a subclass of JComponent. The other important point to note here is that ImagePanel has a setImage method that takes an OFImage as a parameter to display any given OFImage.

11.5.2 Adding the image

Now that we have prepared the classes for dealing with images, adding the image to the user interface is easy. Code 11.4 shows the important differences from previous versions.

Code 11.4

ImageViewer class
with ImagePanel

```
public class ImageViewer
{
    private JFrame frame;
    private ImagePanel imagePanel;

    // Constructor and quit method omitted.

    /**
     * Open function: open a file chooser to select a new
     * image file.
     */
    private void openFile()
    {
        OFImage image = ImageFileManager.getImage();
        imagePanel.setImage(image);
        frame.pack();
    }

    /**
     * Create the Swing frame and its content.
     */
```

Code 11.4
continued
ImageViewer class
with ImagePanel

```
private void makeFrame()
{
    frame = new JFrame("ImageViewer");
    makeMenuBar(frame);

    Container contentPane = frame.getContentPane();

    imagePanel = new ImagePanel();
    contentPane.add(imagePanel);

    // building is done - arrange the components and show
    frame.pack();
    frame.setVisible(true);
}

// MakeMenuBar method omitted.
}
```

When comparing this code with the previous version, we note that there are only two small changes:

- In method makeFrame, we now create and add an ImagePanel component instead of a JLabel. Doing this is not more complicated than adding the label. The ImagePanel object is stored in an instance field so that we can access it again later.

- Our openFile method has now been changed to actually open and display an image file. Using our image-processing classes, this also is easy now. The ImageFileManager class has a method to select and open an image, and the ImagePanel object has a method to display that image. One thing to note is that we need to call frame.pack() at the end of the openFile method, as the size of our image component has changed. The pack method will recalculate the frame layout and redraw the frame so that the size change is properly handled.

Exercise 11.14 Open and test the *imageviewer0-4* project. The folder for this chapter's projects also includes a folder called *images*. Here, you can find some test images you can use. Of course, you can also use your own images.

Exercise 11.15 What happens when you open an image and then resize the frame? What if you first resize the frame and then open an image?

With this version, we have solved the central task; we can now open an image file from disk and display it on screen. Before we call our project "version 1.0," however, and thus declare it finished for the first time, we want to add a few more improvements (see Figure 11.2).

- We want to add two labels: one to display the image filename at the top and a status text at the bottom.

- We want to add a *Filter* menu that contains some filters that change the image's appearance.

- We want to add a *Help* menu that contains an *About ImageViewer* item. Selecting this menu item should display a dialog with the application's name, version number, and author information.

11.5.3 Layout

First, we shall work on the task of adding two text labels to our interface: one at the top that is used to display the filename of the image currently displayed and one at the bottom that is used for various status messages.

Creating these labels is easy—they are both simple JLabel instances. We store them in instance fields so that we can access them later to change their displayed text. The only question is how to arrange them on screen.

A first (naïve and incorrect) attempt could look like this:

```
Container contentPane = frame.getContentPane();

filenameLabel = new JLabel();
contentPane.add(filenameLabel);

imagePanel = new ImagePanel();
contentPane.add(imagePanel);

statusLabel = new JLabel("Version 1.0");
contentPane.add(statusLabel);
```

The idea here is simple: we get the frame's content pane and add, one after the other, all three components that we wish to display. The only problem is that we did not specify exactly how these three components should be arranged. We might want them to appear next to each other, or one below the other, or in any other possible arrangement. As we did not specify any layout, the container (the content pane) uses a default behavior. And this, it turns out, is not what we want.

Swing uses *layout managers* to arrange the layout of components in a GUI. Each container that holds components, such as the content pane, has an associated layout manager that takes care of arranging the components within that container.

> **Exercise 11.16** Continuing from your last version of the project, use the code fragment shown above to add the two labels. Test it. What do you observe?

Swing provides several different layout managers to support different layout preferences. The most important are: FlowLayout, BorderLayout, GridLayout, and BoxLayout. Each of those is represented by a Java class in the Swing library, and each lays out in different ways the components under its control.

Here follows a short description of each layout. The key differences between them are the ways in which they position components and how the available space is distributed between the components. You can find the examples illustrated here in the *layouts* project.

A FlowLayout (Figure 11.6) arranges all components sequentially from left to right. It will leave each component at its preferred size and center them horizontally. If the horizontal space is not enough to fit all components, they wrap around to a second line. The FlowLayout can also be set to align components left or right. Because the components are not resized to fill the available space, there will be spare space around them if the window is resized.

Figure 11.6
FlowLayout

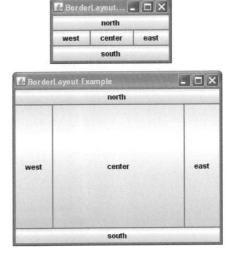

A BorderLayout (Figure 11.7) places up to five components in an arranged pattern: one in the center and one each at the top, bottom, right, and left. Each of these positions may be empty, so it may hold fewer than five components. The five positions are named CENTER, NORTH, SOUTH, EAST, and WEST. There is no leftover space with a BorderLayout when the window is resized; it is all distributed (unevenly) between the components.

Figure 11.7
BorderLayout

This layout may seem very specialized at first—one wonders how often this is needed. But in practice, this is a surprisingly useful layout that is used in many applications. In BlueJ, for example, both the main window and the editor use a BorderLayout as the main layout manager.

When a BorderLayout is resized, the middle component is the one that gets stretched in both dimensions. The east and west components change in height but keep their width. The north and south components keep their height, and only the width changes.

As the name suggests, a GridLayout is useful (Figure 11.8) for laying out components in an evenly spaced grid. The numbers of rows and columns can be specified, and the GridLayout manager will always keep all components at the same size. This can be useful to force buttons, for example, to have the same width. The width of JButton instances is initially determined by the text on the button—each button is made just wide enough to display its text. Inserting buttons into a GridLayout will result in all buttons being resized to the width of the widest button. If an odd number of equal-size components cannot fill a 2D grid, there may be spare space in some configurations.

Figure 11.8
GridLayout

A BoxLayout lays out multiple components either vertically or horizontally. The components are not resized, and the layout will not wrap components when resized (Figure 11.9). By nesting multiple BoxLayouts inside each other, sophisticated two-dimensionally aligned layouts may be built.

Figure 11.9
BoxLayout

Exercise 11.17 Using the *layouts* project from this chapter, experiment with the examples illustrated in this section. Add and remove components from the existing classes to get a proper feel for the key characteristics of the different layout styles. What happens if there is no CENTER component with `BorderLayout`, for instance?

11.5.4 Nested containers

All the layout strategies discussed above are fairly simple. The key to building good-looking and well-behaved interfaces lies in one last detail: layouts can be nested. Many of the Swing components are *containers*. Containers appear to the outside as a single component, but they can contain multiple other components. Each container has its own layout manager attached.

The most-used container is the class `JPanel`. A `JPanel` can be inserted as a component into the frame's content pane, and then more components can be laid out inside the `JPanel`. Figure 11.10, for example, shows an interface arrangement similar to that of the BlueJ main window. The content pane of this frame uses a `BorderLayout`, where the EAST position is unused. The NORTH area of this `BorderLayout` contains a `JPanel` with a horizontal `FlowLayout` that arranges its components (say toolbar buttons) in a row. The SOUTH area is similar: another `JPanel` with a `FlowLayout`.

Figure 11.10
Building an interface using nested containers

JPanel with GridLayout   JPanel with FlowLayout

JPanel with vertical FlowLayout

JPanel with FlowLayout   Content pane with BorderLayout (EAST area empty)

The button group in the WEST area was first placed into a `JPanel` with a one-column `GridLayout` to give all buttons the same width. This `JPanel` was then placed into another `JPanel` with a `FlowLayout` so that the grid did not extend over the full height of the WEST area. The outer `JPanel` is then inserted into the WEST area of the frame.

Note how the container and the layout manager cooperate in the layout of the components. The container holds the components, but the layout manager decides their exact arrangement on screen. Every container has a layout manager. It will use a default layout manager if we do not explicitly set one. The default is different for different containers: the content pane of a `JFrame`, for example, has by default a `BorderLayout`, whereas `JPanels` use a `FlowLayout` by default.

Exercise 11.18 Look at the GUI of the calculator project used in Chapter 7 (Figure 7.6 on page 253). What kind of containers/layout managers do you think were used to create it? After answering in writing, open the *calculator-gui* project and check your answer by reading the code.

Exercise 11.19 What kind of layout managers might have been used to create the layout of BlueJ's editor window?

Exercise 11.20 In BlueJ, invoke the *Use Library Class* function from the *Tools* menu. Look at the dialog you see on screen. Which containers/layout managers might have been used to create it? Resize the dialog and observe the resize behavior to get additional information.

It is time to look again at some code for our `ImageViewer` application. Our goal is quite simple. We want to see three components above each other: a label at the top, the image in the middle, and another label at the bottom. Several layout managers can do this. Which one to choose becomes clearer when we think about resizing behavior. When we enlarge the window, we would like the labels to maintain their height and the image to receive all the extra space. This suggests a `BorderLayout`: the labels can be in the NORTH and SOUTH areas, and the image in the CENTER. Code 11.5 shows the source code to implement this.

Two details are worth noting. First, the `setLayout` method is used on the content pane to set the intended layout manager.[5] The layout manager itself is an object, so we create an instance of `BorderLayout` and pass it to the `setLayout` method.

Second, when we add a component to a container with a `BorderLayout`, we use a different `add` method that has a second parameter. The value for the second parameter is one of the public constants NORTH, SOUTH, EAST, WEST, and CENTER, which are defined in class `BorderLayout`.

---

[5] Strictly speaking, the `setLayout` call is not needed here, as the default layout manager of the content pane is already a `BorderLayout`. We have included the call here for clarity and readability.

Code 11.5

Using a `Border Layout` to arrange components

```
contentPane = frame.getContentPane();

contentPane.setLayout(new BorderLayout());

filenameLabel = new JLabel();
contentPane.add(filenameLabel, BorderLayout.NORTH);

imagePanel = new ImagePanel();
contentPane.add(imagePanel, BorderLayout.CENTER);

statusLabel = new JLabel("Version 1.0");
contentPane.add(statusLabel, BorderLayout.SOUTH);
```

Exercise 11.21 Implement and test the code shown above in your version of the project.

Exercise 11.22 Experiment with other layout managers. Try in your project all of the layout managers mentioned above, and test whether they behave as expected.

11.5.5 Image filters

Two things remain to be done before our first image-viewer version is finished: adding some image filters and adding a *Help* menu. Next, we shall do the filters.

The image filters are the first step toward image manipulation. Eventually, we want not only to be able to open and display images, but also to be able to manipulate them and save them back to disk.

Here, we start by adding three simple filters. A filter is a function that is applied to the whole image. (It could, of course, be modified to be applied to a part of an image, but we are not doing that just yet.)

The three filters are named *darker*, *lighter*, and *threshold*. *Darker* makes the whole image darker, and *lighter* makes it lighter. The threshold filter turns the image into a grayscale picture with only a few preset shades of gray. We have chosen a three-level threshold. This means we shall use three colors: black, white, and medium-gray. All pixels that are in the upper-third value range for brightness will be turned white, all that are in the lower third will be turned black, and the middle third will be gray.

To achieve this, we have to do two things:

■ create menu items for each filter with an associated menu listener

■ implement the actual filter operation

First the menus. There is nothing really new in this. It is just more of the same menu-creation code that we already wrote for our existing menu.

We need to add the following parts:

■ We create a new menu (class JMenu) named *Filter* and add it to the menu bar.

■ We create three menu items (class JMenuItem) named *Darker*, *Lighter*, and *Threshold*, and add them to our filter menu.

■ To each menu item, we add an action listener, using the code idiom for anonymous classes that we discussed for the other menu items. The action listeners should call the methods makeDarker, makeLighter, and threshold, respectively.

After we have added the menus and created the (initially empty) methods to handle the filter functions, we need to implement each filter.

The simplest kinds of filters involve iterating over the image and making a change of some sort to the color of each pixel. A pattern for this process is shown in Code 11.6. More-complicated filters might use the values of neighboring pixels to adjust a pixel's value.

> **Exercise 11.23** Add the new menu and the menu items to your version of the *image-viewer0-4* project, as described here. In order to add the action listeners, you need to create the three methods makeDarker, makeLighter, and threshold as private methods in your **ImageViewer** class. They all have a void return type and take no parameters. These methods can initially have empty bodies, or they could simply print out that they have been called.

Code 11.6

Pattern for a simple filtering process

```
int height = getHeight();
int width = getWidth();
for(int y = 0; y < height; y++) {
    for(int x = 0; x < width; x++) {
        Color pixel = getPixel(x, y);
        alter the pixel's color value;
        setPixel(x, y, pixel);
    }
}
```

The filter function itself operates on the image, so following responsibility-driven design guidelines, it should be implemented in the OFImage class. On the other hand, handling the menu invocation also includes some GUI-related code (for instance, we have to check whether an image is open at all when we invoke the filter), and this belongs in the ImageViewer class.

As a result of this reasoning, we create two methods, one in ImageViewer and one in OFImage, to share the work (Code 11.7 and Code 11.8). We can see that the makeDarker method in ImageViewer contains the part of the task that is related to the GUI (checking that we have an image loaded, displaying a status message, repainting the frame), whereas the darker method in OFImage includes the actual work of making each pixel in the image a bit darker.

Code 11.7

The filter method in the ImageViewer class

```java
public class ImageViewer
{
    // Fields, constructors and all other methods omitted.

    /**
     * 'Darker' function: make the picture darker.
     */
    private void makeDarker()
    {
        if(currentImage != null) {
            currentImage.darker();
            frame.repaint();
            showStatus("Applied: darker");
        }
        else {
            showStatus("No image loaded.");
        }
    }
}
```

Code 11.8

Implementation of a filter in the OFImage class

```java
public class OFImage extends BufferedImage
{
    // Fields, constructors and all other methods omitted.

    /**
     * Make this image a bit darker.
     */
    public void darker()
    {
        int height = getHeight();
        int width = getWidth();
        for(int y = 0; y < height; y++) {
            for(int x = 0; x < width; x++) {
                setPixel(x, y, getPixel(x, y).darker());
            }
        }
    }
}
```

Exercise 11.24 What does the method call `frame.repaint()` do, which you can see in the `makeDarker` method?

Exercise 11.25 We can see a call to a method `showStatus`, which is clearly an internal method call. From the name, we can guess that this method should display a status message using the status label we created earlier. Implement this method in your version of the *imageviewer0-4* project. (*Hint*: Look at the `setText` method in the `JLabel` class.)

Exercise 11.26 What happens if the *Darker* menu item is selected when no image has been opened?

Exercise 11.27 Explain in detail how the `darker` method in `OFImage` works. (*Hint*: It contains another method call to a method also called `darker`. Which class does this second method belong to? Look it up.)

Exercise 11.28 Implement the *lighter* filter in `OFImage`.

Exercise 11.29 Implement the *threshold* filter. To get the brightness of a pixel, you can get its red, green, and blue values and add them up. The `Color` class defines static references to suitable black, white, and gray objects.

You can find a working implementation of everything described so far in the *imageviewer1-0* project. You should, however, attempt to do the exercises yourself first, before you look at the solution.

11.5.6 Dialogs

Our last task for this version is to add a *Help* menu that holds a menu item labeled *About ImageViewer…*When this item is selected, a dialog should pop up that displays some short information.

Now we have to implement the `showAbout` method so that it displays an "About" dialog.

Exercise 11.30 Again add a menu named *Help*. In it, add a menu item labeled *About ImageViewer…*

Exercise 11.31 Add a method stub (a method with an empty body) named `showAbout`, and add an action listener to the *About ImageViewer…*menu item that calls this method.

One of the main characteristics of a dialog is whether or not it is *modal*. A modal dialog blocks all interaction with other parts of the application until the dialog has been closed. It forces the user to deal with the dialog first. Non-modal dialogs allow interaction in other frames while the dialogs are visible.

Dialogs can be implemented in a similar way to our main JFrame. They often use the class JDialog to display the frame.

For modal dialogs with a standard structure, however, there are some convenience methods in class JOptionPane that make it very easy to show such dialogs. JOptionPane has, among other things, static methods to show three types of standard dialog. They are:

- *Message dialog:* This is a dialog that displays a message and has an *OK* button to close the dialog.

- *Confirm dialog:* This dialog usually asks a question and has buttons for the user to make a selection—for example, *Yes, No,* and *Cancel.*

- *Input dialog:* This dialog includes a prompt and a text field for the user to enter some text.

Our "About" box is a simple message dialog. Looking through the JOptionPane documentation, we find that there are static methods named showMessageDialog to do this.

Exercise 11.32 Find the documentation for showMessageDialog. How many methods with this name are there? What are the differences between them? Which one should we use for the "About" box? Why?

Exercise 11.33 Implement the showAbout method in your ImageViewer class, using a call to a showMessageDialog method.

Exercise 11.34 The showInputDialog methods of JOptionPane allow a user to be prompted for input via a dialog when required. On the other hand, the JTextField component allows a permanent text input area to be displayed within a GUI. Find the documentation for this class. What input causes an ActionListener associated with a JTextField to be notified? Can a user be prevented from editing the text in the field? Is it possible for a listener to be notified of arbitrary changes to the text in the field? (*Hint*: What use does a JTextField make of a Document object?)

You can find an example of a JTextField in the *calculator* project in Chapter 7.

After studying the documentation, we can now implement our "About" box by making a call to the showMessageDialog method. The code is shown in Code 11.9. Note that we have introduced a string constant named VERSION to hold the current version number.

Code 11.9

Displaying a modal dialog

```
private void showAbout()
{
    JOptionPane.showMessageDialog(frame,
            "ImageViewer\n" + VERSION,
            "About ImageViewer",
            JOptionPane.INFORMATION_MESSAGE);
}
```

This was the last task to be done to complete "version 1.0" of our image-viewer application. If you have done all the exercises, you should now have a version of the project that can open images, apply filters, display status messages, and display a dialog.

The *imageviewer1-0* project, included in the book projects, contains an implementation of all the functionality discussed thus far. You should carefully study this project and compare it with your own solutions.

In this project, we have also improved the openFile method to include better notification of errors. If the user chooses a file that is not a valid image file, we now show a proper error message. Now that we know about message dialogs, this is easy to do.

11.5.7 Summary of layout management

In this section, we have added some custom classes to deal with images, but more importantly for our GUI, we have looked at the layout of components. We have seen how containers and layout managers work together to achieve the exact arrangement we need on screen.

Learning to work with layout managers takes some experience and often some trial-and-error experimentation. Over time, however, you will get to know the layout managers well.

We have now covered the basics of all important areas of GUI programming. For the rest of the chapter, we can concentrate on fine-tuning and improving what we've got.

11.6 ImageViewer 2.0: improving program structure

Version 1.0 of our application has a useable GUI and can display images. It can also apply three basic filters.

The next obvious idea for an improvement of our application is to add some more-interesting filters. Before we rush in and do it, however, let us think about what this involves.

With the current structure of filters, we have to do three things for each filter:

1 add a menu item

2 add a method to handle the menu activation in ImageViewer

3 add an implementation of the filter in OFImage

Numbers 1 and 3 are unavoidable—we need a menu item and a filter implementation. But number 2 looks suspicious. If we look at these methods in the ImageViewer class (Code 11.10 shows two of them as an example), this looks a lot like code duplication. These methods are essentially the same (except for some small details), and for each new filter we have to add another one of these methods.

As we know, code duplication is a sign of bad design and should be avoided. We deal with it by refactoring our code.

Code 11.10

Two of the filter-handling methods from `ImageViewer`

```
private void makeLighter()
{
    if(currentImage != null) {
        currentImage.lighter();
        frame.repaint();
        showStatus("Applied: lighter");
    }
    else {
        showStatus("No image loaded.");
    }
}

private void threshold()
{
    if(currentImage != null) {
        currentImage.threshold();
        frame.repaint();
        showStatus("Applied: threshold");
    }
    else {
        showStatus("No image loaded.");
    }
}
```

In this case, we want to find a design that lets us add new filters without having to add a new dispatch method for the filter every time.

To achieve what we want, we need to avoid hard-coding every filter-method name (lighter, threshold, etc.) into our ImageViewer class. Instead, we shall use a collection of filters and then write a single filter-invocation method that finds and invokes the right filter. This will be similar in style to the introduction of an act method when decoupling the simulator from individual actor types in the *foxes-and-rabbits* project in Chapter 10.

In order to do this, filters must themselves become objects, rather than just method names. If we want to store them in a common collection, then all filters will need a common superclass, which we name Filter and give an apply method (Figure 11.11 shows the structure, Code 11.11 shows the source code).

Every filter will have an individual name, and its apply method will apply that particular sort of filter to an image. Note that this is an abstract class, as the apply method has to be abstract at this level, but the getName method can be fully implemented so it is not an interface.

Figure 11.11

Class structure for
filters as objects

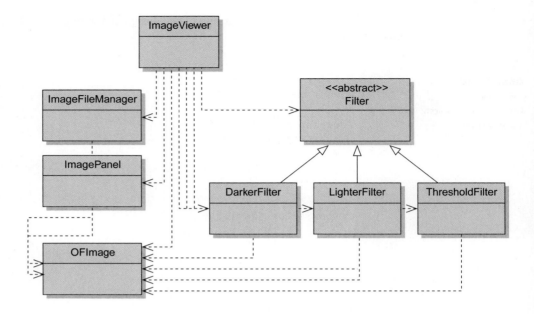

Code 11.11

Abstract class `Filter`:
Superclass for all filters

```java
public abstract class Filter
{
    private String name;

    /**
     * Create a new filter with a given name.
     */
    public Filter(String name)
    {
        this.name = name;
    }

    /**
     * Return the name of this filter.
     *
     * @return The name of this filter.
     */
    public String getName()
    {
        return name;
    }

    /**
     * Apply this filter to an image.
     *
```

Code 11.11
continued
Abstract class `Filter`:
Superclass for all filters

```
        * @param image The image to be changed by this filter.
        */
    public abstract void apply(OFImage image);
}
```

Once we have written the superclass, it is not hard to implement specific filters as subclasses. All we need to do is provide an implementation for the `apply` method that manipulates an image (passed in as a parameter) using its `getPixel` and `setPixel` methods. Code 11.12 shows an example.

Code 11.12
Implementation of a
specific filter class

```
// All comments omitted.

public class DarkerFilter extends Filter
{
    public DarkerFilter(String name)
    {
        super(name);
    }

    public void apply(OFImage image)
    {
        int height = image.getHeight();
        int width = image.getWidth();
        for(int y = 0; y < height; y++) {
            for(int x = 0; x < width; x++) {
                image.setPixel(
                    x, y, image.getPixel(x, y).darker());
            }
        }
    }
}
```

As a side effect of this, the `OFImage` class becomes much simpler, as all of the filter methods can be removed from it. It now only defines the `setPixel` and `getPixel` methods.

Once we have defined our filters like this, we can create filter objects and store them in a collection (Code 11.13).

Code 11.13
Adding a collection
of filters

```
public class ImageViewer
{
    // Other fields and comments omitted.

    private List<Filter> filters;
```

```
public ImageViewer()
{
    filters = createFilters();
    ...
}

private List<Filter> createFilters()
{
    List<Filter> filterList = new ArrayList<Filter>();
    filterList.add(new DarkerFilter("Darker"));
    filterList.add(new LighterFilter("Lighter"));
    filterList.add(new ThresholdFilter("Threshold"));

    return filterList;
}

// Other methods omitted.
}
```

Once we have this structure in place, we can make the last two necessary changes:

■ We change the code that creates the filter menu items so that it iterates over the filter collection. For every filter, it creates a menu item and uses the filter's getName method to determine the item's label.

■ Having done this, we can write a generic applyFilter method that receives a filter as a parameter and applies this filter to the current image.

The *imageviewer2-0* project includes a complete implementation of these changes.

Exercise 11.35 Open the *imageviewer2-0* project. Study the code for the new method to create and apply filters in class ImageViewer. Pay special attention to the makeMenuBar and applyFilter methods. Explain in detail how the creation of the filter menu items and their activation works. Draw an object diagram. Note, in particular, that the filter variable in makeMenuBar has been declared as final, as discussed in Section 11.4.8. Make sure that you understand why this is necessary.

Exercise 11.36 What needs to be changed to add a new filter to your image viewer?

Exercise 11.37 *Challenge exercise* You might have observed that the apply methods of all of the Filter subclasses have a very similar structure: iterate over the whole image and change the value of each pixel independently of surrounding pixels. It should be possible to isolate this duplication in much the same way as we did in creating the Filter class.

Create a method in the Filter class that iterates over the image and applies a filter-specific transformation to each individual pixel. Replace the bodies of the apply methods in the three Filter subclasses with a call to this method, passing the image and an object that can apply the appropriate transformation.

In this section, we have done pure refactoring. We have not changed the functionality of the application at all, but have worked exclusively at improving the implementation structure so that future changes become easier.

Now, after finishing the refactoring, we should test that all existing functionality still works as expected. In all development projects, we need phases like this. We do not always make perfect design decisions at the start, and applications grow and requirements change. Even though our main task in this chapter is to work with GUIs, we needed to step back and refactor our code before proceeding. This work will pay off in the long run by making all further changes easier.

Sometimes it is tempting to leave structures as they are, even though we recognize that they are not good. Putting up with a bit of code duplication may be easier in the short term than doing careful refactoring. One can get away with that for a short while, but for projects that are intended to survive for a longer time, this is bound to create problems. As a general rule: Take the time; keep your code clean!

Now that we have done this, we are ready to add some more filters.

Exercise 11.38 Add a *grayscale* filter to your project. The filter turns the image into a black-and-white image in shades of gray. You can make a pixel any shade of gray by giving all three color components (red, green, blue) the same value. The brightness of each pixel should remain unchanged.

Exercise 11.39 Add a *mirror* filter that flips the image horizontally. The pixel at the top left corner will move to the top right, and vice versa, producing the effect of viewing the image in a mirror.

Exercise 11.40 Add an *invert* filter that inverts each color. "Inverting" a color means replacing each color value x with $255 - x$.

Exercise 11.41 Add a *smooth* filter that "smoothes" the image. A smooth filter replaces every pixel value with the average of its neighboring pixels and itself (nine pixels in total). You have to be careful at the image's edges, where some neighbors do not exist. You also have to make sure to work with a temporary copy of the image while you process it, because the result is not correct if you work on a single image. (Why is this?) You can easily obtain a copy of the image by creating a new `OFImage` with the original as the parameter to its constructor.

Exercise 11.42 Add a *solarize* filter. Solarization is an effect one can create manually on photo negatives by re-exposing a developed negative. We can simulate this by replacing each color component of each pixel that has a value v of less than 128 with $255 - v$. The brighter components (value of 128 or more) we leave unchanged. (This is a very simple solarization algorithm—you can find more-sophisticated ones described in the literature.)

Exercise 11.43 Implement an *edge detection* filter. Do this by analyzing the nine pixels in a three-by-three square around each pixel (similar to the smooth filter), and then set the value of the middle pixel to the difference between the highest and the lowest value found. Do this for each color component (red, green, blue). This also looks good if you invert the image at the same time.

Exercise 11.44 Experiment with your filters on different pictures. Try applying multiple filters, one after another.

Once you have implemented some more filters of your own, you should change the version number of your project to "version 2.1."

11.7   ImageViewer 3.0: more interface components

Before we leave the image-viewer project behind us, we want to add a few last improvements, and in the process look at two more GUI components: buttons and borders.

11.7.1   Buttons

We now want to add functionality to the image viewer to change the size of the image. We do this by providing two functions: *larger*, which doubles the image size, and *smaller*, which halves the size. (To be exact, we double or halve both the width and the height, not the area.)

One way to do this is to implement filters for these tasks. But we decide against it. So far, filters never change the image size, and we want to leave it at that. Instead, we introduce a toolbar on the left side of our frame with two buttons in it labeled *Larger* and *Smaller* (Figure 11.12). This also gives us a chance to experiment a bit with buttons, containers, and layout managers.

Figure 11.12
Image viewer with
toolbar buttons

So far, our frame uses a BorderLayout, where the WEST area is empty. We can use this area to add our toolbar buttons. There is one small problem, though. The WEST area of a BorderLayout can hold only one component, but we have two buttons.

The solution is simple. We add a JPanel to the frame's WEST area (as we know, a JPanel is a container), and then stick the two buttons into the JPanel. Code 11.14 shows the code to do this.

Code 11.14

Adding a toolbar panel with two buttons

```
// Create the toolbar with the buttons
JPanel toolbar = new JPanel();

smallerButton = new JButton("Smaller");
toolbar.add(smallerButton);

largerButton = new JButton("Larger");
toolbar.add(largerButton);

contentPane.add(toolbar, BorderLayout.WEST);
```

Exercise 11.45 Add two buttons labeled *Larger* and *Smaller* to your latest version of the project, using code similar to the one above. Test it. What do you observe?

When we try this out, we see that it works partially but does not look as expected. The reason is that a JPanel uses, by default, a FlowLayout, and a FlowLayout arranges its components horizontally. We would like them arranged vertically.

We can achieve this by using another layout manager. A GridLayout does what we want. When creating a GridLayout, constructor parameters determine how many rows and columns we wish to have. A value of zero has a special meaning here, standing for "as many as necessary."

Thus, we can create a single column GridLayout by using 0 as the number of rows and 1 as the number of columns. We can then use this GridLayout for our JPanel by using the panel's setLayout method immediately after creating it:

```
JPanel toolbar = new JPanel();
toolbar.setLayout(new GridLayout(0, 1));
```

Alternatively, the layout manager can also be specified as a constructor parameter of the container:

```
JPanel toolbar = new JPanel(new GridLayout(0, 1));
```

Exercise 11.46 Change your code so that your toolbar panel uses a GridLayout, as discussed above. Test. What do you observe?

If we try this out, we can see that we are getting closer, but we still do not have what we want. Our buttons now are much larger than we intended. The reason is that a container in a BorderLayout (our toolbar JPanel in this case) always covers its whole area (the WEST area in our frame). And a GridLayout always resizes its components to fill the whole container.

A FlowLayout does not do this; it is quite happy to leave some empty space around the components. Our solution is therefore to use both: the GridLayout to arrange the buttons in a column and a FlowLayout around it to allow some space. We end up with a GridLayout panel inside a FlowLayout panel inside a BorderLayout. Code 11.15 shows this solution. Constructions like this are very common. You will often nest various containers inside other containers to create exactly the look you want.

Code 11.15

Using a nested
GridLayout container
inside a FlowLayout
container

```
// Create the toolbar with the buttons.
JPanel toolbar = new JPanel();
toolbar.setLayout(new GridLayout(0, 1));

smallerButton = new JButton("Smaller");
toolbar.add(smallerButton);

largerButton = new JButton("Larger");
toolbar.add(largerButton);

// Add toolbar into panel with flow layout for spacing.
JPanel flow = new JPanel();
flow.add(toolbar);

contentPane.add(flow, BorderLayout.WEST);
```

Our buttons now look quite close to what we were aiming for. Before adding the finishing polish, we can first work on making the buttons work.

We need to add two methods, named, for instance, makeLarger and makeSmaller, to do the actual work, and we need to add action listeners to the buttons that invoke these methods.

Exercise 11.47 In your project, add two method stubs named makeLarger and makeSmaller. Initially, put just a single println statement into these method bodies to see when they have been called. The methods can be private.

Exercise 11.48 Add action listeners to the two buttons that invoke the two new methods. Adding action listeners to buttons is identical to adding action listeners to menu items. You can essentially copy the code pattern from there. Test it. Make sure your makeSmaller and makeLarger methods get called by activating the buttons.

Exercise 11.49 Properly implement the `makeSmaller` and `makeLarger` methods. To do this, you have to create a new `OFImage` with a different size, copy the pixels from the current image across (while scaling it up or down), and then set the new image as the current image. At the end of your method, you should call the frame's `pack` method to rearrange the components with the changed size.

Exercise 11.50 All Swing components have a `setEnabled(boolean)` method that can enable and disable the component. Disabled components are usually displayed in light gray and do not react to input. Change your image viewer so that the two toolbar buttons are initially disabled. When an image is opened, they should be enabled, and when it is closed, they should be disabled again.

11.7.2 Borders

The last polish we want to add to our interface is some internal borders. Borders can be used to group components or just to add some space between them. Every Swing component can have a border.

Some layout managers also accept constructor parameters that define their spacing, and the layout manager will then create the requested space between components.

The most used borders are `BevelBorder`, `CompoundBorder`, `EmptyBorder`, `EtchedBorder`, and `TitledBorder`. You should familiarize yourself with these.

We shall do three things to improve the look of our GUI:

- add some empty space around the outside of the frame
- add spacing between the components of the frame
- add a line around the image

The code to do this is shown in Code 11.16. The `setBorder` call on the content pane with an `EmptyBorder` as a parameter adds empty space around the outside of the frame. Note that we now cast the `contentPane` to a `JPanel`, as the supertype `Container` does not have the `set-Border` method.[6]

Code 11.16

Adding spacing with gaps and borders

```
JPanel contentPane = (JPanel) frame.getContentPane();
contentPane.setBorder(new EmptyBorder(12, 12, 12, 12));

// Specify the layout manager with nice spacing.
contentPane.setLayout(new BorderLayout(6, 6));

imagePanel = new ImagePanel();
imagePanel.setBorder(new EtchedBorder());
contentPane.add(imagePanel, BorderLayout.CENTER);
```

---

[6] Using a cast in this way only works because the dynamic type of the content pane is already `JPanel`. The cast does not transform the content-pane object into a `JPanel` in any sense.

Creating the BorderLayout with two int parameters adds spacing between the components that it lays out. And finally, setting an EtchedBorder for the imagePanel adds a line with an "etched" look around the image. (Borders are defined in the package javax.swing. border—we have to add an import statement for this package.)

All the improvements discussed in the section have been implemented in the last version of this application in the book projects: *imageviewer3-0*. In that version, we have also added a *Save As* function to the file menu so that images can be saved back to disk.

And we have added one more filter, called *Fish Eye*, to give you some more ideas about what you can do. Try it out. It works especially well on portraits.

11.8   Further extensions

Programming GUIs with Swing is a big subject area. Swing has many different types of components and many different containers and layout managers. And each of these has many attributes and methods.

Becoming familiar with the whole Swing library takes time, and is not something done in a few weeks. Usually, as we work on GUIs, we continue to read about details that we did not know before and become experts over time.

The example discussed in this chapter, even though it contains a lot of detail, is only a brief introduction to GUI programming. We have discussed most of the important concepts, but there is still a large amount of functionality to be discovered, most of which is beyond the scope of this book. There are various sources of information available to help you continue. You frequently have to look up the API documentation for the Swing classes; it is not possible to work without it. There are also many GUI/Swing tutorials available, both in print and on the web.

A very good starting point for this, as so often is the case, is the Java Tutorial, available publicly on Oracle's web site. It contains a section titled *Creating a GUI with JFC/Swing* (http:// download.oracle.com/javase/tutorial/uiswing/index.html).

In this section, there are many interesting subsections. One of the most useful may be the section entitled *Using Swing Components* and in it the subsection *How To...* It contains these entries: *How to Use Buttons, Check Boxes, and Radio Buttons*; *How to Use Labels*; *How to Make Dialogs*; *How to Use Panels*; and so on.

Similarly, the top-level section *Laying Out Components within a Container* also has a *How To...* section that tells you about all available layout managers.

Exercise 11.51 Find the online Java Tutorial section *Creating a GUI with JFC/Swing* (the sections are called *trails* on the web site). Bookmark it.

Exercise 11.52 What do CardLayout and GroupLayout have to offer that is different from the layout managers we have discussed in this chapter?

Exercise 11.53 What is a *slider*? Find a description and summarize. Give a short example in Java code about creating and using a slider.

Exercise 11.54 What is a *tabbed pane*? Find a description and summarize. Give examples of what a tabbed pane might be used for.

Exercise 11.55 What is a *spinner*? Find a description and summarize.

Exercise 11.56 Find the demo application *ProgressBarDemo*. Run it on your computer. Describe what it does.

This is where we shall leave the discussion of the image-viewer example. It can, however, be extended in many directions by interested readers. Using the information from the online tutorial, you can add numerous interface components.

The following exercises give you some ideas, and obviously there are many more possibilities.

Exercise 11.57 Implement an *undo* function in your image viewer. This function reverses the last operation.

Exercise 11.58 Disable all menu items that cannot be used when no image is being displayed.

Exercise 11.59 Implement a *reload* function that discards all changes to the current image and reloads it from disk.

Exercise 11.60 The `JMenu` class is actually a subclass of `JMenuItem`. This means that nested menus can be created by placing one `JMenu` inside another. Add an *Adjust* menu to the menu bar. Nest within it a *Rotate* menu that allows the image to be rotated either 90 or 180 degrees, clockwise or counterclockwise. Implement this functionality. The *Adjust* menu could also contain menu items that invoke the existing *Larger* and *Smaller* functionality, for instance.

Exercise 11.61 The application always resizes its frame in order to ensure that the full image is always visible. Having a large frame is not always desirable. Read the documentation on the `JScrollPane` class. Instead of adding the `ImagePanel` directly to the content pane, place the panel in a `JScrollPane` and add the scroll pane to the content pane. Display a large image and experiment with resizing the window. What difference does having a scroll pane make? Does this allow you to display images that would otherwise be too large for the screen?

Exercise 11.62 Change your application so that it can open multiple images at the same time (but only one image is displayed at any time). Then add a pop-up menu (using class `JComboBox`) to select the image to display.

Exercise 11.63 As an alternative to using a `JComboBox` as in Exercise 11.62, use a tabbed pane (class `JTabbedPane`) to hold multiple open images.

Exercise 11.64 Implement a slide-show function that lets you choose a directory and then displays each image in that directory for a specified length of time (say, 5 seconds).

Exercise 11.65 Once you have the slide show, add a slider (class `JSlider`) that lets you select an image in the slide show by moving the slider. While the slide show runs, the slider should move to indicate progress.

11.9 Another example: MusicPlayer

So far in this chapter, we have discussed one example of a GUI application in detail. We now want to introduce a second application to provide another example to learn from. This program introduces a few additional GUI components.

This second example is a music-player application. We shall not discuss it in any great amount of detail. It is intended as a basis for studying the source code largely on your own and as a source of code fragments for you to copy and modify. Here, in this chapter, we shall only point out a few selected aspects of the application that are worth focusing on.

Exercise 11.66 Open the *musicplayer* project. Create an instance of `MusicPlayerGUI`, and experiment with the application.

The *musicplayer* project provides a GUI interface to classes based on the *music-organizer* projects from Chapter 4. As there, the program finds and plays MP3 files stored in the *audio* folder inside the project folder. If you have sound files of the right format of your own, you should be able to play them by dropping them in the project's *audio* folder.

The music player is implemented across three classes: `MusicPlayerGUI`, `MusicPlayer`, and `MusicFilePlayer`. Only the first is intended to be studied here. `MusicFilePlayer` can be used essentially as a library class; instances are created along with the name of the MP3 file to be played. Familiarize yourself with its interface, but you do not need to understand or modify its implementation. (You are welcome, of course, to study this class as well if you like, but it uses some concepts that we shall not discuss in this book.)

Following are some noteworthy observations about the *musicplayer* project.

Model/view separation

This application uses a better model/view separation than the previous example. This means that the application functionality (the model) is separated cleanly from the application's user interface (the GUI). Each of those two, the model and the view, may consist of multiple classes, but every class should be clearly in one or the other group to achieve a clear separation. In our example, the view consists of a single GUI class.

Separating the application's functionality from the interface is an example of good cohesion; it makes the program easier to understand, easier to maintain, and easier to adapt to different requirements (especially different user interfaces). It would, for example, be fairly easy to write a text-based interface for the music player, effectively replacing the `MusicPlayerGUI` class and leaving the `MusicPlayer` class unchanged.

Inheriting from `JFrame`

In this example, we are demonstrating the alternative popular version of creating frames that we mentioned at the start of the chapter. Our GUI class does not instantiate a `JFrame` object; instead, it extends the `JFrame` class. As a result, all the `JFrame` methods we need to call (such as `getContentPane`, `setJMenuBar`, `pack`, `setVisible`, and so on) can now be called as internal (inherited) methods.

There is no strong reason for preferring one style (using a `JFrame` instance) over the other (inheriting from `JFrame`). It is largely a matter of personal preference, but you should be aware that both styles are widely used.

Displaying static images

It is very common that we want to display an image in a GUI. The easiest way to do this is to include in the interface a `JLabel` that has a graphic as its label (a `JLabel` can display either text or a graphic or both). The sound player includes an example of doing this. The relevant source code is

```
JLabel image = new JLabel(new ImageIcon("title.jpg"));
```

This statement will load an image file named "title.jpg" from the project directory, create an icon with that image, and then create a `JLabel` that displays the icon. (The term "icon" seems to suggest that we are dealing only with small images here, but the image can in fact be of any size.) This method works for JPEG, GIF, and PNG images.

Combo boxes

The sound player presents an example of using a `JComboBox`. A combo box is a set of values, one of which is selected at any time. The selected value is displayed, and the selection can be accessed through a pop-up menu. In the sound player, the combo box is used to select a particular ordering for the tracks—by artist, title, etc.

A `JComboBox` may also be editable, in which case the values are not all predefined but can be typed by a user. Ours is not.

Lists

The program also includes an example of a list (class `JList`) for the list of tracks. A list can hold an arbitrary number of values, and one or more can be selected. The list values in this example are strings, but other types are possible. A list does not automatically have a scrollbar.

Scrollbars

Another component demonstrated in this example is the use of scrollbars.

Scrollbars can be created by using a special container, an instance of class `JScrollPane`. GUI objects of any type can be placed into a scroll pane, and the scroll pane will, if the held object is too big to be displayed in the available space, provide the necessary scrollbars.

In our example, we have placed our track list into a scroll pane. The scroll pane itself is then placed into its parent container. The scrollbars only become visible when necessary. You can try this by either adding more tracks until they do not fit into the available space or by resizing the window to make it too small to display the current list.

Other elements demonstrated in this example are the use of a slider (which does not do much), and the use of color for changing the look of an application. Each of the GUI's elements has many methods for modifying the component's look or behavior—you should look through the documentation for any component that interests you and experiment with modifying some properties of that component.

Exercise 11.67 Change the music player so that it displays a different image in its center. Find an image on the web to use, or make your own.

Exercise 11.68 Change the colors of the other components (foreground and background colors) to suit the new main image.

Exercise 11.69 Add a new component to display details of the current track when one is playing.

Exercise 11.70 Add a *reload* capability to the music player that rereads the files from the *audio* folder. Then you can drop a new file into the folder and load it without having to quit the player.

Exercise 11.71 Add an *Open* item to the file menu. When activated, it presents a file-selection dialog that lets the user choose a sound file to open. If the user chooses a directory, the player should open all sound files in that directory (as it does now with the *audio* directory).

Exercise 11.72 Modify the slider so that the start and end (and possibly other tick marks) are labeled with numbers. The start should be zero, and the end should be the length of the music file. The `MusicPlayer` class has a `getLength` method. Note that the slider is not currently functional.

Exercise 11.73 Modify the music player so that a double click on a list element in the track list starts playing that track.

Exercise 11.74 Improve the button look. All buttons that have no function at any point in time should be grayed out at that time and should be enabled only when they can reasonably be used.

Exercise 11.75 The display of tracks is currently simply a `JList` of `String` objects. Investigate whether there are any Swing components available that would provide greater sophistication than this. For instance, can you find a way to provide a header line and align the artist, title, and other parts of the track information? Implement this in your version.

Exercise 11.76 *Challenge exercise* Have the position slider move as a track is being played.

11.10 Summary

In this chapter, we have given an introduction to GUI programming using the Swing and AWT libraries. We have discussed the three main conceptual areas: creating GUI components, layout, and event handling.

We have seen that building a GUI usually starts with creating a top-level frame, such as a JFrame. The frame is then filled with various components that provide information and functionality to the user. Among the components we have encountered are menus, menu items, buttons, labels, borders, and others.

Components are arranged on screen with the help of containers and layout managers. Containers hold collections of components, and each container has a layout manager that takes care of arranging the components within the container's screen area. Nesting containers, using combinations of different layout managers, is a common way to achieve the desired combination of component size and juxtaposition.

Interactive components (those that can react to user input) generate events when they are activated by a user. Other objects can become event listeners and be notified of such events by implementing standard interfaces. When the listener object is notified, it can take appropriate action to deal with the user event.

We have introduced the concept of anonymous inner classes as a modular, extendable technique for writing event listeners.

And finally, we have given a pointer to an online reference and tutorial site that may be used to learn about details not covered in the chapter.

Exercise 11.77 Add a GUI to the *world-of-zuul* project from Chapter 6. Every room should have an associated image that is displayed when the player enters the room. There should be a non-editable text area to display text output. To enter commands, you can choose between different possibilities: you can leave the input text-based and use a text field (class JTextField) to type commands, or you can use buttons for command entry.

Exercise 11.78 Add sounds to the *word-of-zuul* game. You can associate individual sounds with rooms, items, or characters.

Exercise 11.79 Design and build a GUI for a text editor. Users should be able to enter text, edit, scroll, etc. Consider functions for formatting (font faces, style, and size) and a character/word-count function. You do not need to implement the load and save functions just yet—you may like to wait with that until you have read the next chapter.

Terms introduced in this chapter

GUI, AWT, Swing, component, layout, event, event handling, event listener, frame, menu bar, menu, menu item, content pane, modal dialog, anonymous inner class, final variable

Concept summary

- **components** A GUI is built by arranging components on screen. Components are represented by objects.

- **layout** Arranging the layout of components is achieved by using layout managers.

- **event handling** The term *event handling* refers to the task of reacting to user events, such as mouse-button clicks or keyboard input.

- **image format** Images can be stored in different formats. The differences primarily affect file size and the quality of the image.

- **menu bar, content pane** Components are placed in a frame by adding them to the frame's menu bar, or content pane.

- **event listener** An object can listen to component events by implementing an event-listener interface.

- **anonymous inner classes** Anonymous inner classes are a useful construct for implementing event listeners.

CHAPTER 12

Handling errors

Main concepts discussed in this chapter:

- defensive programming
- exception throwing and handling
- error reporting
- basic file processing

Java constructs discussed in this chapter:

```
TreeMap, TreeSet, SortedMap, assert, exception, throw, throws,
try, catch, File, FileReader, FileWriter, Path, Scanner, stream
```

In Chapter 7, we saw that logical errors in programs are harder to spot than syntactic errors because a compiler cannot give any help with logical errors. Logical errors arise for several reasons, which may overlap in some situations:

- The solution to a problem has been implemented incorrectly. For instance, a problem involving generating some statistics on data values might have been programmed to find the mean value rather than the median value (the "middle" value).

- An object might be asked to do something it is unable to. For instance, a collection object's get method might be called with an index value outside the valid range.

- An object might be used in ways that have not been anticipated by the class designer, leading to the object being left in an inconsistent or inappropriate state. This often happens when a class is reused in a setting that is different from its original one, perhaps through inheritance.

Although the sort of testing strategies discussed in Chapter 7 can help us identify and eliminate many logical errors before our programs are put to use, experience suggests that program failures will continue to occur. Furthermore, even the most thoroughly tested program may fail as a result of circumstances beyond the programmer's control. Consider the case of a web-browser asked to display a web page that does not exist or a program that tries to write data to a disk that has no more space left. These problems are not the result of logical programming errors, but they could easily cause a program to fail if the possibility of their arising has not been taken into account.

In this chapter, we look at how to anticipate potential errors and how to respond to error situations as they arise during the execution of a program. In addition, we provide some suggestions on how to report errors when they occur. We also provide a brief introduction to how to perform textual input/output, as file processing is one of the situations where errors can easily arise.

12.1 The *address-book* project

We shall use the *address-book* family of projects to illustrate some of the principles of error reporting and error handling that arise in many applications. The projects represent an application that stores personal-contact details—name, address, and phone number—for an arbitrary number of people. Such a contacts list might be used on a mobile phone or in an e-mail program, for instance. The contact details are indexed in the address book by both name and phone number. The main classes we shall be discussing are `AddressBook` (Code 12.1) and `ContactDetails`. In addition, the `AddressBookDemo` class is provided as a convenient means of setting up an initial address book with some sample data.

Code 12.1

The `AddressBook` class

```java
import java.util.Iterator;
import java.util.LinkedList;
import java.util.List;
import java.util.Set;
import java.util.SortedMap;
import java.util.TreeMap;
import java.util.TreeSet;

/**
 * A class to maintain an arbitrary number of contact details.
 * Details are indexed by both name and phone number.
 * @author David J. Barnes and Michael Kölling.
 * @version 2011.07.31
 */
public class AddressBook
{
    // Storage for an arbitrary number of details.
    private TreeMap<String, ContactDetails> book;
    private int numberOfEntries;

    /**
     * Perform any initialization for the address book.
     */
    public AddressBook()
    {
        book = new TreeMap<String, ContactDetails>();
        numberOfEntries = 0;
    }

    /**
     * Look up a name or phone number and return the
     * corresponding contact details.
```

```java
 * @param key The name or number to be looked up.
 * @return The details corresponding to the key.
 */
public ContactDetails getDetails(String key)
{
    return book.get(key);
}

/**
 * Return whether or not the current key is in use.
 * @param key The name or number to be looked up.
 * @return true if the key is in use, false otherwise.
 */
public boolean keyInUse(String key)
{
    return book.containsKey(key);
}

/**
 * Add a new set of details to the address book.
 * @param details The details to associate with the person.
 */
public void addDetails(ContactDetails details)
{
    book.put(details.getName(), details);
    book.put(details.getPhone(), details);
    numberOfEntries++;
}

/**
 * Change the details previously stored under the given key.
 * @param oldKey One of the keys used to store the details.
 * @param details The replacement details.
 */
public void changeDetails(String oldKey,
                          ContactDetails details)
{
    removeDetails(oldKey);
    addDetails(details);
}

/**
 * Search for all details stored under a key that starts with
 * the given prefix.
 * @param keyPrefix The key prefix to search on.
 * @return An array of those details that have been found.
 */
```

**Code 12.1
continued**

The AddressBook
class

```java
public ContactDetails[] search(String keyPrefix)
{
    List<ContactDetails> matches =
            new LinkedList<ContactDetails>();
    // Find keys that are equal-to or greater-than the prefix.
    SortedMap<String, ContactDetails> tail =
            book.tailMap(keyPrefix);
    Iterator<String> it = tail.keySet().iterator();
    boolean endOfSearch = false;
    while(!endOfSearch && it.hasNext()) {
        String key = it.next();
        if(key.startsWith(keyPrefix)) {
            matches.add(book.get(key));
        }
        else {
            // As the list is sorted, no more will be found.
            endOfSearch = true;
        }
    }
    ContactDetails[] results =
            new ContactDetails[matches.size()];
    matches.toArray(results);
    return results;
}

/**
 * Return the number of entries currently in the
 * address book.
 * @return The number of entries.
 */
public int getNumberOfEntries()
{
    return numberOfEntries;
}

/**
 * Remove the entry with the given key from the address book.
 * @param key One of the keys of the entry to be removed.
 */
public void removeDetails(String key)
{
    ContactDetails details = book.get(key);
    book.remove(details.getName());
    book.remove(details.getPhone());
    numberOfEntries--;
}
```

**Code 12.1
continued**

The AddressBook
class

```java
/**
 * Return all the contact details, sorted according
 * to the sort order of the ContactDetails class.
 * @return A sorted list of the details.
 */
public String listDetails()
{
    // Because each entry is stored under two keys, it is
    // necessary to build a set of the ContactDetails.
    // This eliminates duplicates.
    StringBuilder allEntries = new StringBuilder();
    Set<ContactDetails> sortedDetails =
            new TreeSet<ContactDetails>(book.values());
    for(ContactDetails details : sortedDetails) {
        allEntries.append(details);
        allEntries.append('\n');
        allEntries.append('\n');
    }
    return allEntries.toString();
}
}
```

New details can be stored in the address book via its addDetails method. This assumes that the details represent a new contact and not a change of details for an existing one. To cover the latter case, the changeDetails method removes an old entry and replaces it with the revised details. The address book provides two ways to retrieve entries: the getDetails method takes a name or phone number as the key and returns the matching details; the search method returns an array of all those details that start with a given search string (for instance, the search string "08459" would return all entries with phone numbers having that area prefix).

There are two introductory versions of the *address-book* project for you to explore. Both provide access to the same version of AddressBook, as shown in Code 12.1. The *address-book-v1t* project provides a text-based user interface, similar in style to the interface of the *zuul* game discussed in Chapter 6. Commands are currently available to list the address book's contents, search it, and add a new entry. Probably more interesting as an interface, however, is the *address-book-v1g* version, which incorporates a simple GUI. Experiment with both versions to gain some experience with what the application can do.

Exercise 12.1 Open the *address-book-v1g* project and create an AddressBookDemo object. Call its showInterface method to display the GUI and interact with the sample address book.

Exercise 12.2 Repeat your experimentation with the text interface of the *address-book-v1t* project.

Exercise 12.3 Examine the implementation of the `AddressBook` class and assess whether you think it has been well written or not. Do you have any specific criticisms of it?

Exercise 12.4 The `AddressBook` class uses quite a lot of classes from the `java.util` package; if you are not familiar with any of these, check the API documentation to fill in the gaps. Do you think the use of so many different utility classes is justified? Could a `HashMap` have been used in place of the `TreeMap`?

If you are not sure, try changing `TreeMap` to `HashMap` and see if `HashMap` offers all of the required functionality.

Exercise 12.5 Modify the `CommandWords` and `AddressBookTextInterface` classes of the *address-book-v1t* project to provide interactive access to the `getDetails` and `removeDetails` methods of `AddressBook`.

Exercise 12.6 The `AddressBook` class defines a field to record the number of entries. Do you think it would be more appropriate to calculate this value directly, from the number of unique entries in the `TreeMap`? For instance, can you think of any circumstances in which the following calculation would not produce the same value?

```
return book.size() / 2;
```

Exercise 12.7 How easy do you think it would be to add a `String` field for an email address to the `ContactDetails` class, and then to use this as a third key in the `AddressBook`? Don't actually try it, at this stage.

12.2 Defensive programming

12.2.1 Client–server interaction

An `AddressBook` is a typical server object, initiating no actions on its own behalf; all of its activities are driven by client requests. Implementers can adopt at least two possible views when designing and implementing a server class:

■ They can assume that client objects will know what they are doing and will request services only in a sensible and well-defined way.

■ They can assume that server objects will operate in an essentially problematic environment in which all possible steps must be taken to prevent client objects from using them incorrectly.

These views clearly represent opposite extremes. In practice, the most likely scenario usually lies somewhere in between. Most client interactions will be reasonable, with the occasional attempt to use the server incorrectly—either as the result of a logical programming error or of misconception on the part of the client programmer. A third possibility, of course, is an intentionally hostile client who is trying to break or find a weakness in the server.

These different views provide a useful base from which to discuss questions such as:

■ How much checking should a server's methods perform on client requests?

■ How should a server report errors to its clients?

■ How can a client anticipate failure of a request to a server?

■ How should a client deal with failure of a request?

If we examine the AddressBook class with these issues in mind, we shall see that the class has been written to trust completely that its clients will use it appropriately. Exercise 12.8 illustrates one of the ways in which this is the case and how things can go wrong.

Exercise 12.8 Using the *address-book-v1g* project, create a new AddressBook object on the object bench. This will be completely empty of contact details. Now make a call to its removeDetails method with any string value for the key. What happens? Can you understand why this happens?

Exercise 12.9 For a programmer, the easiest response to an error situation arising is to allow the program to terminate (i.e., to "crash"). Can you think of any situations in which simply allowing a program to terminate could be very dangerous?

Exercise 12.10 Many commercially sold programs contain errors that are not handled properly in the software and cause them to crash. Is that unavoidable? Is it acceptable? Discuss this issue.

The problem with the removeDetails method is that it assumes that the key passed to it is a valid key for the address book. It uses the supposed key to retrieve the associated contact details:

```
ContactDetails details = book.get(key);
```

However, if the map does not have that particular key, then the details variable ends up containing null. That, of itself, is not an error; but the error arises from the following statement, where we assume that details refers to a valid object:

```
book.remove(details.getName());
```

It is not allowed to call a method on a variable containing null, and the result is a runtime error. BlueJ reports this as a NullPointerException and highlights the statement from which it resulted. Later in this chapter, we shall be discussing exceptions in detail. For now, we can simply say that, if an error such as this were to occur in a running application, then the application would crash—i.e., terminate in an uncontrolled way—before it had completed its task.

There is clearly a problem here, but whose fault is it? Is it the fault of the client object for calling the method with a bad parameter value, or is it the fault of the server object for failing to handle this situation properly? The writer of the client class might argue that there is nothing in the method's documentation to say that the key must be valid. Conversely, the writer of the server class might argue that it is obviously wrong to try to remove details with an invalid key. Our concern in this chapter is not to resolve such disputes, but to try to prevent them from arising in the first place. We shall start by looking at error handling from the point of view of the server class.

Exercise 12.11 Save a copy, to work on, of one of the *address-book-v1* projects under another name. Make changes to the `removeDetails` method to avoid a `NullPointerException` arising if the key value does not have a corresponding entry in the address book. Use an if statement. If the key is not valid, then the method should do nothing.

Exercise 12.12 Is it necessary to report the detection of an invalid key in a call to `remove-Details`? If so, how would you report it?

Exercise 12.13 Are there any other methods in the `AddressBook` class that are vulnerable to similar errors? If so, try to correct them in your copy of the project. Is it acceptable in all cases for the method simply to do nothing if its parameter values are inappropriate? Do the errors need reporting in some way? If so, how would you do it, and would it be the same way for each error?

12.2.2 Parameter checking

A server object is most vulnerable when its constructor and methods receive external values through their parameters. The values passed to a constructor are used to set up an object's initial state, while the values passed to a method will be used to influence the overall effect of the method call and may change the state of the object and a result the method returns. Therefore, it is vital that a server object knows whether it can trust parameter values to be valid or whether it needs to check their validity for itself. The current situation in both the `ContactDetails` and `AddressBook` classes is that there is no checking at all on parameter values. As we have seen with the `removeDetails` method, this can lead to a fatal runtime error.

Preventing a `NullPointerException` in `removeDetails` is relatively easy, and Code 12.2 illustrates how this can be done. Note that, as well as improving the source code in the method, we have updated the method's comment, to document the fact that unknown keys are ignored.

Code 12.2

Guarding against an invalid key in `removeDetails`

```
/**
 * Remove the entry with the given key from the address book.
 * If the key does not exist, do nothing.
 * @param key One of the keys of the entry to be removed.
 */
public void removeDetails(String key)
{
    if(keyInUse(key)) {
        ContactDetails details = book.get(key);
        book.remove(details.getName());
        book.remove(details.getPhone());
        numberOfEntries--;
    }
}
```

If we examine all the methods of AddressBook, we find that there are other places where we could make similar improvements:

- The addDetails method should check that its actual parameter is not null.

- The changeDetails method should check both that the old key is one that is in use and that the new details are not null.

- The search method should check that the key is not null.

These changes have all been implemented in the version of the application to be found in the *address-book-v2g* and *address-book-v2t* projects.

Exercise 12.14 Why do you think we have felt it unnecessary to make similar changes to the getDetails and keyInUse methods?

Exercise 12.15 In dealing with parameter errors, we have not printed any error messages. Do you think an AddressBook *should* print an error message whenever it receives a bad parameter value to one of its methods? Are there any situations where a printed error message would be inappropriate? For instance, do error messages printed to the terminal seem appropriate with the GUI version of the project?

Exercise 12.16 Are there any further checks you feel we should make on the parameters of other methods, to prevent an AddressBook object from functioning incorrectly?

12.3 Server-error reporting

Having protected a server object from performing an illegal operation through bad parameter values, we could take the view that this is all that the server writer needs to do. However, ideally we should like to avoid such error situations from arising in the first place. Furthermore, it is often the case that incorrect parameter values are the result of some form of programming error in the client that supplied them. Therefore, rather than simply programming around the problem in the server and leaving it at that, it is good practice for the server to make some effort to indicate that a problem has arisen, either to the client itself or to a human user or programmer. In that way, there is a chance that an incorrectly written client will be fixed. But notice that those three "audiences" for the notification will often be completely different.

What is the best way for a server to report problems when they occur? There is no single answer to this question, and the most appropriate answer will often depend upon the context in which a particular server object is being used. In the following sections, we shall explore a range of options for error reporting by a server.

Exercise 12.17 How many different ways can you think of to indicate that a method has received incorrect parameter values or is otherwise unable to complete its task? Consider as many different sorts of applications as you can—for instance: those with a GUI; those with a textual interface and a human user; those with no sort of interactive user, such as software in a vehicle's engine-management system; or software in embedded systems such as a cash machine.

12.3.1   Notifying the user

The most obvious way in which an object might respond when it detects something wrong is to try to notify the application's user in some way. The main options are either to print an error message using `System.out` or `System.err` or to display an error message alert window.

The two main problems with both approaches are:

■ They assume that the application is being used by a human user who will see the error message. There are many applications that run completely independently of a human user. An error message, or an error window, will go completely unnoticed. Indeed, the computer running the application might not have any visual-display device connected to it at all.

■ Even where there is a human user to see the error message, it will be rare for that user to be in a position to do something about the problem. Imagine a user at an automatic teller machine being confronted with a `NullPointerException`! Only in those cases where the user's direct action has led to the problem—such as supplying invalid input to the application—is the user likely to be able take some appropriate corrective or avoiding action the next time.

Programs that print inappropriate error messages are more likely to annoy their users rather than achieve a useful outcome. Therefore, except in a very limited set of circumstances, notifying the user is not a general solution to the problem of error reporting.

12.3.2   Notifying the client object

A radically different approach from those we have discussed so far is for the server object to feedback an indication to the client object when something has gone wrong. There are two main ways to do this:

■ A server can use a non-`void` return type of a method to return a value that indicates either success or failure of the method call.

■ A server can *throw an exception* if something goes wrong. This introduces a new feature of Java that is also found in some other programming languages. We shall describe this feature in detail in Section 12.4.

Both techniques have the benefit of encouraging the programmer of the *client* to take into account that a method call could fail. However, only the decision to throw an exception will actively prevent the client's programmer from ignoring the consequences of method failure.

The first approach is easy to introduce to a method that would otherwise have a `void` return type, such as `removeDetails`. If the `void` type is replaced by a `boolean` type, then the method can return `true` to indicate that the removal was successful and `false` to indicate that it failed for some reason (Code 12.3).

Code 12.3
A `boolean` return type to indicate success or failure

```
/**
 * Remove the entry with the given key from the address book.
 * The key should be one that is currently in use.
 * @param key One of the keys of the entry to be removed.
```

Code 12.3 continued

A `boolean` return type to indicate success or failure

```
 * @return true if the entry was successfully removed,
 *         false otherwise.
 */
public boolean removeDetails(String key)
{
    if(keyInUse(key)) {
        ContactDetails details = book.get(key);
        book.remove(details.getName());
        book.remove(details.getPhone());
        numberOfEntries--;
        return true;
    }
    else {
        return false;
    }
}
```

This allows a client to use an if statement to guard statements that depend on the successful removal of an entry:

```
if(contacts.removeDetails("...")) {
    // Entry successfully removed. Continue as normal.
    ...
}
else {
    // The removal failed. Attempt a recovery, if possible.
    ...
}
```

Where a server method already has a non-`void` return type—effectively preventing a `boolean` diagnostic value from being returned—there may still be a way to indicate that an error has occurred through the return type. This will be the case if a value from the return type's range is available to act as an error diagnostic value. For instance, the `getDetails` method returns a `ContactDetails` object corresponding to a given key, and the example below assumes that a particular key will locate a valid set of contact details:

```
// Send David a text message.
ContactDetails details = contacts.getDetails("David");
String phone = details.getPhone();
...
```

One way for the `getDetails` method to indicate that the key is invalid or not in use is to have it return a `null` value instead of a `ContactDetails` object (Code 12.4).

Code 12.4

Returning an out-of-bounds error diagnostic value

```
/**
 * Look up a name or phone number and return the
 * corresponding contact details.
 * @param key The name or number to be looked up.
```

**Code 12.4
continued**

Returning an out-of-
bounds error diagnostic
value

```
 * @return The details corresponding to the key, or
 *            null if the key is not in use.
 */
public ContactDetails getDetails(String key)
{
    if(keyInUse(key)) {
        return book.get(key);
    }
    else {
        return null;
    }
}
```

This would allow a client to examine the result of the call and then either continue with the normal flow of control or attempt to recover from the error:

```
ContactDetails details = contacts.getDetails("David");
if(details != null) {
    // Send a text message to David.
    String phone = details.getPhone();
    ...
}
else {
    // Failed to find the entry. Attempt a recovery, if possible.
    ...
}
```

It is common for methods that return object references to use the `null` value as an indication of failure or error. With methods that return primitive-type values, there will sometimes be an *out-of-bounds value* that can fulfill a similar role: for instance, the `indexOf` method of the `String` class returns a negative value to indicate that it has failed to find the character sought.

Exercise 12.18 Do you think the different interface styles of the *v2t* and *v2g address-book* projects mean that there should be a difference in the way errors are reported to users?

Exercise 12.19 Using a copy of the *address-book-v2t* project, make changes to the `AddressBook` class to provide failure information to a client when a method has received incorrect parameter values or is otherwise unable to complete its task.

Exercise 12.20 Do you think that a call to the `search` method that finds no matches requires an error notification? Justify your answer.

Exercise 12.21 What combinations of parameter values would it be inappropriate to pass to the constructor of the `ContactDetails` class?

> **Exercise 12.22** Does a constructor have any means of indicating to a client that it cannot correctly set up the new object's state? What should a constructor do if it receives inappropriate parameter values?

Clearly, an out-of-bounds value cannot be used where all values from the return type already have valid meanings to the client. In such cases, it will usually be necessary to resort to the alternative technique of *throwing an exception* (see Section 12.4), which does, in fact, offer some significant advantages. To help you appreciate why this might be, it is worth considering two issues associated with the use of return values as failure or error indicators:

- Unfortunately, there is no way to require the client to check the return value for its diagnostic properties. As a consequence, a client could easily carry on as if nothing has happened and could then end up terminating with a `NullPointerException`; or, worse than that, it could even use the diagnostic return value as if it were a normal return value, creating a difficult-to-diagnose logical error!

- In some cases, we may be using the diagnostic value for two quite different purposes. This is the case in the revised `removeDetails` (Code 12.3) and `getDetails` (Code 12.4). One purpose is to tell the client whether its request was successful or not. The other is to indicate that there was something wrong with its request, such as passing bad parameter values.

In many cases, an *unsuccessful* request will not represent a logical programming error, whereas an *incorrect* request almost certainly does. We should expect quite different follow-up actions from a client in these different situations. Unfortunately, there is no general satisfactory way to resolve the conflict simply by using return values.

12.4 Exception-throwing principles

Throwing an exception is the most effective way a server object has of indicating that it is unable to fulfill a call on one of its methods. One of the major advantages this has over using a special return value is that it is (almost) impossible for a client to ignore the fact that an exception has been thrown and carry on regardless. Failure by the client to handle an exception will result in the application terminating immediately.[1] In addition, the exception mechanism is independent of the return value of a method, so it can be used for all methods, irrespective of the return type.

An important point to bear in mind throughout the following discussion is that, where exceptions are involved, the place where an error is discovered will be distinct from where recovery (if any) is attempted. Discovery will be in the server's method, and recovery will be in the client. If recovery were possible at the point of discovery, then there would be no point in throwing an exception.

---

[1] This is exactly what you will have experienced whenever your programs inadvertently died because of a `NullPointerException` or `IndexOutOfBoundsException`.

12.4.1 Throwing an exception

Code 12.5 shows how an exception is thrown using a *throw statement*. Here, the `getDetails` method is throwing an exception to indicate that passing a `null` value for the key does not make sense because it is not a valid key.

Code 12.5

Throwing an exception

```
/**
 * Look up a name or phone number and return the
 * corresponding contact details.
 * @param key The name or number to be looked up.
 * @return The details corresponding to the key,
 *         or null if there are none matching.
 * @throws IllegalArgumentException if the key is invalid.
 */
public ContactDetails getDetails(String key)
{
    if(key == null){
        throw new IllegalArgumentException(
            "null key in getDetails");
    }
    return book.get(key);
}
```

> **Concept:**
>
> An **exception** is an object representing details of a program failure. An exception is thrown to indicate that a failure has occurred.

There are two stages to throwing an exception. First, an exception object is created using the new keyword (in this case, an `IllegalArgumentException` object); then the exception object is thrown using the `throw` keyword. These two stages are almost invariably combined in a single statement:

```
throw new ExceptionType("optional-diagnostic-string");
```

When an exception object is created, a diagnostic string may be passed to its constructor. This string is later available to the receiver of the exception via the exception object's `get-Message` and `toString` methods. The string is also shown to the user if the exception is not handled and leads to the termination of the program. The exception type we have used here, `IllegalArgumentException`, is defined in the `java.lang` package and is regularly used to indicate that an inappropriate actual parameter value has been passed to a method or constructor.

Code 12.5 also illustrates that the `javadoc` documentation for a method can be expanded to include details of any exceptions it throws, using the `@throws` tag.

12.4.2 Checked and unchecked exceptions

An exception object is always an instance of a class from a special inheritance hierarchy. We can create new exception types by creating subclasses in this hierarchy (Figure 12.1). Strictly

Figure 12.1
The exception
class hierarchy

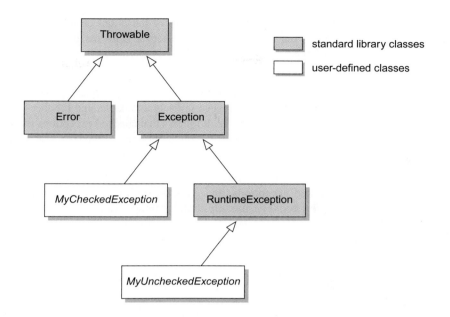

speaking, exception classes are always subclasses of the `Throwable` class that is defined in the `java.lang` package. We shall follow the convention of defining and using exception classes that are subclasses of the `Exception` class, also defined in `java.lang`.[2] The `java.lang` package defines a number of commonly seen exception classes that you might already have run across inadvertently in developing programs, such as `NullPointerException`, `IndexOutOfBoundsException`, and `ClassCastException`.

Java divides exception classes into two categories: *checked exceptions* and *unchecked exceptions*. All subclasses of the Java standard class `RuntimeException` are unchecked exceptions; all other subclasses of `Exception` are checked exceptions.

Slightly simplified, the difference is this: checked exceptions are intended for cases where the client should expect that an operation could fail (for example, if it tries to write to a disk, it should anticipate that the disk could be full). In such cases, the client will be forced to check whether the operation was successful. Unchecked exceptions are intended for cases that should never fail in normal operation—they usually indicate a program error. For instance, a programmer would never knowingly try to get an item from a position in a list that does not exist, so when they do, it elicits an unchecked exception.

Unfortunately, knowing which category of exception to throw in any particular circumstance is not an exact science, but we can offer the following general advice:

■ One rule of thumb is to use unchecked exceptions for situations that should lead to program failure—typically because it is suspected that there is a logical error in the program that will prevent it from continuing any further. It follows that checked exceptions should be used

---

[2] `Exception` is one of two direct subclasses of `Throwable`; the other is `Error`. Subclasses of `Error` are usually reserved for runtime-system errors rather than errors over which the programmer has control.

where there may be a possibility of the client effecting a recovery. One problem with this policy is that it assumes that the server is aware enough of the context in which it is being used to be able to determine whether client recovery is likely or unlikely to be possible.

■ Another rule of thumb is to use unchecked exceptions for situations that could reasonably be avoided. For instance, calling a method on a variable containing `null` is the result of a logical programming error that is completely avoidable, and the fact that `NullPointerException` is unchecked fits this model. It follows that checked exceptions should be used for failure situations that are beyond the control of the programmer, such as a disk becoming full when trying to write to a file or a network operation failing because a wireless network connection has dropped out.

The formal Java rules governing the use of exceptions are significantly different for unchecked and checked exceptions, and we shall outline the differences in detail in Sections 12.4.4 and 12.5.1, respectively. In simplified terms, the rules ensure that a client object calling a method that could throw a checked exception will contain code that anticipates the possibility of a problem arising and that attempts to handle the problem whenever it occurs.[3]

> **Exercise 12.23** List three exception types from the `java.io` package.
>
> **Exercise 12.24** Is `SecurityException` from the `java.lang` package a checked or an unchecked exception? What about `NoSuchMethodException`? Justify your answers.

12.4.3   The effect of an exception

What happens when an exception is thrown? There are really two effects to consider: the effect in the method where the problem is discovered and the exception is thrown, and the effect in the caller of the problem method.

When an exception is thrown, the execution of the current method finishes immediately; it does not continue to the end of the method body. A consequence of this is that a method with a non-`void` return type is not required to execute a return statement on a route that throws an exception. This is reasonable, because throwing an exception is an indication of the throwing method's inability to continue normal execution, which includes not being able to return a valid result. We can illustrate this principle with the following alternative version of the method body shown in Code 12.5:

```
if(key == null) {
    throw new IllegalArgumentException("null key in getDetails");
}
else {
    return book.get(key);
}
```

The absence of a return statement in the route that throws an exception is acceptable. Indeed, the compiler will indicate an error if any statements are written following a throw statement, because they could never be executed.

---

[3] In fact, it is still all too easy for the writer of the client to adhere to the rules in principle but to fail to attempt a proper recovery from the problem, which rather subverts their purpose!

The effect of an exception on the point in the program that called the problem method is a little more complex. In particular, the full effect depends upon whether or not any code has been written to *catch* the exception. Consider the following contrived call to getDetails:

```
AddressDetails details = contacts.getDetails(null);
// The following statement will not be reached.
String phone = details.getPhone();
```

We *can* say that, in all cases, the execution of these statements will be left incomplete; the exception thrown by getDetails will interrupt the execution of the first statement, and no assignment will be made to the details variable. As a result, the second statement will not be executed either.

This neatly illustrates the power of exceptions to prevent a client from carrying on regardless of the fact that a problem has arisen. What actually happens next depends upon whether or not the exception is caught. If it isn't caught, then the program will simply terminate with an indication that an uncaught IllegalArgumentException has been thrown. We shall discuss how to catch an exception in Section 12.5.2.

12.4.4 Using unchecked exceptions

Concept:

An **unchecked exception** is a type of exception whose use will not require checks from the compiler.

Unchecked exceptions are the easiest to use from a programmer's point of view, because the compiler enforces few rules on their use. This is the meaning of "unchecked": the compiler does not apply special checks, either on the method in which an unchecked exception is thrown or on the place from which the method is called. An exception class is unchecked if it is a subclass of the RuntimeException class, defined in the java.lang package. All of the examples we have used so far to illustrate exception throwing have involved unchecked exceptions. So there is little further to add here about how to throw an unchecked exception—simply use a throw statement.

If we also follow the convention that unchecked exceptions should be used in those situations where we expect the result to be program termination—i.e., the exception is not going to be caught—then there is also nothing further to be discussed about what the method's caller should do, because it will do nothing and let the program fail. However, if there is a need to catch an unchecked exception, then an exception handler *can* be written for it, exactly as for a checked exception. How to do this is described in Section 12.5.2.

We have already seen use of the unchecked IllegalArgumentException. This is thrown by a constructor or method to indicate that its parameter values are inappropriate. For instance, the get-Details method might also choose to throw this if the key string passed to it is blank (Code 12.6).

Code 12.6

Checking for an illegal parameter value

```
/**
 * Look up a name or phone number and return the
 * corresponding contact details.
 * @param key The name or number to be looked up.
 * @throws IllegalArgumentException if the key is invalid.
 * @return The details corresponding to the key,
 *         or null if there are none matching.
 */
```

Code 12.6 continued

Checking for an illegal parameter value

```java
public ContactDetails getDetails(String key)
{
    if(key == null) {
        throw new IllegalArgumentException("null key in getDetails");
    }
    if(key.trim().length() == 0) {
        throw new IllegalArgumentException(
                "Empty key passed to getDetails");
    }
    return book.get(key);
}
```

It is well worth having a method conduct a series of validity checks on its parameters before proceeding with the main purpose of the method. This makes it less likely that a method will get part way through its actions before having to throw an exception because of bad parameter values. A particular reason for avoiding this situation is that partial mutation of an object is likely to leave it in an inconsistent state for future use. If a method fails for any reason, the object on which it was called should ideally be left in the state it was before the operation was attempted.

Exercise 12.25 Review all of the methods of the AddressBook class and decide whether there are any additional situations in which they should throw an IllegalArgumentException. Add the necessary checks and throw statements.

Exercise 12.26 If you have not already done so, add javadoc documentation to describe any exceptions thrown by methods in the AddressBook class.

Exercise 12.27 UnsupportedOperationException is an unchecked exception defined in the java.lang package. How might this be used in an implementation of the java.util. Iterator interface to prevent removal of items from a collection that is being iterated over? Try this out in the LogfileReader class of the *weblog-analyzer* project from Chapter 4.

12.4.5 Preventing object creation

An important use for exceptions is to prevent objects from being created if they cannot be placed in a valid initial state. This will usually be the result of inappropriate parameter values being passed to a constructor. We can illustrate this with the ContactDetails class. The constructor is currently fairly forgiving of the parameter values it receives: it does not reject null values but replaces them with empty strings. However, the address book needs at least a name or phone number from each entry to use as a unique index value, so an entry with both name and phone fields blank would be impossible to index. We can reflect this requirement by preventing construction of a ContactDetails object with no valid key details. The process of throwing an exception from a constructor is exactly the same as throwing one from a method. Code 12.7 shows the revised constructor that will prevent an entry from ever having both name and phone fields blank.

An exception thrown from a constructor has the same effect on the client as an exception thrown from a method. So the following attempt to create an invalid `ContactDetails` object will completely fail; it will *not* result in a `null` value being stored in the variable:

```
ContactDetails badDetails = new ContactDetails("", "", "");
```

Code 12.7

The constructor of the `ContactDetails` class

```java
/**
 * Set up the contact details. All details are trimmed to remove
 * trailing white space. Either name or phone must be non-blank.
 * @param name The name.
 * @param phone The phone number.
 * @param address The address.
 * @throws IllegalStateException If both name and phone are blank.
 */
public ContactDetails(String name, String phone, String address)
{
    // Use blank strings if any of the parameters is null.
    if(name == null) {
        name = "";
    }
    if(phone == null) {
        phone = "";
    }
    if(address == null) {
        address = "";
    }

    this.name = name.trim();
    this.phone = phone.trim();
    this.address = address.trim();

    if(this.name.length() == 0 && this.phone.length() == 0) {
        throw new IllegalStateException(
                "Either the name or phone must not be blank.");
    }
}
```

12.5 Exception handling

The principles of exception throwing apply equally to both unchecked and checked exceptions, but the rules of Java mean that exception handling becomes a requirement only with checked exceptions. A checked exception class is one that is a subclass of `Exception` but not of `RuntimeException`. There are several more rules to follow when using checked exceptions, because the compiler enforces checks both in a method that throws a checked exception and in any caller of that method.

12.5.1 Checked exceptions: the throws clause

The first requirement of the compiler is that a method throwing a checked exception must declare that it does so in a *throws clause* added to the method's header. For instance, a method throwing a checked IOException from the java.io package might have the following header:[4]

```
public void saveToFile(String destinationFile)
    throws IOException
```

It is permitted to use a throws clause for unchecked exceptions, but the compiler does not require one. We recommend that a throws clause be used only to list the checked exceptions thrown by a method.

It is important to distinguish between a throws clause in the header of a method and the @throws javadoc comment that precedes the method; the latter is completely optional for both types of exception. Nevertheless, we recommend that javadoc documentation be included for both checked and unchecked exceptions. In that way, as much information as possible will be available to someone wishing to use a method that throws an exception.

12.5.2 Anticipating exceptions: the try statement

The second requirement, when using checked exceptions, is that a caller of a method that throws a checked exception must make provision for dealing with the exception. This usually means writing an *exception handler* in the form of a *try statement*. Most practical try statements have the general form shown in Code 12.8. This introduces two new Java keywords—try and catch—which mark a *try block* and a *catch block*, respectively.

Code 12.8
The try and catch blocks of an exception handler

```
try {
    Protect one or more statements here.
}
catch(Exception e) {
    Report and recover from the exception here.
}
```

Suppose we have a method that saves the contents of an address book to a file. The user is requested in some way for the name of a file (perhaps via a GUI dialog window), and the address book's saveToFile method is then called to write out the list to the file. If we did not have to take exceptions into account, then this would be written as follows:

```
String filename = request-a-file-from-the-user;
addressbook.saveToFile(filename);
```

However, because the writing process could fail with an exception, the call to saveToFile must be placed within a try block to show that this has been taken into account. Code 12.9 illustrates how we would tend to write this, anticipating possible failure.

Any number of statements can be included in a try block, so, in fact, we tend to place there not just the single statement that could fail, but all of the statements that are related to it in some way.

---

[4] Note that the keyword here is throws and not throw.

Code 12.9

An exception handler

```
String filename = null;
try {
    filename = request-a-file-from-the-user;
    addressbook.saveToFile(filename);
    successful = true;
}
catch(IOException e) {
    System.out.println("Unable to save to " + filename);
    successful = false;
}
```

The idea is that a try block represents a sequence of actions we wish to treat as a logical whole but recognize that they might fail at some point.[5] The catch block will then attempt to deal with the situation or report the problem if an exception arises from any statement within the associated try block. Note that, because both the try and catch blocks make use of the `filename` variable, it has to be declared outside the try statement in this example, for reasons of scope.

In order to understand how an exception handler works, it is essential to appreciate that *an exception prevents the normal flow of control from being continued in the caller*. An exception interrupts the execution of the caller's statements, and hence any statements immediately following the problem statement will not be executed. The question then arises, "Where is execution resumed in the caller?" A try statement provides the answer: if an exception arises from a statement called in the try block, then execution is resumed in the corresponding catch block. So, if we consider the example in Code 12.9, the effect of an `IOException` being thrown from the call to `saveToFile` will be that control will transfer from the try block to the catch block, as shown in Code 12.10.

Statements in a try block are known as *protected statements*. If no exception arises during execution of protected statements, then the catch block will be skipped over when the end of the try block is reached. Execution will continue with whatever follows the complete try/catch statement.

1 Exception thrown from here   2 Control transfers to here

Code 12.10

Transfer of control in a try statement

```
try {
    filename = request-a-file-from-the-user;
    addressbook.saveToFile(filename);
    successful = true;
}
catch(IOException e) {
    System.out.println("Unable to save to " + filename);
    successful = false;
}
```

[5] See Exercise 12.30 for an example of what can happen if a statement that might result in an exception is treated in isolation from the statements around it.

A catch block names the type of exception it is designed to deal with in a pair of parentheses immediately following the `catch` word. As well as the exception type name, this also includes a variable name (traditionally, simply e or ex) that can be used to refer to the exception object that was thrown. Having a reference to this object can be useful in providing information that will support recovery from, or reporting of, the problem—e.g., accessing any diagnostic message placed in it by the throwing method. Once the catch block has been completed, control does *not* return to the statement that caused the exception.

Exercise 12.28 The *address-book-v3t* project includes some throwing of unchecked exceptions if parameter values are `null`. The project source code also includes the checked exception class `NoMatchingDetailsException`, which is currently unused. Modify the `removeDetails` method of `AddressBook` so that it throws this exception if its key parameter is not a key that is in use. Add an exception handler to the `remove` method of `AddressBookTextInterface` to catch and report occurrences of this exception.

Exercise 12.29 Make use of `NoMatchingDetailsException` in the `changeDetails` method of `AddressBook`. Enhance the user interface so that the details of an existing entry may be changed. Catch and report exceptions in `AddressBookTextInterface` that arise from use of a key that does not match any existing entry.

Exercise 12.30 Why is the following not a sensible way to use an exception handler? Will this code compile and run?

```
Person p = null;
try {
    // The lookup could fail.
    p = database.lookup(details);
}
catch(Exception e) {
}
System.out.println("The details belong to: " + p);
```

Note that in all the examples of try statements you have seen, the exception is not thrown *directly* by the statements in the try block, which is in the client object. Rather, the exception arises *indirectly*, passed back from a method in the server object, which is called from the statements within the try block. This is the usual pattern, and it would almost certainly be a mistake to enclose a throw statement directly within a try statement.

12.5.3 Throwing and catching multiple exceptions

Sometimes a method throws more than one type of exception in order to indicate different sorts of problems. Where these are checked exceptions, they must all be listed in the throws clause of the method, separated by commas. For instance:

```
public void process()
    throws EOFException, FileNotFoundException
```

An exception handler must cater for all checked exceptions thrown from its protected statements, so a try statement may contain multiple catch blocks, as shown in Code 12.11. Note that the same variable name can be used for the exception object in each case.

Code 12.11

Multiple catch blocks in a try statement

```
try {
    ...
    ref.process();
    ...
}
catch(EOFException e) {
    // Take action appropriate to an end-of-file exception.
    ...
}
catch(FileNotFoundException e) {
    // Take action appropriate to a file-not-found exception.
    ...
}
```

When an exception is thrown by a method call in a try block, the catch blocks are checked in the order in which they are written until a match is found for the exception type. So, if an EOFException is thrown, then control will transfer to the first catch block, and if a FileNotFoundException is thrown, then control will transfer to the second. Once the end of a single catch block is reached, execution continues following the last catch block.

Polymorphism can be used to avoid writing multiple catch blocks, if desired. However, this could be at the expense of being able to take type-specific recovery actions. In Code 12.12, the single catch block will handle *every* exception thrown by the protected statements. This is because the exception-matching process that looks for an appropriate catch block simply checks that the exception object is an instance of the type named in the block. As all exceptions are subtypes of the Exception class, the single block will catch everything, whether checked or unchecked. From the nature of the matching process, it follows that the order of catch blocks in a single try statement matters and that a catch block for one exception type cannot follow a block for one of its supertypes (because the earlier supertype block will always match before the subtype block is checked). The compiler will report this as an error.

Code 12.12

Catching all exceptions in a single catch block

```
try {
    ...
    ref.process();
    ...
}
catch(Exception e) {
    // Take action appropriate to all exceptions.
    ...
}
```

12.5.4 Multi-catch Java 7

A new feature was introduced in Java 7 that allows multiple exceptions to be handled in the same catch block. This reduces the code duplication involved when the same recovery action is required for different exception types. The different exception types are written in front of the exception variable name, separated by the "|" symbol. See Code 12.13.

Code 12.13

Multi-catch in Java 7

```
try {
    ...
    ref.process();
    ...
}
catch(EOFException | FileNotFoundException e) {
    // Take action appropriate to both exceptions.
    ...
}
```

Java 7 also introduced another new feature to the try statement, called "try-with-resources" or "automatic resource management" (ARM). We shall cover this briefly, along with file handling, in Section 12.9.

Exercise 12.31 Enhance the try statements you wrote as solutions to Exercises 12.28 and 12.29 so that they handle checked and unchecked exceptions in different catch blocks.

Exercise 12.32 What is wrong with the following try statement?

```
Person p = null;
try {
    p = database.lookup(details);
    System.out.println("The details belong to: " + p);
}
catch(Exception e) {
    // Handle any checked exceptions ...
    ...
}
catch(RuntimeException e) {
    // Handle any unchecked exceptions ...
    ...
}
```

12.5.5 Propagating an exception

So far, we have suggested that an exception must be caught and handled at the earliest possible opportunity. That is, an exception thrown in a method process would have to be caught and handled in the method that called process. In fact, this is not strictly the case, as Java allows an exception to be *propagated* from the client method to the caller of the client method, and possibly beyond. A method propagates an exception simply by not including an exception handler to protect the statement that might throw it. However, for a checked exception, the compiler requires that the propagating method include a throws clause, even though it does not itself create and throw the exception. This means that you will sometimes see a method that has a throws clause but with no throw statement in the method body. Propagation is common where the calling method is either unable to, or does not need to, undertake any recovery action itself, but this might be possible or necessary from within higher-level calls. It is also common in constructors, where a constructor's actions in setting up a new object fail and the constructor cannot recover from this.

If the exception being propagated is unchecked, then the throws clause is optional, and we prefer to omit it.

12.5.6 The finally clause

A try statement can include a third component that is optional. This is the *finally clause* (Code 12.14), and it is often omitted. The finally clause provides for statements that should be executed whether an exception arises in the protected statements or not. If control reaches the end of the try block, then the catch blocks are skipped and the finally clause is executed. Conversely, if an exception is thrown from the try block, the appropriate catch block is executed and this is then followed by execution of the finally clause.

Code 12.14

A try statement with a finally clause

```
try {
      Protect one or more statements here.
}
catch(Exception e) {
      Report and recover from the exception here.
}
finally {
      Perform any actions here common to whether or not
      an exception is thrown.
}
```

At first sight, a finally clause would appear to be redundant. Doesn't the following example illustrate the same flow of control as Code 12.14?

```
try {
      Protect one or more statements here.
}
catch(Exception e) {
      Report and recover from the exception here.
}
Perform any actions here common to whether or not an exception is thrown.
```

In fact, there are at least two cases where these two examples would have different effects:

■ A finally clause is executed even if a return statement is executed in the try or catch blocks.

■ If an exception is thrown in the try block but not caught, then the finally clause is still executed.

In the latter case, the uncaught exception could be an unchecked exception that does not require a catch block, for instance. However, it could also be a checked exception that is not handled by a catch block but propagated from the method, to be handled at a higher level in the call sequence. In such a case, the finally clause would still be executed.

It is also possible to omit the catch blocks in a try statement that has both a try block and a finally clause if the method is propagating all exceptions:

```
try {
    Protect one or more statements here.
}
finally {
    Perform any actions here common to whether or not
    an exception is thrown.
}
```

12.6 Defining new exception classes

Where the standard exception classes do not satisfactorily describe the nature of an error condition, new, more-descriptive exception classes can be defined using inheritance. New checked exception classes can be defined as subclasses of any existing checked exception class (such as Exception), and new unchecked exceptions would be subclasses of the RuntimeException hierarchy.

All existing exception classes support the inclusion of a diagnostic string passed to a constructor. However, one of the main reasons for defining new exception classes is to include further information within the exception object to support error diagnosis and recovery. For instance, some methods in the *address-book* application, such as changeDetails, take a key parameter that should match an existing entry. If no matching entry can be found, then this represents a programming error, as the methods cannot complete their task. In reporting the exception, it is helpful to include details of the key that caused the error. Code 12.15 shows a new checked exception class that is defined in the *address-book-v3t* project. It receives the key in its constructor and then makes it available through both the diagnostic string and a dedicated accessor method. If this exception were to be caught by an exception handler in the caller, the key would be available to the statements that attempt to recover from the error.

Code 12.15

An exception class with extra diagnostic information

```
/**
 * Capture a key that failed to match an entry
 * in the address book.
 *
 * @author David J. Barnes and Michael Kölling.
 * @version 2011.07.31
 */
```

Code 12.15 continued

An exception class with extra diagnostic information

```java
public class NoMatchingDetailsException extends Exception
{
    // The key with no match.
    private String key;

    /**
     * Store the details in error.
     * @param key The key with no match.
     */
    public NoMatchingDetailsException(String key)
    {
        this.key = key;
    }

    /**
     * @return The key in error.
     */
    public String getKey()
    {
        return key;
    }

    /**
     * @return A diagnostic string containing the key in error.
     */
    public String toString()
    {
        return "No details matching '" + key + "' were found.";
    }
}
```

The principle of including information that could support error recovery should particularly be kept in mind when defining new checked exception classes. Defining formal parameters in an exception's constructor will help to ensure that diagnostic information is available. In addition, where recovery is either not possible or not attempted, ensuring that the exception's toString method is overridden to include appropriate information will help in diagnosing the reason for the error.

Exercise 12.33 In the *address-book-v3t* project, define a new checked exception class: DuplicateKeyException. This should be thrown by the addDetails method if either of the non-blank key fields of its actual parameter is already currently in use. The exception class should store details of the offending key(s). Make any further changes to the user interface class that are necessary to catch and report the exception.

Exercise 12.34 Do you feel that DuplicateKeyException should be a checked or unchecked exception? Give reasons for your answer.

12.7 Using assertions

12.7.1 Internal consistency checks

When we design or implement a class, we often have an intuitive sense of things that should be true at a given point in the execution, but rarely state them formally. For instance, we would expect a `ContactDetails` object to always contain at least one non-blank field, or, when the `removeDetails` method is called with a particular key, we would expect that key to be no longer in use at the end of the method. Typically, these are conditions we wish to establish while developing a class, before it is released. In one sense, the sort of testing we discussed in Chapter 7 is an attempt to establish whether we have implemented an accurate representation of what a class or method should do. Characteristic of that style of testing is that the tests are *external* to the class being tested. If a class is changed, then we should take the time to run regression tests in order to establish that it still works as it should; it is easy to forget to do that. The practice of checking parameters, which we have introduced in this chapter, slightly shifts the emphasis from wholly external checking to a combination of external and internal checking. However, parameter checking is primarily intended to protect a server object from incorrect usage by a client. That still leaves the question of whether we can include some internal checks to ensure that the server object behaves as it should.

One way we could implement internal checking during development would be through the normal exception-throwing mechanism. In practice, we would have to use unchecked exceptions, because we could not expect regular client classes to include exception handlers for what are essentially internal server errors. We would then be faced with the issue of whether to remove these internal checks once the development process has been completed, in order to avoid the potentially high cost of runtime checks that are almost certainly bound to pass.

12.7.2 The assert statement

In order to deal with the need to perform efficient internal consistency checks, which can be turned on in development code but off in released code, an *assertion facility* is available in Java. The idea is similar to what we saw in Chapter 7 with JUnit testing, where we asserted the results we expected from method calls and the JUnit framework tested whether or not those assertions were confirmed.

The *address-book-assert* project is a development version of the *address-book* projects that illustrates how assertions are used. Code 12.16 shows the `removeDetails` method, which now contains two forms of the *assert statement*.

Code 12.16

Using assertions for internal consistency checks

```
/**
 * Remove the entry with the given key from the address book.
 * The key should be one that is currently in use.
 * @param key One of the keys of the entry to be removed.
 * @throws IllegalArgumentException If the key is null.
 */
```

**Code 12.16
continued**

Using assertions for
internal consistency
checks

```java
public void removeDetails(String key)
{
    if(key == null) {
        throw new IllegalArgumentException(
                "Null key passed to removeDetails.");
    }
    if(keyInUse(key)) {
        ContactDetails details = book.get(key);
        book.remove(details.getName());
        book.remove(details.getPhone());
        numberOfEntries--;
    }
    assert !keyInUse(key);
    assert consistentSize() :
                "Inconsistent book size in removeDetails";
}
```

Concept:

An **assertion** is a
statement of a fact
that should be true
in normal program
execution. We can
use assertions to
state our assump-
tions explicitly and
to detect program-
ming errors more
easily.

The `assert` keyword is followed by a boolean expression. The purpose of the statement is to assert something that should be true at this point in the method. For instance, the first assert statement in Code 12.16 asserts that `keyInUse` should return `false` at that point, either because the key wasn't in use in the first place or because it is no longer in use as the associated details have now been removed from the address book. This seemingly obvious assertion is more important than might at first appear; notice that the removal process does not actually involve use of the key with the address book.

Thus, an assert statement serves two purposes. It expresses explicitly what we assume to be true at a given point in the execution and therefore increases readability both for the current developer and for a future maintenance programmer; also, it actually performs the check at runtime so that we get notified if our assumption turns out to be incorrect. This can greatly help in finding errors early and easily.

If the boolean expression in an assert statement evaluates to `true`, then the assert statement has no further effect. If the statement evaluates to `false`, then an `AssertionError` will be thrown. This is a subclass of `Error` (see Figure 12.1) and is part of the hierarchy regarded as representing unrecoverable errors—hence, no handler should be provided in clients.

The second assert statement in Code 12.16 illustrates the alternative form of assert statement. The string following the colon symbol will be passed to the constructor of `AssertionError` to provide a diagnostic string. The second expression does not have to be an explicit string; any value-giving expression is acceptable and will be turned into a `String` before being passed to the constructor.

The first assert statement shows that an assertion will often make use of an existing method within the class (e.g., `keyInUse`). The second example illustrates that it might be useful to provide a method specifically for the purpose of performing an assertion test (`consistentSize` in this example). This might be used if the check involves significant computation. Code 12.17 shows the `consistentSize` method, whose purpose is to ensure that the `numberOfEntries` field accurately represents the number of unique details in the address book.

Code 12.17

Checking for internal consistency in the address book

```java
/**
 * Check that the numberOfEntries field is consistent with
 * the number of entries actually stored in the address book.
 * @return true if the field is consistent, false otherwise.
 */
private boolean consistentSize()
{
    Collection<ContactDetails> allEntries = book.values();
    // Eliminate duplicates, as we are using multiple keys.
    Set<ContactDetails> uniqueEntries =
            new HashSet<ContactDetails>(allEntries);
    int actualCount = uniqueEntries.size();
    return numberOfEntries == actualCount;
}
```

12.7.3 Guidelines for using assertions

Assertions are primarily intended to provide a way to perform consistency checks during the development and testing phases of a project. They are not intended to be used in released code. It is for this reason that a Java compiler will include assert statements in the compiled code only if requested to do so. It follows that assert statements should never be used to perform normal functionality. For instance, it would be wrong to combine assertions with removal of details, as follows, in the address book:

```java
// Error: don't use assert with normal processing!
assert book.remove(details.getName()) != null;
assert book.remove(details.getPhone()) != null;
```

Exercise 12.35 Open the *address-book-assert* project. Look through the `AddressBook` class and identify all of the assert statements to be sure that you understand what is being checked and why.

Exercise 12.36 The `AddressBookDemo` class contains several test methods that call methods of `AddressBook` that contain assert statements. Look through the source of `AddressBookDemo` to check that you understand the tests, and then try out each of the test methods. Are any assertion errors generated? If so, do you understand why?

Exercise 12.37 The `changeDetails` method of `AddressBook` currently has no assert statements. One assertion we could make about it is that the address book should contain the same number of entries at the end of the method as it did at the start. Add an assert statement (and any other statements you might need) to check this. Run the `testChange` method of `AddressBookDemo` after doing so. Do you think this method should also include the check for a consistent size?

> **Exercise 12.38** Suppose that we decide to allow the address book to be indexed by address as well as name and phone number. If we simply add the following statement to the `addDetails` method
>
> ```
> book.put(details.getAddress(), details);
> ```
>
> do you anticipate that any assertions will now fail? Try it. Make any further necessary changes to `AddressBook` to ensure that all of the assertions are now successful.

> **Exercise 12.39** `ContactDetails` are immutable objects—that is, they have no mutator methods. How important is this fact to the internal consistency of an `AddressBook`? Suppose the `ContactDetails` class had a `setPhone` method, for instance? Can you devise some tests to illustrate the problems this could cause?

12.7.4 Assertions and the BlueJ unit-testing framework

In Chapter 7, we introduced the support that BlueJ provides for the JUnit unit-testing framework. That support is based on the assertion facility we have been discussing in this section. Methods from the framework, such as `assertEquals`, are built around an assertion statement that contains a boolean expression made up from their parameters. If JUnit test classes are used to test classes containing their own assertion statements, then assertion errors from these statements will be reported in the test-results window along with test-class assertion failures. The *address-book-junit* project contains a test class to illustrate this combination. The `testAddDetailsError` method of `AddressBookTest` will trigger an assertion error, because `addDetails` should not be used to change existing details (see Exercise 12.33).

12.8 Error recovery and avoidance

So far, the main focus of this chapter has been on the problem of identifying errors in a server object and ensuring that any problem is reported back to the client if appropriate. There are two complementary issues that go with error reporting: error recovery and error avoidance.

12.8.1 Error recovery

The first requirement of successful error recovery is that clients take note of any error notification that they receive. This may sound obvious, but it is not uncommon for a programmer to assume that a method call will not fail and so not bother to check the return value. While ignoring errors is harder to do when exceptions are used, we have often seen the equivalent of the following approach to exception handling:

```
AddressDetails details = null;
try {
    details = contacts.getDetails(...);
}
```

```
    catch(Exception e) {
        System.out.println("Error: " + e);
    }
    String phone = details.getPhone();
```

The exception has been caught and reported, but no account has been taken of the fact that it is probably incorrect just to carry on regardless.

Java's try statement is the key to supplying an error-recovery mechanism when an exception is thrown. Recovery from an error will usually involve taking some form of corrective action within the catch block and then trying again. Repeated attempts can be made by placing the try statement in a loop. An example of this approach is shown in Code 12.18, which is an expanded version of Code 12.9. The efforts to compose an alternative filename could involve trying a list of possible folders, for instance, or prompting an interactive user for different names.

Code 12.18

An attempt at error recovery

```
// Try to save the address book.
boolean successful = false;
int attempts = 0;
do {
    try {
        addressbook.saveToFile(filename);
        successful = true;
    }
    catch(IOException e) {
        System.out.println("Unable to save to " + filename);
        attempts++;
        if(attempts < MAX_ATTEMPTS) {
            filename = an alternative file name;
        }
    }
} while(!successful && attempts < MAX_ATTEMPTS);
if(!successful) {
    Report the problem and give up;
}
```

Although this example illustrates recovery for a specific situation, the principles it illustrates are more general:

■ Anticipating an error, and recovering from it, will usually require a more complex flow of control than if an error cannot occur.

■ The statements in the catch block are key to setting up the recovery attempt.

■ Recovery will often involve having to try again.

■ Successful recovery cannot be guaranteed.

■ There should be some escape route from endlessly attempting hopeless recovery.

There won't always be a human user around to prompt for alternative input. It might be the client object's responsibility to log the error so that it can be investigated.

12.8.2 Error avoidance

It should be clear that arriving at a situation where an exception is thrown will be, at worst, fatal to the execution of a program and, at best, messy to recover from in the client. It can be simpler to try to avoid the error in the first place, but this often requires collaboration between server and client.

Many of the cases where an AddressBook object is forced to throw an exception involve null parameter values passed to its methods. These represent logical programming errors in the client that could clearly be avoided by simple prior tests in the client. Null parameter values are usually the result of making invalid assumptions in the client. For instance, consider the following example:

```
String key = database.search(zipCode);
ContactDetails university = contacts.getDetails(key);
```

If the database search fails, then the key it returns may well be either blank or null. Passing that result directly to the getDetails method will produce a runtime exception. However, using a simple test of the search result, the exception can be avoided and the real problem of a failed zip code search can be addressed instead:

```
String key = database.search(zipCode);
if(key != null && key.length() > 0) {
    ContactDetails university = contacts.getDetails(key);
    ...
}
else {
    Deal with the zipcode error ...
}
```

In this case, the client could establish for itself that it would be inappropriate to call the server's method. This is not always possible, and sometimes the client must enlist the help of the server.

Exercise 12.33 established the principle that the addDetails method should not accept a new set of details if one of the key values is already in use for another set. In order to avoid an inappropriate call, the client could make use of the address book's keyInUse method, as follows:

```
// Add what should be a new set of details to the address book.
if(contacts.keyInUse(details.getName()) {
    contacts.changeDetails(details.getName(), details);
}
else if(contacts.keyInUse(details.getPhone())) {
    contacts.changeDetails(details.getPhone(), details);
}
else {
    Add the details ...
}
```

Using this approach, it is clearly possible to completely avoid a DuplicateKeyException being thrown from addDetails, which suggests that it could be downgraded from a checked to an unchecked exception.

This particular example illustrates some important general principles:

■ If a server's validity-check and state-test methods are visible to a client, the client will often be able to avoid causing the server to throw an exception.

■ If an exception can be avoided in this way, then the exception being thrown really represents a logical programming error in the client. This suggests use of an unchecked exception for such situations.

■ Using unchecked exceptions means that the client does not have to use a try statement when it has already established that the exception will not be thrown. This is a significant gain, because having to write try statements for "cannot happen" situations is annoying for a programmer and makes it less likely that providing proper recovery for genuine error situations will be taken seriously.

The effects are not all positive, however. Here are some reasons why this approach is not always practical:

■ Making a server class's validity-check and state-test methods publicly visible to its clients might represent a significant loss of encapsulation and result in a higher degree of coupling between server and client than is desirable.

■ It will probably not be safe for a server class to assume that its clients *will* make the necessary checks that avoid an exception. As a result, those checks will often be duplicated in both client and server. If the checks are computationally "expensive" to make, then duplication may be undesirable or prohibitive. However, our view would be that it is better to sacrifice efficiency for the sake of safer programming, where the choice is available.

12.9   File-based input/output

An important programming area in which error recovery cannot be ignored is input/output. This is because a programmer may have little direct control over the external environment in which their code is executed. For instance, a required data file may have been accidentally deleted or have become corrupted in some way, before the application is run; or an attempt to store results to the file system may be thwarted by lack of appropriate permissions or exceeding a file-system quota. There are many ways in which an input or output operation could fail at any stage. Furthermore, modern input/output has moved beyond a program simply accessing its local file store to a networked environment in which connectivity to the resources being accessed may be fragile and inconsistent—for example, when in a mobile environment.

The Java API has undergone a number of evolutions over the years, reflecting the increasing diversity of environments in which Java programs have come to be used. The core package for input/output-related classes has always been java.io. This package contains numerous classes to support input/output operations in a platform-independent manner. In particular, it defines the checked exception class IOException as a general indicator that something has gone wrong with an input/output operation, and almost any input/output operation must anticipate that one of these might be thrown. Instances of checked subclasses of IOException may be thrown at times to provide more-detailed diagnostic information, such as FileNotFoundException and EOFException. From Java 7, a shift is taking place from a number of classes in the java.io package to those in the java.nio hierarchy, although without completely superseding everything in java.io. We will introduce some of these new classes alongside the legacy ones.

A full description of the many different classes in the java.io and java.nio packages is beyond the scope of this book, but we shall provide some fundamental examples within the context of several of the projects we have already seen. This should give you enough background to experiment with input/output in your own projects. In particular, we shall illustrate the following common tasks:

- obtaining information about a file from the file system

- writing textual output to a file with the FileWriter class

- reading textual input from a file with the FileReader and BufferedReader classes

- anticipating IOException exceptions

- parsing input with the Scanner class

In addition, we look at reading and writing binary versions of objects as a brief introduction to Java's *serialization* feature.

For further reading on input/output in Java, we recommend Oracle's tutorial, which can be found online at:

```
http://download.oracle.com/javase/tutorial/essential/io/index.html
```

12.9.1 Readers, writers, and streams

Several of the classes of the java.io package fall into one of two main categories: those dealing with text files and those dealing with binary files. We can think of text files as containing data in a form similar to Java's char type—typically simple, line-based, human-readable alphanumeric information. Web pages, written in HTML, are a particular example. Binary files are more varied: image files are one common example, as are executable programs such as word processors and media players. Java classes concerned with processing text files are known as *readers* and *writers*, whereas those concerned with binary files are known as *stream* handlers. In the main, we shall focus on readers and writers.

12.9.2 The File class and Path interface

A file is much more than just a name and some contents. A file will be located in a particular *folder* or *directory* on a particular disk drive, for instance, and different operating systems have different conventions for which characters are used in file pathnames. The File class allows a program to enquire about details of an external file in a way that is independent of the particular file system on which the program is running. The name of the file is passed to the constructor of File. Creating a File object within a program does not create a file in the file system. Rather, it results in details about a file being stored in the File object if the external file exists.

In Java 7, the Path interface in java.nio.file fulfills a similar role. Because Path is an interface rather than a class, a concrete instance of an implementing class is created via a static get method of the Paths class (note the plural name), which is also in the java.nio.file package. When working with legacy code, an equivalent Path object may be created from a File object via the toPath method of File.

We can sometimes avoid getting into situations that require an exception to be handled, by using a File or Path object to check whether or not a file exists. A File object has exists and canRead methods, which make attempting to open a file less likely to fail if we use them first. However, because opening a file that we know exists *still* requires a potential exception to be handled, most people don't bother with checking first.

Path does not itself have equivalent methods. Instead, the Files class (plural, again) provides a large number of static methods for querying the attributes of a Path object; for instance, exists, isReadable, isDirectory, etc.

> **Exercise 12.40** Read the API documentation for the File class from the java.io package. What sort of information is available on files?
>
> **Exercise 12.41** Using a File object, how can you tell whether a file name represents an ordinary file or a directory (folder)?
>
> **Exercise 12.42** Is it possible to determine anything about the contents of a particular file from the information stored in a File object?
>
> **Exercise 12.43** If you are using Java 7, repeat the preceding three exercises using the Path and Files classes.

12.9.3 File output

There are three steps involved in storing data in a file:

1 The file is opened.

2 The data is written.

3 The file is closed.

The nature of file output means that any of these steps could fail, for a range of reasons, many completely beyond the application programmer's control. As a consequence, it will be necessary to anticipate exceptions being thrown at every stage.

In order to write a text file, it is usual to create a FileWriter object, whose constructor takes the name of the file to be written. The file name can be either in the form of a String or a File object. Creating a FileWriter has the effect of opening the external file and preparing it to receive some output. If the attempt to open the file fails for any reason, then the constructor will throw an IOException. Reasons for failure might be that file system permissions prevent a user from writing to certain files or that the given file name does not match a valid location in the file system.

When a file has been opened successfully, then the writer's `write` methods can be used to store characters—often in the form of strings—into the file. Any attempt to write could fail, even if the file has been opened successfully. Such failures are rare, but still possible.

Once all output has been written, it is important to formally close the file. This ensures that all the data really has been written to the external file system, and it often has the effect of freeing some internal or external resources. Once again, on rare occasions the attempt to close the file could fail.

The basic pattern that emerges from the above discussion looks like this:

```
try {
    FileWriter writer = new FileWriter("... name of file ...");
    while(there is more text to write) {
        ...
        writer.write(next piece of text);
        ...
    }
    writer.close();
}
catch(IOException e) {
    something went wrong in dealing with the file
}
```

The main issue that arises is how to deal with any exceptions that are thrown during the three stages. An exception thrown when attempting to open a file is really the only one it is likely to be possible to do anything about, and only then if there is some way to generate an alternative name to try instead. As this will usually require the intervention of a human user of the application, the chances of dealing with it successfully are obviously application- and context-specific. If an attempt to write to the file fails, then it is unlikely that repeating the attempt will succeed. Similarly, failure to close a file is not usually worth a further attempt. The consequence is likely to be an incomplete file.

An example of this pattern can be seen in Code 12.19. The `LogfileCreator` class in the *weblog-analyzer* project includes a method to write a number of random log entries to a file whose name is passed as a parameter to the `createFile` method. This uses two different `write` methods: one to write a string and one to write a character. After writing out the text of the entry as a string, we write a newline character so that each entry appears on a separate line.

Code 12.19

Writing to a text file

```
/**
 * Create a file of random log entries.
 * @param filename The file to write.
 * @param numEntries How many entries.
 * @return true if successful, false otherwise.
 */
public boolean createFile(String filename, int numEntries)
{
    boolean success = false;
    try {
        FileWriter writer = new FileWriter(filename);
        LogEntry[] entries = new LogEntry[numEntries];
```

**Code 12.19
continued**
Writing to a text file

```
            for(int i = 0; i < numEntries; i++) {
                entries[i] = createEntry();
            }
            Arrays.sort(entries);
            for(int i = 0; i < numEntries; i++) {
                writer.write(entries[i].toString());
                writer.write('\n');
            }

            writer.close();
            success = true;
        }
        catch(IOException e) {
            System.err.println("There was a problem writing to " +
                                filename);
        }
        return success;
    }
```

One problem with the pattern shown in Code 12.19 is that failure, once the file has been opened, will leave it open. This wastes a small amount of program resource but, more importantly, leaves the file system in a misleading position, because it must assume that the program is still using the file. See the following section for a way to deal with error situations as a result of changes introduced in Java 7.

12.9.4 The try-with-resource statement

Java 7 introduced a feature to the try statement for dealing with situations where a resource such as an open file should definitely be closed once it is finished with—whether the use of it completed successfully or not. This form is called *try with resource* or *automatic resource management* (ARM). Code 12.20 shows its use with an alternative version of Code 12.19, which you can find in the project *weblog-analyzer-v7*.

Code 12.20
Writing to a text file
using a try-with-
resource statement

```
/**
 * Create a file of random log entries.
 * @param filename The file to write.
 * @param numEntries How many entries.
 * @return true if successful, false otherwise.
 */
```

**Code 12.20
continued**

Writing to a text file
using a try-with-
resource statement

```java
public boolean createFile(String filename, int numEntries)
{
    boolean success = false;
    try(FileWriter writer = new FileWriter(filename)) {
        entry creation omitted

        for(int i = 0; i < numEntries; i++) {
            writer.write(entries[i].toString());
            writer.write('\n');
        }
        success = true;
    }
    catch(IOException e) {
        System.err.println("There was a problem writing to " +
                            filename);
    }
    return success;
}
```

The resource is created in a new parenthesized section immediately after the `try` word. Once the try statement is completed, the `close` method will be called automatically on this resource. This version of the try statement is only appropriate for objects of classes that implement the `AutoCloseable` interface, defined in the `java.lang` package. These will predominantly be classes associated with input/output.

Exercise 12.44 Modify the *world-of-zuul* project so that it writes a script of user input to a text file as a record of the game. There are several different ways that you might think of tackling this:

■ You could modify the `Parser` class to store each line of input in a list and then write out the list at the end of the game. This will produce a solution that is closest to the basic pattern we have outlined in the discussion above.

■ You could place all of the file handling in the `Parser` class so that, as each line is read, it is written out immediately in exactly the same form as it was read. File opening, writing, and closing will all be separated in time from one another (or would it make sense to open, write, and then close the file for every line that is written?).

■ You could place the file handling in the `Game` class and implement a `toString` method in the `Command` class to return the `String` to be written for each command.

Consider each of these possible solutions in terms of responsibility-driven design and the handling of exceptions, along with the likely implications for playing the game if it proves impossible to write the script. How can you ensure that the script file is always closed when the end of the game is reached? This is important to ensure that all of the output is actually written to the external file system.

12.9.5 Text input

The complement to the output of text with a `FileWriter` is the input with a `FileReader`. As you might expect, a complementary set of three input steps is required: opening the file, reading from it, and closing it. Just as the natural units for writing text are characters and strings, the obvious units for reading text are characters and lines. However, although the `FileReader` class contains a method to read a single character,[6] it does not contain a method to read a line. The problem with reading lines from a file is that there is no predefined limit to the length of a line. This means that any method to return the next complete line from a file must be able to read an arbitrary number of characters. For this reason, we usually want to be working with the `BufferedReader` class, which does define a `readLine` method. However, `BufferedReader` cannot open files! Therefore, we must create a `FileReader` first and immediately wrap it in a `BufferedReader` object. Thereafter, we ignore the `FileReader` object and work solely with the `BufferedReader`.

The line-termination character is always removed from the `String` that `readLine` returns, and a `null` value is used to indicate the end of file.

This suggests the following basic pattern for reading the contents of a text file:

```
try {
    BufferedReader reader = new BufferedReader(
                        new FileReader("... name of file ..."));
    String line = reader.readLine();
    while(line != null) {
        do something with line
        line = reader.readLine();
    }
    reader.close();
}
catch(FileNotFoundException e) {
    the specified file could not be found
}
catch(IOException e) {
    something went wrong with reading or closing
}
```

Note that we don't even bother to store the `FileReader` object into a variable, but pass it straight to the constructor of `BufferedReader`. This avoids the confusion of having two `Reader` variables referring to the same source of input, because we should access the file only via the `BufferedReader` object.

With Java 7, we would use a try-with-resources statement here, as above, but also see below for an alternative way to create the `BufferedReader` via the `Files` class.

Code 12.21 illustrates the practical use of a `BufferedReader` in the *tech-support* project from Chapter 5. This has been done so that we can read the system's default responses from a file rather than hardwiring them into the code of the `Responder` class (project: *tech-support-io*).

---

[6] In fact, its `read` method returns each character as an `int` value rather than as a `char`, because it uses an out-of-bounds value, -1, to indicate the end of the file. This is exactly the sort of technique we described in Section 12.3.2.

Code 12.21

Reading from a text file

```java
import java.io.*;
import java.util.*;

public class Responder
{
    // Default responses to use if we don't recognize a word.
    private List<String> defaultResponses;
    // The name of the file containing the default responses.
    private static final String FILE_OF_DEFAULT_RESPONSES =
                            "default.txt";
    ... other fields and methods omitted ...

    /**
     * Build up a list of default responses from which we can pick
     * if we don't know what else to say.
     */
    private void fillDefaultResponses()
    {
        try {
            BufferedReader reader = new BufferedReader(
                    new FileReader(FILE_OF_DEFAULT_RESPONSES));
            String response = reader.readLine();
            while(response != null) {
                defaultResponses.add(response);
                response = reader.readLine();
            }
            reader.close();
        }
        catch(FileNotFoundException e) {
            System.err.println("Unable to open " +
                            FILE_OF_DEFAULT_RESPONSES);
        }
        catch(IOException e) {
            System.err.println("A problem was encountered reading " +
                            FILE_OF_DEFAULT_RESPONSES);
        }
        // Make sure we have at least one response.
        if(defaultResponses.size() == 0) {
            defaultResponses.add("Could you elaborate on that?");
        }
    }
}
```

As with output, the question arises as to what to do about any exceptions thrown during the whole process. In this example, we have printed an error message and then provided at least one response in case of a complete failure to read anything.

With Java 7, the normal way to create a `BufferedReader` is via the static `new-BufferedReader` method of the `Files` class. In addition to a `Path` parameter corresponding to the file to be opened, one complication is that a `Charset` parameter is also required. This is used to describe the character set to which the characters in the file belong. `Charset` can be found in the `java.nio.charset` package. There are a number of standard character sets, such as `US-ASCII` and `ISO-8859-1`, and more details can be found in the API documentation for `Charset`. Code 12.22 shows the use of these features to read a text file.

Code 12.22

Reading from a text file with Java 7

```java
import java.io.*;
import java.nio.charset.Charset;
import java.nio.file.*;
import java.util.*;

public class Responder
{
    ... fields and methods omitted ...

    /**
     * Build up a list of default responses from which we can pick
     * if we don't know what else to say.
     */
    private void fillDefaultResponses()
    {
        Charset charset = Charset.forName("US-ASCII");
        Path path = Paths.get(FILE_OF_DEFAULT_RESPONSES);
        try(BufferedReader reader =
                Files.newBufferedReader(path, charset)) {
            String response = reader.readLine();
            while(response != null) {
                defaultResponses.add(response);
                response = reader.readLine();
            }
        }
        catch(FileNotFoundException e) {
            System.err.println("Unable to open " +
                            FILE_OF_DEFAULT_RESPONSES);
        }
        catch(IOException e) {
            System.err.println("A problem was encountered reading " +
                            FILE_OF_DEFAULT_RESPONSES);
        }
        // Make sure we have at least one response.
        if(defaultResponses.size() == 0) {
            defaultResponses.add("Could you elaborate on that?");
        }
    }
}
```

Exercise 12.45 The file `default.txt` in the project folder contains the default responses read in by the `fillDefaultResponses` method. Using any text editor, change the content of this file so that it contains an empty line between any two responses. Then change your code to work correctly again in reading in the responses from this file.

Exercise 12.46 Change your code so that several lines of text found in the file not separated by an empty line are read as one single response. Change the `default.txt` file so that is contains some responses spanning multiple lines. Test.

Exercise 12.47 Modify the `Responder` class of the *tech-support-io* project so that it reads the associations between keywords and responses from a text file, rather than initializing `responseMap` with strings written into the source code in the `fillResponseMap` method. You can use the `fillDefaultResponses` method as a pattern, but you will need to make some changes to its logic, because there are two strings to be read for each entry rather than one— the keyword and the response. Try storing keywords and responses on alternating lines; keep the text of each response on a single line. You may assume that there will always be an even number of lines (i.e., no missing responses).

12.9.5 Scanner: parsing input

So far, we have treated input largely as unstructured lines of text, for which `BufferedReader` is the ideal class. However, many applications will then go on to decompose the individual lines into component pieces representing multi-typed data values. For instance, comma-separated values (CSV) format is a commonly used way to store text files whose lines consist of multiple values, each of which is separated from its neighbors by a comma character.[7] In effect, such lines of text have an implicit structure. Identifying the underlying structure is known as *parsing*, while piecing the individual characters into separate data values is known as *scanning*.

The `Scanner` class, in the `java.util` package, is specifically designed to scan text and convert composite sequences of characters to typed values, such as integers (`nextInt`) and floating-point numbers (`nextDouble`). While a `Scanner` can be used to break up `String` objects, it is also often used to read and convert the contents of files directly instead of using `BufferedReader`. It has constructors that can take `String`, `File`, or (in Java 7) `Path` arguments. Code 12.23 illustrates how a text file that is to be interpreted as containing integer data might be read in this way.

Code 12.23

Reading integer data with `Scanner`

```
/**
 * Read integers from a file and return them
 * as an array.
 * @param filename The file to be read.
 * @return The integers read.
 */
```

---

[7] In practice, any character can be used in place of a comma; for instance, a tab character is frequently used.

Code 12.23
continued
Reading integer data
with Scanner

```
public int[] readInts(String filename)
{
    int[] data;
    try {
        List<Integer> values = new ArrayList<Integer>();
        Scanner scanner = new Scanner(new File(filename));
        while(scanner.hasNextInt()) {
            values.add(scanner.nextInt());
        }
        // Copy them to an array of the exact size.
        data = new int[values.size()];
        Iterator<Integer> it = values.iterator();
        int i = 0;
        while(it.hasNext()) {
            data[i] = it.next();
            i++;
        }
    }
    catch(FileNotFoundException e) {
        System.out.println("Cannot find file: " + filename);
        data = new int[0];
    }
    return data;
}
```

Note that this method does not guarantee to read the whole file. The `Scanner`'s `hasNextInt` method that controls the loop will return `false` if it encounters text in the file that does not appear to be part of an integer. At that point, the data gathering will be terminated. In fact, it is perfectly possible to mix calls to the different `next` methods when parsing a complete file, where the data it contains is to be interpreted as consisting of mixed types.

Another common use of `Scanner` is to read input from the "terminal" connected to a program. We have regularly used calls to the `print` and `println` methods of `System.out` to write text to the BlueJ terminal window. `System.out` is of type `java.io.PrintStream` and maps to what is often called the *standard output* destination. Similarly, there is a corresponding *standard input* source available as `System.in`, which is of type `java.io.InputStream`. An `InputStream` is not normally used directly when it is necessary to read user input from the terminal, because it delivers input one character at a time. Instead, `System.in` is usually passed to the constructor of a `Scanner`. The `InputReader` class in the *tech-support-complete* project of Chapter 5 uses this approach to read questions from the user:

```
Scanner reader = new Scanner(System.in);
... intervening code omitted ...
String inputLine = reader.nextLine();
```

The `nextLine` method of `Scanner` returns the next complete line of input from standard input (without including the final newline character).

> **Exercise 12.48** Review the `InputReader` class of *tech-support-complete* to check that you understand how it uses the `Scanner` class.
>
> **Exercise 12.49** Read the API documentation for the `Scanner` class in the `java.util` package. What `next` methods does it have in addition to those we have discussed in this section?
>
> **Exercise 12.50** Review the `Parser` class of *zuul-better* to also see how it uses the `Scanner` class. It does so in two slightly different ways.
>
> **Exercise 12.51** Review the `LoglineTokenizer` class of *weblog-analyzer* to see how it uses a `Scanner` to extract the integer values from log lines.

12.9.7 Object serialization

Concept:

Serialization allows whole objects, and object hierarchies, to be read and written in a single operation. Every object involved must be from a class that implements the `Serializable` interface.

In simple terms, serialization allows a whole object to be written to an external file in a single write operation and read back in at a later stage using a single read operation.[8] This works with both simple objects and multi-component objects such as collections. This is a significant feature that avoids having to read and write objects field by field. It is particularly useful in applications with persistent data, such as address books or media databases, because it allows all entries created in one session to be saved and then read back in at a later session. Of course, we have the choice to write out the contents of objects as text strings, but the process of reading the text back in again, converting the data to the correct types, and restoring *the exact state* of a complex set of objects is often difficult, if not impossible. Object serialization is a much more reliable process.

In order to be eligible to participate in serialization, a class must implement the `Serializable` interface that is defined in the `java.io` package. However, it is worth noting that this interface defines no methods. This means that the serialization process is managed automatically by the runtime system and requires little user-defined code to be written. In the *address-book-io* project, both `AddressBook` and `ContactDetails` implement this interface so that they can be saved to a file. The `AddressBookFileHandler` class defines the methods `saveToFile` and `readFromFile` to illustrate the serialization process. Code 12.24 contains the source of `saveToFile` to illustrate how little code is actually required to save the whole address book, in a single write statement. Note too that, because we are writing objects in binary form, a `Stream` object has been used rather than a `Writer`. The `AddressBookFileHandler` class also includes further examples of the basic reading and writing techniques used with text files. See, for instance, its `saveSearchResults` and `showSearchResults` methods.

---

[8] This is a simplification, because objects can also be written and read across a network, for instance, and not just within a file system.

Code 12.24

Serialization of a complete Address Book with all Contact Details

```
public class AddressBookFileHandler
{
    ...fields and methods omitted...

    /**
     * Save a binary version of the address book to the given file.
     * If the file name is not an absolute path, then it is assumed
     * to be relative to the current project folder.
     * @param destinationFile The file where the details
     * are to be saved.
     * @throws IOException If the saving process fails for any reason.
     */
    public void saveToFile(String destinationFile) throws IOException
    {
        File destination = makeAbsoluteFilename(destinationFile);
        ObjectOutputStream os = new ObjectOutputStream(
                                new FileOutputStream(
                                    (destination)));

        os.writeObject(book);
        os.close();
    }
}
```

Exercise 12.52 Modify the *network* project from Chapter 9 so that the data can be stored to a file. Use object serialization for this. Which classes do you have to declare to be serializable?

Exercise 12.53 What happens if you change the definition of a class by, say, adding an extra field and then try to read back serialized objects created from the previous version of the class?

12.10   Summary

When two objects interact, there is always the chance that something could go wrong, for a variety of reasons. For instance:

■ The programmer of a client might have misunderstood the state or the capabilities of a particular server object.

■ A server object may be unable to fulfill a client's request because of a particular set of external circumstances.

■ A client might have been programmed incorrectly, causing it to pass inappropriate parameter values to a server method.

If something does go wrong, a program is likely either to terminate prematurely (i.e., crash!) or to produce incorrect and undesirable effects. We can go a long way toward avoiding many of these problems by using exception throwing. This provides a clearly defined way for an object to report to a client that something has gone wrong. Exceptions prevent a client from simply ignoring the problem, and encourage programmers to try to find an alternative course of action as a workaround if something does go wrong.

When developing a class, assert statements can be used to provide internal consistency checking. These are typically omitted from production code.

Input/output is an area where exceptions are likely to occur. This is primarily because a programmer has little, if any, control over the environments in which their programs are run, but it also reflects the complexity and diversity of the environments in which programs are run.

The Java API supports input/output of both textual and binary data via readers, writers, and streams. Java 7 has brought changes to I/O through the introduction of the `java.nio` packages.

Exercise 12.54 Add to the *address-book* project the ability to store multiple e-mail addresses in a `ContactDetails` object. All of these e-mail addresses should be valid keys. Use assertions and JUnit testing through all stages of this process to provide maximum confidence in the final version.

Terms introduced in this chapter

exception, unchecked exception, checked exception, exception handler, assertion, serialization

Concept summary

- **exception** An exception is an object representing details of a program failure. An exception is thrown to indicate that a failure has occurred.

- **unchecked exception** An unchecked exception is a type of exception whose use will not require checks from the compiler.

- **checked exception** A checked exception is a type of exception whose use will require extra checks from the compiler. In particular, checked exceptions in Java require the use of throws clauses and try statements.

- **exception handler** Program code that protects statements in which an exception might be thrown is called an *exception handler*. It provides reporting and/or recovery code should one arise.

- **assertion** An assertion is a statement of a fact that should be true in normal program execution. We can use assertions to state our assumptions explicitly and to detect programming errors more easily.

- **serialization** Serialization allows whole objects, and object hierarchies, to be read and written in a single operation. Every object involved must be from a class that implements the `Serializable` interface.

Main concepts discussed in this chapter:

- discovering classes
- CRC cards
- designing interfaces
- patterns

Java constructs discussed in this chapter:

(No new Java constructs are introduced in this chapter.)

In previous chapters of this book, we have described how to write good classes. We have discussed how to design them, how to make them maintainable and robust, and how to make them interact. All of this is important, but we have omitted one aspect of the task: finding the classes.

In all our previous examples, we have assumed that we more or less know what the classes are that we should use to solve our problems. In a real software project, deciding what classes to use to implement a solution to a problem can be one of the most difficult tasks. In this chapter, we discuss this aspect of the development process.

These initial steps of developing a software system are generally referred to as *analysis and design*. We analyze the problem, and then we design a solution. The first step of design will be at a higher level than the class design discussed in Chapter 6. We will think about what classes we should create to solve our problem and how exactly they should interact. Once we have a solution to this problem, then we can continue with the design of individual classes and start thinking about their implementation.

13.1 Analysis and design

Analysis and design of software systems is a large and complex problem area. Discussing it in detail is far outside the scope of this book. Many different methodologies have been described in the literature and are used in practice for this task. In this chapter, we aim only to give an introduction to the problems encountered in the process.

We will use a fairly simple method to address these tasks, which serves well for relatively small problems. To discover initial classes, we use the *verb/noun method*. Then we will use *CRC cards* to perform the initial application design.

13.1.1 The verb/noun method

This method is all about identifying classes and objects, and the associations and interactions between them. The nouns in a human language describe "things," such as people, buildings, and so on. The verbs describe "actions," such as writing, eating, etc. From these natural-language concepts, we can see that, in a description of a programming problem, the nouns will often correspond to classes and objects, whereas the verbs will correspond to the things those objects do—that is, to methods. We do not need a very long description to be able to illustrate this technique. The description typically needs to be only a few paragraphs in length.

The example we will use to discuss this process is the design of a cinema booking system.

13.1.2 The cinema booking example

This time, we will not start by extending an existing project. We now assume that we are in a situation where it is our task to create a new application from scratch. The task is to create a system that can be used by a company operating cinemas to handle bookings of seats for movie screenings. People often call in advance to reserve seats. The application should, then, be able to find empty seats for a requested screening and reserve them for the customer.

We will assume that we have had several meetings with the cinema operators, during which they have described to us the functionality they expect from the system. (Understanding what the expected functionality is, describing it, and agreeing about it with a client is a significant problem in itself. This, however, is outside the scope of this book and can be studied in other courses and other books.)

Here is the description we wrote for our cinema booking system:

> *The cinema booking system should store seat bookings for multiple theaters. Each theater has seats arranged in rows. Customers can reserve seats and are given a row number and a seat number. They may request bookings of several adjoining seats.*

> *Each booking is for a particular show (that is, the screening of a given movie at a certain time). Shows are at an assigned date and time and are scheduled for a theater where they are screened. The system stores the customer's telephone number.*

Given a reasonably clear description such as this, we can make a first attempt at discovering classes and methods by identifying the nouns and verbs in the text.

13.1.3 Discovering classes

The first step in identifying the classes is to go through the description and mark all the nouns and verbs in the text. Doing this, we find the following nouns and verbs. (The nouns are shown in the order in which they appear in the text; verbs are shown attached to the nouns they refer to.)

Nouns	**Verbs**
cinema booking system	*stores* (seat bookings)
	stores (telephone number)
seat booking	*has* (seats)
theater	
seat	
row	
customer	*reserves* (seats)
	is given (row number, seat number)
	requests (seat booking)
row number	
seat number	
show	*is scheduled* (in theater)
movie	
date	
time	
telephone number	

The nouns we identified here give us a first approximation for classes in our system. As a first cut, we can use one class for each noun. This is not an exact method; we might find later that we need a few additional classes or that some of our nouns are not needed. This, however, we will test a bit later. It is important not to exclude any nouns straight away; we do not yet have enough information to make an informed decision.

Almost always when we do this exercise with students, some students immediately leave out some nouns. For example, a student leaves out the noun "*row*" from the previous description. When questioned about this, students often say: "Well, that's just a number, so I just use an int. That doesn't need a class." It is really important at this stage not to do this. We really do not have enough information at this point to decide whether *row* should be an int or a class. We can make this decision only much later. For now, we just go through the paragraph mechanically, picking out *all* nouns. We make no judgments yet about which are "good ones" and which are not.

You might like to note that all of the nouns have been written in their singular form. It is typical that the names of classes are singular rather than plural. For instance, we would always choose to define a class as Cinema rather than Cinemas. This is because the multiplicity is achieved by creating multiple instances of a class.

Exercise 13.1 Review projects from earlier chapters in this book. Are there any cases of a class name being a plural name? If so, are those situations justified for a particular reason?

13.1.4   Using CRC cards

The next step in our design process is to work out interactions between our classes. In order to do this, we shall use a method called *CRC cards*.[1]

CRC stands for Class/Responsibilities/Collaborators. The idea is to take cardboard cards (normal index cards do a good job) and use one card for each class. It is important for this activity to do this using real, physical cards, not just a computer or a single sheet of paper. Each card is divided into three areas: one area at the top left, where the name of the class is written; one area below this, to note responsibilities of the class; and one area to the right for writing collaborators of this class (classes that this one uses). Figure 13.1 illustrates the layout of a CRC card.

Figure 13.1
A CRC card

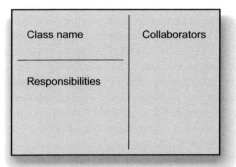

> **Exercise 13.2** Make CRC cards for the classes in the cinema booking system. At this stage, you need only fill in the class names.

13.1.5   Scenarios

Concept:

Scenarios (also known as "use cases") can be used to get an understanding of the interactions in a system.

Now we have a first approximation to the classes needed in our system, and a physical representation of them on CRC cards. In order to figure out necessary interactions between the classes in our system, we play through *scenarios*. A scenario is an example of an activity that the system has to carry out or support. Scenarios are also referred to as *use cases*. We do not use that term here because it is often used to denote a more formal way of describing scenarios.

Playing through scenarios is best done in a group. Each group member is assigned one class (or a small number of classes), and that person plays their role by saying out loud what the class is currently doing. While the scenario is played through, the person records on the CRC card everything that is found out about the class in action: what its responsibilities should be and which other classes it collaborates with.

---

[1] CRC cards were first described in a paper by Kent Beck and Ward Cunningham, titled *A Laboratory For Teaching Object-Oriented Thinking*. This paper is worth reading as information supplemental to this chapter. You can find it online at `http://c2.com/doc/oopsla89/paper.html` or by doing a web search for its title.

We start with a simple example scenario:

> A customer calls the cinema and wants to make a reservation for two seats tonight to watch the classic movie *The Shawshank Redemption*. The cinema employee starts using the booking system to find and reserve a seat.

Because the human user interacts with the booking system (represented by the `Cinema BookingSystem` class), this is where the scenario starts. Here is what might happen next:

■ The user (the cinema employee) wants to find all showings of *The Shawshank Redemption* that are on tonight. So we can note on the `CinemaBookingSystem` CRC card, as a responsibility: *Can find shows by title and day*. We can also record class `Show` as a collaborator.

■ We have to ask ourselves: How does the system find the show? Who does it ask? One solution might be that the `CinemaBookingSystem` stores a collection of shows. This gives us an additional class: the collection. (This might be implemented later by using an `ArrayList`, a `LinkedList`, a `HashSet`, or some other form of collection. We can make that decision later; for now, we just note this as a `Collection`.) This is an example of how we might introduce additional classes during the playing of scenarios. It might happen every now and then that we have to add classes for implementation reasons that we initially overlooked. We add to the responsibilities of the `CinemaBookingSystem` card: *Stores collection of shows*. And we add `Collection` to the collaborators.

> **Exercise 13.3** Make a CRC card for the newly identified `Collection` class, and add it to your system.

■ We assume that three shows come up: one at 5:30 p.m., one at 9:00 p.m., and one at 11:30 p.m. The employee informs the customer of the times, and the customer chooses the one at 9:00 p.m. So the employee wants to check the details of that show (whether it is sold out, which theater it runs at, etc.). Thus, in our system, the `CinemaBookingSystem` must be able to retrieve and display the show's details. Play this through. The person playing the booking system should ask the person playing the show to tell them the required details. Then you note on the card for `CinemaBookingSystem`: *Retrieves and displays show details*, and on the `Show` card you write: *Provides details about theater and number of free seats*.

■ Assume that there are plenty of free seats. The customer chooses seats 13 and 14 in row 12. The employee makes that reservation. We note on the `CinemaBookingSystem` card: *Accepts seat reservations from user*.

■ We now have to play through exactly how the seat reservation works. A seat reservation is clearly attached to a particular show, so the `CinemaBookingSystem` should probably tell the show about the reservation; it delegates the actual task of making the reservation to the `Show` object. We can note for the `Show` class: *Can reserve seats*. (You may have noticed that the notion of objects and classes is blurred when playing through CRC scenarios. In effect, the person representing a class is representing its instances too. This is intentional and not usually a problem.)

■ Now it is the `Show` class's turn. It has received a request to reserve a seat. What exactly does it do? To be able to store seat reservations, it must have a representation of the seats in the theater. So we assume that each show has a link to a `Theater` object. (Note this on the card: *Stores theater*. This is also a collaborator.) The theater should probably know about the exact number and arrangement of seats it has. (We can also note in the back of our heads, or on a separate piece of paper, that each show must have its own instance of the `Theater` object, because several shows can be scheduled for the same `Theater` and reserving a seat in one does not reserve the same seat for another show. This is something to look out for when `Show` objects are created. We have to keep this in mind so that later, when we play through the scenario of *Scheduling a new show*, we remember to create a theater instance for each show.) The way a show deals with reserving a seat is probably by passing this reservation request on to the theater.

■ Now the theater has accepted a request to make a reservation. (Note this on the card: *Accepts reservation request*.) How does it deal with it? The theater could have a collection of seats in it. Or it could have a collection of rows (each row being a separate object), and rows, in turn, hold seats. Which of these alternatives is better? Thinking ahead about other possible scenarios, we might decide to go with the idea of storing rows. If, for example, a customer requests four seats together in the same row, it might be easier to find four adjacent seats if we have them all arranged by rows. We note on the `Theater` card: *Stores rows*. `Row` is now a collaborator.

■ We note on the `Row` class: *Stores collection of seats*. And then we note a new collaborator: `Seat`.

■ Getting back to the `Theater` class, we have not yet worked out exactly how it should react to the seat reservation request. Let us assume it does two things: find the requested row and then make a reservation request with the seat number to the `Row` object.

■ Next, we note on the `Row` card: *Accepts reservation request for seat*. It must then find the right `Seat` object (we can note that as a responsibility: *Can find seats by number*) and can make a reservation for that seat. It would do so by telling the `Seat` object that it is now reserved.

■ We can now add to the `Seat` card: *Accepts reservations*. The seat itself can remember whether it has been reserved. We note on the `Seat` card: *Stores reservation status (free/reserved)*.

> **Exercise 13.4** Play this scenario through on your cards (with a group of people, if possible). Add any other information you feel was left out in this description.

Should the seat also store information about who has reserved it? It could store the name of the customer or the telephone number. Or maybe we should create a `Customer` object as soon as someone makes a reservation, and store the `Customer` object with the seat once the seat has been reserved? These are interesting questions, and we will try to work out the best solution by playing through more scenarios.

This was just the first, simple scenario. We need to play through many more scenarios to get a better understanding of how the system should work.

Playing through scenarios works best when a group of people sit around a table and move the cards around on it. Cards that cooperate closely can be placed close together to give an impression of the degree of coupling in the system.

Other scenarios to play through next would include the following:

■ A customer requests five seats together. Work out exactly how five adjoining seats are found.

■ A customer calls and says he forgot the seat numbers he was given for the reservation he made yesterday. Could you please look up the seat numbers again?

■ A customer calls to cancel a reservation. He can give his name and the show but has forgotten the seat numbers.

■ A customer calls who already has a reservation. She wants to know whether she can reserve another seat next to the ones she already has.

■ A show is canceled. The cinema wants to call all customers that have reserved a seat for that show.

These scenarios should give you a good understanding of the seat lookup and reservation part of the system. Then we need another group of scenarios: those dealing with setting up the theater and scheduling shows. Here are some possible scenarios:

■ The system has to be set up for a new cinema. The cinema has two theaters, each of a different size. Theater A has 26 rows with 18 seats each. Theater B has 32 rows. In this theater, the first six rows have 20 seats, the next 10 rows have 22 seats, and the other rows have 26 seats.

■ A new movie is scheduled for screening. It will be screened for the next two weeks, three times each day (4:40 p.m., 6:30 p.m., and 8:30 p.m.). The shows have to be added to the system. All shows run in theater A.

> **Exercise 13.5** Play through these scenarios. Note on a separate piece of paper all the questions you have left unanswered. Make a record of all scenarios you have played through.
>
> **Exercise 13.6** What other scenarios can you think of? Write them down, and then play them out.

Playing through scenarios takes some patience and some practice. It is important to spend enough time doing this. Playing through the scenarios mentioned here will take several hours.

It is very common for beginners to take shortcuts and not question and record every detail about the execution of a scenario. This is dangerous! We will soon move on to developing this system in Java, and if details are left unanswered, it is very likely that ad hoc decisions will be made at implementation time that will later turn out to be bad choices.

It is also common for beginners to forget some scenarios. Forgetting to think through a part of the system before starting the class design and implementation can cause a large amount of work later, when an already partially implemented system would have to be changed.

Doing this activity well, carefully stepping through all necessary steps, and recording steps in sufficient detail takes some practice and a lot of discipline. This exercise is harder than it looks and more important than you realize.

Exercise 13.7 Make a class design for an airport-control-system simulation. Use CRC cards and scenarios. Here is a description of the system:

The program is an airport simulation system. For our new airport, we need to know whether we can operate with two runways or whether we need three. The airport works as follows:

There are multiple runways. Planes take off and land on runways. Air traffic controllers coordinate the traffic and give planes permission to take off or land. The controllers sometimes give permission right away, but sometimes they tell planes to wait. Planes must keep a certain distance from one another. The purpose of the program is to simulate the airport in operation.

13.2 Class design

Now it is time for the next big step: moving from CRC cards to Java classes. During the CRC card exercise, you should have gained a good understanding of how your application is structured and how your classes cooperate to solve the program's tasks. You may have come across cases where you had to introduce additional classes (this is often the case with classes that represent internal data structures), and you may have noticed that you have a card for a class that was never used. If the latter is the case, this card can now be removed.

Recognizing the classes for the implementation is now trivial. The cards show us the complete set of classes we need. Deciding on the interface of each class (that is, the set of public methods that a class should have) is a bit harder, but we have made an important step toward that as well. If the playing of the scenarios was done well, then the responsibilities noted for each class describe the class's public methods (and maybe some of the instance fields). The responsibilities of each class should be evaluated according to the class design principles discussed in Chapter 6: responsibility-driven design, coupling, and cohesion.

13.2.1 Designing class interfaces

Before starting to code our application in Java, we can once more use the cards to make another step toward the final design by translating the informal descriptions into method calls and adding parameters.

To arrive at more formal descriptions, we can now play through the scenarios again, this time talking in terms of method calls, parameters, and return values. The logic and the structure of the application should not change any more, but we try to note down complete information about method signatures and instance fields. We do this on a new set of cards.

Exercise 13.8 Make a new set of CRC cards for the classes you have identified. Play through the scenarios again. This time, note exact method names for each method you call from another class, and specify in detail (with type and name) all parameters that are passed and the methods' return values. The method signatures are written on the CRC card instead of the responsibilities. On the back of the card, note the instance fields that each class holds.

Once we have done the exercise described above, writing each class's interface is easy. We can translate directly from the cards into Java. Typically, all classes should be created and *method stubs* for all public methods should be written. A method stub is a placeholder for the method that has the correct signature and an empty method body.[2]

Many students find doing this in detail tedious. At the end of the project, however, you will hopefully come to appreciate the value of these activities. Many software development teams have realized after the fact that time saved at the design stage had to be spent many times over to fix mistakes or omissions that were not discovered early enough.

Inexperienced programmers often view the writing of the code as the "real programming." Doing the initial design is seen as, if not superfluous, at least annoying, and people cannot wait to get it over with so that the "real work" can start. This is a very misguided picture.

The initial design is one of the most important parts of the project. You should plan to spend at least as much time working on the design as on the implementation. Application design is not something that comes before the programming—it *is* (the most important part of) programming!

Mistakes in the code itself can later be fixed fairly easily. Mistakes in the overall design can, at best, be expensive to put right and, at worst, fatal to the whole application. In unlucky cases, they can be almost unfixable (short of starting all over again).

13.2.2   User interface design

One part that we have left out of the discussion so far is the design of the user interface.[3] At some stage, we have to decide in detail what users see on the screen and how they interact with our system.

In a well-designed application, this is quite independent of the underlying logic of the application, so it can be done independently of designing the class structure for the rest of the project. As we saw in the previous chapters, BlueJ gives us the means of interacting with our application before a final user interface is available, so we can choose to work on the internal structure first.

The user interface may be a GUI (graphical user interface) with menus and buttons, it can be text based, or we can decide to run the application using the BlueJ method-call mechanism. Maybe the system runs over a network and the user interface is presented in a web browser on a different machine.

For now, we shall ignore the user-interface design and use BlueJ method invocation to work with our program.

---

[2] If you wish, you can include trivial return statements in the bodies of methods with non-`void` return types. Just return a `null` value for object-returning methods and a zero, or `false`, value for primitive types.

[3] Note carefully the double meaning of the term 'designing interfaces' here! Above, we were talking about the interfaces of single classes (a set of public methods); now, we talk about the *user interface*—what the user sees on screen to interact with the application. Both are very important issues, and unfortunately the term *interface* is used for both.

13.3 Documentation

After identifying the classes and their interfaces, and before starting to implement the methods of a class, the interface should be documented. This involves writing a class comment and method comments for each class in the project. These should be described in sufficient detail to identify the overall purpose of each class and method.

Along with analysis and design, documentation is a further area that is often neglected by beginners. It is not easy for inexperienced programmers to see why documentation is so important. The reason is that inexperienced programmers usually work on projects that only have a handful of classes and are written in the span of a few weeks or months. A programmer can get away with bad documentation when working on these mini-projects.

However, even experienced programmers often wonder how it is possible to write the documentation before the implementation. This is because they fail to appreciate that good documentation focuses on high-level issues such as what a class or method does rather than on low-level issues such as exactly how it is done. This is usually symptomatic of viewing the implementation as being more important than the design.

If a software developer wants to progress to more-interesting problems and starts to work professionally on real-life applications, it is not unusual to work with dozens of other people on an application over several years. The *ad hoc* solution of just "having the documentation in your head" does not work anymore.

> **Exercise 13.9** Create a BlueJ project for the cinema booking system. Create the necessary classes. Create method stubs for all methods.
>
> **Exercise 13.10** Document all classes and methods. If you have worked in a group, assign responsibilities for classes to different group members. Use the `javadoc` format for comments, with appropriate `javadoc` tags to document the details.

13.4 Cooperation

> **Pair programming** Implementation of classes is traditionally done alone. Most programmers work on their own when writing the code, and other people are brought in only after the implementation is finished, to test or review the code.
>
> More recently, pair programming has been suggested as an alternative that is intended to produce better-quality code (code with better structure and fewer bugs). Pair programming is also one of the elements of a technique known as *Extreme Programming*. Do a web search for "pair programming" or "extreme programming" to find out more.

Software development is usually done in teams. A clean object-oriented approach provides strong support for teamwork, because it allows for the separation of the problem into loosely coupled components (classes) that can be implemented independently.

Although the initial design work was best done in a group, it is now time to split it up. If the definition of the class interfaces and the documentation was done well, it should be possible to implement the classes independently. Classes can now be assigned to programmers, who can work on them alone or in pairs.

In the remainder of this chapter, we shall not discuss the implementation phase of the cinema booking system in detail. That phase largely involves the sorts of task we have been doing throughout this book in previous chapters, and we hope that by now readers can determine for themselves how to continue from here.

13.5 Prototyping

Instead of designing and then building the complete application in one giant leap, *prototyping* can be used to investigate parts of a system.

Concept:

Prototyping is the construction of a partially working system in which some functions of the application are simulated. It serves to provide an understanding early in the development process of how the system will work.

A prototype is a version of the application where one part is simulated in order to experiment with other parts. You may, for example, implement a prototype to test a graphical user interface. In that case, the logic of the application may not be properly implemented. Instead, we would write simple implementations for those methods that simulate the task. For example, when calling a method to find a free seat in the cinema system, a method could always return *seat 3, row 15* instead of actually implementing the search. Prototyping allows us to develop an executable (but not fully functional) system quickly so that we can investigate parts of the application in practice.

Prototypes are also useful for single classes to aid a team development process. Often when different team members work on different classes, not all classes take the same amount of time to be completed. In some cases, a missing class can hold up continuation of development and testing of other classes. In those cases, it can be beneficial to write a class prototype. The prototype has implementations of all method stubs, but instead of containing full, final implementations, the prototype only simulates the functionality. Writing a prototype should be possible quickly, and development of client classes can then continue using the prototype until the class is implemented.

As we discuss in Section 13.6, one additional benefit of prototyping is that it can give the developers insights into issues and problems that were not considered at an earlier stage.

Exercise 13.11 Outline a prototype for your cinema-system example. Which of the classes should be implemented first, and which should remain in prototype stage?

Exercise 13.12 Implement your cinema-system prototype.

13.6 Software growth

Several models exist for how software should be built. One of the most commonly known is often referred to as the *waterfall model* (because activity progresses from one level to the next, like water in a cascading waterfall—there is no going back).

13.6.1   Waterfall model

In the waterfall model, several phases of software development are done in a fixed sequence:

- analysis of the problem
- design of the software
- implementation of the software components
- unit testing
- integration testing
- delivery of the system to the client

If any phase fails, we might have to step back to the previous phase to fix it (for example, if testing shows failure, we go back to implementation), but there is never a plan to revisit earlier phases.

This is probably the most traditional, conservative model of software development, and it has been in widespread use for a long time. However, numerous problems have been discovered with this model over the years. Two of the main flaws are that it assumes that developers understand the full extent of the system's functionality in detail from the start and that the system does not change after delivery.

In practice, both assumptions are typically not true. It is quite common that the design of a system's functionality is not perfect at the start. This is often because the client, who knows the problem domain, does not know much about computing, and because the software engineers, who know how to program, have only limited knowledge of the problem domain.

13.6.2   Iterative development

One possibility to address the problems of the waterfall model is to use early prototyping and frequent client interaction in the development process. Prototypes of the systems are built that do not do much but give an impression of what the system would look like and what it would do, and clients comment regularly on the design and functionality. This leads to a more circular process than the waterfall model. Here, the software development iterates several times through an *analysis–design–prototype implementation–client feedback* cycle.

Another approach is captured in the notion that good software is not designed, it is *grown*. The idea behind this is to design a small and clean system initially and get it into a working state in which it can be used by end users. Then additional features are gradually added (the software grows) in a controlled manner, and "finished" states (meaning states in which the software is completely usable and can be delivered to clients) are reached repeatedly and fairly frequently.

In reality, growing software is, of course, not a contradiction to designing software. Every growth step is carefully designed. What the software growth model does not try to do is design the complete software system right from the start. Even more, the notion of a complete software system does not exist at all!

The traditional waterfall model has as its goal the delivery of a complete system. The software growth model assumes that complete systems that are used indefinitely in an unchanged state do not exist. There are only two things that can happen to a software system: either it is continuously improved and adapted, or it will disappear.

This discussion is central to this book, because it strongly influences how we view the tasks and skills required of a programmer or software engineer. You might be able to tell that the authors of this book strongly favor the software growth model over the waterfall model.[4]

As a consequence, certain tasks and skills become much more important than they would be in the waterfall model. Software maintenance, code reading (rather than just writing), designing for extendibility, documentation, coding for understandability, and many other issues we have mentioned in this book take their importance from the fact that we know there will be others coming after us who have to adapt and extend our code.

Viewing a piece of software as a continuously growing, changing, adapting entity, rather than a static piece of text that is written and preserved like a novel, determines our views about how good code should be written. All the techniques we have discussed throughout this book work toward this.

Exercise 13.13 In which ways might the cinema booking system be adapted or extended in the future? Which changes are more likely than others? Write down a list of possible future changes.

Exercise 13.14 Are there any other organizations that might use booking systems similar to the one we have discussed? What significant differences exist between the systems?

Exercise 13.15 Do you think it would be possible to design a "generic" booking system that could be adapted or customized for use in a wide range of different organizations with booking needs? If you were to create such a system, at what point in the development process of the cinema system would you introduce changes? Or would you throw that one away and start again from scratch?

13.7 Using design patterns

Concept:

A **design pattern** is a description of a common computing problem and a description of a small set of classes and their interaction structure that helps to solve that problem.

In earlier chapters, we have discussed in detail some techniques for reusing some of our work and making our code more understandable to others. So far, a large part of these discussions has remained at the level of source code in single classes.

As we become more experienced and move on to design larger software systems, the implementation of single classes is not the most difficult problem any more. The structure of the overall system—the complex relationships between classes—becomes harder to design and to understand than the code of individual classes.

---

[4] An excellent book describing the problems of software development and some possible approaches to solutions is *The Mythical Man-Month* by Frederick P. Brooks Jr., Addison-Wesley. Even though the original edition is nearly 40 years old, it makes entertaining and very enlightening reading.

It is a logical step that we should try to achieve the same goals for class structures that we attempted for source code. We want to reuse good bits of work, and we want to enable others to understand what we have done.

At the level of class structures, both these goals can be served by using *design patterns*. A design pattern describes a common problem that occurs regularly in software development and then describes a general solution to that problem that can be used in many different contexts. For software design patterns, the solution is typically a description of a small set of classes and their interactions.

Design patterns help in our task in two ways. First, they document good solutions to problems so that these solutions can be reused later for similar problems. The reuse in this case is not at the level of source code, but at the level of class structures.

Second, design patterns have names and thus establish a vocabulary that helps software designers talk about their designs. When experienced designers discuss the structure of an application, one might say, "I think we should use a Singleton here." *Singleton* is the name of a widely known design pattern, so if both designers are familiar with the pattern, being able to talk about it at this level saves explanation of a lot of detail. Thus, the pattern language introduced by commonly known design patterns introduces another level of abstraction, one that allows us to cope with complexity in ever-more-complex systems.

Software design patterns were made popular by a book published in 1995 that describes a set of patterns, their applications, and benefits.[5] This book is still today one of the most important works about design patterns. Here, we do not attempt to give a complete overview of design patterns. Rather, we discuss a small number of patterns to give readers an impression of the benefits of using design patterns, and then we leave it up to the reader to continue the study of patterns in other literature.

13.7.1 Structure of a pattern

Descriptions of patterns are usually recorded using a template that contains some minimum information. A pattern description is not only information about a structure of some classes, but also includes a description of the problem(s) this pattern addresses and competing forces for or against use of the pattern.

A description of a pattern includes at least:

- a **name** that can be used to conveniently talk about the pattern
- a description of the **problem** that the pattern addresses (often split into sections such as *intent*, *motivation*, and *applicability*)
- a description of the **solution** (often listing *structure*, *participants*, and *collaborations*)
- the **consequences** of using the pattern, including results and trade-offs

In the following section, we shall briefly discuss some commonly used patterns.

---

[5] *Design Patterns: Elements of Reusable Object-Oriented Software* by Erich Gamma, Richard Helm, Ralph Johnson, and John Vlissides, Addison-Wesley, 1995.

13.7.2 Decorator

The *Decorator* pattern deals with the problem of adding functionality to an existing object. We assume that we want an object that responds to the same method calls (has the same interface) as the existing object but has added or altered behavior. We may also want to add to the existing interface.

One way this could be done is by inheritance. A subclass may override the implementation of methods and add additional methods. But using inheritance is a static solution: once created, objects cannot change their behavior.

A more dynamic solution is the use of a Decorator object. The Decorator is an object that encloses an existing object and can be used instead of the original (it usually implements the same interface). Clients then communicate with the Decorator instead of with the original object directly (without a need to know about this substitution). The Decorator passes the method calls on to the enclosed object, but it may perform additional actions. We can find an example in the Java input/output library. There, a `BufferedReader` is used as a Decorator for a `Reader` (Figure 13.2). The `BufferedReader` implements the same interface and can be used instead of an unbuffered `Reader`, but it adds to the basic behavior of a `Reader`. In contrast to using inheritance, decorators can be added to existing objects.

Figure 13.2
Structure of the
decorator pattern

13.7.3 Singleton

A common situation in many programs is to have an object of which there should be only a single instance. In our *world-of-zuul* game, for instance, we want only a single parser. If we write a software development environment, we might want only a single compiler or a single debugger.

The *Singleton* pattern ensures that only one instance will be created from a class, and it provides unified access to it. In Java, a Singleton can be defined by making the constructor private. This ensures that it cannot be called from outside the class, and thus client classes cannot create new instances. We can then write code in the Singleton class itself to create a single instance and provide access to it (Code 13.1 illustrates this for a `Parser` class).

Code 13.1
The Singleton pattern

```
public class Parser
{
    private static Parser instance = new Parser();

    public static Parser getInstance()
```

```
    {
        return instance;
    }

    private Parser()
    {
        ...
    }
}
```

In this pattern:

- The constructor is private so that instances can be created only by the class itself. This has to be in a static part of the class (initializations of static fields or static methods), because no instance will otherwise exist.

- A private static field is defined and initialized with the (sole) instance of the parser.

- A static getInstance method is defined, which provides access to the single instance.

Clients of the Singleton can now use that static method to gain access to the parser object:

```
Parser parser = Parser.getInstance();
```

13.7.4 Factory method

The *Factory method* pattern provides an interface for creating objects but lets subclasses decide which specific class of object is created. Typically, the client expects a superclass or an interface of the actual object's dynamic type, and the factory method provides specializations.

Iterators of collections are an example of this technique. If we have a variable of type Collection, we can ask it for an Iterator object (using the iterator method) and then work with that iterator (Code 13.2). The iterator method in this example is the Factory method.

```
public void process(Collection<Type> coll)
{
    Iterator<Type> it = coll.iterator();
    ...
}
```

From the client's point of view (in the code shown in Code 13.2), we are dealing with objects of type Collection and Iterator. In reality, the (dynamic) type of the collection may be ArrayList, in which case the iterator method returns an object of type ArrayListIterator. Or it may be a HashSet, and iterator returns a HashSetIterator. The Factory method is specialized in subclasses to return specialized instances to the "official" return type.

We can make good use of this pattern in our *foxes-and-rabbits* simulation, to decouple the Simulator class from the specific animal classes. (Remember: In our version, Simulator was coupled to classes `Fox` and `Rabbit`, because it creates the initial instances.) Instead, we can introduce an interface `ActorFactory` and classes implementing this interface for each actor (for example, `FoxFactory` and `RabbitFactory`). The `Simulator` would simply store a collection of `ActorFactory` objects, and it would ask each of them to produce a number of actors. Each factory would, of course, produce a different kind of actor, but the `Simulator` talks to them via the `ActorFactory` interface.

13.7.5   Observer

In the discussions of several of the projects in this book, we have tried to separate the internal model of the application from the way it is presented on screen (the view). The *Observer* pattern provides one way of achieving this model/view separation.

More generally, the Observer pattern defines a one-to-many relationship so that when one object changes its state, many others can be notified. It achieves this with a very low degree of coupling between the observers and the observed object.

We can see from this that the Observer pattern not only supports a decoupled view on the model, but it also allows for multiple different views (either as alternatives or simultaneously). As an example, we can again use our *foxes-and-rabbits* simulation.

In the simulation, we presented the animal populations on screen in a two-dimensional animated grid. There are other possibilities. We might have preferred to show the population as a graph of population numbers along a timeline or as an animated bar chart (Figure 13.3). We might even like to see all representations at the same time.

Figure 13.3
Multiple views of one subject

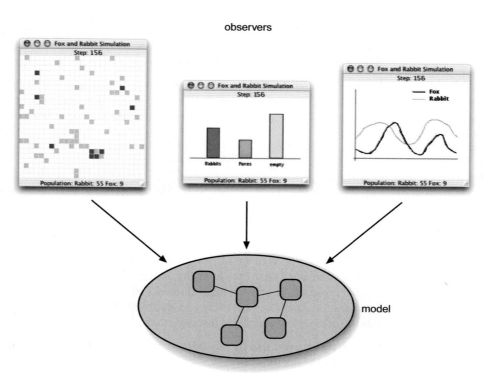

For the Observer pattern, we use two types: Observable and Observer.[6] The observable entity (the Field in our simulation) extends the Observable class, and the observer (SimulatorView) implements the Observer interface (Figure 13.4).

Figure 13.4
Structure of the
Observer pattern

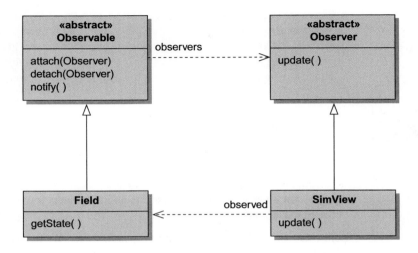

The Observable class provides methods for observers to attach themselves to the observed entity. It ensures that the observers' update method is called whenever the observed entity (the field) invokes its inherited notify method. The actual observers (the viewers) can then get a new, updated state from the field and redisplay.

The Observer pattern can also be used for problems other than a model/view separation. It can always be applied when the state of one or more objects depends on the state of another object.

13.7.6 Pattern summary

Discussing design patterns and their applications in detail is beyond the scope of this book. Here, we have presented only a brief idea of what design patterns are, and we have given an informal description of some of the more common patterns.

We hope, however, that this discussion serves to show where to go from here. Once we understand how to create good implementations of single classes with well-defined functionality, we can concentrate on deciding what kinds of classes we should have in our application and how they should cooperate. Good solutions are not always obvious, so design patterns describe structures that have proven useful over and over again for solving recurring classes of problems. They help us in creating good class structures.

The more experienced you get as a software developer, the more time you will spend thinking about higher-level structure rather than about implementation of single methods.

---

[6] In the Java java.util package, Observer is actually an interface with a single method, update.

Exercise 13.16 Three further, commonly used patterns are the *State* pattern, the *Strategy* pattern, and the *Visitor* pattern. Find descriptions of each of these, and identify at least one example application for each.

Exercise 13.17 Late in the development of a project, you find that two teams who have been working independently on two parts of an application have implemented incompatible classes. The interface of several classes implemented by one team is slightly different from the interface the other team is expecting to use. Explain how the *Adapter* pattern might help in this situation by avoiding the need to rewrite any of the existing classes.

13.8 Summary

In this chapter, we have moved up one step in terms of abstraction levels, away from thinking about the design of single classes (or cooperation between two classes) and toward the design of an application as a whole. Central to the design of an object-oriented software system is the decision about the classes to use for its implementation and the communication structures between these classes.

Some classes are fairly obvious and easy to discover. We have used as a starting point a method of identifying nouns and verbs in a textual description of the problem. After discovering the classes, we can use CRC cards and played-out scenarios to design the dependences and communication details between classes and to flesh out details about each class's responsibilities. For less-experienced designers, it helps to play through scenarios in a group.

CRC cards can be used to refine the design down to the definition of method names and their parameters. Once this has been achieved, classes with method stubs can be coded in Java and the classes' interfaces can be documented.

Following an organized process such as this one serves several purposes. It ensures that potential problems with early design ideas are discovered before much time is invested in implementation. It also enables programmers to work on the implementation of several classes independently, without having to wait for the implementation of one class to be finished before implementation of another can begin.

Flexible, extendible class structures are not always easy to design. Design patterns are used to document generally good structures that have proven useful in the implementation of different classes of problems. Through the study of design patterns, a software engineer can learn a lot about good application structures and improve application design skills.

The larger a problem, the more important is a good application structure. The more experienced a software engineer becomes, the more time he or she will spend designing application structures rather than just writing code.

Terms introduced in this chapter

analysis and design, verb/noun method, CRC card, scenario, use case, method stub, design pattern

Concept summary

- **verb/noun** Classes in a system roughly correspond to nouns in the system's description. Methods correspond to verbs.

- **scenarios** Scenarios (also known as "use cases") can be used to get an understanding of the interactions in a system.

- **prototyping** Prototyping is the construction of a partially working system in which some functions of the application are simulated. It serves to provide an understanding early in the development process of how the system will work.

- **design pattern** A design pattern is a description of a common computing problem and a description of a small set of classes and their interaction structure that helps to solve that problem.

Exercise 13.18 Assume that you have a school management system for your school. In it, there is a class called `Database` (a fairly central class) that holds objects of type `Student`. Each student has an address that is held in an `Address` object (i.e., each `Student` object holds a reference to an `Address` object).

Now, from the `Database` class, you need to get access to a student's street, city, and zip code. The `Address` class has accessor methods for these. For the design of the `Student` class, you now have two choices:

Either you implement `getStreet`, `getCity`, and `getZipCode` methods in the `Student` class—which just pass the method call on to the `Address` object and hand the result back—or you implement a `getAddress` method in `Student` that returns the complete `Address` object to the `Database` and lets the `Database` object call the `Address` object's methods directly.

Which of these alternatives is better? Why? Make a class diagram for each situation and list arguments either way.

CHAPTER

14

A case study

Main concepts discussed in this chapter:

■ whole-application development

Java constructs discussed in this chapter:

(No new Java constructs are introduced in this chapter.)

In this chapter, we draw together many of the object-oriented principles that we have introduced in this book by presenting an extended case study. We shall take the study from the initial discussion of a problem, through class discovery, design, and an iterative process of implementation and testing. Unlike previous chapters, it is not our intention here to introduce any major new topics. Rather, we are seeking to reinforce those topics that have been covered in the second half of the book, such as inheritance, abstraction techniques, error handling, and application design.

14.1 The case study

The case study we will be using is the development of a model for a taxi company. The company is considering whether to expand its operations into a new part of a city. It operates taxis and shuttles. Taxis drop their passengers at their target locations before taking on new passengers, whereas shuttles may collect several passengers from different locations on the same trip, taking them to similar locations (such as collecting several guests from different hotels and taking them to different terminals at the airport). Based on estimates of the number of potential customers in the new area, the company wishes to know whether an expansion would be profitable and how many cabs it would need there in order to operate effectively.

14.1.1 The problem description

The following paragraph presents an informal description of the taxi company's operating procedures, arrived at following several meetings with them.

The company operates both individual taxis and shuttles. The taxis are used to transport an individual (or small group) from one location to another. The shuttles are used to pick up individuals from different locations and transport them to their several destinations. When the company receives a call from an individual, hotel, entertainment venue, or tourist organization, it tries to schedule a vehicle to pick up the fare. If it has no free vehicles, it does not operate any form of queuing system. When a vehicle arrives at a pickup location, the driver notifies the company. Similarly, when a passenger is dropped off at their destination, the driver notifies the company.

As we suggested in Chapter 10, one of the common purposes of modeling is to help us learn something about the situation being modeled. It is useful to identify at an early stage what we wish to learn, because the resulting goals may well have an influence on the design we produce. For instance, if we are seeking to answer questions about the profitability of running taxis in this area, then we must ensure that we can obtain information from the model that will help us assess profitability. Two issues we ought to consider, therefore, are: how often potential customers are lost because no vehicle is available to collect them and, at the opposite extreme, how much time taxis remain idle for lack of passengers. These influences are not found in the basic description of how the taxi company normally operates, but they do represent scenarios that will have to be played through when we draw up the design.

So we might add the following paragraph to the description:

The system stores details about passenger requests that cannot be satisfied. It also provides details of how much time vehicles spend in each of the following activities: carrying passengers, going to pickup locations, and being idle.

However, as we develop our model, we shall focus on just the original description of the company's operating procedures and leave the additional features as exercises.

Exercise 14.1 Is there any additional data that you feel it would be useful to gather from the model? If so, add these requirements to the descriptions given above and use them in your own extensions to the project.

14.2 Analysis and design

As suggested in Chapter 13, we will start by seeking to identify the classes and interactions in the system's description, using the verb/noun method.

14.2.1 Discovering classes

The following (singular versions of) nouns are present in the description: company, taxi, shuttle, individual, location, destination, hotel, entertainment venue, tourist organization, vehicle, fare, pickup location, driver, and passenger.

The first point to note is that it would be a mistake to move straight from this list of nouns to a set of classes. Informal descriptions are rarely written in a way that suits that sort of direct mapping.

One refinement that is commonly needed in the list of nouns is to identify any *synonyms*: different words used for the same entity. For instance, "individual" and "fare" are both synonyms for "passenger."

A further refinement is to eliminate those entities that do not really need to be modeled in the system. For instance, the description identified various ways in which the taxi company might be contacted: by individuals, hotels, entertainment venues, and tourist organizations. Will it really be necessary to maintain these distinctions? The answer will depend upon the information we want from the model. We might wish to arrange discounts for hotels that provide large numbers of customers or send publicity material to entertainment venues that do not. If this level of detail is not required, then we can simplify the model by just "injecting" passengers into it according to some statistically reasonable pattern.

Exercise 14.2 Consider simplifying the number of nouns associated with the vehicles. Are "vehicle" and "taxi" synonyms in this context? Do we need to distinguish between "shuttle" and "taxi"? What about between the type of vehicle and "driver"? Justify your answers.

Exercise 14.3 Is it possible to eliminate any of the following as synonyms in this context: "location," "destination," and "pickup location"?

Exercise 14.4 Identify the nouns from any extensions you have added to the system, and make any necessary simplifications.

14.2.2   Using CRC cards

Figure 14.1 contains a summary of the noun and verb associations we are left with once some simplification has been performed on the original description. Each of the nouns should now be assigned to a CRC card, ready to have its responsibilities and collaborators identified.

Figure 14.1
Noun and verb associations in the taxi company

Nouns	**Verbs**
company	*operates taxis and shuttles*
	receives a call
	schedules a vehicle
taxi	*transports a passenger*
shuttle	*transports one or more passengers*
passenger	
location	
passenger-source	*calls the company*
vehicle	*picks up passenger*
	arrives at pickup location
	notifies company of arrival
	notifies company of drop-off

From that summary, it is clear that "taxi" and "shuttle" are distinct specializations of a more general vehicle class. The main distinction between a taxi and a shuttle is that a taxi is only ever concerned with picking up and transporting a single passenger or coherent group, but a shuttle deals with multiple *independent* passengers concurrently. The relationship between these two vehicles is suggestive of an inheritance hierarchy, where "taxi" and "shuttle" represent subtypes of vehicle.

> **Exercise 14.5** Create physical CRC cards for the nouns/classes identified in this section, in order to be able to work through the scenarios suggested by the project description.
>
> **Exercise 14.6** Do the same for any of your own extensions you wish to follow through in the next stage.

14.2.3 Scenarios

The taxi company does not actually represent a very complex application. We shall find that much of the total interaction in the system is explored by taking the fundamental scenario of trying to satisfy a passenger request to go from one location in the city to another. In practice, this single scenario will be broken down into a number of steps that are followed in sequence, from the initial call to the final drop-off.

■ We have decided that a passenger source creates all new passenger objects for the system. So a responsibility of PassengerSource is *Create a Passenger*, and a collaborator is Passenger.

■ The passenger source calls the taxi company to request a pickup for a passenger. We note TaxiCompany as a collaborator of PassengerSource and add *Request a pickup* as a responsibility. Correspondingly, we add to TaxiCompany a responsibility to *Receive a pickup request*. Associated with the request will be a passenger and a pickup location. So TaxiCompany has Passenger and Location as collaborators. When it calls the company with the request, the passenger source could pass the passenger and pickup location as separate objects. However, it is preferable to associate closely the pickup location with the passenger. So a collaborator of Passenger is Location, and a responsibility will be *Provide pickup location*.

■ From where does the passenger's pickup location originate? The pickup location and destination could be decided when the Passenger is created. So add to PassengerSource the responsibility *Generate pickup and destination locations for a passenger*, with Location as a collaborator; and add to Passenger the responsibilities *Receive pickup and destination locations* and *Provide destination location*.

■ On receipt of a request, the TaxiCompany has a responsibility to *Schedule a vehicle*. This suggests that a further responsibility is *Store a collection of vehicles*, with Collection and Vehicle as collaborators. Because the request might fail—there may be no vehicles free—a success or failure indication should be returned to the passenger source.

■ There is no indication whether the company seeks to distinguish between taxis and shuttles when scheduling, so we do not need to take that aspect into account here. However, a vehicle can be scheduled only if it is free. This means that a responsibility of Vehicle will be *Indicate whether free*.

■ When a free vehicle has been identified, it must be directed to the pickup location. TaxiCompany has the responsibility *Direct vehicle to pickup*, with the corresponding responsibility in Vehicle being *Receive pickup location*. Location is added as a collaborator of Vehicle.

■ On receipt of a pickup location, the behavior of taxis and shuttles may well differ. A taxi will have been free only if it was not already on its way to either a pickup or a destination location. So the responsibility of Taxi is *Go to pickup location*. In contrast, a shuttle has to deal with multiple passengers. When it receives a pickup location, it may have to choose between several possible alternative locations to head to next. So we add the responsibility to Shuttle to *Choose next target location*, with a Collection collaborator to maintain the set of possible target locations to choose from. The fact that a Vehicle moves between locations suggests that it has a responsibility to *Maintain a current location*.

■ On arrival at a pickup location, a Vehicle must *Notify the company of pickup arrival*, with TaxiCompany as a collaborator; TaxiCompany must *Receive notification of pickup arrival*. In real life, a taxi meets its passenger for the first time when it arrives at the pickup location, so this is the natural point for the vehicle to receive its next passenger. In the model, it does so from the company, which received it originally from the passenger source. TaxiCompany responsibility: *Pass passenger to vehicle*; Vehicle responsibility: *Receive passenger*, with Passenger added as a collaborator to Vehicle.

■ The vehicle now requests the passenger's intended destination. Vehicle responsibility: *Request destination location*; Passenger responsibility: *Provide destination location*. Once again, at this point the behavior of taxis and shuttles will differ. A Taxi will simply *Go to passenger destination*. A shuttle will *Add location to collection of target locations* and choose the next one.

■ On arrival at a passenger's destination, a Vehicle has responsibilities to *Offload passenger* and *Notify the company of passenger arrival*. The TaxiCompany must *Receive notification of passenger arrival*.

The steps we have outlined represent the fundamental activity of the taxi company, repeated over and over as each new passenger requests the service. An important point to note, however, is that our computer model needs to be able to restart the sequence for each new passenger as soon as each fresh request is received, even if a previous request has not yet run to completion. In other words, within a single step of the program, one vehicle could still be heading to a pickup location while another could be arriving at a passenger's destination, and a new passenger might be requesting a pickup.

Exercise 14.7 Review the problem description and the scenario we have worked through. Are there any further scenarios that need to be addressed before we move on to class design? Have we adequately covered what happens, for instance, if there is no vehicle available when a request is received? Complete the scenario analysis if you feel there is more to be done.

Exercise 14.8 Do you feel that we have described the scenario at the correct level of detail? For instance, have we included too little or too much detail in the discussion of the differences between taxis and shuttles?

Exercise 14.9 Do you feel it is necessary to address *how* vehicles move between locations at this stage?

Exercise 14.10 Do you think that a need for further classes will emerge as the application is developed—classes that have no immediate reference in the problem description? If so, why is this the case?

14.3 # Class design

In this section, we shall start to make the move from a high-level abstract design on paper to a concrete outline design within a BlueJ project.

14.3.1 Designing class interfaces

In Chapter 13, we suggested that the next step was to create a fresh set of CRC cards from the first, turning the responsibilities of each class into a set of method signatures. Without wishing to de-emphasize the importance of that step, we shall leave it for you to do and move directly to a BlueJ project outline containing stub classes and methods. This should provide a good feel for the complexity of the project and whether we have missed anything crucial in the steps taken so far.

It is worth pointing out that, at every stage of the project life cycle, we should expect to find errors or loose ends in what we have done in earlier stages. This does not necessarily imply that there are weaknesses in our techniques or abilities. It is more a reflection of the fact that project development is often a discovery process. It is only by exploring and trying things out that we gain a full understanding of what it is we are trying to achieve. So discovering omissions actually says something positive about the process we are using!

14.3.2 Collaborators

Having identified collaborations between classes, one issue that will often need to be addressed is how a particular object obtains references to its collaborators. There are usually three distinct ways in which this happens, and these often represent three different patterns of object interaction:

- A collaborator is received as an argument to a constructor. Such a collaborator will usually be stored in one of the new object's fields so that it is available through the new object's life. The collaborator may be shared in this way with several different objects. Example: A PassengerSource object receives the TaxiCompany object through its constructor.

- A collaborator is received as an argument to a method. Interaction with such a collaborator is usually transitory—just for the period of execution of the method—although the receiving object may choose to store the reference in one of its fields, for longer-term interaction. Example: TaxiCompany receives a Passenger collaborator through its method to handle a pickup request.

- The object constructs the collaborator for itself. The collaborator will be for the exclusive use of the constructing object, unless it is passed to another object in one of the previous two ways. If constructed in a method, the collaboration will usually be short term, for the duration of the block in which it is constructed. However, if the collaborator is stored in a field, then the collaboration is likely to last the full lifetime of the creating object. Example: TaxiCompany creates a collection to store its vehicles.

Exercise 14.11 As the next section discusses the *taxi-company-outline* project, pay particular attention to where objects are created and how collaborating objects get to know about each other. Try to identify at least one further example of each of the patterns we have described.

14.3.3 The outline implementation

The project *taxi-company-outline* contains an outline implementation of the classes, responsibilities, and collaborations that we have described as part of the design process. You are encouraged to browse through the source code and associate the concrete classes with the corresponding descriptions of Section 14.2.3. Code 14.1 shows an outline of the Vehicle class from the project.

Code 14.1

An outline of the
Vehicle class

```java
/**
 * Capture outline details of a vehicle.
 *
 * @author David J. Barnes and Michael Kölling
 * @version 2011.07.31
 */

public abstract class Vehicle
{
    private TaxiCompany company;
    // Where the vehicle is.
    private Location location;
    // Where the vehicle is headed.
    private Location targetLocation;

    /**
     * Constructor of class Vehicle
     * @param company The taxi company. Must not be null.
     * @param location The vehicle's starting point. Must not
     *                 be null.
     * @throws NullPointerException If company or location is
     *                              null.
     */
    public Vehicle(TaxiCompany company, Location location)
    {
        if(company == null) {
            throw new NullPointerException("company");
        }
        if(location == null) {
            throw new NullPointerException("location");
        }
        this.company = company;
        this.location = location;
        targetLocation = null;
    }
```

Code 14.1 continued

An outline of the Vehicle class

```java
/**
 * Notify the company of our arrival at a pickup
 * location.
 */
public void notifyPickupArrival()
{
    company.arrivedAtPickup(this);
}

/**
 * Notify the company of our arrival at a
 * passenger's destination.
 */
public void notifyPassengerArrival(Passenger passenger)
{
    company.arrivedAtDestination(this, passenger);
}

/**
 * Receive a pickup location.
 * How this is handled depends on the type of vehicle.
 * @param location The pickup location.
 */
public abstract void setPickupLocation(Location location);

/**
 * Receive a passenger.
 * How this is handled depends on the type of vehicle.
 * @param passenger The passenger.
 */
public abstract void pickup(Passenger passenger);

/**
 * Get the target location.
 * @return Whether or not this vehicle is free.
 */
public abstract boolean isFree();

/**
 * Offload any passengers whose destination is the
 * current location.
 */
public abstract void offloadPassenger();

/**
 * @return Where this vehicle is currently located.
 */
```

**Code 14.1
continued**

An outline of the
`Vehicle` class

```java
public Location getLocation()
{
    return location;
}

/**
 * Set the current location.
 * @param location Where it is. Must not be null.
 * @throws NullPointerException If location is null.
 */
public void setLocation(Location location)
{
    if(location != null) {
        this.location = location;
    }
    else {
        throw new NullPointerException();
    }
}

/**
 * @return Where this vehicle is currently headed, or
 * null if it is idle.
 */
public Location getTargetLocation()
{
    return targetLocation;
}

/**
 * Set the required target location.
 * @param location Where to go. Must not be null.
 * @throws NullPointerException If location is null.
 */
public void setTargetLocation(Location location)
{
    if (location != null) {
        targetLocation = location;
    }
    else {
        throw new NullPointerException();
    }
}

/**
 * Clear the target location.
 */
```

Code 14.1 continued

An outline of the `Vehicle` class

```
public void clearTargetLocation()
{
    targetLocation = null;
}
}
```

The process of creating the outline project raised a number of issues. Here are some of them:

■ You should expect to find some differences between the design and the implementation, owing to the different natures of design and implementation languages. For instance, discussion of the scenarios suggested that `PassengerSource` should have the responsibility *Generate pickup and destination locations for a passenger*, and `Passenger` should have the responsibility *Receive pickup and destination locations*. Rather than mapping these responsibilities to individual method calls, the more natural implementation in Java is to write something like

```
new Passenger(new Location(...), new Location(...))
```

■ We have ensured that our outline project is complete enough to compile successfully. That is not always necessary at this stage, but it does mean that undertaking incremental development at the next stage will be a little easier. However, it does have the corresponding disadvantage of making missing pieces of code potentially harder to spot, because the compiler will not point out the loose ends.

■ The shared and distinct elements of the `Vehicle`, `Taxi`, and `Shuttle` classes only really begin to take shape as we move towards their implementation. For instance, the different ways in which taxis and shuttles respond to a pickup request is reflected in the fact that `Vehicle` defines `setPickupLocation` as an abstract method, which will have separate concrete implementations in the subclasses. On the other hand, even though taxis and shuttles have different ways of deciding where they are heading, they can share the concept of having a single target location. This has been implemented as a `targetLocation` field in the superclass.

■ At two points in the scenario, a vehicle is expected to notify the company of its arrival at either a pickup point or a destination. There are at least two possible ways to organize this in the implementation. The direct way is for a vehicle to store a reference to its company. This would mean that there would be an explicit association between the two classes on the class diagram.

An alternative is to use the *Observer* pattern introduced in Chapter 13, with `Vehicle` extending the `Observable` class and `TaxiCompany` implementing the `Observer` interface. Direct coupling between `Vehicle` and `TaxiCompany` is reduced, but implicit coupling is still involved, and the notification process is a little more complex to program.

■ Up to this point, there has been no discussion about how many passengers a shuttle can carry. Presumably there could be different-sized shuttles. This aspect of the application has been deferred until a later resolution.

There is no absolute rule about exactly how far to go with the outline implementation in any particular application. The purpose of the outline implementation is not to create a fully working project, but to record the design of the outline structure of the application (which has been developed through the CRC card activities earlier). As you review the classes in the *taxi-company-outline* project, you may feel that we have gone too far in this case, or maybe even not far enough. On the positive side, by attempting to create a version that at least compiles, we certainly found that we were forced to think about the Vehicle inheritance hierarchy in some detail: in particular, which methods could be implemented in full in the superclass and which were best left as abstract. On the negative side, there is always the risk of making implementation decisions too early: for instance, committing to particular sorts of data structures that might be better left until later or, as we did here, choosing to reject the *Observer* pattern in favor of the more direct approach.

Exercise 14.12 For each of the classes in the project, look at the class interface and write a list of JUnit tests that should be used to test the functionality of the class.

Exercise 14.13 The *taxi-company-outline* project defines a Demo class to create a pair of PassengerSource and TaxiCompany objects. Create a Demo object and try its pickup-Test method. Why is the TaxiCompany object unable to grant a pickup request at this stage?

Exercise 14.14 Do you feel that we should have developed the source code further at this stage, to enable at least one pickup request to succeed? If so, how much further would you have taken the development?

14.3.4   Testing

Having made a start on implementation, we should not go too much further before we start to consider how we shall test the application. We do not want to make the mistake of devising tests only once the full implementation is complete. We can already put some tests in place that will gradually evolve as the implementation is evolved. Try the following exercises to get a feel for what is possible at this early stage.

Exercise 14.15 The *taxi-company-outline-testing* project includes some simple initial JUnit tests. Try them out. Add any further tests you feel are appropriate at this stage of the development, to form the basis of a set of tests to be used during future development. Does it matter if the tests we create fail at this stage?

Exercise 14.16 The Location class currently contains no fields or methods. How is further development of this class likely to affect existing test classes?

14.3.5   Some remaining issues

One of the major issues that we have not attempted to tackle yet is how to organize the sequencing of the various activities: passenger requests, vehicle movements, and so on. Another is that locations have not been given a detailed concrete form, so movement has no effect. As we further develop the application, resolutions of these issues and others will emerge.

14.4 **Iterative development**

We obviously still have quite a long way to go from the outline implementation developed in *taxi-company-outline* to the final version. However, rather than being overwhelmed by the magnitude of the overall task, we can make things more manageable by identifying some discrete steps to take toward the ultimate goal and undertaking a process of iterative development.

14.4.1 Development steps

Planning some development steps helps us to consider how we might break up a single large problem into several smaller problems. Individually, these smaller problems are likely to be both less complex and more manageable than the one big problem, but together they should combine to form the whole. As we seek to solve the smaller problems, we might find that we need to also break up some of them. In addition, we might find that some of our original assumptions were wrong or that our design is inadequate in some way. This process of discovery, when combined with an iterative development approach, means that we obtain valuable feedback on our design and on the decisions we make, at an early enough stage for us to be able to incorporate it back into a flexible and evolving process.

Considering what steps to break the overall problem into has the added advantage of helping to identify some of the ways in which the various parts of the application are interconnected. In a large project, this process helps us to identify the interfaces between components. Identifying steps also helps in planning the timing of the development process.

It is important that each step in an iterative development represent a clearly identifiable point in the evolution of the application toward the overall requirements. In particular, we need to be able to determine when each step has been completed. Completion should be marked by the passing of a set of tests and a review of the step's achievements, so as to be able to incorporate any lessons learned into the steps that follow.

Here is a possible series of development steps for the taxi company application:

- Enable a single passenger to be picked up and taken to their destination by a single taxi.
- Provide sufficient taxis to enable multiple independent passengers to be picked up and taken to their destinations concurrently.
- Enable a single passenger to be picked up and taken to their destination by a single shuttle.
- Ensure that details are recorded of passengers for whom there is no free vehicle.
- Enable a single shuttle to pick up multiple passengers and carry them concurrently to their destinations.
- Provide a GUI to display the activities of all active vehicles and passengers within the simulation.
- Ensure that taxis and shuttles are able to operate concurrently.
- Provide all remaining functionality, including full statistical data.

We will not discuss the implementation of all of these steps in detail, but we will complete the application to a point where you should be able to add the remaining functionality for yourself.

> **Exercise 14.17** Critically assess the list of steps we have outlined, with the following questions in mind. Do you feel the order is appropriate? Is the level of complexity of each too high, too low, or just right? Are there any steps missing? Revise the list as you see fit, to suit your own view of the project.
>
> **Exercise 14.18** Are the completion criteria (tests on completion) for each stage sufficiently obvious? If so, document some tests for each.

14.4.2 A first stage

For the first stage, we want to be able to create a single passenger, have them picked up by a single taxi, and have them delivered to their destination. This means that we shall have to work on a number of different classes: Location, Taxi, and TaxiCompany, for certain, and possibly others. In addition, we shall have to arrange for simulated time to pass as the taxi moves within the city. This suggests that we might be able to reuse some of the ideas involving actors that we saw in Chapter 10.

The *taxi-company-stage-one* project contains an implementation of the requirements of this first stage. The classes have been developed to the point where a taxi picks up and delivers a passenger to their destination. The run method of the Demo class plays out this scenario. However, more important at this stage are really the test classes—LocationTest, PassengerTest, PassengerSourceTest, and TaxiTest—which we discuss in Section 14.4.3.

Rather than discuss this project in detail, we shall simply describe here some of the issues that arose from its development out of the previous outline version. You should supplement this discussion with a thorough reading of the source code.

The goals of the first stage were deliberately set to be quite modest yet still relevant to the fundamental activity of the application—collecting and delivering passengers. There were good reasons for this. By setting a modest goal, the task seemed achievable within a reasonably short time. By setting a relevant goal, the task was clearly taking us closer toward completing the overall project. Such factors help to keep our motivation high.

We have borrowed the concept of actors from the *foxes-and-rabbits* project of Chapter 10. For this stage, only taxis needed to be actors, through their Vehicle superclass. At each step a taxi either moves toward a target location or remains idle (Code 14.2). Although we did not have to record any statistics at this stage, it was simple and convenient to have vehicles record a count of the number of steps for which they are idle. This anticipated part of the work of one of the later stages.

Code 14.2

The Taxi class as an actor

```
/**
 * A taxi is able to carry a single passenger.
 *
 * @author David J. Barnes and Michael Kölling
 * @version 2011.07.31
 */
```

Code 14.2 continued

The Taxi class as an actor

```java
public class Taxi extends Vehicle
{
    private Passenger passenger;

    /**
     * Constructor for objects of class Taxi
     * @param company The taxi company. Must not be null.
     * @param location The vehicle's starting point.
     *                 Must not be null.
     * @throws NullPointerException If company or location is null.
     */
    public Taxi(TaxiCompany company, Location location)
    {
        super(company, location);
    }

    /**
     * Carry out a taxi's actions.
     */
    public void act()
    {
        Location target = getTargetLocation();
        if(target != null) {
            // Find where to move to next.
            Location next = getLocation().nextLocation(target);
            setLocation(next);
            if(next.equals(target)) {
                if(passenger != null) {
                    notifyPassengerArrival(passenger);
                    offloadPassenger();
                }
                else {
                    notifyPickupArrival();
                }
            }
        }
        else {
            incrementIdleCount();
        }
    }

    /**
     * Is the taxi free?
     * @return Whether or not this taxi is free.
     */
```

Code 14.2 continued

The Taxi class as an actor

```java
public boolean isFree()
{
    return getTargetLocation() == null && passenger == null;
}


/**
 * Receive a pickup location. This becomes the
 * target location.
 * @location The pickup location.
 */
public void setPickupLocation(Location location)
{
    setTargetLocation(location);
}


/**
 * Receive a passenger.
 * Set their destination as the target location.
 * @param passenger The passenger.
 */
public void pickup(Passenger passenger)
{
    this.passenger = passenger;
    setTargetLocation(passenger.getDestination());
}


/**
 * Offload the passenger.
 */
public void offloadPassenger()
{
    passenger = null;
    clearTargetLocation();
}


/**
 * Return details of the taxi, such as where it is.
 * @return A string representation of the taxi.
 */
public String toString()
{
    return "Taxi at " + getLocation();
}
}
```

The need to model movement required the Location class to be implemented more fully than in the outline. On the face of it, this should be a relatively simple container for a two-dimensional position within a rectangular grid. However, in practice, it also needs to provide both a test for coincidence of two locations (equals), and a way for a vehicle to find out where to move to next, based on its current location and its destination (nextLocation). At this stage, no limits were put on the grid area (other than that coordinate values should be positive), but this raises the need in a later stage for something to record the boundaries of the area in which the company operates.

One of the major issues that had to be addressed was how to manage the association between a passenger and a vehicle, between the request for a pickup and the point of the vehicle's arrival. Although we were required only to handle a single taxi and a single passenger, we tried to bear in mind that ultimately there could be multiple pickup requests outstanding at any one time. In Section 14.2.3, we had decided that a vehicle should receive its passenger when it notifies the company that it has arrived at the pickup point. So, when a notification is received, the company needs to be able to work out which passenger has been assigned to that vehicle. The solution we chose was to have the company store a *vehicle:passenger* pairing in a map. When the vehicle notifies the company that it has arrived, the company passes the corresponding passenger to it. However, there are various reasons why this solution is not perfect, and we shall explore this issue further in the exercises below.

One error situation we addressed was that there might be no passenger found when a vehicle arrives at a pickup point. This would be the result of a programming error, so we defined the unchecked MissingPassengerException class.

As only a single passenger was required for this stage, development of the PassengerSource class was deferred to a later stage. Instead, passengers were created directly in the Demo and Test classes.

Exercise 14.19 If you have not already done so, take a thorough look through the implementation in the *taxi-company-stage-one* project. Ensure that you understand how movement of the taxi is effected through its act method.

Exercise 14.20 Do you feel that the TaxiCompany object should keep separate lists of those vehicles that are free and those that are not, to improve the efficiency of its scheduling? At what points would a vehicle move between the lists?

Exercise 14.21 The next planned stage of the implementation is to provide multiple taxis to carry multiple passengers concurrently. Review the TaxiCompany class with this goal in mind. Do you feel that it already supports this functionality? If not, what changes are required?

Exercise 14.22 Review the way in which *vehicle:passenger* associations are stored in the assignments' map in TaxiCompany. Can you see any weaknesses in this approach? Does it support more than one passenger being picked up from the same location? Could a vehicle ever need to have multiple associations recorded for it?

> **Exercise 14.23** If you see any problems with the current way in which *vehicle:passenger* associations are stored, would creating a unique identification for each association help—say a "booking number"? If so, would any of the existing method signatures in the `Vehicle` hierarchy need to be changed? Implement an improved version that supports the requirements of all existing scenarios.

14.4.3 Testing the first stage

As part of the implementation of the first stage, we have developed two test classes: `LocationTest` and `TaxiTest`. The first checks basic functionality of the `Location` class that is crucial to correct movement of vehicles. The second is designed to test that a passenger is picked up and delivered to their destination in the correct number of steps and that the taxi becomes free again immediately afterwards. In order to develop the second set of tests, the `Location` class was enhanced with the `distance` method, to provide the number of steps required to move between two locations.[1]

In normal operation, the application runs silently, and without a GUI there is no visual way to monitor the progress of a taxi. One approach would be to add print statements to the core methods of classes such as `Taxi` and `TaxiCompany`. However, BlueJ does offer the alternative of setting a breakpoint within the `act` method of, say, the `Taxi` class. This would make it possible to "observe" the movement of a taxi by inspection.

Having reached a reasonable level of confidence in the current state of the implementation, we have simply left print statements in the notification methods of `TaxiCompany` to provide a minimum of user feedback.

As testimony to the value of developing tests alongside implementation, it is worth recording that the existing test classes enabled us to identify and correct two serious errors in our code.

> **Exercise 14.24** Review the tests implemented in the test classes of *taxi-company-stage-one*. Should it be possible to use these as regression tests during the next stages, or would they require substantial changes?

> **Exercise 14.25** Implement additional tests and further test classes that you feel are necessary to increase your level of confidence in the current implementation. Fix any errors you discover in the process of doing this.

14.4.4 A later stage of development

It is not our intention to discuss in full the completion of the development of the taxi company application, as there would be little for you to gain from that. Instead, we shall briefly present the application at a later stage, and we encourage you to complete the rest from there.

This more advanced stage can be found in the *taxi-company-later-stage* project. It handles multiple taxis and passengers, and a GUI provides a progressive view of the movements of both (Figure 14.2). Here is an outline of some of the major developments in this version from the previous one.

---

[1] We anticipate that this will have an extended use later in the development of the application as it should enable the company to schedule vehicles on the basis of which is closest to the pickup point.

Figure 14.2

A visualization of
the city

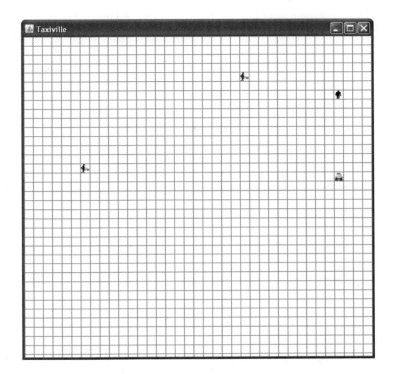

- A `Simulation` class now manages the actors, much as it did in the *foxes-and-rabbits* `project`. The actors are the vehicles, the passenger source, and a GUI provided by the `CityGUI` class. After each step, the simulation pauses for a brief period so that the GUI does not change too quickly.

- The need for something like the `City` class was identified during development of stage one. The `City` object defines the dimensions of the city's grid and holds a collection of all the items of interest that are in the city—the vehicles and the passengers.

- Items in the city may optionally implement the `DrawableItem` interface, which allows the GUI to display them. Images of vehicles and people are provided in the `images` folder within the project folder for this purpose.

- The Taxi class implements the `DrawableItem` interface. It returns alternative images to the GUI, depending on whether it is occupied or empty. Image files exist in the `images` folder for a shuttle to do the same.

- The `PassengerSource` class has been refactored significantly from the previous version, to better fit its role as an actor. In addition, it maintains a count of missed pickups for statistical analysis.

- The `TaxiCompany` class is responsible for creating the taxis to be used in the simulation.

As you explore the source code of the *taxi-company-later-stage* project, you will find illustrations of many of the topics we have covered in the second half of this book: inheritance, polymorphism, abstract classes, interfaces, and error handling.

Exercise 14.26 Add assertion and exception-throwing consistency checks within each class, to guard against inappropriate use. For instance, ensure that a `Passenger` is never created with pickup and destination locations that are the same; ensure that a taxi is never requested to go to a pickup when it already has a target location; etc.

Exercise 14.27 Report on the statistical information that is being gathered by taxis and the passenger source; also on taxi idle time and missed pickups. Experiment with different numbers of taxis to see how the balance between these two sets of data varies.

Exercise 14.28 Adapt the vehicle classes so that records are kept of the amount of time spent traveling to pickup locations and passenger destinations. Can you see a possible conflict here for shuttles?

14.4.5 Further ideas for development

The version of the application provided in the *taxi-company-later-stage* project represents a significant point in the development toward full implementation. However, there is still a lot that can be added. For instance, we have hardly developed the `Shuttle` class at all, so there are plenty of challenges to be found in completing its implementation. The major difference between shuttles and taxis is that a shuttle has to be concerned with multiple passengers, whereas a taxi has to be concerned with only one. The fact that a shuttle is already carrying a passenger should not prevent it from being sent to pick up another. Similarly, if it is already on its way to a pickup, it could still accept a further pickup request. These issues raise questions about how a shuttle organizes its priorities. Could a passenger end up being driven back and forth while the shuttle responds to competing requests, the passenger never getting delivered? What does it mean for a shuttle not to be free? Does it mean that it is full of passengers or that it has enough pickup requests to fill it? Suppose at least one of those pickups will reach their destination before the final pickup is reached: Does that mean it could accept more pickup requests than its capacity?!

Another area for further development is vehicle scheduling. The taxi company does not operate particularly intelligently at present. How should it decide which vehicle to send when there may be more than one available? No attempt is made to assign vehicles on the basis of their distance from a pickup location. The company could use the `distance` method of the `Location` class to work out which is the nearest free vehicle to a pickup. Would this make a significant difference to the average waiting time of passengers? How might data be gathered on how long passengers wait to be picked up? What about having idle taxis move to a central location, ready for their next pickup, in order to reduce potential waiting times? Does the size of the city have an impact on the effectiveness of this approach? For instance, in a large city, is it better to have idle taxis space themselves out from one another rather than have all gather at the center?

Could the simulation be used to model competing taxi companies operating in the same area of the city? Multiple `TaxiCompany` objects could be created and the passenger source allocate passengers to them competitively on the basis of how quickly they could be picked up. Is this too fundamental a change to graft onto the existing application?

14.4.6 Reuse

Currently, our goal has been to simulate the operation of vehicles in order to assess the commercial viability of expanding a business into a new area of the city. You may have noticed that substantial parts of the application may actually be useful once the expansion is in operation.

Assuming that we develop a clever scheduling algorithm for our simulation to decide which vehicle should take which call or that we have worked out a good scheme for deciding where to send the vehicles to wait while they are idle, we might decide to use the same algorithms when the company actually operates in the new area. The visual representation of each vehicle's location could also help.

In other words, there is potential to turn the simulation of the taxi company into a taxi management system used to help the real company in its operations. The structure of the application would change, of course: the program would not control and move the taxis, but rather record their positions, which it might receive from GPS (global positioning system) receivers in each vehicle. However, many of the classes developed for the simulation could be reused with little or no change. This illustrates the power of reuse that we gain from good class structure and class design.

14.5 Another example

There are many other projects that you could undertake along similar lines to the taxi company application. A popular alternative is the issue of how to schedule elevators in a large building. Coordination between elevators becomes particularly significant here. In addition, within an enclosed building, it may be possible to estimate numbers of people on each floor and hence to anticipate demand. There are also time-related behaviors to take account of: morning arrivals, evening departures, and local peaks of activity around lunchtimes.

Use the approach we have outlined in this chapter to implement a simulation of a building with one or more elevators.

14.6 Taking things further

We can only take you so far by presenting our own project ideas and showing you how we would develop them. You will find that you can go much further if you develop your own ideas for projects and implement them in your own way. Pick a topic that interests you, and work through the stages we have outlined: analyze the problem, work out some scenarios, sketch out a design, plan some implementation stages, and then make a start.

Designing and implementing programs is an exciting and creative activity. Like any worthwhile activity, it takes time and practice to become proficient at it. So do not become discouraged if your early efforts seem to take forever or are full of errors. That is normal, and you will gradually improve with experience. Do not be too ambitious to start with, and expect to have to rework your ideas as you go; that is all part of the natural learning process.

Most of all: Have fun!

Working with a BlueJ Project

A.1 Installing BlueJ

To work with BlueJ, you must install a Java Development Kit (JDK) and the BlueJ environment.

You can find the JDK and detailed installation instructions on this book's CD or at `http://www.oracle.com/technetwork/java/javase/overview/index.html`

You can find the BlueJ environment and installation instructions on this book's CD or at `http://www.bluej.org`

A.2 Opening a project

To use any of the example projects included on this book's CD, the projects must be copied to a writable disk. BlueJ projects can be opened but not executed from a CD (to execute, BlueJ needs to write to the project folder). Therefore, it does not usually work to use projects from the CD directly.

The easiest way is to copy the folder containing all of the book's projects (named *projects*) to your hard disk. After installing and starting BlueJ by double-clicking its icon, select *Open ...* from the *Project* menu. Navigate to the *projects* folder and select a project. (You can have multiple projects open at the same time.) Each project folder contains a `bluej.project` file that, when associated with BlueJ, can be double-clicked to open a project directly.

More information about the use of BlueJ is included in the BlueJ Tutorial. The tutorial is on the book's CD, and it is also accessible via the *BlueJ Tutorial* item in BlueJ's *Help* menu.

A.3 The BlueJ debugger

Information on using the BlueJ debugger may be found in Appendix F and in the BlueJ Tutorial. The tutorial is on the book's CD, and it is also accessible via the *BlueJ Tutorial* item in BlueJ's *Help* menu.

A.4 CD contents

On the CD that is included in this book, you will find the following files and directories:

Folder	Comment
bluej/	*The BlueJ system and documentation.*
bluejsetup-305.exe	*BlueJ installer for Microsoft Windows (all versions).*
BlueJ-305.zip	*BlueJ for Mac OS X.*
bluej-305.deb	*BlueJ for Debian-based systems (Debian, Ubuntu).*
bluej-305.jar	*BlueJ for other systems.*
tutorial.pdf	*The BlueJ Tutorial.*
testing-tutorial.pdf	*A tutorial introducing the testing tools.*
teamwork-tutorial.pdf	*The tutorial for use of team work tools.*
repository-setup.pdf	*Information about setting up a CVS or Subversion repository for team work support.*
ReadMe.htm	*CD documentation. Open this file in a web browser to read it. Contains CD content overview, installation instructions, and other useful pointers.*
jdk/	*Contains Java systems (JDK) for various operating systems.*
linux/	*JDK installer for Linux.*
solaris/	*JDK installer for Solaris.*
windows/	*JDK installer for Microsoft Windows (all versions).*
jdk-doc/	*Contains the Java library documentation. This is a single zip file. Copy this file to your hard disk and uncompress to use the documentation.*
projects/	*Contains all projects discussed in this book. Copy this complete folder to your hard disk before using the projects. Contains subfolders for each chapter.*

A.5 Configuring BlueJ

Many of the settings of BlueJ can be configured to better suit your personal situation. Some configuration options are available through the *Preferences* dialog in the BlueJ system, but many more configuration options are accessible by editing the "BlueJ definitions file." The location of that file is *<bluej_home>/lib/bluej.defs*, where *<bluej_home>* is the folder where the BlueJ system is installed.[1]

Configuration details are explained in the "Tips archive" on the BlueJ web site. You can access it at

```
http://www.bluej.org/help/archive.html
```

---

[1] On Mac OS, the *bluej.defs* file is inside the application bundle. See the "Tips archive" for instructions how to find it.

Following are some of the most common things people like to configure. Many more configuration options can be found by reading the `bluej.defs` file.

A.6 Changing the interface language

You can change the interface language to one of several available languages. To do this, open the `bluej.defs` file and find the line that reads

```
bluej.language=english
```

Change it to one of the other available languages. For example:

```
bluej.language=spanish
```

Comments in the file list all available languages. They include at least Afrikaans, Catalan, Chinese, Czech, Danish, Dutch, English, French, German, Greek, Italian, Japanese, Korean, Portuguese, Russian, Slovak, Spanish, and Swedish.

A.7 Using local API documentation

You can use a local copy of the Java class library (API) documentation. That way, access to the documentation is faster and you can use the documentation without being online. To do this, copy the Java documentation file from the book's CD (a zip file) and unzip it at a location where you want to store the Java documentation. This will create a folder named *jdk-7-api-doc*.

Then open a web browser, and, using the *Open File* .... (or equivalent) function, open the file *index.html* inside this folder. Once the API view is correctly displayed in the browser, copy the URL (web address) from your browser's address field, open BlueJ, open the *Preferences* dialog, go to the *Miscellaneous* tab, and paste the copied URL into the field labeled *JDK documentation URL*. Using the *Java Class Libraries* item from the *Help* menu should now open your local copy.

A.8 Changing the new class templates

When you create a new class, the class's source is set to a default source text. This text is taken from a template and can be changed to suit your preferences. Templates are stored in the folders

<bluej_home>/lib/<language>/templates/ and

<bluej_home>/lib/<language>/templates/newclass/

where *<bluej_home>* is the BlueJ installation folder and *<language>* is your currently used language setting (for example, *english*).

Template files are pure text files and can be edited in any standard text editor.

Java data types

Java's type system is based on two distinct kinds of type: primitive types and object types.

Primitive types are stored in variables directly, and they have value semantics (values are copied when assigned to another variable). Primitive types are not associated with classes and do not have methods.

In contrast, an object type is manipulated by storing a reference to the object (not the object itself). When assigned to a variable, only the reference is copied, not the object.

B.1 Primitive types

The following table lists all the primitive types of the Java language:

Type name	Description	Example literals		
Integer numbers				
byte	byte-sized integer (8 bit)	24	-2	
short	short integer (16 bit)	137	-119	
int	integer (32 bit)	5409	-2003	
long	long integer (64 bit)	423266353L	55L	
Real numbers				
float	single-precision floating point	43.889F		
double	double-precision floating point	45.63	2.4e5	
Other types				
char	a single character (16 bit)	'm'	'?'	'\u00F6'
boolean	a boolean value (true or false)	true	false	

Notes:

- A number without a decimal point is generally interpreted as an int but automatically converted to byte, short, or long types when assigned (if the value fits). You can declare a literal as long by putting an L after the number. (l, lowercase L, works as well but should be avoided because it can easily be mistaken for a one (1).)
- A number with a decimal point is of type double. You can specify a float literal by putting an F or f after the number.
- A character can be written as a single Unicode character in single quotes or as a four-digit Unicode value, preceded by "\u".
- The two boolean literals are true and false.

Because variables of the primitive types do not refer to objects, there are no methods associated with the primitive types. However, when used in a context requiring an object type, autoboxing might be used to convert a primitive value to a corresponding object. See Section B.4 for more details.

The following table details minimum and maximum values available in the numerical types.

Type name	Minimum	Maximum
byte	-128	127
short	-32768	32767
int	-2147483648	2147483647
long	-9223372036854775808	9223372036854775807

	Positive minimum	Positive maximum
float	1.4e-45	3.4028235e38
double	4.9e-324	1.7976931348623157e308

B.2 Casting of primitive types

Sometimes it is necessary to convert a value of one primitive type to a value of another primitive type—typically, a value from a type with a particular range of values to one with a smaller range. This is called *casting*. Casting almost always involves loss of information—for example, when converting from a floating-point type to an integer type. Casting is permitted in Java between the numeric types, but it is not possible to convert a boolean value to any other type with a cast, or vice versa.

The cast operator consists of the name of a primitive type written in parentheses in front of a variable or an expression. For instance,

```
int val = (int) mean;
```

If mean is a variable of type double containing the value 3.9, then the statement above would store the integer value 3 (conversion by truncation) in the variable val.

B.3 Object types

All types not listed in Section B.1, *Primitive types*, are object types. These include class and interface types from the Java library (such as String) and user-defined types.

A variable of an object type holds a reference (or "pointer") to an object. Assignments and parameter passing have reference semantics (i.e., the reference is copied, not the object). After assigning a variable to another one, both variables refer to the same object. The two variables are said to be aliases for the same object. This rule applies in simple assignment between variables, but also when passing an object as an actual parameter to a method. As a consequence, state changes to an object via a formal parameter will persist, after the method has completed, in the actual parameter.

Classes are the templates for objects, defining the fields and methods that each instance possesses.

Arrays behave like object types; they also have reference semantics. There is no class definition for arrays.

B.4 Wrapper classes

Every primitive type in Java has a corresponding wrapper class that represents the same type but is a real-object type. This makes it possible to use values from the primitive types where object types are required, through a process known as *autoboxing*. The following table lists the primitive types and their corresponding wrapper type from the java.lang package. Apart from Integer and Character, the wrapper class names are the same as the primitive-type names, but with an uppercase first letter.

Whenever a value of a primitive type is used in a context that requires an object type, the compiler uses autoboxing to automatically wrap the primitive-type value in an appropriate wrapper object. This means that primitive-type values can be added directly to a collection, for instance. The reverse operation—*unboxing*—is also performed automatically when a wrapper-type object is used in a context that requires a value of the corresponding primitive type.

Primitive type	Wrapper type
byte	Byte
short	Short
int	Integer
long	Long
float	Float
double	Double
char	Character
boolean	Boolean

B.5 Casting of object types

Because an object may belong to an inheritance hierarchy of types, it is sometimes necessary to convert an object reference of one type to a reference of a subtype lower down the inheritance hierarchy. This process is called *casting* (or *downcasting*). The cast operator consists of the name of a class or interface type written in parentheses in front of a variable or an expression. For instance,

```
Car c = (Car) veh;
```

If the declared (i.e., static) type of variable veh is Vehicle and Car is a subclass of Vehicle, then this statement will compile. A separate check is made at runtime to ensure that the object referred to by veh really is a Car and not an instance of a different subtype.

It is important to appreciate that casting between object types is completely different from casting between primitive types (Section B.2, above). In particular, casting between object types involves *no change* of the object involved. It is purely a way of gaining access to type information that is already true of the object—that is, part of its full dynamic type.

APPENDIX

C

Operators

C.1 Arithmetic expressions

Java has a considerable number of operators available for both arithmetic and logical expressions. Table C.1 shows everything that is classified as an operator, including things such as type casting and parameter passing. Most of the operators are either binary operators (taking a left and a right operand) or unary operators (taking a single operand). The main binary arithmetic operations are:

+   *addition*
−   *subtraction*
*   *multiplication*
/   *division*
%   *modulus*, or *remainder after division*

The results of both division and modulus operations depend on whether their operands are integers or floating-point values. Between two integer values, division yields an integer result and discards any remainder, but between floating-point values, a floating-point value is the result:

```
5 / 3 gives a result of 1
5.0 / 3 gives a result of 1.6666666666666667
```

(Note that only one of the operands needs to be of a floating-point type to produce a floating-point result.)

When more than one operator appears in an expression, then *rules of precedence* have to be used to work out the order of application. In Table C.1, those operators having the highest precedence appear at the top, so we can see that multiplication, division, and modulus all take precedence over addition and subtraction, for instance. This means that both of the following examples give the result 100:

```
51 * 3 - 53
154 − 2 * 27
```

Binary operators with the same precedence level are evaluated from left to right, and unary operators with the same precedence level are evaluated right to left.

When it is necessary to alter the normal order of evaluation, parentheses can be used. So both of the following examples give the result 100:

```
(205 − 5) / 2
2 * (47 + 3)
```

The main unary operators are −, !, ++, −−, [], and new. You will notice that ++ and −− appear in each of the top two rows in Table C.1. Those in the top row take a single operand on their left, while those in the second row take a single operand on their right.

Table C.1

Java operators, highest precedence at the top

[]	.	·	++	−−	(*parameters*)					
++	−−		+	−	!	~				
new	(*cast*)									
*	/	%								
+	−									
<<	>>	>>>								
<	>	>=	<=	instanceof						
==	!=									
&										
^										
|										
&&										
||										
?:										
=	+=	−=	*=	/=	%=	>>=	<<=	>>>=	&=	|=	^=

C.2 Boolean expressions

In boolean expressions, operators are used to combine operands to produce a value of either true or false. Such expressions are usually found in the test expressions of if statements and loops.

The relational operators usually combine a pair of arithmetic operands, although the tests for equality and inequality are also used with object references. Java's relational operators are:

==	equal to		!=	not equal to
<	less than		<=	less than or equal to
>	greater than		>=	greater than or equal to

The binary logical operators combine two boolean expressions to produce another boolean value. The operators are:

&&	and
||	or
^	exclusive or

In addition,

 !   not

takes a single boolean expression and changes it from `true` to `false` and vice versa.

C.3   Short-circuit operators

Both && and || are slightly unusual in the way they are applied. If the left operand of && is `false`, then the value of the right operand is irrelevant and will not be evaluated. Similarly, if the left operand of || is `true`, then the right operand is not evaluated. Thus, they are known as short-circuit operators.

Java control structures

D.1 Control structures

Control structures affect the order in which statements are executed. There are two main categories: *selection statements* and *loops*.

A selection statement provides a decision point at which a choice is made to follow one route through the body of a method or constructor rather than another route. An *if-else statement* involves a decision between two different sets of statements, whereas a *switch statement* allows the selection of a single option from among several.

Loops offer the option to repeat statements, either a definite or an indefinite number of times. The former is typified by the *for-each loop* and *for loop*, while the latter is typified by the *while loop* and *do loop*.

In practice, it should be borne in mind that exceptions to the above characterizations are quite common. For instance, an *if-else statement* can be used to select from among several alternative sets of statements if the *else* part contains a nested if-else statement, and a for loop can be used to loop an indefinite number of times.

D.2 Selection statements

D.2.1 if-else

The *if-else statement* has two main forms, both of which are controlled by the evaluation of a boolean expression:

```
if(expression) {              if(expression) {
    statements                    statements
}                             }
                             else {
                                 statements
                             }
```

In the first form, the value of the boolean expression is used to decide whether or not to execute the statements. In the second form, the expression is used to choose between two alternative sets of statements, only one of which will be executed.

Examples:

```java
if(field.size() == 0) {
    System.out.println("The field is empty.");
}


if(number < 0) {
    reportError();
}
else {
    processNumber(number);
}
```

It is very common to link if-else statements together by placing a second *if-else* in the *else* part of the first. This can be continued any number of times. It is a good idea to always include a final *else* part.

```java
if(n < 0) {
    handleNegative();
}
else if(number == 0) {
    handleZero();
}
else {
    handlePositive();
}
```

D.2.2 switch

The *switch statement* switches on a single value to one of an arbitrary number of cases. Two possible patterns of use are:

```java
switch(expression) {                switch(expression) {
    case value: statements;             case value1:
                break;                  case value2:
    case value: statements;             case value3:
                break;                      statements;
    further cases possible                  break;
    default: statements;                case value4:
                break;                  case value5:
}                                           statements;
                                            break;
                                        further cases possible
                                        default:
                                            statements;
                                            break;
                                    }
```

Notes:

- A *switch* statement can have any number of `case` labels.
- The `break` statement after every case is needed, otherwise the execution "falls through" into the next label's statements. The second form above makes use of this. In this case, all three

of the first values will execute the first *statements* section, whereas values four and five will execute the second *statements* section.

- The `default` case is optional. If no default is given, it may happen that no case is executed.
- The `break` statement after the default (or the last case, if there is no default) is not needed but is considered good style.
- From Java 7, the expression used to switch on and the case labels may be strings.

Examples:

```java
switch(day) {
    case 1:   dayString = "Monday";
              break;
    case 2:   dayString = "Tuesday";
              break;
    case 3:   dayString = "Wednesday";
              break;
    case 4:   dayString = "Thursday";
              break;
    case 5:   dayString = "Friday";
              break;
    case 6:   dayString = "Saturday";
              break;
    case 7:   dayString = "Sunday";
              break;
    default:  dayString = "invalid day";
              break;
}
switch(dow.toLowerCase()) {
    case "mon":
    case "tue":
    case "wed":
    case "thu":
    case "fri":
        goToWork();
        break;
    case "sat":
    case "sun":
        stayInBed();
        break;
}
```

D.3 Loops

Java has three loops: *while*, *do-while*, and *for*. The *for loop* has two forms. Both *while* and *do-while* are well suited for indefinite iteration. The for-each loop is intended for definite iteration over a collection, and the for loop falls somewhere between the two. Except for the for-each loop, repetition is controlled in each with a boolean expression.

D.3.1 While

The *while loop* executes a block of statements as long as a given expression evaluates to *true*. The expression is tested *before* execution of the loop body, so the body may be executed zero times (i.e., not at all). This capability is an important feature of the while loop.

```
while(expression) {
        statements
}
```

Examples:

```
System.out.print("Please enter a filename: ");
input = readInput();
while(input == null) {
    System.out.print("Please try again: ");
    input = readInput();
}


int index = 0;
boolean found = false;
while(!found && index < list.size()) {
    if(list.get(index).equals(item)) {
        found = true;
    }
    else {
        index++;
    }
}
```

D.3.2 do-while

The *do-while loop* executes a block of statements as long as a given expression evaluates to *true*. The expression is tested *after* execution of the loop body, so the body always executes at least once. This is an important difference from the while loop.

```
do {
    statements
} while(expression);
```

Example:

```
do {
    System.out.print("Please enter a filename: ");
    input = readInput();
} while(input == null);
```

D.3.3 *for*

The *for loop* has two different forms. The first form is also known as a *for-each loop* and is used exclusively to iterate over elements of a collection. The loop variable is assigned the value of successive elements of the collection on each iteration of the loop.

```
for(variable-declaration: collection) {
    statements
}
```

Example:

```
for(String note : list) {
    System.out.println(note);
}
```

No associated index value is made available for the elements of the collection. A for-each loop cannot be used if the collection is to be modified while it is being iterated over.

The second form of for loop executes as long as a *condition* evaluates to *true*. Before the loop starts, an *initialization statement* is executed exactly once. The *condition* is evaluated before every execution of the loop body (so the statements in the loop's body may execute zero times). An *increment statement* is executed after each execution of the loop body.

```
for(initialization; condition; increment) {
    statements
}
```

Example:

```
for(int i = 0; i < text.size(); i++) {
    System.out.println(text.get(i));
}
```

Both types of for loop are commonly used to execute the body of the loop a definite number of times—for instance, once for each element in a collection—although a for loop is actually closer in effect to a while loop than to a for-each loop.

D.4   Exceptions

Throwing and catching exceptions provides another pair of constructs to alter control flow. However, exceptions are primarily used to anticipate and handle error situations rather than the normal flow of control.

```
try {
    statements
}
catch(exception-type name) {
    statements
}
```

```
finally {
    statements
}
```

Example:

```
try {
    FileWriter writer = new FileWriter("foo.txt");
    writer.write(text);
    writer.close();
}
catch(IOException e) {
    Debug.reportError("Writing text to file failed.");
    Debug.reportError("The exception is: " + e);
}
```

An exception statement may have any number of *catch clauses*. They are evaluated in order of appearance, and only the first matching clause is executed. (A clause matches if the dynamic type of the exception object being thrown is assignment-compatible with the declared exception type in the catch clause.) The *finally clause* is optional.

Java 7 introduced two mainstream additions to the try statement: multi-catch and try-with-resources, or automatic resource management (ARM).

Multiple exceptions may be handled in the same catch clause by writing the list of exception types separated by the "|" symbol.

Example:

```
try {
    . . .
    var.doSomething();
    . . .
}
catch(EOFException | FileNotFoundException e) {
    . . .
}
```

Automatic resource management—also known as "try-with-resource"—recognizes that try statements are often used to protect statements that use resources that should be closed when their use is complete, both upon success and failure. The header of the try statement is amended to include the opening of the resource—often a file—and the resource will be closed automatically at the end of the try statement.

Example:

```
try (FileWriter writer = new FileWriter(filename)){
    . . .
    Use the writer  . . .
    . . .
}
catch(IOException e) {
    . . .
}
```

D.5 Assertions

Assertion statements are primarily used as a testing tool during program development rather than in production code. There are two forms of assert statement:

```
assert boolean-expression;
assert boolean-expression: expression;
```

Examples:

```
assert getDetails(key) != null;
assert expected == actual:
       "Actual value: " + actual +
       " does not match expected value: " + expected;
```

If the assertion expression evaluates to *false*, then an AssertionError will be thrown.

A compiler option allows assertion statements to be rendered inactive in production code without having to remove them from the program source.

Running Java without BlueJ

Throughout this book, we have used BlueJ to develop and execute our Java applications. There is a good reason for this: BlueJ gives us tools to make some development tasks very easy. In particular, it lets us execute individual methods of classes and objects easily; this is very useful if we want to quickly test a segment of new code.

We separate the discussion of working without BlueJ into two categories: executing an application without BlueJ and developing without BlueJ.

E.1 Executing without BlueJ

Usually, when applications are delivered to end users, they are executed differently than from within BlueJ. They then have one single starting point, which defines where execution begins when a user starts an application.

The exact mechanism used to start an application depends on the operating system. Usually, this is done by double-clicking an application icon or by entering the name of the application on a command line. The operating system then needs to know which method of which class to invoke to execute the complete program.

In Java, this problem is solved using a convention. When a Java program is started, the name of the class is specified as a parameter of the start command, and the name of the method is main. The name "main" is arbitrarily chosen by the Java developers, but it is fixed—the method must have this name. (The choice of "main" for the name of the initial method actually goes back to the C language, from which Java inherits much of its syntax.)

Let us consider, for example, the following command, entered at a command line such as the Windows command prompt or a Unix terminal:

```
java Game
```

The java command starts the Java virtual machine. It is part of the Java Development Kit (JDK), which must be installed on your system. Game is the name of the class that we want to start.

The Java system will then look for a method in class Game with exactly the following signature:

```
public static void main(String[] args)
```

The method has to be public so that it can be invoked from the outside. It also has to be static, because no objects exist when we start off. Initially, we have only classes, so static methods are all we can call. This static method then typically creates the first object. The return type is `void`, as this method does not return a value.

The parameter is a `String` array. This allows users to pass in additional arguments. In our example, the value of the `args` parameter will be an array of length zero. The command line starting the program can, however, define arguments:

```
java Game 2 Fred
```

Every word after the class name in this command line will be read as a separate `String` and be passed into the main method as an element in the string array. In this case, the `args` array would contain two elements, which are the strings `"2"` and `"Fred"`. Command-line parameters are not very often used with Java.

The body of the main method can theoretically contain any statements you like. Good style, however, dictates that the length of the main method should be kept to a minimum. Specifically, it should not contain anything that is part of the application logic.

Typically, the main method should do exactly what you did interactively to start the same application in BlueJ. If, for instance, you created an object of class Game and invoked a method named `start` to start an application, you should add the following main method to the Game class:

```
public static void main(String[] args)
{
    Game game = new Game();
    game.start();
}
```

Now, executing the main method will mimic your interactive invocation of the game.

Java projects are usually stored each in a separate directory. All classes for a project are placed inside this directory. When you execute the command to start Java and execute your application, make sure that the project directory is the active directory in your command terminal. This ensures that the classes will be found.

If the specified class cannot be found, the Java virtual machine will generate an error message similar to this one:

```
Exception in thread "main" java.lang.NoClassDefFoundError: Game
```

If you see a message like this, make sure that you have typed the class name correctly and that the current directory actually contains this class. The class is stored in a file with the suffix `.class`. The code for class Game, for example, is stored in a file named Game. class.

If the class is found but does not contain a main method (or the main method does not have the right signature), you will see a message similar to this one:

```
Exception in thread "main" java.lang.NoSuchMethodError: main
```

In that case, make sure that the class you want to execute has a correct main method.

E.2   Creating executable .jar files

Java projects are typically stored as a collection of files in a directory (or "folder"). We shall briefly discuss the different files below.

To distribute applications to others, it is often easier if the whole application is stored in a single file. Java's mechanism for doing this is the Java Archive (.jar) format. All of the files of an application can be bundled into a single file, and they can still be executed. (If you are familiar with the "zip" compression format, it might be interesting to know that the format is, in fact, the same. "Jar" files can be opened with zip programs and vice versa.)

To make a .jar file executable, it is necessary to specify the main class somewhere. (Remember: The executed method is always main, but we need to specify the class this method is in.) This is done by including a text file in the .jar file (the *manifest file*) with this information. Luckily, BlueJ takes care of this for you.

To create an executable .jar file in BlueJ, use the *Project—Create Jar File* function, and specify in the resulting dialog the class that contains the main method. (You must still write a main method exactly as discussed above.)

For details with this function, read the BlueJ tutorial, which you can get through the BlueJ menu *Help—Tutorial* or from the BlueJ web site.

Once the executable .jar file has been created, it can be executed by double-clicking it. The computer that executes this .jar file must have the JDK or JRE (Java Runtime Environment) installed and associated with .jar files.

E.3   Developing without BlueJ

If you want not only to execute but also develop your programs without BlueJ, you will need to edit and compile the classes. The source code of a class is stored in a file ending in .java. For example, class Game is stored in a file called Game.java. Source files can be edited with any text editor. There are many free or inexpensive text editors around. Some, such as *Notepad* or *WordPad*, are distributed with Windows, but if you really want to use the editor for more than a quick test, you will soon want to get a better one. Be careful with word processors, though. Word processors typically do not save text in plain text format, and the Java system will not be able to read it.

The source files can then be compiled from a command line with the Java compiler that is included with the JDK. It is called javac. To compile a source file named Game.java, use the command

```
javac Game.java
```

This command will compile the Game class and any other classes it depends on. It will create a file called Game.class. This file contains the code that can be executed by the Java virtual machine. To execute it, use the command

```
java Game
```

Note that this command does not include the .class suffix.

Using the debugger

The BlueJ debugger provides a set of basic debugging features that are intentionally simplified yet genuinely useful, both for debugging programs and for gaining an understanding of the runtime behavior of programs.

The debugger window can be accessed by selecting the *Show Debugger* item from the *View* menu or by pressing the right mouse button over the work indicator and selecting *Show Debugger* from the pop-up menu. Figure F.1 shows the debugger window.

Figure F.1

The BlueJ debugger window

The debugger window contains five display areas and five control buttons. The areas and buttons become active only when a program reaches a breakpoint or halts for some other reason. The following sections describe how to set breakpoints, how to control program execution, and the purpose of each of the display areas.

F.1 Breakpoints

A breakpoint is a flag attached to a line of code (Figure F.2). When a breakpoint is reached during program execution, the debugger's displays and controls become active, allowing you to inspect the state of the program and control further execution.

Figure F.2

A breakpoint attached
to a line of code

```
/**
 * Print the next mail item (if any) for this user to the text
 * terminal.
 */
public void printNextMailItem()
{
    MailItem item = server.getNextMailItem(user);
    if(item == null) {
        System.out.println("No new mail.");
    }
    else {
        item.print();
    }
}
```

Breakpoints are set via the editor window. Either press the left mouse button in the breakpoint area to the left of the source text or place the cursor on the line of code where the breakpoint should be and select *Set/Clear Breakpoint* from the editor's *Tools* menu. Breakpoints can be removed by the reverse process. Breakpoints can be set only within classes that have been compiled.

F.2 The control buttons

Figure F.3 shows the control buttons that are active at a breakpoint.

Figure F.3

Active control buttons
at a breakpoint

F.2.1 Halt

The *Halt* button is active when the program is running, thus allowing execution to be interrupted should that be necessary. If execution is halted, the debugger will show the state of the program as if a breakpoint had been reached.

F.2.2 Step

The *Step* button resumes execution at the current statement. Execution will pause again when the statement is completed. If the statement involves a method call, the complete method call is completed before the execution pauses again (unless the call leads to another explicit breakpoint).

F.2.3 Step Into

The *Step Into* button resumes execution at the current statement. If this statement is a method call, then execution will "step into" that method and be paused at the first statement inside it.

F.2.4 Continue

The *Continue* button resumes execution until the next breakpoint is reached, execution is interrupted via the *Halt* button, or the execution completes normally.

F.2.5 Terminate

The *Terminate* button aggressively finishes execution of the current program such that it cannot be resumed again. If it is simply desired to interrupt the execution in order to examine the current program state, then the *Halt* operation is preferred.

F.3   The variable displays

Figure F.4 shows all three variable display areas active at a breakpoint, in an example taken from the predator–prey simulation discussed in Chapter 10. Static variables are displayed in the upper area, instance variables in the middle area, and local variables in the lower area.

Figure F.4
Active-variable
displays

When a breakpoint is reached, execution will be halted at a statement of an arbitrary object within the current program. The *Static variables* area displays the values of the static variables defined in the class of that object. The *Instance variables* area displays the values of that particular object's instance variables. Both areas also include any variables inherited from superclasses.

The *Local variables* area displays the values of local variables and parameters of the currently executing method or constructor. Local variables will appear in this area only once they have been initialized, as it is only at that point that they come into existence within the virtual machine.

A variable in any of these areas that is an object reference may be inspected by double-clicking on it.

F.4   The Call Sequence display

Figure F.5 shows the *Call Sequence* display, containing a sequence six methods deep. Methods appear in the format `Class.method` in the sequence, irrespective of whether they are static methods or instance methods. Constructors appear as `Class.<init>` in the sequence.

Figure F.5

A call sequence

The call sequence operates as a stack, with the method at the top of the sequence being the one where the flow of execution currently lies. The variable display areas reflect the details of the method or constructor currently highlighted in the call sequence. Selecting a different line of the sequence will update the contents of the other display areas.

F.5   The Threads display

The *Threads display* area is beyond the scope of this book and will not be discussed further.

Unit unit-testing tools

In this appendix, we give a brief outline of the main features of BlueJ's support for JUnit-style unit testing. More details can be found in the testing tutorial that is available from the book's CD and the BlueJ web site.

G.1 Enabling unit-testing functionality

In order to enable the unit-testing functionality of BlueJ, it is necessary to ensure that the *Show unit testing tools* box is ticked under the *Tools-Preferences-Miscellaneous* menu. The main BlueJ window will then contain a number of extra buttons that are active when a project is open.

G.2 Creating a test class

A test class is created by right-clicking a class in the class diagram and choosing *Create Test Class*. The name of the test class is determined automatically by adding `Test` as a suffix to the name of the associated class. Alternatively, a test class may be created by selecting the *New Class ...* button and choosing *Unit Test* for the class type. In this case, you have a free choice over its name.

Test classes are annotated with `<<unit test>>` in the class diagram, and they have a color distinct from ordinary classes.

G.3 Creating a test method

Test methods can be created interactively. A sequence of user interactions with the class diagram and object bench are recorded and then captured as a sequence of Java statements and declarations in a method of the test class. Start recording by selecting *Create Test Method* from the pop-up menu associated with a test class. You will be prompted for the name of the new method. Earlier versions of JUnit, up to version 3, required the method names to start with the prefix "test". This is not a requirement in current versions. The *recording* symbol to the left of the class diagram will then be colored red, and the *End* and *Cancel* buttons become available.

Once recording has started, any object creations or method calls will form part of the code of the method being created. Select *End* to complete the recording and capture the test, or select *Cancel* to discard the recording, leaving the test class unchanged.

Test methods have the annotation `@Test` in the source of the test class.

G.4   Test assertions

While recording a test method, any method calls that return a result will bring up a *Method Result* window. This offers the opportunity to make an assertion about the result value by ticking the *Assert that* box. A drop-down menu contains a set of possible assertions for the result value. If an assertion is made, this will be encoded as a method call in the test method which is intended to lead to an `AssertionError` if the test fails.

G.5   Running tests

Individual test methods can be run by selecting them from the pop-up menu associated with the test class. A successful test will be indicated by a message in the main window's status line. An unsuccessful test will cause the *Test Results* window to appear. Selecting *Test All* from the test class's pop-up menu runs all tests from a single test class. The *Test Results* window will detail the success or failure of each method.

G.6   Fixtures

The contents of the object bench may be captured as a *fixture* by selecting *Object Bench to Test Fixture* from the pop-up menu associated with the test class. The effect of creating a fixture is that a field definition for each object is added to the test class, and statements are added to its `setUp` method that re-create the exact state of the objects as they were on the bench. The objects are then removed from the bench.

The `setUp` method has the annotation `@Before` in the test class and the method is automatically executed before the run of any test method, so all objects in a fixture are available for all tests.

The objects of a fixture may be re-created on the object bench by selecting *Test Fixture to Object Bench* from the test class's menu.

A `tearDown` method, with the annotation `@After`, is called following each test method. This can be used to conduct any post-test housekeeping or clean-up operations, should they be needed.

Teamwork tools

In this Appendix, we briefly describe the tools available to support teamwork.

BlueJ includes teamwork support tools based on a source-code-repository model. In this model, a repository server is set up that is accessible over the Internet from the machines the users work on.

The server needs to be set up by an administrator. BlueJ supports both Subversion and CVS repositories.

H.1 Server setup

The setup of the repository server should normally be done by an experienced administrator. Detailed instructions can be found on the book CD in the document titled *repository-setup.pdf*.

H.2 Enabling teamwork functionality

The teamwork tools are initially hidden in BlueJ. To show the tools, open the *Preferences* dialog and, in the *Miscellaneous* tab, tick the *Show teamwork controls* box. The BlueJ interface then contains three extra buttons (*Update*, *Commit*, *Status*) and an additional submenu titled *Team* in the *Tools* menu.

H.3 Sharing a project

To create a shared project, one team member creates the project as a standard BlueJ project. The project can then be shared by using the *Share this Project* function from the *Team* menu. When this function is used, a copy of the project is placed into the central repository. The server name and access details need to be specified in a dialog; ask your administrator (the one who set up the repository) for the details to fill in here.

H.4 Using a shared project

Once a user has created a shared project in the repository, other team members can use this project. To do this, select *Checkout Project* from the *Team* menu. This will place a copy of the shared project from the central server into your local file system. You can then work on the local copy.

H.5   Update and commit

Every now and then, the various copies of the project that team members have on their local disks need to be synchronized. This is done via the central repository. Use the *Commit* function to copy your changes into the repository, and use the *Update* function to copy changes from the repository (which other team members have committed) into your own local copy. It is good practice to commit and update frequently so that the changes at any step do not become too substantial.

H.6   More information

More detailed information is available in the Team Work Tutorial, which is on the book's CD under the name *teamwork-tutorial.pdf*.

APPENDIX I

Javadoc

Writing good documentation for class and interface definitions is an important complement to writing good-quality source code. Documentation allows you to communicate your intentions to human readers in the form of a natural-language, high-level overview, rather than forcing them to read relatively low-level source code. Of particular value is documentation for the `public` elements of a class or interface, so that programmers can make use of it without having to know the details of its implementation.

In all of the project examples in this book, we have used a particular commenting style that is recognized by the `javadoc` documentation tool, which is distributed as part of the JDK. This tool automates the generation of class documentation in the form of HTML pages in a consistent style. The Java API has been documented using this same tool, and its value is appreciated when using library classes.

In this appendix, we give a brief summary of the main elements of the documentation comments that you should get into the habit of using in your own source code.

I.1 Documentation comments

The elements of a class to be documented are the class definition as a whole, its fields, constructors, and methods. Most important from the viewpoint of a user of your class is to have documentation for the class and its public constructors and methods. We have tended not to provide javadoc-style commenting for fields, because we regard these as private implementation-level details and not something to be relied upon by users.

Documentation comments are always opened with the character triplet "/**" and closed by the character pair "*/". Between these symbols, a comment will have a *main description* followed by a *tag section*, although both are optional.

I.1.1 The main description

The main description for a class should be a general description of the purpose of the class. Code I.1 shows part of a typical main description, taken from the Game class of the *world-of-zuul* project. Note how the description includes details of how to use this class to start the game.

Code I.1

The main description
of a class comment

```
/**
 * This class is the main class of the "World of Zuul".
 * application
 * "World of Zuul" is a very simple, text-based adventure game.
 * Users can walk around some scenery. That's all. It should
 * really be extended to make it more interesting!
 * To play this game, create an instance of this class and call
 * the "play" method.
 */
```

The main description for a method should be kept fairly general, without going into a lot of detail about how the method is implemented. Indeed, the main description for a method will often only need to be a single sentence, such as

```
/**
 * Create a new passenger with distinct pickup and destination
 * locations.
 */
```

Particular thought should be given to the first sentence of the main description for a class, interface, or method, as it is used in a separate summary at the top of the generated documentation.

Javadoc also supports the use of HTML markup within these comments.

I.1.2 The tag section

Following the main description comes the *tag section*. Javadoc recognizes around 20 tags, of which we discuss only the most important here (Table I.1). Tags can be used in two forms: *block tags* and *in-line tags*. We shall only discuss block tags, as these are the most commonly used. Further details about in-line tags and the remaining available tags can be found in the *javadoc* section of the *Tools and Utilities* documentation that is part of the JDK.

Table I.1

Common javadoc
tags

Tag	Associated text
@author	author name(s)
@param	parameter name and description
@return	description of the return value
@see	cross-reference
@throws	exception type thrown and the circumstances
@version	version description

The @author and @version tags are regularly found in class and interface comments and cannot be used in constructor, method, or field comments. Both are followed by free-text, and there is no required format for either. Examples are

```
@author Hacker T. Largebrain
@version 2012.12.03
```

The @param and @throws tags are used with methods and constructors, whereas @return is just used with methods. Examples are

```
@param limit The maximum value allowed.
@return A random number in the range 1 to limit (inclusive).
@throws IllegalLimitException If limit is less than 1.
```

The @see tag has several different forms and may be used in any documentation comment. It provides a way to cross-reference a comment to another class, method, or other form of documentation. A *See Also* section is added to the item being commented. Here are some typical examples:

```
@see "The Java Language Specification, by Joy et al"
@see <a href="http://www.bluej.org/">The BlueJ web site</a>
@see #isAlive
@see java.util.ArrayList#add
```

The first simply embeds a text string with no hyperlink; the second embeds a hyperlink to the specified document; the third links to the documentation for the isAlive method in the same class; the fourth links to the documentation for the add method in the ArrayList class of the java.util package.

I.2   BlueJ support for javadoc

If a project has been commented using the *javadoc* style, then BlueJ provides support for generating the complete HTML documentation. In the main window, select the *Tools/Project Documentation* menu item, and the documentation will be generated (if necessary) and displayed within a browser window.

Within the BlueJ editor, the source-code view of a class can be switched to the documentation view by changing the *Source Code* option to *Documentation* at the right of the window (Figure I.1) or by using *Toggle Documentation View* from the editor's *Tools* menu. This provides a quick preview of the documentation, but will not contain references to documentation of superclasses or used classes.

Figure I.1
The *Source Code* and *Documentation* view option

More details are available at:

```
http://www.oracle.com/technetwork/java/javase/documentation/
index-137868.html
```

APPENDIX

J

Program style guide

J.1 Naming

J.1.1 Use meaningful names

Use descriptive names for all identifiers (names of classes, variables, and methods). Avoid ambiguity. Avoid abbreviations. Simple mutator methods should be named *setSomething(...)*. Simple accessor methods should be named *getSomething(...)*. Accessor methods with `boolean` return values are often called *isSomething(...)*—for example, `isEmpty()`.

J.1.2 Class names start with a capital letter

J.1.3 Class names are singular nouns

J.1.4 Method and variable names start with lowercase letters

All three—class, method, and variable names—use capital letters in the middle to increase readability of compound identifiers, e.g. `numberOfItems`.

J.1.5 Constants are written in UPPERCASE

Constants occasionally use underscores to indicate compound identifiers:

    MAXIMUM_SIZE.

J.2 Layout

J.2.1 One level of indentation is four spaces

J.2.2 All statements within a block are indented one level

J.2.3 Braces for classes and methods are alone on one line

The braces for class and method blocks are on separate lines and are at the same indentation level. For example:

```
public int getAge()
{
    statements
}
```

J.2.4 For all other blocks, braces open at the end of a line

All other blocks open with braces at the end of the line that contains the keyword defining the block. The closing brace is on a separate line, aligned under the keyword that defines the block. For example:

```
while(condition) {
    statements
}
if(condition) {
    statements
}
else {
    statements
}
```

J.2.5 Always use braces in control structures

Braces are used in if-statements and loops even if the body is only a single statement.

J.2.6 Use a space before the opening brace of a control structure's block

J.2.7 Use a space around operators

J.2.8 Use a blank line between methods (and constructors)

Use blank lines to separate logical blocks of code; this means at least between methods, but also between logical parts within a method.

J.3 Documentation

J.3.1 Every class has a class comment at the top

The class comment contains at least:

- a general description of the class
- the author's name(s)
- a version number

Every person who has contributed to the class has to be named as an author or has to be otherwise appropriately credited.

A version number can be a simple number, a date, or other format. The important thing is that a reader must be able to recognize whether two versions are different and to determine which one is newer.

J.3.2 Every method has a method comment

J.3.3 Comments are Javadoc-readable

Class and method comments must be recognized by Javadoc. In other words, they should start with the comment symbol "/**".

J.3.4 Code comments (only) where necessary

Comments in the code should be included where the code is not obvious or is difficult to understand (and preference should be given to make the code obvious or easy to understand where possible) and where comments facilitate understanding of a method. Do not comment obvious statements—assume that your reader understands Java!

J.4 Language-use restrictions

J.4.1 Order of declarations: Fields, constructors, methods

The elements of a class definition appear (if present) in the following order: package statement; import statements; class comment; class header; field definitions; constructors; methods; inner classes.

J.4.2 Fields may not be public (except for final fields)

J.4.3 Always use an access modifier

Specify all fields and methods as either `private`, `public`, or `protected`. Never use default (package private) access.

J.4.4 Import classes separately

Importing statements explicitly naming every class are preferred over importing whole packages. For example:

```
import java.util.ArrayList;
import java.util.HashSet;
```

is better than

```
import java.util.*;
```

J.4.5 Always include a constructor (even if the body is empty)

J.4.6 Always include a superclass constructor call

In constructors of subclasses, do not rely on automatic insertion of a superclass call. Include the `super()` call explicitly, even if it would work without it.

J.4.7 Initialize all fields in the constructor

J.5 Code idioms

J.5.1 Use iterators with collections

To iterate over a complete collection, use a for-each loop. When the collection must be changed during iteration, use an `Iterator` with a while loop or a for loop, not an integer index.

APPENDIX

K

Important library classes

The Java platform includes a rich set of libraries that support a wide variety of programming tasks.

In this Appendix, we briefly summarize details of some classes and interfaces from the most important packages of the Java API. A competent Java programmer should be familiar with most of these. This Appendix is only a summary, and it should be read in conjunction with the full API documentation.

K.1 The `java.lang` package

Classes and interfaces in the `java.lang` package are fundamental to the Java language, as this package is automatically imported implicitly into any class definition.

---

package `java.lang`–Summary of the most important classes

interface `Comparable`	Implementation of this interface allows comparison and ordering of objects from the implementing class. Static utility methods such as `Arrays.sort` and `Collections.sort` can then provide efficient sorting in such cases, for instance.
class `Math`	`Math` is a class containing only static fields and methods. Values for the mathematical constants e and π are defined here, along with trigonometric functions and others such as `abs`, `min`, `max`, and `sqrt`.
class `Object`	All classes have `Object` as a superclass at the root of their class hierarchy. From it, all objects inherit default implementations for important methods such as `equals` and `toString`. Other significant methods defined by this class are `clone` and `hashCode`.
class `String`	Strings are an important feature of many applications, and they receive special treatment in Java. Key methods of the `String` class are `charAt`, `equals`, `indexOf`, `length`, `split`, and `substring`. Strings are immutable objects, so methods such as `trim` that appear to be mutators actually return a new `String` object representing the result of the operation.
class `StringBuilder`	The `StringBuilder` class offers an efficient alternative to `String` when it is required to build up a string from a number of components: e.g., via concatenation. Its key methods are `append`, `insert`, and `toString`.

K.2 The `java.util` package

The `java.util` package is a relatively incoherent collection of useful classes and interfaces.

package `java.util`—Summary of the most important classes and interfaces

interface `Collection`	This interface provides the core set of methods for most of the collection-based classes defined in the `java.util` package, such as `ArrayList`, `HashSet`, and `LinkedList`. It defines signatures for the `add`, `clear`, `iterator`, `remove`, and `size` methods.
interface `Iterator`	`Iterator` defines a simple and consistent interface for iterating over the contents of a collection. Its three methods are `hasNext`, `next`, and `remove`.
interface `List`	`List` is an extension of the `Collection` interface and provides a means to impose a sequence on the selection. As such, many of its methods take an index parameter: for instance, `add`, `get`, `remove`, and `set`. Classes such as `ArrayList` and `LinkedList` implement `List`.
interface `Map`	The `Map` interface offers an alternative to list-based collections by supporting the idea of associating each object in a collection with a *key* value. Objects are added and retrieved via its `put` and `get` methods. Note that a `Map` does not return an `Iterator`, but its `keySet` method returns a `Set` of the keys, and its `values` method returns a `Collection` of the objects in the map.
interface `Set`	`Set` extends the `Collection` interface with the intention of mandating that a collection contain no duplicate elements. It is worth pointing out that, because it is an interface, `Set` has no actual implication to enforce this restriction. This means that `Set` is actually provided as a marker interface to enable collection implementers to indicate that their classes fulfill this particular restriction.
class `ArrayList`	`ArrayList` is an implementation of the `List` interface that uses an array to provide efficient direct access via integer indices to the objects it stores. If objects are added or removed from anywhere other than the last position in the list, then following items have to be moved to make space or close the gap. Key methods are `add`, `get`, `iterator`, `remove`, and `size`.
class `Collections`	`Collections` contains many useful static methods for manipulating collections. Key methods are `binarySearch`, `fill`, and `sort`.
class `HashMap`	`HashMap` is an implementation of the `Map` interface. Key methods are `get`, `put`, `remove`, and `size`. Iteration over a `HashMap` is usually a two-stage process: obtain the set of keys via its `keySet` method, and then iterate over the keys.
class `HashSet`	`HashSet` is a hash-based implementation of the `Set` interface. It is closer in usage to a `Collection` than to a `HashMap`. Key methods are `add`, `remove`, and `size`.
class `LinkedList`	`LinkedList` is an implementation of the `List` interface that uses an internal linked structure to store objects. Direct access to the ends of the list is efficient, but access to individual objects via an index is less efficient than with an `ArrayList`. On the other hand, adding objects or removing them from within the list requires no shifting of existing objects. Key methods are `add`, `getFirst`, `getLast`, `iterator`, `removeFirst`, `removeLast`, and `size`.
class `Random`	The `Random` class supports generation of pseudo-random values—typically, random numbers. The sequence of numbers generated is determined by a *seed value*, which may be passed to a constructor or set via a call to `setSeed`. Two `Random` objects starting from the same seed will return the same sequence of values to identical calls. Key methods are `nextBoolean`, `nextDouble`, `nextInt`, and `setSeed`.
class `Scanner`	The `Scanner` class provides a way to read and parse input. It is often used to read input from the keyboard. Key methods are `next` and `hasNext`.

K.3 The `java.io` and `java.nio.file` packages

The `java.io` and `java.nio.file` packages contain classes that support input and output and access to the file system. Many of the input/output classes in `java.io` are distinguished by whether they are *stream-based* (operating on binary data) or *readers* and *writers (*operating on characters). The `java.nio.file` package supplies several classes that support convenient access to the file system.

package `java.io.file`–Summary of the most important classes and interfaces	
interface `Serializable`	The `Serializable` interface is an empty interface requiring no code to be written in an implementing class. Classes implement this interface in order to be able to participate in the serialization process. `Serializable` objects may be written and read as a whole to and from sources of output and input. This makes storage and retrieval of persistent data a relatively simple process in Java. See the `ObjectInputStream` and `ObjectOutputStream` classes for further information.
class `BufferedReader`	`BufferedReader` is a class that provides buffered character-based access to a source of input. Buffered input is often more efficient than unbuffered, particularly if the source of input is in the external file system. Because it buffers input, it is able to offer a `readLine` method that is not available in most other input classes. Key methods are `close`, `read`, and `readLine`.
class `BufferedWriter`	`BufferedWriter` is a class that provides buffered character-based output. Buffered output is often more efficient than unbuffered, particularly if the destination of the output is in the external file system. Key methods are `close`, `flush`, and `write`.
class `File`	The `File` class provides an object representation for files and folders (directories) in an external file system. Methods exist to indicate whether a file is readable and/or writeable, and whether it is a file or a folder. A `File` object can be created for a nonexistent file, which may be a first step in creating a physical file on the file system. Key methods are `canRead`, `canWrite`, `createNewFile`, `createTempFile`, `getName`, `getParent`, `getPath`, `isDirectory`, `isFile`, and `listFiles`.
class `FileReader`	The `FileReader` class is used to open an external file ready for reading its contents as characters. A `FileReader` object is often passed to the constructor of another reader class (such as a `BufferedReader`) rather than being used directly. Key methods are `close` and `read`.
class `FileWriter`	The `FileWriter` class is used to open an external file ready for writing character-based data. Pairs of constructors determine whether an existing file will be appended or its existing contents discarded. A `FileWriter` object is often passed to the constructor of another `Writer` class (such as a `BufferedWriter`) rather than being used directly. Key methods are `close`, `flush`, and `write`.
class `IOException`	`IOException` is a checked exception class that is at the root of the exception hierarchy of most input/output exceptions.
interface `Path`	The `Path` interface provides the key methods for accessing information about a file in the file system. `Path` is, in effect, a replacement for the older `File` class of the `java.io` package.

package `java.io.file`–**Summary of the most important classes and interfaces**	
class `Paths`	The `Paths` class provides `get` methods to return concrete instances of the `Path` interface.
class `Files`	`Files` is a class that provides static methods to query attributes of files and directories (folders), as well as to manipulate the file system—e.g., creating directories and changing file permissions. It also includes methods for opening files, such as `newBufferedReader`.

K.4   The `java.net` package

The `java.net` package contains classes and interfaces supporting networked applications. Most of these are outside the scope of this book.

package `java.net`–**Summary of the most important classes**	
class URL	The URL class represents a Uniform Resource Locator. In other words, it provides a way to describe the location of something on the Internet. In fact, it can also be used to describe the location of something on a local file system. We have included it here because classes from the `java.io` and `javax.swing` packages often use URL objects. Key methods are `getContent`, `getFile`, `getHost`, `getPath`, and `openStream`.

K.5   Other important packages

Other important packages are:

```
java.awt
java.awt.event
javax.swing
javax.swing.event
```

These are used extensively when writing graphical user interfaces (GUIs), and they contain many useful classes that a GUI programmer should become familiar with.

Index

Oracle Binary Code License Agreement for the Java SE Platform Products

ORACLE AMERICA, INC. ("ORACLE"), FOR AND ON BEHALF OF ITSELF AND ITS SUBSIDIARIES AND AFFILIATES UNDER COMMON CONTROL, IS WILLING TO LICENSE THE SOFTWARE TO YOU ONLY UPON THE CONDITION THAT YOU ACCEPT ALL OF THE TERMS CONTAINED IN THIS BINARY CODE LICENSE AGREEMENT AND SUPPLEMENTAL LICENSE TERMS (COLLECTIVELY "AGREEMENT"). PLEASE READ THE AGREEMENT CAREFULLY. BY SELECTING THE "ACCEPT LICENSE AGREEMENT" (OR THE EQUIVALENT) BUTTON AND/OR BY USING THE SOFTWARE YOU ACKNOWLEDGE THAT YOU HAVE READ THE TERMS AND AGREE TO THEM. IF YOU ARE AGREEING TO THESE TERMS ON BEHALF OF A COMPANY OR OTHER LEGAL ENTITY, YOU REPRESENT THAT YOU HAVE THE LEGAL AUTHORITY TO BIND THE LEGAL ENTITY TO THESE TERMS. IF YOU DO NOT HAVE SUCH AUTHORITY, OR IF YOU DO NOT WISH TO BE BOUND BY THE TERMS, THEN SELECT THE "DECLINE LICENSE AGREEMENT" (OR THE EQUIVALENT) BUTTON AND YOU MUST NOT USE THE SOFTWARE ON THIS SITE OR ANY OTHER MEDIA ON WHICH THE SOFTWARE IS CONTAINED.

1. DEFINITIONS. "Software" means the Java SE Platform Products in binary form that you selected for download, install or use from Oracle or its authorized licensees, any other machine readable materials (including, but not limited to, libraries, source files, header files, and data files), any updates or error corrections provided by Oracle, and any user manuals, programming guides and other documentation provided to you by Oracle under this Agreement. "General Purpose Desktop Computers and Servers" means computers, including desktop and laptop computers, or servers, used for general computing functions under end user control (such as but not specifically limited to email, general purpose Internet browsing, and office suite productivity tools). The use of Software in systems and solutions that provide dedicated functionality (other than as mentioned above) or designed for use in embedded or function-specific software applications, for example but not limited to: Software embedded in or bundled with industrial control systems, wireless mobile telephones, wireless handheld devices, netbooks, kiosks, TV/STB, Blu-ray Disc devices, telematics and network control switching equipment, printers and storage management systems, and other related systems are excluded from this definition and not licensed under this Agreement. "Programs" means Java technology applets and applications intended to run on the Java Platform, Standard Edition platform on Java-enabled General Purpose Desktop Computers and Servers. "Commercial Features" means those features identified in Table 1-1 (Commercial Features In Java SE Product Editions) of the Software documentation accessible at http://www.oracle.com/technetwork/java/javase/documentation/index.html.

   "README File" means the README file for the Software accessible at http://www.oracle.com/technetwork/java/javase/documentation/index.html.

2. LICENSE TO USE. Subject to the terms and conditions of this Agreement including, but not limited to, the Java Technology Restrictions of the Supplemental License Terms, Oracle grants you a non-exclusive, non-transferable, limited license without license fees to reproduce and use internally the Software complete and unmodified for the sole purpose of running Programs. THE LICENSE SET FORTH IN THIS SECTION 2 DOES NOT EXTEND TO THE COMMERCIAL FEATURES. YOUR RIGHTS AND OBLIGATIONS RELATED TO THE COMMERCIAL FEATURES ARE AS SET FORTH IN THE SUPPLEMENTAL TERMS ALONG WITH ADDITIONAL LICENSES FOR DEVELOPERS AND PUBLISHERS.

3. RESTRICTIONS. Software is copyrighted. Title to Software and all associated intellectual property rights is retained by Oracle and/or its licensors. Unless enforcement is prohibited by applicable law, you may not modify, decompile, or reverse engineer Software. You acknowledge that the Software is developed for general use in a variety of information management applications; it is not developed or intended for use in any inherently dangerous applications, including applications that may create a risk of personal injury. If you use the Software in dangerous applications, then you shall be responsible to take all appropriate fail-safe, backup, redundancy, and other measures to ensure its safe use. Oracle disclaims any express or implied warranty of fitness for such uses. No right, title or interest in or to any trademark, service mark, logo or trade name of Oracle or its licensors is granted under this Agreement. Additional restrictions for developers and/or publishers licenses are set forth in the Supplemental License Terms.

4. DISCLAIMER OF WARRANTY. THE SOFTWARE IS PROVIDED "AS IS" WITHOUT WARRANTY OF ANY KIND. ORACLE FURTHER DISCLAIMS ALL WARRANTIES, EXPRESS AND IMPLIED, INCLUDING WITHOUT LIMITATION, ANY IMPLIED WARRANTIES OF MERCHANTABILITY, FITNESS FOR A PARTICULAR PURPOSE OR NONINFRINGEMENT.

5. LIMITATION OF LIABILITY. IN NO EVENT SHALL ORACLE BE LIABLE FOR ANY INDIRECT, INCIDENTAL, SPECIAL, PUNITIVE OR CONSEQUENTIAL DAMAGES, OR DAMAGES FOR LOSS OF PROFITS, REVENUE, DATA OR DATA USE, INCURRED BY YOU OR ANY THIRD PARTY, WHETHER IN AN ACTION IN CONTRACT OR TORT, EVEN IF ORACLE HAS BEEN ADVISED OF THE POSSIBILITY OF SUCH DAMAGES. ORACLE'S ENTIRE LIABILITY FOR DAMAGES HEREUNDER SHALL IN NO EVENT EXCEED ONE THOUSAND DOLLARS (U.S. $1,000).

6. TERMINATION. This Agreement is effective until terminated. You may terminate this Agreement at any time by destroying all copies of Software. This Agreement will terminate immediately without notice from Oracle if you fail to comply with any provision of this Agreement. Either party may terminate this Agreement immediately should any Software become, or in either party's opinion be likely to become, the subject of a claim of infringement of any intellectual property right. Upon termination, you must destroy all copies of Software.

7. EXPORT REGULATIONS. You agree that U.S. export control laws and other applicable export and import laws govern your use of the Software, including technical data; additional information can be found on Oracle's Global Trade Compliance web site (http://www.oracle.com/products/export). You agree that neither the Software nor any direct product thereof will be exported, directly, or indirectly, in violation of these laws, or will be used for any purpose prohibited by these laws including, without limitation, nuclear, chemical, or biological weapons proliferation.

8. TRADEMARKS AND LOGOS. You acknowledge and agree as between you and Oracle that Oracle owns the ORACLE and JAVA trademarks and all ORACLE- and JAVA-related trademarks, service marks, logos and other brand designations ("Oracle Marks"), and you agree to comply with the Third Party Usage Guidelines for Oracle Trademarks currently located at http://www.oracle.com/us/legal/third-party-trademarks/index.html. Any use you make of the Oracle Marks inures to Oracle's benefit.

9. U.S. GOVERNMENT LICENSE RIGHTS. If Software is being acquired by or on behalf of the U.S. Government or by a U.S. Government prime contractor or subcontractor (at any tier), then the Government's rights in Software and accompanying documentation shall be only those set forth in this Agreement.

10. GOVERNING LAW. This agreement is governed by the substantive and procedural laws of California. You and Oracle agree to submit to the exclusive jurisdiction of, and venue in, the courts of San Francisco, or Santa Clara counties in California in any dispute arising out of or relating to this agreement.

11. SEVERABILITY. If any provision of this Agreement is held to be unenforceable, this Agreement will remain in effect with the provision omitted, unless omission would frustrate the intent of the parties, in which case this Agreement will immediately terminate.

12. INTEGRATION. This Agreement is the entire agreement between you and Oracle relating to its subject matter. It supersedes all prior or contemporaneous oral or written communications, proposals, representations and warranties and prevails over any conflicting or additional terms of any quote, order, acknowledgment, or other communication between the parties relating to its subject matter during the term of this Agreement. No modification of this Agreement will be binding, unless in writing and signed by an authorized representative of each party.

SUPPLEMENTAL LICENSE TERMS

These Supplemental License Terms add to or modify the terms of the Binary Code License Agreement. Capitalized terms not defined in these Supplemental Terms shall have the same meanings ascribed to them in the Binary Code License Agreement. These Supplemental Terms shall supersede any inconsistent or conflicting terms in the Binary Code License Agreement, or in any license contained within the Software.

A. COMMERCIAL FEATURES. You may not use the Commercial Features for running Programs, Java applets or applications in your internal business operations or for any commercial or production purpose, or for any purpose other than as set forth in Sections B, C, D and E of these Supplemental Terms. If You want to use the Commercial Features for any purpose other than as permitted in this Agreement, You must obtain a separate license from Oracle.

B. SOFTWARE INTERNAL USE FOR DEVELOPMENT LICENSE GRANT. Subject to the terms and conditions of this Agreement and restrictions and exceptions set forth in the README File incorporated herein by reference, including, but not limited to the Java Technology Restrictions of these Supplemental Terms, Oracle grants you a non-exclusive, non-transferable, limited license without fees to reproduce internally and use internally the Software complete and unmodified for the purpose of designing, developing, and testing your Programs.

C. LICENSE TO DISTRIBUTE SOFTWARE. Subject to the terms and conditions of this Agreement and restrictions and exceptions set forth in the README File, including, but not limited to the Java Technology Restrictions of these Supplemental Terms, Oracle grants you a non-exclusive, non-transferable, limited license without fees to reproduce and distribute the Software, provided that (i) you distribute the Software complete and unmodified and only bundled as part of, and for the sole purpose of running, your Programs, (ii) the Programs add significant and primary functionality to the Software, (iii) you do not distribute additional software intended to replace any component(s) of the Software, (iv) you do not remove or alter any proprietary legends or notices contained in the Software, (v) you only distribute the Software subject to a license agreement that: (a) is a complete, unmodified reproduction of this Agreement; or (b) protects Oracle's interests consistent with the terms contained in this Agreement and that includes the notice set forth in Section G, and (vi) you agree to defend and indemnify Oracle and its licensors from and against any damages, costs, liabilities, settlement amounts and/or expenses (including attorneys' fees) incurred in connection with any claim, lawsuit or action by any third party that arises or results from the use or distribution of any and all Programs and/or Software.

D. LICENSE TO DISTRIBUTE REDISTRIBUTABLES. Subject to the terms and conditions of this Agreement and restrictions and exceptions set forth in the README File, including but not limited to the Java Technology Restrictions of these Supplemental Terms, Oracle grants you a non-exclusive, non- transferable, limited license without fees to reproduce and distribute those files specifically identified as redistributable in the README File ("Redistributables") provided that: (i) you distribute the Redistributables complete and unmodified, and only bundled as part of Programs, (ii) the Programs add significant and primary functionality to the Redistributables, (iii) you do not distribute additional software intended to supersede any component(s) of the Redistributables (unless otherwise specified in the applicable README File), (iv) you do not remove or alter any proprietary legends or notices contained in or on the Redistributables, (v) you only distribute the Redistributables pursuant to a license agreement that: (a) is a complete, unmodified reproduction of this Agreement; or (b) protects Oracle's interests consistent with the terms contained in the Agreement and includes the notice set forth in Section G, (vi) you agree to defend and indemnify Oracle and its licensors from and against any damages, costs, liabilities, settlement amounts and/or expenses (including attorneys' fees) incurred in connection with any claim, lawsuit or action by any third party that arises or results from the use or distribution of any and all Programs and/or Software.

E. DISTRIBUTION BY PUBLISHERS. This section pertains to your distribution of the JavaTM SE Development Kit Software with your printed book or magazine (as those terms are commonly used in the industry) relating to Java technology ("Publication"). Subject to and conditioned upon your compliance with the restrictions and obligations contained in the Agreement, Oracle hereby grants to you a non-exclusive, nontransferable limited right to reproduce complete and unmodified copies of the Software on electronic media (the "Media") for the sole purpose of inclusion and distribution with your Publication(s), subject to the following terms: (i) You may not distribute the Software on a stand-alone basis; it must be distributed with your Publication(s); (ii) You are responsible for downloading the Software from the applicable Oracle web site; (iii) You must refer to the Software as JavaTM SE Development Kit; (iv) The Software must be reproduced in its entirety and without any modification whatsoever (including with respect to all proprietary notices) and distributed with your Publication subject to a license agreement that is a complete, unmodified reproduction of this Agreement; (v) The Media label shall include the following information: Copyright 2011, Oracle America, Inc. All rights reserved. Use is subject to license terms. ORACLE and JAVA trademarks and all ORACLE- and JAVA-related trademarks, service marks, logos and other brand designations are trademarks or registered trademarks of Oracle in the U.S. and other countries. This information must be placed on the Media label in such a manner as to only apply to the Oracle Software; (vi) You must clearly identify the Software as Oracle's product on the Media holder or Media label, and you may not state or imply that Oracle is responsible for any third-party software contained on the Media; (vii) You may not include any third party software on the Media which is intended to be a replacement or substitute for the Software; (viii) You agree to defend and indemnify Oracle and its licensors from and against any damages, costs, liabilities, settlement amounts and/or expenses (including attorneys' fees) incurred in connection with any claim, lawsuit or action by any third party that arises or results from the use or distribution of the Software and/or the Publication; ; and (ix) You shall provide Oracle with a written notice for each Publication; such notice shall include the following information: (1) title of Publication, (2) author(s), (3) date of Publication, and (4) ISBN or ISSN numbers. Such notice shall be sent to Oracle America, Inc., 500

Oracle Parkway, Redwood Shores, California 94065 U.S.A , Attention: General Counsel.

F. JAVA TECHNOLOGY RESTRICTIONS. You may not create, modify, or change the behavior of, or authorize your licensees to create, modify, or change the behavior of, classes, interfaces, or subpackages that are in any way identified as "java", "javax", "sun", "oracle" or similar convention as specified by Oracle in any naming convention designation.

G. COMMERCIAL FEATURES NOTICE. For purpose of complying with Supplemental Term Section C.(v)(b) and D.(v)(b), your license agreement shall include the following notice, where the notice is displayed in a manner that anyone using the Software will see the notice:

> Use of the Commercial Features for any commercial or production purpose requires a separate license from Oracle. "Commercial Features" means those features identified Table 1-1 (Commercial http://www.oracle.com/technetwork/java/javase/documentation/index.html

H. SOURCE CODE. Software may contain source code that, unless expressly licensed for other purposes, is provided solely for reference purposes pursuant to the terms of this Agreement. Source code may not be redistributed unless expressly provided for in this Agreement.

I. THIRD PARTY CODE. Additional copyright notices and license terms applicable to portions of the Software are set forth in the THIRDPARTYLICENSEREADME file accessible at http://www.oracle.com/technetwork/java/javase/documentation/index.html. In addition to any terms and conditions of any third party opensource/freeware license identified in the THIRDPARTYLICENSEREADME file, the disclaimer of warranty and limitation of liability provisions in paragraphs 4 and 5 of the Binary Code License Agreement shall apply to all Software in this distribution.

J. TERMINATION FOR INFRINGEMENT. Either party may terminate this Agreement immediately should any Software become, or in either party's opinion be likely to become, the subject of a claim of infringement of any intellectual property right.

K. INSTALLATION AND AUTO-UPDATE. The Software's installation and auto- update processes transmit a limited amount of data to Oracle (or its service provider) about those specific processes to help Oracle understand and optimize them. Oracle does not associate the data with personally identifiable information. You can find more information about the data Oracle collects as a result of your Software download at http://www.oracle.com/technetwork/java/javase/documentation/index.html.

For inquiries please contact: Oracle America, Inc., 500 Oracle Parkway, Redwood Shores, California 94065, USA.

Last updated May 17, 2011